Property and Dispossession

Allan Greer examines the processes by which forms of land tenure emerged and natives were dispossessed from the sixteenth to the eighteenth centuries in New France (Canada), New Spain (Mexico) and New England. By focusing on land, territory and property, he deploys the concept of "property formation" to consider the ways in which Europeans and their Euro-American descendants remade New World space as they laid claim to the continent's resources, extended the reach of empire and established states and jurisdictions for themselves. Challenging long-held, binary assumptions of property as a single entity, which various groups did or did not possess, Greer highlights the diversity of indigenous and Euro-American property systems in the early modern period. The book's geographic scope, comparative dimension and placement of indigenous people on an equal plane with Europeans make it unlike any previous study of early colonization and contact in the Americas.

ALLAN GREER holds the Canada Research Chair in Colonial North America at McGill University in Montreal, Canada. He has published seven books, including *Mohawk Saint: Catherine Tekakwitha and the Jesuits* (2005) and *La Nouvelle-France et le monde* (2009). He has been the recipient of fellowships from the John Simon Guggenheim Foundation and the Killam Foundation. Greer is a member of the Royal Society of Canada and a former resident fellow at the Institut d'études avancées, Paris.

Studies in North American Indian History

Editors

Frederick Hoxie, *University of Illinois, Urbana-Champaign*
Neal Salisbury, *Smith College, Massachusetts*
Tiya Miles, *University of Michigan, Ann Arbor*
Ned Blackhawk, *Yale University*

This series is designed to exemplify new approaches to the Native American past. In recent years scholars have begun to appreciate the extent to which Indians, whose cultural roots extended back for thousands of years, shaped the North American landscape as encountered by successive waves of immigrants. In addition, because Native Americans continually adapted their cultural traditions to the realities of the Euro-American presence, their history adds a thread of non-Western experience to the tapestry of American culture. Cambridge Studies in North American Indian History brings outstanding examples of this new scholarship to a broad audience. Books in the series link Native Americans to broad themes in American history and place the Indian experience in the context of social and economic change over time.

Also in the Series

Property and Dispossession

Natives, Empires and Land in Early Modern North America

ALLAN GREER

McGill University

CAMBRIDGE
UNIVERSITY PRESS

University Printing House, Cambridge CB2 8BS, United Kingdom

One Liberty Plaza, 20th Floor, New York, NY 10006, USA

477 Williamstown Road, Port Melbourne, VIC 3207, Australia

314–321, 3rd Floor, Plot 3, Splendor Forum, Jasola District Centre, New Delhi – 110025, India

79 Anson Road, #06–04/06, Singapore 079906

Cambridge University Press is part of the University of Cambridge.

It furthers the University's mission by disseminating knowledge in the pursuit of education, learning, and research at the highest international levels of excellence.

www.cambridge.org
Information on this title: www.cambridge.org/9781316613696
DOI: 10.1017/9781316675908

© Allan Greer 2018

First published 2018

Printed in the United States of America by Sheridan Books, Inc.

A catalogue record for this publication is available from the British Library.

Library of Congress Cataloging-in-Publication Data
NAMES: Greer, Allan, author.
TITLE: Property and dispossession : natives, empires and land in early modern North America / Allan Greer, McGill University.
DESCRIPTION: Cambridge ; New York, NY : Cambridge University Press, 2017. |
SERIES: Studies in North American Indian history | Includes bibliographical references and index.
IDENTIFIERS: LCCN 2017038384| ISBN 9781107160644 (Hardback : alk. paper) |
ISBN 9781316613696 (pbk. : alk. paper)
SUBJECTS: LCSH: Indians of North America–Land tenure–History. | Indian land transfers–United States–History. | Indians of North America–Government relations.
CLASSIFICATION: LCC E98.L3 G73 2017 | DDC 323.1197–DC23
LC record available at https://lccn.loc.gov/2017038384

ISBN 978-1-107-16064-4 Hardback
ISBN 978-1-316-61369-6 Paperback

to Kate

Contents

Maps

Illustrations

Acknowledgments

The research underpinning this book was made possible by grants from the Social Science and Humanities Research Council of Canada and the John Carter Brown Library, as well as by a generous fellowship from the John Simon Guggenheim Memorial Foundation. A Killam Fellowship from the Canada Council gave me time to write the manuscript. I'm deeply grateful. Thanks also to the Institut d'études avancées de Paris for a stimulating year as a fellow in residence.

Early in this project, I moved from the University of Toronto to McGill University. Both those great institutions were supportive of my work and my colleagues at both places helped me thrive. I also benefited from a one-year affiliation with the Centre d'études nord américaines at the École des hautes études en sciences sociales in Paris. A number of talented students at Toronto and McGill assisted with the research: Marie-France Barrette, Jennifer Bonnell, Fannie Dionne, Daniel Laxer, Chris Parsons, Renaud Séguin, Graham Splawski and Jonathan Weier. Mike LaMonica worked on illustrations and prepared the index.

I've had the good fortune to present my work to colleagues on various occasions and to get feedback that has helped me work through issues connected with the history of colonial property making. Thanks to all concerned at the Reves Center for International Study at the College of William and Mary; John Carter Brown Library; Harvard International Seminar on the History of the Atlantic World; University of New Brunswick; University of Toronto Legal History Seminar; Concordia University, Montreal; Early Modern Legal History Conference, Newberry Library, Chicago; University of Montreal; Contested Spaces in the Americas Symposium, McNeil Center, Philadelphia; University

College, Dublin; École des hautes études en sciences sociales, Paris; Atlantic World Workshop, New York University; Université du Québec à Montréal; McMaster University, Hamilton; Canada Seminar, Harvard University; French Colonial History Society; and "Property in the Making of the Portuguese Empire" workshop, Lisbon.

It was at one of these gatherings that I met Dr. Chantal Cramaussel of the Colegio de Michoacán. She told me, quite frankly, that the Mexican portion of my work (as it then stood) was overly reliant on English-language works. It was painful to admit, but my critic had a valid point. "Could you suggest some Mexican materials in Spanish?" I asked, hoping for an email with some references. Instead, a box arrived at my office a few weeks later packed with books, articles, photocopied chapters and documents, all of them hard if not impossible to find north of the Rio Grande. Muchas gracias Chantal! Your generosity made a big difference to the shape of this book. I wish I could relate the circumstances in which others helped me, but space constraints force me to simply list names: Miguel Aguilar Robledo, Ida Altman, Bernard Bailyn, Juliana Barr, Frances Berdan, John Bishop, Michael Blaakman, Elizabeth Blackmar, Rafe Blaufarb, Amy Bushnell, Colin Coates, Edward Countryman, Aileen Desbarats, Helen Dewar, Nick Everett, François Furstenberg, Jean-Philippe Garneau, Paul Grant-Costa, Jack Greene, Sally Hadden, Gilles Havard, Rebecca Horn, Michel Lavoie, Leonardo López Luján, Jean-François Lozier, Karen Marrero, Tim Mennel, Toby Morantz, Jeanette Neeson, Herbert J. Nickel, Jason Opal, Jean-François Palomino, Chris Rogers, Richard Ross, José Vicente Serrão, William Taylor, Cécile Vidal and Thomas Wien. My heartfelt thanks to all.

I gratefully acknowledge the helpful comments and corrections of those who read portions of the manuscript: Virginia Anderson, Elizabeth Blackmar, Catherine LeGrand, Leonardo López Luján, Daviken Studnicki-Gizbert and the late Daniel Vickers. Neal Salisbury read the whole work, made countless suggestions and corrections, offered encouragement and even gave his reluctant approval to my use of the neo-ethnonym "Ninnimissinuok." At Cambridge University Press, I'd like to thank editor Deborah Gershenowitz, as well as Kristina Deusch, Stephanie Sakson, Katherine Tengco-Barbaro and Ishwarya Mathavan.

Finally, a rather inadequate word of recognition for all the help and inspiration I've received from Kate Desbarats, my colleague and life partner: her historical knowledge and critical insight never cease to amaze me.

Chapter 7 is a revised version of "Commons and Enclosure in the Colonization of North America," *American Historical Review* 117 (April 2012): 365–86, while excerpts from "Dispossession in a Commercial Idiom: From Indian Deeds to Land Cession Treaties," in *Contested Spaces of Early America*, ed. Juliana Barr and Edward Countryman (Philadelphia: University of Pennsylvania Press, 2014), 69–92, have been incorporated into Chapters 6 and 10.

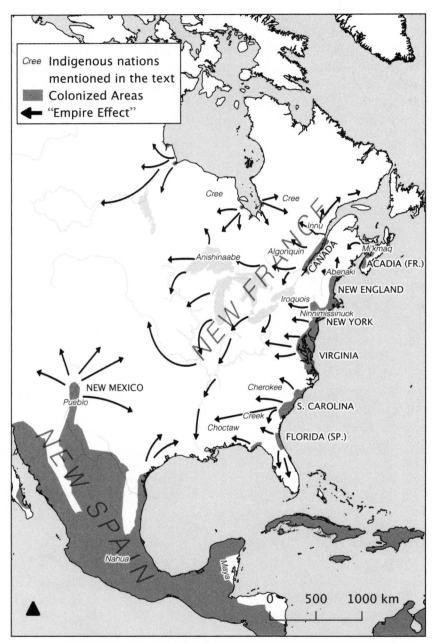

Legend:
- *Cree* Indigenous nations mentioned in the text
- Colonized Areas
- ← "Empire Effect"

Cree *Cree*

Innu

NEW FRANCE

Anishinaabe *Algonquin* *Mi'kmaq*

CANADA ACADIA (FR.)

Abenaki

NEW ENGLAND

Iroquois

Ninnimissinuok NEW YORK

VIRGINIA

NEW MEXICO

Pueblo *Cherokee*

S. CAROLINA

Creek

Choctaw FLORIDA (SP.)

NEW SPAIN

Nahua *Maya*

0 500 1000 km

MAP I.I Empires, colonies and indigenous nations, late seventeenth century

Introduction

Property and Colonization

To sum up, there everywhere appears to be an intimate link between the way in which nature is used and the way in which human beings themselves are used. However, whilst historians have given much thought to the path leading from ways of treating human beings to those of appropriating nature, researchers who have explored the opposite trajectory are still rare.

> Maurice Godelier, "Territory and Property in Some
> Pre-Capitalist Societies"[1]

Every established order tends to produce (to very different degrees and with very different means) the naturalization of its own arbitrariness ...

> Pierre Bourdieu, *Outline of a Theory of Practice*[2]

Parchment domains, leases and freeholds delimited by inky clauses, not by ancient hedges or boundary stones. His [Thomas Cromwell's] acres are notional acres, sources of income, sources of dissatisfaction in the small hours, when he wakes up and his mind explores their geography ... he thinks not of the freedom his holdings allow, but of the trampling intrusion of others, their easements and rights of way, their fences and vantage points, that allow them to impinge on his boundaries and interfere with his quiet possession of his future.

> Hilary Mantel, *Bring up the Bodies*[3]

This book proposes a new reading of the history of the colonization of North America and the dispossession of its indigenous peoples. Land,

[1] Maurice Godelier, *The Mental and the Material* (London: Verso, 1986), "Territory and Property in Some Pre-Capitalist Societies," 116–17.
[2] Pierre Bourdieu, *Outline of a Theory of Practice*, trans. Richard Nice (Cambridge: Cambridge University Press, 1977), 164.
[3] Hilary Mantel, *Bring up the Bodies* (London: HarperCollins, 2012), 102.

territory and property are its central focus and it deploys the concept of "property formation" to consider the ways in which Europeans and their Euro-American descendants remade New World space as they laid claim to the continent's resources, extended the reach of empire and established polities and jurisdictions for themselves. It examines the cases of Mexico (New Spain), New England and Canada (New France) from the sixteenth to the eighteenth century. This selection of zones of colonization shines a comparative spotlight not only on the three principal European empires active in North America, but also on indigenous nations ranging from what are sometimes referred to as agricultural state societies (the Nahua peoples of Mexico), to semi-sedentary villagers (New England Algonquians) to nomadic hunter-gatherers (the Innu of Quebec). Although dispossession of one sort or another was their ultimate fate, these native peoples were not pure victims and accordingly they appear in this account as actors. As Chapter 2 will show, each had its own complex traditions governing territoriality and property, and as later parts of the book reveal, those who survived the colonizers' onslaught had a hand in shaping the course of colonial property formation.

Property and Dispossession challenges a set of assumptions, powerfully entrenched since the time of the Enlightenment, that sees property as a single thing, the hallmark of civilization and modernity.[4] Europeans of the early modern period had "it," according to this view, Native Americans did not, and colonization meant installing this mechanism of progress on New World soil where it had previously been unknown. Historians who would not dream of endorsing such ideological justifications of imperialism still tend to take a rather naive view of property, as though colonists arrived from Europe with a system of property that was somehow complete, fully formed and fundamentally in line with that of the historian's own time. In place of the on/off binary conception of property (and its close cousin, the linear scale leading from "weak" to "strong" property), my book highlights the diversity of indigenous and Euro-American property systems in the early modern period, bringing out their contingent and protean qualities, not to mention their occasional incoherence. It tries to take all forms of landed property seriously on their

---

[4] Emer de Vattel, *Le droit des gens ou principes de la loi naturelle appliqués à la conduite et aux affaires des nations et des souverains*, 4 vols. (London [Neuchatel]: n.p., 1758), vol. 1: 78–79, 195–96; Adam Ferguson, *An Essay on the History of Civil Society* (Edinburgh: A. Kincaid & J. Bell, 1767), 112–64; Robert A. Williams, *Linking Arms Together: American Indian Treaty Visions of Law and Peace, 1600–1800* (New York: Oxford University Press, 1997), 146 n 18.

own terms, including the indigenous American as well as the European-derived versions, and aims at a historicized, cross-cultural understanding of New World property formation.

My objective has been to tell this story without reifying "property" or "land," without naturalizing current arrangements and without falling into whiggish assumptions about progress. Undercurrents in settler-national memory portray the European takeover of America as a vast modernizing operation: a new nation was born and the engines of economic development switched on the moment natives were displaced. Contemporary historiography generally avoids such celebratory readings, but where landed property is concerned, there is still an unreflexive tendency to equate colonization and modernization.[5] A leftist variant on this metanarrative of progress insists on an association between colonization and capitalism stretching back to the earliest encounters with the New World and its inhabitants. "Colonists were moved to transform the soil by a property system that taught them to treat land as capital," declares one influential study of early New England.[6] A more wide-ranging work puts it more strongly: "The form of colonialism that the Indigenous peoples of North America have experienced was modern from the beginning: the expansion of European corporations, backed by government armies, into foreign areas, with subsequent expropriation of lands and resources."[7] One consistent theme of this book will be to emphasize the very limited role of developments associated with capitalism, private property and modernity in the early colonization of North America. Moreover, as Chapter 7 argues,

---

[5] Usually an unspoken assumption structuring historical accounts, that interpretation is occasionally expressed baldly, most often in popular works. See, for example, Tom Bethell, *The Noblest Triumph: Property and Prosperity through the Ages* (New York: St. Martin's Press, 1998); Niall Ferguson, *Civilization: The West and the Rest* (London: Allen Lane, 2011), ch. 3, "Property," 96–140; Andro Linklater, *Owning the Earth: The Transforming History of Land Ownership* (New York: Bloomsbury, 2013). Faith in the wonder-working propensity of property, whether linked to colonization or not, is particularly strong in the field of economic history. See, for example, Douglas C. North and Robert Paul Thomas, *The Rise of the Western World: A New Economic History* (Cambridge: Cambridge University Press, 1973); David S. Landes, *The Wealth and Poverty of Nations: Why Some Are So Rich and Some So Poor* (New York: W. W. Norton, 1998), 31–36.

[6] William Cronon, *Changes in the Land: Indians, Colonists, and the Ecology of New England* (New York: Hill and Wang, 1983), 77.

[7] Roxanne Dunbar-Ortiz, *An Indigenous Peoples' History of the United States* (Boston: Beacon Press, 2014), 6. See also Howard Zinn, *A People's History of the United States: 1492–Present*, revised ed. (New York: HarperCollins, 2003), 16; Ellen Meiksins Wood, *Empire of Capital* (London: Verso, 2003), 73–101.

natives were dispossessed as much by the settler commons as by any sort of colonial version of the Enclosure movement. Though rapacity and exploitation are very much part of the history of empire and colonization, the establishment of settler tenures revolved more around the requirements of residence and subsistence than of profit. While setting the pattern in many respects for later centuries, early modern colonization remained, if I may put it this way, more "early" than "modern."

This book is about the practices by which settlers came to exert control over particular portions of the land at the expense of indigenous peoples. Scholars working in an intellectual history tradition have already examined, with great rigor and thoroughness, the various legal doctrines, "theories of empire" and "ceremonies of possession" by which Europeans expressed their qualms and asserted their justifications for seizing overseas territories.[8] The emphasis here will instead be on concrete on-the-ground actions, actions that had the effect of instituting colonial property for both settlers and surviving indigenous populations. Of course, it is not so easy to concentrate exclusively on what some have called the "history of the real":[9] we cannot escape discursive and conceptual issues merely by dedicating ourselves to the study of practice. The vocabulary evoked here, beginning with the key terms "property" and "land," raises all sorts of questions of definition. To project these words, loaded as they are with contemporary assumptions and ideals, back into the seventeenth century

---

[8] Highlights from a vast literature: L. C. Green and Olive Patricia Dickason, *The Law of Nations and the New World* (Edmonton: University of Alberta Press, 1988); Anthony Pagden, *Lords of All the World: Ideologies of Empire in Spain, Britain and France c. 1500–c. 1800* (New Haven, Conn.: Yale University Press, 1995); Patricia Seed, *Ceremonies of Possession in Europe's Conquest of the New World, 1492–1640* (New York: Cambridge University Press, 1995); David Armitage, *The Ideological Origins of the British Empire* (Cambridge: Cambridge University Press, 2000); Patricia Seed, *American Pentimento: The Invention of Indians and the Pursuit of Riches* (Minneapolis: University of Minnesota Press, 2001); Paul G. McHugh, *Aboriginal Societies and the Common Law: A History of Sovereignty, Status, and Self-Determination* (Oxford: Oxford University Press, 2004); Brian Slattery, "Paper Empires: The Legal Dimensions of French and English Ventures in North America," in *Despotic Dominion: Property Rights in British Settler Societies*, ed. John McLaren, A. R. Buck, and Nancy E. Wright (Vancouver: UBC Press, 2005), 50–78; Anthony Pagden, "Law, Colonization, Legitimation, and the European Background," in *The Cambridge History of Law in America*, vol. 1: *Early America, 1580–1815*, ed. M. Grossberg and Christopher L. Tomlins (New York: Cambridge University Press, 2008), vol. 1: 1–31.

[9] See David Gary Shaw, "A Way with Animals," *History and Theory* 52 (2013): 11. "At this moment," writes Shaw, "history and theory have generally been turning away from the symbolic and the linguistic. Trends are toward sensation and presence, to materiality and space, to the body and its affect."

is to court conceptual disaster. (By way of illustration, we might note that the word "propriété" rarely occurred in connection with land in the French language at that time, while in English people usually spoke of property *in*, rather than property *of*, a piece of land.)[10] But even in the context of today's world, the language of property is anything but transparent. Those who have thought deeply about the topic show that the everyday discourse of property is rife with metaphors, reification, and complex and contradictory assumptions.[11] This chapter will have more to say about the general conceptual problem of property in land and the book as a whole might be read as a set of further reflections on that theme. Meanwhile, another key word, "colonization," needs to be addressed, as it will be used here in a particular way.

EMPIRES, COLONIZATION AND LAND

"The actual geographical possession of land," wrote Edward Said, "is what empire in the final analysis is all about."[12] Where European empires of the early modern world are concerned, this is not a strictly accurate statement. The navigators who ventured across the seas in the "Age of Discovery" were generally more interested in controlling trade, plundering treasure, extending the reach of Christendom and enhancing the glory of their respective monarchs than they were in appropriating territory. As Lauren Benton and others have established, empire in this period was as much about water – trade routes, ports and estuaries – as it was about land. Portuguese, Dutch and, later, English and French fought to control the sea lanes leading to the spice islands and beyond; they each used their superior naval firepower to force Asian rulers to open their ports to trade and to close them to rivals; and they tried to legitimate their monopoly claims in terms of a nascent international law that focused as much on the sea as the land.[13] Their territorial claims along the coasts of Africa and Asia rarely extended

---

[10] G. E. Aylmer, "The Meaning and Definition of 'Property' in Seventeenth-Century England," *Past & Present*, no. 86 (1980): 87–97.

[11] Thomas C. Grey, "The Disintegration of Property," in *Property*, ed. J. Roland Pennock and John W. Chapman (New York: New York University Press, 1980), 69–85; Alain Pottage, "Instituting Property," *Oxford Journal of Legal Studies* 18 (1998): 331–44.

[12] Edward W. Said, *Culture and Imperialism* (New York: Knopf, 1994), 78.

[13] Lauren A. Benton, *A Search for Sovereignty: Law and Geography in European Empires, 1400–1900* (New York: Cambridge University Press, 2010). See also Sanjay Subrahmanyam, *The Portuguese Empire in Asia, 1500–1700: A Political and Economic History*, 2nd ed. (Chichester, UK: Wiley-Blackwell, 2012); Romain Bertrand, *L'histoire à parts égales: récits d'une rencontre Orient-Occident, XVIe-XVIIe siècle* (Paris: Points, 2014).

beyond isolated fortified ports. America was a somewhat different story: beginning at the time of Columbus, Spaniards used ruthless violence to establish control over the large islands of the Caribbean before invading and conquering the Aztec Empire of Mesoamerica and then the Inca Empire of the Andes. Even where Spanish arms prevailed, however, "possession of the land" remained qualified and uncertain (see Chapter 4). Moreover, the largest part of the New World, including coastal areas exposed to the Atlantic, long remained unconquered; through the sixteenth and much of the seventeenth centuries, Europeans probed and traded and established coastal strongholds, but they did not manage to seize and hold very much territory. On sea and on land, the vigorously expansive European overseas empires of the early modern period are best envisioned as webs and nodes rather than as solid blocks of territory.[14]

In place of "empire," Edward Said might better have inserted the word "colonization," for that is indeed a historical process intimately bound up with real "possession of land." The empire/colony distinction, critical for what follows, needs to be highlighted. Influenced by the history of the "high imperialism" of the late nineteenth century, casual discourse tends to confuse the concepts of empires/imperialism on the one hand with colonies/colonization on the other. Colonies tend to be seen basically as subordinate polities, subject to the sovereign authority of a distant imperial metropole: colonization, from this point of view, suggests the subjection of one country to the exploitive rule of another. Put differently, colonies are often viewed as the territorial units of which an empire is composed. But things were never that tidy, even during the heyday of modern imperialism,[15] and certainly not in the sixteenth and seventeenth centuries. Rather than being composed of territorially defined building blocks, overseas empires then were essentially tentacular entities, unbounded whether by sea or by land. They were opportunistic, employing strongholds, fortified ports and enclaves of settlement to influence and lay claim to much broader, but ill-defined, areas over which they exercised varying degrees and different kinds of influence.[16] Colonization was an aspect of empire building, but it was not the same thing as empire building. Certainly, colonies did not define the spatial extent of empire.

---

[14] Benton, *A Search for Sovereignty*.
[15] Ann Laura Stoler, "On Degrees of Imperial Sovereignty," *Public Culture* 18 (2006): 125–46.
[16] Benton, *A Search for Sovereignty*. See also Charles Maier, *Once Within Borders: Territories of Power, Wealth, and Belonging since 1500* (Cambridge, Mass.: Harvard University Press, 2017), 14.

In European languages of the period, "colonization" and its associated vocabulary referred more to demography and agriculture than to political institutions. More so than its English cognate, the French term *colonisation* had (and still has) a specifically agrarian sense, denoting the appropriation of land and its transformation for agricultural purposes. In seventeenth-century English, it was more common to speak of "planting" overseas settlements: what the French referred to as *"une colonie,"* the English called a "plantation"; colonists were typically known as "planters." Over time, "colony" would acquire more of a political sense in English (see Chapter 6). From its earliest stages, however, American colonization north of Mexico was associated with the physical act of tilling the soil to bring it into agricultural production. "Planters" and *"colons"* could be the actual workers in these operations or they could be members of the elite who employed others to do the work, but their use of the land is fundamental to the definition of "colonization" in this period. The Spaniards, with their emphasis on conquering indigenous nations and relying on their tribute and labor, construed colonization somewhat differently. Those who came to dominate New Spain rejected the appellation *"colón"* because of its association with manual labor. They instead wanted to be called *conquistadores* if they had participated in the first wave of invasion, or as *"pobladores"* if they came later; many were proud to be known as *conquistadores/pobladores*, claiming the honor of both subjugating and settling the country.[17] Different, but not utterly different, from English and French discourses, the Spanish language of colonization also evoked the establishment of European settlers on the ground and the cultivation of the soil.[18] Planting people, planting crops and building homes for enduring habitation: these were essential elements of colonization and they implied a deep hold over circumscribed territory in a way that "empire" did not.

The Americas gradually emerged over the early modern period as the one field of European imperial activity where colonization came to predominate.[19] After an initial surge through the Antilles, Mesoamerica and the Andes in the decades following Columbus's voyages, Spanish

---

[17] J. H. Elliott, *Empires of the Atlantic World: Britain and Spain in America* (New Haven, Conn.: Yale University Press, 2006), 9, 121.

[18] On metaphors of gardening in Spanish and English discourses of colonization, see Jorge Cañizares-Esguerra, *The Puritan Conquistadors: Iberianizing the Atlantic, 1550–1700* (Stanford, Calif.: Stanford University Press, 2006), 178–214.

[19] There were a number of – rather small – European overseas settlements in the period that form exceptions to this generalization: the Canaries and other Atlantic islands, Angola

territorial dominion met limits, imposed mainly by indigenous resistance, and its march slowed. Meanwhile, the Portuguese were settling along the coast of Brazil and beginning their probes into the heart of South America. Later, English, French and Dutch colonists would carve out settlements on the shores of North America; here too, imperial penetration and the indirect effects of the European presence raced into the interior, far ahead of actual colonization. In eastern North America, as in Brazil, the patches of colonized territory grew ever larger; over the course of the nineteenth century, these would encompass large portions of the western half of the continent; more recent times saw progressive penetration into Alaska and northern Canada, though the process of colonization has never been complete. Meanwhile, European colonization was claiming other portions of the world: in South Africa, Algeria and other small parts of Africa and in Australia, New Zealand and Hawaii settlers established themselves, imposed a colonial property regime and dispossessed natives.[20] Almost all of this expanded campaign of colonization, including the occupation of western North America, occurred after the end of what American historians call the "colonial period." The early modern colonization of North America therefore stands as an archetypal model that, notwithstanding all its peculiar (from a modern point of view) characteristics, set the pattern for the larger, global land grabs of later centuries.

For centuries, the greater part of North America remained in the possession of indigenous nations; from the time of Cortés to that of the American Revolution, colonization spread rather slowly.[21] However, that does not mean that natives were unaffected by the European enclaves in their midst. Historians are increasingly coming to grips with what might be called the "empire effect," which is to say the profoundly destabilizing impact of imperial penetration that ran far beyond the zones of conquest and settlement. Here the empire/colonization distinction becomes crucial.

---

and the Cape of Good Hope, as well as the Philippines and some small Indian Ocean islands.

[20] John C. Weaver, *The Great Land Rush and the Making of the Modern World, 1650–1900* (Montreal and Kingston: McGill-Queen's University Press, 2003); James Belich, *Replenishing the Earth: The Settler Revolution and the Rise of the Anglo-World, 1783–1939* (Oxford: Oxford University Press, 2009).

[21] Pekka Hämäläinen, "The Shapes of Power: Indians, Europeans, and North American Worlds from the Seventeenth to the Nineteenth Century," in *Contested Spaces of Early America*, ed. Juliana Barr and Edward Countryman (Philadelphia: University of Pennsylvania Press, 2014), 33–38.

Exploratory probes such as Hernando de Soto's *entrada* into the southeast (1539–42) or Jacques Cartier's contemporaneous expeditions up the St. Lawrence River (1534–41) touched off major transformations across a wide indigenous landscape, even though they did not establish lasting colonies.[22] Later, when Spanish, French and English became established on the coastal margins of North America, the indirect effects of their presence rippled across half a continent. Epidemics of Old World origin decimated whole regions. Just as important, trade spread European products far and wide, though always unevenly. Guns and other weapons of war gave a decisive military advantage to those who could gain direct access to colonial traders; the general effect was to exacerbate conflict and to make it much more deadly. The destructive effects of war and disease produced inland "shatter zones," most notably in the Southeast, where raiders armed by South Carolina traders attacked their neighbors and sold them into slavery.[23] The European presence on the edges of the continent created conditions that fostered the emergence of militaristic indigenous empires in the interior, such as those of the Commanches, the Sioux and the Iroquois.[24] In the midst of death and devastation, the "empire effect" gave birth to new empires, though even more than was the case with European empires, these aimed to dominate peoples rather than territories. For native societies, European empires could be hugely consequential even where they did not rest on "the actual geographical possession of land."

Capitalizing on the mayhem created by the empire effect, the French constructed a vast inland empire in North America (Chapter 5) and other

<hr>

[22] Robbie Franklyn Ethridge, *From Chicaza to Chickasaw: The European Invasion and the Transformation of the Mississippian World, 1540–1715* (Chapel Hill: University of North Carolina Press, 2010), ch. 3, "The Aftermath of Soto, ca. 1541–1650"; Bruce G. Trigger, *Natives and Newcomers: Canada's "Heroic Age" Reconsidered* (Kingston and Montreal: McGill-Queen's University Press, 1985), ch. 3, "The Approach of the Europeans, 1497–1600," 111–163.

[23] R. Brian Ferguson and Neil L. Whitehead, "The Violent Edge of Empire," in *War in the Tribal Zone: Expanding States and Indigenous Warfare*, ed. R. Brian Ferguson and Neil L. Whitehead (Santa Fe, N.M.: School of American Research Press, 1992), 1–30; Tom Holm, "American Indian Warfare: The Cycles of Conflict and the Militarization of Native North America," in *A Companion to American Indian History*, ed. Philip J. Deloria and Neal Salisbury (Oxford: Blackwell, 2004), 154–72; Robbie Ethridge, "Introduction: Mapping the Mississippian Shatter Zone," in *Mapping the Mississippian Shatter Zone: The Colonial Indian Slave Trade and Regional Instability in the American South*, ed. Robbie Ethridge and Sheri M. Shuck-Hall (Lincoln: University of Nebraska Press, 2009), 1–62.

[24] Hämäläinen, "The Shapes of Power," 31–68.

imperial powers did likewise, though on a more modest scale. Colonists also made use of roaming herds of cattle and pigs to add another layer to the imperial effect, undermining indigenous subsistence and so paving the way for future colonization. It was through colonization itself, however, that effective European rule was established and settlers were placed in possession of land previously controlled by indigenous peoples.

In spatial terms, dispossession is really the essence of colonization: colonists from Europe and their progeny displacing the original holders of the land. We need to introduce some nuances, however, for dispossession was never undifferentiated, nor was it total. Some scholars speak of an "eliminationist" logic driving settler colonialism toward the utter destruction of natives who stand in its way,[25] and though there are ample instances of deadly violence and forced migration in the annals of colonial North America, such "ethnic cleansing" is not the whole story. In Mexico, where the term "settler colonialism" hardly applies, the thrust of colonization as examined in Chapter 4 was in the direction of incorporating, rather than eliminating, indigenous peoples and lands. Natives also had a place within the English and French colonies, though on a much smaller scale than in Spanish-ruled America. Forming indigenous enclaves within the European enclaves within the larger indigenous/imperial spaces that surrounded them, the "praying Indian" settlements of New England and the mission villages of New France were more than a merely residual presence. Even as they experienced the *imperium* of the colonial power, these communities did their best to maintain a margin of cultural and jurisdictional autonomy, fashioning a colony within a colony. In all cases, indigenous people lived under separate jurisdiction and they held their lands under their own tenures, different from that of the surrounding European settlements. "Indian land" and settler land emerged as legally quite distinct forms of property. Colonial property formation therefore had a dual thrust: in creating property for colonists and property for natives it effectively defined the boundaries, social and political as much as territorial, dividing colonists from "Indians."

For heuristic purposes, I am proposing a rather schematic set of distinctions here: territories that are colonial or indigenous or indigenous-but-subject-to-empire-effect; indigenous people who either live independently outside the colonized zones or who occupy "Indian" lands within them. Such an approach may seem to run counter to major

---

[25] Patrick Wolfe, "Settler Colonialism and the Elimination of the Native," *Journal of Genocide Research* 8 (2006): 387–409.

currents of contemporary historiography emphasizing borderlands, indeterminacy, "people in between," the mixing of cultures and "races." Viewed up close, especially in contested areas but not only there, the basic spatial distinctions between zones of colonization and zones of imperial penetration tend to break down, as do attempts to trace a clear boundary between colonizers and colonized peoples. Instead, what so much recent work reveals is a fascinating cauldron of shifting identities, multiple agents and undefined geographies. I hope it will become clear in what follows that I have no quarrel with fine-grained research that brings out the rich variety of lived experiences in the encounter/clash of Europeans and native Americans: to the contrary. At the same time, I see value in a zooming-out strategy that attempts to discern some basic patterns in the spatial dynamics of colonialism and property formation.

THE PROBLEM OF PROPERTY IN LAND

So pervasive is the language of ownership in today's society – my car, his shirt, her idea, their backyard – that it may not be initially obvious how strange the idea of property in land really is.[26] When it comes to property

---

[26] Some important theoretical works on the concept of property: A. Irving Hallowell, "The Nature and Function of Property as a Social Institution," in *Culture and Experience* (New York: Schocken, 1967), 236–49; Robert Nozick, *Anarchy, State, and Utopia* (New York: Basic Books, 1974); C. B. Macpherson, "Capitalism and the Changing Concept of Property," in *Feudalism, Capitalism and Beyond*, ed. Eugene Kamenka and Ronald Stanley Neale (London: Edward Arnold, 1975), 105–124; James Tully, *A Discourse on Property: John Locke and His Adversaries* (Cambridge: Cambridge University Press, 1980); Alan Ryan, *Property and Political Theory* (Oxford: Blackwell, 1984); Richard A. Epstein, *Takings: Private Property and the Power of Eminent Domain* (Cambridge, Mass.: Harvard University Press, 1985); Alan Ryan, *Property* (Minneapolis: University of Minnesota Press, 1987); Jeremy Waldron, *The Right to Private Property* (Oxford: Oxford University Press, 1988); Laura S. Underkuffler, "On Property: An Essay," *Yale Law Journal* 100 (1990): 127–49; Robert C. Ellickson, "Property in Land," *Yale Law Journal* 102 (1992): 1315–400; Carol M. Rose, *Property and Persuasion: Essays on the History, Theory, and Rhetoric of Ownership* (Boulder, Colo.: Westview Press, 1994); J. E. Penner, *The Idea of Property in Law* (Oxford: Oxford University Press, 1997); C. M. Hann, ed., *Property Relations: Renewing the Anthropological Tradition* (Cambridge: Cambridge University Press, 1998); Marilyn Strathern, *Property, Substance, and Effect: Anthropological Essays on Persons and Things* (New Brunswick, N.J.: Athlone Press, 1999); Robert Castel, *Propriété privée, propriété sociale, propriété de soi: entretiens sur la construction de l'individu moderne* (Paris: Fayard, 2001); Rosa Congost, "Property Rights and Historical Analysis: What Rights? What History?," *Past & Present*, no. 181 (2003): 73–106; Alain Testart, "Propriété et non-propriété de la terre: l'illusion de la propriété collective archaïque (1re partie)," *Études Rurales* (2003): 209–42; Laura Brace, *The Politics of Property: Labour, Freedom, and Belonging*

claims, land is not like concrete objects ("chattels" or "movable property" in the language of the law). It cannot be passed from hand to hand in barter transactions, nor can it be relocated. It is inextricably attached to a specific environment. Water runs over its surface and collects underground; weeds, insects and fires cross its boundaries; the trees that grow on a lot and the buildings erected upon it affect the currents of air and the exposure to sun of neighboring properties; access to roads, waterways and utilities necessitates arrangements that connect different properties and common spaces. Ground may also have sacred significance: even in our modern secular society landowners are not allowed unrestricted control over buried human remains or ancient artifacts found on their property. Land cannot help but be part of a landscape that has natural, social and spiritual dimensions. My land cannot belong to me exclusively, simply because it cannot be fully detached from other lands.[27] And what about this "me" who claims the land? Can I really be completely disconnected for ownership purposes from my spouse, my family, my community and nation? Since land is for all practical purposes eternal, and human life is finite, property in land implies some sort of inheritance arrangements and therefore it implicates lineages as well as individuals. At least that is the case where the owner is a human person, but in today's world, much land is owned by corporations or by offshoots of the state. The superficial view of property as a relationship between a single owning subject and an owned object ("I own this land") is deceptive in several respects. Though it sometimes appears to refer to a relationship between a person and a thing, property is actually very much a social phenomenon. In Karl Marx's pithy phrase, "An isolated individual could no more have property in land and soil than he could speak."[28]

Of landed property in the sixteenth and seventeenth centuries, we might say, in very general terms, that it consisted of multiple claims to the

---

(New York: Palgrave Macmillan, 2004); Peter Garnsey, *Thinking about Property: From Antiquity to the Age of Revolution* (Cambridge: Cambridge University Press, 2007); Margaret Davies, *Property and Critique: Meanings, Histories and Theories* (Abingdon, UK: Routledge-Cavendish, 2008); Nicole Graham, *Lawscape: Property, Environment and Law* (Abingdon: Routledge, 2011).

[27] For concrete cases illustrating the inherent impossibility of absolute property rights, see Eric T. Freyfogle, *The Land We Share: Private Property and the Common Good* (Washington, D.C.: Island Press, 2003), 11–36.

[28] Karl Marx, *Grundrisse*, as quoted in Godelier, "Territory and Property in Some Pre-Capitalist Societies," 84–85. Cf. Wesley N. Hohfeld, "Fundamental Legal Conceptions as Applied in Judicial Reasoning," *Yale Law Journal* 23 (1913): 28–57.

resources of a given territory; that it was bound up in lineage and marital relations and, more generally, embedded in specific societies;[29] that it delineated surface areas in a variety of imprecise ways, none of which resembled current techniques of geometric mapping; that it was not readily salable. These observations apply to landed property in indigenous North America just as much as in Western Europe at the time of initial colonization. For all their fundamental similarities, however, European and Native American approaches to property diverged in one important respect: the former tried to reduce property to a set of formal rules, "the law," while the latter, on the whole, did not.[30] Chapter 2 will look more closely at indigenous property practices in select regions of North America; here there is room only for a brief overview of theories and practices of landed property in the European context.

Ancient Rome has to be the starting point, for Roman law has for millennia exercised outsize influence over Western understandings of landed property. Central to Roman law were the powers and privileges of ownership: *dominium*. "Conceptually," writes Peter Birks, "ownership was absolute: distinct, singular, and exclusive."[31] A free man could own objects, domestic animals, slaves or lands; in theory, he could use any of these as he saw fit, sell them, rent them or offer them as gages of repayment for a debt. The "Twelve Tables," dating back to the early republican period, give the head of household extensive power to dispose as he pleased of objects, slaves, a wife, sons (including the right to sell or kill the latter), as well as land. In a society dominated by the institutions of slavery and the patriarchal household, the emphasis was on the power of the proprietor, normally a free adult male.[32]

[29] On the socially "embedded" nature of landed property, see Karl Polanyi, "The Economy as Instituted Process," in *Trade and Market in the Early Empires: Economies in History and Theory*, ed. Karl Polanyi, Conrad M. Arensberg and Harry W. Pearson (New York: Free Press, 1957): 243–70; Karl Polanyi, *The Great Transformation: The Political and Economic Origins of Our Time* (Boston: Beacon Press, 1957), 178; Rosa Congost and Rui Santos, "Working Out the Frame: From Formal Institutions to the Social Contexts of Property," in *Contexts of Property: The Social Embeddedness of Property Rights to Land in Europe in Historical Perspective* (Turnhout, Belgium: Brepols Publishers, 2011), 16–17.

[30] Timothy Mitchell argues that the law of property is an abstraction that serves to disguise the origin of property rights in the arbitrary and violent transfer of control over land, notably in a modern colonial context. Timothy Mitchell, *Rule of Experts: Egypt, Techno-Politics, Modernity* (Berkeley: University of California Press, 2002), 1–15.

[31] Peter Birks, "Roman Law Concept of Dominium and the Idea of Absolute Ownership," *Acta Juridica* 7 (1985): 31.

[32] A historian of New World slavery, Orlando Patterson, has made the suggestive point that the "hard" property rights built into Roman law were connected to the prominence of

A central characteristic of Roman law contributed to its reputation for rationality and coherence: it made no distinction in principle between land and other forms of property. When goods were sold under early Roman law, the transaction involved a formal handing over of the physical object (*mancipatio*), but where land was concerned the transfer was, of necessity, metaphorical.[33] In this and in other respects, the legal identity of landed and movable property could be maintained only symbolically. Various servitudes applied only to land: for example, *iter* (the right to cross another's land), the duty to maintain a wall supporting a neighbor's roof, the prohibition against erecting buildings that affected someone else's exposure to light.[34] Such servitudes, inescapable consequences of the fact that owned lands are always situated within and have an effect on a wider environment, had the effect of restricting an owner's control over his property and of differentiating land from other forms of property in everyday life. Consequently, we have to understand the commitment to unrestricted ownership, and the equation of land and other property objects, as a Roman ideal rather than as a description of actual practices of property.

With the so-called barbarian invasions and the fall of Rome, Roman law faded into the background in Western Europe, and along with it the notion that land should be configured as the appendage of a singular owning subject. Among the pastoralist invaders, land holdings tended to be provisional and they were attached more to a family than to an individual; wives and female heirs generally counted for more than was the case among the Romans. When it came to passing land from generation to generation, the *pater familias* was dethroned; across much of Europe during the Middle Ages, a man could bequeath movable objects by means of a will, but land belonged after his death to his widow and children.[35]

---

slavery in the Roman Empire. The aspiration toward absolute power over humans, he writes, led to a corresponding desire for absolute power over land. Orlando Patterson, *Slavery and Social Death: A Comparative Study* (Cambridge, Mass.: Harvard University Press, 1982), 29–32.

[33] Alan Watson, *The Law of the Ancient Romans* (Dallas, Tex.: Southern Methodist University Press, 1970), 50–51. See also David Pugsley, *The Roman Law of Property and Obligations* (Cape Town: Juta, 1972).

[34] Watson, *The Law of Property in the Later Roman Republic*, 176–202; Alan Watson, *Roman Law and Comparative Law* (Athens: University of Georgia Press, 1991), 49–50; Max Radin, "Fundamental Concepts of the Roman Law," *California Law Review* 13 (1925): 210–11.

[35] Jean Imbert, *Histoire du droit privé*, 8th ed. (Paris: Presses universitaires de France, 1996), 26. This situation was partially reversed in England with the passage of the Statute of Wills in 1540.

Meanwhile, peasant communities across Europe were developing tenure customs that blended individual allotments with collective practices (open fields, commons, gleaning) that seem to be the antithesis of Roman *dominium*.[36] Feudal lordships added further layers of property, combining both "benefice," the right to draw revenues, and jurisdiction, the right to judge. Landlordism and judicial authority largely coincided in the Middle Ages. Marc Bloch summed up the complexities of medieval land law in his classic work, *Feudal Society*:

> For nearly all land and a great many human beings were burdened at this time with a multiplicity of obligations differing in their nature, but all apparently of equal importance. None implied that fixed proprietary exclusiveness which belonged to the conception of ownership in Roman law. The tenant who – from father to son, as a rule – ploughs the land and gathers in the crop; his immediate lord, to whom he pays dues and who, in certain circumstances, can resume possession of the land; the lord of the lord, and so on, right up the feudal scale – how many persons there are who can say, each with as much justification as the other, "That is my field!" Even this is an understatement. For the ramifications extended horizontally as well as vertically and account should be taken of the village community, which normally recovered the use of the whole of its agricultural land as soon as it was cleared of crops; of the tenant's family, without whose consent the property could not be alienated; and of the families of successive lords.[37]

In the Middle Ages, people "held" land, as opposed to owning it; they claimed property *in* a certain plot rather than the property *of* it; and it was only with the greatest difficulty that land could be sold. In such cases, it was not ownership but rather *seisin* that changed hands. Toward the late Middle Ages, English lawyers developed a system of conveyancing called "livery of seisin," which left aside questions of ultimate ownership and simply transferred existing rights of possession.[38]

In the late medieval and early modern period, Roman law began to make a comeback, at least in the realm of theory. With the rise of law as a learned profession, jurists began to search for consistent principles on

---

[36] Jerome Blum, "The European Village as Community: Origins and Functions," *Agricultural History* 45 (1971): 157–78.

[37] Marc Bloch, *Feudal Society*, trans. L. A. Manyon (London: Routledge & Kegan Paul, 1961), 116. Note that the words "the property" in the last sentence of this quotation is an imperfect translation of the French term "le bien"; "estate" would come closer to the author's meaning.

[38] William Searle Holdsworth, *An Historical Introduction to the Land Law* (Oxford: Clarendon Press, 1927), 110. See also Bloch, *Feudal Society*, 115; A. W. B. Simpson, *A History of the Land Law* (Oxford: Clarendon Press, 1961), 35; David J. Seipp, "The Concept of Property in the Early Common Law," *Law and History Review* 12 (1994): 29–91.

which to ground a rational and supra-regional understanding of law.[39]
Where property was concerned, the abstract doctrine of *dominium*
appeared as an attractive antidote to the tangled and variable property
practices then prevailing across Europe. The impulse to institute a uniform
and rational legal order, one that assimilated land with other forms of
property, one that reinforced the prerogatives of a single owner and that
facilitated buying and selling, found powerful supporters; princes and royal
ministers were inclined to favor the juridical unification of their realms,
entrepreneurs and many profit-hungry aristocrats detected opportunities
in a regime where land might be figured more as a commodity. Yet the
layered claims of communal customs and feudal lordship could not simply
be swept away; peasants as much as seigneurs tended to react ferociously
to rationalizing measures that threatened their respective entitlements.

The Roman law revival had its greatest impact in Mediterranean
countries such as the kingdom of Castile, where a legal code proclaimed
in 1268, the *Siete Partidas*, used the language of *dominium* as though
every piece of land had a proprietor, with unclaimed territory belonging
to the state. In the real world of early modern Spain, however, unrestricted individual ownership of land was rare. Spain stood out in the
European context as the kingdom par excellence of public lands, municipal commons and extensive grazing privileges.[40] France was not juridic-
ally integrated until the Revolution, but regional customary laws were
consolidated and codified in the sixteenth century in a Roman law–
inspired movement of reform and rationalization. Faced with the bewildering array of feudal claims on the land, French legal experts tried to
retrieve a Roman concept of ownership by pretending that all such claims
could be understood as either "*dominium directum*" – the landlord's
title – or "*dominium utile*" – the vassal's right to use the land.[41] Meanwhile, on the ground, seigneurs in early modern France were doing their
best (encouraged perhaps by the theory of *dominium*) to reinforce their
control over the land and its revenues, encroaching on village commons,
expanding demesnes and leasing land to farmers and sharecroppers.

---

[39] Clifford R. Backman, *The Worlds of Medieval Europe*, 2nd ed. (Oxford: Oxford University Press, 2009), 298–302.

[40] See Chapter 7. Spanish commons remained extensive even in more recent centuries.
Francisco J. Beltrán Tapia, "Social and Environmental Filters to Market Incentives: The
Persistence of Common Land in Nineteenth-Century Spain," *Journal of Agrarian Change*
15 (2015): 239–60.

[41] Imbert, *Histoire du droit privé*, 37; Perry Anderson, *Lineages of the Absolutist State*
(London: NLB, 1974), 25.

Many historians find evidence of growing "agrarian capitalism," operating largely within rather than against existing feudal institutions, in the centuries preceding the Revolution.[42] And yet, notwithstanding the revival of Roman law and the inroads of profit-driven agriculture, France remained a country of peasant communities and aristocratic overlords, one where property in land still consisted of multiple overlapping claims, where rights of *retrait* gave families and seigneurs the ability to annul land sales, and where rural *communes* still regulated the agricultural practices of land-holders.[43]

England may have been less directly affected by the revival of Roman law, but here too the drive to standardize law and to favor unitary ownership and transferability of land made itself felt. The common law was the principal vehicle of that shift as lawyers invented a variety of technical procedures and legal fictions to cope with the complexities of feudal land law. "By the early seventeenth century," writes David Seipp, "'property' had been installed, at least in elementary works on the common law, as a fundamental concept applying to land as well as to other things."[44] The consensus among historians is that property relations changed more rapidly in early modern England than in its continental neighbors (except perhaps the Netherlands), making that

---

[42] Marc Bloch, *French Rural History: An Essay on Its Basic Characteristics*, trans. Janet Sondheimer (Berkeley: University of California Press, 1966), 126–49; Jean Meyer, *La noblesse bretonne au XVIIIe siècle* (Paris: Flammarion, 1972), 219–29; Georges Lefebvre, *Les paysans du nord pendant la révolution française*, 2nd ed. (Paris: Armand Colin, 1972); Jonathan Dewald, *Pont-St-Pierre, 1398–1789: Lordship, Community, and Capitalism in Early Modern France* (Berkeley: University of California Press, 1987); Annie Antoine, "Les paysans en France de la fin du moyen age à la révolution: propriétaires? tenanciers? locataires?," in *Ruralité française et britannique, XIIIe-XXe siècles: approches comparées*, ed. Nadine Vivier (Rennes: Presses universitaires de Rennes, 2005), 153–66; Gérard Béaur, "Les rapports de propriété en France sous l'ancien régime," in ibid., 187–200; Guy Lemarchand, *Paysans et seigneurs en Europe: une histoire comparée, XVIe-XIXe siècle* (Rennes: Presses de l'Université de Rennes, 2011), 193–95.

[43] In addition to the works listed in the previous footnote, see Pierre Goubert, *The Ancien Regime: French Society, 1600–1750* (New York: Harper & Row, 1973), 78–152; Robert Mandrou, *La France aux XVIIe et XVIIIe siècles*, 2nd ed. (Paris: Presses universitaires de France, 1974), 76–83; Gérard Béaur, "Le marché foncier éclaté: les modes de transmission du patrimoine sous l'ancien régime," *Annales. Histoire, sciences sociales* 46 (1991): 189–203; Gérard Béaur, "L'accession à la propriété en 1789," in *Un droit inviolable et sacré: la propriété*, ed. Catherine Chavelet (Paris: ADEF, 1991), 21–29; David Parker, "Absolutism, Feudalism and Property Rights in the France of Louis XIV," *Past & Present*, no. 179 (2003): 60–96.

[44] Seipp, "The Concept of Property in the Early Common Law," 80. On the law of estates and interests, see Holdsworth, *Historical Introduction to the Land Law*, 48–77, 102–10; Simpson, *History of the Land Law*, 82.

nation "unique among European counties in the concentration of its landed property, and in the divorce of its peasantry from the soil."[45] A key to that development seems to be the exceptional political power of the English landed aristocracy. Summary accounts tend to focus exclusively on the Enclosure Movement, a phenomenon that reached major proportions only in the late eighteenth century. In the meantime, many other innovations – for example, the growing imposition of leasehold tenancies that made smallholders vulnerable to eviction and rent rises – tended toward the liquidation of the peasantry.[46] Even so, England in the eighteenth century was not exactly a land of freely circulating private property. Though feudal incidents had been simplified by the Tenures Act of 1660, land continued to be held of a lord; dower rights and strict settlements were among the many obstacles to sales; gleaning rights, wasteland grazing and other collective practices still prevailed over much of the countryside.[47]

In sum, there was no such thing as exclusive personal control over land anywhere in Europe at the time of Columbus, and that was still fundamentally the case three centuries later. Major changes had certainly occurred in Old World property law and practice during the time when North America was being colonized, but land had never been extracted from its social and environmental settings. Notwithstanding the inroads of capitalism, the revival of Roman law and the emergence of an ideology of private property (see Chapter 11), property remained a set of multiple claims – communal, familial, aristocratic and state – over the resources of any given tract. Land could not be reduced entirely to a buyable, sellable object.

PROPERTY FORMATION IN COMPARATIVE PERSPECTIVE

In considering Europe or indigenous America, we need to think of property in fluid and dynamic terms and not as a fixed structure that can be "read"

---

[45] R. H. Tawney, *The Agrarian Problem in the Sixteenth Century* (London: Longmans, 1912), 3.

[46] Tawney, *Agrarian Problem*, 287–301; Robert Brenner, "The Agrarian Roots of European Capitalism," *Past & Present*, no. 97 (1982): 30–75; Harold J. Berman, *Law and Revolution II: The Impact of the Protestant Reformations on the Western Legal Tradition* (Cambridge, Mass.: Harvard University Press, 2003), 333.

[47] Holdsworth, *Historical Introduction to the Land Law*, 36–37; Simpson, *History of the Land Law*, 1; E. P. Thompson, "Custom, Law and Common Right," in *Customs in Common* (New York: New Press, 1991), 97–184; J. M. Neeson, *Commoners: Common Right, Enclosure and Social Change in England, 1700–1820* (Cambridge: Cambridge University Press, 1993); Julian Hoppit, "Compulsion, Compensation and Property Rights in Britain, 1688–1833," *Past & Present*, no. 210 (2011): 93–128.

through a set of rules. Similarly, we can hardly understand the colonial takeover of portions of the New World as a simple replacement: a European regime imposed in place of a native one. I prefer the term "property formation" as a means of more fully historicizing matters. The phrase is meant to convey a sense of movement and flux; it evokes a process of becoming that is never complete. As with the concept of "state formation" from which it is obviously derived, it directs attention to the social forces in play where access to land is concerned and resists the attempt to treat property as a thing. Property formation is relational: it implicates both natives and newcomers, together with their respective property forms, in their confrontations and entanglements. It implies a process of mutual engagement through which native property, European property and new colonial property forms could coexist and shape one another. Of course, this was a massively unequal encounter, one in which force and violence were rarely absent; almost invariably people of settler stock flourished at the expense of indigenous populations; yet the triumph of settler tenures was not instantaneous, nor was it completely conclusive, nor was it the outcome of unilateral settler action. Colonial property formation is instead a fully historical process, filled with contingency and driven by multiple actors. Of necessity, it has to be apprehended in the context of larger historical processes.

If land and proprietors appear as the object and the subject of property relations, the property formation approach considers them as mutually constitutive; put differently, the same process that makes land into property makes people into proprietors: subject and object can therefore be considered two sides of the same property coin.[48] To the extent that it plays a part in creating colonial subjects, property formation includes and excludes: it institutes privileges for some while it pushes others to the margins. In a colonial setting, property can be a prime location for the definition of race, tending at times to divide people into those qualified to own ("whites"), those qualified to be owned ("blacks") and those not qualified to own or be owned ("Indians").[49] We will need to be attentive, in the chapters that follow, to the ways in which emergent rules and practices relating to control

[48] For a discussion of subjects and objects more generally, see Bruno Latour, *An Inquiry into Modes of Existence: An Anthropology of the Moderns* (Cambridge, Mass.: Harvard University Press, 2013).

[49] On this subject, see Patrick Wolfe's suggestive essay, "Land, Labor, and Difference: Elementary Structures of Race," *American Historical Review*, 106 (June 2001): 866–905. Needless to say, race formation was never so simple as to correspond exactly to this tripartite model. For one thing, as recent research on the enslavement of indigenous people reveals, "Indians" very frequently became property. Andrés Reséndez, *The*

over land may have functioned to distinguish "settlers" from "natives" and from intermediate categories such as *mestizo* or *métis*. Of course, gender is also typically constructed in and through property regimes, as are family and kin relations. A fuller history of colonial property formation would have more to say than this book does about these fundamental axes of social differentiation and the creation of subjects.

Colonial property formation had devastating consequences for indigenous America, but that is not to say that it was the work of greedy and rapacious colonizers. Wealth and profit could accrue to some proprietors, though that was not actually a major factor impelling colonization in New France or New England through most of our period. More typically, property provided the material and spatial basis for a way of life. This, it might be noted in passing, is the meaning Hannah Arendt attaches to the term "property" in *The Human Condition*, a work in which, inspired by ancient Greek political culture, she meditates on the interplay of the private and the public realms.[50] Whereas "wealth," expansive and unstable, was about the unrestrained accumulation of economic entitlement, "property" underpinned households and assured the participation of household heads in the life of the *polis*. The confusion of "property" and "wealth," Arendt felt, was undermining the public life of post-war America. I would suggest it was otherwise in the early modern period: the colonial property formation examined in this book mainly concerned "property" in Arendt's sense, rather than "wealth." It underlay and secured the existence of settler households. This may sound benign, but it is not. We need to recall that those households were hardly egalitarian, in their internal structures or in their external relations. More to the present point, colonial property formation – even when "wealth" in the Arendt sense is a minor consideration – was certainly expansive and it necessarily entailed dispossession. Establishing the material basis for new settler households and polities undermined the foundations of indigenous households and polities. Its effects were frequently more severe than that: it could destroy life itself by depriving peoples of the means of subsistence.

Questions about sovereignty and legal jurisdiction are closely bound up in the study of property formation – not always and everywhere, for property is not necessarily dependent on the existence of states and formal

Other Slavery: the Uncovered Story of Indian Enslavement in America (Boston: Houghton Mifflin Harcourt, 2016).

[50] Hannah Arendt, *The Human Condition* (Chicago: University of Chicago Press, 1958), esp. ch. 8, "The Private Realm: Property," and ch. 15, "The Privacy of Property and Wealth."

judicial institutions – but where the state does appear, landed property is bound to be affected. Property formation as presented here revolves around the ways in which courts and governments create tenures, but also the ways in which property relations work to create and sustain courts and governments. Making states, making subjects and making space – property formation is intimately involved in all these connected processes.

Property formation has a pronounced spatial aspect. Since it is about the allocation of ground, it raises issues about how the land is to be apprehended and defined. Chapter 8 discusses the implications of the European "spatial revolution" that happened to coincide with the period when North America was being colonized, while Chapter 9 looks particularly at techniques of surveying land. The spaces of indigenous and colonial property were delineated in a wide variety of ways, and not always through a geometry of outer boundaries. Natives, in many cases, defined property more through reference to central points and lines than perimeters. While settlers may have been more inclined to favor a landscape of bounded spaces, their approaches to dividing the land could be strange and imprecise, far removed from the straight-line grid that became the norm in nineteenth-century settler societies.

The examination of property formation that follows is broadly comparative, moving back and forth between three distinct regions: the central uplands of Mesoamerica, where various Nahuatl-language peoples felt the effects of Spanish imperialism and colonization (New Spain); southern New England, where Algonquian-speaking peoples, known collectively as "Ninnimissinuok," faced English colonizers; and the St. Lawrence Valley (Canada), at the heart of the imperial space called New France and home to the Innu and other indigenous nations. This particular selection is not free of an arbitrary quality – the case could be made for a study of, among other possible sites, Virginia, Martinique and Florida – but it does have several advantages. It includes a wide range of indigenous cultures and political organizations, as well as three of the principal colonies of three of the greatest colonizing powers of the period. (Regrettably, Brazil and the Portuguese Empire are neglected.) The combined early modern histories of New Spain, New France and New England provide a rich multiplicity of laws, customs, economies and natural environments for consideration. And of course the three sites have each been the subject of long-established and still vigorous currents of scholarship in history, but also in anthropology, geography, archaeology and other disciplines.

Colonial historiography, traditionally pursued as an aspect of Mexican, United States and Canadian history, has certainly provided a wealth of studies on aspects of colonization and property formation. Taken together, these national literatures provide the substance from which this book is crafted. The practice of examining the histories of New Spain, New England and New France separately, each as a colonial prelude to the history of a nation-state, (a practice in which my previous work has been deeply implicated) is highly problematic. The term "settler-colonial historiography" has been coined to describe this approach and to highlight the way in which the very framing of the field of study carries interpretive weight, tending to naturalize colonization and treat "settlement" as an inevitable step toward the emergence of a future nation-state.[51] Where the history of property formation is concerned, there is an additional reason to be wary of the colonial/national approach. If only one European legal tradition is under consideration, a particular version of property in land can seem a normal and obvious condition, rather than a contingency that begs explanation. Thus, it seems to me, historians of New France may be too inclined to take the emergence of seigneurialism for granted, while historians of New England may be insufficiently curious about the peculiar implications of deeds and treaties of land surrender simply because these are so familiar; historians of New Spain arguably have similar blind spots about *pueblos de indios* and other colonial tenure forms. When these zones of colonization are brought together within a single analytic frame, differences and peculiarities (not to mention unsuspected similarities) come into view. My comparative method, such as it is, is partly a strategy for defamiliarizing the familiar.

What follows is not a systematically comparative analysis. For the most part, it does not involve hypothesis testing of the sort, "If condition A is said to have caused effect B in jurisdiction X, can we find evidence of effect B in jurisdiction Y where A is also present?"[52] Systematic comparative history has been criticized for reifying units of analysis and exaggerating difference.[53] My use of comparison is more casual and circumstantial and

---

[51] Patrick Wolfe, *Settler Colonialism and the Transformation of Anthropology: The Politics and Poetics of an Ethnographic Event* (London and New York: Cassell, 1999); Lorenzo Veracini, "'Settler Colonialism': Career of a Concept," *The Journal of Imperial and Commonwealth History* 41 (2013): 313–33.

[52] William H. Sewell, "Marc Bloch and the Logic of Comparative History," *History and Theory* 6 (1967): 208–18.

[53] Jürgen Kocka, "Comparison and Beyond," *History and Theory* 42 (2003): 39–44; Eliga Gould, "Entangled Histories, Entangled Worlds: The English-Speaking Atlantic as a Spanish Periphery," *American Historical Review* 112 (2007): 764–86.

I hope it gives due recognition to convergent as well as to divergent tendencies. I try to extract the substantive findings of scholarship from the confines of the national and disciplinary silos in which they have typically been produced and bring them into a larger conversation about property and colonization. Putting into play Nahua, Ninnimissinuok, Innu, Spanish, English and French dimensions of the history of property and colonization is not really a "methodological" move in the strict sense of the term; rather, it represents an attempt to deprovincialize this aspect of early modern history. "To call for comparison," writes Raymond Grew, "is to call for a kind of attitude – open, questioning, searching – and to suggest some practices that may nourish it."[54]

---

[54] Raymond Grew, "The Case for Comparing Histories," *American Historical Review* 85 (1980): 776. See also Chris Lorenz, "Comparative Historiography: Problems and Perspectives," *History and Theory* 38 (1999): 25–39.

PART I

THREE ZONES OF COLONIZATION

Indigenous Forms of Property

Native land and property before the arrival of Europeans in North America: this is our somewhat elusive, but nonetheless essential, starting point. However difficult it is to be precise and certain about indigenous property, we are under an obligation to do our best with the available evidence. The latter is indeed spotty and uncertain: archaeological remains reveal little about this subject; native oral traditions can yield valuable, if not precisely datable, information; the writings of early explorers and missionaries can also be useful, especially when they date from the time of earliest contact. Sometimes, evidence from the early colonial period (for example, dictionaries of aboriginal languages compiled by missionaries) can be deployed so as to shed light on earlier times through the ethnohistorical technique of "upstreaming." Sensitively interpreted, such clues can provide glimpses of a world without colonizers and of the almost infinitely various ways in which the land and its resources were allocated to people and to peoples. The nature of the sources is such that there is really no "purely" indigenous information on pre-contact times: we are always watching for, taking into account and attempting to compensate for the European viewpoints that structure the evidence.[1] Moreover, because conquerors and settlers appeared in different parts of the continent at very different times, a panorama of indigenous property forms tends to

---

[1] On the methods of ethnohistory, see Bruce G. Trigger, *The Children of Aataentsic: A History of the Huron People to 1660* (Kingston and Montreal: McGill-Queen's University Press, 1976), 11–21; Matthew Restall, "A History of the New Philology and the New Philology in History," *Latin American Research Review* 38 (2003): 113–34; Pauline Turner Strong, "Ethnohistory," in *International Encyclopedia of the Social and Behavioral Sciences*, 2nd ed. (Amsterdam: Elsevier, 2015): 192–97.

move back and forth in time as well as in space. Thus, there can be no comprehensive guidebook to the entire continent on the eve of contact, no consistent picture of "America in 1491," only glimpses and fragments.

What follows is an examination of aboriginal land tenure among three peoples: the Nahua of central Mexico, the Ninnimissinuok (Massachusett, Narragansett, Wampanoag, Pequot, etc.) of coastal New England and the Innu (Montagnais) of the northern St. Lawrence Valley. Inhabiting widely separated regions with very different climates, these three cases together provide some notion of the diversity of property forms found in North America. For those who favor ethnographic taxonomies, they might be seen as representatives of the three major categories of Native American societies, respectively, the "state society," "semi-sedentary villagers" and "hunter-gatherer" (or "nonsedentary") societies.[2] State societies (such as the Nahua) are characterized by the presence of cities and of surrounding rural districts, all supported by well-established agriculture. They have a pronounced social hierarchy and are ruled over by a government separate from the society as a whole. Semi-sedentary villagers (such as the Ninnimissinuok) practice agriculture in forest clearings, though they also rely on hunting and fishing to a significant degree. Villages house a few hundred people, sometimes up to 2000, and they shift location periodically so that new new fields can be cleared, taking advantage of the fertility of virgin soils. Hunter-gatherers (such as the Innu) subsist through hunting, fishing and gathering and practice little or no agriculture. These peoples normally live in small groups held together by ties of kin and subject to no authority except the band itself. Their seasonal migrations in pursuit of shifting food resources ensures that they occupy extensive territories. The presence and absence of the maize complex is clearly a fundamental factor differentiating the components of this classificatory scheme: the first category of societies subsisted almost entirely from agriculture, the second category partly so and the third category not at all.

Useful in many ways, this typology also distorts through simplifying a complex and varied historical reality. If it were practical to encompass something closer to the full range of North American societies, we might enumerate hundreds more ways of life and modes of claiming land, some of them difficult to fit into this tripartite classification scheme. For example, many of the peoples living in the middle of the continent, on lands drained

---

[2] James Lockhart and Stuart B. Schwartz, *Early Latin America: A History of Colonial Spanish America and Brazil* (New York: Cambridge University Press, 1983), 31–57.

by the Mississippi and its tributaries, could be seen as semi-sedentary villagers at some times, as they cultivated corn and other crops, hunter-gatherers at other times. Moreover, in a terrain of frequent migrations in search of bison herds, territorial attachments shifted and overlapped. Of the Arkansas Valley in the eighteenth century, Kathleen Duval writes, "Most Indians in this era were comfortable with multiple layers of land rights. One group might have the exclusive right to farm a region, others could hunt there seasonally, and still others had no rights there at all."[3] In the Pacific Northwest, an area rich in food resources, especially fish, populous villages dotted the coastline and lined the major rivers. Because agriculture was not practiced here, and because of the importance of salmon, clams and other marine species, property focused more on water than on land. Clans and individual chiefs prided themselves on their wealth in goods and they jealously guarded their control over specific beaches and waters. Particular stretches of rivers as well as delineated portions of the ocean were subject to exclusive fishing rights, whereas terrestrial zones might be shared by different groups.[4] A full account, beyond this limited sample, of all the property regimes on the continent would only reinforce the sense of almost infinite variety. One could make a similar claim about property in Europe at the time of the discovery of America, though the range would perhaps be somewhat narrower. With this great diversity in mind, any attempt to reduce Native American property forms to a single essence (or even to three essences) seems futile; to present such a construction as the antithesis of "European" property seems utterly wrong-headed.

NAHUA (CENTRAL MEXICO)

The central Basin of Mexico, a hot, dry upland situated halfway between the Pacific and the Gulf, was the site where maize was first domesticated at least 7000 years ago. That wonderfully productive and adaptable plant, along with other, slightly less ancient, cultivars such as beans, squash, tomatoes, chiles and avocadoes, provided enough food to support millions of people; this region was indeed home to the densest concentration of population in the Americas by c. 1500. Rainfall could be unreliable,

---

[3] Kathleen Duval, *The Native Ground: Indians and Colonists in the Heart of the Continent* (Philadelphia: University of Pennsylvania Press, 2006), 9.

[4] Daniel W. Clayton, *Islands of Truth: The Imperial Fashioning of Vancouver Island* (Vancouver: UBC Press, 2000), 101; Keith Carlson, *The Power of Place, the Problem of Time: Aboriginal Identity and Historical Consciousness in the Cauldron of Colonialism* (Toronto: University of Toronto Press, 2010), 109–10.

drought always a danger, but a finely calibrated agricultural system combining uplands, irrigated fields and *chinampas*, artificial islands built on
lakes and filled with lake-bottom mud, supported a succession of civilizations over the centuries.[5] In the early sixteenth century, the region was
home to the Nahua people – speakers of the Nahuatl language – though
other ethnic groups and languages were also present. Cities large and small
dominated the landscape; the greatest of all at this time was the Aztec
capital Tenochtitlán, with its huge markets and temple precincts, its
ranked classes of warrior-nobles, priests, commoners and slaves.[6] An
expansive, conquering nation, the Aztecs drew tribute in the form of
gold vessels, weapons of war, salt, corn, beans, fine fabrics and slaves
from defeated enemies far and wide. However, because supplies had to be
carried on the backs of human carriers, Tenochtitlán drew the bulk of its
corn and other produce from the nearby countryside.[7] Triumphant
nations like the Aztec, as well as the defeated and subjected communities
around them, extracted food supplies, as well as occasional labor services,
each from their own local peasantry, through a mechanism that historians
also label "tribute." The vocabulary can be confusing, for under a single
rubric we have both payments from conquered states, mostly composed of
luxury goods, and regular supplies of produce and labor from common
people to local elites. "Tribute" in the second sense has affinities with what
today would be called "rent," as well as with what we call "tax."

To understand how property relations worked, we need to become
acquainted with the main components of prehispanic Nahua society, which
for shorthand purposes we might call the state, the district and the
household. The basic political unit was the *altepetl* (pl. *altepeme*), a term
translated variously by experts as "city-state," "regional state," "ethnic
kingdom" or "lordship." One scholar puts it this way: "The word for city
or town, or more appropriately for community kingdom was *altepetl*, the
word being a combination of *atl*, or 'water,' and *tepetl*, or 'hill.'"[8]

[5] Eric R. Wolf, *Sons of the Shaking Earth* (Chicago: University of Chicago Press, 1959).
[6] Tenochtitlán is vividly evoked in Inga Clendinnen, *Aztecs: An Interpretation* (Cambridge:
   Cambridge University Press, 1991).
[7] Ross Hassig, *Aztec Warfare: Imperial Expansion and Political Control* (Norman: Univer-
   sity of Oklahoma Press, 1995); Ross Hassig, "El Tributo en la economía prehispánico,"
   Arqueología Mexicana 21 (November 2013): 32–39; Frances Berdan, "El tributo a la
   Triple Alianza," *Arqueología Mexicana* 21 (November 2013): 49–55.
[8] Elizabeth Boone, "Glorious Imperium: Understanding Land and Community in Moctezuma's
   Mexico," in *Moctezuma's Mexico: Visions of the Aztec World*, ed. Davíd Carrasco and
   Eduardo Matos Moctezuma (Niwot: University Press of Colorado, 1992), 161. See also

Each *altepetl* had a ruler, always a sacred figure, often a war leader, the *tlatoani*. There were also privileged classes: the nobility, defined by the warrior vocation of its men, and the priesthood. Most numerous in any *altepetl* were the unprivileged artisans and peasants, called *macehualtin*; these commoners held lands in various ways, both in severalty as a household and in common as part of a local community (see Figure 2.1). *Altepeme* typically joined together in alliances; some owed tribute to a hegemonic power; some, such as Tenochtitlán, drew tribute from others; but all were internally autonomous. By and large, the Aztec empire worked as an engine of tribute exaction. When the Aztecs conquered another *altepetl*, they might install a compliant local *tlatoani*, but as long as the subjected community maintained tribute payments, they did not interfere with its social and economic organization.[9]

Every *altepetl* was divided into districts or neighborhoods called *calpulli*, the primary unit of community and the agency under whose auspices land was held and tribute/tax collected. Though the *calpulli* possessed a territorial base, some scholars suggest that its identity was also defined in terms of extended kinship, so that it had some of the qualities of a clan. Finally, there were the constituent households that made up each *calpulli*. There was no Nahuatl term for "family," the experts tell us; instead, the word *calli* can mean either a house or a room in a housing compound, together with the land upon which it stood.[10] Metaphorically, however, *calli* does seem to imply a human grouping that might be called a "family."

Thomas H. Charlton, "The Aztecs and Their Contemporaries: The Central and Eastern Highlands," in *Cambridge History of the Native Peoples of the Americas*, vol. 2: Mesoamerica, ed. Richard W. Adams and Murdo J. MacLeod (Cambridge: Cambridge University Press, 2000), pt. 2, 500–557; Arij Ouweneel, "*Altepeme* and *Pueblos de indios*: Some Comparative Theoretical Perspectives on the Analysis of the Colonial Indian Communities," in *The Indian Community of Colonial Mexico: Fifteen Essays on Land Tenure, Corporate Organizations, Ideology and Village Politics*, ed. Arij Ouweneel and Simon Miller (Amsterdam: CEDLA, 1990), 1–39.

[9] There were exceptions to this pattern: some *altepeme* of central Mexico were ruled collectively by a noble household rather than an individual *tlatoani*; in some instances, such as in the rebellious Toluca Valley, the Aztecs took direct control of certain lands and even introduced colonial settlers. Frederic Hicks, "Land and Succession in the Indigenous Noble Houses of Sixteenth-Century Tlaxcala," *Ethnohistory* 56 (2009): 569–88; Nadine Béligand, "Les communautés indiennes de la vallée de Toluca (Mexique): 1480–1810," doctoral thesis, École des hautes études en sciences sociales, 1998, 52–68.

[10] James Lockhart, *The Nahuas after the Conquest: A Social and Cultural History of the Indians of Central Mexico, Sixteenth through Eighteenth Centuries* (Stanford, Calif.: Stanford University Press, 1992), 59–72; Susan Kellogg, *Law and the Transformation of Aztec Culture, 1500–1700* (Norman: University of Oklahoma Press, 1995), 62.

FIGURE 2.1 Nahua *macehuales* sowing, tilling and harvesting maize.
Source: Fray Bernadino de Sahagún, *The Florentine Codex*, book IV, folio 72. Courtesy Biblioteca Medicea Laurenzia.

The Nahuatl language is the main medium though which researchers have sought to understand Mesoamerican society and they have found the vocabulary surrounding landed property particularly rich and complex. Documents from the pre-Hispanic period are rare, but scholars have made good use of the records, both Spanish and Nahuatl, from the early colonial period to piece together a picture of land use and tenure stretching back into the pre-conquest period. Linguistic analysis has been a precious tool in this endeavor, as has the close examination of judicial records and notarial documents by which native communities settled disputes and defended their collective interests in the face of a threatening colonialism.[11] Under Spanish rule, courts and administrators were at pains to respect native tenure forms (as they imperfectly understood them), though the context changed radically with the destruction of the Nahua priesthood and the decline of the lay elite; moreover, some indigenous practices and concepts seem to have been lost in translation as European magistrates tried to make sense of the ways of the Aztecs. Consequently, the practice of "upstreaming," interpreting pre-conquest tenure on the basis of post-conquest evidence, can be tricky, the findings always subject to debate. Yet compared with other parts of North America where native-authored sources are rare or entirely absent, the tenure history of indigenous central Mexico is remarkably well documented. Sixteenth-century Nahuatl documents come replete with a multitude of words for lands of various sorts: some refer to the intrinsic qualities of the soil, some to the social status of the owner; some terms have to do with community controls over a plot, others indicate whether or not it can be alienated. To make matters more complicated, there are local variations in vocabulary that may reflect underlying differences in practice or simply shifts in linguistic usage. These uncertainties and nuances give rise to scholarly discussion and ever more refined research.

In the record, one encounters words designating "temple lands" (*teotlalli* or *teopantilli*), that is, scattered plots whose produce went to

---

[11] A leading figure in the analysis of Nahuatl sources for historical study is James Lockhart. See Lockhart, *The Nahuas after the Conquest.* Significant contributions to the study of Nahuatl notarial documents from the post-conquest period include Arthur J. O. Anderson, Frances Berdan, and James M. Lockhart, *Beyond the Codices: The Nahua View of Colonial Mexico* (Berkeley: University of California Press, 1976); S. L. Cline, *Colonial Culhuacan, 1580–1600: A Social History of an Aztec Town* (Albuquerque: University of New Mexico Press, 1986); Rebecca Horn, *Postconquest Coyoacan: Nahua-Spanish Relations in Central Mexico, 1519–1650* (Stanford, Calif.: Stanford University Press, 1997).

the support of temples in a neighboring city; after the Spaniards destroyed the temples and slaughtered the pagan priesthood, this type of tenure disappeared.[12] The term *pillalli* and a variety of synonyms designated land set aside for nobles for their personal benefit. Other words designated lands assigned to certain palaces and public offices; unlike *pillalli*, these properties could not be alienated by any individual, because they belonged to the office, not the officeholder.[13] All these elite properties seem to have been worked by slaves and by local commoners conscripted for temporary service through a kind of *corvée* system.

The largest portion of the arable of central Mexico, including both house lots and more distant plots, was designated as *calpullalli*, meaning that it was held by specific households, but under the authority and eminent domain of the local *calpulli* and its officials. Early Spanish observers, along with many later historians, saw the Mexican *calpulli* as communal property. Alonso de Zorita wrote in 1554:

These lands, which they call calpulli, they still possess today. They do not hold them individually but communally. Individuals cannot alienate their lots, but can enjoy their use for life and leave them to their sons and heirs ... If a certain family dies out, the lands remain in the common ownership of the calpulli, and the head or chief elder assigns them to some other member of the same barrio who has need of them.[14]

Calpullalli land could be inherited, but it could not normally be alienated outside the lineage; if the family who held it died out or moved away, their portion reverted to the community to be reallocated to another by the *calpulli* leaders. Notwithstanding these restrictions on ownership, recent scholarship has tended to reject the notion that *calpullalli* can be equated with common lands; specialists insist instead on the ways in which its component parts were held in severalty.[15] Agriculture was managed by individual households, not collectively as it was in open-field Europe.

[12] Charles Gibson, *The Aztecs under Spanish Rule: A History of the Indians of the Valley of Mexico, 1519–1810* (Stanford, Calif.: Stanford University Press, 1964), 258.

[13] Sarah L. Cline, "Native Peoples of Colonial Central Mexico," in *Cambridge History of the Native Peoples of the Americas*, vol. 2: *Mesoamerica*, part 2, 205–9.

[14] Alonso de Zorita, *Life and Labor in Ancient Mexico: The Brief and Summary Relation of the Lords of New Spain*, ed. and trans. Benjamin Keen (New Brunswick, N.J.: Rutgers University Press, 1963), 106. Cf. Gibson, *The Aztecs*, 267.

[15] Lockhart, *The Nahuas after the Conquest*, 141–202; H. R. Harvey, "Aspects of Land Tenure in Ancient Mexico," in *Explorations in Ethnohistory: Indians of Central Mexico in the Sixteenth Century*, ed. H. R. Harvey and Hanns J. Prem (Albuquerque: University of New Mexico Press, 1984), 83–102; Cline, *Colonial Culhuacan*, 125–58; Horn, *Postconquest Coyoacan*, 111–43.

Moreover, there seems to have been no attempt on the part of the *calpulli* to redistribute plots to ensure equality among its members (unlike more fully communal agrarian regimes such as the traditional Russian *mir*); indeed, by the time the Spanish took over, there were wide gaps, within a given community, between the largest and smallest landholders, suggesting a process of accumulation, rather than equalization.[16] Landholders could normally count, in fact if not in theory, on retaining secure tenure, even if they left their lands in the possession of a tenant. In sum, the new scholarship contends, the *calpulli*'s proprietary powers were much less extensive than Zorita realized. Where earlier expert opinion saw communal ownership, with individuals merely "using" community land, the pendulum has now swung in the direction of something more like the "private property" ideal type. As research advances, however, and as specialists bring out more of the quirks and nuances of *calpulli* property forms, a debate framed in dichotomous private versus communal terms seems increasingly outmoded. We might say that lands in a community belonged to the *macehualtin* who cultivated them, but subject to some degree of *calpulli* control.

However important the division of land into *teotlalli*, *pillalli* and *calpulli*, it would be far too simple to say that Nahua tenure consisted of three types of land corresponding to clerical, noble and commoner status. Cross-cutting these designations were other distinctions: between house lands and fields, between arable and wasteland, between land subject to tribute and tribute-free land, between land that could be alienated and land that could not. In the countryside, houses always came with a plot of land inseparably attached; whether held by nobles or by common *macehualtin*, the ground immediately surrounding a dwelling was designated *callalli*, "house land"; this was often the site where essential food crops were grown.[17] Additionally, households normally held several other plots scattered across the community's territory; dispersed holdings allowed cultivators to benefit from a variety of soils and terrain, such that corn might be grown on one parcel, maguey or agave (the cactus-like plant whose fibers were used to weave rough cloth) on

---

[16] Harvey, "Aspects of Land Tenure," 87–88. On the Russian *mir*, see Teodor Shanin, *The Awkward Class: Political Sociology of Peasantry in a Developing Society: Russia 1910–1925* (Oxford: Clarendon Press, 1972).

[17] It has been suggested that this "house land" was actually attached to rooms or apartments within a rural compound, and not necessarily to self-contained dwellings. Kellogg, *Law and the Transformation of Aztec Culture*, 62.

another. Such plots were somewhat less firmly attached to the house and its occupants. In addition to the tilled lands, there was also an indigenous commons in Central Mexico. The mountainous and semi-arid terrain that surrounded their villages and fields were an area of common access where Nahua people gathered firewood, hunted small game and collected roots.

Among the Nahua, a distinction was made between land that had been purchased (*tlalcohualli*) and land held by inheritance or by virtue of membership in the *calpulli*. The latter was inalienable and subject to tribute/taxation, while the former was seen as more fully personal property, largely free from the control of local officials. Land that had been bought could later be sold, which is why post-conquest Nahua deeds of sale carefully specify that the land being transferred had been previously purchased by the seller.[18] It was exempt from the tribute that was levied on *calpullalli*, in proportion to the measured area, for the benefit of local government or the Aztec state.

In indigenous central Mexico, unlike other parts of North America where state structures and taxation were absent, land was bounded and carefully measured. "Local tlaxilacalli officers kept up-to-date records of the land subject to tribute that was held by each household. Sixteenth-century Spanish sources describe these indigenous land records as indicating the names of individual landholders, as well as the number, location, shape, and dimensions of fields in both map and register format."[19] Individual plots were measured and their size and location recorded on a local "glyphic-pictorial" land registry (see Chapter 9). Boundary markers on the ground might take the form of a stake, a pile of stones or a maguey plant; there were laws decreeing the death penalty to anyone who moved a marker.[20]

NINNIMISSINUOK (NEW ENGLAND)

The region known today as southern New England is an area of diverse environments: a coastal zone of rocky shores and sandy beaches, interspersed with protected lagoons and estuaries; several fertile river valleys; rough uplands dotted with ponds and swamps. It was home to several populous nations – Narragansett, Massachusett, Wampanoag and so on; ethnic boundaries could be fluid – all of them speaking related Algonquian languages, and to whom Kathleen Bragdon has given the

---

[18] Horn, *Postconquest Coyoacan*, 122–29   [19] Horn, *Postconquest Coyoacan*, 129.
[20] Lockhart, *The Nahuas after the Conquest*, 143; Cline, *Colonial Culhuacan*, 126–28.

collective name, *"Ninnimissinuok."*[21] Around 1500, some of these peoples lived in semi-sedentary villages of several hundred souls, others moved as migratory foraging bands; some were farming folk, others subsisted from hunting or fishing or from some combination of horticulture and foraging. There were many ways to live in this part of the continent and the ethnohistorical evidence is uncertain, with the result that experts in the field have difficulty situating Ninnimissinuok within the familiar classifications of their profession.

When they zoom out in space and time, scholars sometimes consider New England as the ragged end of the line of an expanding maize revolution that had rolled out across North America over the course of centuries and millennia. From a point of origin in central Mexico, *Zea mays* had slowly diffused northward, spreading up the Mississippi Valley to the Great Lakes in the ca. 500–1000 period. Through patient selective breeding, native women managed to develop new strains of corn that would resist comparatively long winters; the multicolored Northern Flint variety was a particularly important development. It was only in what archaeologists call the "Late Woodland Period" (ca. 1000–1300) that maize was widely adopted in New England and began to serve, along with squash which came earlier and beans that came a little later, as the region's staple crop. Exactly when maize horticulture arrived, how fully it dominated Ninnimissinuok subsistence and what role it played in the rise of "sedentism" (i.e., settled village life) is a matter of controversy among archaeologists as they struggle to interpret the presence or absence of tiny carbonized seeds at different excavation sites.[22] According to a long-accepted narrative convention, the adoption of corn provoked a thoroughgoing transformation as it fostered concentrated, year-round settlements with a social hierarchy and favored the political domination of chiefs (*sachems*). A revisionist school argues that the advent of corn

[21] Kathleen Bragdon, *Native People of Southern New England, 1500–1650* (Norman: University of Oklahoma Press, 1996), xi. Note that this term is not universally accepted.

[22] A sample of recent contributions to the archaeological literature on this topic: Bragdon, *Native People of Southern New England*, 80–91; Elizabeth S. Chilton, "'Towns They Have None': Diverse Subsistence and Settlement Strategies in Native New England," in *Northeast Subsistence-Settlement Change: AD 700–1300*, ed. John P. Hart and Christina B. Rieth, New York State Museum Bulletin 496 (Albany: New York State Education Department, 2002), 289–300; James B. Petersen and Ellen R. Cowie, "From Hunter-Gatherer Camp to Horticultural Village: Late Prehistoric Indigenous Subsistence and Settlement," in ibid., 265–87; John P. Hart and William A. Lovis, "Reevaluating What We Know about the Histories of Maize in Northeastern North America: A Review of Current Evidence," *Journal of Archaeological Research* 21 (June 2013): 175–216.

was not so consequential, that some semi-sedentary villages on the coast drew their living from the sea rather than from cultivating maize, and that the emergence of chiefdoms and social inequality was the effect of contact with Europeans rather than of horticulture. While many issues remain unresolved a few basic points seem clear.

On the eve of European colonization, maize-based agriculture was present among the Ninnimissinuok, but it was a fairly recent innovation, unevenly spread across the region. In upland regions, many groups continued a migratory hunter-gatherer way of life, not unlike that of the Innu (see below). In some estuaries along the coast and on offshore islands such as Nantucket, rich marine resources allowed large concentrations of population to subsist on shellfish, seals and waterfowl without having to rely fully on corn cultivation.[23] Even so, the earliest European visitors to this coast, such as Samuel de Champlain (1605–6), reported that this was farming country:

All the people here are very fond of tilling the soil, and store Indian corn for the winter, which they preserve in the following way: they make trenches on the hillsides in the sand, five or six feet, more or less, deep; put their corn and other grains in big sacks made of grass, and throw them into these trenches and cover them with sand three or four feet above the surface of the earth. They take from their store at need.[24]

Away from the sea, villages on the Connecticut and other rivers seem to have been more fully dependent on horticulture, though they too engaged in hunting and fishing. Whether or not the Ninnimissinuok ever experienced a "maize revolution," they were by this time mostly living in villages housing 300–500 people and subsisting to a significant degree on corn, beans and squash.

Villages usually consisted of a collection of lightly constructed houses made with a framework of bent saplings covered with woven mats (see Figure 2.2). Around the homes were fields dotted with small mounds where women had heaped up topsoil to plant maize; beans ran up the corn stalks while squash vines typically curled round the base, their leaves serving to discourage weeds.[25] There were no fences around fields;

---

[23] Bragdon, *Native People of Southern New England, 1500–1650*, 55–71, 100, 110–11, 122.

[24] Samuel de Champlain, quoted in Petersen and Cowie, "From Hunter-Gatherer Camp to Horticultural Village," 281.

[25] Peter A. Thomas, "Contrastive Subsistence Strategies and Land Use as Factors for Understanding Indian-White Relations in New England," *Ethnohistory* 23 (1976): 1–18; Bragdon, *Native People of Southern New England, 1500–1650*, 107–10.

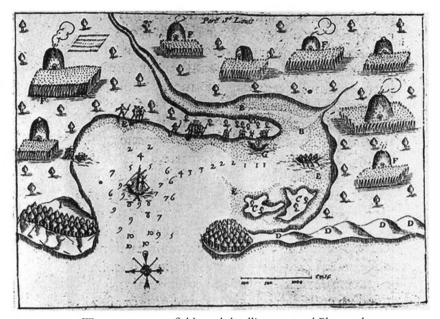

FIGURE 2.2 Wampanoag cornfields and dwellings around Plymouth Harbor, 1605.
Source: H. P. Biggar, ed., *The Works of Samuel de Champlain*, 6 vols. (Toronto: Champlain Society, 1922), vol. 1, plate 74.

instead, children were assigned the task of driving away birds and grazing animals that might damage crops; according to Roger Williams, some Ninnimissinuok also tamed hawks and employed them "to keepe the little Birds from their Corne."[26] Here as in other maize-based villages in North America it seems that women provided all the labor, from planting through harvesting, storing and cooking the food; evidence appears in the patterns of bone wear in skeletons unearthed by archaeologists as well as in the written records of early European contact. Villages tended to relocate every generation or so and clear new land at a nearby location as firewood became scarce and soil fertility declined. Additionally, people often moved seasonally in order to be near fishing or hunting grounds. The ethnographic term "semi-sedentary villagers" reflects the fact that, though they occupied a defined territory, New England Algonquians were not permanently attached to one precise location.

[26] Roger Williams, *A Key into the Language of America* (London: Gregory Dexter, 1643), 166.

More so than Iroquoian peoples to the west, the Ninnimissinuok relied on fish and wild game and they exploited extensive territories for foraging purposes. Adjacent to some coastal villages, especially along Long Island Sound and on the islands off Cape Cod, women harvested the clam beds while their men fished the waters for other marine species. Fishing spots and weirs were also an important element of the subsistence system of the communities that lined the region's rivers. Hunting grounds extended over much larger areas. There were ponds and swamps where men either shot with arrows or captured in nets ducks, geese, swans and turkeys, each in the appropriate season. In winter, small parties ventured into the forest to trap beaver, wolves and deer; they also tracked down and shot moose when snow conditions were favorable. Deer were sometimes rounded up during a collective hunt in which hundreds beat the bushes to drive animals into a corral for slaughter. Environmental historians have emphasized the way in which New England natives "groomed" the land, mostly by igniting fires under the right conditions so as to clear away brush and encourage the growth of young herbage to feed the deer population. Rivers and streams were also dammed in places so as to favor the harvest of shad, alewives and other fish. The forests and the waters were therefore not "primeval"; rather, they were managed and used for the benefit of specific human communities. "Farming, burning, clearing, and encouraging Native flora and fauna created a landscape managed by human hands – a primarily social landscape, which also varied regionally, seasonally, and according to the habits of the local inhabitants."[27]

The indigenous communities in southern New England each had a large and variegated land base. Some zones were more intensively occupied and exploited than others; some were used collectively; others – a clamming beach, a fishing site or a group of corn mounds – were more under the control of a particular woman or man. At the same time, people, places and resources were also subject to the overlordship of a local chieftain or sachem. The tribute-exacting sachem was a special feature of the Ninnimissinuok and of many Atlantic coastal societies, a figure that had no equivalent among Iroquoian horticultural villagers. It is not clear when sachemships first arose in this region or how extensive their powers had been during the pre-contact period. Some scholars

---

[27] Bragdon, *Native People of Southern New England, 1500–1650*, 116–18, 128–29 (quotation 128–29). On the management of hunting lands, see William Cronon, *Changes in the Land: Indians, Colonists, and the Ecology of New England* (New York: Hill and Wang, 1983), 48–53.

maintain that early contact with Europeans, in the decades before settlers began arriving, had reinforced the power of coastal sachems, partly thanks to the latters' control over the burgeoning trade in furs and wampum; some suggest that sachemships arose entirely out of the indirect effects of this irregular European presence. Be that as it may, when Ninnimissinuok sociopolitical organization comes into historical focus in the early seventeenth century, sachems and tribute are a prominent and uncontested fact.

In a frequently cited passage, the Plymouth colonist Edward Winslow describes the situation of a New England sachem in terms derived from his own experience of English landlords:

Every sachim knoweth how far the bounds and limits of his own country extendeth; and that is his own proper inheritance. Out of that, if any of his men desire land to set their corn, he giveth them as much as they can use, and sets them their bounds. In this circuit whosoever hunteth, if they kill any venison, bring him his fee; which is the fore parts of the same, if it be killed on the land, but if in the water, then the skin thereof ... Once a year the pnieses [warrior elite] use to provoke the people to bestow much corn on the sachim. To that end, they appoint a certain time and place, near the sachim's dwelling, where the people bring many baskets of corn, and make a great stack thereof. There the pnieses stand ready to give thanks to the people, on the sachim's behalf; and after acquaint the sachim therewith, who fetcheth the same, and is no less thankful, bestowing many gifts on them.[28]

The sachemship was normally inherited as Winslow implies, usually by a son, sometimes by a daughter of the deceased incumbent, but there could be uncertainty over succession and legitimacy. In spite of his or her exalted status, a sachem remained part of the society, expected to take advice from a village elite and to make proper use of his or her wealth. A sachem had to be a generous giver of gifts, and so his economic function was largely one of redistribution. He could hardly dispose of lands and people any way he wished. On the whole, men and women were entitled to a subsistence and could claim by right the resources they needed. Marshall Sahlins's generalization about chieftainships no doubt applies to the sachems of New England: their property "is an 'ownership' more inclusive than exclusive, and more political than economic: a derived claim on the product and productive means in virtue of an

---

[28] Edward Winslow, "Good Newes from New England: Or a True Relation of Things Very Remarkable at the Plantation of Plimoth in New-England" [1624], in *Chronicles of the Pilgrim Fathers of the Colony of Plymouth, from 1602 to 1625*, ed. Alexander Young (Boston: C. C. Little and J. Brown, 1844), 361–62.

inscribed superiority over the producers."[29] The land was the sachem's, but it was also the people's.

Tribute from his own community provided the sachem with food and other goods to distribute as gifts that served to enhance his or her influence and status. If he was a man, it also enabled him to support a large household, multiple wives and numerous descendants, forming another component of his power and glory. War making, yet another dimension of male status, served as a means by which a people and its sachem forced others to acknowledge their superiority through the payment of tribute. Hierarchies of communities, with some villages turning over regular tribute payments to the sachem of a stronger neighbor, were characteristic of the coastal region at the time Europeans began to settle there. Writers of the early colonial period tended to assimilate Ninnimissinuok tribute, both internal (from community members) and external (from subjugated communities), to landlord rent: people owed a sachem so many deer-skins and baskets of corn "for the use of the land." But the giving of corn may have had more layers of meaning than is implied in any impersonal concept of rent payment: it might also have represented support for the sachem and the ethnic group he or she represented; perhaps it sealed a connection with the community and its living personification. Similarly, external tribute suggested peace and mutual support between former enemies; it was asymmetrical and even somewhat humiliating for the givers, but it implied some obligations – notably military protection – for the recipient. In sum, though it concerned lands and territories, tribute was about social and diplomatic connections between people and between peoples.[30]

The English colonists that historians rely on for information on Ninnimissinuok property developed a bias that led them to look for signs of strong individual ownership, firm sovereignty, defined boundaries and, above all, alienability.[31] After all, they were generally interested in acquiring native lands for themselves and wanted firm and definite title to clearly defined tracts. Hence Winslow's language of bounds, limits and "proper inheritance"; hence also Roger Williams's remark about the Narragansetts: "I have knowne them to make bargaine and sale amongst themselves for a small piece, or quantity of ground." Of course, Winslow and Williams dealt with natives who were willing to deal with Englishmen and they interpreted Ninnimissinuok land tenure in light of their own

---

[29] Marshall D. Sahlins, *Stone Age Economics* (Chicago: Aldine-Atherton, 1972), 92.
[30] See Bragdon, *Native People of Southern New England, 1500–1650*, 140–55.
[31] Ibid., 138.

backgrounds and preoccupations. In our own time, scholars have tried to reinterpret this evidence through analysis of the indigenous languages of the area and in light of broader anthropological knowledge. Kathleen Bragdon has looked closely at the language of possession in early Massachusett documents, evoking "the subtleties of notions of intimate possession in southern New England." Land was associated with self, house and close kin and ownership might be expressed through a meta-phor of eating. To say that a specified tract was inheritable property, a document put it in words that could be transliterated as, "We have eaten it all, I and my children . . . we have used it all my children and I." Bragdon's gloss on this passage: "To eat of the fruits of the land was to own it, to use it was to establish proprietary links extending to one's children." She continues: "For these people, lived space was constituted through life activity, through the intimacy of shared lodging and consumed food."[32] The individual and the kin-group possessed the land that fed them, while at the same time, the sachem was, in a sense, proprietor of the whole country. The sachem also claimed a proprietorial stake in the countries of defeated neighbors, even though these were nevertheless "owned" by their respective sachems, and "eaten" by the families that occupied and possessed them. We have to recognize that tribute relations were highly mutable; through the fortunes of war and diplomacy, the lines of tribute subjection from village to village could change rapidly. Internally, sachems did not stand above and outside the community. In sum, "power and authority were always in flux, and the English tendency to think hierarch-ically about power was a constant source of misunderstanding in Native-English relationships."[33] The layers and nuances of territory and social relations in southern New England were indeed complex, and when we catch sight of them in early colonial writings, they were in rapid evolution.

INNU (QUEBEC)

In late summer, around the time the blueberries ripened, small groups of Innu converged on the shores of the St. Lawrence, at a place they called Kâ Mihkwâwahkâšič ("where there is red sand"), close to the point where the broad river widens into an immense estuary. There were birch trees here to provide materials for making canoes and storage vessels; seals

---

[32] Ibid., 136.
[33] Kathleen Bragdon, *Native People of Southern New England, 1650–1775* (Norman: University of Oklahoma Press, 2009), 113.

could be hunted on the offshore islets; salmon streams emptied into the river; migrating geese and ducks would soon cover the nearby marshes and provide targets for Innu arrows. Food was plentiful here in the early autumn, enough to support a village of several hundred people, living together in their conical birch-bark shelters. The biggest attraction of this place, however, was the facilities it offered for the eel fishery. Every year, millions of American eels migrated from the Great Lakes down the St. Lawrence to the sea, traveling at night and hugging the shoreline. At Kâ Mihkwâwahkâšič, the Innu found shallows, tidal even though the water was fresh, together with rocks and boulders, deposited during the last ice age, that could be arranged into dams and weirs. All had to be in readiness when the eels finally swarmed through; the idea was to allow the animals to enter the enclosure at high tide while impeding their escape at low tide. During turbulent weather, Innu men could catch hundreds per day in underwater traps; in calm conditions it was better to spear them, working at night from canoes and using the light of birch torches. On shore, the women cleaned the eels, removed their heads and slit through the fat flesh of the backs to prepare them for curing over a smoky fire. Smoked eel, produced in great quantities in September, would last for the better part of a year; it would serve as a vital source of provisions during the long winter months, especially at times when hunting conditions were poor or when the band was traveling.[34]

Every year the eel dams had to be rebuilt because storms and moving ice dislodged rocks over the course of the winter. With such powerful and unpredictable natural forces at work in their absence, the Innu often had to locate their fishery and village at different points along the shore from one year to the next. Collectively, they certainly owned Kâ Mihkwâwahkâšič, but its precise location varied slightly. Similarly, their winter hunting grounds in the interior displayed a degree of spatial fluidity and indeterminacy.

After the end of the eel run, and as the weather turned colder, the Innu began to depart from Kâ Mihkwâwahkâšič in small winter hunting bands.[35] These bands were structured around kin relations, but

---

[34] This description of the Innu eel fishery summarizes portions of John Bishop, "'Oblige moy de m'en donner le Massinahigan': Land, Knowledge, and Montagnais-French Relations in the 17th Century," PhD dissertation, McGill University, in progress. My thanks to the author for allowing me to draw on his research. See also H. P. Biggar, ed., *The Works of Samuel de Champlain*, 6 vols. (Toronto: Champlain Society, 1922), 2: 44–46.

[35] Some early seventeenth-century accounts speak of a fall hunt, then a return to the coast, followed by a winter hunt; others suggest the Innu departed for the entire winter. *Works of Samuel de Champlain*, 2: 44–46.

sometimes included unrelated individuals and even a sprinkling of Algonquins and other non-Innu. Ethnic and political distinctions were not sharply drawn in the small-scale and loosely organized societies of the boreal forest. The French spoke of "nations" – the "Montagnais," as they called the Innu, occupied a vast region in what is now northeastern Quebec, the "Algonquins" lived further to the west, and the "Cree" to the north, near James Bay and Hudson Bay – but recent scholarship suggests that these labels and identities are largely the product of colonization. These hunter-gatherers understood identities mainly in terms of family and clan rather than "nation" or "tribe."[36] Families, it should be added, were not exclusively human entities: they encompassed animal spirits. Each hunting band had a (male) leader, but his authority was not coercive and he did not exact tribute. The country of the Innu was immense and it provided rich food resources, but not all in the same place and not at the same time of year. Like other "foragers" or "hunter-gatherers," the Innu had to travel with the seasons in order to harvest the bounty of the land. Consequently, their ingenuity was directed toward the technology of mobility and travel: canoes, snowshoes and toboggans were among the devices that enabled them to travel great distances over a rough landscape that was frozen half the year.

We are fortunate in having a fairly detailed report, written by the Jesuit missionary Paul Le Jeune, of the travels and experiences of one Innu hunting band in the winter of 1633–34.[37] The party was led by Mestigoït ("my host," Le Jeune calls him) and included two of his brothers plus other unnamed men, women and children to a total of twenty. They set off on 18 October, heading down the St. Lawrence in boats and carrying a supply of smoked eel as well as some French provisions; the latter were quickly consumed. They spent almost a month moving through the islands of the lower St. Lawrence, hunting wildfowl as they went. With the freeze-up approaching in mid-November, they

---

[36] Heidi Bohaker, "'Nindoodemag': The Significance of Algonquian Kinship Networks in the Eastern Great Lakes Region, 1600–1701," *William and Mary Quarterly* 63 (January 2006): 23–52. This claim needs to be qualified slightly where the context of diplomacy and war are concerned; clans came together to forge alliances with, or prosecute war against, outsiders.

[37] Paul Le Jeune, "Relation de ce qui s'est passé en la Nouvelle-France" [1634], in *Monumenta Novae Francia*, 9 vols., ed. Lucien Campeau (Rome and Quebec City: Monumenta Historica Soc. Iesu and Presses de l'Université Laval, 1967–2003) (hereafter MNF), vol. 2: 663–728. Excerpts in English translation can be found in Allan Greer, ed., *The Jesuit Relations: Natives and Missionaries in Seventeenth-Century North America* (Boston: Bedford Books, 2000), 23–26.

prepared to strike off inland. But where exactly within the vast Innu domain would they go? They had originally planned to hunt south of the great river, but they heard that other Innu parties had gone there, and since the whole purpose of dispersing in small bands was to limit the population of hunters in any one area, they decided to cross over to the northern shore. However, on the way, they encountered another hunting party paddling in the opposite direction. Hunting was bad in the north, these others reported, and so Mestigoït's band reverted to their original plan.

Storing their canoes at the mouth of a stream, the Innu band loaded snowshoes and other equipment onto their backs, along with the remaining provisions of smoked eels, and began the march inland; they made camp where the hunting was good and stayed as long as it remained so. Paul Le Jeune summarizes the season in these terms: "From the twelfth of November of the year 1633, when we entered these vast forests, to the twenty-second of April of this year 1634, when we returned to the banks of the great river St. Lawrence, we camped at twenty-three different places. Sometimes we were in deep valleys, then upon lofty mountains, sometimes in the low flat country; but always in the snow."[38] While women tended fires, processed carcasses and skins and sewed and decorated clothing, men went in search of game. For subsistence food supplies, moose and caribou were the most prized quarry; moose were best pursued in deep snow where hunters on snowshoes could chase them to exhaustion as the animals wallowed in the drifts until they succumbed to spear thrusts. Beaver were also part of the food supply, along with porcupines and other small game, but they were especially valuable for their glossy pelts, which could be traded to the French for brass pots, iron axes and even guns. (Mestigoït possessed an arquebus that had proved useful in hunting wildfowl.) Beaver were sometimes taken in traps and nets, sometimes hunted with bow and arrow. Famine and feast alternated over the course of an Innu winter, depending mainly on changing weather and snow conditions. Le Jeune seems to have chosen a particularly difficult year to share the life of these hunter-gatherers for he describes several periods of severe food shortage when gaunt and listless people boiled up scraps of leather and ate needles from the evergreen trees. There was occasional contact with other Innu bands in the vicinity: a joint feast when hunting was good, shared emergency rations at times of desperate

---

[38] Greer, ed., *Jesuit Relations*, 23.

hunger. The presence of "neighbors," even if they were miles away in a different river valley, may have played a part in saving some Innu from utter starvation.

Paul Le Jeune's account says little about property, apart from an anecdote about bargaining with an Innu boy to buy a piece of moose hide to sleep on. As far as territory is concerned, he gives an impression of almost aimless wandering – just what Europeans of the time expected of "savage" hunters – rather than of exclusive hunting grounds. However, the missionary was more focused on religious than on property matters, and his knowledge of the Innu language was still quite rudimentary. He indicates that food was shared, but doesn't seem to know whether the meat was owned in common or was the gift of the hunter. In hunter-gatherer societies, such matters are frequently of central importance: hunters may be socially obligated to share, but their prestige derives from their generosity, which in turn depends on an initial recognition of ownership.[39] Likewise, Le Jeune says little about the ownership of moose hides and beaver pelts, the latter already a salable commodity in 1634; nor does he think to explain how trapping zones may have been allocated to individual Innu around each camping site. He may not have known about these things or he may not have had room to discuss them in his narrative of adventures, hardships and efforts at religious conversion.

Other early-contact sources on people with customs similar to those of the Innu suggest that, even within a given band's hunting range, there were individual family territories. Baron Lahontan, who frequented northern hunters in the Great Lakes region, reported that they "agree among themselves as they are travelling, to allot each Family a certain compass of Ground."[40] Writing of the Mi'kmaq of eastern Canada (he calls them "Gaspesiens"), the French Recollet Chrestien Le Clercq drew on a European vocabulary of property and political authority: "It is the right of the head of the nation, according to the customs of the country, which serve as laws and regulations to the Gaspesians, to distribute the places of hunting to each individual. It is not permitted to any Indian to overstep the bounds and limits of the region which shall have been assigned him in the assemblies of the elders. These are held in

---

[39] Alan Barnard and James Woodburn, "Property, Power and Ideology in Hunting and Gathering Societies: An Introduction," in *Hunters and Gatherers*, vol. 2: *Property, Power and Ideology*, ed. Tim Ingold, David Riches and James Woodburn (Oxford: Berg, 1988), 4–31.

[40] Quoted in Nancy Shoemaker, *A Strange Likeness: Becoming Red and White in Eighteenth-Century North America* (New York: Oxford University Press, 2004), 18.

autumn and spring expressly to make this assignment."[41] This missionary
certainly had a good knowledge of the northern hunters and no doubt he
did his best to describe their property practices, but when he speaks of
"laws and regulations" in relation to a noncoercive stateless society, and
when he invokes "bounds and limits" in the context of a vast forest,
unmarked by fences and survey lines, we begin to wonder if he is trans-
lating Mi'kmaq property practices into a foreign idiom that cannot
accommodate its subtleties.

It is difficult for the historian to gain a sense of hunter-gatherer territoriality and property practices on the basis of European documents
from the early contact period. It is not simply that missionaries such as
Le Jeune and Le Clercq were biased in favor of agriculture and fixed
residence and prejudiced against the nomadic way of life. The problem
runs deeper: they and the colonizers who accompanied them to America
brought with them an ingrained sense, the product of an agrarian way of
life with all its attendant customs, legal principles and spatial concepts,
of what land, land holding and property were. It was difficult, if not
impossible, to find a place for indigenous approaches to land within that
European mental universe. Consequently, early reports often treat the
migrations that were a necessary part of forager existence as the aimless
wanderings of restless savages, while they dismiss the notion that people
such as the Innu had any legitimate claim to their hunting grounds.
Needless to say, this view could function as a convenient justification
for colonial appropriation. However, there was a minority report from
some colonizers, mostly those who, like Chrestien Le Clercq, had taken
the time to gain some acquaintance with hunters' territorial practices,
who insisted that hunting zones were indeed property in much the way
that other kinds of lands were. The implicit disagreement of Paul LeJeune
and Chrestien Le Clercq parallels a similar divergence (quite explicit in
this case) in the views of John Winthrop and Roger Williams concerning
the foraging territories of New England natives. The Winthrop/Williams
debate was really mostly about strategies of dispossession: Winthrop
thought that Indians had a legitimate claim only to their "planting
grounds" and that colonists need not hesitate to occupy the territories
where they hunted; Williams, for his part, was inclined to recognize
hunting grounds as authentic property, land that could be purchased by

---

[41] Chrestien Le Clercq, *New Relation of Gaspesia, with the Customs and Religion of the
Gaspesian Indians*, ed. and trans. William F. Ganong (Toronto: Champlain Society,
1910), 237.

settlers as part of the business of establishing the foundations of a colonial tenure regime (see Chapter 3). These polarized positions on the hunting territories are less contradictory than they seem. While some missionaries and colonists tended to exaggerate difference, others exaggerated similarity, even as both parties predictably measured hunter-gatherer property systems against the cultural norms and legal categories of their own society. As a consequence, the documentary sources that historians habitually draw on when they study this period provide conflicting evidence about hunting grounds and scholars are tempted to lean toward the position that seems most politically congenial. Now as in the past, arguments tend to be structured around an outsider's notion of what constitutes genuine property.

Can the hunting grounds of mobile and nomadic peoples like the Innu be considered part of a property system? If it was in any sense property, should it be understood as "private property" or communal property? In other words, did the foraging zones Paul Le Jeune visited belong to Mestigoït himself or were they the band's? As a means of reframing the issues while expanding our understanding of property in ways that make room for the land practices of foragers as well as cultivators, we might usefully draw on the work of anthropologists who have studied Innu and other, similar hunting-gathering societies of the present day. Many modern-day Innu, along with their neighbors the Algonquins and Cree, continue to hunt for a living in more or less the same northern Quebec environment that sustained their ancestors centuries ago. The rough terrain and severe climate of their country kept agrarian settlers at bay and it was only in comparatively recent historical times that timber and mining companies invaded portions of their territory; extensive flooding associated with the giant James Bay hydroelectric projects produced more severe dislocation for the Cree in the 1970s. As hunting peoples maintaining traditional land practices in modern North America, and as litigants pressing their claims in the face of capitalist resource extraction, the Innu, Cree and Algonquins have attracted the attention of numerous scholarly researchers. Anthropologists, geographers and linguists have displayed particular interest in native customs surrounding property and territoriality. Tapping into the discussions over the land tenure of hunter-gatherers of the twentieth century can perhaps help us better understand the property ways of their seventeenth-century ancestors. This ethnohistorical procedure of "upstreaming" presents well-known pitfalls as well as opportunities. Obviously, information and analysis developed in an era of snowmobiles, bureaucratic states and global capitalism cannot be projected, directly and literally, onto the seventeenth century. On the other hand, when deployed sensitively, ethnographic research on what contemporary Innu say and do about hunting territories, as well as linguistic analysis of their language, can help to open up our own conceptual vocabulary and guide our interpretation of the historical sources.

Sylvie Vincent and José Mailhot, anthropologists working with Innu hunters (they use the French term "Montagnais"), have taken a linguistic approach in their attempt to convey a full sense of the terms in which the latter talk about land and belonging. Their work is particularly precious to historians since language is always shaped by historical traditions as well as current practices.

In the Montagnais language, the same terms are used to refer to the relationship of the Amerindians to the land, whether one speaks of a family hunting territory, rivers and portage trails, a band territory, land claimed by a political association, or even Canada as a whole. These terms are, in essence, two verbs: *tipenitam* and *kanauenitam*. Both have the derivational final *-enit* which conveys the idea of mental activity on the part of the subject of the verb and both belong to the extensive paradigm of Montagnais verbs of thinking. *Tepenitam* refers to the legal relationship between the Montagnais and their lands, that is, the title they claim to the land. *Kanauenitam* refers to the exercise of that title, in other words, the effective daily use of these lands.

The verb *tipenitam*, which refers to title over land, translates literally as "he matches, fits it to, his thinking." An idiomatic English translation would be "he has control, mastery over it." Far from being restricted to the context of territory, this term is commonly used whenever notions of "power" and "control" are implied. It is used to refer to the relationship of a mayor to his city ... parents to their children, God to men and, in the context of Montagnais religion, Master-spirits to the animal species they control. Examination of these contexts indicates that *tipenitam* combines the English meanings of to manage, to be responsible for, to have power over, to control, to direct, to be the master or boss of. The same verb is used to refer to the legal relationship of an individual to a certain number of goods: his house, his car, his money, land he bought or inherited.[42]

"Power" and "control" are prominent among the connotations of the Innu vocabulary of territorial entitlement, but so is productive use of resources. This language of particular attachments applies in a variety of contexts, including religion, politics, personal possessions; it applies within a social universe that includes animals and spiritual entities. It does also apply to land, however, such that territory is spoken of not simply as neutral environment, but as something subject to control by human agents.

---

[42] Sylvie Vincent and José Maihot, "Montagnais Land Tenure," *Interculture* 15 (1982): 63.

In addition to the linguistic approach, several researchers have engaged in on-the-ground ethnographic observation. Examining different communities across the vast and varied landscapes of northern Quebec, their work in the aggregate suggests a diverse pattern of land practices. Some anthropologists report the presence of individualized hunting territories, whereas others do not. One study of the James Bay Cree draws a distinction between commercial hunting and food hunting, insisting that spatial practices are quite different for these two activities. Another observes a tendency in recent historical times for particular families to attach themselves to a certain trading post and to maintain hunting grounds in the vicinity.[43] Research has found that individualized hunting allocations can actually shift location from one year to the next. Based on his work among the Mistassini Cree, Adrian Tanner suggests that personal claims to hunting areas are based more on a relationship with the animals than with "the land" per se; accordingly, the location of a hunter's range can shift somewhat over time, for example, when forest fires provoke migrations.[44]

In hunting-gathering societies, such as that of the Innu, human and other species are not seen as completely separate, and thus the networks of kinship and affiliation that define property relations can extend into the animal world as well as the spiritual sphere. Though humans are in practice the agents of appropriation and land management, animals and mythic figures may well be implicated in the social relations that define tenure. Thus, people in more than one foraging society around the world often speak of the land owning the people rather than the people owning the land.[45] These considerations obviously complicate notions of property and land tenure, but they are not incompatible with specific human claims to particular territories. Adrian Tanner insists on the need to

---

[43] Colin Scott, "Frontières et territoires: Mode de tenure des terres des Cris de l'Est dans la région frontalière Québec/Ontario," *Recherches amérindiennes au Québec* 34 (2004): 25.

[44] Adrian Tanner, "The Significance of Hunting Territories Today," in *Native People, Native Lands: Canadian Indians, Inuit and Metis*, ed. Bruce Alden Cox (Ottawa: Carleton University Press, 1987), 60–74; Adrian Tanner, "The New Hunting Territory Debate: An Introduction to Some Unresolved Issues," *Anthropologica* 28 (1986): 19–36. On the impact of forest fires, see Harvey Feit, "Les territoires de chasse algonquiens avant leur 'découverte'? Études et histoires sur la tenure, les incendies de forêt et la sociabilité de la chasse," *Recherches amérindiennes au Québec* 34 (2004): 5–22.

[45] Tanner, "The Significance of Hunting Territories Today," 60–74. On hunter-gatherers in a very different setting, see Allen Abramson, "Bounding the Unbounded: Ancestral Land and Jural Relations in the Interior of Eastern Fiji," in *Land, Law, and Environment: Mythical Land, Legal Boundaries*, ed. Allen Abramson and Theodossopoulos Dimitrios (London: Pluto Press, 2000), 189–210.

expand conceptions of land tenure to accommodate the norms of northern hunter-gatherers. "In the cases I am aware of," he notes, "Algonquian territories are never 'owned' by anyone other than those who work on them; they cannot be sold, accumulated, or used by the owner to accumulate surplus production."[46] A hunter may enjoy personal "control" over a given territory, but that control is defined within the context of an egalitarian society pursuing a foraging existence in cooperation with the area's fauna. Alienating land is decidedly not part of what it means to "control" a hunting ground.

While Adrian Tanner makes us reconsider the nature of ownership, another anthropologist, Colin Scott, problematizes the figure of the proprietor. Based on his research among the eastern Cree of James Bay, Scott considers the nature of the "control" exercised by a hunter in charge of a given territory. Is this a matter of a beneficial right enjoyed by an individual for himself or is this in the nature of a managerial authority exercised on behalf of a larger collectivity? Scott comes down in favor of the latter view; hunters that earlier ethnographers would not have hesitated to label "proprietors" he refers to instead as "hunting bosses":

The basic unit of land tenure among eastern Cree is a hunting ground or territory ... used by an extended kin network comprising as few as two but as many as a dozen households in an actual production unit. As a production unit, it is permeable, often incorporating people who are primarily or seasonally affiliated with other grounds. The leader of the group is the steward of such a ground. The relationship of the leader (*uuchimaau*) to his land (*utaschiim, -aschii-/* "hunting ground," "land," "world," "creation") centres on his relationship to the animals he uses from it, and to his fellow humans ... The leader's activity is commonly expressed by the verb *tapaiitam* ("he decides," "controls" or "is in charge of it," or more literally, "he matches it to his thinking") ...

There are echoes here of Vincent and Mailhot's linguistic work on the closely related Innu language: a verb – *tapaiitam* in this instance – implying intentionality and control comes to the fore when Cree people speak of hunting grounds. The subject might be a specific man, but his powers are not unlimited and his territory is not his alone: on the contrary, the individual and the land are embedded in a larger social network. Such authority as he enjoys is exercised on behalf of a group and not for his personal benefit. "Customary rights in the land, living resources and products may be specified," Scott writes, "but these relate to the technical and political relations of managing and sharing resources – resources in

---

[46] Tanner, "The New Hunting Territory Debate," 28.

which no one, in the last analysis, retains exclusive or absolute rights."[47] What he describes might be seen as a commons, with constituent zones allocated to particular hunting bands, under the direction of hunting bosses, to ensure that hunting is dispersed in the interests of short-term efficiency and long-term sustainability.

Colin Scott's work also alerts us to the fact that northern hunters speak differently about hunting territories depending on whether they are addressing other Cree or nonindigenous outsiders. When dealing with government agencies or forestry corporations, representatives of a world dominated by capitalism, Quebec Cree tend to refer to hunting lands as personal properties within the territory of the Cree nation, this in spite of a strongly communal aspect to actual practices within their respective communities. Their approach might be seen as a strategic response to the real challenge of communicating between fundamentally different concepts and languages of space and property entitlement. The language of private property arises when the Cree confront state authorities seeking access to their territory for hydroelectric and other forms of development. Negotiations then take place through a discourse of analogies that attempts to bridge the gap between native customs and nonnative legal categories.[48] When the time comes to defend indigenous lands against white outsiders, it becomes necessary to present a case to officialdom and the courts in the language of territorial sovereignty and private property, even if these do not exactly reflect native land practices.

What do we learn from this excursion into the world of modern hunters of the boreal forest? Through studies of the Innu and Cree languages we catch glimpses of a complex of ideas surrounding the vocabulary of "control" that applies in different ways to a variety of objects, places and resources of the land. Ethnographic research acquaints us with territorial allocations that are real and consequential, even where land is not delineated by precise and stable boundaries. We encounter a situation where a given hunting ground might be held and controlled by an individual hunter, even though it also remained the collective property of a band. In this context, the opposition of "communal" and "private"

---

[47] Colin Scott, "Property, Practice and Aboriginal Rights among Quebec Cree Hunters," in Ingold et al., eds., *Hunters and Gatherers*, vol. 2: *Property, Power and Ideology*, 38–40.

[48] Ibid.; Colin Scott, "Hunting Territories, Hunting Bosses and Communal Production among Coastal James Bay Cree," *Anthropologica* 28 (1986): 163–73. In a similar vein, see Paul Nadasdy, "'Property' and Aboriginal Land Claims in the Canadian Subarctic: Some Theoretical Considerations," *American Anthropologist* 104 (March 2002): 247–61.

property (or "collective" versus "personal") seems inadequate, if not meaningless. The only way to salvage these terms would be to treat them, not as poles in a dichotomy, but as different aspects of a single regime. Finally, we learn that hunting peoples often feel the need to offer a simplified, and therefore somewhat distorted, account of their land practices when they communicate with state agencies and other outsiders. It is hardly helpful to add that claims to land and resources were not "absolute," since property rights are never absolute.[49] Similarly, to say that hunting bosses/proprietors were not isolated individuals with exclusive personal control over the resources of their hunting grounds, while true, does not distinguish them from proprietors in other property regimes, since marital and kin connections are always built in to the meaning of property in land. In the infinitely varied spectrum of human property systems, what seems particular to these northern hunters (and by extension perhaps to other foraging peoples) is the way property prerogatives inhere in individuals seamlessly integrated into kin networks. Equally characteristic are the territorial practices by which the Cree and Innu configure space, with landscape understood in terms of central places and waterways rather than being defined by outer boundaries. We will return for a closer look at this spatial aspect of hunting territories in Chapter 8.

Circling back now to the Innu of the early seventeenth century, we can apply some of the lessons derived from ethnographic research on modern hunters and hunting territories. Those lessons are of course suggestive rather than conclusive, since no one would argue that patterns observed in the late twentieth century could be read directly onto an early-contact setting. That said, the observations of ethnographers among northern hunters of our own time indicate that the Innu that Paul Le Jeune accompanied into the bush may well have disposed of multiple hunting territories with shifting locations. Moreover, keeping in mind modern research on the proprietor/hunting boss helps us avoid the trap of an overpolarized conception of private versus collective property. We can better contemplate the notion that trap lines, hunting areas and the game animals that traversed them simultaneously belonged to Mestigoït as

---

[49] The anthropologists cited above – Vincent, Mailhot, Tanner and Scott, whose research and insights have shaped my sense of the property regimes of northern hunters – are all opposed to the use of the term "property" in that context. Vincent and Mailhot, "Montagnais Land Tenure," 63; Tanner, "The New Hunting Territory Debate," 28; Scott, "Property, Practice and Aboriginal Rights," 40.

band leader and to the band itself. Access to the food resources of the hunting territory was inseparably dependent on kin and social relations focusing on Mestigoït, but contemporary ethnography suggests that outsiders could be integrated into the band through fictive kin connections. Le Jeune clearly benefited from the headman's personal sponsorship. Anxious to maintain good relations with the French, this band had conferred an Innu name on the missionary ("Nicanis") and that gesture seems to have implied honorary kinsman status, and as a consequence, a share in the produce of the hunt. From modern ethnography as well we get a sense of the geography of hunter-gatherer property, a landscape defined more by rivers, lakes and watersheds than by terrestrial boundaries. Perhaps it did not occur to Paul Le Jeune to ask by what right his hosts hunted waterfowl on and around the islands of the St. Lawrence, but we can be confident that Mestigoït knew what he was doing in this respect.

THE ANTHROPOLOGY OF HUNTING GROUNDS

Study of the land practices of Innu and related northern hunting peoples has turned out to be an intellectual launching pad for more general reflections on the nature of property in a variety of disciplines. Since these disciplines are all rooted in a culture whose norms, expectations, laws and even languages, as they relate to land and entitlement, were shaped by an agricultural way of life, mobile peoples and their foraging territories serve as important food for reflection. Can unbounded forests whose resources are available in different ways and at different seasons to individuals embedded in kin networks really be considered property? Territoriality and entitlement among hunter-gatherers seems to form a kind of intellectual boundary case, suggesting a need either to limit the term "property" to agriculturally based societies or to extend its definition to encompass foraging zones and perhaps other forms of territorial entitlement unfamiliar to Europeans. Research on the hunting grounds of northern hunters has supplied empirical material to fuel debates about the nature of property in anthropology, law and economics. These more general inquiries and the theories they have generated are of obvious importance for the present study, all the more so to the extent that they revolve around hunting grounds, for the latter are a feature of most indigenous North American societies, including semi-sedentary villagers like the Ninnimissinuok as well as the Innu. It therefore seems worthwhile to embark on a brief tangent to explore some of the ways in which such non-European land practices have been integrated into (or explicitly banished from) theories of property.

For one of the founders of modern anthropology, Lewis Henry Morgan, property provided the key to charting the evolution of human society:

The idea of property was slowly formed in the human mind, remaining nascent and feeble through immense periods of time. Springing into life in savagery, it required all the experience of this period and of the subsequent period of barbarism to develop the germ, and to prepare the human brain for the acceptance of its controlling influence. Its dominance as a passion over all other passions marks the commencement of civilization. It not only led mankind to overcome the obstacles which delayed civilization, but to establish political society on the basis of territory and of property. A critical knowledge of the evolution of the idea of property would embody, in some respects, the most remarkable portion of the mental history of mankind.[50]

Morgan's field research focused on the Iroquois of New York State, but he also assembled information on societies around the globe and probed the literature on ancient civilizations to construct a general theory on the progress of humanity. He was convinced that the world's cultures all progressed, some more quickly than others, by way of the same stages: from savagery, through lower, middle and upper barbarism, to civilization. Technological innovations – notably the adoption of agriculture and mastery of metallurgy – drove the process along, but it was the distinctive property regimes that most clearly marked off one stage from another. "Savage" societies – what later scholars would call hunter-gatherers – and "barbarian" society – a broad rubric under which Morgan places semi-sedentary villagers like the Ninnimissinuok as well as diverse peoples such as the ancient Hebrews and Aztecs – each had their particular customs for controlling the possession and intergenerational transmission of personal property and land. Unlike movable wealth, land was never owned by an individual in savage and barbarian societies. On this point, Morgan was insistent, not to say dogmatic: prior to the advent of civilization, land was communally owned. When a barbarian chief was regarded as the owner of all his people's lands, he argues, this was a fiction masking the fact that the tribe itself, personified by its chieftain, actually owned the territory in common. Morgan used the Latin term *gens* to cover a variety of extended or fictive kin groups that held land in savage and barbarian societies: from the archaic Roman *gens* to the Iroquoian clan and the Nahua *calpulli*. When such a communal property regime was finally superseded in favor of individual property, the shift constituted a major watershed,

---

[50] Lewis Henry Morgan, *Ancient Society* (Cambridge, Mass.: Belknap Press of Harvard University Press, 1964 [1877]), 13.

bringing in its wake monogamy, patriarchy and inheritance by offspring. "The idea of absolute individual ownership of land was a growth through experience, the complete attainment of which belongs to the period of civilization."[51] In other words, civilization, the summit of cultural development, is defined by private property.

Lewis Morgan's views on property and kinship found an enthusiastic audience in Karl Marx and his collaborator Friedrich Engels; the latter fashioned from Morgan's theory the concept of "primitive communism."[52] In Marx and Engels's evolutionary model, the communalism of the "savage" stage demonstrated that humans have a capacity for cooperation and sharing that could be resurrected after capital, under a regime of private property, had completed the task of enhancing productivity and wealth; the universal prosperity of advanced socialism would ensue. Some Marxist anthropologists have continued to refine the concept of primitive communism down to the present day.[53]

Meanwhile, Franz Boas and his followers were busy turning the discipline of anthropology against the general idea, pervaded, as they believed, by racist and imperialist assumptions, that humanity advanced by stages from an inferior to a superior state.[54] In the early twentieth century, two Boas students, Robert H. Lowie and Frank Speck, took the lead in refuting what they called the "myth of primitive communism." Lowie, the more theoretically minded of the two, surveyed the ethnographic literature and concluded that particular claims to land and resources were a feature of all societies, including so-called primitive ones.[55] The bulk of the empirical ammunition for this argument came from the tireless field research of Frank Speck, an anthropologist who mounted a series of summer expeditions to Innu, as well as Abenaki and

---

[51] Ibid., 249.

[52] Friedrich Engels, *The Origin of the Family, Private Property, and the State, in the Light of the Researches of Lewis H. Morgan* (New York: International Publishers, 1972 [German original 1884]).

[53] See, for example, Richard B. Lee, "Reflections on Primitive Communism," in *Hunters and Gatherers*, vol. 1: *History, Evolution and Social Change*, ed. T. Ingold, D. Riches and J. Woodburn (Oxford: Berg, 1988), 252–68. Another noteworthy Marxist contribution to the anthropology of landed property makes less extensive use of the language of "primitive communism": Maurice Godelier, "Territory and Property in Some Pre-Capitalist Societies," in *The Mental and the Material* (London: Verso, 1986), 71–121.

[54] Regna Darnell, "North American Traditions in Anthropology: The Historiographic Baseline," in *A New History of Anthropology*, ed. Henrika Kuklick (Malden, Mass., and Oxford: Blackwell, 2008), 35–51.

[55] Robert H. Lowie, *Primitive Society* (New York: Boni and Liveright, 1920), 205–55.

Cree, communities of Quebec and Labrador.[56] Since he visited in what was, for these hunters, the off-season, he did not actually experience the winter hunt or traverse their often-remote northern hunting grounds. Nevertheless, through intensive interviews with the people concerned, Speck managed to map the contours of hunting and trapping territories belonging to individual families. Critics would later charge that his cartography corresponded to the ideals of how people thought the tenure regime *should* function, rather than how land was actually used on the winter hunts. They also note that Speck's main informants were at the time engaged in disputes with timber companies and, in an effort to defend their rights in terms that corresponded to the "white man's law," they were exaggerating the degree to which their tenure conformed to the dominant culture's sense of "private property."[57] Be that as it may, Speck was convinced that the northern hunting economy was organized on the basis of stable and clearly bounded individual hunting grounds. And although Speck's research was not particularly historical, other anthropologists contributed evidence gleaned from missionary and fur-trade writings from across northeastern North America in the colonial era that seemed to support the notion that hunting grounds were, and had always been, private property, plain and simple.[58]

An important Marxist riposte to the Lowie–Speck interpretation of hunting territories arrived in 1954 when Eleanor Leacock attempted to salvage the primitive communism thesis by combining it with the then-current anthropological concept of "acculturation." Like Speck before

[56] Frank G. Speck, "The Family Hunting Band as the Basis of Algonkian Social Organization," *American Anthropologist* 17, no. 2 (1915): 289–305; Frank G. Speck, "Mistassini Hunting Territories in the Labrador Peninsula," *American Anthropologist* 25 (1923): 452–71; Frank G. Speck and Loren C. Eiseley, "Montagnais-Naskapi Bands and Family Hunting Districts of the Central and Southeastern Labrador Peninsula," *Proceedings of the American Philosophical Society* 85, no. 2 (January 1942): 215–42. See also Janet Chute, "Frank G. Speck's Contribution to the Understanding of Mi'kmaq Land Use, Leadership and Land Management," *Ethnohistory* 46 (1999): 481–540.

[57] See Harvey Feit, "The Construction of Algonquian Hunting Territories: Private Property as Moral Lesson, Policy Advocacy, and Ethnographic Error," in *Colonial Situations: Essays on the Contextualization of Ethnographic Knowledge*, ed. George W. Stocking, Jr. (Madison: University of Wisconsin Press, 1991), 109–35.

[58] John M. Cooper, "Land Tenure among the Indians of Eastern and Northern North America," *Pennsylvanian Archaeologist* 8 (1938): 55–59; John M. Cooper, "Is the Algonquian Family Hunting Ground System Pre-Columbian?," *American Anthropologist* 41 (1939): 66–90; Loren C. Eiseley, "Land Tenure in the Northeast: A Note on the History of a Concept," *American Anthropologist* 49 (1947): 680–81; Anthony F. C. Wallace, "Political Organization and Land Tenure among the Northeastern Indians, 1600–1830," *Southwestern Journal of Anthropology* 13 (1957): 301–21.

her, Leacock concentrated on the case of the Innu and related northern hunters, but she combined research in an ethnohistorical vein with fieldwork in northern Quebec. Central to her historical argument is evidence from Paul Le Jeune's account of his experiences accompanying Mestigoït's band through the frozen forests in the winter of 1633–34. That hunting expedition, she observes, had an improvised quality quite incompatible with the highly regulated system Speck discerned three centuries later. Until the moment of departure, both the composition and the destination of the winter hunting party seemed uncertain. Rather than returning annually to their own respective grounds, hunters adjusted their course, moving toward reported concentrations of game and away from other hunting parties. The stable private hunting territories that Speck described were therefore not primordial, but rather the product of a fundamental historical change. "Traditional" primitive communism gave way to private property, and the agent of change, Leacock argues, was the fur trade. Once the Innu had become integrated into the Atlantic economy and dependent on imported European goods, they established individualized hunting grounds on which to trap beaver for trade. Even so, these exclusive property rights applied only to commercial fur trapping, not to the food hunt. Thus, she concludes, the advent of commodity production brought about the momentous shift from the open-access primitive communism of the aboriginal stage to the private property in land characteristic of a world dominated by capital.[59]

Leacock's before-and-after narrative rests quite heavily on a particular reading of the Le Jeune text, supported by a few other passages from the early *Jesuit Relations*. It also depends on the accuracy of Speck's claim that twentieth-century hunting territories represented private property of an unproblematic sort. In light of the more recent research cited above, however, both poles of that stark contrast seem grossly oversimplified. Northern hunters of the present day manage hunting territories in complex ways that cannot be reduced to either "private property" or "primitive communism." Moreover, the mechanism of change that Leacock proposes – "acculturation" through the effects of commercial fur production – also raises questions. Current historical scholarship on the early fur trade hardly supports the assumption that the Innu of the St. Lawrence were commodity virgins in Mestigoït's day. These people

---

[59] Eleanor Burke Leacock, *The Montagnais "Hunting Territory" and the Fur Trade* (Menasha, Wis.: American Anthropological Association, 1954).

had a long-standing connection with Atlantic commercial circuits. French, English and other European traders had been visiting them on a regular basis for at least fifty years by that time; trapping for commercial purposes was, by all indications, a well-established part of the Innu economy before Mestigoït was born.[60] All this to say that the compelling tidiness of Leacock's story of a fundamental transformation of property relations through the influence of commodity production breaks down when the constituent elements of the thesis are examined closely. The evidence no longer supports the notion that Innu property systems corresponded to the ideal type of primitive communism in 1634 or to that of private property in 1915; nor is there firm support for the assertion that the fur trade effected a shift from one state to the other.

Notwithstanding these difficulties, the Leacock thesis was accepted in many quarters as a full and conclusive account of property transformation among northern hunting peoples. The study's influence extended well beyond Marxist circles in anthropology. For some, the Innu shift to private property under the influence of commodity production would take on the quality of a paradigmatic case with universal significance. The economist Harold Demsetz (anything but a Marxist) drew on Leacock's work to fashion a general theory accounting for changes in property systems.[61] Under what circumstances and according to what calculations of advantage, Demsetz asked, do societies make transitions between common property, state property and private property? The list of categories in this morphology is rather limited and their respective characteristics summarily sketched, but Demstetz felt confident that he had demonstrated how the move from communal to private property allows "externalities" to become "internalities" and the case of the Innu is his one illustrative example. Communal hunting grounds worked well as long as people hunted only to satisfy their own needs for food and skins, but when beaver pelts became a salable product, every hunter had an incentive to kill as many animals as possible. To prevent such unsustainable overhunting, the Innu reached a societal decision to create individualized territories so that each hunter could

---

[60] Marcel Trudel, *Histoire de la Nouvelle France*, vol. 1: *Les vaines tentatives, 1524–1603* (Montreal: Fides, 1963), 213–44; Bruce G. Trigger, *Natives and Newcomers: Canada's "Heroic Age" Reconsidered* (Kingston and Montreal: McGill-Queen's University Press, 1985), 135–44; Bernard Allaire, *Pelleteries, manchons et chapeaux de castor: les fourrures nord-américaines à Paris, 1500–1632* (Sillery, QC: Septentrion, 1999), 57–93.

[61] Harold Demsetz, "Toward a Theory of Property Rights," *The American Economic Review* 57 (May 1967): 347–59.

then manage the resources of his respective zone to ensure a sustained yield. This was certainly a weighty conclusion to hang on Eleanor Leacock's rather tenuous interpretation of the *Jesuit Relations* and of Frank Speck's field studies. Interestingly, Demsetz's view of the advantages of private over communal property displays affinities with Garrett Hardin's hugely influential article, "The Tragedy of the Commons," published at about the same time as Demsetz's paper.[62] Hardin, an ecologist, argued that common property, such as a collective pasture in a pastoral community or a forest used by many woodcutters, is subject to overexploitation because each user has an interest in maximizing her or his take and no one has an incentive to limit harvests in the interests of long-term sustainability. Written in forceful, nontechnical prose, Hardin's essay generated widespread interest in the general public. Both Hardin and Demsetz came down strongly in favor of private property, but it was the economist who enjoyed a more lasting influence within social scientific circles. Demsetz's theoretical piece would come to be regarded as a cornerstone text in the emergence of the field known as the "new institutional economics." A later contribution to that field, *The Rise of the Western World*, by Nobel prize winner Douglas C. North and his co-author Robert Thomas, traces the progressive implantation of private "property rights" as a basic foundation of capitalism and modernity.[63] Whereas nineteenth-century anthropology had once posited a metanarrative of modernity with private property marking the threshold of fundamental change, a hundred years later a similar schematic history of human progress found a home in economics.

---

[62] Garrett Hardin, "The Tragedy of the Commons," *Science* 162 (1968): 1243–48. Fabien Locher situates Hardin's theory in the context of cold war science: Fabien Locher, "Les pâturages de la Guerre froide: Garrett Hardin et la 'tragédie des communs,'" *Revue d'histoire moderne et contemporaine* 60 (2013): 7–36.

[63] Douglas C. North and Robert Paul Thomas, *The Rise of the Western World: A New Economic History* (Cambridge: Cambridge University Press, 1973). It is important to note that the new institutional economics, under the influence of another Nobel Prize winner, Elinor Ostrom, moved on from a rather uncritical celebration of private property to an appreciation of the importance and value of common property and open-access resources. What remains, however, is a continuing attachment to the Platonic ideal of "full ownership of land" as a meaningful analytic concept; "commons" and "private property" still form a stark dichotomy in the work of this school of thought. See, for example, Daniel H. Cole and Elinor Ostrom, eds., *Property in Land and Other Resources* (Cambridge, Mass.: Lincoln Institute of Land Policy, 2012).

Meanwhile, anthropology had moved on. Anthropologists continued to wrestle with the challenges posed by hunter-gatherer societies and their land regimes, tending always toward more complex understandings. As early as the 1940s, Ojibway specialist Irving Hallowell was challenging the common-versus-individual terms in which debates about hunting grounds had been conducted. His discussion of hunting territories led him to more probing reflections on the concept of landed property more generally. Hallowell's fieldwork was conducted in north-central Canada, among hunters whose way of life and property regime closely resembled those of the Innu, and his conclusion was that territories did not correspond to either of the ideal-types of "private" or "communal" property. Instead, he argued, property is always embedded in social relations. "Considered from a functional point of view, property rights are institutionalized means of defining *who* may control various classes of valuable objects for a variety of present and future purposes and the *conditions* under which this power may be exercised."[64] The Africanist Max Gluckman would later develop this point more fully. Property rights, according to Gluckman, tend to have both personal and community dimensions, and so the Morgan versus Lowie confrontation hinged on a false dichotomy.[65]

But do these observations apply only to "tribal societies" or hunter-gatherers? What about us? What about property in the Euro-American "West"? When they tried to characterize property systems like those of the Innu or the Ninnimissinuok, anthropologists frequently ended up implicitly commenting on the property systems of their own society and that of their imagined reader. This is most obvious in Morgan's complacent view of savage and barbarian property as "communal" and therefore the negation of modern, "civilized" private property. "Our" property defines "their" property as its opposing counterpart; in a similar fashion,

---

[64] A. Irving Hallowell, "The Nature and Function of Property as a Social Institution," in his *Culture and Experience* (New York: Schocken, 1967), 236–49 (originally published 1943).

[65] "We say that a person or a group 'owns' a piece of land or some item of property. We are speaking loosely when we use this sort of phrasing: what is owned in fact is a claim to have power to do certain things with the land or property, to possess immunities against the encroachment of others on one's rights in them, and to exercise certain privileges in respect of them. But in addition other persons may have certain rights, claims, powers, privileges and immunities in respect of the same land or property." Gluckman goes on: "Property law in tribal society defines not so much rights of persons over things, as obligations owed between persons in respect of things." Max Gluckman, *Politics, Law and Ritual in Tribal Society* (Oxford: Blackwell, 1965), 36, 46.

"their" property defines "ours." Later generations of anthropologists deliberately rejected Morgan's hierarchical view of inferior and superior cultures, but they did not find it easy to escape from a we/they binary opposition where such matters as property were concerned. Moreover, disciplinary traditions about the location of field research created an imbalance between the two components of the comparison: information on Ojibway or Ashanti property (and culture more generally) derived from close and careful ethnographic investigation, whereas data on the modern West were gathered through more casual observation. The danger of essentializing, the attribution of exaggerated, fundamental difference, was ever-present.

Since the late twentieth century, anthropologists have been bringing a higher degree of self-reflexivity to studies of indigenous land tenure and property. Having felt the influence of postmodernism's suspicion of binary oppositions, the new anthropology of property tends to embrace complexity and to challenge simple oppositions of individual versus collective property, usufruct versus ownership, modern versus premodern, nature versus culture, even subject versus object. We cannot hope to apprehend the property systems of hunting or pastoral societies, it implies, if we are besotted with the provincialism and collective self-delusions of our own society. Ethnography directed at the other therefore tends to go hand-in-hand with critical inquiry directed at the anthropologist's own culture. The work of Marilyn Strathern nicely exemplifies this intellectual orientation. Strathern specializes in what she and others call research in a "double location." Initially she followed the traditions of ethnographic fieldwork in selecting for close scrutiny a nonstate society, the Mt. Hagen people of the New Guinea highlands; among other aspects of their complex property system, she wrote on bridewealth, gifts, men's and women's claims to lands, pigs and labor. In this context, she found, individuals did not appear as integrated subjects, but rather as fragmented entities, simultaneously owners and owned objects in variegated kin, marital and social relations. At a certain point in her investigations, Strathern turned her attention to emergent property forms in her own society, especially to the legal and ethical issues raised by new reproductive technologies and the patenting of gene sequences. The western individual, it turned out, was just as divided as the New Guinea highlander, and in somewhat similar ways: for now frozen embryos and human genetic matter had become, actually or potentially, property. Different aspects of a single person could be simultaneously owner and owned, in this respect following the lead of the ostensibly "primitive" Hagens. By moving her gaze back and forth between supposedly "modern" and "premodern" settings, the ethnographer subverts the favored dichotomies of modern thought.[66]

Some anthropologists remain convinced that the vocabulary of "property" has no place in discussions of nonstate peoples pursuing a foraging way of life.[67] Other scholars take a contrary view, arguing that, in spite of the almost universal ethic of sharing, a rule that works against the accumulation of wealth, foragers inhabit a world built upon intricate systems of property relations. Write Alan Barnard and James Woodburn, "*Property rights*, arguably, are the foundation of hunter-gatherer society."[68] Another scholar redefines property in the following terms: "The word 'property' is best seen as directing attention to a vast field of cultural as well as social relations, to the symbolic as well as the material contexts within which things are recognized and personal as well as collective identities made."[69] Indeed, there was a revival in anthropological studies on landed property in the wake of the fall of European communism and the spread of capitalism across previously remote parts of the Third World. With collective farms being privatized, while agrobusiness and mining corporations fence off lands previously used by poor villagers in Africa and Latin America, ethnographers find abundant opportunities to study the social implications of property regimes and their transformations.[70]

---

[66] Marilyn Strathern, *Property, Substance, and Effect: Anthropological Essays on Persons and Things* (New Brunswick, N.J.: Athlone Press, 1999). In a very different way, Alain Testart also examines property in a "double location." His essay, synthetic and much more historical than Strathern's work, compares African and European traditions of land tenure. Alain Testart, "Propriété et non-propriété de la terre. L'illusion de la propriété collective archaïque (1re partie)," *Études rurales* (2003): 209–42.

[67] In addition to the works cited in note 49, see Paul Nadasdy, "'Property' and Aboriginal Land Claims in the Canadian Subarctic: Some Theoretical Considerations," *American Anthropologist* 104 (March 2002): 247–61.

[68] Barnard and Woodburn, "Property, Power and Ideology in Hunting and Gathering Societies," 4 (emphasis in original).

[69] C. M. Hann, "Introduction: The Embeddedness of Property," in *Property Relations: Renewing the Anthropological Tradition*, ed. C. M. Hann (Cambridge: Cambridge University Press, 1998), 5.

[70] See the essays collected in Hann, ed., *Property Relations*.

3

Early Contacts

This chapter examines the first years of colonial contact in our three zones, maintaining the focus, to the extent possible, on the indigenous experience of this novel situation. When Spaniards, French and English intruded into indigenous spaces and decided to make themselves at home there, existing territorial and property arrangements could not help but be affected. And yet, the immediate effects were not necessarily transformative. More than one might expect, the newcomers formed their settlements within established native tenurial regimes. However aggressive they may have been in asserting their ways of government and religion, the conquerors and empire builders could be quite tentative and pragmatic when it came to establishing landed property.

NAHUA

"First contact" in central Mexico quickly turned into a bloody cataclysm. After a long and exceptionally destructive siege by a force of Spaniards and native allies commanded by Hernán Cortés, the Aztec capital of Tenochtitlán finally surrendered on day One Serpent in the year Three House (13 August 1521). With their city in ruins, the gaunt and bewildered Mexica survivors awaited their fate, while Spanish attention turned to the spoils of war. The pillaging of Aztec gold and silver had begun well before Cortés was assured of victory, as had the forcible enlistment of natives to labor in support of the besieging army. The moment of victory only signaled a fuller orgy of rape and pillage. Soldiers searched for gold vessels hidden under the skirts of refugees fleeing shattered Tenochtitlán, notes a Nahuatl account of the defeat; it continues: "A few of the men were separated from the others. These men were the bravest and strongest warriors ... The Spaniards immediately branded them with hot irons, either on the cheek or the lips."[1] Precious metals apart, it was people that they wanted: men to transport supplies for new expeditions of conquest and to build the new capital, Mexico City, women and children for domestic service and sexual servitude. Nahua people who remained in the surrounding countryside had to bring in food and other supplies. Conquistadors took what they wanted, but title to land was not their target, as opposed to the products of Indian effort exerted on Indian land.

Armed bands of Spaniards spread across the landscape, seemingly unstoppable now that the indigenous power of the region had been crushed. In the bloodshed and destruction of the conquest period, some elements of Nahua society suffered more severely than others. Priests, seen as instruments of the devil, were massacred without mercy; the noble warrior class also perished disproportionately, though some of the indigenous elite survived, their numbers and power diminished. Peasants would predominate numerically in this largely decapitated native society. Likewise, the peaks of the built landscape crashed to the ground as temples were demolished and palaces looted; indigenous Mexico was already beginning to take on a strictly rural character. A deadly epidemic that broke out shortly after Cortés's first arrival in 1519 proved to be the precursor of a series of lethal contagions that would reduce the native population to a fraction of its pre-conquest level. Amazingly, and in spite of all these assaults, the Nahua peoples survived and even managed to preserve much of their language, culture, community life and lands.

In the immediate aftermath of the conquest, Cortés struggled to control the chaos and establish stable Spanish rule; in addition to assuring discipline and military security, this meant, above all, finding ways to replace random, violent pillage with a system of regular, predictable exploitation of natives. (He had only to think of the utter devastation of the Caribbean Taino under predatory Spanish rule to realize how quickly colonization *à outrance* could self-destruct.) Such a transition entailed challenges that countless other conquerors had faced before him: how to intimidate and pacify the conquered without destroying their capacity to produce,

---

[1] Miguel Leon-Portilla, ed., *The Broken Spears: The Aztec Account of the Conquest of Mexico* (Boston: Beacon Press, 1992), 118–20. See also Bernal Díaz del Castillo, *The Conquest of New Spain*, trans. J. M. Cohen (London: Penguin Books, 1963), 408; Stuart B. Schwartz, ed., *Victors and Vanquished: Spanish and Nahua Views of the Conquest of Mexico* (Boston: Bedford/St. Martin's, 2000).

how to control his own warriors without forfeiting their loyalty, how to invoke the legitimate authority of a distant monarch without surrendering the advantages of on-the-spot power. Faced with these dilemmas, Cortés experimented with various strategies. He sent some of his followers off to conquer lands that had been beyond the reach of the Aztec armies, while he rewarded others with domains in central Mexico. He wrote to Charles V, presenting him with a rich overseas kingdom and then proceeded to ignore the king's orders to turn over the revenues attached to that prize. As for the indigenous population, defeated and injured but still very numerous, Cortés dealt with them as a conqueror, drawing on both Nahua and Spanish cultural scripts as he improvised systems of subjugation. It would not be about taking lands away from people, but rather about incorporating a populated and productive territory, previously dominated by Moctezuma, into a new imperial order.

As soon as Charles V learned that Mexico had been won in his name, he ordered Cortés to secure for the royal treasury all revenues the inhabitants owed to their deposed rulers. "They will give and pay to us for each year as much revenue and tribute as were given and paid until now to their priests and lords."[2] It is noteworthy that, at the imperial center, the first response to conquest should be an impulse to take over the Aztec *tlatoani*'s position in the Mesoamerican tribute system. Cortés, happy to invoke the king's sovereignty to legitimize his authority, had other plans for the riches of Mexico and he was in no mood to surrender these quietly. Such a rich country, with a large population accustomed to obedience and to the exactions of conquerors, was a prize worth fighting for.[3] By the time the king's orders reached Cortés, he had, in fact, already divided up most of the country into lucrative estates for his followers (the biggest reserved for himself, needless to say), and, in blatant defiance of royal authority, he resisted all attempts to interfere with his jurisdiction and with his and his underlings' privileges. With no other forces in New Spain to enforce compliance, the king had to give ground. Eventually, a viceroy would be installed and a colonial bureaucracy

---

[2] Quoted in Hanns J. Prem, "Spanish Colonization and Indian Property in Central Mexico, 1521–1620," *Annals of the Association of American Geographers* 82 (1992): 445.

[3] The aboriginal nations colonized by the English and the French were quite different in that respect, which is one reason why neither New England nor New France was built upon tribute relations. (The English and French did occasionally demand tribute from defeated Indians, but the practice was hardly foundational to the colonial relationship.) See Anthony Pagden, *Lords of All the World: Ideologies of Empire in Spain, Britain and France c. 1500–c. 1800* (New Haven, Conn.: Yale University Press, 1995), 65–66 and passim.

would begin to bring the conquistadors to heel, but it would be a difficult, protracted struggle, punctuated with compromises.

Meanwhile, Cortés took the first formal steps to regularize his conquest by summoning indigenous rulers from across the Aztec-dominated territories to come and submit to him at his temporary quarters in Coyoacan, where he lived during the construction of the colonial capital of Mexico City. The only Spanish record of this meeting is a brief and somewhat enigmatic passage from a bill of indictment, drawn up years later when Cortés stood accused of corruption and misrule; it does not specify a date, but the context suggests it was likely in 1522.[4] This seems to have been an important moment in the initial consolidation of Spanish rule, though the sources do not allow much certainty about exactly how the event unfolded. It is said that the "lords of the land" presented Cortés with rich presents of gold and featherwork. Gifts usually confer obligations and cement relations and so it seems likely that the Nahua leaders were desperately hoping that their presents would serve to moderate Spanish violence and establish a more predictable regime. At the same time, they may also have wished to demonstrate their own political importance. Cortés accordingly confirmed the internal authority of each submissive ruler over his respective *altepetl*, effectively recognizing the autonomy of the indigenous communities. Henceforth, local communities would be known as "pueblos" ("villages" in Spanish) instead of *altepeme*, and the Caribbean Taino word "cacique" (chief) would designate the ruler formerly known as *tlatoani*.

After affirming this basic continuity of status, Cortés then "gave" each pueblo so constituted to a Spaniard from among his followers or, in some cases, reserved it for himself in his personal capacity. There were gifts, there was submission, there was confirmation of local rule: all this would have been readily understandable to both Spaniards and Nahua. But what did it mean to "give" a community to a particular Spaniard in a case where the local *tlatoani* had just been recognized as lord and vassal of his

---

[4] *Colección de Documentos Inéditos relativos al descubrimiento, conquista y organización de las antiguas posesiones españolas de América y Oceanía*, 42 vols. (Madrid: Manuel G. Hernández, 1864–84), vol. 27: 22–23, 260. For interpretations of this source, see Rebecca Horn, *Postconquest Coyoacan: Nahua-Spanish Relations in Central Mexico, 1519–1650* (Stanford, Calif.: Stanford University Press, 1997), 10; René García Castro, "Los Pueblos de Indios," in *Gran Historia de Mexico Ilustrada* (Mexico City: Planeta DeAgostini, 2001), vol. 8: 143; María Cristina Torales Pacheco, *Tierras de Indios, tierras de españoles: Confirmación y composición de tierras y aguas en la jurisdicción de Cholula (siglos XVI-XVIII)* (Mexico City: Universidad Iberoamericana, 2005), 17.

majesty the king? The cryptic primary account speaks of events "at the time of dividing up the land"; elsewhere the indictment says that Cortés divided up "Indians and lots" unfairly, reserving to himself "large numbers of Indians and provinces."[5] At first glance, it might almost seem that these phrases referred to a distribution of slaves, landed estates and territorial jurisdictions ("provinces"), but that would be a misreading. It would be more accurate to say that Cortés was conferring upon his associates a form of property that entailed the power to exploit the native population of a given territory. We seem to be witnessing the beginning of the *encomienda* system in New Spain.

Encomienda was not exactly a landed estate as contemporaries in Europe would understand that term: although each grant came with a certain sense of locality and territory, it was not really a precise spatial designation; *encomiendas* were measured in terms of population, not surface area. An entire community, with its existing internal government and property arrangements, was to be subjected to the exactions of the *encomendero*. The system was sometimes justified in paternalistic terms as an institution through which a Spaniard would protect "his" Indians and guide them toward a Christian way of life, but in practice it was baldly exploitive:

The record of the first encomienda generation, in the Valley [of Mexico] as elsewhere, is one of generalized abuse and particular atrocities. Encomenderos used their Indians in all forms of manual labor, in building, farming, and mining, and for the supply of whatever the country yielded. They overtaxed and over-worked them. They jailed them, killed them, beat them, and set dogs on them. They seized their goods, destroyed their agriculture, and took their women ... The first encomenderos, without known exception, understood Spanish authority as provision for unlimited personal opportunism.[6]

This was not "appropriation of native land" as seen in later versions of American colonization and it was not like the more orderly style of pre-Hispanic Aztec tribute collection, but it had in common with the latter a tendency to extract value without transforming the internal tenure systems and political organization of conquered communities.

Encomienda in New Spain had Mesoamerican as well as European and Atlantic-world roots. In its Old World setting, the institution and the

---

[5] *Colección de Documentos Inéditos*, 27: 22–23, 260. "Al tiempo que se rrepartió la Tierra"; "que rrepartió los indios e solares"; "mucha suma de yndios e provincias."

[6] Charles Gibson, *The Aztecs under Spanish Rule: A History of the Indians of the Valley of Mexico, 1519–1810* (Stanford, Calif.: Stanford University Press, 1964), 78.

underlying idea that tribute was the proper way to express the subjugation of defeated non-Christians, while rewarding warriors who had
fought to extend the king's dominions, goes back to the Reconquista
of the Middle Ages, when the Iberian peninsula was a battleground
between contending Christian and Muslim principalities. In the kingdom
of Castile, the large Christian state that eventually formed the core of
consolidated Spain, *encomienda* was the favored term for the lucrative
privileges accorded to the leaders of conquering armies as well as to
ecclesiastical bodies and others active in colonizing newly won territories.
The king asserted his own dominion over the resources of lands conquered in his name, but he usually bowed to the alignment of forces on
the ground and granted control over land, jurisdiction and revenues to a
trusty vassal. These privileges had a feudal flavor characteristic of the
period, such that jurisdiction and landlordism intertwined; exactions
that a later age would distinguish as taxes, rents, and labor service tended
to be mixed together.[7] In this earlier Iberian context, warriors were
rewarded, religious adversaries were humiliated and the king's authority
was recognized in principle. When Spain took possession of the islands
of the West Indies following Columbus's voyages, *encomienda* emerged
as a device for rewarding conquistadors by extracting revenue from
subjugated non-Christian peoples, "Indians" in this case, rather than
Moors. The religious logic of Iberian *encomienda* – disabilities designed
to provide an incentive to religious conversion – evaporated in the New
World setting: natives who became Christian did not escape from the
burdens of the system.

Tribute and labor service were at the core of the Mexican *encomienda*,
an arrangement that tended, in the early decades of Spanish rule, to
follow established Mesoamerican patterns. As under the Aztecs, tribute
could take many forms, with maize, cloth, chiles, construction materials
and handicraft products numbering among the goods accepted. Households, as represented by married men, were liable for tribute; widows
and the unmarried were not assessed directly; indigenous nobles seem to
have been entirely exempt. Tribute levels corresponded roughly to the
size of land-holdings. In addition to their regular payments in kind,
Indians also had to supply labor, to the *encomendero* as well as to
colonial officials, especially for the construction of churches and public
buildings. Generally, tribute and labor service requirements resembled

---

[7] Robert S. Chamberlain, "Castilian Backgrounds of the Repartimiento-Encomienda,"
Contributions to American Anthropology and History 5 (1939): 23–70.

pre-conquest practices, though they seem to have been more severely burdensome under the Spanish.

Even as he confirmed native property and local government under Spanish rule, Cortés was also creating lands and jurisdictions for Spaniards. The process of establishing islands of Spanish jurisdiction actually began before the Aztecs had been defeated. Shortly after landing on the shores of the Gulf of Mexico in 1519, Cortés set up the town of La Villa Rica de Vera Cruz, complete with municipal officers and magistrates; his object at the time was to improvise a judicial body that could provide a cover of legality for his dubiously legitimate expedition.[8] Later, during the course of the conquest, he instituted *cabildos* (town councils) wherever Spanish arms prevailed and groups of conquerors settled down to enjoy the fruits of victory. "Now that this land had been pacified," he writes of one region, "... I chose the site which seemed best and founded there a town, to which I gave the name Santistevan del Puerto; and to the people who wished to remain there as settlers, I assigned those villages in Your Majesty's name, for their sustenance."[9] As Spanish towns became more fully established, they acquired judicial powers as well as the authority to distribute lands. Local citizens (*vecinos*) were each entitled to a building lot in the town (*solar*) as well as access to the municipal commons (*ejido*). Spanish-American *cabildos* were also able – at least in the early years, before the viceroy monopolized land grants – to grant pieces of land to individuals. These grants, along with the urban lots and commons, were for "Spaniards" only, and they were held, inherited and sold under terms and conditions quite unlike those prevailing in a *pueblo de indios*. Needless to say, this property did not carry an obligation to pay tribute. As of the time of the conquest, Spanish municipalities were beginning to appear as so many islands in the midst of what were still predominantly indigenous Mexican lands.[10]

Before long, Crown-owned lands and lands held by virtue of grants from the Crown would also make their appearance. The Castilian monarchy had a long tradition, dating back to the Reconquista, of asserting direct ownership claims over conquered territories, even when it was not

---

[8] J. H. Elliott, "Cortés, Velásquez and Charles V," in Hernán Cortés, *Letters from Mexico*, ed. and trans. Anthony Pagden, rev. ed. (New Haven, Conn.: Yale University Press, 1986), xix.

[9] Cortés, *Letters from Mexico*, 296.

[10] Richard M. Morse, "Some Characteristics of Latin American Urban History," *American Historical Review* 67 (1962): 317–38; Lyle N. McAlister, *Spain and Portugal in the New World, 1492–1700* (Minneapolis: University of Minnesota Press, 1984), 136–37.

able to enforce those claims fully and immediately. Basically, the theory was that, in zones of conquest, the Crown was entitled to the property of the defeated prince (hence Charles V's claim to Moctezuma's tribute), "treasure" including mines of precious metals, and unoccupied or abandoned land (*tierras baldías*).[11] Of course the king could not be a proprietor like any other, and this was only partly for practical reasons. The government was not equipped to conduct mining operations, for example, nor could it prospect for new deposits, and therefore it adopted the practice of according licenses to prospectors and mining entrepreneurs, reserving a royalty of one-fifth of the silver produced, the "*quinto real*."[12] Initially, the Crown also had to tolerate Cortés's *encomienda* arrangements, channeling tribute to individual conquistadors, though it treated these as rewards, provisionally bestowed, to meritorious vassals. Over time, the viceroys of New Spain would struggle to regain control over tribute, and, at the same time, they would make efforts to give practical effect to the theory of Crown ownership over "empty" lands. Eventually, the regulation, licensing and granting of *tierras baldias* would come to shape property formation in colonial Mexico.

It is important to notice that although the Spanish Crown formulated some strong property claims over New World territories, these were not unlimited in their spatial extent. English and French monarchs later developed the habit of granting vast domains to individuals and chartered companies in recently discovered regions of America, as though they themselves already owned these lands from the moment of "discovery." In their basically feudal construction of territorial control, *imperium*, the field of sovereignty, and *dominium*, the field of ownership, tended to merge. By way of contrast, sovereign claims and ownership claims did not coincide spatially in the Spanish empire: the former encompassed broad, theoretically unlimited, areas, whereas the latter were much less extensive.[13] This is because the Spanish Crown, unlike its European

---

[11] J. H. Elliott, *Imperial Spain, 1469–1716* (Harmondsworth: Penguin, 1970), 67; Mariano Peset and Margarita Menegus, "Rey propietario o rey soberano," *Historia Mexicana* 43 (1994): 563–99. For an alternative interpretation, one stressing more extensive Crown property claims, see José María Ots Capdequí, *El Régimen de la tierra en la América Española durante el período colonial* (Ciudad Trujillo: Universidad de Santo Domingo, 1946).

[12] Peter Bakewell, "Mining," in *Colonial Spanish America*, ed. Leslie Bethell (Cambridge: Cambridge University Press, 1987), 232.

[13] Anthony Pagden, "Law, Colonization, Legitimation, and the European Background," in *The Cambridge History of Law in America*, ed. Michael Grossberg and Christopher L. Tomlins, 3 vols. (New York: Cambridge University Press, 2007), vol. 1: 9.

rivals, recognized indigenous property. Cortés did not grant land to the Indian pueblos and their caciques, nor did Charles V: they both basically accepted the prior existence and legitimacy of native property. In principle, indigenous title would be accepted as primordial through the first half of the history of New Spain, such that courts would not require documentary proof from Indians, as they would from Spaniards claiming title. Indeed, the Crown set itself up as defender and protector of Indian land rights.

Central Mexico was a conquered country, its lands and indigenous peoples subject to the tribute exactions, first of Aztec conquerors, later of Spaniards. The Spanish conquest and the processes of colonization that followed it shook Nahua civilization to its foundations: the priesthood was decimated, temples leveled, secular rulers laid low; laws, institutions and ceremonies were transformed to accommodate the Spanish ascendancy. And yet land tenure in the native countryside retained much of its indigenous character. However, in addition to setting up a regime of unprecedented harshness for the indigenous communities, the Spanish established settlements of their own, with separate jurisdictions and property regimes in the midst of the Nahua landscape, something the Aztecs had rarely done. Colonization meant that, from the start, New Spain had two distinct land laws, both under the authority of the Crown: one for Spaniards and one for Indians.

INNU

Looking back to the distant past of his ancestors, an Innu man named Charles Katush interpreted the founding of New France in the following terms: "The French were looking for something that they could own. They were looking for a place where they could be the masters ..." His recollection had a somewhat speculative quality, for he went on to add, "They must have come here for that reason."[14] Charles Katush's historical memory seems at odds with conventional textbook accounts of the beginnings of New France, the latter stressing fur trade, alliance and mutual respect between natives and newcomers, rather than appropriation and domination. In the vast spaces of the St. Lawrence Valley and

---

[14] Quoted in Sylvie Vincent, "The Uepishtikueiau Narrative: The Arrival of the French at the Site of Québec City According to Innu Oral Tradition," in *Aboriginality and Governance: A Multidisciplinary Perspective*, ed. Gordon Christie (Penticton, Canada: Theytus Books, 2006), 6.

its hinterland, there was ample room for indigenous hunter-gatherers and agricultural colonists to coexist; moreover, the numbers of settlers and natives were comparatively small, and instead of competing for the same terrain, they tended to rely on different natural environments. The standard settler-national historiography of gentle, mutually beneficial colonization does have some merit in that the French colonization of Canada did not proceed *primarily* through the destruction of native property. And yet, the Innu oral tradition as expressed by Charles Katush is not wrong: there was indeed dispossession.

The establishment of Quebec in 1608, conventionally considered the inauguration of Canadian or Quebec history, was hardly a turning point for the Innu of the Lower St. Lawrence. A trading post manned by a crew of 16 to 28 men on temporary contracts, early Quebec scarcely qualified as a colonial society in its first few years.[15] The Frenchmen who overwintered there were simply the latest in a series of visitors who had been coming to these shores for almost a century. Contact had intensified in the late sixteenth century when vessels, mostly French, began to arrive every summer to trade for beaver pelts and other furs. This economic relationship generally took the form of ritual gift exchanges and therefore it suggested connections of friendship and alliance between the parties. The Innu were keen to trade, not only because they coveted for their own use and ornamentation the copper pots, iron blades and glass beads the visitors purveyed, but also because of the way their privileged access to the French enhanced their leverage in relations with other indigenous nations who wanted to get some of these wonderful products of overseas origin. They were not powerful enough to prevent Algonquins, Hurons and Abenakis from also trading with the French, but their position empowered them in their regional alliances.

Whereas it was once thought that the advent of the fur trade revolutionized indigenous life, turning hunting from a subsistence into a commercial activity, with all that implied about individual competition and intensive exploitation of salable species (specifically beaver), recent scholarship suggests that change for the Innu was much less abrupt. The fur trade developed quite gradually and it did not require major changes in the native way of life. Since European felt makers made use of the soft inner fur of the beaver, the traders prized pelts that had been used as clothing or as blankets, long enough for the coarse outer hairs to have

---

[15] Allan Greer, "1608 as Foundation," *Thèmes canadiens/Canadian Issues*, (fall 2008), 20–23.

fallen out. For the Innu therefore, the fur trade was less a matter of producing for a market than of disposing of their old clothes for metal wares and other valuable merchandise. The French post at Quebec brought almost nothing but benefits at first: a convenient source of trade goods, it also strengthened security in the face of enemy Mohawk raids; additionally, the French sometimes provided emergency rations when hunting conditions were poor. Moreover, the Innu were initially spared the scourge of Old World diseases for the sailors and trading company employees they dealt with were all mature men who would have been exposed to smallpox and acquired immunity earlier in their lives.[16]

The situation changed over the course of the 1620s and 1630s with the arrival of a handful of Jesuit missionaries and a few hundred settlers. There seemed to be more than enough land for the latter to establish farms in the vicinity of Quebec without interfering with Innu resource requirements. Colonists received title to their respective plots from the Company of New France (1627–63), a corporation that claimed virtually all of North America as a fief under the Crown of France; the basically feudal title of the company and of the individual settler/vassals could coexist with native property, which is why there was no talk of buying Indian lands in New France. However, it did imply an assertion of territorial power that would justify Charles Katush's sense that the French wanted to "be the masters." At the same time, the Jesuits were making efforts to gain an ascendancy over the Innu for the purpose of bringing them under the rule of God; their ministry would eventually take on a central role in the dispossession of the Innu of Kâ Mihkwâwahkâšič. In 1639 these same Innu suffered a terrible smallpox epidemic,[17] the result of increased contact with a more varied European population, a tragedy that weakened them just when they needed all the strength they could summon to cope with the challenges of colonization.

In the wake of Father LeJeune's harrowing attempt to follow the Innu on their winter hunt, the Jesuits decided to try to induce the Innu and their western cousins, the Algonquins, to renounce their "nomadic" ways and settle down. Inspired by the model of the Jesuit *reducciones* of South America, LeJeune and his colleagues experimented with an aggressive

---

[16] Bruce G. Trigger, *Natives and Newcomers: Canada's "Heroic Age" Reconsidered* (Montreal and Kingston: McGill-Queen's University Press, 1986), 164–225; Dean R. Snow and Kim M. Lanphear, "European Contact and Indian Depopulation in the Northeast: The Timing of the First Epidemics," *Ethnohistory* 35 (1988): 15–33.

[17] Rémi Savard, "La 'réduction' de Sillery 1638–1660," *Recherches amérindiennes au Québec* 38 (2008): 128.

approach to disciplining and "civilizing" the natives. (In later decades, after the failure of this Innu mission, they would turn to the more flexible and sensitive methods of evangelizing that we associate with the French Jesuits.)[18] In 1637 they inaugurated a mission station, complete with wooden houses, a chapel and a hospital, close to Kâ Mihkwâwahkâšič, the Innu eel-fishing place; they named it Sillery, after a French donor who funded the enterprise. Rudimentary stone fortifications were added to protect the Innu and Algonquins from Mohawk raids, an increasingly deadly menace in the late 1640s and early 1650s. Many natives accepted baptism and adopted some elements of Catholicism, but they showed little taste for agriculture and sedentary existence, preferring to continue their hunting, gathering and seasonal relocation.[19] Sillery emerged as a space partly controlled by the Jesuits, partly by the Innu and Algonquins. By the late 1640s, French settlers were beginning to establish themselves in the immediate vicinity and, more ominously, colonists were becoming interested in the eel fishery.

"The eel constitutes a manna exceeding all belief," enthused the Jesuits in a publication intended to stimulate immigration by portraying Canada as a land of plenty; forest and field provide an abundance of products, they concluded, but "to tell the truth, this country is the Kingdom of water and of fish."[20] Secular colonists echoed this view: eels harvested near Quebec, wrote Pierre Boucher, "are fatter and much better tasting than those of France ... We catch them in such great quantities that you would have to see it to believe it."[21] Having learned the Innu techniques of catching eels, the French too were becoming reliant on that fish for winter provisions. Instead of smoking them, however, they preserved them, salted, in barrels. There are even indications that smoked and salted

---

[18] James Axtell, *The Invasion Within: The Contest of Cultures in Colonial North America* (New York: Oxford University Press, 1985), 61–90.

[19] James P. Ronda, "The Sillery Experiment: A Jesuit-Indian Village in New France, 1637–1663," *American Indian Culture and Research Journal* 3 (1979): 1–18; Alain Beaulieu, *Convertir les fils de Caïn: Jésuites et amérindiens nomades en Nouvelle-France, 1632–1642* (Québec City: Nuit blanche, 1990); Marc Jetten, *Enclaves amérindiennes: les 'réductions' du Canada 1637–1701* (Quebec City: Septentrion, 1994), 34–60; R. Cole Harris, ed., *Historical Atlas of Canada*, 3 vols., vol. 1: *Beginnings to 1800* (Toronto: University of Toronto Press, 1987), plate 47.

[20] Relation of 1652–53, in *The Jesuit Relations and Allied Documents*, 73 vols., ed. Reuben Thwaites (Cleveland: Burrows Brothers, 1896–1900) (hereafter JR), 40: 213–15. See also Relation of 1642–43, JR 23: 305; Relation of 1659–60, JR 45: 191.

[21] Pierre Boucher, *Histoire véritable et naturelle des moeurs et productions du pays de la Nouvelle-France, vulgairement dite le Canada* (Paris: Florentin Lambert, 1664), 78. My translation.

eels had become a commercial commodity sold to provision ships' crews and newly arrived colonists. "They caught, this year, forty thousand eels," states the Jesuits' journal for 1646, "most of which were sold at half an écu the hundred."[22] The Jesuits were themselves involved in the eel business, as were many other religious orders and enterprising colonists. Though the fish themselves remained plentiful, rocky shallows suitable for weirs were in limited supply, the best being concentrated around Quebec and Kâ Mihkwâwahkâšič. With French fishers, many of them working for the colony's nascent ecclesiastical and secular elite, crowding the shoreline during the season of eel migration, the Innu struggled to retain access to this vital resource.

From the 1630s on, a seigneurial tenure regime was incrementally taking shape in the St. Lawrence Valley, as the colony's feudal overlord, the Company of New France, granted plots of land to settlers willing to make their homes there (see Chapter 5). Agricultural rents could not be more than a pittance at this stage, when colonists were hard pressed to grow enough to feed themselves, but money was being made in the eel fishery. The company therefore began charging rent for the use of the foreshore, invoking feudal law that accorded control over the shore between high tide and low tide marks to the superior seigneur, regardless of any grants of adjoining land.[23] From Quebec up to Sillery and beyond, the Company of New France granted carefully measured stretches of shoreline, charging an annual rent in barrels of eels; some of the grantees leased out the fishing rights to a third party, charging an additional portion of the catch. Natives were not immediately affected by these measures: they, along with some religious orders, remained exempt from seigneurial fishing charges. However, by the late 1640s, the main Innu eel grounds at Kâ Mihkwâwahkâšič were hemmed in by settler fisheries above and below Sillery. Their neighbor to one side was the governor of New France himself and his shore allotment extended right up to Kâ Mihkwâwahkâšič (Pointe de Puiseaux to the French). In an effort to curry favor, the Jesuits even allowed Governor Montmagny's servants to set a few traps alongside those of the Innu to supply the governor's table. In return, the grateful Montmagny donated barrels of flour and biscuit to supplement the

---

[22] JR 28: 237; Lucien Campeau, ed., *Monumenta Novae Francia*, 9 vols. (Rome and Quebec City: Monumenta Historica Soc. Iesu and Presses de l'Université Laval, 1967–2003) (hereafter MNF), 6: 734.

[23] See Marcel Trudel, *Les Débuts du régime seigneurial au Canada* (Montreal: Fides, 1974), 194–95.

natives' provisions. However, in 1648 he was replaced by a new governor, Louis d'Ailleboust, who adopted the view that exclusive fishing rights at Pointe de Puiseaux were one of the perquisites of his office; with eels now very much a commercial product, d'Ailleboust was able to farm out the fishing spot to contractors at a high rent. The Innu, their numbers depleted by disease and war, were powerless to resist. When they arrived to set up their traps in the summer of 1650, the governor's tenants threw rocks at them and violently chased them away.[24]

It was the Jesuits, familiar with the ways of French law and already feuding with the governor for various other reasons, who took it upon themselves to protest this appropriation. They petitioned the governor and the courts, laying out a detailed set of legal arguments. Father Jean Dequen, the Sillery superior, presented himself as guardian and attorney to the Innu converts; repeatedly the Jesuits claimed to be acting under an "obligation to look out for the interests of these poor Christians."[25] In these documents, the natives are always "pauvres sauvages" and the word "poor" here is more than simply an economic term: it implies humility, vulnerability and religious ignorance. This is fairly standard paternalist discourse for the period: the powerful have an obligation to help and guide the "poor" (the "savage," the female, the young) and the latter should submit to their superiors. The poor and the indigenous also have some basic entitlements beginning with the right to subsistence. "They draw their food supply from this fishery, not only during the season of fishing but also for the winter." Furthermore, they have "a right that nature has given them in their own country, which they have enjoyed peacefully in the past and of which there can be no excuse for despoiling them."[26] Two kinds of rights were invoked in favor of Innu property: the right of the poor to their subsistence and the right to continue in possession of land and resources that have been occupied unchallenged and used continuously for a long time. These two principles,

---

[24] "Requête d'opposition à la prise de possession de la pêcherie d'anguilles, par le P. Jean Dequen *ca* octobre 1650," in MNF, 7: 681–82; "Mémoire du P. Paul Ragueneau sur la pêche de l'anguille, octobre 1650," in ibid., 7: 684–88.

[25] Ibid., 7: 682, 688. "... ceux qui ont obligation d'avoir l'oeil aux interests de ces pauvres chrestiens ..." On the history of Sillery and its contested lands, see Michel Lavoie, *C'est ma seigneurie que je réclame: la lutte des Hurons de Lorette pour la seigneurie de Sillery, 1650–1900* (Montreal: Boréal, 2010), 19–69.

[26] MNF, 7: 685, 686. "Car ils tirent leur nourriture de ceste pesche, non seulement tout le temps qu'elle dure, mais mesme pour tout leur hyver ..." "Les pauvres sauvages de jouir d'un droit que la nature leur a donné en leur proper pais, dont ils on jouy paisiblement par le passé et dont on ne peut avoir aucune raison de les despouiller."

long established in the European legal and ethical tradition, were hardly controversial in the seventeenth century. Versions of them were invoked in debates over the proper treatment of indigenous Americans in the Spanish and English empires, less commonly in French America where the ideas seem to have been simply taken for granted. But note that when "the rights of the Indian" did come up in New France, it was in a context of tutelage: native property under French ascendancy.

Within Canada, the Jesuits' protests fell on deaf ears, so powerful was Governor d'Ailleboust's influence in the small colony, and so Father Jérôme Lalemant decided to go over the governor's head. In September 1650 he traveled to France and went straight to the top, approaching the regent, Anne d'Autriche, then doing her best to rule the turbulent kingdom in the name of her young son Louis XIV. Lalement secured the dismissal of Governor d'Ailleboust and then set about securing lasting control over the lands and waters of Sillery for the Innu and their priests. The Jesuit requested that the whole area be erected into a fief for the use of the Christian Innu, including fishing privileges along the entire riverfront. The ongoing dispute with d'Ailleboust seems to have had the effect of sharpening the thrust of Lalemant's polemics. Like his contemporary Roger Williams (see below), and in somewhat similar terms, he set out the case for an indigenous seigneurie. A seigneurial grant to natives was not at all the same as grants to French settlers, Lalemant maintained:

For the latter are a gift of something the recipient did not have, whereas the former [i.e., a grant to natives], to all appearances the gift of something already possessed from time immemorial, is not so much a gift and genuine concession to the Indians: instead it is, in its practical effects, a proscription barring the French from taking that which remains to the Indians of the lands that we have usurped.[27]

The company duly issued a grant creating the fief of Sillery comprising an area one league in width along the St. Lawrence and three leagues in depth, a considerable area encompassing Kâ Mihkwâwahkâšič, the Jesuit mission with adjacent Innu and Algonquin villages, as well as several French habitant farms. To make it clear that the tenure would be truly

---

[27] [Jérôme Lalemant], "Remarques sur la concession des terres aux sauvages de Sillery," 11 September 1650, in ibid., 7: 673. "Il faut remarquer que cette concession est d'une nature bien différente des autres qui se font aux François, car celles-cy sont un don d'une chose qu'on n'avoit pas, et celle-là, estant en apparence un don d'une chose qu'on possédoit de temps immémorial, est plustost en effet une défense aux François de ne point toucher à ce qui est laissé de reste aux Sauvages de leurs terres qu'on a usurpées qu'un don et une concession véritable faicte aux Sauvages."

seigneurial, the document specifies that settlers "will hold their lands under the Christian captain of the Indians just as they held them under us before this grant."[28] The queen mother, signing in Louis XIV's name, provided royal confirmation of the feudal grant, evidently at Father Lalemant's urging since the ratification echoes his proposition that this was already Innu land. Europeans who settle in Sillery "will be and will remain dependents of the Christian Captains," and as for feudal dues demanded of the settlers, continues the queen, "these small emoluments drawn from their own country" will help them to give up their wandering ways and adopt a good Christian life.[29]

As a rule, the French respected native lands in practice, though not in theory. This invocation on the part of the Jesuits and the queen of a principle that would later be known as "aboriginal title" is unique in the annals of the first French empire. There was a catch, however, as there usually was whenever colonizers announced that indigenous people were the rightful proprietors of land. The title deed to the new fief of Sillery specified that it would belong to the Christian *sauvages*, "under the guidance and direction of the Jesuit fathers."[30] What this meant in practice is that the missionaries managed the seigneurie and collected the rents owed by French colonists. As on other Jesuit seigneuries, natives were exempt from rents and other charges; in this case, the Innu were titular landlords rather than tenants, but they were not really in control of the seigneurie of Sillery. With the support of the secular French authorities, the Jesuits treated them as wards, incapable of administering their own property and in need of firm "guidance and direction."

Sillery was, in fact, the site of an exceptionally severe mission regime by New France standards. Neophyte Christians were to be whipped and imprisoned for behavior that the missionaries deemed "adultery" or "blasphemy." It became a singularly inhospitable environment for the Innu families that had survived the lethal epidemics and bloody wars that had taken such a toll since the arrival of the French. Their eel fishing site had been saved, but the price proved to be too steep. Over the course of

---

[28] Concession of Sillery by the Compagnie de la Nouvelle-France, 13 March 1651, in *Pièces et documents relatifs à la tenure seigneuriale* (Quebec City: E. R. Fréchette, 1852), 50–51. "... releveront du capitaine chrestien des sauvages comme ils relevaient de nous avant cette donation ..."

[29] Archives nationales du Québec, E21, S66, SS3, "Ratification par Louis XIV de la concession de Sillery," July 1651, typed transcript. Sincere thanks to Michel Lavoie for providing me with a photocopy of this and other documents on Sillery.

[30] Concession of Sillery, *Pièces et documents*, 50–51.

the 1650s, fewer and fewer hunters gathered for the summer rendezvous at Kâ Mihkwâwahkâšič. Their country was large, its resources varied. They would instead pass the summer at other points along the St. Lawrence and up the Saguenay, far to the northeast, where the climate was more severe and eels less plentiful. French fur traders would follow them, supplying foodstuffs as well as hardware in return for beaver skins. They had not been expelled from Sillery at gunpoint, nor had they sold their lands, but they had certainly been dispossessed. By the 1660s, there were no more Innu at Sillery. For a time, the Jesuits accommodated other displaced native nations there, but on the long run it turned out to be more profitable to grant lands to rent-paying colonists. Eventually, they succeeded in changing their status from trustees managing the seigneurie in the name of the "Christian Indians" to legal seigneur in their own right. Sillery then emerged in the eighteenth century as a fully Jesuit estate entirely colonized by French-Canadian settlers.

The case of Sillery stands out in the history of New France in two ways: it represents a singular instance of indigenous property rights being officially and explicitly recognized; it was also the site of a coercive mission regime that effectively drove the Innu from this resource-rich part of the St. Lawrence Valley. This juxtaposition may seem surprising, even paradoxical. It can serve as a warning that the formal recognition of aboriginal title to land may not be at odds with dispossession.

NINNIMISSINUOK

Whereas central Mexico was the scene of a sudden eruption of Europeans followed by a rapid conquest and subjugation of the native population, most parts of North America experienced a more protracted period of irregular contact prior to colonization. Along the coasts of New England Ninnimissinuok peoples such as the Narragansetts and Wampanoags had repeated visits from English, Dutch and French fishermen, traders and explorers in the early seventeenth century. There were friendly exchanges of furs for metal goods as well as some violent skirmishes; the captain of one vessel reportedly kidnapped twenty natives to sell into slavery. Wampum made from seashells was used to procure furs from inland hunting peoples and the furs bought axes, knives and other valuable goods from seaborne traders; a sachem who controlled supplies of these exotic products could distribute them in ways that enhanced his power and influence. At the same time, contact with outsiders brought infectious disease epidemics that swept through the region in 1616–19 and again in

1633, bringing suffering and death on a massive scale. The fact that the diseases struck selectively – the Massachusetts were decimated while the Narragansetts were initially spared – further destabilized power relations among the nations of southern New England. Some sachems and their peoples were on the rise (for example, the Pequots of present-day Connecticut) and others were weakening and finding themselves subjected to stronger neighbors.[31] In the midst of these economic and demographic upheavals, and with patterns of alliance and tribute relations shifting rapidly, it seems unlikely that the arrival of a ship loaded with English families at Plymouth Harbor in December 1620 struck anyone as a momentous event.

The newcomers, and the larger numbers who would land at nearby Massachusetts Bay in the following decades, did not come seeking quick riches like so many of those who had gone to New Spain and early Virginia. Nor did they give the impression of aiming to take full control of the country and subjugate its inhabitants. Instead they were looking for a place to live. They tended to compare themselves to the Israelites who had wandered into the land of Canaan and there made a home for themselves. As a point of national and religious pride, they were determined to avoid the "cruelty" they associated with the Papist conquerors of New Spain. Yet they still came armed, for they were frightened of "the Indians" and they wished to reassure themselves and, if possible, overawe natives. As a chosen people, carriers of true religion, they tended to assume a right to occupy a country of "heathen savages." It was not an unqualified or unlimited right, however; when pressed, they might justify their appropriation of North American space in terms of a patent by which their king granted them the country; some, such as John Winthrop, preferred to argue that New England was empty land and, therefore, apart from the small areas actively cultivated by indigenous farmers, open to all; occasionally, early leaders would propose to acquire land from natives by gift or purchase. Thinking on the topic was casual and inconsistent; the question of legitimate title to land became a pressing issue only at a later stage when colonists were crowding into New England and when territorial boundaries – between settlers, between

---

[31] Bert Salwen, "Indians of Southern New England and Long Island: Early Period," in William C. Sturtevant and Raymond J. DeMallie, eds., *Handbook of North American Indians*, vol. 15: *Northeast*, ed. Bruce Trigger (Washington, D.C.: Smithsonian Institution, 1978), 160–76; Kathleen Bragdon, *The Columbia Guide to American Indians of the Northeast* (New York: Columbia University Press, 2001), 28–29.

colonies, and between English zones and Ninnimissinuok zones – became a focus of attention. For all their dogmatism in the religious realm, the Mayflower Pilgrims and the Massachusetts Bay Puritans were, like most colonizers, remarkably pragmatic about the business of appropriating and occupying territory.

The dominant tone of William Bradford's chronicle of the first months of the Plymouth colony is one of anxiety: though the settlers had no direct contact with natives at first, they knew they were intruding and they expected trouble. The Wampanoags sent a series of emissaries to visit them in March 1621, in an effort first to ascertain what the strangers were up to (the presence of women and children was probably viewed as a good sign) and then to calm and reassure the visibly nervous English. One native spoke some English. "He told us the place where we now live is called Patuxet, and that about four years ago all the inhabitants died of an extraordinary plague, and there is neither man, woman, nor child remaining, as indeed we have found none, so as there is none to hinder our possession, or to lay claim unto it." Bradford's concluding comment is characteristically pragmatic: a simple observation about the practical implications of local depopulation. Eventually the sachem Massasoit came, in state and surrounded by an escort, to conclude an agreement with the settlers.

As reported by Governor Bradford, the pact was of a purely military-diplomatic nature, establishing peace and mutual assistance in war.[32] Both parties were visibly wary and suspicious in the wake of nasty incidents that saw settlers looting native stores of corn and Wampanoags stealing English tools. The treaty seems to have been part of a larger ongoing effort, involving meetings and gift exchanges, to cultivate a relationship of coexistence, if not of perfect understanding. Both parties had an interest in establishing habits and procedures for addressing points of friction, nipping conflict in the bud and easing tensions. If the English were going to stay, Massasoit seems to have reasoned, better to have them as allies than as enemies; the English must have felt similarly. It is not clear whether he regarded the English gifts as tribute implying recognition of his superiority or as exchanges between equals; given the shifting

[32] William Bradford, *Of Plymouth Plantation, 1620–1647: The Complete Text*, ed. S. E. Morison (New York: Alfred A. Knopf, 1952), 80–81. On the Massasoit–Plymouth treaty and its context, see Neal Salisbury, *Manitou and Providence: Indians, Europeans, and the Making of New England, 1500–1643* (New York: Oxford University Press, 1982), 111–25; Daniel K. Richter, *Before the Revolution: America's Ancient Pasts* (Cambridge, Mass.: Harvard University Press, 2011), 153–57.

and uncertain circumstances, he may have left that question to be resolved in the future as power relations clarified. Like the English, he was improvising to make the best of an unfamiliar and rapidly evolving situation. Meanwhile, the Plymouth colonists were receiving expressions of hostility from Canonicus, the powerful Narragansett sachem who viewed Massasoit as a subject who owed him tribute. From the start, relationships in New England were multipolar and the number of players would continue to grow with the establishment of New Netherlands, the Massachusetts Bay colony and other European and indigenous polities. Massasoit's arrangements with the English appear to have had everything to do with his strategies vis-à-vis Canonicus and other native power brokers. To view the treaty of 1621 as some sort of grand intercultural settlement between "English" and "Indians" would be to overlook its very limited and specific scope as an alliance between two small regional powers.

Moreover, the agreement Massasoit negotiated with Plymouth, as recorded by the English, makes no mention of any territorial arrangements, nothing suggestive of a transfer of property or a surrender of sovereignty. Implicitly, the sachem seems to accept that the English would occupy space to live and to farm within Wampanoag territory, but he would have no reason then to think of this as a matter of relinquishing land. A Ninnimissinuok sachem was rich and powerful in proportion to the size and wealth of the populations who owed him tribute and so the new English village was a potential asset rather than a territorial loss. Unresolved issues remained about the nature of his relationship with the English: for a time he apparently tried to treat them as subjects, but before long the reinforced Plymouth colony would be strong enough to turn the tables and treat the Wampanoags as subjects. As they sized one another up in 1621, however, neither Massasoit nor his English counterpart displayed any inclination to consider land/territory as something to be abstracted from the larger context of relationships of alliance or enmity.

In the 1630s, the English presence in the area was massively reinforced with the rapid arrival of thousands of Puritan immigrants and the establishment of new townships in Massachusetts and then in the offshoot colonies of Rhode Island and Connecticut. The burgeoning population put pressure on space and resources, with the result that "land" became more of a preoccupation, both within and among the English settlements and in their relations with the Ninnimissinuok. Colonists would increasingly describe their dealings with natives in the language of property and territory and they would begin to make a fetish of written documents, the "deeds" and "treaties" that were supposed to settle the allocation of space with the stroke of a pen. In reality, native–settler relations long remained multidimensional and far more fluid than anything that might be captured in a simple deed of sale. A closer look at the history of property around Narragansett Bay (today's state of Rhode Island) at the time of initial colonization will help to illustrate this point.

Most of our information on this subject comes from the pen of the dissident Puritan Roger Williams, who played a central part in establishing a colony here. A remarkable figure in many respects, Williams is remembered in American history mainly as the founder of Rhode Island, as a proponent of religious toleration and as a staunch advocate of native property rights. He rejected the royal patent on which the Massachusetts Bay colony based its territorial claims, and insisted that indigenous residents were the rightful owners of the region, including their hunting grounds as well as their "planting grounds." It is therefore worth noting that, for all his insistence on procedural justice in dealings with natives, Williams was unwavering in his basic commitment to the cause of English colonization. In acquiring native territory, he pronounced himself proud "to further and advance that great end of planting and subduing this barbarous Countrey to English Industrie and Civilitie."[33] On the other hand, he also cultivated friendship with indigenous people, especially the sachems of the Narragansetts, and learned their language. A classic imperial go-between figure, Williams could consider natives both friends and dangerous "barbarians." Working with Ninnimissinuok people in their environment, in their language and in a situation of rough parity of power, he came to know them as few of his fellow-countrymen did. Furthermore, his disputatious nature led him to become embroiled in a series of conflicts over "Indian policy" and from these battles issued a stream of polemical writings; the polemics reveal a great deal of what he knew from first-hand experience of Ninnimissinuok property ways. For our purposes, Williams is remarkable mainly as a window onto the property encounter in early New England. Because he wrote prolifically and because he became acquainted with native people from an initial position of comparative weakness, Roger Williams, like the Jesuit missionaries of New France, is a wonderful source of information on topics that would otherwise be lost to the historical record.

---

[33] Quoted in Anne Keary, "Retelling the History of the Settlement of Providence: Speech, Writing, and Cultural Interaction on Narragansett Bay," *New England Quarterly* 69, no. 2 (June 1996): 277.

Williams's early dealings were mostly with the dual sachems of the Narragansetts, Canonicus and his nephew Miantonomi. Because they had escaped the first epidemics of Old World disease, the Narragansetts had emerged in the early 1630s as one of the most populous and powerful nations of New England (though they would soon be devastated, along with all their neighbors, by the epidemic of 1633–34). Midway between the settlements of the English and those of the Dutch, they did their best to stay aloof from Europeans. On the other hand, they wanted – and increasingly they needed – the imported textiles, metal wares and weapons that only the newcomers could provide. Moreover, locked in conflict with the powerful Pequot nation to the west, the Narragansetts knew they needed allies, settler and indigenous, to avoid the perils of diplomatic isolation. Thus, with some misgivings, they welcomed Dutch and English traders who came offering European goods in exchange for corn and furs.[34] Among the traders frequenting Narragansett Bay at the time was Roger Williams. Williams learned the Narragansett language and developed a personal relationship with the two sachems. Aware of his fame among the English as an orator, Canonicus and Miantonomi seem to have considered Williams a man worth cultivating; his generosity with presents suggested not only goodwill but also a sachem-like status that might make him a valuable advocate of Narragansett interests.[35] While developing a relationship with the Narragansetts, Williams fell afoul of Massachusetts Bay authorities because of his outspoken views on religious doctrine and politics. Banished from the colony in 1636, he nevertheless remained on close terms with Governor John Winthrop, who encouraged him to establish a settlement on Narragansett Bay. Thus, in spite of appearances to the contrary, Canonicus and Miantonomi may have made a savvy choice in selecting Roger Williams as their ally and intermediary with Massachusetts. At the same time, they were right to be wary, for like any go-between, Williams had divided loyalties: his friendship was both sincere and contingent.

[34] Elisha Reynolds Potter, *The Early History of Narragansett: With an Appendix of Original Documents, Many of Which Are Now for the First Time Published* (Providence, R.I.: Marshall, Brown, 1835), 16–17.

[35] Roger Williams, *The Correspondence of Roger Williams*, ed. Glenn W. LaFantasie, 2 vols. (Providence: Rhode Island Historical Society, 1988), 2: 751. On Williams and the Narragansetts, see Salisbury, *Manitou and Providence*, 193–99, 212–14; Keary, "Retelling the History of the Settlement of Providence," 250–286; Jeffrey Glover, "Wunnaumwáyean: Roger Williams, English Credibility, and the Colonial Land Market," *Early American Literature* 41, no. 3 (January 2006): 429–53.

In the summer of 1636, Williams led a party of thirteen settler families from Massachusetts to Narragansett Bay. It took some time to find a suitable site for the little settlement, as there were many contending claimants to the region. Plymouth Colony asserted that the eastern shore of the bay fell within the limits of their patent. The Wampanoag sachem Massasoit claimed this same area, but both Plymouth and the Narragansetts claimed Massasoit as their tributary. In this tense and complex situation, Roger Williams later testified, "I was forced to travel between them three [Massasoit, Canonicus and Miantonomi], to pacify, to satisfie all their [*sic*], and their independent spirits, of my honest intentions to live peaceably by them."[36] Shuttling between Wampanoags and Narragansetts and lavishing gifts upon both parties, Williams may have played an instrumental role in negotiating the hegemony of Canonicus/Miantonomi over the Wampanoags. A Narragansett ascendancy suited his purposes given what he had already spent over the years in time and money to secure the sachems' friendship. "I had the frequent promise of Miantenomy (my Kind friend)," he later wrote, "that It should not be Land that I should want about those Boundes mentioned, provided, that I satisfied the Indians there inhabeting; I having made Covenantes of a peacable Neighbour-hood with all the Sachims. And Natives Round about us." On that basis, Williams secured a space for the English settlement between two small rivers at the head of the Narragansett Bay, a place he called Providence. There his small party organized itself into a township, laid out lots, one for each family, and collected thirty shillings from each household, in "loving consideration and gratuitye," to help defray Williams's expenses.[37]

As the colonists set to work clearing forest and building houses, Canonicus and Miantonomi finalized their agreement with Williams, specifying a set of boundaries on the landscape that would enclose a site with ample space for homes and fields to house and sustain the thirty initial colonists. There was even space for the additional settlers that Williams expected to attract to Providence, but the grant remained modest in extent. The sachems explained that their generosity was constrained by the presence of other tributary villages in the vicinity, "because they would not

---

[36] Potter, *The Early History of Narragansett*, 3–4.
[37] Howard Millar Chapin, *Documentary History of Rhode Island, Being the History of the Towns of Providence and Warwick to 1649 and of the Colony to 1647* (Providence, R.I.: Preston and Rounds, 1916), 27; Williams to Winthrop, 25 August 1636, *Correspondence of Roger Williams*, 1: 54.

intrench upon the Indians inhabiting round about us for the prevention of strife between us."[38] Williams still described the grant as "an abundant Sufficiencie for my selfe and my Friends."[39] Following Ninnimissinuok practice, the agreement was verbal and it was embedded within a preexisting and ongoing alliance/tribute relationship. Williams produced no written record and gave no measurements of the land acquired, though two years later he did ask the Narragansett sachems to sign a "confirmatory deed" that recorded their understanding in writing; Canonicus, the older sachem with preeminent status at home, drew a bow on the document while Miantonomi, his emissary to the outside world, drew an arrow. When the settlers later needed pasture to graze their livestock and meadows to gather hay, Canonicus and Miantonomi agreed to an extension of Providence southward to the Pawtuxet River, plus upriver grazing rights: "up the streame of Pautuckett and Pautuxet without limmets wee might have for our use of Cattell."[40] The spatial references were not to measured distances and acreage, but to a known landscape; at the time, Narragansetts and English seem to have had a shared understanding of what land had been designated.

Providence as English space was taking shape through ongoing, multipolar negotiations, involving a series of gifts, grants, agreements and amendments to those agreements. Occasionally, the settlers introduced a written document to keep track of the proceedings, using the format of the "Indian deed" then becoming common in New England. Indian deeds were rather simple instruments (simple because usually drawn up by colonists without legal training) modeled on the English common law deed of conveyance. Be that as it may, Roger Williams would later insist that his agreement with Canonicus had been anything but a purchase and sale.

'Tis true he recd presents and gratuities many of me: but it was not thousands nor ten thoughsands of mony could have bought of him an English Entrance into this Bay. Thouhsands could not have bought of him Providence or Pawtuxit or Aquedenick or any other Land I had of him. I made him and his Youngest bro. Son Miantunnomu gifts of 2 Sorts: First formr Presents from Plymmouth and

---

[38] Roger Williams to John Whipple, Jr., 8 July 1669, *Correspondence of Roger Williams*, 2: 587.

[39] Roger Williams to John Whipple, Jr., 24 August 1669, *Correspondence of Roger Williams*, 2: 596.

[40] Providence Town Evidence, 24 March 1637/38, as quoted in Glenn W. Lafantasie, "Conflict over Land in Providence: Editorial Note," in *Correspondence of Roger Williams*, 2: 507. See also Keary, "Retelling the History of the Settlement of Providence," 269.

Salem 2 I was here their Councellour and Secretary in all their Wars with Pequts, Munhiggins, Long Ilanders, Wompanoogse. They had my person, my shallop and Pinnace and hired servant etc. at Command on all occasions, transporting 50 at a time, and lodging 50 at a time at my howse. I never denied them ought [ie., aught] [lawfully?] they desired of me.[41]

This passage comes from a submission Williams presented in 1677 as part of his response to political enemies who suggested that he had profited from his land transactions at the time of the founding of Providence. His contention was that, rather than "flipping" real estate, he had gone into personal debt to finance his campaign to secure the goodwill of the Narragansett sachems; then, once the Providence settlement was established, he received voluntary contributions from the community that only amounted to enough to defray a portion of his expenses. What he had received of Canonicus and Miantonomi by means of gifts and negotiations, he maintained, was not real estate but "an English Entrance into this Bay." Furthermore, that objective was achieved through an alliance relationship that developed over time and that involved gifts, services and hospitality. According to Williams, his dealings with the Providence settlers, as well as with the Narragansetts, took place outside the bounds of a market economy, that is to say they derived from personal relations, neighborliness and a sense of moral obligation, rather than from legal contracts. Interestingly, even Williams's political enemies of later years, men like William Harris, who stood for strong settler property rights and the aggressive appropriation of Indian lands, seemed to think that it would have been illegitimate for Williams to buy lands from the Narragansetts and then sell them at a profit to colonists.[42]

When he argues, as in the quotation above, against a market transaction conception of settler–native relations, we hear the voice of Roger Williams the self-righteous radical, but we can also detect that of Roger Williams the knowledgeable cross-cultural broker. Because of his intimate familiarity with Ninnimissinuok ways, he was able to draw on what he knew to be the Narragansett conception of arrangements surrounding the establishment of Providence. However, in other contexts, Williams would adopt the prevailing idiom among New England colonizers and speak of "buying land of the Indians"; indeed, he boasted of his role in securing

[41] Roger Williams to an assembly of commissioners, 17 November 1677, *Correspondence of Roger Williams*, 752. (Bracketed glosses are from the published edition.)

[42] On William Harris and his protracted conflicts with Williams, see Glenn W. Lafantasie's informative "Editorial Notes" in ibid., 506–13, 556–70.

space and furthering colonization by that means. In other contexts, Williams clearly accepted that land could be the object of purchase and sale; for example, he speaks of raising funds to acquire Providence by mortgaging his house in Salem, an operation that treats land as a merchantable asset. Land could function as a commodity, but it was not always a commodity; it worked differently in different contexts. We might say that Williams wanted it both ways as far as property is concerned. In that respect he was not alone: other, more aggressive colonizers, fixated though they seemed on appropriation through deeds, also sought to subdue and subjugate the very natives who were construed legally as autonomous agents voluntarily selling property.

War drums, both English and Ninnimissinuok, form the audible background to the colonization of Narragansett Bay, not to mention New England as a whole. Canonicus, Miantonomi and Massasoit led nations that used violence and the threat of violence to defend their independence and, where possible, to dominate other groups. The English colonists, from the moment the Mayflower landed, behaved similarly. Roger Williams saw himself as a man of peace, but the friendly relations he cultivated with the Narragansett sachems had a pronounced military dimension ("I was here their Councellour and Secretary in all their Wars"). Moreover, just at the time he was securing "an English entrance into this Bay," he was also playing a crucial diplomatic role on behalf of the United Colonies in their campaign to defeat and exterminate the Pequots. Armed conflict and power rivalries were not peripheral matters: they were at the heart of the negotiations by which the English secured a place in New England. Both Providence and Plymouth were initially established through alliances with local indigenous actors, and "alliance" presupposes conflict. Williams is quite clear on this point: his friendship with Canonicus and Miantonomi did not institute universal peace; instead, it strengthened the Narragansetts vis-à-vis native rivals. They also faced the dangerous and rapidly growing power of the English colonies and Williams was a useful ally in that context too. Canonicus and Miantonomi seem to have realized that they would need to admit more settlers to their midst in order to reinforce their connections with the dangerous powers surrounding them and they placed their faith in Roger Williams as chief negotiator of territorial arrangements with the English.

Williams was thus able to arrange for a group of Antinomian religious refugees led by William Coddington to acquire Aquidneck (soon to be known as Rhode Island) in 1637. The deed written up on that occasion indicates that Coddington presented Canonicus and Miantonomi with forty fathoms of white beads (wampum) for the island. However, the transaction was far more complicated than a straight wampum-for-land exchange. Coddington also gave Wanamatraunemit, tributary sachem of the Narragansetts actually residing on the island, five additional fathoms to induce him to vacate Aquidneck. As part of the bargain with Canonicus and Miantonomi, the purchasers also received the right to harvest hay from natural meadows on most of the islands of Narragansett Bay. Williams and Coddington also had Massasoit to contend with for the Wampanoag sachem still aspired to independence and tribute rights in the area and so, four months after concluding the Narragansett deed, they added a clause on the back indicating that Massasoit had received five fathoms of wampum in return for haying privileges on the eastern side of the bay. In acknowledging receipt of the wampum, the deed says, Massasoit took the opportunity to "promise loveinge and just carriage of myselfe and all my men to the said Mr. Coddington and English his friends united to him."[43] This is a very brief document, but it contains multiple layers of complexity. In addition to witnesses, it mentions six main protagonists; four of them, Canonicus, Miantonomi, Wanamatraunemit and Massasoit, are cast in the role of sellers, though their territorial claims were actually at odds with one another from the point of view of English law. Needless to say, we do not know exactly what arrangements these sachems felt had been concluded, nor do we know exactly what the gesture of drawing an arrow or a bow on a piece of paper implied for them. But we do know that Coddington, guided by Roger Williams, was prepared to "buy" the same island from three different sellers and that what he wished to "purchase" was a basket of goods and benefits that included exclusive occupancy of one island, use-rights in dispersed and vaguely delineated locations, plus peaceful and positive relations with indigenous polities in the area. "Land" as a valuable object abstracted from its social and political setting is not what the Ninnimissinuoks were selling, nor was it what the settlers were buying. The more closely we look at the various agreements concerning territory and colonization in 1630s Narragansett Bay the more difficult it becomes to accept the conventional wisdom about Indian deeds in early New England: the idea that the natives and settlers had sharply divergent, even incommensurable, understandings of what these transactions meant. Indigenous people thought

---

[43] "Narragansett and Wampanoag Deed for Aquidneck Island," in Alden T. Vaughan, ed., *Early American Indian Documents: Treaties and Laws, 1607–1789,* 20 vols. (Washington, D.C.: University Publications of America, 1979–85), 19: 49–50.

they were relinquishing use-rights, so the story goes, whereas the English thought they were buying "the land itself."[44] The Rhode Island treaty suggests that English approaches to territory and property were more complex than this simple formula admits; at the conceptual level they were not entirely incompatible with those of the Ninnimissinuok.

In 1638, Roger Williams went into partnership with John Winthrop to acquire the uninhabited Prudence Island in Narragansett Bay for the purpose of raising pigs. In this case, we seem to be looking at something more like a business deal. Though this transaction, like the Rhode Island treaty, involved the presentation of wampum and other goods to the Narragansett sachems and the granting of territorial rights, Williams emphasized in a letter to Winthrop that these were not really purchases. "Neither of them were sold properly, for a thousand fathom would not have bought either, by strangers. The truth is, not a penny was demanded for either, and what was paid was only gratuity, though I chose, for better assurance and form, to call it a sale." Years later he wrote, "Yet since there is so much sound and noyse of Purchase and Purchasers, I judge it not unseasonable to declare the Rise and bottome of the planting of Rode Iland in the fountaine of it. It was not price nor Money that could have purchased Rode Iland. Rode Iland was obtained by Love."[45] By "love" Williams did not mean intimate affection – Williams describes Canonicus as "most shie of all English to his last breath,"[46] and there is no reason to think the Narragansett sachems were under any illusions about the currents of antagonism that ran beneath the surface of their alliance – he was referring to the personal relationship that underlay his transactions with Canonicus, Miantonomi and Massasoit.

To summarize, small parties of English colonists came to Plymouth Harbor and later to Narragansett Bay, seeking a place to live. In Roger Williams's words, they wanted "an entrance," meaning acceptance of their presence on the part of the indigenous population, and "a Sufficiencie," meaning access to resources with which they could feed and sustain

---

[44] This view pervades contemporary historiography. Strong versions can be found in Francis Jennings, *The Invasion of America: Indians, Colonialism, and the Cant of Conquest* (Chapel Hill: University of North Carolina Press, 1975), 128–45; Keary, "Retelling the History of the Settlement of Providence," 261.

[45] Chapin, *Documentary History of Rhode Island*, 52; Roger Williams to General Court of Commissioners of Providence Plantations, 25 August 1658, *Correspondence of Roger Williams*, 485.

[46] Roger Williams to an Assembly of Commissioners, 17 November 1677, *Correspondence of Roger Williams*, 2: 751.

their settlement. The Ninnimissinuok sachems of these two localities do not appear to have found these aspirations altogether mysterious. They would have understood that newcomers, if they were to stay, would need space for their houses and for their fields; they would also need access to the forest and shoreline for their hunting, fishing and fuel gathering (a concept of a shared commons that could be adapted to the needs of grazing animals). This spatial accommodation could only work if the newcomers linked themselves, as tributaries or allies, to the existing native powers of the locality. Colonists and natives had a common interest in cultivating allies to strengthen their respective positions in the wider region and both needed peaceful, predictable relations with their immediate neighbors to guarantee their own security. There was a natural basis for a strategic alliance involving geographic proximity and rituals of gift giving. In what might be called the "Middle Ground" phase of the colonization of New England, Ninnimissinuok and English could accommodate one another's expectations even in the absence of a perfect meeting of minds.[47]

Of course, the Middle Ground stage was short lived, for the tidal wave of English immigration, along with the heavy disease mortality suffered by the indigenous population, tipped the power balance decisively in favor of the English. First in some coastal enclaves and then progressively over the entire region, settlers were strong enough to occupy territories and trample over the prerogatives of Ninnimissinuok sachems. "Indian deeds" in these circumstances often had nothing to do with genuine negotiated agreements. However, throughout the seventeenth century there were always places where circumstances favored accommodation. When settlers were few in number to begin with and when they were unable to count on the backing of a strong colonial state, they seem to have adapted to the expectations of their Ninnimissinuok neighbors. Examples that come to mind include the early settlers of Martha's Vineyard, under the uncertain manorial jurisdiction of Thomas Mayhew, as well as those who set themselves up on Long Island in an area in dispute between the Dutch and the British.[48] As settlement moved

---

[47] Cf. Richard White, *The Middle Ground: Indians, Empires, and Republics in the Great Lakes Region, 1650–1815* (New York: Cambridge University Press, 1991).

[48] David J. Silverman, *Faith and Boundaries: Colonists, Christianity, and Community among the Wampanoag Indians of Martha's Vineyard, 1600–1871* (New York: Cambridge University Press, 2005); Faren Siminoff, *Crossing the Sound: The Rise of Atlantic American Communities in Seventeenth-Century Eastern Long Island* (New York: New York University Press, 2004), 8, 21–22.

inland, colonists on the edges of European-controlled territory could not necessarily dictate terms to the natives of the place, and so, to avoid trouble and violence, they took the pragmatic course involving gifts, negotiation and alliance.[49] Sometimes these arrangements gave rise to a written text in the form of an "Indian deed," sometimes they were purely verbal.[50] We can be pretty sure, in light of Roger Williams's testimony, that agreements developed over time, even when the laconic documents of the period give the impression they were concluded on a single occasion.

The Indian deed, born out of the living agreements that sachems negotiated with colonists during the initial stage of New England colonization, would go on, like a lethal virus escaping from a scientific laboratory, to pursue a career of its own in the emergent colonial property regime. New deeds and treaties would be concluded in circumstances of coercion and deceit that made a mockery of the formal trappings of a voluntary, mutually advantageous contract. Yet it is important to avoid reading later developments back into the early period when agreements were a more meaningful expression of both Ninnimissinuok and English approaches to territory, property and alliance. Treaties involving land were a native as much as they were an English invention.[51]

Indeed, that observation might be generalized. In all three cases of early colonization examined here, Spanish, French and English, the "property encounter" was shaped to a considerable extent by indigenous customs and land practices. Even the hyperaggressive conquerors of Mexico adapted to Nahua tribute systems, while leaving agricultural lands in the hands of natives and subject to indigenous tenures. The French established settlements in the St. Lawrence Valley with indigenous permission and encouragement; scandal arose when Innu were squeezed out

---

[49] For examples, see Jennings, *Conquest of America*, 131; Salisbury, *Manitou and Providence*, 192, 226–27; Emerson W. Baker, "A Scratch with a Bear's Paw: Anglo-Indian Land Deeds in Early Maine," *Ethnohistory* 36 (1989): 235–56; Peter S. Leavenworth, "'The Best Title That Indians Can Claime': Native Agency and Consent in the Transferal of Penacook-Pawtucket Land in the Seventeenth Century," *The New England Quarterly* 72, no. 2 (June 1999): 275–300; Gail D. MacLeitch, "'Red' Labor: Iroquois Participation in the Atlantic Economy," *Labor: Studies in Working-Class History of the Americas* 1 (2004): 78.

[50] It is in the nature of undocumented agreements that they are hard to verify. However, there are many indications in the record of colonists claiming to have purchased land from natives without a written deed. See, for example, Vaughan, ed., *Early American Indian Documents*, 19: 217.

[51] See Robert A. Williams, *Linking Arms Together: American Indian Treaty Visions of Law and Peace, 1600–1800* (New York: Oxford University Press, 1997).

of one vital fishing site and French authorities were driven to affirm that natives had a natural right to their territories. In a somewhat similar vein, the earliest settlers of New England negotiated, largely on Ninnimissinuok terms, permission to establish themselves in the country. Of course, the colonizers had their own characteristic ways of understanding the issues of land and territoriality and these did not coincide with those of the Nahua, Ninnimissinuok and Innu. Moreover, Spanish, French and English approaches diverged, if only because the legal traditions of the three imperial powers were so different.

Colonists could not simply impose European versions of landed property in North America, and not only because they were constrained to take account of indigenous peoples and indigenous tenures. There was no such thing as a coherent "Spanish" or "French" or "English" version of landed property. As noted in the Introduction, Old World tenure remained a vast patchwork of regional laws and customs, featuring scalar, overlapping and complex property claims; moreover, all was in historical flux as landlords, peasants, magistrates and princes struggled to redefine the meaning of property. Given this tenure pluralism, colonizers arrived on American shores armed with a diversified toolbox of land laws, institutions and procedures (sometimes imperfectly understood) that they used to claim the land. Improvisation and *bricolage* were inevitable as they attempted to secure spaces for themselves in a Native American property universe, taking the first steps in the direction of new colonial property forms.

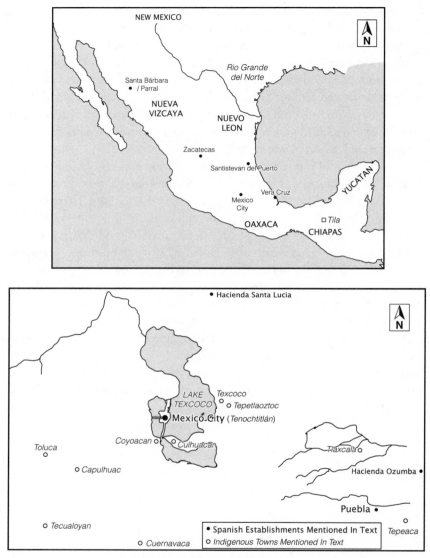

MAP 4.1 New Spain/Mexico

4

New Spain

Over the years and decades that followed the fall of Tenochtitlán, a colonial regime took shape in the central basin of Mexico and then spread north and southward well beyond the territories that had been dominated by the Aztecs. A brief sketch of the major sixteenth-century developments in New Spain would have to begin with the horrifying decline of the indigenous population, the combined result of imported pathogens and an environment of war, dislocation and impoverishment. Specialists dispute the numbers (from 25 million in 1519 to 750,000 a century later?), but no one doubts the reality of a dramatic fall.[1] Meanwhile, immigrants from Spain came streaming into the country and they eventually brought in substantial numbers of enslaved Africans to serve them. So populous was pre-conquest Mexico, however, that natives never ceased to outnumber all other racial designations within New Spain's population; moreover, the demographic decline reversed itself at some point in the seventeenth century and Indian population grew through the second half of Mexico's colonial period. In New Spain, indigenous people were always numerically preponderant, in striking contrast to the areas of North America colonized by France and England. At the same time, so-called racial mixing became a massive phenomenon in Mexico with the emergence of large numbers of people whose parentage, appearance and

---

[1] Noble David Cook, *Born to Die: Disease and New World Conquest, 1492–1650* (New York: Cambridge University Press, 1998); Alfred Crosby, "Virgin Soil Epidemics as a Factor in the Aboriginal Depopulation in America," *William and Mary Quarterly*, 3rd ser., 33 (1976): 289–99; David S. Jones, "Virgin Soils Revisited," *William and Mary Quarterly*, 3rd ser., 60 (2003): 703–42.

culture ceased to match the categories of "Spaniard," "negro" and "Indian" supplied by the dominant colonial ideology of difference.

Within three years of the military conquest, Christian missionaries arrived in New Spain to begin the wholesale integration of indigenous society into the Catholic Church. Before long, this religious change had placed its mark on the Nahua landscape, as a church sprang up at what was, or would become, the center of each pueblo. Parochial boundaries tended to coincide with, and therefore to reinforce, those of pueblo and *encomienda*. And yet, in a context of population decline, growing pressures from Spanish neighbors, as well as various campaigns on the part of Church and state to rationalize the administration of Indians, communities were not altogether stable and stationary. Dispersed settlements were, in many cases, forcibly displaced and their inhabitants concentrated in pueblos through the process of *"congregación."* Furthermore, individuals and families increasingly left their villages of origin, seeking to earn a living in some distant mining camp or Spanish city.

Post-conquest colonization was a dynamic affair, disruptive of all sorts of settled relations. In 1546 a major silver deposit was discovered at Zacatecas; other strikes followed in the region north of Mexico City and large-scale mining operations increasingly drove the economic and environmental transformation of New Spain. Many indigenous people were recruited to work in the mines, either as "free laborers" or as part of the rotation of labor service. Native communities were not as severely affected in Mexico (thanks partly to the importation of African slaves), as were the indigenous peoples of Peru, drawn in through the hellish operations of the Potosí *mita*. However, they were severely affected by depopulation and migration. At the same time, the surging demand for food and other supplies for the mining camps placed new pressures on native pueblos, already overtaxed by the demands of *encomienda*. Prices ran high for products that indigenous agriculture, organized around hand tillage on small plots, was ill-equipped to supply in quantity: wheat, meat, sheep's wool, horses and mules. Enterprising Spaniards inevitably turned their attention to agriculture, especially stock raising, and sought land, as well as Indian labor, to pursue these activities. The conflicts that ensued would undermine the conquest/tribute regime and menace the very survival of native communities.

Meanwhile, the conquest period witnessed political/administrative turmoil as Cortés's personal rule was first established and then overthrown to the benefit of his rivals. New courts, notably the *audiencia*, were set up and the Catholic clergy established its institutions and authority. In 1535, New Spain was reorganized as a kingdom with a viceroy exercising sovereign power in the name of the king of Spain. A corps of regional governors (*corregidores*) aided by other royal administrators would help establish something resembling stable rule and bring the conquistadors to heel. Successive viceroys would struggle to maintain order, moderate the exploitation of the indigenous population and safeguard the Crown's material interests (principally in land, minerals and native tribute) against the inroads of the Spanish colonial elite and its Creole descendants. In New Spain as in other colonial formations, there were chronic tensions between the state and the colonists, though these were complicated by the fact that government officials were often busy lining their own pockets rather than advancing the interests of the Crown. Moreover, these same officials tended to assimilate into the colonial upper class they were supposed to be controlling: particularly where natives and native lands were concerned, white racial solidarity frequently bridged the gap separating imperial government and the creole elite.

RISE AND DECLINE OF THE CONQUEST TRIBUTE REGIME

Conquest and the distinction between conquerors and conquered were defining features of the colonial society that developed in Mexico under Spanish rule. In this respect, New Spain was not entirely unique for, as Anthony Pagden notes, "all European empires in America were empires of expansion, all, at one stage or another, had been based upon conquest and had been conceived and legitimized using the language of warfare."[2] In order to bring out the specificity of the Spanish colonial order, we need to introduce some distinctions in the concept of "conquest." That term can be meaningful in several different ways: descriptively to designate military relations, ideologically as a justification for hierarchy, and politically/legally as the basis for differential rights and duties. Conquest in the first two senses was a reality that shaped New England and New France as well as New Spain. All these colonization projects began with the arrival of armed men from Europe, and although they did not all witness the kind of spectacular and bloody battles that accompanied Cortés's assault on Tenochtitlán, all involved lethal violence and the constant

[2] Anthony Pagden, *Lords of All the World: Ideologies of Empire in Spain, Britain and France c. 1500–c. 1800* (New Haven, Conn.: Yale University Press, 1995), 63. Note that, as late as the 1760s, the jurist William Blackstone was still describing the British American colonies as conquered lands. John H. Elliott, *Empires of the Atlantic World: Britain and Spain in America* (New Haven, Conn.: Yale University Press, 2006), 136.

FIGURE 4.1 Indians performing agricultural labor service for a Spanish encomendero.
Source: Pintura del gobernador, alcaldes y regidores de México [Codice Osuna], 1565. Courtesy Biblioteca Nacional de España.

threat of war to guarantee the colonial presence. Moreover, there was a widespread sense, rooted in the male aristocratic values of the period, that valor and military strength made Euro-Americans superior to Indians; such attitudes can be found among the English and French colonists as well as those of Spain. Sometimes the rights of the conqueror were cited, along with other justifications, to legitimize European territorial claims. What made New Spain special in this context is the degree to which conquest was institutionalized in law, governance and land tenure.

Tribute, initially integrated into the *encomienda* system, became a crucial defining feature of *indio* status in the Spanish kingdoms of America. "The payment of tribute, in specie or in kind, or in a combination of the two, was obligatory on the Indians under Spanish rule almost from the conquest until its abolition during the wars of independence at the beginning of the nineteenth century."[3] While the *encomienda* system was gradually phased out, tribute remained, and it was redirected toward the colonial state. Likewise, labor service was sometimes viewed as an integral element of tribute, sometimes treated separately, but always built in to what it meant to be an Indian in New Spain (see Figure 4.1). If tribute was to be paid and if natives were to support themselves between periods

---

[3] J. H. Elliott, "Spain and America in the Sixteenth and Seventeenth Centuries," in *The Cambridge History of Latin America*, 11 vols., ed. Leslie Bethell (Cambridge: Cambridge University Press, 1984), vol. 1: 311.

of labor service, they needed a secure land base. Accordingly, public discussion tended to treat the subject of native lands as a conservation issue.[4] The logic of the tribute complex led to an attitude toward indigenous land and property in Spanish America different from that which would prevail in other European colonies: the Spanish state generally guaranteed native lands. It did so more wholeheartedly during the early period when tribute was economically significant than it would later when its relative value declined. Moreover, the commitment to protect Indian lands was constantly undercut by the self-serving actions of Spaniards, government officials, *encomenderos* and others, facilitated by the colonial racial hierarchy.

For along with tribute, the conquest regime was built upon the structural disempowerment of *indios*. Scorned initially as "pagans," most natives quickly accepted Christian baptism, and so their inferiority was attributed to other cultural characteristics such as language and costume; over time, a notion of "impure blood" replaced religion as the central element of colonialist ideology.[5] Racialism gained ground even as the introduction of African slaves and the massive growth of a "mixed" population made it more and more difficult to define racial boundaries. In this context, the colonial regime took steps to inscribe *indio* status in legal restrictions and customs of denigration. Indians were not allowed to ride horses, wear European-style clothes or carry swords. "In the Americas, Spaniards required from the Indians those respectful behaviors that they had become accustomed to receiving from Spanish Muslims. In their demeanor, Indians were to be 'obedient, submissive, subdued, humble, servile, and yielding.' They were to give way to Spaniards on the streets and to indicate their subservience openly."[6] Indian testimony, when it was accepted in the courts, was greatly discounted; legislation in Peru, generally followed across Spanish America, specified that, in view of their feeble judgment, seven Indian witnesses counted the same as a single Spaniard.[7] At the same time, *indios* were entitled to paternalistic protection by virtue

---

[4] My thanks to Daviken Studnicki-Gizbert for suggesting this point.

[5] J. H. Sweet, "The Iberian Roots of American Racist Thought," *William & Mary Quarterly* 54 (1997): 143–66.

[6] Patricia Seed, *American Pentimento: The Invention of Indians and the Pursuit of Riches* (Minneapolis: University of Minnesota Press, 2001), 82. See also *Recopilación de Leyes de Los Reynos de Las Indias*, 3 vols. (Madrid: Julian de Paredes, 1681), libro 6, Titulo 1, law of 19 July 1568.

[7] Juan de Solórzano Pereira, *Política Indiana* [1648], 3 vols. (Madrid: Fundación José Antonio de Castro, 1996), 1: 583–84 (libro II, capitulo 28, paragraphs 34–35).

of their "humility" and vulnerability. The Church and the colonial government in particular took upon themselves the duty of ensuring that the
"poor Indians" were not exploited excessively. Accordingly, natives were
not entirely without recourse in this colonial polity, which officially recognized them and guaranteed their property. On the other hand, they were as
a group permanently vulnerable to the violence of Spanish ranchers and the
machinations of corrupt officials; in a thousand instances of conflict – over
land, for example – their voices did not carry as much weight as those of the
settler elite. "Protection" was not a hoax, but neither was it a fully effective
bulwark against exploitation and dispossession.

Where native lands were concerned, the obligations of Christian
benevolence were reinforced by the dictates of sensible policy. As long
as tribute remained an important element in the colonial economy – as it
did through the first century of New Spain's existence – good administrators could see that the indigenous population needed a secure land base
in order to grow the crops with which to pay its exactions, as well as to
sustain itself between periods of labor service. Over the years, the viceroy
issued dozens of royal *cédulas* (edicts) forbidding nonnatives to occupy,
encroach upon, or even buy, Indian lands. Ranchers were supposed to
keep their livestock well away from native cornfields. "The Indians shall
continue to possess their lands, both arable tracts and grazing lands,"
declared a 1532 edict, "so that they do not lack what is necessary."[8]
Colonial courts respected native property and even did their best to
observe indigenous tenure regimes and inheritance customs. When
unoccupied land was granted to colonists, formal inquiries were held to
ensure that no prior Indian claims were infringed upon. Such measures
guaranteeing Indian property were integral to the logic of the tribute
regime.

Gradually, over the course of the sixteenth century, the Spanish state
managed to rip tribute and labor service from the clutches of the conquistadors and their descendants. First the "New Laws" of the 1540s ordered
a reduction in the size of the biggest *encomiendas* and prohibited the
inheritance of *encomiendas*. To head off the emergence of a class of
landed magnates the state prohibited land grants to *encomenderos* within
their *encomienda* territories. These regulations against land grants and
heredity were often honored in the breach, however, partly because the

---

[8] Royal cédula of 1532 translated and quoted in William B. Taylor, *Landlord and Peasant
in Colonial Oaxaca* (Stanford, Calif.: Stanford University Press, 1972), 67. See also
Recopilación de Leyes, libro 4, titulo 12, "de la vente y composicion de tierras."

encomenderos and government officialdom intermingled. Over the long run, however, native depopulation and the changing economy of New Spain made *encomienda* less attractive and the government finally succeeded in phasing out the institution. In the campaign to control and eliminate *encomienda*, the growth of a colonial bureaucracy played a crucial part, taking over the administration of native tribute and labor for the benefit of the government. The office of *corregidor* (magistrate, or literally, "corrector") and the institution of the *corregimiento* as a unit of local governance were central to the colonial state formation that allowed the Spanish monarchy to tame the *encomenderos*. By the late sixteenth century, the institution had disappeared from central Mexico, though some *encomiendas* persisted on the edges of Spanish America.

As a sidebar to the history of *encomienda*, we should insert a word on the unique feudal domain that Hernán Cortés established for himself and his descendants as a device to maintain some prestige and wealth at a time when his political enemies were preventing him from securing control over all of New Spain. Having acquired the title of marquis, he assembled a large territory, centered on Cuernavaca but encompassing Coyoacan and many other areas south of the capital, all of which would be under his and his successors' lordship as the *"marquesado del Valle."* It functioned as a kind of super-*encomienda* with the marquis controlling the distribution of Indian tribute; however, he also exercised feudal jurisdiction and claimed some of the state's powers of eminent domain, including the right to grant unoccupied lands. This sort of feudal privatization of the Crown's territorial prerogatives was by no means rare in *Reconquista* Spain,[9] but it did not sit well with the king or the viceroy. The latter chipped away at the privileges of the *marquesado* over the years and tried to limit its heritability, choosing, as with the anti-*encomienda* campaign, a gradual approach rather than a head-on confrontation with powerful colonial interests. After a long and difficult series of lawsuits between 1610 and 1644, the government finally succeeded in suppressing this feudal experiment.[10]

Long before it had succeeded in eliminating either the *marquesado* or the *encomiendas*, the government had managed to bring about major reforms in the administration of tribute and labor service. Whereas through the first half of the sixteenth century, there were many exemptions from tribute on grounds of noble status or because people paid tribute to a

---

[9] James Casey, *Early Modern Spain: A Social History* (London: Routledge, 2002), 87–110.
[10] François Chevalier, *Land and Society in Colonial Mexico: The Great Hacienda*, trans. Alvin Eustis (Berkeley: University of California Press, 1963), 127–34.

local *cacique* or paid as members of kin and neighborhood collectivities, reforms enacted in the 1550s made every Indian individual liable. The general effect was to equalize and universalize tribute within native society. It also detached tribute from land holdings and made the exaction more like a head tax. Around the same time, the form of payment narrowed to only two acceptable commodities, maize and money; instead of following the contours of local indigenous economies, tribute now forced natives to conform to the requirements of the colonial economy. Universalizing tribute (with *caciques* excepted) contributed to the leveling down of the native social hierarchy. All Indians (with the exception of a few surviving members of ruling families) had the same legal/fiscal status and that status denoted subjugation and inferiority to Spaniards.[11]

As tribute came to be treated more like a tax, it also tended to part company with the labor service requirements that had been an integral part of what *macehuales* owed their native lords and later their *encomenderos*. Subjection to forced labor did remain a part of what it meant to be an "Indian" in New Spain: until the end of the colonial period Indians had to be available to work (for a low wage) on a temporary basis. However, this obligation was detached from *encomienda* in 1549; henceforth, *corregidores*, aided by native officials at the local level, would organize drafts of workers and contract them out to farmers, construction entrepreneurs and other colonists who needed cheap, unskilled labor. Labor service, now referred to as "*repartimiento*," was another defining characteristic of what it meant to be part of a conquered race. In that sense it remained an integral element, along with annual payments of corn and money, of the larger system of tribute that was the hallmark of Spanish colonialism in the New World.

The *Códice tributos de Coyoacan*, painted by a native artist in the early 1550s, provides a record of changing tribute assessments in the pueblo of Coyoacan, near Mexico City, over the three decades following the conquest (Figures 4.2 and 4.3).[12] It is a fascinating document, combining Nahua and Spanish practices of record-keeping. Mesoamerican

---

[11] The most lucid account of sixteenth-century tribute, and the main source for this paragraph, is Rebecca Horn, *Postconquest Coyoacan: Nahua-Spanish Relations in Central Mexico, 1519–1650* (Stanford, Calif.: Stanford University Press, 1997), 86–100.

[12] The original is held in the Achivo General de Simancas (Spain). A fine facsimile edition, together with an introductory essay, has been published: *Códice Tributos de Coyoacan*, ed. Juan José Batalla Rosada (Madrid: Editorial Brokarte, 2002). I have drawn on the interpretations of Batalla Rosada as well as those of Rebecca Horn (*Postconquest Coyoacan*, 97–99).

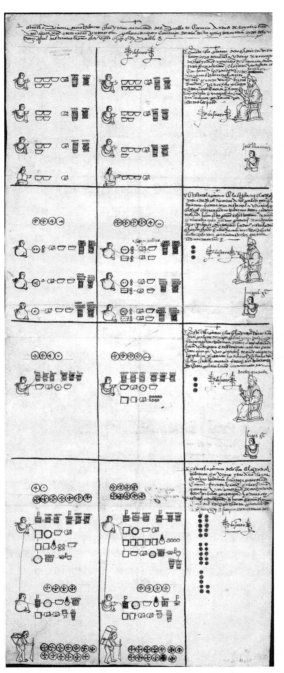

FIGURE 4.2 *Códice Tributos de Coyoacan*: a record of the tribute owed by residents of the pueblo of Coyoacan, near Mexico City, in the mid-sixteenth century.
Source: Archivo General de Simancas (Spain), Sección de Mapas, Planos, y Documentos, XII-35. E. 8334-21. Courtesy Archivo General de Simancas.

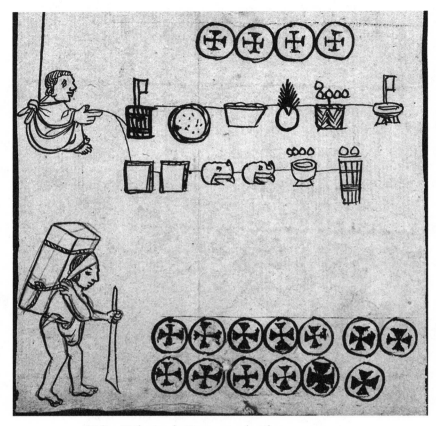

FIGURE 4.3 *Códice Tributos de Coyoacan*, detail.
Source: Archivo General de Simancas (Spain), Sección de Mapas, Planos, y Documentos, XII-35. E. 8334-21. Courtesy Archivo General de Simancas.

pictographs, some of them apparently mnemonic reminders that modern scholars cannot read precisely, others more transparently meaningful, are at the heart of the codex; a Spanish scribe who signed as Alonso de Suero has added a Spanish gloss. The three columns and four rows of the document proceed in time upward, from the immediate wake of the conquest at the bottom to, at the top, a visit by the magistrate Gómez de Santillán in 1553 to revise tribute schedules at Coyoacan. The right-hand column shows Santillán and his predecessor judge, aided in each case by a native magistrate ("*juez*"), ruling on tribute rates, while Indians are depicted in the other two columns, sitting in the midst of symbols indicating the products and the quantities of each that they owe their *encomendero*. Distinctions are made between those who pay at a higher or lower rate, depending on the size of their land holdings. Among the products enumerated are traditional Mesoamerican tribute items, such as corn, bundles of firewood, cacao beans, cloth, salt and mats; chickens, a new species of fowl that took the place of native turkeys, are indicated by a rather reptilian-looking head. The small circles above each item signify the number of each required, with a small flag indicating twenty and a tuft of hairs (with the appearance of a miniature pine tree) indicating four hundred. In the earlier (lower) quadrants, a mortar and pestle represents labor service; a man carrying a heavy load on his back indicates that tribute items had to be delivered to the *encomendero*. Mortars and pestles are nowhere to be found in the upper frames and the Spanish text states specifically that "personal service" has been done away with. (Work duty had not actually been done away with, but it no longer formed part of *encomienda*.) Most of the frames contain disks with crosses, signifying a number of pesos: these indicate the money value of all the tribute. It will be noted that the range of products assessed narrows over time (bottom to top) and that the total amount of tribute demanded lessens. The sequence of tribute revisions was, in fact, a response to the fact that native population was plummeting and communities were simply unable to maintain tribute levels.

Just because official tribute schedules were being revised downward and labor service was being detached from *encomienda* does not mean that the lot of the native peasantry was improving. Even as the worst excesses of the *encomenderos* were curbed, other privileged actors stepped up to ensure that the *macehuales* continued to be overtaxed. There were reports of grasping *corregidores* overburdening natives with work for their own benefit: writes Charles Gibson, "The early corregidores received their daily food, fodder, fuel, and Indian service as an additional portion of their salaries, just as encomenderos received theirs in the form of extra tribute."[13] Meanwhile, several court cases arose pitting native pueblos against their own *caciques* (otherwise known as *principales*) in the wake of the elimination of tribute exemptions. At Tepeaca and Tlaxcala, residents had owed their native rulers a form of tribute known locally as "*terrazgo*," the elements of which have been summarized in these terms:

[13] Charles Gibson, *The Aztecs under Spanish Rule: A History of the Indians of the Valley of Mexico, 1519–1810* (Stanford, Calif.: Stanford University Press, 1964), 58–97 (quotation at 83).

Every *terrazguero* was obliged to work a plot of specified dimensions, apart from the land he worked for his own subsistence. The *terrazgueros* had to transport the yield of these tribute lands to the house of the *principal*. In addition they were supposed to provide the *principal* in question three or four times a year with hens (*gallinas*) and a number of cacao beans. They also had to fulfill personal services of a week in the house of a *principal* a few times a year. At the onset of the week of services they had to bring firewood and water. The wives of the *terrazgueros* took part in the services in the house of the *principal*. They also supplied products of the domestic industries – in Tepeaca this included for example semi-processed cotton. Finally the *terrazgueros* had to repair the house of the *principal* whenever necessary.

In the 1560s, they were ordered to pay tribute to the state, seemingly instead of to their respective native rulers. However, the *principales* insisted that they had to continue the *terrazgo* even as they took on these new obligations, for the *terrazgo*, they insisted, was actually a rent rather than a tax, applying to land the *principales* argued was their own property. The *audiencia* of Mexico decided in favor of the *principales*; the Indians were thus subjected to double exploitation, with state exactions piled on top of older native tribute.[14]

It seems that the Nahua peasantry, long accustomed to suffering exploitation before the Spaniards arrived, found themselves burdened even more heavily after the conquest, though there are no precise data on that point. More readily verifiable is the fact that changing practices of tribute and labor service were now creating a new sociopolitical landscape after the conquest. Whereas Nahua conquerors normally imposed tribute on a vanquished polity as such, Spaniards generally exacted it from vanquished religious enemies as individuals (even if these were sometimes grouped together in corporate bodies). There was a certain continuity linking tribute flows within an *altepetl*, up from peasant to noble and ruler, and tribute flows from a defeated *altepetl* to a victorious one. At the local level, within the *altepetl*, tribute had been assessed in proportion to the extent of assessable land. In the Spanish tradition, however, tribute tended to be assessed on the basis of population rather than land holdings; moreover, it was associated with religious and ethnic status. The reforms of the mid-sixteenth century imposed this Spanish

---

[14] Rik Hoekstra, "A Different Way of Thinking: Contrasting Spanish and Indian Social and Economic Views in Central Mexico (1550–1600)," in *The Indian Community of Colonial Mexico: Fifteen Essays on Land Tenure, Corporate Organizations, Ideology and Village Politics*, ed. Arij Ouweneel and Simon Miller (Amsterdam: CEDLA, 1990), 60–85 (quotation at 62).

model on Mexico, reinforcing a fundamental bifurcation of colonial society into native and European/Creole spheres.

Protective legislation rested on the assumption that New Spain was made up of two distinct components: "Indians" and "Spaniards." Of course, the notion that society can be neatly divided into colonizers and colonized is fundamental to any colonial regime,[15] but compared with many other colonial regimes, New Spain had a notably frank ideology of difference. Different in costume as well as skin color, Indians and Spaniards spoke different languages, pursued different occupations and, in theory, lived in different locations. Many distinctions, such as the right to bear arms, ride horses and enter certain professions, were proscribed by law. The kingdom was imagined as being composed of two realms: the *"republica de indios"* and the *"republica de españoles,"* the latter relying on the dutiful support of the former. Mixing and "contamination" were discouraged, to the point where Spaniards were forbidden to live in native villages. Of course, strict separation was impossible in practice. When the prerogatives of the conqueror included having native servants to perform household tasks and occasionally to sleep with the master, how could "purity" be ensured? Moreover, it turned out that individuals of native birth could, with enough money and cultural adaptation, be accepted as Spaniards. As is generally the case, "race" was a complex and somewhat unstable social construction, built upon the fiction of simple biological difference. However, the incoherence of racial categories did not prevent the establishment of a basic duality of corporate status. For all its social complexity, New Spain was composed legally of two collectivities: *indio* communities for the subjugated indigenous population and the "Spanish" sphere for everyone else.

Land tenure played a central role in defining the boundaries dividing the indigenous and the Spanish realms. There may have been many kinds of people in New Spain, but there really were only two basic property systems. Natives held land as members of a "pueblo de indios" and subject to the eminent domain of their respective pueblos. The pueblo was both a unit of landholding subject to tribute and a jurisdiction (more on this shortly). As of the 1560s, Indians who paid tribute were ipso facto entitled to a share of pueblo lands.[16] Tribute, native property and Indian

[15] Jan Vansina, *Being Colonized: The Kuba Experience in Rural Congo, 1880–1960* (Madison: University of Wisconsin Press, 2010), 35.
[16] Arij Ouweneel, "*Altepeme* and *Pueblos de indios*: Some Comparative Theoretical Perspectives on the Analysis of the Colonial Indian Communities," in *The Indian*

status were thus intimately connected. Moreover, in the early colonial period, courts treated Indian community lands as primordial; whereas Spaniards were supposed to document their property claims, no evidence beyond occupancy was required to prove Indian ownership.[17] Spaniards acquired title to land through grant or by purchase; such land was held under tenure quite different from that of Indian lands and it was subject to a different jurisdiction. Thus, Spanish status also was rooted in a particular property regime.

This picture of a bifurcated conquest/tribute regime neatly divided by "race," civic status and land tenure never corresponded precisely to reality, though it functioned as a very real organizing principle through the sixteenth century and into the seventeenth. Over time, however, a variety of developments worked to diminish the importance of tribute and to reduce the saliency of the "two republics" and their respective property regimes. Native depopulation reduced the aggregate value of tribute in New Spain, while the growth of Spanish, African and mixed-origin populations complicated the racial bifurcation. The mining and ranching boom that began in the mid-sixteenth century placed tribute further into the shade economically, even as it fueled a massive assault on Indian land holdings. The Spanish Crown's commitment to preserving native property became ever more ineffectual in the face of pressures to expand "Spanish" holdings. By the eighteenth century, with the tribute system now only of vestigial economic importance, the government seemed more interested in promoting "development" (on the part of nonnatives) than in guaranteeing the lands of indigenous pueblos. Though diminished in extent, the protected domain left to the tribute-paying conquered population would remain a basic element of New Spain's territorial organization until the end of the colonial era, and well beyond.

PUEBLOS DE INDIOS

The government of New Spain recognized about two thousand *pueblos de indios* in the second half of the sixteenth century.[18] These autonomous

Community of Colonial Mexico: Fifteen Essays on Land Tenure, Corporate Organizations, Ideology and Village Politics, ed. Arij Ouweneel and Simon Miller (Amsterdam: CEDLA, 1990), 8.

[17] Brian P. Owensby, *Empire of Law and Indian Justice in Colonial Mexico* (Stanford, Calif.: Stanford University Press, 2008), 92

[18] René García Castro, "Los Pueblos de Indios," in *Gran Historia de Mexico Ilustrada* (Mexico City: Planeta DeAgostini, 2001), vol. 8: 143.

units of residence and jurisdiction were both pre-Hispanic survivals and colonial creations. Initially based on the Nahua *altepetl*, ruled by a *tlatoani*, the pueblo gradually acquired, during the post-conquest decades, institutional layers of Spanish origin: first the *encomienda* was imposed as a mechanism of tribute exaction; then the parish was added as communities accepted Christianity and built churches in their midst (which added a further exaction in the form of the tithe); finally a version of the *cabildo* was introduced as a corporate instrument of local jurisdiction and administration. Typically, a given territory and human community appeared simultaneously in the guise of an *encomienda*, a Catholic parish and a municipality. Pueblos still retained much of their pre-conquest indigenous identity, even as they adapted to new procedures and incorporated new, Spanish vocabulary into the language of community life.

The trappings of municipal corporations began to appear in native central Mexico in the 1530s.[19] Each pueblo was dominated by a "governor" (*gobernador*, sometimes known as *cacique*), either elected by the population or appointed by the viceroy, but usually chosen from the dynasty of indigenous *tlatoque*; he carried a staff of office, symbolizing his authority. Each *cabildo* also acquired a corps of council members and local judges (*alcaldes* and *regidores*) and these too, though elected annually, were typically drawn from the traditional noble families. Judges and councilors in Coyoacan generally represented the constituent *calpulli* of the pueblo, yet another instance of Spanish institutions adapting to pre-existing Nahua community organization. There was also a contingent of minor officials: *fiscales* to manage church affairs, tribute collectors, scribes and notaries; their offices too seem to have long been dominated by descendants of the pre-conquest elite. Indian pueblos handled significant economic resources, especially in the wake of the tribute reforms of the mid-sixteenth century; *cabildos* were then charged with the responsibility of collecting local tribute for the *encomendero* or the colonial regime; they also assessed one and a half *fanegas* of corn per resident to nourish the municipal treasury out of which salaries and other expenses

---

[19] This paragraph is based mainly on Horn, *Postconquest Coyoacan*, 44–66. See also García Castro, "Los Pueblos de Indios," 141–60; James Lockhart, *The Nahuas after the Conquest: A Social and Cultural History of the Indians of Central Mexico, Sixteenth through Eighteenth Centuries* (Stanford, Calif.: Stanford University Press, 1992), 28–58; Ethelia Ruiz Medrano, *Mexico's Indigenous Communities: Their Lands and Histories, 1500–2010*, trans. Russ Davidson (Boulder: University Press of Colorado, 2010), 126–27.

were paid.[20] Native notaries, continuing the indigenous tradition of the pictorial record-keeper (*amatlacuilo*), used Latin alphabetic writing – learned from Franciscan missionaries – to produce legal documents in the Nahuatl language.

More clearly than the pre-Hispanic *altepetl*, which referred more to human hierarchies than to topographical spaces, the colonial pueblo was a territorial unit. However, its boundaries could be and were contested, both by encroaching Spaniards and by neighboring native communities. Dwindling population, the result of disease mortality and out-migration, made it difficult for some pueblos to defend their lands. The colonial state stepped in in the late sixteenth century to forcibly relocate many depopulated communities, concentrating people in locations that were more conveniently supervised by Church and state authorities. As part of this policy of *congregación*, the government ordered whole settlements demolished to prevent any surreptitious return; Indians were left to rebuild their houses in a new location and to reconstruct a merged pueblo community.[21] In theory, *congregación* was not supposed to deprive natives of their property in the old location, but in practice it often proved impossible to cultivate and maintain active possession of lands that were far from the new village of residence. Forced relocation was one of the more dramatic ways in which colonization remade indigenous Mexican space, but it was the fate of only a minority of pueblos. However, all communities faced pressures that modified their land base, almost always in a downward direction.

To live in a *pueblo de indios* was to be subject to the *cabildo*'s jurisdiction; it was also to be subject to tribute, both as a kind of local rate and as an exaction betokening the submission of the conquered. At the same time, being on the tribute list gave one a legal right to a share of pueblo lands.[22] Tribute, jurisdiction and property were fully and intimately connected. But what if a Spaniard were to acquire a piece of land within the territory of a pueblo? In that case, and of course such cases did occur, the new owner, a member of the conquering rather than of the conquered race, would not be subject to tribute payment or to the

---

[20] García Castro, "Los Pueblos de Indios," 156.

[21] Bernardo García Martínez, *Los Pueblos de la sierra: el poder y el espacio entre los indios del norte de Puebla hasta 1700* (México City: Colegio de México, Centro de Estudios Históricos, 1987), 175–79; Gibson, *The Aztecs under Spanish Rule*, 281–85; Hanns J. Prem, "Spanish Colonization and Indian Property in Central Mexico, 1521–1620," *Annals of the Association of American Geographers* 82 (1992): 451–52.

[22] Ouweneel, "*Altepeme* and *Pueblos de indios*," 8.

jurisdiction of the *cabildo de indios*. Consequently, the land would no longer form part of the pueblo.[23] The conjunction of land tenure with civic/racial status ensured that Indian lands, once extracted from the indigenous sphere, became for evermore property of a different nature.

Within the pueblo, land was held through a multitude of complex tenures, some of these reflecting the continuing ascendancy through much of the sixteenth century of the indigenous elite. As in the pre-conquest past, some lands were attached to a particular office. For example, in Culhuacan, a substantial plot, worked by local *macehuales*, was set aside for the benefit of the *gobernador*; the produce was his as long as he held office.[24] Some documents refer to *"tecpantlalli,"* meaning land attached to a palace or noble house. Does this imply that plots so designated were permanently owned by a noble lineage; were they exempt from tribute; did commoners rent them or work them as part of traditional labor service? Scholars are unsure about the answers to these questions, though they note that *tecpantlalli* disappears from the records a generation or two after the conquest.[25] Better known is the hybrid tenure, *cacicazgo*, a kind of seigneurial estate belonging to members of the indigenous elite and composed of lands both within and outside Indian pueblos;[26] significant through the first half of the sixteenth century, *cacicazgo* later became rare in central Mexico. Certain lands might be dedicated to the church; bearing no real connection with the old temple lands, these were mainly plots bequeathed by individuals to fund masses for the repose of their souls.[27]

The largest portion of pueblo lands had always been in the possession of the *macehuales* (common peasants), and with the disappearance of various temple and palace estates at the conquest, and then the subsequent decline of *cacicazgo*, such unprivileged, tribute-paying tenures predominated even more fully. However, "commoner" land was not all the same; far from it. The wills and deeds of sale recorded by Nahua notaries refer to lands within the pueblo by a variety of terms, all containing the suffix *"tlalli,"* meaning land: *huehuetlalli*, inherited land;

[23] García Martínez, *Los Pueblos de la Sierra*, 240–41.
[24] S. L. Cline, *Colonial Culhuacan, 1580–1600: A Social History of an Aztec Town* (Albuquerque: University of New Mexico Press, 1986), 141–42.
[25] Cline, *Colonial Culhuacan*, 145; Horn, *Postconquest Coyoacan*, 121.
[26] On *cacicazgo*, see Tomás Jalpa Flores, *Tierra y sociedad: la apropiación del suelo en la región de Chalco durante los siglos XV–XVII* (Mexico City: Instituto Nacional de Antropología e Historia, 2008), 120–24.
[27] Cline, *Colonial Culhuacan*, 144.

tlalcohualli, purchased land; *cihuatlalli*, woman land; *calpullalli*, *calpulli* land; *tequitlalli*, tribute land; *callalli*, house land. Sampling this rich and varied vocabulary helps to demonstrate the complexity of indigenous tenure, but it is important that the terms not be erected into a system of mutually exclusive categories.[28] Notaries seem to have chosen their words so as to emphasize a particular aspect of a land parcel's identity in light of the legal purposes of the documents they were preparing. For example, in a deed of sale, it was important to underline the nonpatrimonial nature of the land by identifying it as "purchased land." The distinction predates the conquest, but it may have gained prominence as a result of colonial protective legislation designed to ensure that Indians were not pressured into selling off their essential land base to Spaniards.

Under Spanish rule, as in the Aztec period, the nuances of native property practices escape any simple "private property" versus "communal lands" opposition. Most pueblo lands would be considered *calpullalli*, meaning they owed tribute and belonged to a specific household, but were subject to varying degrees of oversight on the part of the *calpulli* (neighborhood). "Calpollalli was considered both inalienable and subject to taxation. It could be inherited, but reverted to the calpolli for reallocation if there were no heirs."[29] Households still typically held land immediately attached to their home as well as detached plots scattered across the *calpulli*.

A pictographic document, apparently submitted as part of a lawsuit (possibly an inheritance case: the picture was preserved without any accompanying text to explain its purpose) shows the holdings of a native woman named Juliana Flanco of Huexocolco (Figure 4.4).[30] The wrapped corpses represent ancestors from whom she inherited her various properties. A two-story house is depicted in collapsed form as though the floors lay next to one another; as is normally the case, it sits in the midst of a compound, the nucleus of the household's holdings and inseparably connected to the house itself. There are eight scattered plots, five in her home community as indicated by the tree glyph (Huexocolco means "place of the twisted willow tree"), and three in the nearby pueblo of Chalchiuhquayaco (meaning "place of the round jade beads" and designated by the glyph over the middle lot). The lines linking these two groupings with the house land indicate that they all belong to the same

---

[28] Lockhart, *The Nahuas after the Conquest*, 155–63.
[29] Horn, *Postconquest Coyoacan*, 116.
[30] "Pièce d'un procès," Bibliothèque nationale de France, manuscrits mexicains, 33.

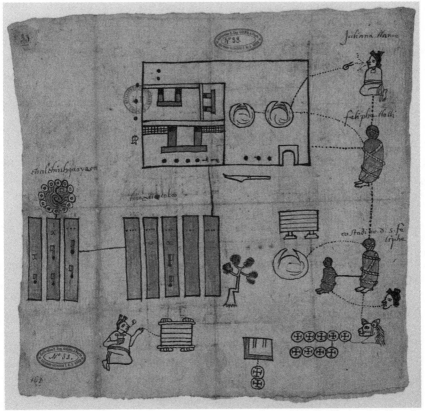

FIGURE 4.4 Pictographic record of the land holdings of Juliana Flanco of Huexocolco. This undated, post-conquest document seems to have been prepared for a legal case. It shows Juliana Flanco in the upper right, connected to the deceased ancestors from whom she inherited these lands. The two-story house and attached house lot appear at the top. Eight holdings scattered across two pueblos are shown as shaded rectangles (green in the original); this is a schematic diagram, not drawn to proportion, but the size of each lot is indicated by number glyphs. Symbols below refer to tribute rates.

Source: "Pièce d'un procès: plan et titre d'une propriété sise à Huexocolco près de Texcoco, au nom de Juliana Flanco," Département des Manuscrits, Mexicain 33. Courtesy Bibliothèque nationale de France.

owner. The different lots are shown schematically, without regard to their actual location or relative size. We can tell that, in spite of appearances, the scattered plots are actually much larger than the home compound because their dimensions are specified in the pictogram. Round black dots indicate the number of linear units (these varied from locality to locality, so we can discern only relative, not absolute, sizes) and the small "flags" pictured in three of the scattered lots stand for twenty of these units; thus the scattered plots measure forty by three units as compared with a house lot that appears to be only three by seven units. Two bins are pictured here, of a type normally used to indicate tribute as a quantity of corn or other agricultural produce. There is also some cloth in the bottom center, connected to symbols for two pesos; this is also tribute, the money probably indicating the value of the cloth. One of the tribute bins is linked to a woman, who may be Juliana herself or possibly a tenant of hers. Both women have speech scrolls, alluding perhaps to the words of a statement recorded on a now-lost accompanying text, or possibly indicating more generally Juliana Flanco's rights and authority. Much about this picto-graph, including the three circular objects with "ears," cannot be inter-preted, even by experts in the field; it is not clear what the horse and nine pesos connected to Juliana's dead ancestor are all about. Nevertheless, this document provides a good sense of how land holdings were under-stood and depicted in a post-conquest Nahua setting.[31]

Along with pictorial documents such as the one recording Juliana Flanco's property, scholars have made good use of the wills, deeds of sale and other legal records drawn up by the native notaries to illuminate the land tenure practices of central Mexico in the post-conquest period.[32] These fascinating sources are written in the Nahuatl language, with a sprinkling of Spanish legal vocabulary; they show traces of indigenous scribal/pictorial practices, but their medium is often European-style paper, ink and lettering. (The Juliana Flanco document was actually drawn on agave paper.) In content as well as in form, the products of the native notaries display a hybrid quality, blending indigenous and Spanish property practices. They show that Indians bought and sold and rented plots of land within the pueblo. The location and dimensions of the land in question were carefully noted in the deed, and a detailed narrative of the chain of ownership leading to the current owner was usually included as well, for it was a matter of consequence to know if the property was patrimonial (i.e., inherited) or acquired by purchase.

---

[31] This paragraph was written under the guidance of two leading Nahuatl scholars, Rebecca Horn and Frances Berdan. Although I take responsibility for the interpretation offered here, I am very grateful for their generous assistance. Rebecca Horn, personal communi-cation, 8 May 2014; Frances Berdan, personal communications, 8 and 28 May 2014.

[32] Arthur J. O. Anderson, Frances Berdan and James M. Lockhart, *Beyond the Codices: The Nahua View of Colonial Mexico* (Berkeley: University of California Press, 1976); Cline, *Colonial Culhuacan*; Horn, *Postconquest Coyoacan*.

Recurrent mortality crises ensured that complicated inheritance arrangements occurred, with widows, daughters and distant relatives often inheriting land. It may well be that the notarial documents, by their very nature, give an exaggerated impression of the frequency with which land changed hands. Nonetheless, they do make it clear that Indian pueblos were not exactly "communal," even if the *calpulli* did enjoy something like "eminent domain" over individual holdings.

Though they were not simply communal in the aggregate, pueblos did have commons. Beyond the house lots and the other cultivated fields of each community were common lands, located both in their midst and on their fringes. Sometimes referred to as *altepetlalli*, these included *calpulli* that had been abandoned, perhaps because a family line had died out without heirs (not unusual in epidemic periods) or because the owner had moved away. In such cases, an individual could approach the *cabildo* and ask for a formal grant of the plot. Another important part of the pueblo's land base was the uncultivated commons, often rough mountainous areas, that surrounded many settlements. These were places for gathering wood for fuel, reeds for basketry, wild fruits and various other natural products. When indigenous people began raising sheep and goats, the pueblo commons provided them with pasture. Pueblos had to be vigilant to protect their outer commons, for as uncultivated land it was vulnerable to encroachment. When a Spaniard applied for a land grant in the mountains behind the pueblo of Tecualoyan in 1607, the Indian *cabildo* protested that this area formed part of their commons. "Fruits grow there which they use for their sustenance and to pay their tributes," read the petition, carefully worded to appeal to colonial authorities.[33]

SPANISH LANDS

If the conquest ideal required that Indians retain land for their own subsistence and to enable them to pay tribute, it also presupposed a Spanish presence, and therefore a zone of exclusive property and jurisdiction for the conquerors (in addition to the property rights *encomenderos* enjoyed over Indian pueblos). The *"republica de españoles"* was

---

[33] Alessandra Russo, *El realismo circular: tierras, espacios y paisajes de la cartografía indígena novohispana, siglos XVI y XVII* (Mexico City: Universidad Nacional Autónoma de México, Instituto de Investigaciones Estéticas, 2005), 183 ("... alli tienen frutales con los que se sustenta y pagan sus tributos"). See also Taylor, *Landlord and Peasant*, 72; Horn, *Postconquest Coyoacan*, 117–18.

territorially small and scattered at first, but it grew steadily in extent as the demographic balance shifted, as the colonial economy changed and as a colonial state took shape and strengthened its grip over Mexico.

Initially, it was the colonial municipality, rather than the Crown, that played a central role in instituting settler property in Mexico. The towns – quintessentially Mexico City – emerged as places of residence for Spaniards and centers of military, ecclesiastical and administrative power.[34] In the Spanish tradition, towns were corporate bodies, each with its own constitution that ensured its legal autonomy. In the early modern Hispanic world, corporations such as guilds, colleges, religious confraternities and, above all, cities were part and parcel of the state system. They "formed an integral part of the mode of government and were consubstantial with the institution of monarchy."[35] The founding of new towns in territory wrested from Moorish control had been a feature of the Iberian *Reconquista*; through the instrumentality of the municipal corporation, order and good Christian government were to be established. The town was a place, but it was also a legal jurisdiction, embodied in that capacity by the town council, or *cabildo*. Essential features of this legal-political culture, together with the institution of the *cabildo*, were introduced into Mexico from the earliest stages of the conquest; they predated the establishment of royal rule by a decade.

Like its native counterpart, the *pueblo de indios*, the Spanish town council in Mexico exercised authority over land and acted to create, define and guarantee property.[36] As mentioned in the previous chapter, a municipal citizen (*vecino*) was entitled to a house lot within the town (*solar*) as well as use-rights over the commons (*ejido*). The basic layout of colonial towns in Hispanic America featured a square grid of streets with ample *plazas*, a church, public buildings and lots for private residences. The commons formed a belt around the city; its extent was not always clearly delimited. This land was available to citizens for their games and recreation, as well as to pasture their livestock; sometimes individuals

---

[34] However, as Barbara Mundy demonstrates, all around its central core, Mexico City remained a predominantly indigenous settlement in the early colonial period. Barbara E. Mundy, *The Death of Aztec Tenochtitlan, the Life of Mexico City* (Austin: University of Texas Press, 2015).

[35] Annick Lempérière, *Entre Dieu et le roi, la république: Mexico, XVIe-XIXe siècles* (Paris: les Belles lettres, 2004), 18. My translation.

[36] Richard M. Morse, "Some Characteristics of Latin American Urban History," *American Historical Review* 67 (1962): 317–38; Lyle N. McAlister, *Spain and Portugal in the New World, 1492–1700* (Minneapolis: University of Minnesota Press, 1984), 136–37.

were also allowed to fence off a portion of the commons for orchards or to grow crops, and these allotments could evolve into permanent, inheritable property. In some cases, the city of Mexico rented out portions of its commons on a "*censo enfitéutico.*" All these urban and extra-urban spaces of property were designed, as the legislation surrounding them makes explicit,[37] to provide a residence for Spaniards, together with the pastures, gardens and orchards needed to sustain the population and its domestic animals. In the context of the colonial municipality, property functioned, originally and ideally, in ways that call to mind Hannah Arendt's view of the ancient Greek *polis*, to provide a physical place and a means of sustenance for urban households. It was about assuring a presence rather than accumulating a fortune.

Of course, from the indigenous perspective, the Spanish town was hardly a benign institution. *Vecinos* depended on conscripted Indian labor to work in their garden plots and orchards and their food supply came also from Indian tribute payments. Moreover, the colonial cities – most notably Mexico – were typically erected on indigenous lands. The *Codice Osuna* shows an urban magistrate laying out lots for the city of Mexico right in the midst of a Nahua family compound.[38] Originally, the city claimed a belt of common lands running two leagues beyond its walls, but later, as the Spanish population burgeoned, it extended its *ejido* deeper into the indigenous countryside. The Nahua community of Tlatelulco took the city to court for encroaching on its territory. The case was appealed all the way up to the Council of the Indies in Spain and that body eventually ruled in favor of Tlatelulco, ordering Mexico City to withdraw from Indian lands.[39] Undeniably, the establishment of colonial cities entailed the dispossession of some natives, but the territorial footprint of the Spanish municipalities was actually quite limited; as long as its land requirements revolved around residence and basic sustenance, intrusions into native property were highly localized.

In the real world of sixteenth-century New Spain, the territorially limited "Spanish republic," made up of a few towns and their immediate surroundings, could not be contained. The developments mentioned at the beginning of this chapter unleashed an inexorable expansion into

---

[37] Guadalupe Rivera Marín de Iturbe, *La propriedad territorial en México: 1301–1810* (Mexico City: Siglo veintiuno, 1983), 204–9.
[38] Luis Chávez Orozco, ed., *Códice Osuna, reproducción facsimilar de la obra Orozco* (Mexico City: Ediciones del Instituto indigenista interamericano, 1947), 194.
[39] Ibid., 207.

native lands. With the indigenous population collapsing and the "Spanish" sector growing through immigration and *mestizaje*, tribute supplies shrank and pressure grew to transfer agricultural lands to Spanish control. Furthermore, Spaniards wanted many products of the soil other than the maize, chiles, cacao and cotton that indigenous cultivation was capable of providing. Hungering for familiar European foods, the colonizers introduced wheat, olives and orchard fruits, as well as cattle, horses, sheep and other domestic ruminants. Where they saw advantageous opportunities, native cultivators did integrate some of these Old-World crops and domestic animals into their agriculture, but only to a limited extent. Wholesale conversion to European-style plough tillage combined with livestock raising was out of the question, even supposing the Indians could have afforded the investments required. Mesoamericans had developed a finely tuned agrarian system that sustained dense populations in Mexico's dry environment; it would have been folly to jettison it. Settlers wanting bread, beef and wool therefore had to organize their own farming operations, on such land as would support these enterprises. Of course they looked to native pueblos for labor, but they also wanted land beyond the confines of their urban settlements.

How did Spaniards come into possession of agricultural land? In many cases, powerful individuals (typically *encomenderos*) simply occupied terrain, unceremoniously expelling any indigenous inhabitants who might stand in their way. This was particularly characteristic of the chaotic period immediately following the conquest. Forcible occupation does not create a property regime, however, even if many specific property claims, in Mexico or anywhere, originated with just such arbitrary actions. As Spanish law became established in New Spain, actual possession and productive use would come to weigh heavily in the courts as prima facie evidence of legitimate ownership, regardless of the means by which possession had been acquired; but simple occupation was not enough, in the absence of legal apparatus and procedures, to transform usurpation into anything resembling secure property. As colonial administration and law were established and reinforced in New Spain, Spaniards were able to secure, through a variety of procedures that will be outlined below, more legally durable claims to portions of Mexican soil through the developing processes of property formation.

One way of solidifying title was to secure a land grant (*merced*) from a municipal government or from the Crown. Sometimes a Spaniard would request a grant first and then occupy the land; sometimes it was the other way around, such that the grant signified official approval of the act of occupying a given tract. A *merced* by itself did not confer anything like full and definitive title: most sixteenth-century grants contained a clause making them revocable in the event that the king wanted the land back to found a city.[40] Moreover, they were always hedged with conditions; most important was the requirement to occupy and develop the land within a specified period of time, failing which the grant would be revoked. Also, land was granted for a particular purpose, as an orchard, a watermill site, a cattle ranch, etc.; theoretically, land granted for the purpose of raising sheep could not be used for mules. There were restrictions also on a grantee's ability to alienate; a sale of land granted by the viceroy was valid only if the deed of sale was officially approved.[41] Grants of most sorts were free of charge, but loaded with conditions.

The earliest grants (apart from those made by Cortés on his personal authority) were issued by Spanish *cabildos* for neighboring lands beyond the perimeter of their municipal commons. In 1528–30, Mexico City's council awarded 83 orchard plots (*huertas*) in the Tacuba–Coyoacan region alone; the majority of grantees were *encomenderos* who, by virtue of that status, would have had access to Indian labor.[42] After 1535, the viceregal regime would claim a monopoly on behalf of the Crown over land granting. Efforts to stamp out municipal grants were not entirely successful, however. Through the procedure of *composición* (see Chapter 10), some towns in the seventeenth century paid the Crown to secure control over land in their respective regions, thus giving municipal grants a new lease on life.[43] Meanwhile, within the *Marquesado del Valle*, the large stretch of territory over which Hernán Cortés had established a kind of seigneurial regime, it was the feudal lord who issued land grants. In the early seventeenth century, Don Pedro Cortés, the fourth Marqués del Valle, was imposing an annual rent on lands granted to Spaniards through what were called "*mercedes a censo*."[44]

Though it was not the only authority granting lands, the viceregal regime was certainly the most active. Even before the conquest of Mexico, the Crown had established a set of procedures designed to encourage colonization by regularizing occupation of the soil. Imagining

---

[40] Jalpa Flores, *Tierra y Sociedad*, 129–31.

[41] Rivera Marín de Iturbe, *La propriedad territorial en México*, 186.

[42] Horn, *Post-Conquest Coyoacan*, 168, 262–64.

[43] José María Ots Capdequí, *El Régimen de la Tierra en la América Española durante el período colonial* (Ciudad Trujillo: Universidad de Santo Domingo, 1946), 145–50; Prem, "Spanish Colonization and Indian Property in Central Mexico," 448.

[44] Horn, *Post-Conquest Coyoacan*, 190, 193–96.

Roman-style military colonies scattered across "the Indies," Charles V ordered that grants of different sizes be provided to support gentlemen-officers and soldiers, each at an appropriate level of existence. There was the *"peonía"* for infantrymen and the *"caballería,"* a larger grant designed to support a mounted gentleman. Since few settlers arrived in New Spain willing to work a modest plot with their own labor, *peonías* became rare and the *caballería* emerged as the standard grant. Hundreds of *caballerías* were granted over the course of the sixteenth century in the Nahua country of central Mexico as demand for European-style agriculture and stock raising grew. In some cases, the beneficiary actually worked the land himself, usually with the aid of a few Indian laborers or African slaves. Such *labradores*, Spanish settler-proprietors tilling the soil and populating the country, were the class that Charles V seems to have had in mind when he originally authorized land grants, but they did not prevail in New Spain. Instead, granted land increasingly fell under the control of Church bodies and secular elites who did not work the land themselves, but instead formed estates manned by unfree laborers.[45]

The consistently reiterated policy of the viceroys, as well as the Cortés family who handled *mercedes* within the *marquesado*, was to ensure that only "unoccupied" land could be granted to Spaniards; Indian pueblos were not to be interfered with. But what that should mean in practice was not entirely obvious. The prehispanic Nahua had quite precise systems of land measurement and recording, but in the chaos of the conquest period, records were lost, elders died and whole communities were uprooted. The Spanish did not institute systematic surveying and cadastral mapping to replace Aztec procedures and so land granting in the first century of Spanish rule retained a slapdash quality. With people on the move and epidemics snuffing out lineages and leaving many native properties ownerless, it was genuinely difficult to know which land was vacant and which belonged to a pueblo. Further complicating matters was the fact that Indians and Spaniards used land differently and therefore did not always have the same sense of which places were vacant. In the absence of systematic information on holdings and boundaries, the colonial administration attempted to head off incursions by subjecting land grants to a judicial procedure called *"vista de ojo,"* an on-site inspection. Accompanied by a local magistrate, and after proper public notification, the holder of a provisional *merced* would visit the land requested; residents of the

---

[45] Ibid., 173–74; Prem, "Spanish Colonization and Indian Property," 447, 451.

area, both natives and Spaniards, could come forward and object if the grant infringed on their property. In the absence of protests the magistrate deemed valid, the grant would be laid out using a long cord to measure distances. The new proprietor normally walked the perimeter of the holding, uprooting plants and throwing stones, in a ritual of taking possession with distant Iberian roots.

In addition to acquiring supposedly "vacant" land by *mercedes*, Spaniards also bought land from native owners. In the central valley of Mexico, and especially around the capital, there are many records of such transactions during the sixteenth century, and this in spite of the general opposition of native community leaders, who rightly feared the permanent loss of pueblo lands, and of government officials, who worried that alienating lands would detract from the Indians' ability to pay tribute.[46] In many cases, sales were linked to native mortality crises: in Coyoacan, there was a spurt of sales following the terrible epidemics of 1576–81, with executors selling off plots to Spaniards when there was no native heir (this in spite of a viceregal edict ordering that Indian lands without heirs must revert to the pueblo). Around the same time, nobles and town officials in Culhuacan, its population similarly depleted, were active in selling off uplands on the periphery of the pueblo to Spanish ranchers. The deeds of sale in all these cases include elaborate explanations insisting that the land being alienated was not really needed, noting that it had been purchased in the past and that the seller had other lands that would assure both subsistence and tribute. Alienating land, the documents imply, and all the more so when the purchaser was a nonnative, could be legitimate only under special circumstances. Moreover, such sales concerned an entire community and not just the seller. A Nahua deed from 1738 by which "Senor don Antonio Gonsales, Franciscan," bought a lot from two native brothers contains a report on a pueblo meeting called by the governor and other local officials to consult town residents, "to see if they have demands concerning the aforementioned Castilian's purchased land, if it was truly the property of the sellers of the land, or if perhaps it was someone else's property or was district land." The typical pattern in this part of Mexico seems to have been for a single Spaniard or a religious order to buy up a number of small Indian holdings in order to consolidate or expand an existing estate. The generally low prices suggest that native sellers may have been

---

[46] Hanns J. Prem, *Milpa y hacienda: Tenencia de la tierra indígena y española en la cuenca del Alto Atoyac, Puebla, México (1520–1650)* (Wiesbaden: Steiner, 1978), 182–85.

desperate for cash to pay tribute obligation and/or that they had been subject to other forms of pressure and coercion.[47]

By these various means, the zone of Spanish property reached out beyond the circumscribed zones of Mexico City, Puebla and their respective suburban belts into the Nahua heartland of central Mexico. Shrinking in population, native communities progressively lost portions of their territory to the colonizers, such that, "by the 1620s only vestiges of Indian property remained."[48] One historian estimates that 80 to 90 percent of pueblo lands in the vicinity of the major cities had fallen into Spanish hands by the early eighteenth century.[49] The circumscribed sphere of Spanish property, centered on the new colonial towns, had burst its banks and leaked out into the surrounding Nahua territories. Across the rest of New Spain, indigenous property held out much longer and more effectively. Even close to Mexico City, some areas such as Texcoco where the terrain was inhospitable to European agriculture maintained their indigenous integrity, but further from centers of Spanish population hundreds of pueblos remained substantially intact, though subject to tribute.[50] Over time, conquests would extend further, especially to the north, bringing new lands and additional peoples into the grip of the tribute-labor service regime. At the same time, and as an integral part of the conquests, new forms of Spanish property, large estates revolving around livestock raising, would inundate many of these previously remote indigenous territories.

Great landed estates had begun to emerge in central Mexico in the mid-sixteenth century, as it had become clear that Indian tribute could not satisfy the burgeoning demand for food and other products of the soil. Well-placed *encomenderos* and government officials began acquiring multiple *caballerías* and other lands to create large-scale farms worked by gangs of conscripted native laborers. Sugar plantations also arose in some localities – these required major investments in irrigation facilities,

---

[47] Horn, *Post-Conquest Coyoacan*, 177–78; García Castro, "Los pueblos de Indios," 150; S. L. Cline, *Colonial Culhuacan, 1580–1600: A Social History of an Aztec Town* (Albuquerque: University of New Mexico Press, 1986), 155–56; Lockhart, *The Nahuas after the Conquest*, 171; Arthur J. O. Anderson, Frances Berdan and James Lockhart, *Beyond the Codices: The Nahua View of Colonial Mexico* (Berkeley: University of California Press, 1976), 100–109 (quotation at 103).

[48] Prem, "Spanish Colonization and Indian Property," 448.

[49] García Castro, "Los pueblos de Indios," 154.

[50] For example, Oaxaca as described in William B. Taylor, *Landlord and Peasant in Colonial Oaxaca*.

machinery and black slaves as a permanent core of skilled workers; Cortés himself was a pioneer in the sugar industry. Sugar plantations and other large-scale agricultural enterprises occupied extensive consolidated blocks of land, dominating both natives and Spanish settler-farmers in the vicinity. They formed a generally expanding concentration of power and profit – "wealth" in Hannah Arendt's schema – that represented a major departure from the model of colonial settlement implied by Charles V's policy on land grants, which had envisioned urban islands for Spaniards occupying enough land to assure residence and subsistence.

Much more expansionist than these agricultural plantations were the livestock ranching operations that were taking shape around the same time. Pigs, sheep, horses, cattle, chickens and donkeys were the most important among the domestic creatures imported to Mexico from the Spanish West Indies; here they found an environment that allowed them to thrive and multiply at amazing rates.[51] Across New Spain, it is estimated that "Spanish ranchers maintained herds of 7 to 10 million animals that grazed over 125,000 square kilometers" a century after the conquest.[52] Natives and Spanish *labradores* acquired a few of these beasts (though Indians were not allowed horses), but some rich and well-connected Spaniards invested in huge flocks and herds. Those who opted for sheep found a ready market for their meat in the cities of New Spain, while their wool supplied textile workshops (*obrajes*) staffed by drafts of indigenous women from the pueblos. Horses and mules could also be profitably raised for sale to urban buyers and northern miners. Cattle ranching on a grand scale turned out to be the most popular investment, however. Not only did cattle raising enjoy a certain prestige derived from its prominence in Iberian Spain, it was also lucrative as long as the colonial market for beef and the overseas demand for hides and tallow remained good. Moreover, whereas sheep were vulnerable to predators and required close supervision, cattle could take care of themselves; wandering far and wide in search of pasture, they could be rounded up periodically (*"rodeo"*) and identified by brand. Stock raising was mostly carried out on the common lands of the open range; government grants conferred on ranchers only the right to graze over a vaguely defined

[51] Alfred W. Crosby, *The Columbian Exchange: Biological and Cultural Consequences of 1492* (Westport, Conn.: Greenwood, 1972), 75–113; Alfred W. Crosby, *Ecological Imperialism: The Biological Expansion of Europe, 900–1900* (New York: Cambridge University Press, 1986), 171–94.

[52] John F. Richards, *The Unending Frontier: An Environmental History of the Early Modern World* (Berkeley: University of California Press, 2003), 346.

territory. Eventually those ranchers managed to expand limited usufruct rights into exclusive property over large and bounded domains (see Chapter 7).

INVASION OF THE NORTH

The various regions of Mexico experienced the colonial transformation differently and according to a differentiated timetable. The fertile and heavily populated lands of the central basin, especially those in the vicinity of the new cities of Mexico and Puebla, naturally felt the Spanish presence early and heavily. The south of New Spain, including Yucatan, Oaxaca and Guatemala, was mostly subjugated within a few years of the fall of Tenochtitlán (though some pockets of Mayan resistance survived for more than a century).[53] Mayans and other native peoples of the region found themselves subject to tribute and labor service, but with Europeans more thinly distributed on the ground, they did not lose possession of their lands to anything like the same extent as their Nahua counterparts. In Oaxaca, as William Taylor demonstrates, indigenous property survived to the end of the colonial era: ranching was certainly a threat to pueblos, but many of the largest cattle operations were owned by the native elite.[54] Something resembling the classic conquest regime of Indian property burdened by tribute obligations prevailed across the southern region and lasted much longer than it did in the center.

North of central Mexico, it was a very different story. This was a vast country of mountains, deserts and steppes, punctuated by fertile river valleys. There were no great pre-Hispanic cities here or extensive cornfields; instead, a comparatively sparse population of small-scale cultivators and migratory hunter-gatherers subsisted in the arid and semi-arid landscape. The Aztecs called the northern peoples "Chichimecas" and viewed them as ferocious barbarians who periodically raided their "civilized" neighbors and who, because of their mobility, were impossible to conquer. That warlike reputation, along with the inhospitable natural environment, certainly slowed Spanish penetration into the northern region and might even have discouraged it altogether had it not been

---

[53] Nancy M. Farriss, *Maya Society under Colonial Rule: The Collective Enterprise of Survival* (Princeton, N.J.: Princeton University Press, 1984); Inga Clendinnen, *Ambivalent Conquests: Maya and Spaniard in Yucatan, 1517–1570*, 2nd ed. (New York: Cambridge University Press, 2003).

[54] Taylor, *Landlord and Peasant in Colonial Oaxaca*.

for the discovery of rich silver deposits. The lure of precious metal, together with the presence of extensive grazing ranges across the northern steppes, provided an obvious motive for expansion, and these economic impulses only served to reinforce the natural expansionist tendencies of a Christian empire dedicated to incorporating lands and peoples into the kingdom and into the Church.

It started with a major silver strike and subsequent mining rush at Zacatecas in 1546. Other discoveries followed, pulling miners as far north as Santa Bárbara by 1567. Mining camps (reales) sprang up overnight and in some cases grew into cities. They were fairly compact, but they drew on a broad hinterland for supplies: forests were consumed for charcoal and river valleys were occupied to raise mules and to grow food supplies for the workers. Cattle advanced northward alongside the miners. At first it was mostly feral animals wandering over the dry grasslands and these became the prey for cattle hunters who sold their meat at the reales; ranching haciendas with branded herds followed in their wake.[55] These intrusions into indigenous territories naturally provoked conflict with the inhabitants and it tended to be all the more intense when the ranchers and miners tried to force natives to work for them. Thus, the northward expansion took place in a context of endemic though intermittent warfare, with some groups forming strategic alliances with the Spaniards, others resisting actively through guerrilla raids on colonists and their allies. Like the Aztecs before them, the new invaders found it impossible to subjugate all these flexibly organized societies fully and conclusively.

The Spaniards who played a leading role in the mining and ranching enterprises came to the north with a retinue of armed men: lower class Spaniards, natives detached from central Mexican pueblos, mestizos and blacks. In the absence of any "official" military force, power was wielded by private armies of cowboy-conquistadors. Their commanders frequently secured appointments as captains, governors or corregidores from the viceroy, but in their ability to unleash violence, they were only partially and loosely constrained by central authorities. They led an extended conquest that was all about subduing natives, turning them into obedient Christian subjects and forcing them to work for the conquerors. In pursuit of this objective, the northern warlords had the basic

[55] Chevalier, Land and Society in Colonial Mexico, 38–39; Chantal Cramaussel, Poblar la frontera: la provincia de Santa Bárbara en Nueva Vizcaya durante los siglos XVI y XVII (Zamora: El Colegio de Michoacán, 2006), 306–12.

support of the secular and ecclesiastical authorities of New Spain, even if the latter disapproved of excessive brutality and exploitation. The sense that the "wild" Indians needed to be tamed and the belief that Spanish enterprise required a subservient labor force led to the revival of the institution of *encomienda* here, just when it was being phased out in the rest of New Spain.

In the northern province that the Spanish named Nueva Vizcaya, indigenous peoples such as the Concho, Tarahumara and Tepehuan began to feel the effects of colonial contact even before Spaniards gained a solid foothold in their countries. Epidemics struck, cutting populations in half, European goods worked their way into native commercial circuits and horses, often feral, became available, allowing people to travel great distances to hunt and to make war. When the Spaniards did show up in force, their aim was to conduct bands to the vicinity of *reales* and haciendas and to subject them to the regime of colonial labor service. Meeting with resistance, they enlisted native allies and attacked the "rebels" relentlessly; according to Chantal Cramaussel, wars were often waged with the express purpose of capturing workers. Surviving warriors, along with women and children, would then be sold into slavery. Others who could be persuaded to surrender were relocated and, most frequently, placed under the tutelage of Jesuit missionaries.[56]

As missionaries, the Jesuits were latecomers to New Spain and so, while other religious orders concentrated on quieter zones, they took up the challenge of converting the nomadic peoples of the north.[57] They established missions and welcomed natives who had been weakened and traumatized by disease and war, offering an assured food supply and protection from enemies to those who would accept baptism and live as colonial subjects. As part of the bargain, hunter-gatherers and semi-sedentary cultivators had to adapt to a new way of life built around field agriculture at a fixed location. Mission communities were modeled on the *pueblos de indios* of central Mexico, with their municipal institutions, their common lands and individual plots and their obligation to provide

---

[56] Cramaussel, *Poblar la frontera*, 280; Susan Deeds, *Defiance and Deference in Mexico's Colonial North: Indians under Spanish Rule in Nueva Vizcaya* (Austin: University of Texas Press, 2003), 12–61; Salvador Álvarez, "El Pueblo de indios en la frontera septentrional Novohispana," *Relaciones* 24, no. 95 (2003): 113–64.

[57] The title of a chronicle of the evangelizing activities nicely expresses the Jesuit view of northern natives: Andrés Pérez de Ribas, *History of the Triumphs of Our Holy Faith amongst the Most Barbarous and Fierce Peoples of the New World*, trans. Daniel T. Reff, Maureen Ahern and Richard K. Danforth (Tucson: University of Arizona Press, 1999).

workers in rotation to Spaniards in the vicinity. Tribute was not part of the *encomienda* system revived for the northern frontier, but labor service was a basic feature. Historians have noted that the missions where Indians were congregated were always located close to ranches and mines where labor was required.[58]

All this was much more foreign to the traditions of the nonsedentary northern peoples than it had been for Nahua farmers of the center. Once they had experienced the full rigors of life in those dubious havens, many escaped the missions and made their way to the mountains. The *encomenderos'* forces would do their best to hunt down these fugitives and return them to their duties. Insofar as the Jesuits succeeded in attracting and retaining natives, it was mostly thanks to the ambient context of terror and violence; here as in many other parts of Spanish America, missions seemed like the lesser evil when death or enslavement threatened on all sides. The missionaries did their best to protect "their" Indians and to temper the violence of the colonizers, and yet they basically worked hand-in-glove with the secular invaders.

In "reducing" indigenous people to what they considered a civil, Christian existence, the Spanish were imposing a version of colonial property formation that, in theory, conferred benefits as well as obligations. In place of the extensive territorial claims they exercised in the past, mission Indians would now possess, and exploit more intensively, a narrowly circumscribed zone surrounding a new church and plaza; moreover, their right to this property would be guaranteed by the state and the Jesuit order. It was a grim bargain: subjection to authority and the acceptance of hard labor in return for protection from violence and a land base that ensured subsistence. If only that land base really were secure! In the event, with more Spaniards and mestizos pouring into the north and with the expansion of the hacienda regime over the course of the seventeenth century, there were more and more incursions into the mission lands that had been set aside for the use of indigenous Christians.

The northward march of humans, cattle and other animals exerted pressures on the dwindling native populations of more and more regions; in 1598 the sedentary, and relatively populous, agricultural villages of the upper Rio Grande were conquered and renamed "New Mexico"; even the dry and silver-poor region east of the Sierra Madre Oriental was incorporated in 1596 as the frontier province of Nuevo Leon. Meanwhile, the

---

[58] Deeds, *Defiance and Deference in Mexico's Colonial North*, 19–22.

mining entrepreneurs and hacienda owners of Nueva Vizcaya were finding the rotating drafts conscripted from the Jesuit missions inadequate to satisfy their voracious appetite for cheap labor. They had come to the region with a diversified assortment of retainers – indigenous people detached from the pueblos of central Mexico (*naborios*), black slaves, mestizo *vaqueros*, natives enslaved in the frontier wars – and they generally found this comparatively stable, on-the-spot workforce more useful than mission Indians who each worked only a few weeks per year.[59] Over the course of the seventeenth and eighteenth centuries, hacendados turned to debt peonage – the hacienda store providing goods at inflated prices and on credit, ensuring that debts could never be paid off – to tie down indigenous workers. Another device was to provide laborers with small houses and plots of ground to raise subsistence crops, both as a means of keeping workers alive at no cost during seasonal slack periods and in order to attach these same workers to the estate as quasi-feudal tenants. Eventually, it became difficult to distinguish slaves from notionally "free" laborers. Historians find evidence that, when haciendas changed hands, the workers were often sold along with the land and the livestock; natives born on a hacienda were treated as bound to the soil of that estate.[60] The land had come to possess the very people who had once possessed it.

Mission Indians were among those entrapped within the toils of the haciendas, especially when the latter undermined the subsistence lands allowed them under the mission/*encomienda* regime. Writes Susan Deeds of the region of Parral in the seventeenth century:

As miners and other Spaniards acquired properties in nearby areas, some mission pueblos began to feel the effects of unfenced cattle encroaching on their milpas [fields]. Increasingly, they found their access to irrigation water or floodplains blocked. In addition, wilderness areas used for hunting and gathering were occasionally incorporated for both grazing and charcoal making by Spanish hacendados ... These early – seventeenth century – conflicts over land resulted

---

[59] Forced migration on a massive scale was central to the colonization of the north. Chantal Cramaussel, "The Forced Transfer of Indians in Nueva Vizcaya and Sinaloa: A Hispanic Method of Colonization," in *Contested Spaces of Early America*, ed. Juliana Barr and Edward Countryman (Philadelphia: University of Pennsylvania Press, 2014), 184–207.

[60] Chevalier, *Land and Society in Colonial Mexico*, 285. This paragraph mostly follows François Chevalier's classic thesis on the growth of the hacienda. For a critical discussion that nuances Chevalier's argument by introducing a number of regional and temporal differences in the incidence of such phenomena as debt peonage, see Eric Van Young, "Mexican Rural History since Chevalier: The Historiography of the Colonial Hacienda," *Latin American Research Review* 18, no. 3 (January 1983): 5–61.

in part from a growing non-Indian population, but they also reflected the influence exercised by a few powerful landowners.[61]

Missionaries were supposed to defend the interests of their native flocks, but when natives and latifundists clashed over land, they usually negotiated arrangements completely favorable to the latter.[62] "Usurpation" of pueblo lands advantaged the great landowners doubly: first, it increased the resources they could draw on for tillage or pasture; second, in undermining the mission Indians' subsistence, it created landless workers who could be recruited for full-time employment on the hacienda. The great estates were swallowing up people as well as land.

First, northern Indians were forced into a colonial property regime that required them to gain a living by tilling the soil while working part of the year for miners or ranchers; then, before long, even the modest stake that had been left them under the colonial order began to be hedged in and undermined by the growing influence of latifundia. The growth of great estates at the expense of pueblo lands and independent Indian subsistence was not a phenomenon limited to Nueva Vizcaya alone; similar developments occurred to one degree or another in all the regions of New Spain in the seventeenth and eighteenth centuries, though the process of property concentration was most brutal and most pronounced in the lawless north.[63]

THE STRUGGLE FOR INDIAN LANDS

In the wake of the Conquest, two distinct but interpenetrating colonial tenures developed in New Spain. There was Indian pueblo land, held under tenures that reflected both continuity with pre-Hispanic ways and an ongoing adaptation to Spanish rule and to the shifting conditions of colonial life. Native property was, in a general sense, primordial, and

---

[61] Deeds, *Defiance and Deference in Mexico's Colonial North*, 73.

[62] Salvador Alvarez, *El indio y la sociedad colonial norteña: siglos XVI–XVIII* (Durango, Mexico: Instituto de Investigaciones Históricas/UJED, 2009), 270–72.

[63] Chevalier, *Land and Society in Colonial Mexico*, 172; Prem, "Spanish Colonization and Indian Property"; Herman W. Konrad, *A Jesuit Hacienda in Colonial Mexico: Santa Lucia, 1576–1767* (Stanford, Calif.: Stanford University Press, 1980), 163–72; Eric Van Young, *Hacienda and Market in Eighteenth-Century Mexico: The Rural Economy of the Guadalajara Region, 1675–1820* (Berkeley: University of California Press, 1981), 297–307; Miguel Aguilar-Robledo, "Formation of the Miraflores Hacienda: Lands, Indians, and Livestock in Eastern New Spain at the End of the Sixteenth Century," *Journal of Latin American Geography* 2 (2003): 87–110.

imperial authorities accepted the fact that its existence and legitimacy pre-dated any European property. At the same time, the Crown, as heir to the Aztec emperors, assumed an overlord's right to collect tribute from native lands. Whether or not this right was gifted to an *encomendero*, there was always a Spanish element in the multilayered property regime (which also included family, *calpulli* and pueblo layers) of the colonial *pueblo de indios*. Thus, the Crown had a material stake in the preservation of Indian lands, a situation that was in harmony with its ethical commitment to guaranteeing the integrity of native property and protecting the "poor Indian" against dispossession; considerations of justice and consider-ations of interest tended to be mutually reinforcing in this context.

There was also a Spanish property regime, which emerged at the time of the Conquest and evolved over the centuries: the very nature of Spanish tenure changed, even as its territorial scope expanded. Property making within the Spanish sphere proceeded through the complex interplay of individual appropriations by private parties and the development of a colonial state that asserted Crown *dominium* with increasing efficacy. Government officials awarded land grants, regulated the grazing com-mons, issued licenses for stock-raising sites, administered water rights and established procedures for inheritance. These actions helped to establish landed property for Spaniards while it simultaneously placed limits on the prerogatives of ownership. Individual Spaniards gave substance to the emergent colonial property regime by using native labor to plow fields, dam streams and release cattle to range over the countryside, often claiming more than the law allowed. The legal/regulatory framework established by the state and the environmental transformations and appropriations undertaken by private initiative on the ground were both integral aspects of a single process of property formation, but they worked in tension, the state both empowering and restraining land-owners. Property making for Spaniards took shape in tandem with the emergence of a colonial political regime. The rise of a class of great landowners was very much a product of this dual development, for these privileged parties were almost always closely connected with influential state officials when they were not high officials themselves. One final point about "Spanish" property: in material, environmental terms, it was largely created by indigenous people, since colonial agricultural and pastoral enterprises almost invariably depended on cheap and unfree Indian labor.

The Spanish property zone proved to be expansive in a way native land never was. The demographic growth of the nonnative sector, at a time when Indians were declining in numbers, ensured that there would be a demand for ever more living space; the rise of the hacienda/latifundia made the drive to incorporate territory into the Spanish property system into a powerful and relentless force. With wealth and power as the objective, and not just land to support settler households, the appetite for land became insatiable. More pronounced in the north than in other regions, there was a tendency to encroach on the indigenous sphere, not only to maximize profits, but also to dominate regions and to undermine native economic autonomy. As of the second half of the sixteenth century, indigenous pueblos had to be on constant guard against what was referred to as "usurpation."

The main threat, as we have seen, came from stock-raisers hungry for extensive grazing lands. In spite of legislation ordering ranchers to keep their animals away from natives' crops, pueblo lands were still vulnerable. Not only were Indians as such structurally disempowered under colonial rule, as cultivators they faced a set of Iberian laws and customs about land use that systematically favored animal husbandry and the right to graze. Another feature of Spanish law that worked against native tenure was the emphasis on possession, meaning "'the act of placing the feet' on a piece of land, as a sign of a person's 'will to obtain it' and 'enter it and hold it.'"[64] Thus, if a rancher could gain a toehold, perhaps grazing his cattle on the uncultivated commons that formed the outer periphery of a pueblo, then he might eventually invoke the laws of "prescription" or "presura" to defend himself against any legal attempt to evict him.[65] And of course powerful hacendados disposed of a range of techniques for gaining a toehold within Indian lands, including violence, intimidation and deception. Brian Owensby lists some of the stratagems:

Spanish ranchers or sheep farmers might release livestock on targeted land, claiming it was open to public grazing. If crops were trampled several years running and if residents fled, a usurper might claim the land as vacant or abandoned. Another ploy involved taking land in rent from Indian villages, cultivating it and years later claiming the same land outright as having been held from "time imme-morial." Alternatively, opportunistic tenants might conclude a rental arrangement

---

[64] Owensby, *Empire of Law*, 91. The author is quoting from the *Siete Partidas*.

[65] Presura "conceded proprietary rights to those who occupied and cultivated public, or even private, land," while prescription amounted to "a mechanism whereby time, not original title, becomes a valid basis for substantive rights ..." Jonathan D. Amith, *The Mobius Strip: A Spatial History of Colonial Society in Guerrero, Mexico* (Stanford, Calif.: Stanford University Press, 2005), 98.

orally and hope that actual possession and cultivation would later win the day in court when the owners could not offer proof that they owned the land.[66]

Why, one might well ask, would pueblos rent out land to Spaniards when they ran the risk of losing it permanently? The conquest/tribute regime had a role to play here, for the pressure to meet tribute payments, even in lean years, was what forced some communities to sell or rent out land. Labor service through *repartimiento* only reinforced that economic vulnerability by making it more difficult for an Indian community to find the time to cultivate its lands.[67] On the one hand, colonial law insisted on the integrity of native land holdings; on the other hand, it gave Spanish ranchers the opportunity to intrude into the Indian sphere in the name of common grazing rights. Furthermore, it provided them abundant opportunities to convert intrusion into something like exclusive ownership (see Chapter 10).

The wonder is that, in spite of everything, indigenous lands did survive, more so in some regions and remote localities than in others. By the end of the period of Spanish rule there were still substantial zones of native control, many of which persist down to the present day. That outcome has to be attributed to the many modest victories natives were able to score in their struggles to defend their lands. There were violent revolts, as well as more subtle and covert practices of resistance; sometimes natives petitioned colonial power-holders, sometimes they challenged usurpers in the courts. The most successful strategies generally involved adapting to the ways of the conqueror, seeking out influential allies and taking advantage of legal and extra-legal possibilities for resisting dispossession.

There was, of course, no united "Indian" front against dispossession. In the chaotic conditions created by war, depopulation and forced relocation, each pueblo had to be vigilant to defend its own lands. And whereas holdings within a given Nahua community were quite precisely delineated, the outer edges of each *altepetl*/pueblo tended to be vague. Typically, they shaded off into a buffer zone between communities, sometimes a mountainous hunting-gathering commons, sometimes a bottomland area of heavy soils that were unsuitable for Mesoamerican agriculture. These buffer zones, particularly the bottomlands, sometimes provided an opening for Spaniards to intrude.[68] They could also become the object

---

[66] Owensby, *Empire of Law*, 117.
[67] Prem, "Spanish Colonization and Indian Property in Central Mexico," 452.
[68] Richards, *Unending Frontier*, 343.

of conflict between neighboring pueblos in the unstable and competitive conditions of the post-conquest period. Central Mexican indigenous societies were also divided by class, and the interests of ordinary *macehuales* and those of the surviving aristocracy did not always coincide. Land conflict in the early colonial period sometimes arose from *caciques'* attempts to set themselves up as exclusive proprietors, renting out land to their subjects or selling parcels to Spaniards. Thus, threats to *calpulli* land could come from at least three different sources: local notables, neighboring pueblos and intruding Spaniards. The first two threats were most common in the early period, whereas nonnative incursions, particularly on the part of haciendas, became the major issue in the seventeenth and eighteenth centuries.

Though not perfectly united, native communities did possess a certain coherence thanks to their corporate institutions. The *pueblo de indios*, set up under the conquest regime, combined elements of Spanish law and municipal practices with indigenous traditions of collective life to create a vibrant institutional framework that could, however imperfectly, adjudicate internal conflicts and represent the community in dealings with the outside world. The pueblo was recognized as a corporate person capable of pursuing legal action and, as such, it sometimes functioned as a vitally important instrument of defense. *Cabildo* officers included native scribes and artists skilled in the preparation of textual documents and maps. *Gobernadores* or *alcaldes* were authorized to represent their community before the courts, and they could even draw on municipal coffers, filled by local tribute contributions, to cover their travel and other expenses. Of course, these financial resources were quite limited at the best of times, nonexistent in bad years, and impoverished pueblos were no match for hacendados with deep pockets who could use appeals to prolong legal cases for years. Moreover, *cabildo* officers could be corrupt or negligent or simply unfamiliar with Spanish law. However, without idealizing matters, we have to recognize what an important instrument indigenous Mexicans disposed of in their institutions of local government.

Of course, the effectiveness of their efforts to preserve their lands depended greatly on their ability to locate sympathetic allies in high places. In the mid-sixteenth century, many pueblos discovered in the first two viceroys of New Spain, Antonio de Mendoza and Luis de Velasco, powerful advocates who could be persuaded to take action against "usurpers." "Mendoza set aside two mornings a week for listening to Indians' complaints; Velasco embarked upon a systematic defense of their rights and personally supervised execution of his orders whenever he could."[69] Learning of the opportunity for redress, many pueblos dispatched deputations of native *alcaldes* to invoke the aid of His Majesty's representative – and they were not always disappointed. Henry Hawks, an English merchant who spent five years in Mexico in the late 1560s, wrote that natives "receive most favorable treatment from justice officials."[70] In 1574, a special tribunal, the Juzgado General de Indios, was established, with an official acting as "attorney for the general defense of the natives of this kingdom."[71] It is important to remember that these champions of indigenous property rights were defending the integrity of a system that demanded of Indians tribute, work and submission. Moreover, their practical ability to regulate the behavior of Spanish landowners was not unlimited. Nevertheless, they did provide communities with some recourse when cattle destroyed their crops or when farmers interfered with their water supplies.

Later viceroys had less time for representatives of indigenous communities and, more generally, the preservation of Indian lands became a less pressing priority in ruling circles, just at a time – the turn of the seventeenth century – when haciendas were becoming a much greater menace. Natives could still fight to preserve their lands in the colonial courts, and many of them did just that in spite of the obstacles arrayed against them. The economic barriers mentioned above, especially the cost of travel to distant seats of justice, were prominent among these; to be Indian was to be poor and therefore disadvantaged when it came to litigation. Natives also had to contend with the stigma of inferior status as a conquered people; concretely, this meant that the testimony of Indian witnesses was officially devalued. Moreover, judges were Spanish and, when not major landowners themselves, they tended to be closely connected to the landowning class and therefore inclined to see things from the hacendado point of view. Even so, and in spite of these and other disadvantages, the record shows that natives often sued and that they did not always lose.[72]

The basic colonial pact recognizing indigenous property as legitimate and as prior to any Spanish claims remained central to Indian legal strategies (and extra-legal direct action). The Crown and the courts never renounced this fundamental commitment, but over time, there seem to have been some discernible shifts – changes that were invariably

---

[69] Chevalier, *Land and Society in Colonial Mexico*, 190.   [70] Ibid., 203.
[71] Ibid., 204.
[72] See, for example, Van Young, *Hacienda and Market in Eighteenth-Century Mexico*, 338–42.

unfavorable to natives – in areas such as the burden of proof and the spatial definition of Indian property. For example, while fields currently under cultivation were always sacrosanct, lands that had been abandoned for a time due to depopulation or forced relocation were more problematic; likewise, the outer commons, vital as a source of reeds, firewood, game animals and the like, might or might not be recognized as valid pueblo property. Spaniards in conflict with native communities frequently claimed that the lands under dispute had been abandoned and were therefore "*tierras baldías*," available for grazing. Historians note a growing tendency in the seventeenth and eighteenth centuries for courts to lean toward the rancher's view, the one that minimized the extent of pueblo property.

The colonial regime never renounced its duty to protect Indian lands from the incursions of Spaniards and their creatures, but over the centuries, the protective measures in place evolved in ways that ceded more and more ground. From the start, royal grants for cultivation and pasturing had included clauses against "prejudicing" others, particularly Indians: *mercedes* were not supposed to infringe on existing land rights, on pain of nullification. But what did that mean in practice, when fences were rare, surveys inadequate and when Indian horticulture and Spanish pastoralism used land quite differently? A royal *cedula* of 1550 ordered ranchers to keep their livestock well away from pueblo fields, seemingly placing the responsibility on stock-raisers to know where Indian lands were located and to make sure their animals did not roam there.[73] Needless to say, enforcement was not effective. Later legislation began specifying distances, but the precision was illusory: one sixteenth-century decree said that grants to Spaniards had to be at least one league (4.2 kilometers) from the nearest pueblo, another banned ranches within one and a half leagues of any Indian community. The (theoretically) protected perimeter tended to shrink over the course of the seventeenth century. A 1687 law set the perimeter where grants were prohibited at 600 *varas* (503 meters), a measurement that remained the reference point through the rest of the colonial period.[74] From the native point of view, the problem – apart from lax enforcement – was that what began as a

---

[73] *Recopilación de leyes*, tomo 2, libro 4, 103v, Carlos, 24 March and 2 May, 1550. See also ibid., 103, Felipe II, 11 June 1594; ibid., Felipe III, 3 December 1607.

[74] Sergio Eduardo Carrera Quezada, "Las composiciones de tierras en los pueblos de indios en dos jurisdicciones coloniales de la Huasteca, 1692–1720," *Estudios de Historia Novohispana* 52 (January 2015): 37–38.

zone of protection gradually evolved into an effective outer limit. Soon any land more than 600 *varas* from an Indian village was unprotected and therefore potentially available to haciendas. Natives took action to secure their interests, erecting houses overnight beyond the outer edge of their communities in order to extend the perimeter. Under pressure from hacendados, the authorities countered this tactic with new legislation specifying that the 600 *varas* were to be measured from the village church rather than from the last house.[75] By the early eighteenth century, conflict shifted to the shape of the protected area: should the lines of 600 *varas* radiating out from the church provide the center for a square with sides 1200 *varas* long or should it describe a smaller diamond shape? There was something slightly absurd about this pseudo-precise geometry, though the intensity of the struggles underline how much was at stake. They also show how legislation originally aimed at protecting existing native lands morphed into a device for confining pueblos within limited territories.

Meanwhile, there was also the question of how Indians could prove that their land was really theirs. In the early colonial period, the basic presumption was that territory occupied and used by a given community was its legitimate property. If challenged, a pueblo could invoke the principle of *primitivo patrimonio*, asserting that it had possessed the ground in question "since time immemorial."[76] As the seventeenth century wore on, however, courts seemed less satisfied with this argument, and that placed natives in the difficult position of having to come up with documentary proof. Whereas hacienda owners could usually brandish a sheaf of *mercedes* and deeds of sale, pueblo lands were normally primordial and, for that reason, had never been granted or sold. By this time, more than a century after the Conquest, hardly any genuine pre-Hispanic records survived. Indians therefore manufactured documents, drawing on oral tradition, knowledge of the landscape and sense of place. By the second half of the seventeenth century, the strongboxes of many central Mexican pueblos contained a package of ancient-looking papers covered with pictures and writing in the Nahuatl language. These "primordial

---

[75] Gibson, *The Aztecs under Spanish Rule*, 285–87; Gonzalo Aguirre Beltrán, *El Señorío de Cuauhtochco: Luchas agrarias en México durante el Virreinato* (Mexico City: Ediciones Frente cultural, 1940), 75–76; Stephanie Wood, "The *Fundo Legal* or Lands *Por Razón de Pueblo*: New Evidence from Central New Spain," in Ouweneel and Miller, *The Indian Community of Colonial Mexico*, 117–29.

[76] Taylor, *Landlord and Peasant in Colonial Oaxaca*, 79; Owensby, *Empire of Law*, 101.

titles" (*"titulos primordiales"*) took the form of a local history with an emphasis on community lands; typically, they featured an exhortation in the voice of unnamed ancestors calling on their descendants to preserve their territory. To quote from one example, "Spaniards come to seize what we have justly won ... We urge our sons to know, guard, and keep the water, monte, streets, and houses of the town ... Sons of the town, guard the lands ... Here are its limits and its boundaries ... Do not forget ... Guard this paper."[77] Some scholars have dismissed *titulos primordiales* as "forgeries" concocted for the purpose of winning lawsuits, but Stephanie Wood, a leading expert, argues that they were prepared mainly for an indigenous readership – and the passage quoted above seems to support that position.[78] They were sometimes presented to government officials and judges in the apparently sincere belief that they provided an accurate description of pueblo territories. The fact that some *titulos* celebrated the establishment of Christianity and that many harked back to a grant to the community by a viceroy or by the conqueror Cortés leads some historians to conclude that they represent evidence of a colonized mind.[79] Better, perhaps, to see them as productions of vibrant indigenous traditions struggling to survive in a colonial setting where defense of community territory was a central concern. Above all, *titulos primordiales* seem to represent an exercise in translation, recording indigenous local knowledge in a form that could be expected to have meaning for outsiders as well as for the community itself as it imagined future generations trying to survive under colonial rule.

In addition to textual documents, many pueblos possessed painted cloth with graphic images of the community and its lands. Called *lienzos*, these chorographic representations pictured and mapped the landscape in typically Nahua style: schematically and abstractly. Some seem to have been of genuinely pre-Hispanic manufacture, but many appear to have been produced in colonial times for the purpose of

---

[77] Gibson, *The Aztecs under Spanish Rule*, 271.

[78] Stephanie Wood, "The Social vs. Legal Context of Nahuatl Títulos," in *Native Traditions in the Postconquest World*, ed. Elizabeth Hill Boone and Tom Cummins (Washington, D.C.: Dumbarton Oaks Research Library and Collection, 1998), 201–31. Cf. Robert Haskett, "Indian Community Land and Municipal Income in Colonial Cuernavaca: An Investigation through Nahuatl Documents," in Ouweneel and Miller, *The Indian Community of Colonial Mexico*, 130–41.

[79] Serge Gruzinski, *The Conquest of Mexico: The Incorporation of Indian Societies into the Western World, 16th–18th Centuries*, trans. Eileen Corrigan (Cambridge: Polity Press, 1993), 98–145.

bolstering territorial claims. They have sometimes been dismissed as "crude" and nonrepresentational, but modern scholars suggest that they were actually quite accurate when properly "read" with an understanding of the pictorial language of Nahua art. European land mapping could also be quite stylized in the sixteenth century, not so far removed from indigenous Mexican ways of representing landscape and ownership; indeed, the authorities in New Spain often employed Indian artists, using Nahua chorographic styles, to paint maps of Spanish land grants in New Spain.[80]

Titulos and pseudo-ancient *lienzos* did not always impress colonial courts, particularly when Spanish landowners or their representatives were on hand, actively seeking to discredit them. Presenting these materials as evidence in colonial courts might be seen as a desperate measure to fend off threats to native land at a time when legal documents were assuming more and more importance as the basis of landed property. To the extent that these maps and texts did sometimes help secure favorable judgments in support of land claims, they represent a triumph of native ingenuity. But the very fact that written documents were increasingly gaining an edge over *primitivo patrimonio* in property disputes was a menacing development for Mexican Indians.

In addition to documents of their own manufacture, indigenous communities also occasionally deployed royal *mercedes* to defend their lands. Land grants to Indians were an anomaly since *mercedes* were supposed to be only for terrain that was not already native property and that had therefore fallen into the king's domain. However, grants were nevertheless awarded, particularly in cases where communities were forcibly relocated through the process of *congregación*. From the 1590s, pueblos were also able to secure legal protection against threats to their lands in the form of an "*amparo*" (protective order) issued by the *audiencia* of Mexico City. Traveling to the capital and petitioning the court, community delegates could secure implicit confirmation of what they knew to be manifestly true: their collective lands were really theirs and they should not be deprived of them. Not exactly a title deed, an *amparo* was at least a legal document, and in addition to fending off an immediate threat, it could serve on the long run to bolster a community's claim to legitimate possession of its

[80] Barbara Mundy, *The Mapping of New Spain: Indigenous Cartography and the Maps of the Relaciónes Geográphicas* (Chicago: University of Chicago Press, 1996), 183–87. See also Haskett, "Indian Community Land," 133; Elizabeth Boone, "Glorious Imperium: Understanding Land and Community in Moctezuma's Mexico," in *Moctezuma's Mexico: Visions of the Aztec World*, ed. David Carrasco and Eduardo Matos Moctezuma (Niwot: University Press of Colorado, 1992), 159–73.

territory.[81] At the same time, the very popularity of *amparos* is indicative of the vulnerability of indigenous lands at a time when written title was becoming more and more powerful. A colonial state that once assumed that indigenous title took precedence, even over the claims of the Crown, was now edging in the direction of a presumption that Indian lands were somehow a gift of the government. By the end of the seventeenth century, native pueblos were obtaining *composiciónes*, another legal device for solidifying title (see Chapter 10). Stronger than an *amparo* in its legal punch, but also much more costly, a *composición* was a deed by which, in return for a substantial payment, the Crown transformed doubtful or illegal possession into legal title. It may have been a wise investment for a pueblo anxious to defend its property rights, but it represented another step away from reliance on *primitivo patrimonio*. Eighteenth-century practice was increasingly implying that natives owned their lands only by the grace of the monarch. The gradual strengthening of imperial *dominium* that accompanied the growth of Spanish landholding had as its counterpart the long-term erosion of respect for primordial indigenous property.

Around 1640, after a century of dispossession and at a time when Mexico's indigenous population had sunk to its lowest level, natives still controlled more of New Spain's surface area than Spaniards. The geographer Karl Butzer estimates their share at 45 percent, versus 25 percent in nonnative hands (the remaining 30 percent he calls "public lands").[82] In southern Mexico, native land holding remained overwhelmingly predominant through to the end of the colonial period and beyond. Exploited and dispossessed though they were, the indigenous peoples of New Spain did not lose their territories to anything like the degree that their counterparts did within the settler-dominated zones of New France and New England.

Notwithstanding the progressive expansion of settler property at the expense of native lands, and even though the nature of landed property changed greatly for both natives and nonnatives between the sixteenth

---

[81] Ots Capdequí, *El Régimen de la tierra en la América Española*, 74; Owensby, *Empire of Law*, 98, 124.

[82] Karl W. Butzer, "The Americas before and after 1492: An Introduction to Current Geographical Research," *Annals of the Association of American Geographers* 82 (1992): 354. Needless to say, figures of this sort – even when presented as "estimates" – give a misleading sense of precision. Not only are sources incomplete, the diverse spatial practices of property do not lend themselves to statistical comparison. Still, the basic idea that indigenous lands were more extensive than Spanish-held land accords with what other scholars have found working at a regional level.

and the eighteenth centuries, land tenure in New Spain never lost its dual character. Spanish ideologues of the period liked to represent colonial society as a composite of two self-contained elements, a *republica de indios* and a *republica de españoles*, a view that historians generally see more as a colonialist fiction than an accurate sociological description. Yet as far as land tenure is concerned, the bifurcation was real and, I think, consequential. In very general terms, the colonization of New France and New England proceeded similarly: as we shall see, separate tenures took shape in both places for settlers and for colonized natives. However, New Spain still stands out as a special case in this context, for nowhere else was colonized Indian territory so extensive and nowhere else was native property so fully elaborated in law.

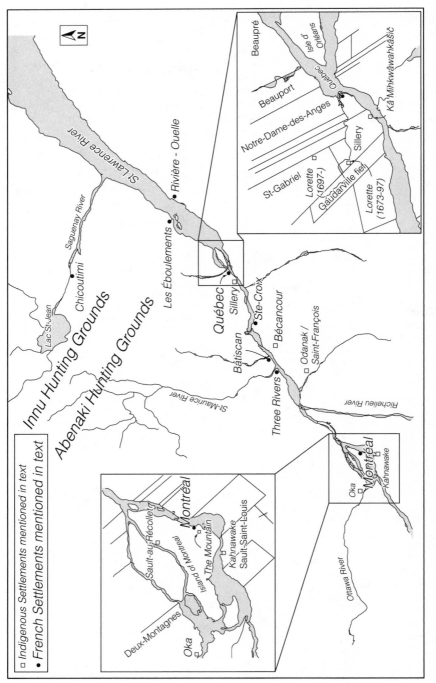

MAP 5.1 Canada (within New France)

5

New France

The St. Lawrence River gave the French access to the interior of North America and it was along the edge of that broad waterway that they established the settlement colony they usually referred to as "Canada." Circumstances favored their colonizing enterprise in the early seventeenth century because, like eastern Massachusetts where the Puritans would find empty fields and abandoned villages, this was a "widowed land," depopulated at least partly because of earlier European incursions. The French navigator Jacques Cartier had explored this region in the 1530s and found the riverside thickly populated with thriving agricultural villages. Archaeologists call these people the "St. Lawrence Iroquoians," noting similarities in their language and culture to the Iroquois proper of northern New York State. A new generation of French colonizers returned sixty years later to find that the St. Lawrence Iroquoians had completely disappeared. Exactly what happened in the interim remains one of the great mysteries of early Canadian history. Did epidemic disease introduced by the Cartier expeditions wipe out the villages? Was climate change the culprit, rendering the corn cultivation that villagers depended on for food too unreliable? Or did the introduction of European goods and weapons, supplied by visiting fishermen in the second half of the sixteenth century, provoke war and upheaval as nations vied for control over trade?[1]

---

[1] See Roland Tremblay, *The Saint Lawrence Iroquoians: Corn People* (Montreal: l'Homme, 2006).

Unless climate change was the only factor at work, which seems unlikely, it is apparent that the French proto-colonial presence bore a significant degree of responsibility for the demographic clearing out that created a space for colonization in the St. Lawrence Valley.

And of course it was not really empty space when colonization began. Mobile peoples navigated its waters and camped on its banks, drawn by its rich fish and wildfowl resources, but also by opportunities to trade with Europeans and with other natives. Innu, Algonquins and other northern hunters frequented the region but they traveled warily, for fear of lethal encounters with their enemies, the Mohawks, a populous and powerful nation, one of the five nations that constituted the Iroquois Confederacy (Haudenosaunee) based in northern New York. Whether or not the Mohawks were descended from the St. Lawrence Iroquoians, they seem to have considered the middle St. Lawrence as part of their security zone and felt justified in attacking intruders. Thus, New France was established in a war zone, a contested indigenous borderland of violence, commerce and fleeting encounters where no one could live securely. Colonists drew Mohawk/Iroquois ire by aligning themselves with the latters' enemies, by establishing settlements without Mohawk permission and by spurning commercial overtures. The 1642 founding of Montreal, not far from the Mohawks' heartland and well within their security perimeter, was a special provocation. The Mohawks never launched a frontal attack on the fortified post, but they harassed colonists in the vicinity with sudden raids and deadly ambushes; for a time, settlers hardly dared to venture outside the town walls to urinate.[2] The French only began to feel secure with the arrival of a large contingent of troops in 1665. The reinforced colony was able to inflict defeats on the Iroquois, and though the latter were never truly conquered, they did agree to a peace and to tolerate the French as neighbors; indeed, many Iroquois went so far as to align themselves closely with the colonists, migrating north to live side-by-side with their erstwhile enemies.

While the French made the St. Lawrence Valley a place of relative strength and security for themselves and their indigenous allies, turmoil reigned all around them. The French presence in Canada, along with that of the growing Dutch and English colonies to the south, may have been territorially modest, but the associated "empire effect" spread waves of death and disruption far and wide across the indigenous

---

[2] François Dollier de Casson, *A History of Montreal, 1640–1672*, ed. Ralph Flenley (London and Toronto: J.M. Dent & Sons, 1928 [original French manuscript ca. 1672]).

northeast. Epidemics of Old World origin decimated populations and the uneven introduction of European weapons and other products had the effect of disrupting power balances and unleashing increasingly deadly cycles of war.[3] Whole nations migrated to new homes or simply disappeared, while other polities, either newly created out of the wreckage or, like the Iroquois, reinforced by the assimilation of war captives to replace epidemic losses, prospered through a combination of violence and astute diplomacy. The impacts were profound, and mostly negative, but they unfolded over time and space in complex and unpredictable ways.

The French-Canadian colony took root in the eye of this storm of disease, migration and violence, and almost from the start, it became an active participant in the region's shifting conflicts. Never very numerous, the French had no choice but to forge alliances in order to survive, and through their alliances, they inevitably acquired enemies (notably the Iroquois) as well as friends. The upheavals that surrounded them may have been ultimately attributable to their presence (and to that of other colonizers), but that does not mean that the French planned or controlled, or even understood, the processes at work. However, fur traders, missionaries and adventurers were quick to seize opportunities to pursue their interests in the disturbed North American interior, using the St. Lawrence settlements as their base. In the process, they spread French influence far and wide. By the 1660s–70s, French missions and trading posts dotted the Great Lakes and the upper Mississippi Valley; by the turn of the eighteenth century, an imperial network ran from Quebec to the Gulf of Mexico, arcing around the more compact British establishments on the Atlantic Coast. Later decades saw the French penetrating westward onto the Great Plains, with posts appearing on the Missouri and Saskatchewan Rivers. A few hundred venturers fanning out across half a continent were taking advantage of the instability produced by the empire effect to forge advantageous relations with indigenous peoples, even as their expeditions served to spread dislocation further and further afield.

---

[3] See Bruce G. Trigger, *Natives and Newcomers: Canada's "Heroic Age" Reconsidered* (Montreal and Kingston: McGill-Queen's University Press, 1986), passim; Daniel K. Richter, "War and Culture: The Iroquois Experience," *William and Mary Quarterly* 40 (1983): 528–59; Daniel K. Richter, *The Ordeal of the Longhouse: The Peoples of the Iroquois League in the Era of European Colonization* (Chapel Hill: University of North Carolina Press, 1992).

This was neither conquest nor colonization, for beyond the St. Lawrence Lowlands the French could not begin to enforce jurisdiction and rule, and except for a few small enclaves around Detroit and in the Illinois country, they did not really occupy the land. The missionaries, traders and soldiers, adapting to indigenous cultural expectations, were nevertheless able to construct an alliance system, tenuous and uncertain though it always was, that Richard White labeled the "Middle Ground" in his classic work of that title.[4] In relationships characterized by what White calls "creative misunderstanding," natives acknowledged the governor of New France as their "father" (meaning mediator and dispenser of gifts), while imperial officials convinced themselves that this implied submission to the authority of the French Empire. This pattern of ambiguous engagement along the disturbed edges of empire was not unique to New France. Something of the sort developed in the hinterlands beyond the British colonies as well, and in South America, as Tamar Herzog demonstrates, the Portuguese and Spanish engaged in competitive empire-building of a similar sort – trade, gift-giving, alliance – in the contested zones that separated their settlements.[5] What made New France unique in this context was the sheer size, extending over half a continent, of its "peripheral" quasi-empire, and the very modest size, spatially and demographically, of the colonial settlement that anchored it.

In official Bourbon discourse – that is, in pronouncements, maps and diplomatic correspondence addressed to rival European imperialists – the extended version of "New France" was treated as French sovereign territory: broad, unbounded, continually expanding, and closed to other empires. As much *bricolage* and opportunism went into the construction of these official claims in Europe as went into the elaboration of quasi-imperial alliance networks on North American ground. Spokesmen for the French state never suggested that it fully and exclusively possessed the claimed territories or that it exercised unmediated sovereignty over their populations. (They could not really make that claim about France itself, never mind "French" America.) Magically transforming the alliances

[4] Richard White, *The Middle Ground. Indians, Empires, and Republics in the Great Lakes Region, 1650–1815* (Cambridge: Cambridge University Press, 1991). For another view of French imperial penetration into the North American interior, see Gilles Havard, *Empire et métissages: Indiens et français dans le pays d'en haut, 1660–1715* (Sillery and Paris: Septentrion and Presses de l'Université de Paris – Sorbonne, 2003).

[5] Tamar Herzog, *Frontiers of Possession: Spain and Portugal in Europe and the Americas* (Cambridge, Mass.: Harvard University Press, 2015), ch. 2, pp. 70–134.

by which independent indigenous nations aligned themselves with the French into "submission" to their king, these imperial ideologues felt justified in counting such territories as part of New France, frequently adding distant peoples allied to or defeated in war by their allies. A basically feudal sense of territorial authority underlay the notion that such a loose and tenuously connected array of independent native polities could be construed as a field of empire subject to a distant monarch.[6]

A map of New France prepared by the royal hydrographer at Quebec at the end of the seventeenth century nicely illustrates the prevailing conception of imperial geography[7] (Figure 5.1). In Jean-Baptiste-Louis Franquelin's cartographic vision, the large letters spelling out "New France" hover over North America with no lines to indicate any outer boundary. Yet, across most of the space depicted, native nations are shown as not only present, but fully in control of their respective territories. The map-maker is at pains to acknowledge their independence and territoriality: rather than indicating, for example, the Sioux, as a mere feature of the landscape, he indicates "the country, land and nation of the western Sioux"; likewise for other indigenous nations. French sovereignty is being constructed here, not to the exclusion of native sovereignty, but *through* native sovereignty. Similarly, indigenous property in the land is emphatically recognized. As a general rule, the French did not seek to create colonial property for settlers in the vast interior domain. To the contrary: they repeatedly affirmed that the land was property of the natives, which is why their territories became part of the French empire when they received presents and accepted the king as their "father." Claiming what is now the state of Wisconsin in 1689, Nicolas Perrot declared, "in the name of the king, [I] take possession of the lands and rivers where these said nations live and of which they are the proprietors"; he did not imply that those nations ceased to be proprietors when the king "took possession."[8] In an earlier "ceremony of

---

[6] Gilles Havard and Cécile Vidal, *Histoire de l'Amérique Française* (Paris: Flammarion, 2003), 189–91; Gilles Havard, "'Les forcer à devenir cytoyens': État, sauvages et citoyenneté en Nouvelle-France (XVIIe-XVIIIe siècle)," *Annales. Histoire, sciences sociales* 64, no. 5 (2009): 985–1018; Catherine Desbarats and Allan Greer, "Où est la Nouvelle-France?," *Revue d'histoire de l'Amérique française* 64, 3–4 (hiver 2011): 31–62.

[7] Catherine Desbarats and Allan Greer, "North America from the Top Down: Visions of New France," *Journal of Early American History* 5 (fall 2015): 7–10.

[8] Perrot quoted in Arnaud Balvay, *L'épée et la plume: amérindiens et soldats des troupes de la marine en Louisiane et au pays d'en haut (1683–1763)* (Quebec City: Presses de l'université Laval, 2006), 86. "Au nom du Roy prendre possession des Terres et rivières où les d nations habitent et desquelles Elles sont propriétaires."

FIGURE 5.1 A late seventeenth-century map of New France, by J.-B. Franquelin, king's cartographer at Quebec. The lettering for "La Nouvelle-France" suggests a claim to most of the continent, with minimal recognition of the English colonies. Indigenous nations, on the other hand, are a prominent feature of the map. Their territorial integrity is at once recognized and subsumed under the banner of "New France."

Source: Jean-Baptiste Franquelin, *Carte de la Nouvelle France où est compris la Nouvelle Angleterre, Nouvelle Yorc, Nouvelle Albanie, Nouvelle Suède, la Pensilvanie, la Virginie, la Floride.* Bibliothèque nationale de France, département Cartes et plans, CPL GE DD-2987. Courtesy Bibliothèque nationale de France.

possession," another officer simultaneously staked a French claim to the Great Lakes region and "gave to the Indians as a present those lands of which he had taken possession."[9] These arcane proceedings, intended

---

[9] Jean Talon's report on the expedition to Sault Ste-Marie of Daumont de Saint-Lusson: France, Archives nationales d'outre-mer, colonies (hereafter ANOM), C11A, vol. 3: fol. 171–71v, Talon au roi, 2 November 1671. Needless to say, the indigenous people who witnessed these ceremonies were far from consenting to any territorial surrender. D. Peter Macleod, "The Anishinabeg Point of View: The History of the Great Lakes Region to 1800 in Nineteenth-Century Mississauga, Odawa, and Ojibwa Historiography," *Canadian Historical Review* 78 (1992): 207–8; Michael Witgen, "The Rituals of Possession: Native

for possible use in future inter-imperial negotiations and largely meaning-less to the people who witnessed them, demonstrate that the French legal case for imperial expansion tended to proceed not through dispossession, but through the incorporation of autonomous indigenous nations, fully in possession of their respective territories, into a network of commercial, religious and diplomatic affiliations.

Colonial property formation was confined to the Laurentian Low-lands: indeed, it formed a defining feature that distinguished the colony of Canada from the larger imperial project known as New France.[10] I have nevertheless been at pains to evoke that broader zone of disturbed and war-torn indigenous space and French empire-building because its history and that of the Canadian settlement are inextricably linked. The French colonial presence had profound effects on native nations far and wide, and, reciprocally, French Canada was shaped by that wider indi-genous context. Not only did the colony draw wealth from the interior through the fur trade, it also depended on its allies for military support, first against the Iroquois and later against the more powerful British. Furthermore, Canada drew demographic reinforcements from native spaces beyond the edge of colonization. For a variety of reasons, immi-gration from France was always quite modest, but it was supplemented over the second half of the seventeenth century by a substantial stream of indigenous migration into the St. Lawrence Valley.[11]

In a context of war and upheaval, many natives gravitated to the emerging Canadian settlements in search of security and/or commercial opportunity. Missionaries welcomed them and did their best to integrate them into the Catholic Church, while military leaders encouraged them to strengthen the colony's offensive and defensive capabilities. Innu and Algonquin bands adhered for a time to the French settlements of Quebec and Three Rivers, though as we saw in Chapter 3, the Innu eventually departed from the oppressive regime the Jesuits tried to

Identity and the Invention of Empire in Seventeenth-Century Western North America," *Ethnohistory* 54 (2007): 639–68.

[10] Geo-political usage could be inconsistent in the early modern period: sometimes "Canada" and "New France" were treated as synonyms, but most commonly "Canada" was the term reserved for the more or less Europeanized landscape of the St. Lawrence Valley, while "New France" designated the larger field of French aspirations to sover-eignty across North America. See Desbarats and Greer, "North America from the Top Down," 10–26.

[11] Allan Greer, *The People of New France* (Toronto: University of Toronto Press, 1997), 12–19.

institute at Sillery. These two peoples nevertheless maintained a presence along the river that had always been a central part of their territory. Others came to the St. Lawrence after the French had become established there. Refugee Hurons (Wendat) from the west established a village at Lorette, near Quebec City, after their homeland had been destroyed by the Iroquois in 1649. After the Iroquois themselves made peace with the French in 1667, a substantial faction, especially from the Mohawk nation, relocated to lands near Montreal. Toward the end of the century, "Abenakis," an amalgam of peoples from northern New England, many of them refugees from King Philip's War and the frontier struggles of Maine, relocated their villages to Canada. Actually, none of these migrants were truly newcomers without prior connections to the St. Lawrence Valley: the Mohawks had a long-standing relationship with the region, particularly the island of Montreal and its surroundings, while the Abenakis had long been in the habit of trapping and trading on the St. Maurice, a tributary of the St. Lawrence.[12]

Each group willingly settled close to the French, adapting to some extent to French law, religion and land tenure, without abandoning their cultures or giving up their independence. Most people accepted Catholic baptism and built their villages close to mission churches.[13] Three of the largest missions were sponsored by the Jesuits: Kahnawake (Sault St-Louis), a Mohawk/Iroquois community near Montreal; Lorette, the Huron village near Quebec; and Odanak (St-François), the most important Abenaki village, located midway between Quebec and Montreal. After the failed Sillery experiment, the Jesuits renounced coercion, tacitly accepting a degree of cultural and political autonomy that

---

[12] For a fuller account of these migrations and on the locations of new indigenous communities in Canada, see R. Cole Harris, ed., *Historical Atlas of Canada* (3 vols.), vol. 1: *Beginnings to 1800* (Toronto: University of Toronto Press, 1987), plate 47. On the early seventeenth-century Abenaki presence, see "Relation de ce qui s'est passé en la Nouvelle-France en l'année 1637," in *Monumenta Novae Francia*, 9 vols., ed. Lucien Campeau (Rome and Quebec City: Monumenta Historica Soc. Iesu and Presses de l'Université Laval, 1967–2003) (hereafter MNF), vol. 2: 658–59; Sylvie Savoie and Jean Tanguay, "Le noeud de l'ancienne amitié: la presence abénaquise sur la rive nord du Saint-Laurent aux XVIIe et XVIIIe siècles," *Recherches amérindiennes au Québec* 33 (2003): 30–36.

[13] On the mission communities, see James Axtell, *The Invasion Within: The Contest of Cultures in Colonial North America* (New York: Oxford University Press, 1985), 43–127; Marc Jetten, *Enclaves amérindiennes: les "réductions" du Canada 1637–1701* (Quebec: Septentrion 1994); Allan Greer, "Conversion and Identity: Iroquois Christianity in Seventeenth-Century New France," in Kenneth Mills and Anthony Grafton, ed., *Conversions: Old Worlds and New* (Rochester: University of Rochester Press, 2003), 175–98.

would have been unthinkable to Latin American missionaries. A fourth major mission settlement was established by the Sulpician order for Iroquois (mostly Mohawk) converts; it occupied a series of locations in the vicinity of Montreal before coming to rest at the seigneurie of Deux-Montagnes (Oka) in 1721. The colonial administration was just as resigned as the missionary clergy when it came to the independence of resident natives; this was especially the case after 1689 when recurrent wars against British America had the effect of elevating the status of resident natives as Canada's most important military force. Church and state in French Canada wanted natives to stay close by and they were painfully aware of their inability to retain them by force; accommodation was the only option.

At these mission-associated locales in the midst of the French-Canadian settlements, Hurons, Iroquois and Abenakis established their villages and, to borrow the New England expression, their "planting grounds." The land and climate were not ideal for native horticulture, however, and so people experimented to some degree with European styles of agriculture, combining indigenous hand tillage with plowing and some livestock raising. Inevitably, the villagers of the St. Lawrence did become enmeshed to some degree in the ongoing processes of colonial property formation, a subject to which we will return toward the end of this chapter. Parallels with the "praying towns" of New England and with the *congregaciónes* of Mexico suggest themselves, though the native communities of the St. Lawrence were generally much more independent, culturally, economically and politically, than these other communities. As in the other two cases, the general pattern was a succession of two distinct stages: first indigenous enclaves were established within the emergent colonial property regime, and then a contrary process of settler encroachment shrank and undermined these native properties. First, colonizers incorporate mobile or semi-nomadic peoples, encouraging them to "settle"; then later they dispossess them.

In the Canadian case, however, there was much more to the story beyond what this schematic narrative implies. Land in the colonized zone was only one element in the property system that the St. Lawrence villagers fashioned for themselves. In addition to the security and commercial contacts that residence close to the French entailed, the Iroquois and Abenakis who moved northward also sought access to the rich fur-trapping lands of northern Quebec. This was a time (second half of the seventeenth century) when beaver had been hunted almost to extinction across much of New York and New England and so the vast boreal forests beckoned. What ensued was a grab for northern hunting territories, largely at the expense of the Innu and Algonquins, nations whose numbers – and therefore ability to defend extensive hunting ranges – had dwindled. With French encouragement, the Abenaki, Iroquois and Huron "settlers" bound themselves in peaceful alliance with the Innu and Algonquins; the latter were therefore obligated to make room for the newcomers.[14] But how much space were the latter entitled to and where exactly would it be located? The fact that all parties were officially friends and allies did not preclude friction and strong-arm tactics. All indications are that a massive process of dispossession and property remaking occurred in the northern hinterland, mostly beyond the ken of the colonial authorities (see Chapter 8).

FEUDAL NEW FRANCE IN CONTEXT

New France was legally constituted as a fief. By its 1627 charter, the Company of New France was granted all of North America, from Florida to the Arctic Circle, as one vast fief, "in full property, jurisdiction and seigneurie." The company held this feudal estate from the Crown and was required to pledge homage (*foi et hommage*) and present a gold crown when a new monarch took the throne. The grant conferred the right of "subinfeodation," meaning that the company could subgrant portions of its estate as subordinate fiefs. Indeed, the charter allowed the company to distribute lands "to people who shall settle that country and others as they see fit"; it could grant land "at whatever charges, reserves and conditions that they find proper."[15] Eight years after this charter was issued for New France, Cardinal Richelieu set up a "Compagnie des Isles de l'Amérique" to regularize French occupation of several West Indian islands; the land tenure provisions of this charter were essentially the same as those prescribed for the northern colony, though property formation in the French Caribbean would follow a course very different from that

---

[14] Jean Tanguay, "Les règles d'alliance et l'occupation Huronne du territoire," *Recherches amérindiennes au Québec* 30 (2002): 21–34; Savoie and Tanguay, "Le noeud de l'ancienne amitié."

[15] *Édits, ordonnances, déclarations et arrêts relatifs à la tenure seigneuriale, demandés par une adresse de l'assemblée législative, 1851* (Quebec: E. R. Fréchette, 1852), 5 (my translation). On the charter and its implications for colonial tenure in New France, see R. Cole Harris, *The Seigneurial System in Early Canada; a Geographical Study* (Madison: University of Wisconsin Press, 1966), 21–22.

in Canada.[16] Three decades after the founding of the New France and the American islands companies, Louis XIV's great minister, Jean-Baptiste Colbert, folded these companies, amalgamating their colonial possession under a giant Compagnie des Indes Occidentales (1664). The new company inherited all French territories across the Atlantic world, together with existing "seigneurial rights" in these colonies.[17] Ten years after this integrating move, Colbert wound up the Compagnie des Indes Occidentales and repossessed its colonial dominions in Louis XIV's name. From 1674 on, the French Crown would hold New France directly, without the mediation of a corporation, but still as a fief.

An eighteenth-century legal dictionary defined "fief" as "an estate held from the king or from another lord in homage and subject to other charges. The person who possesses it is called vassal, and the person under whom the estate is held is called seigneur."[18] The language here harks back to the Middle Ages, when land tenure and jurisdiction were inseparable and when vassal lords were authorized to exploit local peasantries in return for loyalty to and military service on behalf of their respective overlords. The concepts of fief and lordship retained a prominent place in French land law long after feudalism as a military-political syndrome had passed from the scene. It is important to recognize that other European legal systems of the early modern period were also marked by their medieval feudal origins. France, and especially northern and western France, the regions of the country most involved in overseas colonization, had been the heartland of medieval feudalism. Here most visibly, but also in England and Spain, the law and vocabulary of land tenure retained a feudal flavor through the early modern period.

In European historiography, "feudal" and, a fortiori, "feudalism" are tricky terms, long surrounded by controversy. Marxists extended their meaning into an all-encompassing socioeconomic order, the "feudal mode

---

[16] "Contrat de rétablissement de la Compagnie des Isles de l'Amérique," 12 February 1635, in *Loix et constitutions des colonies françaises de l'Amérique sous le vent*, 6 vols., ed. Médéric Moreau de Saint Méry (Paris: Saint Méry, 1785–90), vol. 1: 29, 33; Nicole Nimar, *Propriété et exploitation en Martinique et en Guadeloupe* (Bordeaux: Biscaye Frères, 1971), 29.

[17] *Édits, ordonnances, déclarations et arrêts relatifs à la tenure seigneuriale*, 17.

[18] Claude-Joseph de Ferrière, *Dictionnaire de droit et de pratique contenant l'explication des termes de droit, d'ordonnances, de coutume & de pratique avec les jurisdictions de France*, 4th ed., 2 vols. (Paris: Chez Joseph Saugrain, 1758), vol. 1: 633. "Fief, est un héritage tenu du Roi ou d'autre Seigneur à foi & hommage, & à la charge de quelques autres droits. Celui qui le possede, est appellé Vassal; & celui de qui l'héritage releve est appellé Seigneur."

of production,"[19] leading to a reaction on the part of many medievalists who insisted on greater precision and specificity. The French historian Marc Bloch understood feudalism in basically political terms: it had to do with the networks of personal loyalty and dependence that bound together the different ranks of a warrior elite at a time, the Middle Ages, when sovereignty was fragmented and uncertain.[20] But by the time New France was founded, that sort of political/military feudalism was a thing of the past, largely suppressed by the centralizing Bourbon monarchs. What remained by the seventeenth century was landed estates with some rights of jurisdiction, what Jean Gallet calls "civic feudalism," as opposed to the older "military feudalism."[21] In this chapter, I would like to revert to the original meaning of "feudal" as part of the vocabulary of land tenure: strictly speaking, it is simply the adjective that corresponds to the noun "fief."[22] For current purposes, we can dispense with the totalizing concept "feudalism" and talk instead about landed property systems centered on the legal category of fief, which can be called "feudal" by virtue of this fact.

In a seventeenth-century context, there is nothing unusual about the feudal language of the Company of New France charter. Not only was it standard across the French empire, it also resembled the legal idiom of contemporary British colonial grants. Colonial charters generally specified more or less feudal tenures partly because these were the norm in both France and England themselves.[23] Colonies constructed in legal

---

[19] Karl Marx, *Capital: A Critique of Political Economy* (3 vols.) (Moscow: Progress Publishers, 1954), vol. 3, ch. 47; Perry Anderson, *Passages from Antiquity to Feudalism* (London: NLB, 1974); Centre d'études et de recherches marxistes, *Sur le féodalisme* (Paris: Éditions sociales, 1974); Alain Guerreau, *Le féodalisme: un horizon théorique* (Paris: le Sycomore, 1980); Guy Lemarchand, *Paysans et seigneurs en Europe: une histoire comparée, XVIe-XIXe siècle* (Rennes: Presses de l'Université de Rennes, 2011).

[20] Marc Bloch, *Feudal Society*, trans. L. A. Manyon (London: Routledge & Kegan Paul, 1961); A. R. Brown, "The Tyranny of a Construct: Feudalism and Historians of Medieval Europe," *American Historical Review* 79 (1974): 1063–83.

[21] Jean Gallet, *Seigneurs et paysans en France, 1600–1793* (Rennes: Editions Ouest-France, 1999), 7.

[22] It was in this sense that "feudalism" was criticized in eighteenth-century France and eventually "abolished" on the night of 4 August 1789. See Alexis de Tocqueville, *The Old Regime and the French Revolution*, trans. Stuart Gilbert (New York: Doubleday, 1955), 31; J. Q. C. Mackrell, *The Attack on "Feudalism" in Eighteenth-Century France* (London: Routledge and Kegan Paul, 1973); Jean Bastier, *La féodalité au siècle des lumières dans la région de Toulouse (1730–1790)* (Paris: Bibliothèque nationale, 1975). Bastier cites (p. 23) the definition of feudal ("*féodalité*") offered by the *Encyclopédie*: "la qualité de fief, la tenure d'un héritage à titre de fief."

[23] On the basically feudal nature of English land law, especially before the passage of the 1660 Statute of Tenures, see William Searle Holdsworth, *An Historical Introduction to*

terms as fiefs were well suited to the task of asserting *dominium* over distant lands through the delegated sovereignty of a proprietor or company. Declaring proprietors or colonizing corporations to be their vassals, monarchs gave these agents an incentive to establish and defend practical control over American territory; feudal tenure allowed sovereign and proprietor, as well as inferior vassals and settlers, all to play their part in establishing *dominium*; each could claim their respective stake in the property of the land. Acknowledging the king as the ultimate source of state power and landed property contributed to colonists' sense of security and legitimacy in their often-precarious overseas establishments. Even the precociously modern Dutch republic, when it got around to establishing a legal framework for the colonization of New Netherland in 1629, instituted essentially feudal "patroonships" whose landlords ("patroons") would "own and possess and hold from the company as a perpetual fief of inheritance" their respective estates, together with "high, middle, and low jurisdiction, rights of fishing, fowling, and grinding, to the exclusion of all others."[24] Thus, in framing their claims to New World land, the Dutch Republic, like the monarchies of France and England, had recourse to legal instruments that associated property, rule, jurisdiction and honor. Feudal in different ways and to varying degrees, these foundational texts all established colonial land tenure on the base of the sovereign's claims as supreme landlord.

Though New France was not unique in being constituted as a fief, it developed additional layers of feudal qualities that did come to distinguish it from all other colonial jurisdictions of the Americas. To start with, it was the site of extensive subinfeodation. Other French colonizing enterprises, not to mention the proprietors of Maryland, the Carolinas, Newfoundland and the British West Indies, were similarly authorized to endow colonial landlords with subordinate fiefs within their respective territories and under their overlordship.[25] Feudal estates were indeed

---

the Land Law (Oxford: Clarendon Press, 1927), 36–37; A. W. B. Simpson, A History of the Land Law, 2nd ed. (Oxford: Clarendon Press, 1986), 1–22; Alan Watson, Roman Law and Comparative Law (Athens: University of Georgia Press, 1991), 141–43.

[24] Jaap Jacobs, *New Netherland: A Dutch Colony in Seventeenth-Century America* (Leiden: Brill, 2005), 112–32 (quotation at 114). See also Clarence White Rife, "Land Tenure in New Netherland," in *Essays in Colonial History Presented to Charles Mclean Andrews by His Students* (New Haven: Yale University Press, 1931), 41–73.

[25] On Maryland, see Debra A. Meyers, "Calvert's Catholic Colony," in *Constructing Early Modern Empires: Proprietary Ventures in the Atlantic World, 1500–1750*, ed. L. H. Roper and Bertrand Van Ruymbeke (Leiden: Brill, 2007), 370–71. On the Carolinas, see Marion Eugene Sirmans, *Colonial South Carolina: A Political History, 1663–1763*

granted within all these English colonies, as well as in the French establishments of St-Christophe, Martinique, Guadeloupe and Acadia.[26] However, subinfeodation was spotty and, on the whole, short-lived in these colonial jurisdictions. Both English and French settlers were resistant to the interposition of a layer of exactions and jurisdiction between the occupying landholder and the colonial regime; in Maryland and Martinique, violent revolts sealed the fate of seigneurialism.[27] What distinguishes New France in this setting is the thoroughness with which the colonized zone of the St. Lawrence Lowland was covered with subordinate fiefs, more commonly known as "seigneuries."[28] There were 210 seigneuries here by the end of French rule in 1760 and they blanketed virtually all the ground available for settlement. In land tenure terms, it would be the presence of seigneuries that defined the legal geography of the colony of Canada within the larger imperial space known as New France.

Approaching the topic from a legal viewpoint, we might say that a seigneurie was land held "*en fief*," one of the tenure forms provided by French imperial law. Where civil law is concerned, seventeenth-century

---

(Chapel Hill: University of North Carolina Press, 1966), 11–12; L. H. Roper, "Conceiving an Anglo-American Proprietorship: Early South Carolina History in Perspective," in Roper and Van Ruymbeke, ed., *Constructing Early Modern Empires*, 389–410.

[26] See James S. Pritchard, *In Search of Empire: The French in the Americas, 1670–1730* (Cambridge: Cambridge University Press, 2004), 78–88; Allan Greer, "A Feudal Empire? Land Tenure in the French Atlantic," Law and the French Atlantic Conference, Newberry Library, Chicago, October 2012. The agrarian settlements of Acadia (present-day Nova Scotia) form an uncertain exception to this generalization. Definitely fiefs were granted here and seigneurs certainly tried to subject settlers to their exactions, but how fully and consistently did they succeed in imposing their feudal claims? Unfortunately, the surviving source materials are very sparse, which makes it difficult to draw any definitive conclusions. The scholarly consensus long held that seigneuries in that contested territory, repeatedly captured by the English and restored to the French, remained empty shells. (See Andrew Hill Clark, *Acadia: The Geography of Early Nova Scotia to 1760* (Madison: University of Wisconsin Press, 1968), 113–21.) However, a revisionist work by Gregory Kennedy argues that settlers in the region did actually pay rents and other seigneurial exactions. Gregory M. W. Kennedy, *Something of a Peasant Paradise?: Comparing Rural Societies in Acadie and the Loudunais, 1604–1755* (Montreal: McGill-Queen's University Press, 2014), 128–67.

[27] Meyers, "Calvert's Catholic Colony," 370–87; Pierre Pluchon, *Histoire des Antilles et de la Guyane* (Toulouse: Privat, 1982), 76–77; Nimar, *Propriété et exploitation*, 37, 44–45.

[28] In the medieval European setting, according to Marc Bloch, "fief" and "seigneurie" were quite distinct entities, with different histories. There seems to have been a tendency for the two institutions to merge in the early modern period, however. Certainly in the New France setting "fief" and "seigneurie" were treated as synonymous terms. See Bloch, *La société féodale*, 389.

France was a patchwork of diverse customary laws, each of which had been codified in the previous century under the influence of the Renaissance revival of Roman law. One of the regional *coutumes*, the "Custom of Paris," enjoyed a certain supraregional prestige,[29] and so, when France established colonies in America, the Crown made efforts to establish it as the sole reference for regulating and adjudicating matters such as inheritance, debt and property. In the early years, Canadian notaries occasionally framed contracts subject to the custom of Brittany, but the Custom of Paris soon predominated.[30] The latter is often considered one of the most feudal of the *ancien régime* customs: fiefs do indeed occupy the lion's share of its provisions relating to real estate.

Under the Custom of Paris, *en fief* is one of three modes of holding land; a fief is always held from a superior seigneur in a chain of vassalage leading up to the king. The second mode is called *"en censive."* *Censive* land is always located within a fief (the adage *"nul terre sans seigneur"* – no land without a seigneur – appears frequently in the pages of the Custom of Paris); in other words, a given tract would be held simultaneously by two parties under two different tenures: *en censive* and *en fief*. The distinguishing mark of *censive* tenure is the obligation to pay a small annual sum, the *cens*, symbolizing subjection to the fief; the person paying the *cens* was thus known as the *"censitaire."* The *cens* also implied subjection to a mutation fine, the *lods et ventes*, and additional rents and other charges could be added to the *cens* by contractual agreement. An individual lot under *censive* tenure is usually called a *"roture,"* which suggests commoner status. However, while *en fief* was considered a noble tenure and *censive* had inferior status, the Custom states explicitly that these qualities are "real" rather than "personal," attaching to the land, not its holder. As a result, there could be a discrepancy between the status of the land and the status of its proprietor: inheritance or sale could, for example, lead to a situation where a noble paid *cens* to a commoner

---

[29] Jean Imbert, *Histoire du droit privé*, 8th ed. (Paris: Presses universitaires de France, 1996), 58.

[30] Legislation in 1664 removed any trace of ambiguity: the Custom of Paris was formally pronounced the exclusive law of the French Empire (though colonial jurisdictions were notorious for their selective enforcement of some provisions of the Custom, while quietly ignoring others). Marcel Trudel, *Histoire de la Nouvelle-France*, 4 vols. (Montreal: Fides, 1963–96), vol. 3, *La seigneurie des Cent-Associés 1627–1663*, tome 1, *Les événements*, 408; John Dickinson, "New France: Law Courts and the Coutume de Paris, 1608–1760," in *Canada's Legal Inheritances*, ed. DeLloyd J. Guth and W. Wesley Pue (Winnipeg: Canadian Legal History Project, 2001), 38. On the French West Indies, see Louis-Philipe May, *Histoire économique de la Martinique, 1635–1763* (Paris: M. Rivière, 1930), 251.

seigneur. The third tenure recognized by the Custom of Paris was the
"*franc alleu*," otherwise known as "allodial" tenure. This was land free of
cens and other obligations to a seigneur.[31] Allodial tenure soon became
the norm in the French West Indies, whereas the *fief/censive* duo came to
dominate in Canada.

The St. Lawrence settlements within New France stand out, not only as
the most thoroughly seigneurialized colony in America, the place where
fiefs most fully blanketed the terrain; it was also the site of a unique
historical development, one by which seigneuries bore down with ever-
increasing weight on settlers and natives alike. Far from fading away,
feudal exactions tended to become ever more numerous and more intense
over time.

This is not to say that the habitants of the St. Lawrence Valley were the
only colonists on the continent who found themselves burdened by rents
and under the thumb of landlords – far from it. Rent-paying tenancies
were common in all the English colonies, including New England; the
best-known example there is the Springfield, Massachusetts region,
where William and John Pynchon were the dominant landlords in the
seventeenth century.[32] New York was the colony with the most significant and long-lasting manorial regime.[33] For a time, Hudson Valley
settlers felt the burden of a variety of feudal-type restrictions as landlords
claimed judicial powers, the right to appoint local clergymen, corvée
labor, a monopoly over grist milling; some even asserted control over
the marketing of their tenants' surplus grain. However, by the eighteenth
century simpler tenure practices had come to prevail, with limited-term
leases and monetized rents. Throughout British America, there was a

---

[31] François Bourjon, *Le droit commun de la France et la Coutume de Paris réduits en
    principes, tirés des loix, des ordonnances, des arrêts, des jurisconsultes & des auteurs,
    & mis dans l'ordre d'un commentaire complet & méthodique sur cette coutume*, revised
    ed., 2 vols. (Paris: Grangé et Cellot, 1770); Yves Zoltvany, "Esquisse de la coutume de
    Paris," *Revue d'histoire de l'Amérique française* 25 (1971): 365–84. On the Custom of
    Paris in the French West Indies, see Edith Géraud-Lloca, "La coutume de Paris outre-mer:
    L'habitation antillaise sous l'ancien régime," *Revue historique de droit français et étran-
    ger* 60 (1982): 207–59.

[32] Stephen Innes, *Labor in a New Land: Economy and Society in Seventeenth-Century
    Springfield* (Princeton, N.J.: Princeton University Press, 1983).

[33] Sung Bok Kim, *Landlord and Tenant in Colonial New York: Manorial Society,
    1664–1775* (Chapel Hill: University of North Carolina Press, 1978). Other British
    American colonies also saw the establishment of landed estates. Prince Edward Island
    became the site in 1767 of a particularly thoroughgoing experiment in landlord–tenant
    colonization. See J. M. Bumsted, *Land, Settlement, and Politics on Eighteenth-Century
    Prince Edward Island* (Kingston and Montreal: McGill-Queen's University Press, 1987).

rather clear distinction between landlords, considered full proprietors of their respective estates, and tenants, who could make use of land for a specified period and at a specified price. Rents may well have been every bit as burdensome in their economic effects – if not more so – as all the seigneurial exactions demanded of Canadian habitants, but the property relations were fundamentally different from those characterizing a genuinely seigneurial regime, where *censive* tenure was permanent, rather than temporary, and where the distinction between proprietors and tenants was not clear-cut. In seigneurial New France, property formation proceeded on its own particular track, with settlers and seigneurs enjoying different and overlapping stakes in a given piece of land.

New France was legally constructed as a fief; the Canadian settlements within that larger whole were divided into subordinate fiefs/seigneuries; and those seigneuries were a consequential feature of agrarian relations. The colonization of the St. Lawrence Valley was thus feudal in three distinct ways. Moreover, those three feudal dimensions were not necessarily connected, for other colonies displayed some but not all of these characteristics. It is important to stress these distinctions, as historians of early Canada have an unfortunate tendency to roll the disparate feudal aspects of property into a single monolithic object, known as the "seigneurial system."[34] Running through the literature on the subject is an exaggerated sense of coherence, as though the complex, layered and constantly evolving tenure forms constituted, if not a concrete object, then at least a fully integrated package. There is a further tendency to assume that this "system" was somehow transported from France holus-bolus. Timeless as well as seamless, the system simply became, more or less, what it already was at the point of inception. In the more conspiratorial versions of this view, seigneurialism was "imposed" on the colony as part of a social engineering agenda intended to shape settler society along authoritarian lines.[35] The phrase "seigneurial system" then functions as a totalizing concept, eradicating distinctions between the various aspects

---

[34] In addition to Harris, *The Seigneurial System*, see William Bennett Munro, *The Seigniorial System in Canada: A Study in French Colonial Policy* (New York: Longmans Green and Co., 1907); Marcel Trudel, *The Seigneurial Regime* (Ottawa: Canadian Historical Association, 1956); Benoît Grenier, *Brève histoire du régime seigneurial* (Montréal: Boréal, 2012).

[35] Sigmund Diamond, "An Experiment in 'Feudalism': French Canada in the Seventeenth Century," *William and Mary Quarterly*, 3rd ser., 18 (1961): 3–34; Jean-Pierre Wallot, "Le régime seigneurial et son abolition au Canada," *Canadian Historical Review* 50 (1969): 367–93.

of land tenure, but also between law, colonial society, economy and imperial policy.[36] We need to disaggregate the various phenomena and levels of analysis that are habitually jumbled together under the "seigneurial system" heading in order grasp the dynamics at work as fiefs spread across the St. Lawrence Valley and put their mark on evolving property making. This was a historical process that unfolded within the colony; impulses emanating from the settler society and the indigenous presence turn out to have shaped that evolution at least as much as the decrees of distant European rulers.

THE EMERGENCE OF SEIGNEURIAL TENURE IN CANADA

The earliest grants of land to French settlers in the enclave surrounding the post at Quebec actually pre-dated the feudal charter of the Company of New France.[37] These, together with the grants accorded by the company after 1627 in that central area, were made directly to settlers without any feudal intermediary. Each of the three tenures recognized by the Custom of Paris was represented in these early grants: some lands were given *en fief*, some *en censive* and others *en alleu*; in some cases, no particular tenure was specified in the records.[38] The largest number of grants was *en censive*, but at a very low rate, mostly six *deniers* per *arpent*, a trifling monetary payment, hardly worth the expense of collection; nor was much else demanded beyond the requirement for land-holders occasionally to present their titles and swear homage to a representative of the company (later of the Crown). These were still not onerous requirements; had settlers been numerous and influential enough, one could well imagine them falling into disuse – after the fashion of quitrents in many of the English colonies. The company granted some *allods* as well, using the

---

[36] Some writers, trapped in the schematic model of universal evolution through well-defined stages, do not hesitate to describe New France as a "feudal society" with a "feudal mode of production." H. Clare Pentland, *Labour and Capital in Canada, 1650–1860* (Toronto: J. Lorimer, 1981); Robert C. H. Sweeny, "What Difference Does a Mode Make? A Comparison of Two Seventeenth-Century Colonies: Canada and Newfoundland," *William and Mary Quarterly* 63 (April 2006): 281–304.

[37] Actually, Canada's first agricultural settler, Louis Hébert, came in 1617 as an employee of a fur-trading company, then in control of the post at Quebec. He was granted the use of lands to farm, but the company retained full proprietorship of the land, plus any improvements. See Marcel Trudel, *Le Comptoir, 1604–1627*, vol. 2: *Histoire de la Nouvelle France* (Montreal: Fides, 1966), 243–44.

[38] Pierre Georges Roy, ed., *Papier terrier de la compagnie des indes occidentales, 1667–1668* (Beauceville, QC: L'Eclaireur, 1931), passim.

Custom of Paris's "free" tenure. For noble settlers, ecclesiastical bodies and others deemed to be of high status, the company sometimes exercised its power of subinfeodation and, for purely honorific reasons, declared grants to be *en fief*.

Regardless of tenure, some land grants were large and some were small. Some fiefs were quite large, while others were the size of a modest family farm. At a later stage, it became the pattern that fiefs would be large and that their seigneurs would grant *rotures* to ordinary settlers, each *roture* nested within its seigneurie – the arrangement historians have in mind when they speak of "the seigneurial system" – but that was not the consistent pattern in the first half of the seventeenth century. Fiefs and *rotures* frequently stood side-by-side, each held directly from the Company of New France. Moreover, some *rotures* and *allods* were much bigger than many fiefs. The larger land grants, in whatever tenure, seem to have been intended, like similar large grants to elite colonists in New Spain and New England, to be developed as agricultural estates worked by subservient labor. As the Laurentian colony struggled to feed itself, some comparatively well-off colonists employed indentured servants to clear land and raise crops on their grants, while others subgranted *rotures* to independent settlers. It was not initially clear how large landed endowments would be exploited and for a time it hardly mattered since both servants and settlers were in short supply, given the very limited immigration from France. The most economically consequential grants of the 1640s were the narrow strips of shoreline at Quebec, granted out as *allods* for commercial eel-fishing purposes, mainly to the benefit of religious houses.[39]

The Jesuits held an estate called Notre-Dame-des-Anges, measuring one league by four (approximately 3.9 by 15 kilometers). It was originally granted in 1626 and later confirmed by the Company of New France in 1637 as allodial land, held subject to the obligation of an annual mass for the repose of the souls of deceased shareholders in the Company of New France.[40] The Jesuits preferred this tenure to the more honorific *en fief* because it relieved them of the trouble and expense of periodically paying homage.[41] The 1637 grant mentions the expectation that the

[39] Marcel Trudel, *Les débuts du régime seigneurial au Canada* (Montreal: Fides, 1974), 195; Roy, *Papier terrier de la compagnie des indes occidentales*, 160.
[40] Notre-Dame des-Anges, nouvel acte de concession, 15 January 1637, in MNF, vol. 3: 469–72.
[41] "Remarques sur la prise de possession de nos terres par le P. Jérome Lalemant, 24 juillet 1646," in MNF, vol. 6: 484–86; Jesuits' journal, June 1646, in MNF, vol. 6: 720.

reverend fathers would "bring over such persons as they choose to work [this land]" and that they would report the number of sponsored immigrants. The company was required by the terms of its own proprietorship to ensure that 4000 French, Catholic colonists were brought to the St. Lawrence within the space of fifteen years. For a time, it hoped to offload this populating responsibility to large colonial landlords, but the Jesuits managed to recruit only a handful of indentured servants and other seigneurs and proprietors could do little more in that regard, and so the company soon gave up on the notion that immigration responsibilities could be delegated in this way. Working the land themselves and with hired hands, the Jesuits could clear only a tiny portion of Notre-Dame-des-Anges, enough to grow some crops and raise a few animals to help feed the mission station, but this could not be a paying proposition, given the shortage of labor. By the late 1640s, the colonial governor was pressuring them to open up Notre-Dame-des-Anges to settlers. The Jesuits demurred, however, since canon law forbade the unauthorized alienation of ecclesiastical property. They wrote to the general in charge of the Society of Jesus in Rome asking permission to grant lands to settlers, "per modum feudi," as they expressed it in Latin:

We possess here a great deal of land, most of it forested, that our fathers received long ago as a free gift from the lords of this country ... In fact, this estate is utterly useless to us and it stands as an obstacle to colonists who would like to settle here but who are prevented from doing so by the lack of conveniently situated land. Indeed, it harms us as we need colonists more than we need land, men who would settle close to us. It is for this reason that I ask your paternity to grant us the power to detach and alienate portions of our immense territories.[42]

In characterizing Notre-Dame-des-Anges as "utterly useless," the Jesuits were exaggerating to make a point: in the absence of exportable crops, Canadian land was a poor economic investment, but it was vitally important as a subsistence base for settlers who would bolster the tenuous

---

[42] Barthélémi Vimont to Mutius Vitellschi, 1 September 1639, in MNF, vol. 4: 256. "Possidemus hic multa terrarum seu sylvarum spatia, quae Patres nostri nescio qua spe seu redituum magnorum seu domorum aedificandarum obtinuere olim ab huius loci dominis idque sine ullo pretio. Caeterum, hoc nobis inutile penitus est et nocet pluribus incolis qui hic habitare vellent, nec possunt defectu loci commodi. Imi et nocet nobis qui magis egemus incolis et hominibus qui iuxta nos consistere possint quam terris. Quare peto a Vestra Paternitate an velit nobis concedere facultatem dandi et alienandi aliquam partem spatiorum eiusmodi immensorum, nobis prorsus inutilium." See also follow-up correspondence dated "September 1640," in ibid., 501–7. My thanks to Fannie Dionne for help with Latin translation.

French presence here. Even so, the European Jesuit authorities were reluctant to allow "alienation" and so no grants were made for some years. Eventually, the institution of the fief provided the Jesuits with a solution to their problem: by turning Notre-Dame-des-Anges into a seigneurie, they could put lands in the hands of settlers without actually alienating it: the overall size of the estate would not be diminished as portions were subgranted as *rotures*. In 1651 the Company of New France obligingly regranted Notre-Dame-des-Anges, changing its legal status from allodial to seigneurial. The Jesuits did not wait for the official transformation of tenure to begin granting lots to settlers, the latter anxious to begin farming on these prime lands close to the safety of the fort at Quebec. However, the alteration in tenure freed them from concerns about violating canon law as they allowed their estate to be recruited into the company's strategy of delegating to seigneurs the job of granting land to settlers. Feudal tenure, with its ambiguities and layered entitlements, nicely served the purpose of keeping this ecclesiastical estate intact while making land available for colonization.[43]

Like its French Caribbean counterpart that downloaded property affairs to the governors of each of its islands, like the General Court of Massachusetts that encouraged colonists to group themselves into townships and distribute land at a local level, the New France company welcomed the idea that colonial notables might take over land-granting duties through the institution of the fief. In all three cases, this move to delegate settler-level property-making was more a pragmatic response to circumstances than the outcome of a preexisting plan. In a similar spirit, the company farmed out colonization in the eastern marchlands of Acadia to a subsidiary proprietorship.[44] The company continued to issue grants *en censive* for small building lots in and around the towns of Quebec and Three Rivers, but everywhere else it would award large fiefs and leave retail land-granting to the seigneurs so endowed. The latter would have to distribute *rotures* to settlers, issue title, arrange surveys and provide local judicial facilities. In fact, seigneurs were not always conscientious in the discharge of these duties, especially the provision of courts; as in seventeenth-century France, the royal state tended over time to put seigneurial courts out of business.

---

[43] On Notre-Dame-des-Anges, see, in addition to the Jesuit sources cited above, Trudel, *Les débuts du régime seigneurial*, 122–23.

[44] Helen Dewar, "'Y establir nostre auctorité': Assertions of Imperial Sovereignty through Proprietorships and Chartered Companies in New France, 1598–1663," PhD dissertation, University of Toronto, 2012, 207–47.

Be that as it may, the company was still glad to offload its duties. Even if initial hopes that seigneurs would act as immigration agents were soon dashed, it did manage to free itself from detailed management of grants and titles. The company was relieved of some onerous responsibilities, while the seigneurs gained the prestige of a feudal estate and the hope of landed revenues in the future. The emphasis in early feudal grants was less on the lucrative benefits conferred than on the religious and patriotic duty to contribute to the noble project of Catholic colonization. In several early grants, the company spelled out its motives for creating vassals: it sought to involve other parties in the development of New France, "distributing the lands of this country to those who join with us in this worthy design and who have the means of clearing them and bringing them under cultivation in order to attract Frenchmen [to settle there]."[45]

Commoners, nobles and clerical bodies all received seigneuries, but the bulk of grants went to the privileged first and second estates. Several early grants of fiefs, like the allodial grants nearer Quebec, were given to ecclesiastical institutions. The Jesuits alone had six large seigneuries by the time the Company of New France was dissolved and they acquired additional estates after 1663, making them by far the largest feudal proprietor in the colony. Other early grants went to the Augustinian nuns of the Hôtel-Dieu and the Ursulines of Quebec. The whole island of Montreal was given first to an association of lay Catholic settlers, the *Société notre-dame*, before coming under the control of the Sulpician order. The Quebec seminary acquired the oversize seigneurie of Beaupré by purchase in 1680. The Church's seigneuries numbered only twenty-three out of 210 fiefs enumerated at the end of the French régime, but they tended to be the largest and choicest of Canada's feudal estates.[46] The bulk of feudal grants to Church bodies occurred during the formative period of seigneurial property-making.[47] The Company

---

[45] Seigneurial concession to Robert Giffard, 1634, quoted in Trudel, *Les débuts du régime seigneurial*, 9 (my translation).

[46] Figures on clerical holdings derive from the map on the back endpaper of Harris, *The Seigneurial System*. Statistics on fief ownership are problematic because seigneuries changed hands on the long run. Also, many fiefs were granted by the state and never settled. For indications of value and degree of development of the respective fiefs, see Jacques Mathieu and Réal Brisson, "La vallée laurentienne au XVIIIe siècle: un paysage à connaître," *Cahiers de géographie du Québec* 28 (1984): 117. Additional data can be found in Fernand Ouellet, "Propriété seigneuriale et groupes sociaux dans la vallée du Saint-Laurent (1663–1840)," *Revue de l'Université d'Ottawa* 47 (1977): 159–76; Harris, ed., *Historical Atlas*, plate 51, "The Seigneuries."

[47] See Harris, *The Seigneurial System*, 42–44.

of New France favored clerical bodies partly out of pious motives. The royal charter establishing the company and awarding it feudal ownership of New France had proclaimed the purpose of the enterprise in religious terms: "Our aim in establishing these colonies is principally the glory of God in procuring the salvation of the Indians and savages."[48] In time, the Church would become more oriented toward the settler population, but when the Jesuits and the nuns received the bulk of their endowments, it was still very much a missionary enterprise, focused mainly on the conversion of the "*sauvages.*" Ecclesiastical feudal holdings were therefore partly intended to subsidize the clergy's effort to attach natives to the Lawrentian colony, even as they also provided a property framework for French settlers.

However, there were also mundane, practical reasons for a connection between clerics and seigneurial property. Religious bodies had a particularly high demand for grain, chickens, firewood and other rural produce and these were products that could be exacted from *censitaire*/colonists once the latter had become established on the land. Provisions are what a seigneurie offered to its proprietor and religious orders had a lot of mouths to feed: the priests and nuns themselves, but also those whom they cared for, and in the early years, that meant natives. The Jesuits ran a boarding school for Huron boys near Quebec, while the Ursulines housed and educated indigenous girls.[49] Until the eighteenth century, Canadian fiefs would generate very little in the way of money revenues, simply because there were no exportable staple crops comparable to the tobacco or sugar that were making tropical plantations such lucrative investments. Running landed estates and managing them with an eye to sustenance rather than profit was something religious orders had long experience with; their Old World institutional experience may have equipped them to get the most out of agrarian fiefs in a poor and underpopulated colony. The prevalence of Catholic orders in early New France distinguished that colony from other

[48] *Édits, ordonnances, déclarations et arrêts relatifs à la tenure seigneuriale*, 13, my translation. "Nous regardons dans l'établissement des dites colonies principalement la gloire de Dieu en procurant le salut des Indiens et Sauvages."

[49] Even before the Ursulines arrived in Canada, the fief of Sainte-Croix had been granted them for the express purpose of furnishing "leur nourriture et entretien et de leurs domestiques et nourriture et entretien des d. petites filles des Sauvages qui leur seront données à élever." Grant of Sainte-Croix, 15 January 1637, in *Inventaire des concessions en fief et seigneurie, fois et hommages et aveux et dénombrements conservés aux archives de la province de Québec*, 6 vols., ed. Pierre-Georges Roy (Beauceville, QC: L'Eclaireur, 1927), 5: 139. See also Natalie Zemon Davis, *Women on the Margins: Three Seventeenth-Century Lives* (Cambridge, Mass.: Harvard University Press, 1995), 63–139.

French possessions and this peculiarity goes a long way to explaining why the Company of New France turned so readily to subinfeodation.

When Louis XIV dissolved the Company of New France and took direct control over the colony in 1663, he and his chief minister, Jean-Baptiste Colbert, became convinced that the Jesuits and the Church generally had grown too dominant in Canada and they sought to curtail land grants to religious orders. Their priority was reinvigorating the colony's economy and bolstering its defenses. The accent on military concerns helped to bring the colonial nobility to the fore as the primary recipient of feudal land grants after the 1660s. Seigneurial property did not, in itself, confer nobility, though it was part of a recognized noble style of life; authorities considered it fitting and proper that any colonist of noble status should have a fief. However, the Canadian nobility was initially few in number and rarely of ancient lineage. Thus nobility and seigneurial property functioned in the early decades as distinct but associated devices for enhancing the prestige of the nascent colonial elite. All this changed after the 1660s when the population of nobles, and particularly representatives of the old "nobility of the sword," increased rapidly and government authorities felt pressure to provide them with feudal estates appropriate to their elevated station and birth.

This modest surge in noble immigration occurred in the wake of a long and costly series of wars with the Five Nations of the Iroquois League. Louis XIV had dispatched the Carignan-Salières regiment, a thousand strong, to defend the colony and he now wanted to make Canada militarily self-sufficient. Instead of rotating the regiment back to France at the conclusion of the campaign, the colonial government conceived the idea of encouraging the officers and men to stay in New France through a program of early discharges, subsidies and land grants. The plan was that soldiers would take wives and found families, and so establish a permanent reservoir of fighting capacity to be called on in future wars; at the same time, the officers and their offspring would constitute a leadership cadre for generations to come. Officers in Louis XIV's army generally either came from French noble families or, thanks to the prestige of their position, could pass themselves off as virtually noble ("vivant noblement"). So confident were the authorities in the natural bravery of the *noblesse* that they took steps to bring additional noblemen over from France.[50] These warrior-aristocrats,

---

[50] "Correspondance échangée entre la cour de France et l'intendant Talon pendant ses deux administrations dans la Nouvelle-France," *Rapport de l'archiviste de la province de Québec pour 1930–1931* (Quebec City: Rédempti Paradis, 1931), 84, 86, 100–101,

together with the veterans they once commanded in the field, were supposed to settle the rich lands of Canada's vulnerable southwestern flank, near the mouth of the Richelieu River. Intendant Jean Talon conceived his plan for the new settlements in conscious imitation of Roman models of military colonization, advising against excessive seigneurial exactions that might discourage men trying to adapt to the ways of the ax and the plow.[51] But even Talon soon came to see that nobles had to live nobly, and that meant seigneuries and revenues from the land. Thus a series of fiefs was granted to the noble ex-officers, and around their crude manor houses settled habitant *censitaires*, frequently men who had served in the seigneur's company. Because they happened to be located in a region of fertile soils, these military fiefs would eventually develop into self-sustaining, and indeed quite prosperous, estates.

Meanwhile, many of the sons and grandsons of the original noble seigneurs would make military careers for themselves in a newly founded colonial military force, the *troupes de la marine*, established in Canada in 1683, at a time when conflict with the Iroquois Five Nations was resuming and just before the long struggle with Great Britain broke out. Whereas the rank-and-file of this professional force were recruited in France, the officer corps came to be dominated by the colonial nobility. Descendants of the Carignan officers-turned-seigneurs now acquired commissions, salaries and, when stationed at interior posts, the opportunity to make lucrative side deals in the fur trade. This military-seigneurial *noblesse* came to play a leading role in New France's eighteenth-century campaigns against the British, specializing particularly in frontier raids conducted with native allies. Their style of war-making owed as much to indigenous as to European practices. There was some basis in fact for Francis Parkman's venomous characterization of the Canadian *gentilhomme*:

He was at home among his tenants, at home among the Indians, and never more at home than when, a gun in his hand and a crucifix on his breast, he took the war-path with a crew of painted savages and Frenchmen almost as wild, and pounced like a lynx from the forest on some lonely farm or outlying hamlet of New England.[52]

138–39; Louise Dechêne, *Le peuple, l'état et la guerre au Canada sous le régime français* (Montreal: Boréal, 2008), 137–39.

[51] Munro, *Seigniorial System*, 67–70; Allan Greer, *Peasant, Lord, and Merchant: Rural Society in Three Quebec Parishes, 1740–1840* (Toronto: University of Toronto Press, 1985), 6–15; Marcel Trudel, *La seigneurie de la Compagnie des Indes Occidentales, 1663–1674* (Montreal: Fides, 1997), 342–46.

[52] Francis Parkman, *The Old Régime in Canada* (London: Macmillan, 1899), 210. For less partisan treatments of this topic, see Dechêne, *Le peuple, l'état et la guerre au Canada,*

Putting it more kindly, we might observe that the colonial aristocracy (at least its male component), like the Catholic clergy earlier in the century, functioned as a collective go-between connecting the French colony and allied indigenous nations, even as it stood as a pillar of feudal land-holding.

About the time conflict with the Iroquois died down, the imperial struggle between France and Britain heated up, dominating the history of New France from the late seventeenth century to the end of the Seven Years' War. The result was a progressive militarization of Canada,[53] a tendency that had the effect of reinforcing the colony's aristocratic character. The nobility's proclivity for large families, joined to the French practice of recognizing all the legitimate sons of a nobleman as noble, created a burgeoning privileged class. An eighteenth-century visitor from France complained that "in New France there are more nobles than in all the other colonies put together."[54] Whereas Louis XIV's monarchy took steps to limit the number of nobles in France by insisting on proof of noble status, in New France his administration was much more permissive on that point. A colonial intendant explained his reluctance to investigate claims to nobility, noting that such probing would be unwise, "because of the war."[55]

Many seigneuries were either granted to, or purchased by, lay commoners: bureaucrats, merchants and even habitants. Even though purchasers owed a mutation fine, fiefs could be bought and sold. Seigneurial property, though it was considered a "noble" tenure, was not the exclusive monopoly of the privileged estates (nor was it in Old France). Yet it is clear that the clergy and the nobility predominated and that they played a crucial role, the former in the first half of the seventeenth century,

---

137–48; Evan Haefeli and Kevin Sweeney, *Captors and Captives: The 1704 French and Indian Raid on Deerfield* (Amherst: University of Massachusetts Press, 2003), 39–49; Balvay, *L'épée et la plume*, 41–42; Christian Ayne Crouch, *Nobility Lost: French and Canadian Martial Cultures, Indians, and the End of New France* (Ithaca, N.Y.: Cornell University Press, 2014), 27–31.

[53] W. J. Eccles, "The Social, Economic and Political Significance of the Military Establishment in New France," *Canadian Historical Review* 52 (March 1971): 1–22.

[54] Pierre-François-Xavier de Charlevoix, *Journal d'un voyage fait par ordre du roi dans l'Amérique Septentrionale*, ed. Pierre Berthiaume, 2 vols. (Montréal: Presses de l'Université de Montréal, 1994), 1: 401. On the colonial nobility, see Lorraine Gadoury, *La Noblesse de Nouvelle-France: familles et alliances* (Montreal: Hurtubise HMH, 1991); François-Joseph Ruggiu, "La noblesse du Canada aux XVIIe et XVIIIe siècles," *Histoire, économie et société* 27 (2008): 67–85.

[55] Havard and Vidal, *Histoire de l'Amérique française*, 365.

the latter in the second half, in deepening the feudal nature of tenure in Canada. France could not have established its vast and amorphous imperial space across the middle of North America without the liaison activities of missionaries and military officers (as well as fur traders) connecting the French and the indigenous spheres. Clergy and nobility were centrally involved in the creation and maintenance of this empire of alliances, along with the indigenous nations with whom they cultivated close relations. The prominence of the two privileged orders in constructing New France's broad imperial space largely accounts for the exceptional profusion of fiefs in New France seigneurialism. Similarly, the prestige and influence of the noble officers, joined with the continuing power of the Church, made it difficult for reforming officials to follow metropolitan instructions when the latter called for severe limitations on seigneurial exactions.

SEIGNEURS AND HABITANTS

As the peri-urban zone around the town of Quebec, where the company had granted plots directly, filled up and as rural fiefs were established all up and down the St. Lawrence Valley, it became impossible for new colonists and their Canadian-born offspring to procure land except as a *roture* in someone's seigneurie. Custom, backed by colonial and imperial legislation, required a seigneur to grant a farm-sized piece of land to any genuine settler who asked for it, free of any initial purchase price. By occupying land within a seigneurie, a settler became, as far as tenure relations are concerned, the seigneur's "*censitaire*," required by law to pay the annual *cens*; equally automatically, the land would henceforth be subject to *lods et ventes*, meaning that, if the *censitaire* sold it to anyone outside his direct lineage, the buyer would owe the seigneur one-twelfth of the price (land and improvements included). Further restrictions, such as the *banalité* (obligation to grind grain at the seigneurial mill), connected to the seigneur's judicial authority, were also prescribed by the Custom of Paris and existed independent of any explicit agreement between seigneur and *censitaire*. However, other tenure conditions and exactions could be added, by contractual agreement, to the baseline conditions legally applicable to all *censive* holdings.

The tenure regime that emerged in New France was, in fact, heavily dependent on written documents in contractual form. Grants to settlers were supposed to be recorded in a "concession deed," a notarized document that set out the conditions of tenure; normally, the seigneur received one copy, the settler got a second copy, and the notary retained a third. A proper survey was also supposed to be one of the formalities that accompanied the grant and that generated another piece of property documentation. The *censitaire* was generally responsible for the notary's and the surveyor's charges. The concession deed served the habitant as a title deed, useful when the land was sold or inherited, or when it became the subject of a legal dispute. Seigneurs came to like concession deeds for their own reasons: they allowed supplementary charges and tenure conditions to be added to those specified in the law. Finally, concession deeds were also valued by the colonial state, which ordered seigneurs to insert clauses requiring grantees to occupy and develop their *rotures* (*"tenir feu et lieu"*) within a year or forfeit these for noncompliance; another mandatory clause reserved oak and pine trees for the use of naval shipyards. Along with the seigneur's estate roll (*papier terrier*), which served as a kind of local land registry, concession deeds formed a crucial portion of New France's archive of property.

Sometimes this document was known as a "grant" (*concession*), sometimes as a *"bail à cens"* (a phrase containing the word "lease") and sometimes as a "contract": the varying vocabulary connected with deeds reflects the ambiguous nature of *censive* tenure. These documents bore some similarities to a lease of land from a landlord, except that they provided for tenure in perpetuity and on unchanging terms; *censitaires* enjoyed basic security of tenure and could not normally be evicted. In this respect, their situation was quite different from that of leaseholders in England or tenant-farmers in colonial New York and New England. Regardless of inflation or other economic changes, the seigneur could never (at least in theory) change the level of *cens et rentes*, even as the *roture* was inherited, sold or subdivided over the years. The title deed was a "contract" in that both parties voluntarily signed it and formally agreed to its provisions. The notionally contractual aspect of the title allowed the seigneur to add an annual rent on top of the token *cens*; this rent, again invariable in perpetuity, was typically expressed as a combination of money, wheat or other produce; *censitaires* also signed on for additional charges for the right to cut hay on the commons, fish in the river and whatever else the document specified. Settlers accepted these conditions since there was no other way to procure title. Moreover, since the usual practice was to settle on the strength of an informal location ticket, habitants found themselves subject to tenure terms that were spelled out only long after they had invested substantial labor and capital into a piece of seigneurial land.

In some contexts, *censitaires* were referred to as "tenants" or "vassals" since they held land from a landlord and paid rent; on other occasions they were known as "proprietors," for they enjoyed essentially unlimited security of tenure. Socially (as opposed to tenancy status), agricultural settlers became known as "habitants," a seemingly neutral term, but one that implied the civic status of landed proprietor. "Habitant" became the designation for plantation owners in the French West Indies, whereas in Canada it carried some of the connotations of "peasant." Lawyers in *ancien régime* France, trying to square the definitive categories of Roman law with the ambiguous realities bequeathed to the country by medieval feudalism, argued over whether the seigneur or the *censitaire* was the true owner of a given tract, and historians continue to debate the issue.[56] This may be a false issue, for surely the point is that the attributes of proprietorship remained fragmented and overlapping in the seventeenth century.

Though the terms for each *roture* were set forever at the time of granting, the wording of concession deeds evolved over time, meaning that even within a given seigneurie, lands distributed in 1750 would have conditions attached to them different from those granted a century earlier. The amount of rent attached to the minuscule annual *cens* tended to be substantially greater in later concession deeds than in earlier ones. Seventeenth-century concessions typically specified a rate proportional to the land's river frontage: one *livre* plus a live capon or a barrel of salted eels for every linear *arpent* of land (see Chapter 9 on units of measure). Concession deeds became more elaborate over time, with clauses appearing regarding fishing rights, timber reserves, common pasture charges and other reserves, monopolies and lucrative charges.

By the early eighteenth century, the charges for *censive* land were no longer trivial. Over time, seigneurs added new charges, set rents at ever-higher rates on new concessions and enforced their prerogatives and collected their dues with more and more rigor.[57] Government officials

---

[56] On the *censitaire* as proprietor, see Bourjon, *Le droit commun de la France et la Coutume de Paris*, 1: 292. On the history and historiography of proprietorship in pre-revolutionary France, see Gérard Béaur, *Histoire agraire de la france au XVIIIe siècle: inerties et changements dans les campagnes françaises entre 1715 et 1815* (Paris: Sedes, 2000), 17–21; Gérard Béaur, "Les rapports de propriété en France sous l'ancien régime," in *Ruralité française et britannique, XIIIe-XXe siècles: approches comparées. Actes du colloque franco-britannique du Mans, 12–14 Septembre 2002*, ed. Nicole Vivier (Rennes: Presses universitaires de Rennes, 2005), 187–200.

[57] The general increase in exactions has been examined in detail in several monographs: Dechêne, "L'évolution," 149–73; Greer, *Peasant, Lord and Merchant*, 122–25; Sylvie

and popular opinion insisted that exactions should remain moderate and that no seigneur could demand more than his neighbors, and so increases often took place through subterfuge: grain substituted for money rents at a time when food prices were rising; French currency demanded for rents once set in less valuable colonial currency; land measured in terms of area rather than frontage, but with a rate of conversion skewed in the seigneur's favor. Though there were no lawyers in New France, Canadian seigneurs, especially members of transatlantic religious orders, had access to the burgeoning French legal literature on how to use fine points of law to get enhanced revenues from rural estates.[58] A parallel movement to tighten the screws on the Early Modern French peasantry has been labeled a "seigneurial reaction."[59] Conditioned by demographic and economic circumstances and shaped by evolving configurations of power, this incremental ratcheting up of feudal exactions had the effect of transforming settler tenure in New France from an arrangement almost indistinguishable from freehold in its practical effects to one more closely resembling the situation of European peasants of the time. Louise Dechêne looked closely at the evolution of the seigneurial regime in the Montreal region between 1642 and 1730 and concluded:

In the beginning, seigneurial power was paternal and timid. Its demands mirrored the difficult environment ... The authorities had no need to intervene as the seigneurs quite on their own adapted to the prevailing circumstances: nothing could be extracted from those [the habitants] who had nothing ... But as the population grew and as more land was cleared, the regime looked for ways to benefit from all the rights conferred by the Custom [of Paris], while adding other

Dépatie, Mario Lalancette and Christian Dessureault, *Contributions á l'étude du régime seigneurial canadien* (Montreal: Hurtubise HMH, 1987), passim.

[58] Religious orders, notaries and some lay seigneurs owned legal textbooks that would have kept them abreast of the work of French *feudistes*. See Antonio Drolet, "La bibliothèque du collège des Jésuites," *Revue d'histoire de l'Amérique française* 14 (March 1961): 487–544; Mario Robert, "Le livre et la lecture dans la noblesse canadienne 1670–1764," *Revue d'histoire de l'Amérique française* 56 (2002): 19.

[59] Once thought to be a phenomenon of the second half of the eighteenth century, the trend to find new ways to extract revenues from the peasantry (and to resurrect ancient exactions) is now seen as a prevalent tendency from the sixteenth century to the Revolution. Marc Bloch, *French Rural History: An Essay on Its Basic Characteristics*, trans. Janet Sondheimer (Berkeley: University of California Press, 1966), 126–49; Béaur, *Histoire agraire de la France au XVIIIe siècle*, 229–33; David Parker, "Absolutism, Feudalism and Property Rights in the France of Louis XIV," *Past & Present*, no. 179 (2003): 60–96; Guy Lemarchand, *Paysans et seigneurs en Europe: une histoire comparée, XVIe-XIXe siècle* (Rennes: Presses de l'Université de Rennes, 2011), 193–95.

exactions of its own devising ... A century later, the seigneurie had become more rigid, more invasive; it had no reason to envy the French seigneurie.[60]

Why did the habitants tolerate these escalating exactions? A reforming intendant explained in a 1707 memorandum that seigneurs habitually distributed lands on the basis of a verbal assurance or an informal "ticket" that did not enumerate the conditions of tenure; the concession deed only made its appearance some years later. "Great abuses result: habitants who had worked [the land] without a valid title are subjected to very heavy rents and dues; since the seigneurs would only give them contracts on these conditions, they are obliged to accept them for otherwise they would lose all their [land clearing] efforts."[61] Habitants were rather vulnerable to such schemes, if only because most were illiterate. Moreover, the isolation of New France was such that settlers did not have the option, open to their counterparts in the English colonies, of seeking land in an adjacent colony under better tenure conditions. There were no violent peasant uprisings in New France, largely because nonseigneurial charges – the main cause of agrarian revolts in old France – were so low: tithes consumed only a moderate one-twenty-sixth of harvests and direct state taxation was nonexistent. Settlers were not passive victims, however. They took grasping seigneurs to court; they sometimes openly refused excessive charges and, more commonly, they evaded, avoided and delayed payment, much to the frustration of the seigneurs.

More relevant to the themes of this book than the purely economic aspects of seigneurial tenure are the complicated ways in which property was configured in the French settler sphere. Every fief was in fact composed of varying proportions of three distinct types of land: the demesne; the *censive*, meaning the expanding zone that had been granted out as *rotures* to *censitaires*; and the unconceded domain, which is to say the remaining part of the fief's territory. All these areas "belonged to" the

---

[60] Dechêne, "L'évolution," 172 (my translation). "Dans les commencements, le pouvoir seigneurial est paternel et timide. Ses exigences sont à l'inverse des difficultés ... Les autorités n'ont pas à intervenir car d'eux-memes les seigneurs se plient aux circonstances: on ne peut rien exiger de ceux qui n'ont rien ... Mais à mesure que le peuplement et la mise en valeur progressent, le régime cherche à tirer parti de tous les droits conférés par la coutume, à leur ajouter quelques autres de son crû ... Au bout d'un siècle, la seigneurie est devenue plus rigide, plus envahissante; elle n'a rien à envier à la seigneurie française ..."

[61] Memoir of Jacques Raudot, 10 November 1707, in *Documents Relating to the Seigniorial Tenure in Canada, 1598–1854*, ed. William Bennett Munro (Toronto: Champlain Society, 1908), 73 (my translation; notwithstanding the title of this collection, the documents are published in the original French).

seigneur, but in quite different ways. Only the demesne was fully under the seigneur's control. Within the *censive*, he or she shared the attributes of property with the *censitaires*, while land in the unconceded domain was the seigneur's only in highly qualified ways. He could not sell any part of it, nor could he rent it out, as a New York landlord or a Dutch patroon could, on a limited-term lease. He had legal grounds for preventing others from cutting timber on "his" unconceded domain, but he did not have the right to harvest timber there himself. Whether or not he could exercise control over hunting and fishing in this area was unclear; certainly, he possessed no legal means of ejecting any natives who might be living and hunting there. Property *en fief* was distinct from *censive* property in a variety of ways, including the rules of inheritance: whereas the latter was to be divided equally among legitimate heirs, the former was subject to a form of modified primogeniture designed to keep estates intact.

Through their privileged access to feudal property, the nobility and the clergy had played a central part in making the colonized portion of New France into a land of fiefs, and through their aggressive pursuit of revenue they had, by the eighteenth century, made the seigneurie a significant institution for extracting revenue from the emergent Canadian peasantry. Questions remain about the role of the French imperial state in this process of feudal property formation. Louis XIV and his minister Colbert were actually quite ambivalent about the unusual prominence of the first and second estates in New France and about the prevalence of feudal property. Of course, the king and his advisers were hardly opposed to the clergy and the *noblesse* per se: it was the fact that these privileged orders had an automatic right to preferment and assistance that made them such a troublesome and expensive presence. In another context, Colbert had observed that "families can only keep up their position if they are backed by substantial properties in land";[62] how then could the Canadian nobility be denied their fiefs?

Insofar as the French state could be said to have had a policy on colonial land tenure, it was never consistently pro-feudal, particularly after Louis XIV took charge of the monarchy. At several points, colonial authorities were urged to consider a commutation from seigneurial to allodial tenure.[63]

---

[62] Quoted in Bloch, *French Rural History*, 138.
[63] In establishing the Compagnie de l'Occident in 1664, the Crown turned over to that body all feudal rights owned by the now-defunct Company of New France, but the edict added an option: "unless the company is inclined to commute [this tenure] for the relief of the said habitants" ("si ce n'est que la compagnie trouve à propos de les commuer en autres droits pour le soulagement des dits habitants"). *Édits, ordonnances, déclarations et arrêts*

Whereas the rulers of the Spanish empire opposed feudal tendencies out of concerns over the potential defiance of the colonial elite, as well as over the latter's tendency to oppress Indians, the Bourbon masters of New France worried about obstacles to the growth of a settler population and to the development of the colony's economy. Accordingly, they issued innumerable edicts threatening to rescind seigneurial grants for failure to settle and develop the lands; likewise, seigneurs were required to repossess lots that were neglected by their *censitaires*.[64] The colonial minister was also insistent that rents and other feudal charges be kept at a minimum so as not to oppress or discourage settlers. But even as the king's officials called for allodial tenure, more seigneuries were being granted in New France; and while Versailles insisted feudal charges stay low and stable, Quebec was allowing them to rise steadily. The explanation may lie in the fact that colonial officials such as the governor and the intendant, though not usually seigneurial proprietors themselves, were surrounded by a Canadian elite that were. Effective political management often required them to keep the colonial seigneurs happy and to use fiefs as patronage rewards.[65] More generally a basic *ancien régime* respect for feudal property rights sometimes battled with the impulse to promote agrarian development.[66]

NATIVES AND SEIGNEURIALISM

In a regime of overlapping claims to land, one in which property rights were fragmented and variable in their intensity, feudal property did not

---

relatifs à la tenure seigneuriale, 17. Years later Louis XIV declared, "It would be desirable that all the lands in New France should be *en roture*," meaning essentially allodial tenure, with no fiefs. ("Il serait à souhaiter que toutes les terres de la Nouvelle-France fussent en roture.") Quoted in Dechêne, "L'évolution," 145.

[64] For data on seigneurs' seizure of *rotures* for nonsettlement, see Jacques Mathieu, "Les réunions de terres au domaine du seigneur 1730–1759," in *Sociétés villageoises et rapports villes-campagnes au Québec et dans la France de l'ouest, XVIIe–XXe siècles*, ed. François Lebrun and Normand Séguin (Trois-Rivières, Quebec: Université du Québec à Trois-Rivières, 1987), 79–100. The basic policy that treated land grants as contingent on development was common to all American colonial empires; uncertain enforcement of such rules was equally universal.

[65] Dechêne, "L'évolution," 146–48.

[66] Similar tensions were at the heart of agrarian politics in *ancien régime* France. On repeated occasions, the Bourbon monarchy attempted to limit seigneurial exactions, mainly in the interests of "protecting" the peasantry, the better to subject it to royal taxation. Yet, time and again, enforcement proved ineffectual, partly because the monarchy and its agents were themselves so deeply implicated in feudal/seigneurial property relations. Gallet, *Seigneurs et paysans en France, 1600–1793*, 167–91.

necessarily nullify native property. The Company and then the government of New France granted fiefs to seigneurs without reference to any prior indigenous claims to the land; likewise, seigneurs granted *rotures* to settlers with documents that made no mention of what would come to be known as "aboriginal title." This does not mean that the French, any more than the Spanish and English, were indifferent to indigenous occupation and territorial possession. To the contrary: they constructed a vast inland empire on the basis of alliances that incorporated sovereign indigenous proprietors; when officers wanted to build a fort in the *pays d'en haut*, they normally asked permission and frequently paid a price.[67] Moreover, in the Canadian settlements, colonial authorities were warned to avoid interfering with native-occupied lands. Royal instructions to the governor of New France in 1665 urged him to ensure that colonists "treat the natives with kindness, justice and fairness"; above all, "the lands which they inhabit are not to be usurped on the pretext that these are better or more convenient for the French."[68] This was fairly standard imperial policy, comparable to the pious declarations emanating from the centers of the Spanish and British empires. What distinguished French procedures of property-making from those of the English was the fact that the latter sought exclusive rights, while the former imposed layers of partial and limited claims. The colonists of New England accorded formal recognition to native property in order to eliminate it and institute settler property in its place, but a New France seigneur had no need to extinguish prior indigenous property in order to enjoy the rights of a feudal proprietor within his estate. This divergence has given rise to chronic misunderstanding: when historians take British procedures of treaty and purchase as the universal norm, and when they privilege ideas and "policies" over actual behavior, the French approach to native property appears somehow deviant and retrograde.[69]

---

[67] See, for example, W. J. Eccles, *Essays on New France* (Toronto: Oxford University Press, 1987), 169; Denys Delâge and Jean-Pierre Sawaya, *Les traités des Sept-Feux avec les Britanniques: droits et pièges d'un héritage colonial au Québec* (Montréal: Septentrion, 2001), 230.

[68] Quoted in Michel Morin, *L'usurpation de la souveraineté autochtone: le cas des peuples de la Nouvelle-France et des colonies anglaises de l'Amérique du nord* (Montreal: Editions Boréal, 1997), 71 (my translation).

[69] See, for example, Alain Beaulieu, "The Acquisition of Aboriginal Land in Canada: The Genealogy of an Ambivalent System (1600–1867)," in *Empire by Treaty: Negotiating European Expansion, 1600–1900*, ed. Saliha Belmessous (New York: Oxford University Press, 2015), 105–7.

On the whole, Innu and Algonquins continued to occupy, move through and exploit the resources of the St. Lawrence Lowlands land-scape, even as territories were allocated to the French as seigneuries. No one remarked on this fact, since there was no presumption that feudal estates were incompatible with native property; however, we do get some glimpses in the colonial records of the coexistence of seigneuries and native hunting and gathering territories. On the eighteenth-century frontier of settlement along the Chaudière River, an Abenaki village sat right beside the seigneurial manor of St. Joseph, and villagers hunted over the lands of the seigneurie with no objection on the part of the seigneur. Similarly, indications surface of native hunting, fishing and foraging on the unconceded domains of seigneuries near "mission" settlements of Lorette, Oka and St-François. Even though some seigneurs zealously defended their hunting and fishing rights where French *censitaires* were concerned, they would have had no legal recourse against natives.[70]

Of course, where land or water was wanted for colonists' immediate purposes, native control could be in jeopardy, as the Innu of Kâ Mihkwâwahkâšič discovered in the 1640s when the governor's tenants tried to expel them from their eel-fishing sites (see Chapter 3). As in New Spain, the colonial regime of New France, though committed in principle to respecting indigenous property, could not always prevent private inter-ests – including those of the highest officials in the land – from undermin-ing that ideal through their encroachments on native space. Different protective measures were taken in an effort to guard indigenous lands from colonists' incursions. At Sillery, the Jesuits, backed by the royal family, secured the grant of a fief in favor of the Christian Innu. As we saw in Chapter 3, this measure recognizing their property did not, in the end, protect the Innu from dispossession. Moreover, the experiment in granting feudal estates directly to natives ended in the late 1660s, as the surviving Innu were drifting away from Sillery. It was at this time that New France was transferred from the Company of New France to the Compagnie des Indes occidentales, and the new colonial proprietors were

---

[70] On this general point, see Havard and Vidal, *Histoire de l'Amérique Française*, 190. For specific examples, see Brian Young, *Patrician Families and the Making of Quebec: The Taschereaus and McCords* (Montreal and Kingston: McGill-Queen's University Press, 2014), 35; Pierre-Georges Roy, *Inventaire des concessions en fief et seigneurie, fois et hommages et aveux et dénombrements conservés aux archives de la province de Québec*, 6 vols. (Beauceville, QC: L'Eclaireur, 1927), 5: 290; Colin Coates, *The Metamorphoses of Landscape and Community in Early Quebec* (Montreal: McGill-Queen's University Press, 2000), 11.

reviewing the titles of all seigneuries. An official report recommended the transfer of Sillery to direct Jesuit ownership on the grounds that it was "ridiculous that savages should be seigneurs."[71]

Yet the fief form remained the favored legal device for formalizing indigenous property within the predominantly French zone along the St. Lawrence. Since the Hurons, Iroquois and Abenaki who arrived in the second half of the seventeenth century were seen as immigrants, the French found it less awkward to "give" them land than was the case with the Innu and Algonquin, whose preexisting property rights simply needed to be "protected." The fief of Sault St-Louis was granted to the Jesuits for the benefit of the Christian Iroquois of Kahnawake in 1680, while another group of Iroquois and Algonquins later received the seigneurie of Deux-Montagnes (Oka) under Sulpician auspices. These seigneurial grants, unlike routine feudal grants, were discussed and authorized from Versailles; since they concerned indigenous allies rather than French settlers, these territorial arrangements fell mainly under the heading of diplomacy and military security in the eyes of imperial authorities. It was not at all clear whether the missionaries named as titular seigneurs in these grants were anything more than trustees for the natives whom the Crown saw as the beneficiaries of the grants. In a different tenurial arrangement with similar purposes, land was allocated in the early 1700s to Abenakis and Sokokis displaced by warfare from their homes in New England. Settling in an area largely neglected by French settlers that lay south of the St. Lawrence near Three Rivers, they found themselves within the confines of the seigneuries of Bécancour and St-François. No one objected; to the contrary. The governor of New France, with the agreement of the seigneur of St-François (happy to gain favored access to the trade in furs with the Abenakis), formally ceded a large tract to the Abenakis and Sokokis (the Jesuits in this case were named as trustees, though they were not seigneurs).[72] As was the case in Sault St-Louis and Deux-Montagnes, the tenure under which the natives would hold these lands was not spelled out in the documents; the omission of all the clauses setting out obligations, dues and restrictions, which were completely

---

[71] "Estat de ce qu'il plaise à messieurs de la compagnie des indes occidentalles regler et faire ensuitte des ordonnances, incluses en leur papier terrier composé par assises tenues par le lieutenant general en leur justice le Sieur Chartier," 1667, ANOM, C11E, vol. 11: fol. 12.

[72] David Gilles, "La souplesse et les limites du régime juridique seigneurial colonial: les concessions aux Abénaquis durant le régime français," in *Nouveaux regards en histoire seigneuriale*, ed. Benoît Grenier and Michel Morissette (Quebec City: Septentrion, 2016), 49–58.

standard at the time in grants to white settlers, signals the peculiar nature of indigenous land tenure within New France's seigneurial zone.

Though the colonial regime drew on the legal language of feudalism to formalize title to the indigenous enclaves of Canada (no doubt because the fief had become the norm in the St. Lawrence Valley), these native villages were not really seigneurial. Seigneurs, whether lay or religious, never treated native residents as *censitaires*. They collected no *cens* or other charges for the use of the land or access to the water. A seigneurie such as Sault St-Louis was not broken down into individual *rotures*; instead, natives occupied the entire tract as a self-regulating community, and particular allocations to Iroquois women had nothing to do with French tenure and were invisible to the legal seigneur. A kind of gazetteer of the Laurentian settlements prepared by a government engineer/geographer in 1712 offered the following description of "the mission of Sault St-Louis," where "Indians from the five Iroquois nations are settled":

These nations are extremely proud. They have chiefs who lead them, although they are accustomed to follow their caprices, since there is no subordination among the Indians. The women here are devout ... Across the full extent of this land grant there are many large trees of all species. The Indians have clearings along the St Lawrence where they plant corn, beans, squash, melons and sunflowers. They sell the surplus of their harvests in Montreal. In addition, they make a quantity of maple sugar and gather grasses [for basketry], which they also sell in the town. Ordinarily, it is the women who do the agricultural work, while the men devote themselves to hunting, fishing and war. Some time ago, they opened up a commercial connection with the English at Orange [Albany, N.Y.], where they take their furs and then bring back textiles and other merchandise that they sell from their homes and at Montreal. The authorities have not been able to make them obey the law.[73]

Iroquois in their way of life, the residents of Kahnawake defied all attempts to subject them to colonial rule and jurisdiction. By the same token, it seems clear that they considered their territory not a "mission" or a seigneurie, but a homeland.

We cannot know the exact content of the discussions and negotiations that led to the Hurons, Iroquois and Abenaki coming into possession of substantial tracts within the seigneurial heartland of Canada, but we have every indication that they came away from these talks with the understanding that these territories were fully theirs, with rights of

---

[73] Gédéon de Catalogne, "Report on the Seigniories and Settlements in the Districts of Québec, Three Rivers, and Montreal," 7 November 1712, in Munro, ed., *Documents Relating to the Seigniorial Tenure in Canada*, 108 (my translation).

property and jurisdiction. Erecting villages and clearing fields, they gave every signal that they understood the lands to be for their use, and that they viewed French missionaries and government officials as allies, not dictators or landlords. French officialdom would maintain the fiction that the *"sauvages domiciliés"* occupied lands held from the Crown and subject to the management of the missionary orders; after the British conquest, when tenurial ambiguity was no longer in fashion, lawyers would debate the question of whether such territories belonged ultimately to the natives or to the missionaries. For the Hurons, Iroquois and Abenakis, however, there was never any doubt. For them, arcane legal documents to which they had no access did not take precedence over the arrangements they had negotiated when they agreed, at French urgings, to make their residence close to the colonists.

Much about these land transactions and the divergent interpretations of the native and European parties involved call to mind the situation of English colonists arriving in America, believing that earlier explorations and discoveries, as well as a royal charter, authorized them to settle in the country. Even if they thought the land was, in a sense, already theirs, they frequently accepted the need to negotiate with indigenous authorities to secure permission to establish their homes in a given location. Similarly, native colonists coming to establish villages in Canada seem to have felt basically entitled to claim lands there, though they appeared willing to adapt, at least partially, to French expectations. The object, in both these cases of colonization, English among natives and natives among French, was to avoid conflict and cultivate a mutually beneficial relationship. As a general rule, indigenous people seeking to live in the midst of the French settlements were prepared to cement the connection by adhering to a version of Catholic Christianity and by acknowledging the king and his representative in New France as their "father." Thanks to Richard White, we know that they did not attach the same meaning to these gestures as the French did, and we know further that what the colonizers chose to interpret as "submission" did not entail, for the natives involved, a surrender of independence or an acceptance of colonial jurisdiction.[74] Similarly, where land is concerned, the Iroquois considered Kahnawake entirely theirs notwithstanding the letters patent by which the Jesuits claimed to hold that land *en fief*.

[74] White, *Middle Ground*.

Whereas natives followed their own tenure forms on the territories they held within the Lawrentian settlements, they were not welcome to take up lands in the seigneuries established for French habitants. There were exceptions to this rule, but the exceptions often underlined the basic principle that *censive* tenure was intended for French settlers, not for indigenous people. In one case, Hurons from the Jesuit mission of Lorette cleared new fields in a forested area near their village (it was the custom of Iroquoian cultivators to relocate their fields periodically) that turned out to be outside the bounds of their seigneurie, and within the unconceded domain of the Gaudarville fief. When this was brought to the attention of the governor, he decreed that they could make use of the land they had brought into cultivation for twelve years. At the end of that period (about the length of a typical Huron agricultural occupation), they would have to return it to the seigneur, "unless the said Indians would rather pay rent for the [additional] time they wish to continue making use of it, as if it were granted to French people."[75] Another anomalous case, equally telling in its implications, appears among the concession deeds of the Jesuit seigneurie of St. Gabriel. In a standard eighteenth-century concession deed enumerating the various *cens, lods et ventes*, rents, restrictions and monopolies, the Jesuits granted a small *roture* to a man named "Jean Langlois, *sauvage* [i.e., Indian]." What distinguishes this deed from hundreds of others of the type is a brief clause inserted at the end: "All the clauses, charges and conditions above are for the French in case the said grantee should transfer to them the rights to this concession; and insofar as it remains his and his Indian heirs and devisees, they will only be required to pay, as total seigneurial *cens et rentes*, two partridges each year."[76]

[75] Grant by Louis de Buade and Jean Bochard to Hurons of Lorette, 5 December 1696, in *Pièces et documents relatifs à la tenure seigneuriale* (Quebec City: E. R. Fréchette, 1852), 428–29. On this particular case, see also Roy, *Inventaire des concessions en fief et seigneurie*, 5: 296; Benoît Grenier, *Marie-Catherine Peuvret, 1667–1739: Veuve et seigneuresse en Nouvelle-France* (Sillery, Québec: Septentrion, 2005), 128, 218. On the general question of native ineligibility for grants *en censive*, see Jean-Philippe Garneau, "Réflexions sur la régulation juridique du régime seigneurial canadien," in *Le régime seigneurial au Québec 150 ans après. Bilans et perspectives de recherches à l'occasion de la commémoration du 150e anniversaire de l'abolition du régime seigneurial*, ed. Alain Laberge and Benoît Grenier (Quebec: Centre interuniversitaire d'études québécoises, 2009), 75.

[76] "Acte de concession d'une terre située dans la seigneurie Saint-Gabriel, par les révérends pères jésuites à Jean Langlois sauvage," notary Pinguet, 15 September 1745, Bibliothèque et Archives nationales du Québec (hereafter BANQ), E21, S64, SS5, SSS6, D381.

As in New Spain, land tenure in New France served to mark out zones and differentiate peoples, dividing colonists from aboriginals. But whereas Indian land in Spanish America was subject to tribute, native lands within the Canadian colony were largely (give or take a partridge or two) exempt from the exactions that burdened settlers. The exact nature of native tenure was not spelled out, presumably since it was considered prior to and largely independent of the colonial tenure regime, notwithstanding the fact that indigenous lands coincided with missionary feudal pretensions. Similarly, native communities were effectively exempt from French jurisdiction, in spite of their location in the heart of the colony. Comparisons with Mexican pueblos again come to mind, though in the Canadian case there was nothing like the quasi-colonial magistracy and native *cabildo*; instead, communities managed themselves according to their own customs and institutions. The missionary fiefs of the Jesuits and Sulpicians enfolded natives within the colonial property regime, even as they left them a wide margin of political and proprietorial autonomy. The layered qualities of feudal tenure are on display here, and so are the inconsistencies and awkward improvisations generally associated with colonialism.

Recognizing aboriginal property, and at the same time trying to place it within a feudal framework, the French strove to incorporate native communities into the Laurentian colony. The effort may be seen as a more intensive version of the incorporative imperial strategy that sought to fashion a New France of continental dimensions out of independent indigenous territories. From time to time, there were attempts to institute seigneuries in the native-dominated *pays d'en haut*, but they generally came to naught as a result of native resistance.[77] One particularly ambitious attempt to regulate land and people through feudal tenures occurred at Detroit, where the French worked to assemble the indigenous nations of the Great Lakes in 1701. Antoine La Mothe Cadillac was the driving force behind this project, which involved a fort and a contingent of French-Canadian settlers, as well as several new indigenous villages. With the backing of New France's government, Cadillac set himself up as

---

[77] On an early attempt to establish a Jesuit seigneurie in the land of the Onondaga Iroquois, see ANOM, C11E, vol. 11: fol. 9–9v, "Concession aux Jésuites d'une seigneurie au pays des Iroquois supérieurs dits Onnontgeronons," 12 April 1656. On Robert Cavalier de la Salle's short-lived feudal empire on the upper Mississippi, see Havard, *Empire et métissages*, 85–87. French seigneuries on the shores of Lake Champlain had to be abandoned, in part because of Mohawk objections. Morin, *L'usurpation de la souveraineté autochtone*, 73–74.

seigneur and began allocating lands both to colonists and to natives. There was no question of demanding rents from the latter; rather, it was a matter of exerting authority and regulation. As Cadillac proudly reported to the minister in charge of colonies, he solemnly and publicly marked out a site for the Hurons to build their village and clear their fields, another place for the Ottawas, a third for the Miamis, etc. "I placed all the nations in the position of having to ask me for lands and for permission to settle." This scene of the king's loyal vassal literally putting indigenous tribes in their place may have flattered the minister's sense of the proper imperial order of things, but the inevitable sequel quickly deflated imperial pretentions. The natives essentially ignored Cadillac's instructions and set up their villages where they judged best, leaving the post commander vainly struggling to assert his authority as seigneur. In one memorable confrontation with a Huron leader whom the French called "Quarante Sols," Cadillac shouted, "This land belongs to me." Quarante Sols shot back, "This land is not yours, it is ours, and we will depart if we wish and go wherever we please."[78] So much for the project of using fiefs to bind western natives into the French orbit.

It is worth lingering over the angry exchange between Cadillac and his Huron counterpart. At first glance it resembles countless confrontations on the Anglo-American frontier between natives and colonizers fighting for control over territory: "This land is mine," asserts the settler; "No, it is mine," replies the native. But notice that in this case the struggle does not revolve around exclusive control over land and resources; it is mostly a question of freedom and authority. The natives are not vowing to stay and defend ancestral hunting, fishing or planting territories: they are instead threatening to go away. Leaving is what Anglo-American frontiersmen typically wanted indigenous people to do, but Cadillac is intent on attracting and retaining them. Like the Jesuits on their St. Lawrence missions, his greatest fear is that natives will simply walk away. In this respect, the French strategy of empire building and property making has more in common with that of the Spanish and Portuguese on the edges of their respective colonial establishments in South America.[79] In New France, fiefs were to incorporate natives, not to displace them; and in this they were not always successful. Indigenous resistance ensured that

---

[78] Quoted in Havard, *Empire et métissage*, 487.
[79] See David J. Weber, *Bárbaros: Spaniards and Their Savages in the Age of Enlightenment* (New Haven, Conn.: Yale University Press, 2005), 205–20; Herzog, *Frontiers of Possession*, 70–133.

the feudal apparatus of colonial power would wither and die beyond the confines of the St. Lawrence Valley. The effect was to reinforce a boundary dividing colonized space dominated by seigneuries (Canada) from a surrounding imperial space that would remain essentially free of fiefs.

Even natives who had moved to the Laurentian Lowlands and closely aligned themselves with the French were far from accepting the rigors of seigneurial tenure. If natives were never charged the *cens* and other seigneurial charges (much less the tribute and labor service demanded of the colonized natives of New Spain), it was because seigneurs, missionaries and officials knew they would not tolerate them. Resident natives were vigilant in defending their lands and their liberties, repeatedly warding off attempts by the colonial courts to subject them to the laws and regulations that applied to French colonists. However, they were not always successful in preventing settler encroachments on their territories. This became a problem in the second quarter of the eighteenth century when the expansion of the habitant population put pressure on lands with agricultural potential that were situated close to colonial centers. In the vicinity of Montreal, land hunger focused particularly on the Iroquois territories that fell under the legal auspices of the Jesuit and Sulpician orders.

At a time when rates of seigneurial rent for newly granted *rotures* were on the rise, ecclesiastical seigneurs had difficulty resisting the temptation to grant out to habitants portions of the land originally set aside for natives. The fact that they were legally inscribed as seigneurs, they claimed, entitled them to dispose of lots as they saw fit; and when it was objected that the government had granted them seigneuries such as Sault St-Louis in trust for the natives who resided there, they insisted that the seigneurial revenues they collected from French-Canadian settlers would be dedicated to the support of their mission work. The different agricultural customs of natives and settlers made this reallocation of land from one to the other seem perfectly appropriate from the missionaries' point of view: Iroquoian peoples practiced swidden agriculture, which entailed the intensive cultivation of maize for one or two decades, at which point fields would be left on a very long fallow and the village would relocate to newly cleared forest. However, land that would no longer support indigenous hoe cultivation was perfectly suitable for the use of settlers equipped with plows; it was indeed premium land since the natives had already cut down the trees. Thus, missionary-seigneurs began to regrant the sites of "abandoned" native fields to rent-paying settler-*censitaires*. The Sulpicians had an especially lucrative approach: they sponsored an Iroquois village on the side of the mountain above Montreal and declared that the land it occupied was part of their seigneurial demesne. When the village relocated to Sault-au-Récollet on the north side of the island of Montreal in 1698, they were able to *sell* the recently vacated village site, charging settlers an initial price (strictly forbidden under Canadian land law, except where the property was developed and therefore part of the seigneur's demesne) on top of the usual yearly seigneurial dues. Twenty years later, it was time for the villagers to move once again, and the Sulpicians used their plight to persuade the government to grant them a new seigneurie (Deux-Montagnes) of valuable land on the Ottawa River. Meanwhile, they declared the Sault-au-Récollet site a developed part of their demesne and sold it off to habitants. The pattern continued on Deux-Montagnes, to the profit of the religious order and at the expense of the natives for whose benefit the new seigneurie had supposedly been granted.[80]

Meanwhile, the Jesuits were also nibbling away at native lands, transforming portions of "their" fiefs into settler *rotures*. Substantial portions of Kahnawake/Sault St-Louis were turned over to habitants in the 1720s and 1730s. Huron lands in Lorette were similarly alienated; and in 1757 the Abenakis of St-François were afraid that the Jesuits would try to deport them to the Ohio Valley in order to make room for habitants.[81] The natives took none of this treatment lying down, though it was harder to resist in the mid-eighteenth century than it would have been earlier, since the threat to emigrate was less plausible than in the past. People had sunk roots in the Laurentian Lowlands; moreover, Abenakis, Iroquois and Hurons alike had valuable hunting territories to the north. Relocation to the south was no longer a viable option, given the spread of English settlement and the growing prevalence of war. These unfavorable circumstances did not prevent the natives from protesting and mobilizing the support of colonial officials who understood the importance of the indigenous contribution to the military defense of New France. On the eve of the Seven Years' War, the governor of Canada ordered the Jesuits to stop granting lands to nonnatives in Kahnawake; the missionaries

---

[80] Louise Tremblay, "La politique missionnaire des sulpiciens au XVIIe et début du XVIIIe siècle, 1668–1735," MA thesis, Université de Montréal, 1981.

[81] Louis Lavallée, *La Prairie en Nouvelle-France, 1647–1760: étude d'histoire sociale* (Montréal: McGill-Queen's University Press, 1992), 74–76; petition of Lanoullier de Boisclerc, 15 October 1736, in Roy, *Inventaire des concessions en fief et seigneurie*, 5: 289–97; Maxime Boily, "Les terres amérindiennes dans le régime seigneurial: les modèles fonciers des missions sédentaires de la Nouvelle-France," MA thesis, Université Laval, 2006, 122–25.

complied, but in the confusion attending the fall of New France, they seized the opportunity to alienate more Iroquois land. However, as British rule over Canada became established, the Iroquois of Kahnawake found new (anti-Jesuit) allies and unprecedented legal recourse. An important decision in 1762 by the military governor, Thomas Gage, eliminated the Jesuit proprietorship and recognized the Iroquois residents as, in effect, their own seigneurs[82] (see Chapter 11).

The fiefs of Sillery, Sault St-Louis and Deux-Montagnes were set up to accommodate natives and integrate them into the Canadian colony. This feudal institution, combining property and jurisdictional powers, served to preserve the political autonomy and economic stability of indigenous communities that were affiliated with New France and located in the midst of the colonized zone of the Laurentian Lowlands. Over the long term, however, the growth of a French settler population and the spread of colonization placed heavy pressure on the territories of these native enclaves. In this context the religious orders, set up as legal guardians of indigenous property by the government, betrayed their trust and presided over a partial transfer of native lands to settler control. As had been the case in Mexico, measures initially devised to guarantee and protect indigenous landed property ended up functioning as instruments of dispossession.

---

[82] Alain Beaulieu, *La question des terres autochtones au Québec, 1760–1860* (Varennes, QC: Ministère de la Justice et Ministère des Ressources naturelles du Québec, 2002), 101–17; Denys Delâge, "Les Iroquois chrétiens des 'réductions,' 1667–1770," *Recherches amérindiennes au Québec* 21 (1991): 59–78; Arnaud Decroix, "Le conflit juridique entre les jésuites et les Iroquois au sujet de la seigneurie du Sault Saint-Louis: analyse de la décision de Thomas Gage (1762)," *Revue Juridique Thémis* 41 (2007): 279–97.

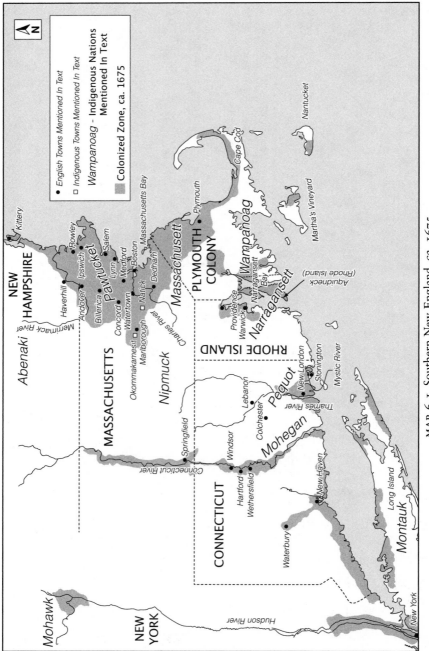

MAP 6.1 Southern New England, ca. 1675

6

New England

Land! Land! hath been the Idol of many ... Idolatry brings the Sword.
Increase Mather, *An Earnest Exhortation to the Inhabitants of
New-England* (Boston, 1676)[1]

In the history and the historiography of colonial New England,[2] "land" does seem to serve as something of a fetish. Idolatry and fetishism are all about mistaking ideas for things and, of course, at one level land really is a material reality, but it is never *only* that. Only when construed as landscape, environment, property, political territory and habitat – that is to say, only in the context of human societies – can the term "land" convey any real historical meaning. Yet the tendency in Early American history is to treat land as a thing, invoking only its material aspect to explain a variety of phenomena. In its abundance, "land" accounts for the kind of settler society that emerged in New England, its agricultural practices, its inheritance arrangements, its egalitarianism and so on. In its scarcity ("land hunger"), land explains speculation, competition and conflicts with natives, such as King Philip's War (1675–76), the conflagration that occasioned Rev. Increase Mather's jeremiad quoted above. Interestingly enough, "land" was rarely invoked in discourses of colonialism, pro or con, concerning New Spain and New France. In the searching critiques of Spanish imperialism in the Americas formulated in

---

[1] Quoted in Daniel K. Richter, *Before the Revolution: America's Ancient Pasts* (Cambridge, Mass.: Harvard University Press, 2011), 369.
[2] With apologies to Maine, New Hampshire and Vermont, I have to admit that the term "New England" is used throughout this chapter and the rest of the book mainly to designate the southern portion of that region.

the sixteenth century, most famously by Bartholomé de las Casas, the accent was mainly on cruelty and exploitation.[3] Las Casas did go out of his way to defend Indians' right to their property, but he seems to have been more concerned about the conquistadores' looting than with any seizure of native lands. In New France, colonists were far more likely to become the targets of ecclesiastical thunderbolts for selling alcohol to natives than for hankering after their land. Obviously "land" was more of an issue in New England because of the large number of settlers who sought accommodation there. Even so, we have seen that settler encroachment on indigenous territories went on apace in New Spain and New France, but there the language of official and public discourse did not rely heavily on "la tierra" or "la terre" as a metonym for colonization. Across the Americas, colonial regimes came to dominate peoples and spaces through a complex set of processes and relationships, some of them violent and lethal, others not directly so. To treat all this as if it were a simple matter of transferring an object – land – from one group to another is to slip into reification, something I'll try to avoid in the account that follows.

COLONIES

A fleet carrying 700 English Puritans arrived on the shores of Massachusetts Bay in the summer of 1630; an advance party had settled at Salem earlier, but the bulk of these migrants would gravitate to the Charles River at the head of the bay. Compared with the Pilgrims who founded Plymouth, these migrants were numerous and well equipped: successive annual waves of reinforcements arriving over the course of the following decade eventually brought 13,000 to Massachusetts before the English Civil War broke out.[4] Despite some disarray and death from disease and hunger at the beginning, the newcomers almost immediately

---

[3] Bartolomé de las Casas, *A Short Account of the Destruction of the Indies*, trans. Nigel Griffin (London: Penguin Books, 1992); Lewis Hanke, *The Spanish Struggle for Justice in the Conquest of America* (Philadelphia: University of Pennsylvania Press, 1949); Anthony Pagden, "Dispossessing the Barbarian: The Language of Spanish Thomism and the Debate over the Property Rights of the American Indians," in *The Languages of Political Theory in Early-Modern Europe*, ed. Anthony Pagden (Cambridge: Cambridge University Press, 1986), 79–98.

[4] Virginia DeJohn Anderson, "New England in the Seventeenth Century," in *The Origins of Empire: British Overseas Enterprise to the Close of the Seventeenth Century*, ed. Nicholas Canny (Oxford: Oxford University Press, 1998), 197–98.

outnumbered their near indigenous neighbors. The Massachusetts Bay colony soon emerged as the most formidable power in southern New England. Mi'kmaq raiders from the north took note and ceased attacking the weakened Ninnimissinuok nations south of the Merrimack. The Massachusett and Pawtucket peoples, for their part, beleaguered by their enemies and depleted in numbers after the terrible plague of 1616–18, welcomed the newcomers as suppliers and potent allies, offering no opposition as the latter began to occupy terrain. The Puritan minister Francis Higginson was probably not indulging in the usual colonizer's self-delusions when he wrote, "They doe generally professe to like well of our comming and planting here; partly because there is abundance of ground that they cannot possess nor make use of, and partly because our being here will be a meanes both of reliefe to them when they want, and also a defence from their Enemies, wherewith (I say) before this Plantation begun, they were often indangered."[5] It was therefore quite easy for the Puritans to secure a foothold where Salem and Boston and their satellites would grow. Their immediate concern was to get crops in the ground and make themselves self-sufficient in food. Colonists therefore dispersed in small groups, seeking out abandoned Ninnimissinuok fields and forming distinct "plantations"; nine of these communities, otherwise known as "townships," had sprung up around Boston by 1634.[6]

The Bay townships bore a strong resemblance to the plantation established at Plymouth a decade earlier, as well as to other early village-like settlements in coastal New England. What made them politically distinctive, however, was the fact that they were established under the auspices of a larger territorial quasi-state, the Massachusetts Bay Colony. Before setting sail for the New World, the founders of Massachusetts had taken the precaution of securing a territorial grant and a royal patent making them a legal corporation. There were some complications because New England had already been awarded to another body, the New England Council, but the Council was willing to grant the would-be colonizers a portion of its domain, a territorial award that was confirmed by a royal charter in 1629. The leading Puritan colonizer, John Winthrop, a lawyer, was clever enough to carry that document with him when he

---

[5] [Francis Higginson], *New-Englands Plantation. Or a short and true Description of the Commodities and Discommodities of that Countrey* (London: Michael Sparke, 1630), 13. See Neal Salisbury, *Manitou and Providence: Indians, Europeans, and the Making of New England, 1500–1643* (New York: Oxford University Press, 1982), 184.

[6] Gloria L. Main, *Peoples of a Spacious Land: Families and Cultures in Colonial New England* (Cambridge, Mass.: Harvard University Press, 2001), 42.

sailed for New England, helping to solidify the virtual independence of the enterprise. By its terms, the king incorporated the Massachusetts Bay Company as a "Body corporate and politique," with a governor, a deputy governor and eighteen assistants, meeting weekly as a court, together with an annual assembly, or general court, to be attended by all "freemen" of the company. The charter also confirmed the Council of New England's grant of territory, stretching along the coast from the Merrimack River to the Charles, plus three miles beyond in both directions, and from the Atlantic to the Pacific Oceans. (There was, of course, no mention of Dutch claims to the Hudson Valley, which formed a westward barrier well short of the Pacific.) The territory granted, for "the plantation therof, and the government of the people there," entailed jurisdiction and property rights. According to the terms of this document, the Bay Company would be self-governing, subject only to the requirement that its laws "be not contrarie or repugnant to the Lawes and Statuts of this our Realme of England." It was also, most emphatically, to be recognized as proprietor of "all Landes and Groundes, Place and Places Soyles, Woodes, and Wood Groundes, Havens, Ports, Rivers, Waters, and Hereditaments whatsoever, lyeing within the said Boundes and Lymytts, and every Parte and Parcell thereof." The language of territorial possession, simultaneously detailed and all-encompassing, recalls the contemporaneous charter of the Company of New France. However, unlike that other document, indigenous peoples are nowhere mentioned in the Massachusetts charter.[7]

In those parts of North America claimed by the English, the colony was emerging as the prime instrument of jurisdiction, territorial sovereignty and property-making. Several had been projected and chartered over a

---

[7] "The Charter of Massachusetts Bay: 1629," Yale Law School, The Avalon Project: Documents in Law, History and Diplomacy, http://avalon.law.yale.edu/17th_century/mass03.asp. The extensive literature on English colonial charters includes Charles McLean Andrews, *The Colonial Period of American History*, 4 vols. (New Haven, Conn.: Yale University Press, 1964), passim; Viola F. Barnes, "Land Tenure in English Colonial Charters of the Seventeenth Century," in *Essays in Colonial History Presented to Charles McLean Andrews by His Students*, [no editor named] (New Haven, Conn.: Yale University Press, 1931), 4–40; John T. Juricek, "English Claims in North America to 1660: A Study in Legal and Constitutional History," PhD dissertation, University of Chicago, 1970; Elizabeth Mancke, "Chartered Enterprises and the Evolution of the British Atlantic World," in *The Creation of the British Atlantic World*, ed. Elizabeth Mancke and Carole Shammas (Baltimore: Johns Hopkins University Press, 2005), 237–62; Christopher L. Tomlins, *Freedom Bound: Law, Labor, and Civic Identity in Colonizing English America, 1580–1865* (New York: Cambridge University Press, 2010), 133–90.

quarter-century, but after Virginia (1607), Massachusetts was the first to take tangible shape on North American soil; Maryland, Connecticut, Rhode Island and New Hampshire soon followed in the 1630s.[8] But what did the word "colony" mean in this historical setting? A British writer offered this definition in 1630: "By a colony we mean a society of men drawn out of one state or people, and transplanted into another country."[9] Actually, seventeenth-century usage was confusingly variable and shifting: at first "colony" and "plantation" were treated as synonymous terms to designate small, village-scale settlements, such as those established by organized groups along the rivers of Virginia. Later the word was applied to larger, politically autonomous territories with authority over multiple constituent "plantations" or "townships." To confuse matters further, some of these larger entities were known officially as "commonwealths" or "provinces," but they were still fundamentally similar and we may as well call them all "colonies," following established usage. Ancestors of today's states, they can be seen as emergent territorial polities, self-governing but ultimately dependent on a distant imperial authority; they designated a territory and a governed population of colonists. Colonies understood in this sense were, in this period, a British specialty.

New Spain and New France were never referred to as "colonies," though both were certainly overseas polities subject to a European monarch. The French did often refer to the Canadian settlements along the St. Lawrence as a "colonie," but they were using the word in a purely descriptive sense to designate an area of predominantly French population that was effectively governed by French laws. However, "Canada" was politically and legally inseparable from the much larger North American territory claimed by the imperial sovereign as New France, an expansive and unbounded zone of many nations, differently governed and each in possession of its own lands. Similarly, New Spain contained "Spanish" towns, though these were not independent of the broader viceregal state. New France and New Spain were literally boundless: when conquerors and discoverers claimed new lands for their respective

---

[8] The vague term "several" is used here because precise counting is impossible. Christopher Tomlins lists 28 major colonial charters for the seventeenth century, but that figure includes three successive Virginia charters, three charters for different colonies in Newfoundland, none of which survived to the end of the century, and one (Plymouth, 1629) that some scholars characterize as a simple land grant. Tomlins, *Freedom Bound*, 157–58 n 80.

[9] Quoted in J. H. Elliott, *Empires of the Atlantic World: Britain and Spain in America* (New Haven, Conn.: Yale University Press, 2006), 9.

monarchs, they always specified natural features before them – the Great Lakes or the Rio Grande – then added, "and beyond," so as not to limit the future reach of empire. The Catholic monarchies worked to construct expansive imperial spaces that encompassed multiple countries and indigenous nations, as well as European settlements. England's kings, ultimately no less ambitious in their claims to New World space, tended to rely on a particular politicolegal structure, the colony, to assert their claims. Sponsoring or authorizing colonizing projects and giving them a modest portion of a potentially vast North American realm, the Crown provided a legal basis for emergent polities such as Massachusetts, Connecticut, Rhode Island and New Hampshire; these were imagined as fully English and wholly possessed of a delimited territory. These colonies were plural, and therefore spatially limited by the presence of near neighbors. Compared with the basically unitary imperial polities of French and Spanish America, territorially open-ended and culturally inclusive,[10] the English colonies belonged to a distinct species.

Approaching this topic from a different angle, the legal historian Christopher Tomlins identifies a "peculiarity of the English" in early seventeenth-century public discussions about overseas expansion. No more nor less arrogant than other European nations in assuming a right to assert control over "savage" lands and to wage "just war" against indigenous peoples who resisted their intrusions, the English nevertheless developed a variant discourse stressing the creation of fully English enclaves on American shores. That discourse, as Tomlins sees it, "elevated land over people as the primary object of the colonizer's attention. It rearranged both the legalities and the institutional mechanisms of colonizing accordingly."[11] He quotes an early propagandist for the Virginia Company, Edward Crashaw, declaring that what the English sought in the New World was "*land and roome* for us to plant in,"[12] which is not the way Crashaw's continental European contemporaries would have

---

[10] The imperial entities that France and Spain projected onto the map of America, by way of contrast, were generally suggestive of uncontained aspirations to dominate. Both French and Spanish America were indeed composed of distinct "kingdoms" and territorial units of administration – New France, Louisiana, Acadia, the viceroyalites of Peru and New Spain – but the boundaries separating these were rather indistinct and fuzzy; each had ample room for expansion, New Spain mainly to the north, Peru to the south, New France to the west. The New England colonies, on the other hand, quickly found themselves boxed in, with the ocean on one side and other colonies all around. See Catherine Desbarats and Allan Greer, "North America from the Top Down: Visions from New France," *Journal of Early American History* 5 (fall 2015), 109–36.

[11] Tomlins, *Freedom Bound*, 133.   [12] Ibid., 152.

expressed their imperial desires and ambitions. The Catholic powers tended to covet a populated landscape, overseas countries defined by their political and cultural geography as much as by their natural terrain, while the English were more inclined to express their claims in nonhuman spatial terms. The distinction is largely discursive: it is not so much that the French and Spanish had no interest in "land and roome," but rather that they understood imperial expansion in different terms than the English, the latter tending to abstract "land" from its human and political context. On the other hand, the English did sometimes seem bent on remaking American spaces in line with their conception of desocialized "land."

One related peculiarity of New England in this connection is that the colonies purported to own all the lands within the boundaries assigned to them. The royal charters that gave the colonies legal standing promised as much, for they were generally feudal in form, combining delegated political authority and landed property. More generally, under English law property and sovereignty tended to converge at the summit, with all political authority and all land tenure deriving ultimately from the king. "The monarch was lord, ultimately, of all the tenants in the realm, and, therefore, was supreme landlord over all lands occupied by English subjects."[13] When English sovereignty was asserted over portions of America, it therefore seemed natural to claim that the king was the rightful proprietor to all these territories and that legitimate property rights descended from him, through the colonies he endowed, and on down to the settler at the end of the great chain of tenure.

This does not mean that indigenous peoples were absent from the English colonial imagination. Acknowledging that the "land and roome" the English sought on the Chesapeake might be claimed by natives, Edward Crashaw had a peremptory response: "These things they have, these they may spare, these we neede, these we will take."[14] Rather than a populated landscape, the English preferred the vision of a depopulated territory. The 1620 charter by which James I had granted the region between the fortieth and the forty-eighth parallels of latitude to the Council of New England made this explicit. "Within these late Yeares there hath by God's Visitation reigned a wonderfull Plague, together with

[13] Ken MacMillan, *Sovereignty and Possession in the English New World: The Legal Foundations of Empire, 1576–1640* (Cambridge: Cambridge University Press, 2006), 31. See also A. W. B. Simpson, *A History of the Land Law* (Oxford: Clarendon Press, 1961), 1–2.

[14] Tomlins, *Freedom Bound*, 153.

many horrible Slaugthers, and Murthers, committed amoungst the Sauages and brutish People there, heertofore inhabiting, in a Manner to the utter Destruction, Deuastacion, and Depopulacion of that whole Territorye." As a consequence of these providential developments, "large and goodly Territoryes, deserted as it were by their naturall Inhabitants, should be possessed and enjoyed by such of our Subjects and People as heertofore have and hereafter shall by his Mercie and Favour, and by his Powerfull Arme, be directed and conducted thither."[15] A merely residual presence in this patent, natives appeared in some other charters of the period as potential enemies, lurking on the margins of rightfully English territory.[16] More frequently, indigenous peoples were not mentioned at all. The consistent implication of all the English charters is that a colony is a space for colonists.

The colonial charters and the public discussions that surrounded them expressed the legal fictions by which the English tried to make sense of their territorial incursions into North America: as if the king really did own and rule all these countries, as if he could delegate his control to the Massachusetts Bay Company and other similar bodies and as if the latter could really exercise property and jurisdictional rights over every square inch of the territories delineated in their respective charters. Colonies as constructed in these documents were imaginatively projected onto politically empty space. However, the real-world colony of Massachusetts, as opposed to the fictive realm projected in the charter of 1629, was carved out of Ninnimissinuok territory, slowly, uncertainly and unevenly. Even if there was no serious opposition to the establishment of the first townships, the Bay Colony still occupied only a fairly small patch of territory. The far greater part of its theoretical domain (even if the latter is seen as extending westward only as far as the Dutch settlements starting to appear in the Hudson Valley and not all the way to the Pacific) remained under indigenous control. Even as new townships formed and larger areas were integrated into the colony, natives continued in possession of more extensive lands until they were defeated in King Philip's War. Setting great stock by the charter's unambiguous grant, the lawyer John Winthrop was on principle opposed to negotiating with Indians, yet reality drove him to relent and authorize some treaties and "purchases." Not only were natives a significant demographic and

---

[15] "The Charter of New England, 1620," Avalon Project, http://avalon.law.yale.edu/17th_century/mass01.asp; Tomlins, *Freedom Bound*, 175.

[16] Tomlins, *Freedom Bound*, 175–77.

military presence across most of the region assigned to Massachusetts by the terms of its charter, they were also a major factor in broader currents of spatial politics that were determining the shape of New England and therefore of Massachusetts.[17]

The multiplicity of English colonial grants, joined to the schematic geography of their assigned boundaries, ensured that there would be squabbling over territory. Massachusetts was soon surrounded by other colonies, all jockeying for commercial, diplomatic and territorial advantage. There was of course Plymouth, originally a village enclave in the Wampanoag country; it sponsored new plantations in the vicinity and grew to be a regional government asserting authority over an extensive zone on Cape Cod and the adjoining mainland. This expanded Plymouth organized itself into a colony modeled on the institutions of Massachusetts.[18] Meanwhile, with the Bay colony's settler population burgeoning, and with political/ecclesiastical dissention erupting among the idealistic Puritans, some began relocating outside the colony's jurisdiction, especially along the Connecticut River and around Narragansett Bay. The search for better meadows to support settlers' livestock added an agrarian impulse to this hiving-off movement. Recognizing that a territorial state conferred power and ensured their survival, the nascent communities banded together and organized themselves into colonies, again variations on the Massachusetts model, and eventually secured English charters for Connecticut and Rhode Island.

These colonial states defined themselves territorially through their interrelations with one another and through their conflicts and alliances with native nations. The Connecticut settlements constituted an affront both to the Dutch who claimed the area and to the Pequots who were the region's preeminent indigenous power. An alliance with Massachusetts and Plymouth, as well as with the Narragansetts, allowed the Connecticut settlers to defeat the Pequots in a conflict that culminated in a dreadful massacre on the Mystic River (1637). This war was crucial to the establishment of Connecticut as a colony. Even though Roger Williams's settlement did not take part in the fighting, he himself was deeply involved in the diplomacy surrounding the conflict; in some respects, the emergence of Rhode Island as a colony was also a product of the Pequot War.

[17] See Salisbury, *Manitou and Providence*; Jenny Hale Pulsipher, *Subjects unto the Same King: Indians, English, and the Contest for Authority in Colonial New England* (Philadelphia: University of Pennsylvania Press, 2005).
[18] Andrews, *The Colonial Period of American History*, 1: 279–99.

Taking advantage of the power vacuum caused by the crushing of the
Pequots, another group of Puritans from England established the nucleus
of a new colony at New Haven in 1638. And Massachusetts Bay, though
it was the dominant power in New England at the time, did not stand
aloof from the complex interplay of alliances and animosities.

The New England colonies were not conquest regimes in quite the
same way that New Spain was. Puritans did not enter the region waging
offensive war and they did not usually rely heavily on the concept of
"conquest" to elaborate and justify the colonial order. Here the clash of
arms typically came after colonization was under way, rather than as a
prelude. The Pequot War stands, along with the later King Philip's War,
as a case in point. It led not only to the seizure of land, but also to the
imposition of tribute payments and the enslavement of men, women and
children from among the vanquished. However, the predominant tendency was more in the direction of eliminating native space rather than
of subjugating natives. English and Hispanic imperial styles may have
diverged in this respect, but the fact remains that the English colonies
were forged in war.[19] In New England as in New France and New Spain,
armed force would prove essential to the reconstitution of space and the
creation of settler property; indeed, the capacity for organized violence
was one of the defining attributes of the colony as institution.

From the start, the New England colonies took on the character of
military powers.[20] When Plymouth plantation was still a small village and
had never been attacked, it was defended by a fort armed with six cannon
plus a stockade mounted with four mortars.[21] There and in all the other
colonies, male settlers were expected to serve as required in a militia force;
even if these were largely untrained and loosely organized units, they were
powerful enough to make them intimidating enemies and valued allies in
native eyes. Diplomacy, the pendant to war in a multipolar competitive
environment, was another defining function of the colonial quasi-states.
Alliances, both tacit and explicit, connected different colonies and different Ninnimissinuok nations at various times up to and including King
Philip's War. Native allies – for example, the Narragansetts when they

---

[19] Jennings, *The Invasion of America*, 202–27.
[20] Salisbury, *Manitou and Providence*, 189–90. See the chapter entitled "How the People of
Christ Ought to Behave Themselves in War-like Discipline," in the 1630 promotional
tract, *Wonder-Working Providence*. Edward Johnson, *Johnson's Wonder-Working
Providence, 1628–1651*, ed. J. Franklin Jameson (New York: C. Scribner's Sons, 1910),
33–36.
[21] Main, *Peoples of a Spacious Land*, 23.

joined Massachusetts forces in their assault on the Pequots – almost all inhabited regions theoretically covered by one or another colonial grant, but they generally insisted on their independence of colonial governments, even as they professed allegiance to the king of England.[22] By treating military arrangements as a matter of diplomacy, the colonial authorities involved were tacitly accepting native independence. Their diplomatic as much as their military activities demonstrated that the colonies were exercising sovereign powers and that their sovereignty remained uncertain and spatially limited.

The colonies also exercised powers of jurisdiction. The court of assistants, an institution inscribed into the colonial charters themselves, represented the highest judicial body in each colony. By 1636, Massachusetts had also instituted a network of six county courts as tribunals of first instance.[23] By and large, these courts dealt with the civil and criminal affairs of the colonists; in disputes with settlers, indigenous people were usually represented by their sachems, which had the effect of situating their participation in the judicial system in a context of intersocietal relations rather than that of internal order.[24] Within the settler sphere, land and property affairs generally dominated the civil-law agenda of the county courts. Not only did the courts adjudicate conflicts over contested inheritance and disputed boundaries, they provided facilities for registering title and recording sales and mortgages. These judicial functions – centrally, though not exclusively to do with property formation – came to be discharged mainly at the county level, but under the auspices of the colonial state.

Meanwhile, colonial legislatures (general courts) were passing laws regulating the purchase of indigenous lands, assigning responsibility to build and maintain fences, laying down regulations for the management of common fields, establishing procedures for the conveyance of land, requiring surveying, authorizing the construction of highways and so on.[25]

[22] Pulsipher, *Subjects unto the Same King.*

[23] Michael S. Hindus, "A Guide to the Court Records of Early Massachusetts," in *Law in Colonial Massachusetts 1630–1800*, ed. Daniel R. Coquillette (Boston: Colonial Society of Massachusetts, 1984), 520.

[24] Salisbury, *Manitou and Providence*, 186–87; Katherine Hermes, "'Justice Will Be Done Us': Algonquian Demands for Reciprocity in the Courts of European Settlers," in *The Many Legalities of Early America*, ed. Christopher L. Tomlins and Bruce H. Mann (Chapel Hill: University of North Carolina Press, 2001), 123–49.

[25] See, for example, Nathaniel Bradstreet Shurtleff, *Records of the Governor and Company of the Massachusetts Bay*, 5 vols. (Boston: W. White printer to the Commonwealth,

Most of these enactments depended on the cooperation of local officers at the township level, but then townships were the offspring of colonies.[26] Authorizing the creation of new townships by granting tracts of lands to organized groups of would-be settlers became a crucial function of colonial government in New England. Here again, the colony's role was one of providing a legal framework for property making: it is at the level of the township and of its constituent households that property would be fully constituted. Delegating, regulating and coordinating the process of property making, while providing the military muscle that guaranteed land occupation, each colony played its part in creating English-owned and English-ruled space and in extending that space ever outward into Ninnimissinuok territory. Colonies to that degree made property.

At the same time, property made colonies. It was the micro-level actions of settler families in the local townships that defined the geography of colonial sovereignty and charted the spatial expansion of each colony. Felling trees, moving stones, building houses, introducing pigs and cattle, physically occupying the land, they marked the face of the earth as English, while the deeds, mortgages and litigation-related records accumulating in the courts constituted a growing archival edifice of property and jurisdiction.

TOWNSHIPS

Early planning for the Massachusetts Bay Company had envisioned individual land grants proportional to household size, along the lines of the Virginia "headright" system,[27] and indeed the colonies always made some grants directly to individuals; however, group settlements sprang up spontaneously, gathering together a few dozen settler families each to create agrarian communities. Massachusetts Colony soon came to accept towns as the collective intermediary between individual households and the colonial state and thenceforth the bulk of grants would be awarded

---

1853), 1: 112, 116, 201, 215, 280, 306–7, 333; 2: 39, 49, 115; 3: 113; 4: 22, 101; 5: 470–71, 374–75.

[26] Connecticut might be a partial exception to this rule, townships having taken root along the Connecticut River Valley prior to the creation of the colony. Legally, however, every township owed its existence to a colony. Michael Zuckerman argues that the New England townships were politically very much under the thumb of the colonies in the seventeenth century. *Peaceable Kingdoms: New England Towns in the Eighteenth Century* (New York: Knopf, 1970), 10–16.

[27] Richter, *Before the Revolution*, 190.

"wholesale" as the waves of English immigration kept arriving and as new townships formed. The colony would authorize, regulate and militarily defend the towns. In return, the towns gave the colony a real presence on New England's soil.

Dozens of new townships were established in the 1630s, as immigrants poured in from England; by 1650, there were more than forty of them, with a total population of 23,000.[28] In an environment punctuated by swamps and rocky terrain, the pockets of good land with adequate hay meadows around Massachusetts Bay, Narragansett Bay and the Connecticut River were quickly occupied. The fact that every township was also a church only accelerated the general mobility, as people settled in one place and then moved on if they found they disagreed with their neighbors on points of religion. There also seems to have been a tendency for immigrants from particular regions of England to gravitate to towns populated by others of the same origin. As the dry land counterpart of the "Great Migration," says Virginia Anderson, came the "great reshuffling," a period of short-term instability that eventually led to more integrated, stable communities.[29] To put this reshuffling in perspective, it is important to note that a similar pattern prevailed in Catholic New Spain and New France, where newly arrived immigrants tended to relocate as they became acclimatized to the colonial scene and moved to correct beginners' mistakes and pursue new opportunities. In all cases, the upshot of this initial instability may have been, as Anderson suggests, more coherent communities, but along the way a lot of more or less undeveloped lands changed hands. Notwithstanding the communal characteristics of early New England property creation, these colonies were the site of what by European standards would be considered a hyperactive real estate market.

Following an initial stage of improvisation, Massachusetts Bay colony legislated a legal framework for its townships in 1636:

Whereas particular townes have many things wch concern onely themselves, & the ordering of their owne affaires ..., it is therfore ordered, that the ffreemen of e[ver]y towne, or the maior pte of them, shall onely have power to dispose of their owne lands, & woods, with all the previlidges & appurtenances of the

---

[28] Anderson, "New England in the Seventeenth Century," 200.
[29] Virginia DeJohn Anderson, *New England's Generation: The Great Migration and the Formation of Society and Culture in the Seventeenth Century* (Cambridge: Cambridge University Press, 1991), 92.

said townes, to graunt lotts, & make such orders as may concerne the well ordering of their owne townes . . .[30]

This law authorized townships to appoint constables and other local officials, to assess local rates and to levy fines up to twenty shillings for noncompliance with bylaws. The colony left it to each town to provide for its own local government, to hire a minister and to assign land holdings. A township therefore had the character both of an institution of local government and of a corporate landed proprietor. Historians often note similarities with the English parish and the English manor, but in contrast to Old World local institutions, a New England town functioned as an active creator of new landed property; it might better be compared to the Spanish-American municipality or, better yet, to the Canadian seigneurie. In many respects – the distribution of individual holdings, the oversight of surveying and boundaries, the management of common pastures – the two institutions were similar; what distinguished the New England township was the way the townsmen acted as their own collective seigneur.

Townships were vernacular institutions, essentially corporations,[31] formed through the initiative of colonists. There were usually leading figures, sometimes a clergyman, often an individual, such as Roger Williams in the case of Providence, who disposed of enough wealth to underwrite the finances of the nascent community. To take one example, Concord, Massachusetts, was founded in 1635–36 at a place originally called Musketaquid, an area of wet bottomland on the Concord River, inhabited by a Ninnimissinuok people, probably of the Pawtucket nation. Settlers newly arrived from England appear to have been led here by a fur trader named Simon Willard, who knew the area west of Boston and presumably used his ties with the indigenous population, in much the way Roger Williams did his, to secure an opening for the settlers. Together with Reverend Peter Bulkeley, reputed to have 4000 pounds at his disposal, and a dozen other families who initially signed on for the venture, he petitioned the General Court for a township grant. The court obliged, establishing the petitioners and other founders who might join them in the

---

[30] Shurtleff, *Records of the Governor and Company of the Massachusetts Bay*, 1: 172, 3 March 1635/36.

[31] According to the strict letter of the law, they were pseudo-corporations; as David Konig points out, only Parliament could create corporations. David Konig, "English Legal Change and the Origins of Local Government in Northern Massachusetts," in *Town and County: Essays on the Structure of Local Government in the American Colonies*, ed. Bruce Daniels (Middletown, Conn.: Wesleyan University Press, 1978), 29–30.

future, as a legal township and awarding them Musketaquid, together with a surrounding "6 myles of land square to belonge to it."[32] Governor John Winthrop considered an area six miles on each side to be ideal for a township, such that a meeting house placed at the center would never be beyond walking distance for any resident.[33] Thirty-six square miles was far more than the initial two or three dozen settler families would ever need to support themselves; the intention was to leave ample room for newcomers and for future generations to expand into.

After the Massachusetts Bay colony had given its approval and the first colonists had begun to occupy clearings at the center of the vaguely sketched township, the General Court authorized the town "to purchase the ground within the limits of the Indians, to wit, Atawans & Squa Sachim."[34] No "Indian deed" survives; however, half a century after the fact, at a time when British imperial officials were questioning the legality of township grants and towns were scrambling to document their legal origins, depositions were taken from two elderly settlers and one aged native, all claiming to have been present when the purchase was concluded. Each witness declared that an area "six miles square" was surrendered (and of course one wonders what that phrase might have meant to Pawtucket people at the time), centering on Peter Bulkeley's house, where the agreement was concluded.[35] We have no way of knowing exactly when this ceremony took place or what negotiations, gift exchanges and other gestures might have preceded it. All we know for certain is that the town fathers of Concord wanted to prove, in 1684,

---

[32] Lemuel Shattuck, *A History of the Town of Concord, Middlesex County, Massachusetts: From Its Earliest Settlement to 1832: and of the Adjoining Towns, Bedford, Acton, Lincoln, and Carlisle, Containing Various Notices of County and State History Not Before Published* (Acton, Mass.: Russell, Odiorne, and Company, 1835), 4; Brian Donahue, *The Great Meadow: Farmers and the Land in Colonial Concord* (New Haven, Conn.: Yale University Press, 2004), 77. Because of all the coming and going, the exact number of Concord founding colonists cannot be specified. It has been suggested that the first colonists who established Dedham, Massachusetts, numbered "about thirty families." Kenneth A. Lockridge, *A New England Town: The First Hundred Years, Dedham, Massachusetts, 1636–1736* (New York: Norton, 1970), 4.

[33] John Winthrop, "Essay on the Ordering of Towns [ca. 1635]," in *Winthrop Papers*, 5 vols. (Boston: Massachusetts Historical Society, 1943), 3: 181–85. Winthrop disapproved of the much larger grants that some townships had already requested and received.

[34] Shurtleff, *Records of the Governor and Company of the Massachusetts Bay*, 1: 196 (17 May 1637).

[35] Depositions from 1684 transcribed in Alfred Sereno Hudson, *The History of Concord, Massachusetts*, 2 vols. (Concord, Mass.: Erudite Press, 1904), 1: 275–76.

that their predecessors had bought the township's territory from natives at the time of first settlement. Thus Concord, like many New England townships, derived its property rights from two different sources: a grant from a colony that claimed full ownership of the country and a deed (in this case virtual) of purchase from natives.

The historiography of New England rarely confronts the strangely contradictory nature of this double origin story. That may be because historians are inclined to take colonial grants seriously as the "real" foundation of township and settler property, while dismissing agreements with natives with the condescending phrase "clearing title." The official position of most of the colonies (Rhode Island is the exception here) was that a grant came first, while Indian deeds came later, and the latter had force because the General Court authorized them. Native purchases, according to this theory, were supposed to be subordinate to the colony's superior jurisdiction. But often the "Indian deed" came first, adherence to a colony later. This was the case not only for Plymouth and Providence, but also for the original townships of Connecticut, as well as for the town of Springfield, which William Pynchon established on land he acquired from natives and then later attached to Massachusetts Bay.[36] Many other towns never did conclude an agreement with any Ninnimissinuok. Because some native agreements seem to have been lost and others were purely verbal, it is not clear what percentage of town founders came to terms with sachems of their respective regions the way the men who began Plymouth and Providence did, offering gifts and pledging friendship to secure permission to settle. We do know of "Indian deeds" for the following towns in Connecticut alone: Hartford, Lebanon, Waterbury, Wethersfield and Windsor.[37] While Roger Williams and John Winthrop argued over the legitimacy of native purchases versus Crown-authorized grants as valid justification for English colonization, most New Englanders seemed to want it both ways. To be clear, the question here is not What constitutes a valid procedure for dispossessing indigenous peoples?

---

[36] Andrews, *The Colonial Period of American History*, 2: 67–143.

[37] John Frederick Martin, *Profits in the Wilderness: Entrepreneurship and the Founding of New England Towns in the Seventeenth Century* (Chapel Hill: University of North Carolina Press, 1991), 151. As another indicator of the frequency of such documents, one local historian compiled sixty-four Indian deeds from western Massachusetts alone. Harry A. Wright, ed., *Indian Deeds of Hampden County: Being Copies of All Land Transfers from the Indians Recorded in the County of Hampden, Massachusetts, and Some Deeds from Other Sources, Together with Notes and Translations of Indian Place Names* (Springfield, Mass.: n.p., 1905).

but rather, How can we best understand the township as a landed proprietor? The fact that many townships derived their tenure from two different sources certainly complicates matters.

Whether townships claimed title to land by virtue of a colonial grant, an Indian deed or both, a number of questions still arise about the nature of their proprietorship. These are issues connected to what might be called the where, how and who of property. How exactly was a township defined territorially? What was the nature of its control over the lands within that territory? And what precisely was the nature of the township, that is, who constituted the township as proprietor?

Beginning with the "where" question: if we try to nail down the exact spatial meaning of the township of Concord early in its history, we find we are dealing with a very uncertain territorial entity. Natives presumably would have had a sense of the kind and quantity of resources that would be needed by the settlers who stood before them, but we cannot know what and how much they may have felt they ceded to the settlers at the time of the purchase. The General Court's grant did specify a quantity of land, but gave no indication of how its six miles square should be laid out. Natives and colonial legislators did agree, however, in anchoring the township to a known central place on the Concord River, a location the settlers had already staked out and occupied it seems. Concord was the first town granted in inland Massachusetts and so the colony had no need to take previous claims into account. Dedham's grant, more typical in this respect, had to be inserted into a landscape beginning to be dotted with other settlements. It concerned "all that land on the Easterly and Southerly side of the Charles River not formerly granted unto any Town or particular person, and also to have five miles square on the other side of the River."[38] As was the case with Concord's grant, the topographical specifications remain quite vague. Outer edges did not matter much in the early years when most of the land claimed by any township was open commons, but eventually, with the growth of settlement, boundary issues would arise. At that point, lines would have to be traced dividing adjoining townships. The procedure was hardly an exercise in applied geometry, however: even had the necessary surveying expertise been available, there would have been little or no documentary basis to guide the process. Instead, the colonial authorities authorized a kind of ad hoc local boundary commission; a committee of men from the

---

[38] Dedham grant of 10 July 1636, quoted in Herman Mann, *Historical Annals of Dedham: From Its Settlement in 1635 to 1847* (Dedham, Mass.: H. Mann, 1847), 55.

communities involved would then negotiate their way across the land-scape, setting up markers as they went.[39]

Thus, a township began life as a location with a somewhat amorphous surrounding territory attached. In this respect, it looked like a microcos-mic version of a colony. Both entities started out as an aspirational space projected onto a vaguely sketched map. Colonies and townships took shape on the ground, gradually and incrementally and mainly by means of the property-making efforts of settlers, as the latter set up habitations and altered the land's ecology. To the question of where the lands of a given township originally lay, there was rarely a stable and precise answer, whether or not Indian deeds were a factor.

Turning from the "where" to the "how" question, we ask: in what sense did the township possess the lands within its territory-in-formation? It has to be said that that tenure was conditional rather than absolute. Grants to townships, like grants to individuals in New England (or, for that matter, in New Spain or New France), had to lead to occupation and use or they could be rescinded.[40] Furthermore, a town was obligated, like a New France seigneur, to subgrant its domain to settlers. Where Indian deeds are concerned, use-rights for hunting, fishing or planting were sometimes reserved to the natives, placing further limits on the town's control over "its" lands. Township territories were therefore tenures, property held subject to particular conditions.

More significantly, a town did not own all its lands in the same way. The fundamental distinction in a developing township is between the portion, small at first but growing, that had been allocated to settler families for their use, and the initially much larger portion left over for future expansion, the "undivided commons." The lands awarded as house lots, open fields, meadows and pastures of course became property of the town's constituent members, some of it in severalty, some held in common; yet the township as corporation did not entirely cease to exer-cise property rights over this section of its territory. The latter's propri-etary stake was comparable to what later came to be known as eminent domain. It meant, for one thing, that parcels of land previously granted to individuals could revert to the town if abandoned by the owner.

---

[39] See Shurtleff, *Records of the Governor and Company of the Massachusetts Bay*, passim; Massachusetts Historical Society, Ms. N-1845, Billerica (Mass.) Records, 1658 [*sic*]–1816 (hereafter Billerica Records), p. 19.

[40] Roy Hidemichi Akagi, *Town Proprietors of the New England Colonies* (Gloucester, Mass.: P. Smith, 1963), 31–32; Main, *Peoples of a Spacious Land*, 52.

Many townships forbade landowners from selling or renting their lots without permission; sometimes an individual grant was subject to stringent conditions, as when Billerica allocated a lot under the following terms: "granted to Heney Jests by the Towne for a Cituation to build upon and for the saide Henry to Live in: & for no othr use nor improvemente whatevr."[41]

Furthermore, towns had the power to make use of granted lands within their borders for local roads. (The colony had similar powers where highways were concerned.) That ability to command private lands for public purposes was not quite the same as the modern power of expropriation, for when a road was laid out across a farmer's field, the roadway in a sense still belonged to the farmer. Colonial legislation relating to roads is ambiguous by modern standards: in the absence of a fully developed notion of "public lands," it was not at all clear that a roadway running over individual lands ceased to be property, even though the owner was required to keep it open to the public and even though the town (or the colony in the case of highways) normally compensated him or her for the loss of its productive capacity.[42] Road legislation serves to remind us that township property rights coexisted with personal property rights over land ceded to individuals.

The town also levied "rates" on allotted lands in the core zone of settlement. These exactions might be considered "taxes," levied with the authorization of the General Court (rates were actually levied partly to contribute to the coffers of the colonial government, partly to finance local expenses), and thus deriving from a delegated share of the colony's sovereignty. On the other hand, they also look very much like rents of the sort one would encounter on an English manor or a Canadian seigneurie, though they were collected for the use of the community rather than for

---

[41] Billerica Records, pp. 5, 26, 48.

[42] Shurtleff, *Records of the Governor and Company of the Massachusetts Bay*, 1: 280, 2: 115; Billerica Records, p. 19; David Konig, *Law and Society in Puritan Massachusetts: Essex County, 1629–1692* (Chapel Hill: University of North Carolina Press, 1979), 49–50; William Michael Treanor, "The Origins and Original Significance of the Just Compensation Clause of the Fifth Amendment," *Yale Law Journal* 94 (1985): 694–716. An English legal treatise of 1657 explains: "He that hath the Land on both sides of the Highway, hath the Property of the soils of the Highway in him, although the King hath the priviledge for his people to pass through it at their pleasures; for the Law presumes that the way was at the first taken out of the Lands of the party that ownes the Lands that lye upon both sides of the way." William Style, *Regestum practicale: Or The Practical Register* (London, 1657), quoted in G. E. Aylmer, "The Meaning and Definition of 'Property' in Seventeenth-Century England," *Past & Present*, no. 86 (1980): 94.

the benefit of a landlord. Additionally, the town meetings regulated land use to a considerable degree. This was particularly the case in open-field areas, where dates of sowing, reaping and grazing had to be coordinated,[43] but even in enclosed communities there were multiple rules about fencing, renting and selling land. Billerica, for example, ruled in 1654 that poles could not be exported to any other township.[44] From the modern point of view, these were all governmental functions, but in the seventeenth century the distinction between the township-as-proprietor and township-as-municipality is far from clear-cut.

In the undivided commons, the area beyond the arable and meadow lands assigned to settlers, the town was more visibly and less ambiguously the proprietor, even though the outer boundaries of this zone remained indistinct in the early years. These lands, typically uncleared forest and swamp, formed a reserve for future agricultural expansion; in this respect, they are the counterpart of the Canadian seigneurial unconceded domain. Even as they awaited subdivision, they were far from useless. Settlers gathered wild fruits and hunted small game here; they cut wood for fuel, building material and fencing; they turned their pigs and cattle loose to forage. This was a genuine commons, comparable to the "waste" (typically moors and woodlands) that formed a vital component of the rural economy of many English villages; it was distinct from, and often formed a complement to, the enclosed and carefully maintained common pastures that were a feature of many New England townships. Undivided internally, the "undivided commons" were also not clearly separated from other towns' commons. Even when boundary lines had been run to divide adjoining townships, there is no reason to think that hunters, wood gatherers, and wandering livestock would have been deterred by these.[45]

---

[43] "In good open-field fashion, a whole set of complicated town orders was passed, year by year, involving pasturage of the common herd, designation of the fields which were to be planted and which were to be left fallow, the dates by which the fences had to be made following the plowing and harrowing, and appointment of the various town officers to supervise all these operations." Sumner Chilton Powell, *Puritan Village: The Formation of a New England Town* (Middletown, Conn.: Wesleyan University Press, 1963), 121–22.

[44] Billerica Records, pp. 2, 5.

[45] By law, the ponds and rivers of Massachusetts were open to all as far as fishing was concerned; the General Court also decreed that anyone could "fetch wood" from any swamps. By custom and practice, the larger colonial commons seems to have been open to all. *The General Laws and Liberties of the Massachusets Colony* (Cambridge: Samuel Green, 1672), 90–91; Shurtleff, *Records of the Governor and Company of the Massachusetts Bay*, 1: 111.

Thus the outer commons of one township tended to merge with those of other townships and to overlap with the indigenous commons of the Ninnimissinuok peoples (see Chapter 7).

The uncertain status and fuzzy edges of the outer commons were resolved over time as the undivided commons was divided. With the growth of population in a given township, townsmen would eventually decide on a "second division," transforming a portion of the undivided commons into a new set of fields and house lots, in order to accommodate new arrivals as well as the children of the original settlers as they reached adulthood. Each township proprietor was entitled to a share of the lands opened up by the second and subsequent divisions. Following a division, colonists would clear the new lands and integrate them into the town's agricultural system. By this means, legally and environmentally peripheral spaces were progressively incorporated into the core zone of colonial property. But who would be entitled to benefit from these successive allocations of land? (And since shares were not equal, what would determine the size of each allotment?) Divisions invariably raised issues about the makeup of a given town: in its guise as corporate land-owner, who exactly formed part of the township?

There was nothing simple or obvious about the composition of these collective proprietorships. Most of the records enumerate a list of individual men when referring either to a town's proprietors as a collectivity or to the owners of lands within the town; and yet we know that wives, sons and daughters were all implicated: they had some legal claims even while the husband/father lived, and they, or some among them, would be entitled to "his" lands and shares in the commons after he died. John Winthrop obliquely acknowledged as much in a journal entry relating to the founding of Concord. A tract was granted, he noted, to "Mr. Buckly ... and about twelve more families, to begin a town."[46] The interplay of marriage, lineage and family was central to the definition of property in land, in New England as in all property regimes, and deserves a fuller examination in another study. Suffice it to say that there was a basic ambiguity from the moment of conception as to whether a township was owned by an association of men or a collection of family lineages.[47] On the other hand, there was nothing ambiguous about the status of servants and slaves: they might in some cases become members

---

[46] Quoted in Shattuck, *A History of the Town of Concord*, 5.
[47] In the interests of simplifying the exposition in this chapter, I will continue to use the conventional language that treats owners as singular male subjects.

of the local church, and thus religiously full members of the community, but for property purposes, they remained appendages of other people's households.

The adult householders, who were recognized as the "freemen" of a township, were entitled to an active voice in local affairs, including matters relating to the regulation of land use, as well as to a vote for representatives to the General Court. It was they who received land allocations within the town in their respective names. In the early years, "freeman" and "proprietor" were basically synonymous terms, meaning that anyone who had lived in the town and held lands there was entitled to a share in future land distributions when portions of the undivided commons were divided. Moreover, this entitlement could be inherited or purchased. Newcomers admitted to the community were usually awarded lands like the original settlers and, like them, recognized as freemen and proprietors with a stake in future divisions. Sooner or later, however, most townships declared themselves "closed." From then on, new arrivals could be resident freemen, but not town proprietors; they would be granted land to farm and a voice in community affairs, but they would have no claim on the undivided commons.[48] The proprietors then emerged as an exclusive circle within each township and the undivided commons was their domain and not the community's as a whole. By 1665 it was becoming common in Connecticut for proprietors to assemble separately from the regular town meeting, as their views and interests were beginning to diverge from those of the larger group of residents.[49] One historian has argued that township proprietors soon became profit-seeking investors, while other scholars, noting that the proprietor and freeman categories continued to coincide to a considerable extent, if not completely, suggest that motives were more complex and communities not so divided.[50] Whoever may be right on this issue, the growing divergence between the status of resident land-owner, on the one hand, and township proprietor, on the other, introduces a new layer of complexity to the overall picture of property formation in colonial New England.

[48] Anderson, *New England's Generation*, 97–99.
[49] Bruce Daniels, "The Political Structure of Local Government in Colonial Connecticut," in *Town and County: Essays on the Structure of Local Government in the American Colonies*, ed. Bruce Daniels (Middletown, Conn.: Wesleyan University Press, 1978), 54.
[50] For the divergence argument, see Martin, *Profits in the Wilderness*, 186–216. For the riposte, to my mind convincing, see Daniel Vickers, *Farmers and Fishermen: Two Centuries of Work in Essex County, Massachusetts, 1639–1830* (Chapel Hill: University of North Carolina Press, 1994), 21.

SETTLERS

Two decades after the fact, the townspeople of Andover, Massachusetts recalled their settlement's 1646 founding in the following terms:

> Ye persons impowred by the Genll. Court wth such others as they associated to themselves, did Covenant and agre at their first planting of this towne [to] give every Inhabitant whome they received as a Townsman an house lott proportionable to his estate, or otherwise as he should reasonably desire, with suteable accomodations therunto of meadow, and all other divisions of upland & plouging ground, that should afterwards be divided.[51]

Allocations to settlers were generally quite small in early New England – Dedham's first generation received an average of about forty acres per household[52] – and they were also unequal. "Proportionable to his estate" meant that ministers and other men of means got more than ordinary townsmen; other factors such as occupation and family size also came into play in determining what was a "reasonable" amount of land to "desire." Uneven distribution partly reflected the prevailing sense of social hierarchy of the times, but it also derived from the assumption that land was granted to be used: men with larger herds and with the money to hire laborers merited more extensive allocations because they possessed the means to make those additional acres fruitful. Also stemming from that emphasis on productive use were the rules requiring that lands be occupied and developed within a specified period (typically three years) on pain of confiscation. As we have seen, similar "use-it-or-lose-it" regulations also applied to land grants in New Spain and New France. There, as in New England, these rules were not always consistently enforced, but they stood as a reminder that land grants were conditional and never constituted anything like absolute title.

A decade before Andover was established, Concord had begun similarly, settlers staking out small "house lots" of a few acres each on a former native cornfield near the center of their grant. There they would build their houses and barns, establish their gardens and, eventually, orchards; they might even plow patches of a house lot to grow crops. Occupied, possessed and ecologically reconfigured to suit the new human residents and their domestic animals, house lots formed only one part of the colonists' holdings. "Each was but the focal point of a much larger

---

[51] Quoted in Philip J. Greven, *Four Generations: Population, Land, and Family in Colonial Andover, Massachusetts* (Ithaca, N.Y.: Cornell University Press, 1970), 45.
[52] Main, *Peoples of a Spacious Land*, 55.

constellation of lands and privileges, including planting rights in the general fields, mowing lots in the meadows, and grazing and other rights in the commons."[53] General fields were large expanses of plowland divided into component strips, each assigned to an individual house-holder. A fence surrounded the whole to protect crops from ruminants, but only unobtrusive stakes indicated internal boundaries between strips. Agriculture in the general fields had to proceed by an agreed-upon sea-sonal rhythm, so that everyone planted, harvested and then grazed their animals on the stubble at the same time. Some large meadows were also jointly managed, even as individuals claimed particular component areas where they gathered their hay. Beyond the house lots and general fields, settlers were sometimes granted individual lots scattered across the "upland." Though assigned to a particular person, an upland lot remained effectively part of the township commons until such time as the owner cleared and fenced it.

A founding settler named William Hartwell ended up with a nine-acre house lot in Concord, three acres in one general field, four and a half in another, plus another twenty-four acres in three scattered upland lots (see Figure 6.1). Additionally, he had access to the town commons, which in the early years simply meant the unassigned and uncultivated lands beyond the fields and meadows. In New England, such common lands were used "for wood pasturing, logging, hunting, haying, quarry-ing, thatch cutting, peat digging, and foraging, all performed under the watchful eye of town wardens."[54] As the town became more established, separate pastures were set aside in the riverside lowlands for cattle and sheep; Hartwell could send his animals there every day, where they would be watched over by the village herdsman. William Hartwell's property in Concord was, like that of all his neighbors, fragmented and dispersed; it was made up of different kinds of land, useful for different agricultural purposes. Moreover, he held it in quite different ways – a share in the commons or an allotment in a general field was not his to do with as he pleased in the way that a house lot was – and so his property was legally, as well as ecologically and agriculturally, plural. Add to that the fact that Hartwell was a proprietor of the township of Concord, and therefore held an inheritable entitlement to future allocations of the large undivided commons: this was a real asset, though it was not "land" in any tangible

---

[53] Donahue, *The Great Meadow*, 80. See also Main, *Peoples of a Spacious Land*, 53.
[54] Richard Judd, *Second Nature: An Environmental History of New England* (Amherst: University of Massachusetts Press, 2014), 74.

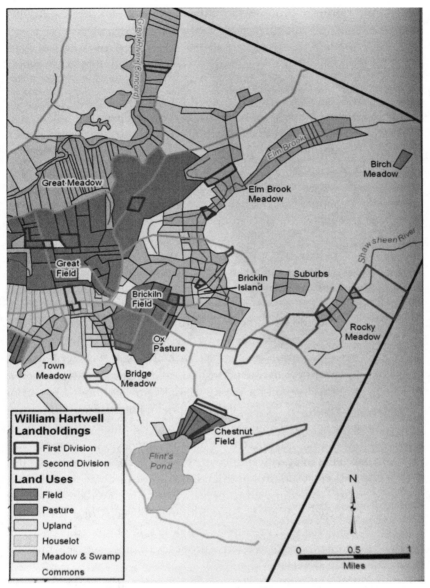

FIGURE 6.1 William Hartwell's land-holdings in the town of Concord,
Massachusetts, acquired through the first (1635 or 1636) and second (1653)
divisions. Hartwell's nine-acre house lot is highlighted here, just under the "Great
Field." Brian Dohahue's map of his holdings indicate twenty-two additional
tracts: "lots in the Great Field, the Bricklin Field, and the Chestnut Field; and
mowing in the Great Meadow, Elm Brook Meadow, and Rocky Meadow."
Source: Brian Donahue, *The Great Meadow: Farmers and the Land in Colonial Concord*
(New Haven: Yale University Press, 2004), plate 2. Courtesy Yale University Press.

sense, but rather a promise of future considerations in terrain that was to become individualized property at a later date.

To call property in Concord and the other early townships of New England "communal" is to get it only partly right. Plymouth Plantation in its first few years had actually functioned on a communistic basis, its lands and produce being shared by the colonists without exclusive claims, but the experiment was short lived. However, open-field tillage and common pasturing of livestock was a feature, to one degree or another, of most seventeenth-century townships. Watertown, Massachusetts, close to the markets of Boston, moved rapidly to consolidate scattered lots into self-contained farms, whereas the enclosure process took place over half a century at Dedham. In spite of extensive enclosure in seventeenth-century Concord, an open "Great Field," together with various collective agricultural practices, survived there until the eve of the Revolution.[55] There were extensive common pastures in Rowley, Massachusetts, their use regulated by "gates" (stints) that determined how many beasts an individual could graze there; when cattle-raising became profitable, a lively market in gates developed (demonstrating that "the commons" could be compatible with a certain form of capitalism). Billerica had a town pasture, but allowed residents to graze their livestock anywhere beyond the arable: "... all such uplands, wch ly unfenced, which are the propriety of any perticuler person or prsons what so ever, shall be accounted Comon for the fre feed of Cattell without any Lett or hinderance from any of the perticuler proprietors of the same." This was not the only town where one man's cattle had legitimate access to what was, in other respects, supposed to be another man's land.[56] Property was not just one thing in seventeenth-century New England: it never implied fully exclusive private control over land. But nor was it entirely collective. Property rights tended instead to be variegated and layered: individuals had different degrees of control over different portions of a township's surface. No doubt something similar could be said of landed property in England and other parts of Western Europe at the time, but New England

---

[55] Powell, *Puritan Village*, 92; Lockridge, *A New England Town*, 82; Donahue, *The Great Meadow*, 117–27.

[56] Billerica Records, p. 39; David Konig, "Community Custom and the Common Law: Social Change and the Development of Land Law in Seventeenth-Century Massachusetts," *American Journal of Legal History* 18 (1974): 168; David Grayson Allen, *In English Ways: The Movement of Societies and the Transferal of English Local Law and Custom to Massachusetts Bay in the Seventeenth Century* (Chapel Hill: University of North Carolina Press, 1981), 33–37, 126–28.

displayed some special characteristics reflective of the fact that settler tenures were just emerging and expanding rapidly.

The variegated property rights associated with different patches of territory that a colonist such as William Hartwell enjoyed within his township were all held conditionally. Lands were given out for a specific purpose, to provide homes and livelihoods for families, and the settler who failed to occupy his land and begin preparing it for agricultural purposes risked having his grant revoked.[57] There was an ecological imperative, both to transform the environment so as to make it suitable for the kind of convertible husbandry that had shaped the European landscape over the centuries and to care for the land so as to maintain its fruitfulness. In his "Essay on the Ordering of Towns," John Winthrop recalled God's "Grand Charter" with Adam: "Replenish the earth and subdue it." Winthrop (who himself owned large undeveloped tracts) goes on: "And therfore I cannot yet se that any man hath Theologicall Right unto any possession without a faithfull practicall care of the performance of this principall Condicion of that Grand Covenant assigned unto him: what pretence of Civell Right soever he may challenge unto himselfe concerneing the same."[58] Land ownership, according to Winthrop's view, implied responsibility as well as benefits; humans owed obligations to the Maker of the universe as well as to one another. That idea of "property as propriety," to borrow a phrase from the legal scholar Carol Rose, was widely shared in the European world of the period.[59] In early New England (as well as in New Spain and New France), it was actually built in to the rules of land granting, making property theoretically contingent on a certain environmental rectitude.

Of course the settler's rectitude could be, and usually was, at odds with the environmental practices of indigenous peoples. Historians tend to dwell on the ecological aggression implied by the biblical injunction to "subdue the earth" – and with good reason. As William Cronon has demonstrated, the colonists' axes and plows, not to mention the sharp hooves of their cattle and the burrowing snouts of their hogs, tore up the earth and disturbed its ecosystems in ways that played havoc with native subsistence systems.[60] Note however that the injunction also calls on

---

[57] Cronon, *Changes in the Land*, 73.
[58] Winthrop, "Essay on the Ordering of Towns," in *Winthrop Papers*, 3: 182.
[59] Carol M. Rose, "Property as Propriety," in *Property and Persuasion: Essays on the History, Theory, and Rhetoric of Ownership* (Boulder, Colo.: Westview Press, 1994), 58–65.
[60] Cronon, *Changes in the Land*.

settlers to "replenish the earth," which implies maintaining its fertility by tilling and manuring fields, removing weeds, pruning fruit trees and so on. This, by the way, was not an exclusively Puritan ideal; the great agricultural treatises of sixteenth- and seventeenth-century Europe were filled with practical advice about making proper use of the land's bounty for the support of families, reflecting a conception of *oeconomia* that went back to the ancient Greeks and that continued to dominate thinking about agriculture until the nineteenth century.[61] Brian Donahue's careful research on agricultural practices in colonial Concord suggests that the colonists of New England were indeed closely attentive to their natural environments and that they labored to fashion a way of using the land that was sustainable: for themselves, their families and their communities.[62]

Settler property formation, and the rules and customs that surrounded it, revolved primarily around the material needs of families. Land allocations within a township seem designed to serve, in the first instance, to grow food for subsistence, to provide fuel and building materials and to support domestic animals. With time, hard work and good luck, these same lands would enable settlers to produce a marketable surplus so that they could acquire "comforts" beyond a bare subsistence. The ideal, writes Daniel Vickers, was a level of economic independence he calls a "competency."[63] How much land did a household need to maintain a competency? That had to be an elastic quantity, depending on the level of "comfort" a colonial family aspired to, but also on the number of children it needed to provide for. If he had growing children, a responsible colonist like William Hartwell had to think about acquiring upland lots beyond his immediate agricultural needs; he would also take a keen interest in the next township "division" and might even watch for an opportunity to acquire land in another town. Property was instituted in New England mainly to support households, but those households just kept growing and multiplying, with the consequence that it could be hard to determine precisely how much land a given family required to maintain its "competency" over the long run. As in Europe, land was attached, through individuals, to evolving and mutating families, but here the supply of both people and land seemed, at times, almost infinitely expandable.

---

[61] See Keith Tribe, *Land, Labour and Economic Discourse* (London: Routledge, 1978), 53–79.
[62] Donahue, *The Great Meadow*. See also Judd, *Second Nature*, 80–83.
[63] Vickers, *Farmers and Fishermen*, 14–23.

Thus, a seemingly modest, self-limiting approach to property-making, one that tied land entitlements to the needs of a household economy, nevertheless served to drive on relentless territorial expansion.

English colonies in the Caribbean and around Chesapeake Bay developed profitable export-oriented agricultures that drove up the value of land and quickly made the latter a lucrative investment; in New England, on the other hand and in spite of the emergence of some pockets of commercially oriented agriculture, it was mainly the growth of the settler population that powered demand for property. Even after immigration tapered off in the 1640s, natural demographic increase continued to fuel expansion, with new townships being created and successive divisions filling in existing towns with more and more fields and meadows. Even if first-generation townships like Concord were developing a new ecological equilibrium based on mixed husbandry, with humans, cattle, croplands, orchards, meadows and waterways coexisting in a sustainable relationship, property making continued on apace as long as the settler population kept growing.

Several historians have detected a general shift in attitudes and practices concerning property in the older English settlements around the 1660s, as entitlements to land came to be more highly prized. Driving this change was no great agricultural boom comparable to the tobacco export economy that was fueling growth in the Chesapeake region. Instead, land pressure came mainly from demographic expansion, with capital imported by immigrants and generated from colonial activities such as shipping and fishing helping to push up land prices. Signs of these changed circumstances can be seen in the behavior of the second and third generation of colonists. Open-field practices declined in many townships as a process of enclosure brought scattered plots together to form consolidated farmsteads and as new divisions were made in severalty, with no provision for new general fields.[64] Developed land near port towns commanded a substantial price. At the same time, professional surveying began to emerge; neighbors took one another to court in disputes over boundaries and rights of way far more frequently than in earlier decades.[65] Finally, townspeople became far more careful about rights in the undivided commons. With more and more reason to think of these undeveloped tracts

---

[64] Lockridge, *A New England Town*, 82; Greven, *Four Generations*, 51–57; Donahue, *The Great Meadow*, 117–27.

[65] Konig, *Law and Society in Puritan Massachusetts*, 50–53; Jonathan M. Chu, "Nursing a Poisonous Tree: Litigation and Property Law in Seventeenth-Century Essex County, Massachusetts – The Case of Bishop's Farm," *American Journal of Legal History* 31 (1987): 221–52.

not only as a potential home for their grown children, but also as a valuable and potentially profitable asset, township proprietors moved to restrict membership and shut out new residents from future divisions.

COMMODIFICATION

Though instituted as a basis for householding and not primarily as an instrument for producing revenue, settler property in early New England was nevertheless highly vendible. Recall that land is not naturally a commodity to be exchanged through a physical act of removal the way movable goods are. When land is held, as it generally was in early modern Europe, subject to multiple overlapping lordships, it could be very difficult to sell a piece of land in such a way as to ensure that the buyer would not later be challenged by other stakeholders. Though basically free of such feudal complications, New England property was still subject to the claims of colony, township, spouse and kin. Nevertheless, in the context of those times, New England developed an unusually effective and streamlined system to facilitate land transactions. However, the phrase "land transactions" masks some degree of heterogeneity, for separate markets developed for different sorts of property: directly exploited plowlands, shares of townships, "gates" or grazing quotas on the commons. To speak precisely, it was not "land," plain and simple, that became salable, but rather diverse claims to territory and resources, present and future.

As one element of the emergent property system, records were supposed to be kept of all properties at the local level. As early as 1634, the Massachusetts General Court required townships to maintain a systematic listing of all "the howses backeside, corne feildes, moweing ground, & other lands, improved, or inclosed ... of every ffree inhabitant," in order to provide "assurance" to the proprietors and to prevent fraudulent claims. Additionally, a system was established for recording deeds in registries that would be open to public view. Massachusetts instituted registries in 1640, with the announced purpose of "avoyding all fraudulent conveyances, & that every man may know what estate or interest other men may have in any houses, lands, or other hereditaments they are to deale in." The aim of these measures was to eliminate uncertainty about title in a situation of rapid growth and mobility; the effect was to make the buying and selling of land comparatively frictionless.[66]

---

[66] *The General Laws and Liberties of the Massachusets Colony*, 32–33; Shurtleff, *Records of the Governor and Company of the Massachusetts Bay*, vol. 1: 116, 137, 201, 306–7;

It is easy to exaggerate the uniqueness and precocious modernity of the New England deed and record system. In fact, townships apparently dragged their feet about maintaining systematic land records, forcing the Massachusetts General Court to reiterate its orders repeatedly. Moreover, even at their best, township land records were light years removed from modern cadastral systems. Holdings were described rather vaguely by "metes and bounds" rather than precise coordinates (see Chapter 9). Little wonder that the courts were filled with land disputes occasioned by ambiguous and conflicting titles. And though the New England system had many advantages from the point of view of vendibility of land, it was not entirely unique. Virginia boasted a land register as early as 1619. In New France, seigneurs maintained *livres terriers* that, along with their primary function of recording rents, also served as a listing of all properties and proprietors in the *censive*; additionally, notaries kept meticulous records of sales and other mutations of ownership (though these were not open to public scrutiny). Such facilities were not unknown in the Old World: land registration may have been unsystematic and geographically spotty in Great Britain, but it was highly developed in the seventeenth-century Netherlands.[67]

It may have been somewhat easier to buy and sell land in New England than in New France and New Spain, but what really distinguishes the English colonies from those of France and Spain is the legal institution of the mortgage. Other jurisdictions used land holdings as security for debts, but only as one part of the debtor's total assets, all of which could be seized in the course of judicial action. Only in British America was it possible for a creditor to tie debt to a specific plot of land with the assurance that no other claimant could touch that asset in the event of a

---

vol. 4, pt. 1: 22, 101; John Noble, ed., *Records of the Court of Assistants of the Colony of the Massachusetts Bay, 1630–1692*, 3 vols. (Boston: County of Suffolk, 1901), 2: 45; George L. Haskins, "The Beginnings of the Recording System in Massachusetts," *Boston University Law Review* 21 (1941): 281–304; Richard Brandon Morris, *Studies in the History of American Law, with Special Reference to the Seventeenth and Eighteenth Centuries*, 2nd ed. (Philadelphia: J. M. Mitchell Co., 1959), 69–73; Peter Charles Hoffer, *Law and People in Colonial America* (Baltimore: Johns Hopkins University Press, 1992), 70–71; Bruce H. Mann, "The Transformation of Law and Economy in Early America," in *The Cambridge History of Law in America*, vol. 1: *Early America, 1580–1815*, ed. M. Grossberg and Christopher L. Tomlins (New York: Cambridge University Press, 2008), 368–69.

67 Marshall Harris, *Origin of the Land Tenure System in the United States* (Ames: Iowa State College Press, 1953), 331–37; Konig, *Law and Society in Puritan Massachusetts*, 40–42.

default. Publicly accessible registers recording mortgages as well as sales were crucial to this procedure, heading off the possibility that a dishonest borrower could use the same land to secure multiple loans. Thanks to these state-provided facilities, simple and secure mortgages emerged as a genuine New England innovation. Mostly mortgages were closely tied to the purchase of the mortgaged property itself: they gave the seller security while the buyer paid off the purchase price in installments. Sometimes, however, money raised on established properties served to finance the expansion of colonization into new areas, as when Roger Williams mortgaged his Salem house to buy the gifts that secured Narragansett approval of the establishment of the new township of Providence (see Chapter 3). It seems apparent that the deed and register system, in its mortgage as well as its sale/purchase function, contributed to the rapid expansion of colonial property formation in this part of the world.

Mortgages also functioned as a device to document and legitimize the seizure of native land. They were particularly useful to fur traders who advanced merchandise to native hunters and, when beaver stocks collapsed, as they inevitably did, and the hunters were unable to discharge their debts, forced them to sign mortgages on large tracts of land. Later, the merchant would foreclose and claim the territory as his property, now firmly within the colonial tenure regime. It was primarily by this means that John Pynchon amassed a large estate in western Massachusetts. The same strategy lay behind many an Indian deed all across New England.[68] It was of course absurd to place a mortgage on land that was, at that point, still Ninnimissinuok property subject to indigenous tenure and therefore neither salable nor mortgageable. In such transactions, the mortgage served a more important function than merely securing a debt; it documented an assertion of jurisdiction over indigenous lands. With fur-trade mortgages, as with cross-cultural purchases, the trick was to pretend that territory was already part of the settler property regime, and by that fiction to make it so.

Mortgages certainly facilitated both native dispossession and settler property-making, but they also complicated the latter by adding a new layer of ownership. A mortgage, in effect, transfers ownership, albeit

---

[68] Peter A. Thomas, *In the Maelstrom of Change: The Indian Trade and Cultural Process in the Middle Connecticut River Valley, 1635–1665* (New York: Garland Publishing, 1990), 324–28; Southern Essex County Register of Deeds, vol. 1, fol. 13; vol. 10, fol. 16; Yasuhide Kawashima, *Puritan Justice and the Indian: White Man's Law in Massachusetts, 1630–1763* (Middletown, Conn.: Wesleyan University Press, 1986), 61; Pulsipher, *Subjects unto the Same King*, 56.

provisionally and conditionally, to the creditor; the property in question remains under the control of the debtor, but only so long as he or she pays off the debt according to the specified terms. Defaulting debtors in New France also stood to lose their land if a court judged against them, but up to the point where assets were liquidated, the property in the French colony still belonged fully to the proprietor, which was not the case for mortgaged land in New England. A mortgagor held an actual share in the land's title until such time as the debt was discharged. Lands in New France were held subject to the claims of a seigneur, whereas lands in New England were held subject to the claims of township, spouse, kin and, in some cases, mortgagor. In neither colony can we find anything that corresponds to the ideal of simple, unitary private property.

At the same time, it is perfectly true that land in New England's fully colonized zone was, thanks to the institutions of mortgage and title registration, rapidly acquiring the quality of convertibility. More readily than in other parts of North America, landed property could be transformed into credit, money and other valuable goods. "Commodification" is the term frequently attached to this phenomenon and it is not misplaced. However, since this word might evoke in some readers' minds visions of the forces of capitalism advancing across the colonial scene and sweeping all before them, a word of caution is in order. Unless we subscribe to a teleological view of history, one in which the only meaningful developments are those that anticipate or contribute to the "transition to capitalism," seventeenth-century property-making has to be understood in different, more complex, terms. It may well be the case that the legal facilities that facilitated land transactions eventually contributed to the industrialization of New England by mobilizing the capital of small proprietors (though that contribution was likely dwarfed by capital amassed through overseas trade), but significant industrial development only occurred much later, after the American Revolution. Through the colonial period, this remained predominantly a society of independent smallholders interspersed with growing commercial centers; capitalist production based on wage labor was not at the heart of this economy.

For more than a century, property formation and the concomitant dispossession of indigenous people proceeded primarily through the establishment of small holdings to support resident family households, each of them embedded in a local community. Territories came into the colonial tenure regime mostly as holdings for settlers. That was the principal means by which townships and colonies grew as governed spaces.

There were indeed many exceptions to this generally prevalent pattern, however: places such as the middle Connecticut Valley in Massachusetts where landlord–tenant relations became common, or the rich pasture lands on Narragansett Bay where some large-scale cattle-raising operations employed hired hands and even slaves to produce for distant markets. Small grants, made under township auspices for the establishment of households, had never accounted for all the land entitlements in colonial New England. From the beginning, some individuals secured claims to wide tracts that seemed to authorize larger economic ambitions. Colonies had used such grants to reward influential individuals, such as Governor John Winthrop, who received 1000 acres in Medford from the Massachusetts General Court; the town of Ipswich later gave his son 300 acres to secure his support for the infant settlement.[69] Other colonial notables who helped establish towns by contributing capital or by exercising political influence received large tracts from their grateful fellow-proprietors. It was easy to be generous in allocating undeveloped acres when these were worth next to nothing; such endowments were really a promise for the future and an enticement to keep the recipient interested in the fate of the region. In most cases, these elite landholders never lived in the townships where their endowments were located (some never even left England), but some took steps to develop their holdings and bring them into the English colonial ecological sphere. Usually located on the edges of growing townships, these plots were often known as "farms," reflecting the prevailing expectation that they would be rented to a tenant and/or operated as an agricultural enterprise employing waged workers ("servants"). Winthrop was among those who did manage to draw some revenue from his land-holdings in this way.[70] Similarly, there were a few colonization entrepreneurs who acquired rights directly from indigenous owners to extensive areas that they subsequently made available to settler families. Roger Williams was one of these, and he claimed he never profited personally from his efforts in launching the town of Providence. William Pynchon represents another case: he acquired substantial holdings along the Connecticut River from natives and then rented out plots to colonists. Although it was settler families creating homes, fields and meadows that did the most to bring Springfield fully into the colonial

---

[69] Main, *Peoples of a Spacious Land*, 191; Anderson, *New England's Generation*, 94.

[70] Adjacent to Winthrop's grant, on the edges of Concord and Billerica townships, the Blood family assembled a number of smaller holdings to create "Blood's Farm." See Shattuck, *A History of the Town of Concord*, 13–14, 64–65; Donahue, *The Great Meadow*, 106.

property regime, the entrepreneurial Pynchon, together with his son John, also made their contribution in documenting title and providing infrastructure for the community.[71]

A decade or so before the outbreak of King Philip's War, full-fledged land speculation made its appearance on the New England scene with the formation of syndicates organized for the purpose of generating profits for nonresident investors. Some of these companies endeavored to exploit the territorial ambiguities in colonial charters and native cessions to claim large tracts, hoping to divide these up and sell them to settlers. An early example is the Atherton Company, which numbered the younger Winthrop among its shareholders, organized in 1659 to secure a huge tract on the uncertain edges of Rhode Island, Connecticut and Narragansett country.[72] Such strictly entrepreneurial land speculation remained somewhat marginal in seventeenth-century New England, where townships created mainly by actual settlers were still the norm. Much later, however, toward the middle of the eighteenth century, land development companies would move to front and center in the process of incorporating space in Maine and the trans-Appalachian west into the colonial sphere (see Chapter 11). Then, as in the earlier period, speculative activity was parasitic, a matter of "rent-seeking" in the language of economics. Property formation in the colonial period depended centrally on the efforts of settler families transforming the environment.

Many ordinary colonists were indeed laying claim to lands beyond their immediate needs and in excess of what they could actually develop. Partly this was a matter of reserving space for the coming generation to colonize, and it led freemen not only to claim their due in township divisions, but also, in many cases, to invest as proprietors in new townships as they were created in the hinterland. At the same time, land in the more established townships, now quite desirable compared with the new settlements because of its convenient location and developed infrastructure, was increasingly likely to be treated as a lucrative entitlement rather than simply a home. People inherited shares in a township and then went

---

[71] Alden T. Vaughan, ed., *Early American Indian Documents: Treaties and Laws, 1607–1789*, 20 vols. (Washington, D.C.: University Publications of America, 1979), 19: 48–49; Stephen Innes, *Labor in a New Land: Economy and Society in Seventeenth-Century Springfield* (Princeton, N.J.: Princeton University Press, 1983), 44–71; Martin, *Profits in the Wilderness*, 47–49.

[72] Martin, *Profits in the Wilderness*, 62–73. For other examples of land speculation companies, see ibid., 73–110. Martin's informative work has to be read with caution, as the author is inclined to find signs of corporate capitalism everywhere and at all times.

to sea or moved to another colony, leaving unoccupied land for rent or for sale to others, thus fueling a kind of low-level, "innocent" speculation that, even when not driven by pure motives of profit, still helped drive a wedge between ownership and residence.[73]

Speculative tendencies, both large and small scale, only added to the pressures on indigenous territories, already squeezed by the ongoing expansion of settler colonization. The Ninnimissinuok were finally driven to violent resistance in the war of 1675–76, and in the wake of that exceedingly destructive conflict, Puritan ministers struggled to understand its meaning. Assuming that this calamity had been a transaction between God and His chosen people, with natives acting only as the instrument of divine chastisement, they asked themselves, what violations of godly justice had led to such severe punishment? A sermon by Rev. Increase Mather pointed the finger of blame at land hunger, which had reached sinful proportions in the years leading up to the war:

Land! Land! hath been the Idol of many in New-England: whereas the first Planters here that they might keep themselves together were satisfied with one Acre for each person, as his propriety, and after that with twenty Acres for a Family, how have Men since coveted after the earth, that many hundreds, nay thousands of Acres, have been engrossed by one man, and they that profess themselves Christians, have forsaken Churches, and Ordinances, and all for land and elbow-room enough in the World.

A Massachusetts synod of 1679–80 echoed this judgment: "Farms and merchandising have been preferred before the things of God."[74]

Land, Mather implies, was not an "idol" in the early stages of colonization, when claims were small and calibrated to settlers' needs: "to keep [i.e., sustain or support] themselves together." Even when they sought more, "for a Family," their aspirations remained legitimate. But beyond the modest claims of subsistence and reproduction lies a realm of sinful covetousness. The preacher dwells on a spiritual/moral distinction (satisfaction versus covetousness), but hints also at a contrast between two different kinds of property. There is the (small) "propriety" that "keeps" individuals, families and communities, and there is the "elbow-room" that some strive to "engross." In the first case "land" is a space that is

---

[73] Konig, *Law and Society in Puritan Massachusetts*, 65–66.

[74] Increase Mather, *An Earnest Exhortation to the Inhabitants of New-England* (Boston: John Foster, 1676), 12 (online edition edited by Reiner Smolinski, Electronic Texts in American Studies, http://digitalcommons.unl.edu/etas/31, reference found in Pulsipher, *Subjects unto the same King*, 72); Main, *Peoples of a Spacious Land*, 193.

possessed and used to sustain people, in the second it is a zone of exclusion. Engrossed, it is held as an investment and not put into production for the support of households. Speculators do eventually have to sell or rent to actual settlers in small parcels in order to realize a profit, but it is the holding of an unproductive entitlement that makes land engrossment unchristian from Mather's point of view. Needless to add, he sees fellow colonists, rather than indigenous people, as the victims of engrossment.

Modern historians tend to follow Increase Mather's spiritual/moral analysis, even as they transpose it into a secular idiom. Did the New England colonists have a capitalistic/entrepreneurial mentality ("coveted after the earth"), they ask, or were they more community-minded ("satisfied")? The subjective, psychological approach focuses, like the Puritan's sermon, on the settler population, probing for the essential inner qualities that characterize them as a group. It lends itself nicely to historical discourses about national character. Historians have shown less interest in what might loosely be called the "objective" content of Mather's jeremiad. Whatever we might imagine to have been going on within the minds of New England's early colonists, a settler family's small holding and the extensive claims of speculators such as the Atherton Company were quite different things. In one case, Mather declares, "land" consists mainly of acres possessed, plowed, planted and grazed; in the other it consists of paper entitlements, by virtue either of colonial grants or of Indian deeds, to zones where possession and use are currently excluded. Economically, socially and ecologically, these are quite different kinds of spaces, and yet we are in the habit of calling them all "land." Increase Mather knew better.

NATIVES

Until their defeat in King Philip's War, Ninnimissinuok peoples continued to control the largest part of the region: not only to the west and north of the colonized zones, but also in substantial enclaves near the coast, often cheek-by-jowl to the Puritan settlements. Amid epidemics, wars and the onrushing flood of immigrants into their homeland, natives were doing their best to survive, maintaining a margin of independence while preserving their access to vital resources. They resisted colonization where possible; some migrated westward or north into Canada, others developed strategies of adaptation. Inevitably, approaches to land and territory changed as natives adopted some English ways and worked out techniques for dealing with the growing settler regimes.

The early peace-and-coexistence agreements that Massasoit, Canonicus and other sachems had negotiated eventually turned out to be an ineffective defense against an English takeover of Ninnimissinuok space. Colonists and their courts were ignoring the treaties' complexities and nuances, focusing only on the brutally simplified formulas recorded in the written "Indian deeds" that supposedly summarized agreed-upon arrangements. In cases where there was no such Indian deed or where the original had been lost, a formal text could always be produced after the fact in the form of signed depositions attesting that a given tract had indeed been sold by "the Indians." By just such means, a 1637 oral agreement allowing colonists to settle Concord was turned into a legal record and virtual deed in 1684.[75] Indian deeds, whether "real," "virtual" or retrospective, had an important role to play within the colonists' legal universe, but we should not fetishize them as though they were the *cause* of native dispossession. English power made itself felt in a thousand ways, ensuring that territory would be absorbed, with or without indigenous agreement, into the colonial property zone.

As the divergence between English and native conceptions of territorial accommodation was progressively revealed, both sides tended to become cynical about purchases and deeds. Colonists had recourse to various forms of fraud and coercion to secure deeds. At the time of a war scare in 1642, the founders of Haverhill, Massachusetts, took advantage of a militia expedition to disarm supposedly hostile Pentuckets, forcing the helpless natives to conclude a gun-point sale of a large tract of land along the Merrimack River. Elsewhere, unscrupulous purchasers would look for a sachem who could be bribed with liquor to sell out his people's birthright. If a chief refused to sell land, complained Wampanoag sachem Metacom, the English would "make a nother king that wold give or seell them there land." On the other hand, it would be wrong to imply that land surrenders were all the product of direct and immediate fraud or

---

[75] Hudson, *The History of Concord, Massachusetts*, 1: 275–76. Such after-the-fact documents are fairly common, leading Francis Jennings to the conclusion that many treaties were fabricated from whole cloth. Such fraud may have been perpetrated in some cases, but the depositions connected with the Concord treaty seem quite plausible. That is to say, I am convinced that an agreement was concluded at about the time Concord was founded. The issue for me is not so much one of documents pretending to record agreements that never took place, but rather of treaties that gave a distorted sense of verbal negotiations and that came to be deployed in ways the native signatories did not intend. See Francis Jennings, "Virgin Land and Savage People," *American Quarterly* 23 (1971): 519–41.

coercion. The sources give the impression that many natives, faced with powerful and relentless pressure for their land, concluded that it would be better to accept a few pounds and sign a paper when dispossession seemed inevitable regardless. There also seem to have been cases where impoverished indigenous people living near the settlements engaged in shakedown operations. That may (or may not) have been the nature of a visitation Christopher Lindsie received from a group of natives shortly after he had bought a house in Lynn, Massachusetts. The sachem Poquanum, Lindsie testified, "Asked me what I would give him for the Land my house stood upon, itt beinge his Land, and his ffathers wigwame stood their abouts."[76]

Around Massachusetts Bay, where Ninnimissinuok populations had been severely affected by the epidemics and wars of the pre-colonization period, a certain political disintegration set in, making it easier for settlers to find self-styled sachems who could be bought off with alcohol and other goods. Such tactics served only to accelerate the disaggregation of native societies. By the 1640s, somewhat desocialized families and small bands could be found on the edges of many townships, selling baskets and other handicrafts and working as hired hands for local settlers. Yet there was no real place for them in colonial society or on colonial lands, township property being, almost by definition, land that had been removed from native control. In 1644, five Massachusett sachems were forced to agree "to put ourselves, our subjects, lands, and estates under the government and jurisdiction of the Massachusets [colonial government]."[77] Still, the Puritans had some hesitation about utterly supplanting and rejecting people who were, after all, children of God (not to mention useful workers and, if pushed to the brink, potentially dangerous enemies). If settler colonialism can be said to vacillate between the impulse to assimilate and the impulse to eliminate the indigene, then it seems unsurprising that the early New England tendency to exclude natives would generate a countercurrent in the form of the "praying town" experiment.

This was originally a strictly Massachusetts phenomenon, largely the brainchild of Rev. John Eliot, a minister who became convinced that, two decades after Puritans had come bringing Christianity to America, it was

---

[76] Sidney Perley, *The Indian Land Titles of Essex County, Massachusetts* (Salem, Mass.: Essex Book and Print Club, 1912), 31–34, 49–50; Virginia DeJohn Anderson, *Creatures of Empire: How Domestic Animals Transformed Early America* (New York: Oxford University Press, 2004), 233

[77] Pulsipher, *Subjects unto the Same King*, 27.

high time to launch an effort to convert the Ninnimissinuok. With financial support from England and with the encouragement of the General Court, he set out to learn the Massachusett language and to communicate the word of God to indigenous people in the vicinity of the English settlements. Between 1651 and 1674, fourteen praying towns were established. As a good Calvinist, Eliot asked natives to conform to European ways of living and working, a much more thoroughgoing cultural transformation than what Catholic missionaries of the period demanded. But like the evangelists of Mexico and Canada, he focused on gathering natives together, under missionary supervision, on specially designated tracts of land. His praying-town project had much in common with the campaign of *congregación* in New Spain, and like the earlier program, it received the support of secular authorities partly for quite secular reasons having to do with the management of natives and their labor and their lands. Though settlers in the immediate vicinity were quite hostile to the Indian presence, English supporters of praying towns defended them on the grounds that they confined native land claims to delimited areas.[78]

To a striking degree, Massachusetts legislation and public discourse surrounding the praying towns is couched in the language of property and jurisdiction. A preliminary measure in 1646 established a committee headed by the surveyor-general to apply charitable donations from England to the purchase of land "for ye incuragmt of ye Indians to live in an orderly way amongst us." Then, in 1652, after Natick had been set up next to Dedham as the first praying town, came more comprehensive legislation. The law first affirmed that "what landes any of the Indians, within this jurisdiction, have by possession or improvement, by subdueing the same, they have just right thereunto, accordinge to that Gen: 1: 28, chap: 9: 1, Psa: 115, 16." This was actually a principle long accepted in the colony, though frequently honored in the breach. The Puritans certainly applied a very restricted definition of "possession," accepting only rights to planting grounds currently cultivated, but within that narrow conception, they did seem prepared to give official recognition to native property. Thus, the Massachusetts General Court, having awarded 3000 acres at the mouth of the Concord River to the widow of Governor

---

[78] On praying towns, see Neal Salisbury, "Red Puritans: The 'Praying Indians' of Massachusetts Bay and John Eliot," *William and Mary Quarterly*, 3rd ser., 31 (1974): 27–54; James Axtell, *The Invasion Within: The Contest of Cultures in Colonial North America* (New York: Oxford University Press, 1985), 131–48; Jean M. O'Brien, *Dispossession by Degree: Indian Land and Identity in Natick, Massachusetts, 1650–1790* (Lincoln: University of Nebraska Press, 1997).

Winthrop, later offered her an additional thirty acres in compensation, "because wee find the Indians possessed of severall parcells of land within the said 3000 acres."[79] However, the 1652 law went on to provide for "the further encouragmt of the hopeful worke amongst them for the civillizinge & helping them forward to Christianitie," by permitting indigenous people who have been "brought to civillitie" to share in township allotments (something that, to my knowledge, never actually happened); of more consequence was the provision that natives "brought to civilitie" might apply for a township of their own and "have graunt of landes undisposed off for a plantation, as the English have." Having established that natives could be "given" lands by the colony, the bill goes on to assert the corollary, namely, that "all the tract of land within the jurisdiction of this Court ... (not being under the qualification of right to the Indians fore recited) is & shalbe accompted the just right of such English as already have or hereafter shall have graunt of landes from this Court & authority thereof." Provision within the colonial sphere of lands for natives judged "civil" thus served as an occasion to bolster English property claims.[80]

Notwithstanding the dreams of Christian universalism that accompanied European empire-building generally, and that found expression in the announcement that natives would be integrated into the emergent colonial society, praying towns were never the same as the self-governing, collectively owned townships established for colonists. Local regulations (mostly concerned with the punishment of "idleness" and the suppression of pagan practices) were devised and enacted by John Eliot, not by the residents themselves. In 1656, superintendent of Indian affairs Daniel Gookin established a system of courts with native magistrates for the praying towns, but ultimate jurisdictional power rested with Gookin himself. As units of land-holding and jurisdiction, the towns resembled a Mexican *pueblo de indios*, but with considerably less autonomy for indigenous people. As in New Spain and New France also, native property rights were hedged about with restrictions, especially concerning sales. Whereas alienability was the one property right the English consistently recognized when dealing with independent indigenous nations, natives living within the colonial sphere in praying towns were not

---

[79] Shurtleff, *Records of the Governor and Company of the Massachusetts Bay*, 2: 12, 14 June 1642.
[80] Ibid. 3: 281–82, 19 October 1652.

permitted to sell land to colonists.[81] Moreover, Eliot's local regulations – designed to transform "savages" into English peasants – left little room for natives to make use of land as they saw fit. All in all, the land tenure of the praying towns was quite distinct from both indigenous Ninnimissin-uok property and New England settler tenure; the praying towns did not belong to their inhabitants in anything like the same way English town-ships belonged to theirs. In the colony but not of it, these closely regulated spaces of exception serve to point up the basic fact that the colonial property system was devised for colonists and not for natives.

For many settlers, particularly those living in areas adjoining a praying town, good, conveniently located land in the possession of Indians con-stituted ipso facto an affront. The original praying town, Natick, grew up on land along the Charles River that had long been occupied by some of the Ninnimissinuok people Eliot persuaded to accept a Christian life, yet its boundaries were never fully respected by neighboring settler town-ships. The town of Dedham maintained that one corner of Natick lay within the bounds of its own grant. Over the years, the dispute generated petitions, lawsuits and compromises, but it was also marked by a series of nasty actions in which Dedham settlers invaded disputed lands, ripping down fences and forcing natives to cease working the soil.[82] A similar situation arose when ambiguous township grants placed portions of the praying town of Okommakamesit in the midst of lands claimed by the town of Marlborough, Massachusetts. The natives planted a thriving apple orchard there but were later forced to abandon it, "because the Englishmen's cattle, &c. devour all in it, because it lies open and unfenced; and while the Indians planted there, it was in a sort fenced by them." This is the report of superintendant Daniel Gookin, about the closest approximation to an advocate for indigenous people to be found

[81] Daniel Gookin, *Historical Collections of the Indians in New England: Of Their Several Nations, Numbers, Customs, Manners, Religion and Government, before the English Planted There: Also a True and Faithful Account of the Present State and Condition of the Praying Indians (or Those Who Have Visibly Received the Gospel in New England) Declaring the Number of That People, the Situation and Place of Their Towns and Churches, and Their Manner of Worshipping God ... : Together with a Brief Mention of the Instruments and Means, That God Hath Been Pleased to Use for Their Civilizing and Conversion, Briefly Declaring the Prudent and Faithful Endeavours of the Right Honourable the Corporation of London, for Promoting That Affair: Also Suggesting Some Expedients for Their Further Civilizing and Propagating the Christian Faith among Them* (Boston: Belknap and Hall, 1792), 179.
[82] O'Brien, *Dispossession by Degree*, 39. On the Dedham–Natick conflict, see also Lock-ridge, *A New England Town*, 83–84.

in mid-century Massachusetts; as he continues, however, Gookin proceeds to blame the Christian natives for their own victimization: "yet by their improvidence and bad fences, they reaped little benefit in those times; and that was one cause of their removal."[83] Thus, lands set aside for compliant Indians were subsequently nibbled at and encroached upon by settlers because the supposedly "protected" natives were largely powerless to resist. Jean O'Brien aptly labels this "dispossession by degrees," and the phenomenon seems strangely reminiscent of patterns set in New Spain and later reproduced in New France.

By and large, it was only the most demoralized and atomized indigenous societies that agreed to accept the praying-town regime, hoping thereby to maintain a foothold in their own country.[84] Until 1676, the stronger, more tightly organized Ninnimissinuok polities of southern New England were able to keep somewhat aloof from the colonial regimes and from the religion and jurisdiction of the English, though their margin of maneuver was increasingly constrained by the growing hegemony of the colonies. Theirs was hardly a story of traditionalism or of static "survival"; rather, existing political organizations were changing and new entities arising in the rapidly shifting conditions provoked by colonization. Powerful, charismatic leaders rose to prominence: Uncas who shaped the Mohegans into a dominant power in eastern Connecticut after the destruction of the Pequots; Ninigret, who gathered villages in western Rhode Island to form the Niantics; and Metacom/King Philip, the son of Massasoit, who forged the Wampanoags into a dominant power east of Narragansett Bay. Before 1675, these polities were not openly opposed to the English. On the contrary, in a context of tensions between the colonies and between the English and the Dutch, they typically did their best to harness the power of the colonial governments to advance their own influence and increase their tribute collections. Uncas aligned the Mohegans with Connecticut, and in 1640 he formally ceded to the colony his lands and those of his tributaries. This measure reinforced both Connecticut's territorial pretentions (the colony had no real charter at this point) and his own, without any expectation that the Mohegans would actually vacate their lands. English help also allowed Uncas to kill Miantonomi and gain the advantage over his rivals, the Narragansetts.[85] In some respects, the Mohegans, Niantics and Wampanoags of this period

---

[83] Gookin, *Historical Collections of the Indians in New England*, 220. See also Pulsipher, *Subjects unto the Same King*, 76–77.
[84] Salisbury, "Red Puritans," 38.   [85] Salisbury, *Manitou and Providence*, 226.

resemble the "coalescent societies" that emerged along the edges of imperial expansion in many parts of North and South America, where the destabilizing effects of a European presence led to the rise of new indigenous powers, aggressively absorbing weaker neighbors.[86] In southern New England, however, these expansive native polities were almost surrounded by settlers as of the mid-seventeenth century, and, as a consequence, their margin of independent maneuver was limited compared with that of their Iroquois, Carib or Catawba contemporaries.

Strong enough to keep the English colonies at bay, these rising chiefdoms were nevertheless constrained to accept the hegemony of the latter. The better to overawe Ninnimissinuok, Massachusetts Bay, Plymouth, Connecticut and New Haven formed an alliance, the United Colonies, in 1643 and used their enhanced power to impose asymmetrical treaties on the leading sachems of southern New England. Culturally accustomed to accepting tributary status under a regional hegemon, those Ninnimissinuok who had avoided the fate of the praying Indians were still able to maintain considerable autonomy, even as they accepted the theoretical sovereignty of the English king. Over time, however, they saw that autonomy increasingly undermined by the economic and environmental effects of the settler presence. By mid-century, the fur/wampum trade that had brought so much wealth to coastal New England was collapsing due to the decline of beaver stocks. Worse still, their very subsistence practices were coming under threat, from the extensive foraging of settler livestock (see Chapter 7) as well as from the colonists' transformation of forests into farmlands.[87]

Not long before his death, the Narragansett sachem Miantonomi attempted to create a united Ninnimissinuok front in opposition to the colonies of southern New England. According to English reports,

[86] The term "coalescent societies" is mentioned in Robbie Ethridge, *From Chicaza to Chickasaw: The European Invasion and the Transformation of the Mississippian World, 1540–1715* (Chapel Hill: University of North Carolina Press, 2010), 2. See also Daniel K. Richter, "War and Culture: The Iroquois Experience," *William and Mary Quarterly* 40 (1983): 528–59; James H. Merrell, "The Indians' New World: The Catawba Experience," *William and Mary Quarterly*, 3rd ser., 41 (1984): 537–65; Stuart B. Schwartz and Frank Salomon, "New Peoples and New Kinds of People: Adaptation, Readjustment, and Ethnogenesis in South American Indigenous Societies (Colonial Era)," in *The Cambridge History of the Native Peoples of the Americas*, vol. 3: *South America*, part 2, ed. Frank Salomon and Stuart B. Schwartz (Cambridge and New York: Cambridge University Press, 1999), 443–501; Ned Blackhawk, *Violence over the Land: Indians and Empires in the Early American West* (Cambridge, Mass.: Harvard University Press, 2006).

[87] For a fascinating comparison of native and settler patterns of land use in the early colonial period, see Peter A. Thomas, "Contrastive Subsistence Strategies and Land Use as Factors for Understanding Indian-White Relations in New England," *Ethnohistory* 23 (1976): 1–18.

he expressed himself in the following terms in a 1642 speech to the Montauks of Long Island:

You know our fathers had plenty of deer and skins, our plains were full of deer, as also our woods, and of turkies, and our coves full of fish and fowl. But these English having gotten our land, they with scythes cut down the grass, and with axes fell the trees; their cows and horses eat the grass, and their hogs spoil our clam banks, and we shall all be starved.[88]

The time was not ripe when Miantonomi preached concerted resistance, but by 1675 matters had reached a desperate pass. It was then that, under the leadership of Metacom/King Philip, most of the independent Ninnimissinuok of southern New England, as well as some Nipmucks from the praying towns, rose up and attacked the English settlements. King Philip's War raged for two years, one of the bloodiest conflicts in North American history. Thousands died and innumerable native villages, as well as fourteen English settlements, were completely destroyed. For much of the struggle, the Ninnimissinuok had the advantage, but their mobile armies eventually ran out of supplies, just as the colonists managed to rally the powerful Mohawks to their side, and the insurgents had to surrender. In the aftermath, the revenge of the English was merciless and indiscriminate: unoffending praying Indians were interned under lethal conditions, prisoners were massacred, noncombatant natives were sold into slavery in large numbers. Racial hatred rose to a high pitch and surviving Ninnimissinuok found themselves virtually defenseless.[89]

In these circumstances, and notwithstanding the setback to settler population growth occasioned by the war, it was open season on Indian land, with speculators leading the way. By the end of the century, only four of the fourteen praying towns of Massachusetts survived and these had all lost lands. Of the large sachemships of southern New England, some fell into the hands of land companies, while others were acquired piecemeal by settlers. Remnant Ninnimissinuok communities persisted in tiny enclaves, especially on Cape Cod and Martha's Vineyard, through the colonial period and down to the present.[90]

[88] Quoted in Salisbury, *Manitou and Providence*, 13.
[89] Ian K. Steele, *Warpaths: Invasions of North America* (New York: Oxford University Press, 1994), 99–108; Jill Lepore, *The Name of War: King Philip's War and the Origins of American Identity* (New York: Knopf, 1998).
[90] Theodore B. Lewis, "Land Speculation and the Dudley Council of 1686," *William and Mary Quarterly*, 3rd ser., 31 (1974): 264; David J. Silverman, *Faith and Boundaries:*

One nation, the Mohegans, by virtue of their close alliance with the English during King Philip's War and during subsequent conficts with the French, had managed to preserve a comparatively large domain for themselves in eastern Connecticut. Astute use of prominent English protectors had also worked in their favor. But by the turn of the eighteenth century, and in spite of their services to the colony, they were under siege in their own homeland. Settlers from Colchester and New London were invading their lands, moving boundary markers and terrorizing the Mohegans to the point where men were afraid to go out hunting. A surveyor named Nicholas Hallam tried in the winter of 1703 to establish a clear line between New London Township and the Mohegan lands. Proceeding to a rock beside the Thames River that had long served as a boundary marker,

[i]t being a cold snowy day, he met with about thirty or forty Moheagan Indians, men, women, and children, in a very poor and naked condition, many of them crying lamentably ... who told this deponent, that the governor [Fitz-John Winthrop] had been up with them that day, and had drove them from their planting land, which they had enjoyed ever since the English came into the country.

Faced with this brutal eviction, the Mohegans were initially reduced to tears and lamentations, but they managed to rally sufficiently to mount a legal challenge against Connecticut's land-grab that went all the way to the Privy Council in London.[91]

Colonists, Christianity, and Community among the Wampanoag Indians of Martha's Vineyard, 1600–1871 (New York: Cambridge University Press, 2005); Main, *Peoples of a Spacious Land*, 194–202; Timothy H. Ives, "Reconstructing the Wangunk Reservation Land System: A Case Study of Native and Colonial Likeness in Central Connecticut," *Ethnohistory* 58 (2011): 65–89.

[91] *Governor and Company of Connecticut, and Moheagan Indians, by Their Guardians: Certified Copy of Book of Proceedings before Commissioners of Review, MDCCXLIII* (London: W. and J. Richardson, 1769), 55. On the Mohegan case, see Joseph Henry Smith, *Appeals to the Privy Council from the American Plantations* (New York: Columbia University Press, 1950), 422–42; Mark D. Walters, "Mohegan Indians v. Connecticut (1705–1773) and the Legal Status of Aboriginal Customary Laws and Government in British North America," *Osgoode Hall Law Journal* 33 (1995): 785–829; Amy E. Den Ouden, *Beyond Conquest: Native Peoples and the Struggle for History in New England* (Lincoln: University of Nebraska Press, 2005); Paul Grant-Costa, "The Last Indian War in New England: The Mohegan Indians v. The Governour and Company of the Colony of Connecticut, 1703–1774," Ph.D. dissertation, Yale University, 2008; Lisa Brooks, *The Common Pot: The Recovery of Native Space in the Northeast* (Minneapolis and London: University of Minnesota Press, 2008), 64–86; Craig Bryan Yirush, "Claiming the New World: Empire, Law, and Indigenous Rights in the Mohegan Case, 1704–1743," *Law and History Review* 29 (2011): 333–73.

Connecticut provided a particularly egregious instance of naked appropriation. Other colonies took a generally more incremental approach. Most enacted protective legislation establishing white "guardians" to supervise native lands and prevent irregular sales. A Massachusetts act of 1746 charged local guardians with ensuring that the inhabitants of an Indian community had enough land to support themselves using English agricultural practices; any surplus land was to be rented to settlers with the proceeds to be used for the good of the natives.[92] With reduced indigenous territories, legally situated outside the colonial tenure system, and subject to paternal supervision, the Ninnimissinuok of southern New England were well on their way toward that property regime of permanent exception that is the reservation system.

---

[92] Vaughan, ed., *Early American Indian Documents*, 17: 197–98. On the guardian system, see Kawashima, *Puritan Justice and the Indian*, 32–33, 55; Wendy B. St. Jean, "Inventing Guardianship: The Mohegan Indians and Their Protectors," *New England Quarterly* 72 (1999): 362–87; Kathleen Bragdon, *Native People of Southern New England, 1650–1775* (Norman: University of Oklahoma Press, 2009), 128–31.

PART II

ASPECTS OF PROPERTY FORMATION

7

The Colonial Commons

There is a strong tendency, when thinking about colonization and dispossession in an Atlantic world setting, to imagine a great Enclosure Movement taking shape, first in England and western Europe and then extending overseas to the New World, bringing survey lines, fences and legal rules fostering exclusive access to delimited portions of the landscape. More than one historian has pointed in the direction of such an extended conception of enclosure, though none has so far made the case in detail. "When the English took possession of lands overseas, they did so by building fences and hedges, the markers of enclosure and private property," write Peter Linebaugh and Marcus Rediker.[1] In relation to the eighteenth and nineteenth centuries, E. P. Thompson also pointed to a

---

[1] Peter Linebaugh and Marcus Rediker, *The Many-Headed Hydra: Sailors, Slaves, Commoners, and the Hidden History of the Revolutionary Atlantic* (Boston: Beacon Press, 2000), 44. Similar views of enclosure and colonization can be found in the following works: Francis Jennings, *The Invasion of America: Indians, Colonialism, and the Cant of Conquest* (Chapel Hill: University of North Carolina Press, 1975), 82–83; Thomas Flanagan, "The Agricultural Argument and Original Appropriation: Indian Lands and Political Philosophy," *Canadian Journal of Political Science* 22 (1989): 589–602; Gary B. Nash, *Red, White and Black: The Peoples of Early North America*, 4th ed. (Upper Saddle River, N.J.: Prentice Hall, 2000), 23; Patricia Seed, *American Pentimento: The Invention of Indians and the Pursuit of Riches* (Minneapolis: University of Minnesota Press, 2001), 32–34; Nancy Shoemaker, *A Strange Likeness: Becoming Red and White in Eighteenth-Century North America* (New York: Oxford University Press, 2004), 20–22; Stuart Banner, *How the Indians Lost Their Land: Law and Power on the Frontier* (Cambridge, Mass.: Harvard University Press, 2005), 37–39, 258–59; Charles Geisler, "Disowned by the Ownership Society: How Native Americans Lost Their Land," *Rural Sociology* 79 (March 2014): 56–78; Derek Wall, *The Commons in History: Culture, Conflict, and Ecology* (Cambridge, Mass.: MIT Press, 2014), 79–86.

connection between enclosure within England and the imposition of "private property" across the overseas British Empire, notably in India, where the Permanent Settlement of Bengal (1793) represented a particularly brutal and doctrinaire attempt to establish unitary proprietorship over land. Thompson's argument about enclosure and colonization appeared in an essay published late in his life and it touches on North America, New Zealand and Africa as well as India.[2] Richly suggestive, it remains schematic and preliminary, pointing to a long-term global movement to privatize the commons that emanated outward from the British Isles. Certainly, there is an intriguing, if rough, coincidence of peak periods of enclosure in England – the Tudor period and the late eighteenth century – with times of imperial expansion and reinvigoration.[3]

Moreover, settlers did normally erect fences, since "enclosure" in that mundane sense of the term played an important part in separating ruminants and crops, the two main elements of typically European "convertible husbandry." If cattle and corn are to be raised in close proximity, then there had better be a fence (or a wall or a ditch or a human cowherd) between them. Marking boundaries and setting up barriers was indeed a crucial part of the process of property formation in colonial North America (though more in some regions than others). Sometimes, this kind of enclosure was the agent immediately responsible for dispossessing native people, but more often indigenous property had already been largely eliminated from a given locality when enclosure occurred. While the long-run outcome of colonization was typically the establishment of a regime of bounded properties, along the way to that destination various forms of commons frequently played a decisive role in depriving natives of their lands. Common property formed a central feature of both native and settler land tenures of the early modern period and, as this chapter will argue, dispossession came about to a significant degree through the clash of an indigenous commons and a colonial commons. It is an

---

[2] E. P. Thompson, "Custom, Law and Common Right," in *Customs in Common* (New York: New Press, 1991), 164–75. See also Ranajit Guha, *A Rule of Property for Bengal: An Essay on the Idea of Permanent Settlement* (Durham, N.C.: Duke University Press, 1996).

[3] On English enclosure, see R. H. Tawney, *The Agrarian Problem in the Sixteenth Century* (London: Longmans, 1912); Joan Thirsk, ed., *The Agrarian History of England and Wales*, vol. 4: *1500–1640* (Cambridge: Cambridge University Press, 1967), 200–255; J. A. Yelling, *Common Field and Enclosure in England, 1450–1850* (London: Macmillan, 1977); J. M. Neeson, *Commoners: Common Right, Enclosure and Social Change in England, 1700–1820* (Cambridge: Cambridge University Press, 1993).

argument that comes up against the lingering, but still potent, influence of John Locke, proponent of both enclosure and colonizing and preeminent philosopher of property in land.

JOHN LOCKE'S DEER HUNT

In the fifth chapter of his *Second Treatise of Civil Government*, a brief but powerfully argued essay entitled, "Of Property," Locke has much to say about commons, enclosure and, at least by implication, colonization.[4] If the world and nature's bounty were created for all of humanity, Locke asks, how can anyone claim exclusive rights to a specific portion of the earth? His answer is that labor provides the ultimate basis for legitimate property. Thus, the "wild Indian" who shoots a deer somewhere in "America" has a perfect right, by virtue of his hunting skill and efforts, to enjoy the meat and leather that its carcass provides, but he has no particular claim on other deer in the forest, much less on the forest itself. Property in land similarly derives from purposeful effort: in the state of nature, acorns are mine when I take the trouble to collect them, and land is mine when I clear, cultivate and fence it. Once government and laws make their appearance, property becomes subject to contractual agreements, but the original appropriation of the universal commons took place through the operation of labor.

Modern commentators note that this chapter of the *Second Treatise* is about property generally and not specifically *private* property, insisting that Locke's logic applies equally to collective and individual property.[5] (Philosophers tend to accept the phrase "private property" as fully meaningful.) However, if we consider the rhetoric of "On Property," the author's preference for enclosure and private property is abundantly clear. There are repeated references to the poverty of "commoners" and to the superiority of enclosures; the question is whether the productivity of one exceeds that of the other by a factor of ten or a hundred. "For I ask

[4] John Locke, *Two Treatises of Government*, ed. Peter Laslett (Cambridge: Cambridge University Press, 1960), 133–46.

[5] James Tully, *A Discourse on Property: John Locke and His Adversaries* (Cambridge: Cambridge University Press, 1980); James Tully, "Differences in the Interpretation of Locke on Property," in *An Approach to Political Philosophy: Locke in Contexts* (Cambridge: Cambridge University Press, 1993), 118–36. Tully's argument challenges C. B. Macpherson's view of Locke as the philosopher of capitalist property relations. C. B. Macpherson, *The Political Theory of Possessive Individualism: Hobbes to Locke* (Oxford: Clarendon Press, 1962), 194–262; C. B. Macpherson, "Capitalism and the Changing Concept of Property," in *Feudalism, Capitalism and Beyond*, ed. Eugene Kamenka and Ronald Stanley Neale (London: Edward Arnold, 1975), 105–24.

whether in the wild woods and uncultivated waste of America, left to
nature, without any improvement, tillage, or husbandry, a thousand acres
yield the needy and wretched inhabitants as many conveniences of life as
ten acres of equally fertile land do in Devonshire, where they are well
cultivated." A few pages later, an acre producing twenty bushels of wheat
in England is compared with an acre of equally good American land; the
former produces revenues of five pounds, the latter hardly a penny, "if all
the profit an Indian received from it were to be valued and sold here."
Quite apart from Locke's reasoning about original appropriation in
the state of nature, the association of words gives his chapter a definite
pro-enclosure rhetorical thrust. Linked together in consistently negative
contexts are the words "commons," "waste," "commoner," "Indian,"
"America," and "poverty."

What is this "America," the haunt of "wild Indians" and unclaimed
resources, an instructive domain filled with lessons on the meaning of
property in land? Is it a time, a place or a concept? An imagined state
of nature put forward as a device for reasoning about humanity in the
absence of government and money? A time in the distant past when these
conditions prevailed everywhere? ("Thus in the beginning all the world
was America," wrote the philosopher.) Or was it the actual New World,
home of "Indians" and site, at the time Locke penned "Of Property," of
active colonizing endeavors on the part of England and other European
powers? The verdict of current scholarship on this issue seems to be
"all of the above." Whereas Locke specialists once tended to treat the
numerous allusions to "America" as pure figures of speech, recent commentators have argued with increasing insistence that the philosopher's
thinking was by no means unrelated to the dispossession of natives in
North America at the time. Locke, they point out, was deeply involved in
colonial projects, particularly with the establishment of Carolina; moreover, although he never personally crossed the Atlantic, he possessed a
substantial collection of books on American topics. He was well informed
on and intensely interested in colonial matters, and his writings reflect a
concern to justify the appropriation of American lands.[6]

---

[6] James Tully, "Rediscovering America: The Two Treatises and Aboriginal Rights," in
An Approach to Political Philosophy: Locke in Contexts, 137–76; Barbara Arneil,
John Locke and America: The Defence of English Colonialism (Oxford: Clarendon
Press, 1996). Addressing an apparent temporal disjunction between Locke's employment
with one of the Carolina proprietors (1669–75) and the publication of the *Two Treatises*
(1689), David Armitage suggests that the composition of the "Of Property" chapter

John Locke's career was shaped by engagement with both the domestic and the overseas colonial spheres and so, it has been argued, was his liberal philosophy. The real world in which Locke's vision developed was an Atlantic world composed of both English and American elements. In his hands, and in those of his liberal heirs down through the centuries, universal principles of individual autonomy, self-government and freedom of contract came with escape clauses that effectively exempted colonized peoples. Liberty at home linked to "imperial exclusions," some say, constituted the hallmark of the Lockean tradition.[7] But what about the specific topic of property? It is in the property chapter of the *Second Treatise* that by far the largest number of references to "Indians" and "America" occur. Where land, commons and enclosures are concerned, does the same logic apply on both sides of the Atlantic, constraining and empowering colonizers and colonized equally?

By referring to indigenous peoples as "commoners" living off the unenclosed bounty of the New World, Locke seems to assimilate them, as far as issues of productivity are concerned, to the cottagers and smallholders of the Old World. "The fruit or venison which nourishes the wild Indian, who knows no enclosure and is still a tenant in common, must be his ... before it can do him any good for the support of his life."[8] An impression is created: "improvement" is equally at odds with common fields in England and uncleared forests in America. Later pro-enclosure propagandists would take up this same equation, comparing poor fen-dwellers in East Anglia with Native Americans who foraged for a living from land that ought ideally to be converted to private property.[9] However, while he emphasizes similarity in the economic implications of commons and enclosure on the two sides of the Atlantic, Locke

---

coincides closely with the period in 1682 when Locke was busy revising the "Fundamental Constitutions" of Carolina. It is noteworthy that the Fundamental Constitutions prohibit colonists from acquiring land through purchase from natives. Taking a hard line against aboriginal title, in striking contrast with their contemporary William Penn, but consistent with Locke's view that "wild Indians" had no property rights, the Carolina proprietors insisted that they, not the indigenous inhabitants, owned the country. David Armitage, "John Locke, Carolina, and the Two Treatises of Government," *Political Theory* 32 (2004): 602–27.

[7] Uday Singh Mehta, *Liberalism and Empire: A Study in Nineteenth-Century British Liberal Thought* (Chicago: University of Chicago Press, 1999), 46–64.

[8] Locke, *Two Treatises*, 134.

[9] "Forests and great Commons make the Poor that are upon them too much like the *Indians*," wrote John Bellers in 1714 (quoted in Thompson, "Custom, Law and Common Right," 165). See also Neeson, *Commoners*, 30.

introduces a radical distinction between the village commons of the Old World and the open lands of the New when he turns to questions of justice and rights.

"Land that is common in England or any other country where there is plenty of people under government who have money and commerce" is perfectly legitimate, collectively owned property, according to Locke. In this setting, unlike the state of nature, "no one can enclose or appropriate any part without the consent of all his fellow-commoners; because this is left common by compact, *i.e.*, by the law of the land, which is not to be violated. And though it be common in respect of some men, it is not so to all mankind, but is the joint property of this country or this parish."[10] America represents a different sort of commons, wide open and available to all: not the collective property of a community, but rather the antithesis of property. Enclosure at home and enclosure overseas may be equally desirable ends, but they have to come about by very different means according to Locke. In England voluntary agreement (and presumably compensation) is a must, whereas enclosure in America requires no one's permission.[11] This procedural divergence over enclosure, critical to Locke's implied theory of colonial property formation, rests on the elision of two different criteria. Legitimate common property is local/particular and it is instituted in law, whereas pre-colonial America knows no law and its lands constitute a commons of universal scope: it corresponds to nature itself.

The notion that pre-Columbian America formed a universal commons and that colonization took the form of a massive program of enclosure, establishing property in land where no such thing had been known before, has had a long life.[12] A pro-colonialist, pro-enclosure variant can be traced from Locke and his predecessors through the Scottish Enlightenment to the modern notion that "property rights" (i.e., strong and exclusive individual claims to land) are essential to economic development. Many writers on the left are just as inclined to subscribe to Locke's view of colonization-as-enclosure, though in this case the valences of commons and enclosure are reversed. The association of "commons" with the poor in England and the indigenous peoples of America, not to

---

[10] Locke, *Two Treatises*, 137.

[11] Locke's insistence on the right of unilateral appropriation in the state of nature, appropriation requiring no one's consent, is a feature that distinguishes his theory of property from that of Grotius. Arneil, *John Locke and America*, 61–62.

[12] To cite one example from a recent reference work: Paul C. Rosier, "Land Tenure," in *Encyclopedia of World Environmental History*, ed. Shepard Krech, John Robert McNeill and Carolyn Merchant (New York: Routledge, 2004), 751–52.

mention its overtones of sharing and cooperation, can lead to a romantic view that emphasizes the *collective* aspects of commoning to the neglect of the *exclusionary* nature of most commons known to history. The political thrust of Locke's essay "Of Property" is inverted as the commons and unenclosed "America" are idealized rather than denigrated, but the basic understanding of colonization is still traceable to Locke.[13] A clearer sense of colonial property formation, purged of colonialist ideology, requires us to jettison the concept of the universal open commons as a figment of the imperial imagination and to explore the ways in which different property systems, each with its particular practices of commoning, confronted one another in an unequal struggle.

VARIETIES OF COMMON PROPERTY

Before turning to the history of commons and enclosure in New Spain, New France and New England, some clarifications and distinctions are in order. Modern scholarship on common property – and this is an area of intense activity bringing together economists, sociologist and anthropologists – does not support the Lockean view that "particular commons" are necessarily the product of law and the sovereign state. Researchers interested in the commons, both those who focus on the history of the agricultural commons and those who examine other versions of "the commons" in today's world would agree with Locke on the need to distinguish particular commons from what they term "open-access resources." The former, specialists tell us, are jointly owned and, in most cases, collectively managed; the latter are portions of the environment – the oceans, the air, the Internet, the continent of Antarctica – that are not property. Yet there would be little empirical support for Locke's notion that particular commons somehow require the prior existence of "government," "law," and "money" in forms that would be recognizable as such by a European observer. Contemporary research has shown that common property does not necessarily depend on legal formalities, but is more typically an organic aspect of fishing, hunting, grazing or wood-cutting communities: a matter of local custom rather than law.[14] That common property of this

[13] See, for example, Peter Linebaugh, *The Magna Carta Manifesto: Liberties and Commons for All* (Berkeley: University of California Press, 2008).

[14] Elinor Ostrom, *Governing the Commons: The Evolution of Institutions for Collective Action* (New York: Cambridge University Press, 1990), 58–102; David Feeny, Fikret Berkes, Bonnie J. McCay and James M. Acheson, "The Tragedy of the Commons: Twenty-Two Years Later," *Human Ecology* 18 (1990): 1–19; Bonnie J. McCay and

sort might be found in pre-Columbian North America, might even have been the norm, is a possibility that John Locke never entertained. His reasoning rests too heavily on a basic ontological division between civil societies and their antithesis, natural humanity: on one side were civilized communities where land could be owned, individually or communally, on the other, unorganized spaces occupied by uncivilized peoples, where land and resources were open to all. In erasing the distinction, where American natives were concerned, between particular commons and open-access resources, Locke effectively disqualified them as proprietors.[15]

Common property was, in fact, a fundamental feature of landholding in both the New World and the Old in the early modern centuries. Commons came in myriad forms, varying from one environmental setting and subsistence regime to the next, shaped in some areas by legal codes and customs, shaped in their particulars also by the factors cited by Locke: population density, government and commerce. Though the commons are perhaps best apprehended in their local specificity, we might still venture some general observations.

In western Europe, where agriculture typically involved the raising of livestock and the growing of crops in close proximity, many communities set aside a delimited area, usually in a place of wet, heavy soils near a body of water, as a communal pasture. Typically, this space was literally "enclosed" by a wall or fence. In "open field" regions, such as the English Midlands and north-central France, grain fields were used as a supplementary pasture for the village herd between harvest and planting time; this meant that individually held plots in the arable became open to everyone's livestock at certain times of year. Additional communal practices were a feature of most rural communities in the early modern period. "Gleaning" is one of these: the almost universal right of the local poor to gather up stray stalks of grain on other people's land after the harvesters

---

Svein Jentoft, "Market or Community Failure? Critical Perspectives on Common Property Research," *Human Organization* 57 (1998): 21–29; Elinor Ostrom and Charlotte Hess, "Private and Common Property Rights," unpublished paper, Workshop in Political Theory and Policy Analysis, Indiana University, 2007 (http://papers.ssrn.com/sol3/papers.cfm?abstract_id=1304699); Daniel H. Cole and Elinor Ostrom, "The Variety of Property Systems and Rights in Natural Resources," in *Property in Land and Other Resources*, ed. Daniel H. Cole and Elinor Ostrom (Cambridge, Mass.: Lincoln Institute of Land Policy, 2012), 37–64. In refuting Garrett Hardin, "The Tragedy of the Commons," *Science* 162 (1968): 1243–48 (see ch. 2), the research cited here demonstrates that fishery, forest and pasture-land commons in the contemporary world are typically regulated, by custom or explicit rules, in the interests of sustainability.

[15] Tully, "Rediscovering America."

had done their work. Thus, "the commons" was both one specific place (the permanent pasture) and a set of practices governing land use across a community's territory.[16]

So far, the focus here has been on commoning within the tillage zone of a European agrarian community: it might be designated the "inner commons." There were also areas on the periphery of a village's croplands where resources were collectively owned and communally managed: let's call this the "outer commons." In England, such areas were known as "the waste": the zone of moor, mountain, marsh or forest that rural folk used as rough pasture for their livestock as well as for cutting wood or peat for fuel, gathering herbs, taking rushes for basketry or thatching, felling timber for construction and so on. A variety of rules and customs, some of them local, others regional or national, governed access to these common resources. Attempts to quantify the percentage of land that was common in any given period and place are misleading because "the commons" was in a sense everywhere. Inner commons, outer commons, stubble grazing customs and gleaning rights blurred the distinction between private holdings and collective resources. The commons was a set of practices and rules as much as it was a location.[17]

Spain was a special case within Europe by virtue of the importance of common property in its laws and its agricultural practices. The medieval Castilian law code, the *Siete Partidas*, had given particular attention to common property, and across the peninsula outer commons were, in fact, very extensive.[18] Every town and rural municipality possessed common lands (*ejidos*), some of it used as collective pastureland, some of it leased to local cultivators for farming. Township boundaries could be indistinct, frequently merging at the edges with unclaimed areas, the "*tierras baldías*," of mountainous and arid land. In theory, the king claimed ownership of these notionally "empty" zones, which in the rough terrain of the Iberian Peninsula were quite extensive.[19] In effect, the *baldías*

[16] Joan Thirsk, "The Common Fields," *Past & Present*, no. 29 (1964): 3–25; Martina de Moor, Leigh Shaw-Taylor and Paul Warde, eds., *The Management of Common Land in North West Europe, c. 1500–1850* (Turnhout, Belgium: Brepols, 2002); Guy Lemarchand, *Paysans et seigneurs en Europe: une histoire comparée, XVIe-XIXe siècle* (Rennes: Presses de l'Université de Rennes, 2011), 51–52, 192–93.

[17] See Thompson, *Customs in Common*.

[18] Robert I. Burns, ed., *Medieval Law: Lawyers and Their Work*, 5 vols., vol. 3: *Las Siete Partidas* (Philadelphia: University of Pennsylvania Press, 2001), 820–22.

[19] James Casey, *Early Modern Spain: A Social History* (London: Routledge, 2002), 47–51. On the geography of enclosed and open-field agriculture in central Spain, see Jesus García

formed a vast national commons, supposedly open to all but actually dominated by powerful interests engaged in large-scale sheep- and cattle-raising. Right around the time that New Spain was conquered and colonized, the Hapsburg monarchs were supporting the formation of a great ranching consortium, the "Mesta," which enjoyed wide-ranging grazing privileges across peninsular Spain. Stock raisers tended to rely on open ranges and seasonal migrations and the law gave them almost unlimited access to water and pasture along transhumance routes. It "guaranteed the right to use 'deserted and uncultivated lands' without distinguishing between privately owned and public lands." Spanish farmers complained constantly of the damage done by migrating herds in this uneven Cain-and-Abel conflict.[20]

Though commons never ceased to be an important feature of the rural scene in early modern Europe, developments in a contrary direction – dividing commons, suppressing communal rights and favoring exclusive control of the land – can be detected in various places. In the sixteenth century, the Spanish monarchy began selling off exemptions to the *derrota de mieses*, the regime that obligated cultivators to allow passing livestock to graze on their stubble. Later, the Crown sold off portions of the *baldias* to raise revenue.[21] In France, it was the seigneurs, rather than the monarch, who tended to monopolize lands once shared by a community. The legal practice of "triage" allowed lords to seize one-third of a community's common pasture and add it to their demesne.[22] England was of course the site of the classic "Enclosure Movement." That phrase, evoking images of open fields being fenced in, while poor peasants are forced off the land to make way for profitable sheep raising, masks a wide range of changes in land holding that varied greatly over time and from region to region. From the fifteenth to the seventeenth century, it was mostly a matter of arable being transformed into pastureland, while in the later eighteenth century (a peak period for enclosure) common pasture was typically

Fernández, "Champs ouverts, champs cloturés en Vieille Castille," *Annales: économies, sociétés, civilisations* 20 (1965): 692–718.

[20] David E. Vassberg, *Land and Society in Golden Age Castile* (Cambridge: Cambridge University Press, 1984), 11, 36, 79–83.

[21] Ibid., 169–72; Casey, *Early Modern Spain*, 50

[22] Gérard Béaur, *Histoire agraire de la France au XVIIIe siècle: inerties et changements dans les campagnes françaises entre 1715 et 1815* (Paris: Sedes, 2000), 71–74; Lemarchand, *Paysans et seigneurs en Europe*, 193–95; Jean-Michel Sallmann, "Les biens communaux et la 'réaction seigneuriale' en Artois," *Revue du Nord* 58 (1976): 209–23.

transformed into arable.[23] The common theme is the triumph of large, exclusive property over the collective property rights of smallholders. These changes were facilitated by the political power of the English landlord class, much greater than that of its French counterpart.[24]

While our language of commons derives from European settings and practices, versions of common property were also present right across indigenous North America at the time of contact. There was, of course, agriculture in the pre-Columbian New World – one of John Locke's big lies was his portrayal of Indians as entirely devoted to hunting[25] – but it was purely crop-based: potatoes, maize, beans, squash and other cultigens were grown without a significant component of animal husbandry. Because crops did not share space with domestic animals, fences and hedges were largely unnecessary and in that literal sense, the land was not enclosed. Whether we consider the cultivators of central Mexico or the semi-sedentary villagers of northeastern North America, we generally find individual families or lineages working particular plots of their own, subject to varying degrees of community control; at the same time, these cultivators drew vital resources from the hills, forests and wetlands beyond their village clearings (see Chapter 2). For all the obvious differences separating European and Native American land use and property, we have to recognize some basic similarities as well. Forms of individual allocation, inner commons and outer commons analogous to European property patterns were a feature of indigenous American property.

Around the great cities of Mesoamerica, agricultural plots were carefully measured and marked off, displaying some of the characteristics associated with "enclosed" areas of England, as well as some characteristics of what Locke would call legal, particular commons. In the terms put forward above, this was a zone of particular allotments and "inner commons." Beyond the houselots and scattered cornfields lay an outer

[23] H. P. R. Finberg and Joan Thirsk, *The Agrarian History of England and Wales*, 8 vols., vol. 4: *1500–1640*, ed. Joan Thirsk (Cambridge: Cambridge University Press, 1967), 200–55; Yelling, *Common Field and Enclosure*.

[24] Marc Bloch, *French Rural History: An Essay on Its Basic Characteristics*, trans. Janet Sondheimer (Berkeley: University of California Press, 1966), 133–35; Robert Brenner, "Agrarian Class Structure and Economic Development in Pre-Industrial Europe," *Past & Present*, no. 70 (1976): 30–75.

[25] As Vicki Hsueh has shown, Locke must have been aware of indigenous American agriculture as his personal library contained numerous, well-thumbed volumes of travel and ethnographic literature on the subject. V. Hsueh, "Cultivating and Challenging the Common: Lockean Property, Indigenous Traditionalisms, and the Problem of Exclusion," *Contemporary Political Theory* 5 (2006): 193–214.

commons of mountainsides and bottomlands. Areas of forest or mountains (all designated *"montes"* under Spanish rule) provided members of a local *calpulli* with supplies of firewood, wild herbs and berries, game and other resources. Frequently areas of moist, heavy soils at the edges of rivers and lakes also formed part of the Nahua outer commons, a source of reeds, fish and wildfowl. As mentioned in Chapter 4, such zones typically formed the indistinct borderline dividing neighboring *altepeme*. Whereas the Spaniards would prize such humid lands as plowlands or pastures for livestock, the soils were too heavy for indigenous hand cultivation methods; besides, as borderlands exposed to enemy attack, they could be too dangerous for permanent residence. Like the *montes*, these bottomlands formed part of the common property of the local *calpulli*, not a universal commons, but rather territory and resources belonging to a particular community. In that respect, the situation was roughly similar to the moors, mountains and forests of Europe: common property but neither unregulated nor open to the entire human race.[26]

In the semi-sedentary villages of southern New England, as in open-field Europe, decisions about the timing of seasonal activities like sowing and reaping would have been made at the level of the community. Women tilled their own plots and reaped the produce, though they were under an obligation to turn over a share to the sachem and to be generous with needy fellow-villagers. Like the Iroquoian peoples who lived further to the west, the Ninnimissinuok also exploited an extensive outer commons of hunting and foraging territory. Modern historians sometimes describe such practices in terms of "usufruct," as opposed to genuine ownership,[27] but the seventeenth-century missionary Gabriel Sagard had no hesitation in drawing on the language of common property when referring to Wendat (Huron) claims to land and resources:

[26] H. R. Harvey, "Aspects of Land Tenure in Ancient Mexico," in *Explorations in Ethnohistory: Indians of Central Mexico in the Sixteenth Century*, ed. H. R. Harvey and Hanns J. Prem (Albuquerque: University of New Mexico Press, 1984), 91; Nadine Béligand, "Les communautés indiennes de la vallée de Toluca (Mexique): 1480–1810," doctoral thesis, École des hautes études en sciences sociales, 1998, 76–80; René García Castro, "Los Pueblos de Indios," in *Gran Historia de Mexico Ilustrada* (Mexico City: Planeta DeAgostini, 2001), vol. 8: 148.

[27] William Cronon, *Changes in the Land: Indians, Colonists, and the Ecology of New England* (New York: Hill and Wang, 1983), 60–68. Creek land, says Claudio Saunt, "was not owned as much as used." Claudio Saunt, *A New Order of Things: Property, Power, and the Transformation of the Creek Indians, 1733–1816* (New York: Cambridge University Press, 1999), 40–42.

It is their custom for every family to live on its fishing, hunting, and planting, since they have as much land as they need; for all the forests, meadows, and uncleared land are common property, and anyone is allowed to clear and sow as much as he will and can, and according to his needs; and this cleared land remains in his possession for as many years as he continues to cultivate and make use of it. After it is altogether abandoned by its owner, then anyone who wishes uses it, but not otherwise.[28]

As we learned in Chapter 2, the private/communal distinction sits awkwardly in any description of the land practices of nonagricultural hunting-gathering peoples such as the Innu. Even in these cases, however, there was interplay between particular allocations of hunting grounds or trap lines and collective control over land and resources.

The upshot of this recapitulation of different Native American patterns of land use and collective property is to show that North America on the eve of colonization was a quilt of common properties, each governed by the land use rules of a specific human society. The notion that the continent was a universal, open-access commons – Locke's "America" – has to be recognized as a colonialist fiction. In the New World as in the Old, the commons was not so much a location (though it usually had a territorial dimension) as a set of rules and customs governing access to and management of resources. In the context of European colonization, we might speak of an "indigenous commons" to distinguish these places and practices from the forms of commoning introduced by settlers. With the founding of colonies came not only cleared, plowed and more or less enclosed farms, but also a "colonial commons," with different varieties of inner commons and outer commons. The theme of the rest of this chapter is the establishment of colonial commons in New Spain, New France and New England, and the clash of the settlers' outer commons with existing indigenous commons. In a colonial setting, the indigenous commons and the colonial (outer) commons typically coexisted in space; they were not so much different places as different customs of access and resource management. Conflict inevitably arose over a number of basic issues: who could make use of given territories, what sorts of benefits they could extract from them and, above all, who defined the terms of access. When colonists introduced domestic animals that they regarded as property no matter where those beasts might wander, these became a bone of

---

[28] Gabriel Sagard, *The Long Journey to the Country of the Hurons*, ed. and trans. G. M. Wrong and H. H. Langton (Toronto: Champlain Society, 1939), 103. Note the way the missionary transposes the language of land and agriculture from the feminine to the masculine gender.

contention with natives who had a very different sense of where nonhuman creatures fit into common property arrangements.

NEW SPAIN

Following Iberian precedents, the towns founded by colonists in New Spain always surrounded themselves with extensive commons (*ejido*). A royal ordinance of 1573 on the founding of new settlements made a point of reinforcing these communal traditions; it required that any new town established on conquered territory must be provided with an *ejido* as well as ample common pastures for the grazing of residents' livestock. Indian pueblos also had commons under Spanish rule. In at least one case, natives and Spaniards shared a municipal *ejido*. Moreover, the government always maintained the principle that the wider commons of the unoccupied wasteland (*montes*) was equally open to Indians and Spaniards for hunting, foraging and firewood collection.[29] In practice, of course, the indigenous commons was never on an equal footing with the colonial commons, and with the rise of livestock raising and the eventual emergence of the *hacienda* regime, a Spanish ranching commons came to dominate ever vaster regions of Mexico, threatening, if not destroying, native livelihoods as it expanded.

The peninsular regulatory framework applied in New Spain, meaning that stock-raising initially depended not on exclusive property rights, but rather on access to the commons and to other people's land. There was a colonial version of the Spanish Mesta to protect the interests of ranchers. The latter claimed the right to move their herds, grazing along the way on *baldías*, pueblo lands and privately owned tracts, as long as no crops were currently growing there. Cattle and sheep raisers each needed a central

[29] "Ordenanzas hechas para los descubrimientos, nuevas poblaciónes y pacificaciónes," 13 July 1573, in *Cedulario de Tierras: Compilación de legislación agraria colonial, 1497–1820*, ed. Francisco de Solano (Mexico City: Universidad Nacional Autónoma de México, 1991), 220–21; Gilberto Rafael Cruz, *Let There Be Towns: Spanish Municipal Origins in the American Southwest, 1610–1810* (College Station: Texas A&M University Press, 1988), 112–13; David J. Weber, *The Spanish Frontier in North America* (New Haven, Conn.: Yale University Press, 1992), 320; Stephanie Wood, "The *Fundo Legal* or Lands *por razón de pueblo*: New Evidence from Central New Spain," in *The Indian Community of Colonial Mexico: Fifteen Essays on Land Tenure, Corporate Organizations, Ideology and Village Politics*, ed. Arij Ouweneel and Simon Miller (Amsterdam: CEDLA, 1990), 119; *Recopilación de leyes de los reynos de las Indias*, 3 vols. (Madrid: Julian de Paredes, 1681), vol 2: 113–113v, laws of n.d. 1533, 25 December 1536, 7 October 1559.

place with an assured water supply to build their corrals and to assemble their herds and flocks periodically. Thus, municipalities, and later the viceroy, would grant ranchers *mercedes* for specific "sites." The grant was called a *"sitio,"* but the corral and other facilities came to be known as an *"estancia,"* a term "coined in the West Indies and used extensively to designate the point where wanderers and their flocks finally came to rest." The vocabulary of *"sitio"* and *"estancia"* reflects the initial status of stock raising as transient and nonexclusive in its use of land. Over time, ranchers would succeed in broadening and deepening their claim to the land, transforming a right of limited access into a much more exclusive form of property.[30]

Grants for livestock-raising involved areas that were supposed to be unoccupied. They were generally quite large – a standard *"sitio de ganado mayor"* (cattle or horses) was over 4000 acres, while a *"sitio de ganado menor"* (sheep, goats) was about 2000 acres[31] – but they did not imply anything resembling "full" ownership of the soil. For example, the Jesuit *hacienda* of Santa Lucia, a collection of several sheep *estancias*, was described in 1576 as comprising grass, springs, ponds and watering holes scattered over seventy square kilometers. However, neighboring Indian pueblos, which had long used these areas to gather roots, grasses and salt and to hunt wild ducks and geese, retained control over those particular resources.[32] Elsewhere, some pastures were granted as *"agostaderos,"* meaning that they could be used only between December and May, when natives living in the area were supposedly not growing crops.[33] The grant of a *sitio* thus gave little more than grazing rights and only for a specific class of livestock; these property rights were exclusive only insofar as they kept out other ranchers. And even these restricted rights could be difficult to enforce since *estancias* lacked clearly designated boundaries. "Mercedes [grants] invariably specified a place and stipulated a size. Borders, even in the rare event that recipients limited

---

[30] François Chevalier, *Land and Society in Colonial Mexico: The Great Hacienda* (Berkeley: University of California Press, 1963), 86–90 (quotation at 88).

[31] Charles Gibson, *The Aztecs under Spanish Rule: A History of the Indians of the Valley of Mexico, 1519–1810* (Stanford, Calif.: Stanford University Press, 1964), 275–79. Since rocky and swampy land was not counted toward the total, *estancias* generally covered much larger areas than what the law specified.

[32] Herman W. Konrad, *A Jesuit Hacienda in Colonial Mexico: Santa Lucia, 1576–1767* (Stanford, Calif.: Stanford University Press, 1980), 28–34.

[33] Ibid., 62, 85; Jonathan D. Amith, *The Mobius Strip: A Spatial History of Colonial Society in Guerrero, Mexico* (Stanford, Calif.: Stanford University Press, 2005), 164.

themselves to the terms of the grant, were often the painful result of *practice* of occupation, the equilibrium point between two forces pushing in opposite directions. When the state formally conveyed a merced, the focus was on the site named in the document, where symbolic possession was given of land at best only vaguely delimited."[34]

Estancia grants were therefore more in the nature of licenses to make particular use of portions of the commons. The territorial coordinates were rather vague and, in practice, quite elastic. Given the absence of fences and the expansive tendencies of grazing herds, the tracts granted by colonial officials served as a central base for ranching that depended on a broader commons. Writes William Taylor: "The Spanish custom of moving livestock between mountain and lowland pastures, and the principle of common pasturage, whereby unoccupied lands were open for all private cattle, meant that Spanish holdings were fluid and without specific boundaries. Often they were not confirmed in writing for a number of years."[35] A Spanish version of the commons, one based primarily on ranging livestock, was being superimposed on a preexisting native commons. The Santa Lucia example makes it perfectly clear that judicial authorities recognized the spatial overlap of indigenous and colonial commons.

New Spain legislation on grazing and land grants always took the interests of native peoples into account. From the earliest years of colonial rule, the latter were guaranteed not only their cultivated fields, but also an equal right, along with Spaniards, to the resources of the mountains, waters and forests that constituted the common wasteland of Mexico.[36] Again and again over the course of the colonial centuries, laws and orders came down calling on ranchers to ensure that their stock did not undermine native livelihoods and threatening to revoke grants that infringed on Indian lands.[37] These regulations were not a dead letter – cases arose where natives successfully pursued legal redress – but neither did they form a barrier sufficient to prevent widespread incursions into indigenous territories. Demographic decline and the general disempowerment of natives created conditions favorable to the ambitions of ruthless ranchers determined to expand their enterprises at the Indians' expense. To make

[34] Amith, *The Mobius Strip*, 186–88 (emphasis in original).
[35] William B. Taylor, *Landlord and Peasant in Colonial Oaxaca* (Stanford, Calif.: Stanford University Press, 1972), 117.
[36] *Recopilación de leyes*, 2: 113
[37] See, for example, Solano, ed., *Cedulario de tierras*, 173, 177, 198.

matters worse, great herds of feral cattle and horses spread northward in advance of human conquerors, damaging the fragile ecology, and thus undermining indigenous subsistence, across northern New Spain.[38]

With unlimited forage always available beyond the horizon and with few predators to control their numbers, the cattle, sheep and goats introduced by Spanish ranchers thrived and reproduced at an astonishing rate. Elinor Melville refers to the explosion of herbivores in such virgin environments as an "ungulate irruption" and in a study of sheep raising in the Valle del Mezquital she charts the thoroughgoing ecological effects of this rapid ovine takeover of the landscape. The before-and-after contrast could not be more striking. "When Europeans first entered these wide, flat valleys and plains they saw a landscape that had been shaped by centuries of human occupation. It was a fertile, densely populated, and complex agricultural mosaic composed of extensive croplands, woodlands, and native grasslands; of irrigation canals, dams, terraces, and limestone quarries. Oak and pine forests covered the hills, and springs and streams supplied extensive irrigation systems." Once sheep were admitted, however, the fragile flora was quickly decimated: ground eroded and the region was transformed into a semi-desert of cactus and mesquite, barely supporting a handful of destitute natives, "eaters of beetles, bugs, and the fruit of the nopal cactus."[39] In other regions, the environmental effects of grazing were less dramatic, but wherever cattle and sheep wandered the landscape changed and indigenous livelihoods were affected.

Across the dry grasslands, and in some tropical forest regions as well,[40] a colonial commons was taking form and its spatial extent kept growing. This commons was shaped by colonial legislation and land-granting practices, as well as by the effects of ecological change and demographic shifts. The wasteland commons was not supposed to be for the use of

---

[38] Chantal Cramaussel, *Poblar la frontera: la provincia de Santa Bárbara en Nueva Vizcaya durante los siglos XVI y XVII* (Zamora, Mexico: El Colegio de Michoacán, 2006), 309–10; Gisela von Wobeser, *La Formación de la hacienda en la época colonial: el uso de la tierra y el agua* (Mexico City: UNAM, 1989), 28.

[39] Elinor G. K. Melville, *A Plague of Sheep: Environmental Consequences of the Conquest of Mexico* (Cambridge: Cambridge University Press, 1994), quotations at 31, 115.

[40] Bernardo García Martínez, *Los pueblos de la Sierra: el poder y el espacio entre los indios del norte de Puebla hasta 1700* (México City: El Colegio de México, Centro de Estudios Históricos, 1987), 142; Andrew Sluyter, "The Ecological Origins and Consequences of Cattle Ranching in Sixteenth-Century New Spain," *Geographical Review* 86 (1996): 161–77; Miguel Aguilar-Robledo, "Formation of the Miraflores Hacienda: Lands, Indians, and Livestock in Eastern New Spain at the End of the Sixteenth Century," *Journal of Latin American Geography* 2 (2003): 87–110.

Spaniards alone: the law was explicit as to natives' right to the resources of the mountains and the *tierras baldias*. Of course, these areas beyond the intensely cultivated valley lands were already part of the commons of one indigenous community or another, the use of their timber, water, game and medicinal plants and roots governed by local rules of access. The colonial commons did not necessarily nullify the indigenous commons, but it could undermine it very severely. Melville nicely sums up the crux of the conflict: "Then as today, common grazing only works when all parties agree to the rules governing the use of specified areas of land; but the Spaniards regarded all land not sown with crops as potential grazing lands, and, as conquerors, Spanish pastorialists could afford to ignore their own laws and customs when it suited them."[41] As Indians fought to protect their crops and their access to the dwindling resources of the rough lands, they were, in effect, engaged in an unequal struggle to preserve their indigenous commons against the aggressive expansion of the colonial commons.

In the wake of this clash of commons came a subsequent stage in the process of property formation, one that bore some resemblance to enclosure. This is the story of the rise and consolidation of the Mexican *hacienda*. The term "*hacienda*" originally had a financial meaning and in sixteenth-century Mexico it came to be attached to commercial livestock raising enterprises. Insofar as "*hacienda*" had a concrete object, it designated not a tract of land, but rather a herd of cattle or *ganado menor*. As stock-raising on a large scale became increasingly profitable and as the grazing lands in a given region began to fill to capacity, ranchers took steps to assert fuller control over portions of the colonial commons, by both legal and extra-legal means, and frequently at the expense of local indigenous communities. Central to the process of *hacienda* formation was the territorialization of property and an intensification of its exclusionary aspects; as a corollary, there was a progressive removal of land from the colonial commons. It was not simply a matter of accumulating land, but of transforming what started out as little more than a collection of licenses to graze into much more exclusive property. At one level, hacendados' grip over the land seems to have tightened through a thousand and one small usurpations, most of them invisible to the historical record, that kept other ranchers at bay and infringed upon the established customs of Indian communities. For example,

---

[41] Melville, *A Plague of Sheep*, 154.

natives were supposed, by explicit decree of the government, to have the right to gather firewood from rough lands (*"montes"*), whether or not these lay within Spanish estates; however, numerous court cases attest to the fact that *hacienda* owners tried to bar access to this resource or to charge Indians a fee to cut wood.[42] It was a classic case of the rich prevailing, regardless of formal regulations, over the poor, the weak and the racially stigmatized. Even as these processes of micro-dispossession continued, changes to the legal framework of property in New Spain served to accelerate the triumph of the *hacienda*. A legal procedure known as *composición*, first introduced in 1591 by a financially strapped Spanish Crown and progressively strengthened over the course of the seventeenth and eighteenth centuries, had the effect of reinforcing and legitimating informal techniques of dispossession. For a price, *hacendados* could transform illegal or dubious occupation into exclusive property (see Chapter 11).

An expansionist phase relying on the colonial commons was followed by a phase of consolidation in the form of wide-scale enclosure, and by this means the *hacienda* came to dominate major portions of Mexico, particularly in the north. *Haciendas*, it should be added, were never about "land" alone. They represented a system of control over space, water and people.[43] By depriving indigenous populations of the means of subsistence, they created their own cheap and compliant labor force in an involuted version of the more familiar effects of the English enclosure movement.

NEW ENGLAND

The importance of commons to property formation within the settlements of early New England is well understood and was touched on in the previous chapter. Township pastures were the norm, as were open-field practices, though the latter varied in form and degree and, in the long run, faded in the face of a colonial enclosure movement. These aspects of the inner commons had only a limited impact on the region's indigenous inhabitants, as they concerned fully colonized spaces from which natives had already been largely excluded. However, even as they busied themselves with property-making in their settlement enclaves, New England's

---

[42] Eric Van Young, *Hacienda and Market in Eighteenth-Century Mexico: The Rural Economy of the Guadalajara Region, 1675–1820* (Berkeley: University of California Press, 1981), 332–33.

[43] Von Wobeser, *La Formación de la hacienda en la época colonial*, 49–56.

settlers were also claiming a colonial outer commons that affected Ninnimissinuok over a broad and expanding front.

Certainly, there was nothing in the northeastern part of North America quite like the intrusion of ranging livestock and the rise of the *hacienda* in Mexico, and yet here too a clash of commons was central to the dispossession of native populations. When export-oriented cattle raising developed here, it depended mainly on lush coastal meadows fenced in as farms or as the inner commons; this region's wooded environment was not suitable for open-range ranching on a commercial scale. On the other hand, forest foraging would still support enough domestic animals, hogs above all but also cattle, to contribute significantly to colonial subsistence. Faced with the heavy demands of land clearing and house building, early settlers tended to let their animals wander off and fend for themselves, trusting they could later round up those that survived. Inevitably, some animals reproduced in the wild and went feral. Such practices were particularly widespread in the Chesapeake region where the forests were comparatively open, the climate was mild and the rewards for cultivating tobacco discouraged careful husbandry; however, New England settlers also allowed animals to roam.[44]

As habits of open-range husbandry took root, the new colonies quickly passed legislation that overthrew a long-standing English legal tradition governing liability for crop damage due to livestock depredation. Human herders and village pastures were among the devices used to control grazing beasts, but if a cow did get loose in a cornfield, English law held that liability lay with the cow's owner. The latter was responsible for keeping his animals confined, failing which he could be sued for damages. In 1643 the Virginia House of Burgesses decreed that henceforth it would be up to the owners of croplands to erect fences to keep out marauding ruminants, effectively taking the onus off stock-raisers for keeping their animals fenced in. Similar legislation was passed in the New England colonies.[45] This inversion of Old World legal norms naturally tended to encourage free-range husbandry and, by that means, to transform the commons.

---

[44] Virginia DeJohn Anderson, *Creatures of Empire: How Domestic Animals Transformed Early America* (New York: Oxford University Press, 2004), 107–40.

[45] Ibid., 114; Richard Brandon Morris, *Studies in the History of American Law, with Special Reference to the Seventeenth and Eighteenth Centuries*, 2nd ed. (Philadelphia: J. M. Mitchell Co., 1959), 208–10; David Thomas Konig, *Law and Society in Puritan Massachusetts: Essex County, 1629–1692* (Chapel Hill: University of North Carolina Press, 1979), 118.

Whereas English observers of the time deplored as a kind of partial reversion to nature the American tendency to allow animals to wander while concentrating efforts on developing the arable, Virginia Anderson demonstrates that this practice played a significant part in dispossessing natives along the edges of English North America.[46] Depending on the numbers of Old World animals at large, the effects on indigenous subsistence could range from the merely annoying to the utterly devastating. Cattle sometimes ate standing crops, while hogs stole stored food or dug up clam beds along the beaches. As in Mexico, trampling hooves and excessive grazing could bring about environmental changes that affected deer and other game populations, while spreading weeds and contributing to soil erosion. To make matters worse, livestock acted as a vector to spread Old World diseases among humans and other animals.[47] Natives complained bitterly of the injuries they suffered through casual settler husbandry. In New England, efforts were made in the early decades to assist Indians in fencing their fields and courts sometimes awarded compensation for crop damage; though the effects of these measures may have been slight, they did imply a sense of settler responsibility, something that was almost entirely absent in the southern colonies.[48] Moreover, with the passage of time and the rise of native–colonist tensions in New England and the Chesapeake, settler regimes grew less and less concerned about the effects of their animals on native livelihoods, to the point where some actually directed their horses and cows toward Ninnimissinuok fields in a deliberate effort to drive natives away and take over their lands.[49]

Allowing cattle and hogs to forage in the forest was clearly more than just a transaction between a settler and the natural environment. Crucial to the viability of this unsystematic system was the assumption that a cow or pig remained property wherever it might roam. In practice, identification of specific beasts could be uncertain and theft was rife, in spite of the severe penalties prescribed by colonial laws; moreover, many animals went completely feral, creating uncertainty about the boundary between wild game and chattels. But these anomalies, as Virginia Anderson observes, only made settlers all the more insistent on livestock's status

[46] Anderson, *Creatures of Empire.*

[47] Ibid., 185–90; Cronon, *Changes in the Land*, 141–50.

[48] *The General Laws and Liberties of the Massachusets Colony* (Cambridge, Mass.: Samuel Green, 1672), 76–77.

[49] David J. Silverman, *Faith and Boundaries: Colonists, Christianity, and Community among the Wampanoag Indians of Martha's Vineyard, 1600–1871* (New York: Cambridge University Press, 2005), 149.

as property; she notes further that open grazing represented a claim to the land itself: "Colonists in effect appropriated Indian common lands to serve as their own commons."[50]

The point deserves to be underlined. Colonists were claiming more than just the livestock that they themselves had introduced to this region. The territory where their animals ranged was already a commons of sorts; in an intricate geography that we catch only obscure glimpses of through European sources, indigenous families, bands and tribes maintained access rights to the resources of this region. When settlers proclaimed, in effect, that the natives' deer, fish and timber were open to all, colonists included, yet the hogs and cattle roaming these same woods remained private property, they were indeed attempting a wholesale appropriation. Beyond the limited clearings occupied and farmed by the English, they were asserting control over a larger zone and treating it as the "wasteland" of rural Europe. Ninnimissinuok were allowed to live here and to support themselves as best they could, but the rules governing access to resources would be those of the colonists. In practice, the margin of subsistence could shrink to the vanishing point for indigenous peoples living on the colonial commons. In Maryland, a native leader named Mattagund addressed authorities in these terms: "Your cattle and hogs injure us you come too near to us to live and drive us from place to place. We can fly no further let us know where to live and how to be secured for the future from the hogs and cattle."[51] Here, as in New Spain, the commons functioned as a prime instrument of dispossession.

One crucial difference distinguishing Europe's common "waste" of mountains and marshes from the colonial commons of America was the basic stability of the former and the relentlessly expansionist dynamic of the latter. Mattagund's sense of being pursued was no illusion. Over the centuries, indigenous peoples over a broad and ever-moving front would feel the effects of the advent of four-legged invaders even before the two-legged variety became a settled presence. The process, one aspect of the larger "empire effect" evoked earlier, is familiar in its broad outlines – waves of immigrants, accompanied by their livestock, seeking more and more lands to settle – but Virginia Anderson points out that, quite apart from the demographic explosion, the foraging of the animals itself

---

[50] Anderson, *Creatures of Empire*, 139–40, 171.
[51] Ibid., 221. See also James D. Rice, *Nature and History in the Potomac Country: From Hunter-Gatherers to the Age of Jefferson* (Baltimore: Johns Hopkins University Press, 2009), 108–29.

produced expansionist tendencies as the environmental damage inseparable from overgrazing induced them to range further and further afield in search of succulent herbage. A multispecies assault on the native commons really was under way as the colonial commons advanced across the face of the continent, bringing in its wake a colonial enclosure movement that left virtually no room for indigenous people.

Complicating the picture somewhat is the fact that some Ninnimissinuok people experimented with animal husbandry over the course of the seventeenth century. They generally found that cattle were incompatible with their mobile way of life. Pigs, on the other hand, were easier to accommodate – like the dogs that were already a part of village life, they could fend for themselves – and so they took their place as a source of meat that could compensate for dwindling returns in the deer hunt. Wampanoags even seem to have produced a surplus of preserved pork to market in colonial cities.[52] Native-owned hogs then became denizens of the extensive, uncultivated territory from which Wampanoag villages drew their livelihood. No sooner did indigenous people begin adapting to English agricultural practices, however, than colonists accused them of stealing livestock and – in a breathtaking turning of the tables – allowing their animals to damage settler crops! The town of Warwick, Rhode Island, passed legislation forbidding natives to "marke" pigs (with ear-marks) and the colony of Massachusetts passed a similar law in 1672.[53] The effect was to ensure that Algonquian people could never prove ownership of a hog at large. The colonial commons, it seems clear, was to be for colonists, not "Indians."

Needless to say, natives did not give up their commons without a fight. There is no way of knowing how often stray pigs and cows were killed, either for their meat or in retaliation for damaging crops or food caches. Ninnimissinuok made efforts to negotiate shared use of the land, but when colonists refused to cooperate and when local tensions rose, domestic animals were often targeted for destruction. The most dramatic and best-documented instances occurred in times of colonial wars when natives slaughtered livestock with a zest that suggested accumulated resentment. During the Powhatan resistance of 1622, natives "fell uppon

---

[52] Virginia DeJohn Anderson, "King Philip's Herds: Indians, Colonists, and the Problem of Livestock in Early New England," *William and Mary Quarterly*, 3rd ser., 51 (1994): 613–17.

[53] Ibid., 615–17; Joshua Micah Marshall, "'A Melancholy People': Anglo-Indian Relations in Early Warwick, Rhode Island, 1642–1675," *The New England Quarterly* 68 (September 1995): 420.

the poultry, Hoggs, Cowes, Goats and Horses whereof they killed great nombers." King Philip's War broke out in New England in 1675 partly because of native grievances over livestock; as in the earlier conflict on the Chesapeake, domestic beasts became a prime target.[54]

NEW FRANCE

The histories of the colonial commons in New Spain and New England display some similar themes: a vibrant inner commons played a central part in property formation within the respective settler zones, while an expansive outer commons, mostly driven by grazing livestock, penetrated into adjacent native territories, functioning as an advance agent of dispossession. In this connection, the colonization of New France stands as a contrasting case where common property had a much less prominent role to play. French towns in Canada may have had small common pastures, but nothing comparable to the *ejidos* of Mexico; and though there were some collective practices in the rural settlements of the St. Lawrence Lowlands, large open fields, like those of early New England, were unknown. After early experiments in communal agriculture on the part of the Counter-Reformation idealists who founded Montreal in the 1640s, and in defiance of government exhortations to gather in nucleated villages with outlying fields, the French settlers quickly settled on a pattern of "agricultural individualism." By and large, habitant farms were self-contained, comprising fields, house, barn, woodlot and (usually) pasture in a single elongated lot. An agrarian pattern made up of consolidated homesteads, each of them combining family residence and all the components of agricultural production, is usually associated with modernity. To those devoted to a modernist schema of progress from communal to private property it may seem strange that the most "feudal" of our cases of property formation is also the least communal.

Before attaching some important qualifications to this characterization of "agricultural individualism," we should recognize some environmental factors that help account for the relative weakness of communal property in and around the French settlements. Here climate, terrain and demography combined to ensure that the colonial outer commons remained a rather insignificant factor, at least as far as grazing cattle and pigs are concerned. During the long, cold winters that conditioned life and

---

[54] Anderson, *Creatures of Empire*, 179, 224–40; Anderson, "King Philip's Herds," 601–24.

agriculture in the St. Lawrence Valley, livestock had to be stall-fed. This constraint, combined with the small population and correspondingly limited market for meat and dairy products, tended to keep herds comparatively small, rarely more than a few head of cattle, pigs and horses: enough to supply the modest needs of an habitant family.[55] Many habitant farms, especially those that fronted on the St. Lawrence or one of its tributaries, offered enough pasture and meadow to provide both grazing in the warmer seasons and hay for the winter, enough perhaps to maintain a few oxen, milk cows and other domestic beasts (depending on whether or not the local seigneur had monopolized pasture lands). The outer commons, so important to livestock-raising in other parts of colonial North America, played a minor role in early Canada. By and large, the thick coniferous forest outside the cultivated zones offered little in the way of acorns, grasses and edible leaves to attract domestic herbivores. Consequently, one searches in vain through the New France records for indications of settler commoning affecting indigenous subsistence. Complaints, such as there are, come not from natives but from habitants, protesting that the natives' dogs are slaughtering their sheep.[56]

There was actually a version – attenuated in comparison to what we've seen in the Spanish and English colonies – of an inner commons in French Canada. Farms here may have been consolidated tracts, but they were not necessarily enclosed in the physical sense of the term. Custom consecrated by colonial regulations required only that hay meadows be fenced. Otherwise, it was up to the owners of livestock to keep their animals supervised and out of grain fields during the growing season, a point on which Canada's laws diverged sharply from those of the British colonies.[57] After the crops were harvested, the custom of *"vaine pâture"* prevailed, meaning that animals could roam across the fields grazing on the stubble and dropping their manure. As a legal commentator of Louis XIV's time

---

[55] Allan Greer, *Peasant, Lord, and Merchant: Rural Society in Three Quebec Parishes, 1740–1840* (Toronto: University of Toronto Press, 1985), 40–42. On the way climatic conditions shaped agricultural practices, see Thomas Wien, "Les 'travaux pressants': Calendrier agricole et régime d'assolement au Canada au XVIIIe siècle," *Revue d'histoire de l'Amérique française* 43 (1990): 293–317.

[56] Denys Delâge, "Microbes, animaux et eau en Nouvelle-France," *Globe: Revue internationale d'études québécoises* 9 (2006): 126; Library and Archives Canada, MG8, A6, Ordonnances des intendants de la Nouvelle-France, 29 May 1751.

[57] Règlements de police, 11 May 1676, in *Ordonnances, commissions, etc., etc., des gouverneurs et intendants de la Nouvelle-France, 1639–1706*, 2 vols., ed. Pierre-Georges Roy (Beauceville, QC: l'Éclaireur, 1924), 1: 197. Similar arrangements prevailed across much of *ancien-régime* France: Bloch, *French Rural History*, 46–47.

remarked, "Under the general law of France the plots are under care and protection only while the crops are showing; once they have been taken in, the ground becomes as it were subject to the law of nations and the common property of all, rich and poor alike."[58] Fences were incompatible with *vaine pâture*. The season of open grazing was short, however, two months or so between harvest and the onset of deep snow. Then, with the coming of the spring thaw, plowing and sowing became urgent priorities and animals were officially banned from the fields. In some localities, it was the seigneur who announced the dates at which animals could be turned loose on the harvested fields and when they needed to be confined. After the grain had been sown in the spring, however, the owners of livestock were supposed to keep their animals from damaging crops.[59] In practice, even though they had the right to impound marauding cattle and shoot pigs on their property, farmers began erecting fences across the front of their narrow farms to prevent incursions from the roadway. In 1725, the colonial administration called for habitants to fence their fields, though livestock owners remained liable for damages even on unenclosed lands. More and more fields were fenced, but many lands remained unenclosed at the time of the British conquest of Canada.[60]

As another qualification to the "agricultural individualism" characterization, we need to recognize the importance of common pastures in some, but by no means all, parts of the Laurentian colony. One study enumerated only thirty-six seigneuries equipped with common pastures in the first half of the eighteenth century and many of these served only a portion of the community's residents. The majority were located in the Montreal and Three Rivers regions, reflecting the greater prevalence there of islands and low-lying riverside areas subject to flooding, and therefore best suited to use as pasture and meadow.[61] These commons were mainly used to graze cattle, but habitants sometimes harvested hay or cut firewood on the commons. Ordinarily, the riverfront commons was open only to those who held adjacent *censives*, not to more distant habitants,

[58] Eusèbe Laurière, quoted in Bloch, *French Rural History*, 46–47. Bloch notes that this generalization did not actually apply to all regions of France.

[59] Louise Dechêne, *Habitants and Merchants in Seventeenth-Century Montreal* (Montreal and Kingston: McGill-Queens University Press, 1992), 175–77.

[60] Ordinance of Superior Council, 13 August, 1725, in *Inventaire des jugements et délibérations du conseil supérieur de la Nouvelle-France de 1717 à 1760*, 7 vols., ed. Pierre-Georges Roy (Beauceville, QC: l'Éclaireur, 1932), 1: 261; Dechêne, *Habitants and Merchants*, 177.

[61] Benoît Grenier, *Brève histoire du régime seigneurial* (Montréal: Boréal, 2012), 77–78.

and it was usually inseparable from land tenure; in other words, grazing rights could not be sold or leased to outsiders as was the case in some New England towns.

In most regions of France, commons were the collective property of the local population. The latter usually had an ancient claim to the land and seigneurs encroached on them only with great difficulty. Encroach they did, however, with the result that contests between peasant communities protecting their commons against the pretentions of seigneurs claiming a portion of the land became a fundamental axis of agrarian conflict under the *ancien régime*.[62] Not so in French Canada. Since the institution of the *seigneurie* preceded settlement, it was normally the seigneur, rather than the peasant community, who designated common lands; and of course seigneurs made a point of constructing that commons legally as their property, land to which they granted access to settlers only as a usufruct right. In actual practice, it was frequently the habitants who selected lands as commons, performed the work of fencing and maintaining the ground and elected trustees to regulate collective use,[63] but as far as the government and the law were concerned, this was the seigneur's land. In several fiefs, seigneurs cordoned off a strip of marshy land along the riverfront before granting *rotures* behind it; every *concession* deed to a settler then included a charge for the use of this commons. Sometimes it was an annual charge in produce or money, assessed on a per-head-of-livestock basis (one seigneur required half a pound of butter per cow per year); in other cases, the seigneur demanded a day of *corvée* labor. Over the years, many seigneurs found it convenient to convert these charges to a single, standard money assessment, typically two or three *livres* per year.[64] Like most conversions and adjustments, the effect of a flattened commons

[62] Bloch, *French Rural History*, 185–89; Gérard Béaur, *Histoire agraire de la France au XVIIIe siècle: inerties et changements dans les campagnes françaises entre 1715 et 1815* (Paris: Sedes, 2000), 71–74; Lemarchand, *Paysans et seigneurs en Europe*, 51, 195.

[63] On the island of Montreal, at least one small common pasture was established entirely on habitant initiative. Ordonnance de Duchesneau, 20 June 1680, in Roy, ed., *Ordonnances, commissions, etc., etc., des gouverneurs et intendants de la Nouvelle-France*, 2: 266–75. On the governance of commons, see Colin Coates, "Collective and State Authority: Governing the Commons in the St Lawrence Valley, Canada, 1660s–1990s," unpublished conference paper, 2016, 9–10.

[64] R. Cole Harris, *The Seigneurial System in Early Canada; a Geographical Study* (Madison: University of Wisconsin Press, 1966), 71–72; Marcel Trudel, *Les débuts du régime seigneurial au Canada* (Montreal: Fides, 1974), 115–19; Greer, *Peasant, Lord and Merchant*, 11–12; Colin Coates, *The Metamorphoses of Landscape and Community in Early Quebec* (Montreal and Kingston: McGill-Queens University Press, 2000), 35.

charge was to increase the weight of seigneurial exactions for most users. Inevitably, commons charges proved to be a bone of contention between habitants and their landlords. The court records of New France contain numerous disputes in which *censitaires* either contested the level of exaction or rejected the commons fee altogether.[65]

Such as it was, Canada's common property was mostly of the "inner commons" variety; consequently, conflict over the commons in the main pitted seigneurs against habitants. Extensive grazing was quite limited and its effects on indigenous peoples minimal. The most significant native–settler confrontation over the resources of the St. Lawrence Valley concerned eel-fishing facilities (see Chapter 3) and here it was more a matter of "enclosure," the privatization of a collectively managed resource. The Innu doubtless suffered other kinds of dispossession, even if these left no trace in the written historical record. Their aboriginal commons included wildfowl hunting and egg-gathering areas on the islands and marshy coves of the St. Lawrence, humid zones that settlers would likely have claimed as pastures and meadows. Nevertheless, and in spite of the acute impact on one band of Innu, the colonial commons of New France does not seem to have had the kind of far-reaching effects that accompanied commoning in New Spain and New England. To the various explanations that have been advanced in the past for the comparatively peaceful relationship between natives and settlers in early Canada (fur trade, low populations, Catholic approach to cultural diversity, etc.), we might then add one additional consideration, the absence of an aggressively expansive outer commons.

* * *

Ruminant herds of cattle, horses and sheep, foraging pigs and other exotic animals set loose on indigenous landscapes: these four-legged pioneers of colonization played a part in dislodging indigenous peoples in many quarters of the globe. Whether attended to by herders or completely feral, animals spread the colonial commons well in advance of settlement. This was the case in South Africa as well as in North America in the seventeenth and eighteenth centuries. A similar pattern developed across Australia in the nineteenth century, where sheep-raisers drove their herds

---

[65] Requête de Joseph Crevier, seigneur de St François, contre Pierre Gamelin, habitant, 7 July 1704, BANQ, juridiction royale de Trois-Rivières, TL3, S11, P2712; TL3, S11, P2944, 28 August 1713.

onto what was regarded as a great interior common pasture, regardless of the prior claims of aboriginal foragers. The western plains of North America were another site of dispossession-by-commons. Here a complicated set of circumstances, including the introduction of horses, led to the extinction of the bison and the consequent starvation of native populations, preparing the way for enclosure and colonization. The expansion from the east of open-range cattle-ranching played a part in these developments, especially by blocking access to the moister zones where bison would otherwise have found sustenance in times of drought.[66]

In the real world of colonial North America, the destruction of indigenous property forms and the establishment of new, colonial property regimes did not follow the pattern that John Locke and countless other theorists suggest. America (not to mention Australia, South Africa and New Zealand) did not welcome Europeans as an open-access universal commons and settlers did not necessarily establish control over the land through procedures resembling enclosure. In the long run, of course, fences, surveys, registry offices and other developments associated with enclosed property made their appearance and stabilized new property regimes from which native peoples were largely excluded. But privatization of land was not the only – or even the most important – mechanism through which indigenous territory came into the possession of colonizers; by the time that sort of enclosure occurred in many places, dispossession was already an accomplished fact, thanks in large measure to the intrusions of the colonial commons.

John Locke's misdescription of colonial property formation as the enclosure of a great universal commons was anything but an innocent mistake. It served both to erase native property in land at the outset and to

---

[66] John C. Weaver, *The Great Land Rush and the Making of the Modern World, 1650–1900* (Montreal and Kingston: McGill-Queens University Press, 2003), 264–308; Leonard Guelke and Robert Shell, "Landscape of Conquest: Frontier Water Alienation and Khoikhoi Strategies of Survival, 1652–1780," *Journal of Southern African Studies* 18 (1992): 803–24; Henry Reynolds, *Dispossession: Black Australians and White Invaders* (St. Leonards, NSW: Allen & Unwin, 1989), 66–95; Robert Foster, "Coexistence and Colonization on Pastoral Leaseholds in South Australia, 1851–99," in *Despotic Dominion: Property Rights in British Settler Societies*, ed. John McLaren, A. R. Buck and Nancy E. Wright (Vancouver, BC: UBC Press, 2005), 248–65; Pekka Hamalainen, "The Rise and Fall of Plains Indian Horse Cultures," *Journal of American History* 90 (December 2003): 833–62; Andrew C. Isenberg, *The Destruction of the Bison: An Environmental History, 1750–1920* (New York: Oxford University Press, 2000), 130–43; Irene Spry, "The Great Transformation: The Disappearance of the Commons in Western Canada," in *Man and Nature on the Prairies*, ed. Richard Allen (Regina, Saskatchewan: Canadian Plains Research Centre, University of Regina, 1976), 21–45.

assimilate colonial appropriation with "improvement," that last word to be understood both in its specialized agricultural sense and in its more general meaning. Placing the focus on pioneers, with their log cabins, axes and plows, rather than on the cattle, hogs and sheep they sent roaming across native common lands, has the effect of obscuring the central business of colonizing "new" lands, which is to say the dispossession of indigenous peoples and the imposition of new property regimes.

8

Spaces of Property

Does Britannia, when she sleeps, dream? Is America her dream? ... Earthly
Paradise, Fountain of Youth, Realms of Prester John, Christ's Kingdom,
ever behind the sunset, safe till the next Territory to the West be seen and
recorded, measur'd and tied in, back into the Net-Work of Points already
known, that slowly triangulates its Way into the Continent, changing all
from subjunctive to declarative, reducing Possibilities to Simplicities that
serve the ends of Governments.

Thomas Pynchon, *Mason and Dixon*[1]

Did the colonization and dispossession of indigenous Americans result
from some inadequacy in their ability to understand territory and space?
A rapid reading of the history of imperial claims and colonial property
formation can give the impression that Europeans took over, in part,
because they had a superior ability to represent space. Mapping, naming
and claiming territory on an extended scale, they could integrate the land
under their feet and before their eyes, but also distant territories beyond
the horizon, by projecting lines and coordinates out through other people's
homelands. The influential historian of cartography, Brian Harley, put it
this way in relation to the cartography of early New England: "In a
European culture, where land was conveyed by precise measurement and
with a fixing of position by latitude and longitude, the Indians' maps,
as we shall see, put them at a technological disadvantage."[2] It is

---

[1] Thomas Pynchon, *Mason and Dixon* (New York: Henry Holt, 1997), 345.
[2] J. B. Harley, "New England Cartography and the Native Americans," in *The New Nature of Maps: Essays in the History of Cartography*, ed. Paul Laxton (Baltimore: Johns Hopkins University Press, 2001), 178.

noteworthy that Harley refers to "conveying" land, associating ownership and alienation with mapping, while implying at the same time that natives became the hapless victims of objective, mathematical techniques for designating territory. Since scholars have paid so much attention to early modern developments in European science generally, and particularly to the mathematization of space and the emergence of powerful new techniques of surveying and cartography, it is understandable that the impression would take hold that these developments played a central part in the appropriation of overseas territories. Europeans' impersonal, mathematical sense of space equipped them to integrate distant territories into their view of the world and to claim new lands by assimilating them to familiar terrain; meanwhile, aboriginal peoples, so the literature seems to imply, remained stuck in a strictly local landscape that was clothed in mythic and spiritual meanings. Science arrived from over the sea and placed its mark upon Nature. This narrative of a spatial confrontation between rational, far-seeing colonizers and culturally blinkered natives recalls other instances of the ideological folklore of imperialism – stories featuring clear-eyed explorers, conquerors and missionaries facing bewildered savages – and it is equally misleading.

When it comes to apprehending and representing territory and space, there were indeed differences between European and indigenous American approaches, but then there were equally important differences among Europeans and among native Americans. Moreover, space was dealt with differently in different circumstances and in pursuit of particular purposes. Philosophers plumbing the secrets of the universe, mariners looking for routes across the ocean, soldiers defining perimeters of security, governments asserting territorial sovereignty, hunters claiming hunting zones, herders occupying grazing ranges, cultivators fencing in fields: all these functions, and many more, had their distinctive spatial practices and each of them varied and evolved over time. It would make for a simpler and, perhaps to some, a more satisfying story if we could say that the Scientific Revolution provided Europeans with the basic spatial concepts and the precise techniques of representation that allowed them to take over the world – if colonial property-making were a matter of extending geometric grids into the trackless wilderness.

The image of the Mason–Dixon surveying expedition "triangulat[ing] its way into the continent" seems to symbolize the forward march of science bringing clarity and precision to a shadowy American landscape. However, the shiny instruments and advanced techniques used by George Mason and Jeremiah Dixon when they traced the boundary between

Maryland and Pennsylvania in the 1760s stand in marked contrast with the rough-and-ready practices of colonial surveyors in New England, New France and New Spain. Scientific cartography and precise land measurement would play a central part in native dispossession in the post-Enlightenment period, with the result that native Americans, quite reasonably, attacked surveyors in the US West, while the appearance of Canadian surveyors in the Red River Valley provoked a violent insurrection on the part of the region's Métis population; Mason and Dixon were themselves halted in their tracks due to the opposition of western Delawares into whose territories they had intruded.[3] These conflicts were characteristic of the late eighteenth and the nineteenth century, when great efforts were made to engineer colonization according to the laws of geometry. Things did not work in anything like the same way during the early modern period. From the sixteenth to the late eighteenth century, European science and technology had a limited and equivocal effect on the colonial recasting of North American space. On the other hand, they did arguably play a part in fostering the kind of dreaming of which Thomas Pynchon writes.

SPATIAL UTOPIAS

The sixteenth and seventeenth centuries saw the emergence of theories of infinite, abstract space, together with techniques of measurement and mapping that transformed European understandings of the world. Michel Foucault has pointed to a perceptual/epistemological shift at the time that amounted to a general "spatialization of knowledge."[4] New instruments – the telescope, the compass, the astrolabe – and new techniques in drawing, trigonometry and cartography – advanced alongside new views of the cosmos, the position of the Earth and the motion of the planets and stars. Developments in the area of land and property were not immune to the effects of these shifting intellectual and artistic currents. Moreover, as has been frequently noted, Europe's first era of overseas exploration and colonization coincided exactly with the age of Copernicus, Galileo and

---

[3] Dwight L. Agnew, "The Government Land Surveyor as a Pioneer," *Mississippi Valley Historical Review* 28 (1941): 377–78; Gerald Friesen, *The Canadian Prairies: A History* (Toronto: University of Toronto Press, 1987), 119–28; Cameron B. Strang, "The Mason-Dixon and Proclamation Lines: Land Surveying and Native Americans in Pennsylvania's Borderlands," *The Pennsylvania Magazine of History and Biography* 136 (2012): 5–23.

[4] The phrase appears in an interview with Foucault published in Paul Rabinow, ed., *The Foucault Reader* (New York: Pantheon 1984), 254. Foucault refers here to his book, *The Order of Things: An Archaeology of the Human Sciences* (London: Routledge, 2002).

Newton; nor was this a simple coincidence. We cannot ignore the connections between colonial property formation and native dispossession, on the one hand, and the immense changes then transforming European spatial conceptions and practices, on the other. However – and this will be the main point of this chapter – the impact of the "mathematization of space" (to sum up complex developments with a shorthand phrase) on North American colonization was far less direct and immediate than might be expected.

To begin with the European background, one area where these early modern spatial transformations are most apparent is in the history of art. The development of linear perspective during the Renaissance, with a vanishing point and invisible radiating lines giving the illusion of depth and solidity, was a crucial part of this shift.[5] Momentous as the breakthroughs of Filippo Brunelleschi and Leon Battista Alberti may have been, revisionist art historians note that Renaissance artists still depict a closed world; their pictures have a frame and a fixed viewpoint; their themes are typically narrative, intelligible only in relation to the Bible, the Lives of the Saints, or some other text. In a much later development, Svetlana Alpers argues, Dutch landscape artists of the seventeenth-century managed to perfect a God's-eye view without a fixed vantage point; furthermore, their pictures convey a sense of space extending out beyond the frame, so that the painted scene seems to be a particular instance within a wider world that existed prior to its depiction, and independent of any story or text.[6] Paintings of towns and countryside bore some resemblance to maps of the time – the latter, as much pictorial as abstract, often showing a horizon line – and benefited from some of the instruments and techniques of surveying and cartography. Emphasizing the close connection between landscape and "the mapping impulse" at this time,

---

[5] Samuel Y. Edgerton, *The Renaissance Rediscovery of Linear Perspective* (New York: Basic Books, 1975). On the conjunction of artistic, scientific and technological approaches to space in this period, see Giorgio de Santillana, "The Role of Art in the Scientific Renaissance," in *Critical Problems in the History of Science*, ed. Marshall Clagett (Madison: University of Wisconsin Press, 1962), 33–65; Jean-Marc Besse, "Entre modernité et postmodernité: la représentation paysagère de la nature," in *Du milieu à l'environnement. Pratiques et représentations du rapport homme/nature depuis la renaissance*, ed. M. C. Robic (Paris: Economica, 1992), 89–121. On the connections linking linear perspective in art and new conceptions of landscape and property, see Denis Cosgrove, "Prospect, Perspective and the Evolution of the Landscape Idea," *Transactions of the Institute of British Geographers* 10 (1985): 45–62.

[6] Svetlana Alpers, *The Art of Describing: Dutch Art in the Seventeenth Century* (Chicago: University of Chicago Press, 1983).

Alpers quotes a Dutch treatise on art to this effect: "How wonderful a good map is, in which one views the world as from another world thanks to the art of drawing."[7]

The plenitude of "worlds" and the uniform regularity of space, in scales ranging from the microscopic to the local to the global to the cosmic, was a broad theme that artists shared with philosophers of the period. From the heretical speculations of Giordano Bruno in the sixteenth century to the equations of Isaac Newton in the late seventeenth, the idea that the universe extended infinitely in all directions was gaining adherents. Of science and philosophy in the sixteenth and seventeenth century, Alexandre Koyré writes: "During this period human, or at least European, minds underwent a deep revolution which changed the very framework and patterns of our thinking and of which modern science and modern philosophy are, at the same time, the root and the fruit." Essentially that change amounted to "the replacement of the Aristotelian conception of space – a differentiated set of innerworldly places – by that of Euclidean geometry – an essentially infinite and homogenous extension."[8] Blaise Pascal, a brilliant mathematician deeply implicated in the new outlook, but also a devout Catholic, found these intellectual developments at once bracing and terrifying. "Nature is an infinite sphere," he wrote, "the center of which is everywhere, the circumference nowhere."[9] Independent of any human presence, space existed as a fundamental reality. It seemed to follow that, on Earth as well as in the outer cosmos, position was neither absolute nor inherently meaningful: locations were simply points best defined by coordinates.

The applied sciences of navigation, cartography, surveying and ballistics all made great strides in this era, largely by inserting mathematics into the study of position, size and movement. Geometry was much more widely studied after John Dee's translation of Euclid in 1570; the early seventeenth century saw a vigorous development in applied mathematics generally.[10]

---

[7] Ibid., 141. See also Monique Pelletier, "Representations of Territory by Painters, Engineers, and Land Surveyors in France during the Renaissance," in *Cartography in the European Renaissance*, ed. David Woodward and J. B. Harley, vol. 3, pt. 2: *The History of Cartography* (Chicago: University of Chicago Press, 2007), 1522–37.

[8] Alexandre Koyré, *From the Closed World to the Infinite Universe* (Baltimore: Johns Hopkins University Press, 1957), vii–viii.

[9] Pascal quoted in Jorge Luis Borges, "Pascal's Sphere," in *Selected Non-Fictions*, ed. Eliot Weinberger, trans. Esther Allen, Suzanne Jill Levine and Eliot Weinberger (New York: Penguin, 1999), 353.

[10] Jacques Beauroy, "La représentation de la propriété privée de la terre: Land surveyors et estate maps en Angleterre de 1570 à 1660," in *Terriers et plans-terriers du XIIIe au XVIIIe siècle. Actes du colloque de Paris (23–25 septembre 1998)*, ed. Ghislain Brunel,

Instruments such as the cross-staff, the quadrant and the telescope played a part in the techniques of space, but the technology involved remained fairly simple: this was mostly a matter of refined measurement of angles, together with mathematical techniques to derive length measurements from the qualities of triangles. Military engineers were at the forefront of much innovation, measuring distances by triangulation, calculating the trajectory of cannon balls, designing fortifications and mapping terrain. At sea, the compass gave mariners a sense of orientation, while instruments such as the cross-staff and astrolabe allowed them to use the angle between the horizon and a star, or in daytime the sun at its zenith, to estimate their position on a north–south axis between the pole and the Equator. Latitude could thus be determined, if approximately, but longitude eluded precise measurement until the late eighteenth century. On land, measurement relied heavily on triangulation and trigonometry, for example, to estimate the distance to a visible church tower of known height. In mapping local areas, practitioners increasingly relied on instruments such as the theodolite, a sixteenth-century invention that placed a finely calibrated simple sighting mechanism (telescopic sights were added only in the mid-eighteenth century) on adjust-able vertical and horizontal axes to measure angles exactly (Figure 8.1). Poles and cords for measuring distance over the ground gave way to the more exact chain of interlinked brass sections devised by Edmund Gunter in the 1620s (Figure 8.2). A good surveyor, aided by such instruments, could gather field measurements, then calculate elevations, distances and surface areas and execute a good plan or "plat" of the area. Property mapping became the main application of these techniques in England, but there (and more so in France) they were also used for military and civic purposes. Map-making developed in close association with the techniques of applied geometry and with those of landscape art as well. Indeed, surveyors and cartographers were frequently referred to as "artists" in this period.

As part of the general "spatialization of knowledge," maps became much more numerous in the early modern period; many of them were published and widely distributed. From the sixteenth century to the eighteenth, maps became more "accurate," but also more abstract. They were at first highly decorated with illustrations and cartouches, and if landscape pictures looked much like maps, local-scale maps looked a lot like pictures. Gradually, however, the embellishments disappeared, leav-ing maps as coded symbolic images that indicate mountains, coasts and

Olivier Guyotjeannin and Jean-Marc Moriceau (Rennes: Association d'histoire des soci-étés rurales – Ecole nationale de chartes, 2002), 94–100.

FIGURE 8.1 A surveyor's theodolite, English, from the late sixteenth century.
The instrument is adjusted on horizontal and vertical planes. With a basic sighting
mechanism (telescopic sights were introduced only in the second half of the
eighteenth century), it allows a sharp-eyed surveyor to measure angles accurately.
Source: Altazimuth Theodolite, by Humfrey Cole, London, 1586, Inv. 55130. © Museum of
the History of Science, University of Oxford.

boundaries, without pretending to resemble the actual landscape. This
abstraction derives from a mathematical conception of space, even if early
modern maps were not, in reality, entirely the product of measurement
and geometry.[11]

Some scholars speak of a "cartographic revolution" that began in late
sixteenth-century Europe and that placed maps at the center of learned
understandings of the universe. Long before they could map the Earth and
seas with exactitude, the educated and the powerful had become habitu-
ated to conceiving of the world and the state, not to mention the cosmos
and the microcosm, by means of spatial symbols inscribed on paper. The
metaphor of "mapping" spread through the sciences to suggest practices
of framing fields and orienting inquiries. In the strictly geographic sphere,

[11] This and the following paragraph draw heavily on David Turnbull, "Tricksters and
Cartographers: Maps, Science and the State in the Making of a Modern Scientific
Knowledge Space," in *Masons, Tricksters and Cartographers: Comparative Studies in
the Sociology of Scientific and Indigenous Knowledge* (Amsterdam: Harwood Academic,
2000), 89–129.

FIGURE 8.2 Gunter's chain, ca. 1700. Since the early seventeenth century, the brass Gunter's chain, with its hundred 7.92-inch links, provided accurate linear measurement along the ground. Unlike a cord, it did not stretch when wet and unlike a pole – another cheap alternative much used in the colonies – it had rings at either end that allowed it to pivot on a pin to measure the next 66 feet with minimal loss of accuracy at the transition point.
Source: Gunter's chain, English, ca. 1700, Inv. 57576. © Museum of the History of Science, University of Oxford.

early modern maps increasingly gave the impression of uniform space integrating distant locations into a single picture of the world. In the words of the historian of cartography Christian Jacob, "Maps allow the assemblage of a multitude of heterogeneous inputs in order to subject them to the same mathematical logic and to erase their differences through the coherence of the visual codes."[12] They also seem to have encouraged the sense that terrestrial space could be sliced, divided and bounded. When viewed through the intermediary of a map, it seemed to make sense, whether the topic was sovereignty or property, to draw a line and say, "On this side is mine, on that side is yours." No coincidence then that the age of cartography corresponded with the rise of territorial states, not to mention overseas empires and transformed property.

---

[12] Quoted in Turnbull, "Tricksters and Cartographers," 100.

In the political history of Europe, the early modern period saw the emergence of "a more territorialized notion of monarchy and, by extension, a more cartographic approach to governance itself."[13] Feudal political authority had been articulated more in personal terms, whereas the emergent new monarchies aspired to exercise full and uniform control over a geographically defined realm with definite borders. Sovereignty came to be understood as a fundamentally territorial phenomenon. Increasingly, states were taking on the appearance of discrete, self-contained and internally uniform spaces, sharply divided from adjacent states. At least that was the ideal, frequently expressed in maps of the period. The reality is that, with the partial exception of England/Britain, an island bounded by nature, the territorial state remained an unrealized ideal. Most states of the sixteenth and seventeenth centuries were internally differentiated spaces with ambiguous outer limits. "Spain" was still very much a composite monarchy made up of Castile, Aragon and various appendages within and beyond the Iberian Peninsula. The king of France ruled over provinces that had been acquired variously by conquest, treaty or dynastic marriage and that, in many cases, retained their own laws, customs and tariffs; even on the eve of the Revolution, the component parts of "France" were not subject to the monarch's sovereignty to the same extent or in the same way. Moreover, the kingdom's boundaries were never clear-cut, in spite of Louis XIV's best efforts to establish solid frontiers. There were still internal enclaves such as Avignon and the Comtat Venaissin, which were owned by the pope. The northern city of Arras owed allegiance to the Hapsburgs. The Duchy of Lorraine was occupied by French troops in the seventeenth century even though only a portion of its territory was legally French and even though the entire duchy belonged to the Holy Roman Empire. As for mountain villages in the Pyrenees, sometimes it was anyone's guess whether they fell under French or Spanish jurisdiction.[14]

---

[13] Richard L. Kagan and Benjamin Schmidt, "Maps and the Early Modern State: Official Cartography," in *Cartography in the European Renaissance*, ed. David Woodward and J. B. Harley, vol. 3, part 1: *The History of Cartography* (Chicago: University of Chicago Press, 2007), 661–79.

[14] James B. Collins, *The State in Early Modern France* (Cambridge: Cambridge University Press, 1995), 30–33; Peter Sahlins, *Boundaries: The Making of France and Spain in the Pyrenees* (Berkeley: University of California Press, 1989). On the chronic indeterminacy of the Spain–Portugal border, see Tamar Herzog, *Frontiers of Possession: Spain and Portugal in Europe and the Americas* (Cambridge, Mass.: Harvard University Press, 2015), 135–242.

Though early modern states and cartographic representations of early modern states emerged in tandem, the irony is that it proved impossible to map an entire nation using the new mathematical spatial technologies. The problem was that, while map-making could be very precise within a given visual horizon, it was difficult to maintain exact proportions at the scale of a kingdom. In the absence of really precise measures of latitude and longitude, geographers could not fully integrate local maps from far-flung parts of a country as large as, for example, France. Under Louis XIV, Jean-Dominique Cassini arrived at a partial solution to the problem through the technique of continuous triangulation, a painstaking and expensive method of surveying a series of interlocking triangles from one end of France to the other, and using it as a backbone to tie together local topographical surveys to create a unified national map. Preliminary results in the 1680s indicated that the area of the kingdom was smaller than previously thought, which led Louis to remark, "I paid my academicians well and they have diminished my kingdom." Cassini's son and grandson oversaw the surveying of a more complete network of triangles, finishing their national map in 1744. An even more precise, geodetic survey followed, this one requiring expeditions to Lapland and Peru to determine whether the Earth was perfectly round or slightly flattened toward the poles (as Newton's theory predicted); it was completed on the eve of the French Revolution.[15] Britain was slower to produce a standardized, consistent set of maps for the whole country; work began on the ordinance survey series in 1791 and concluded only in 1895. Mathematically grounded cartography had been a theoretical possibility for centuries, but as a practical program for representing national spaces, it proved an elusive ideal throughout the early modern period.

The same can be said of systematic property mapping, a procedure – or rather an objective – intimately connected with state formation. With the example of the Roman empire and its regional cadastres before them, and inspired by the technological capabilities now at their disposal, some early modern rulers dreamed of establishing a record of all the properties and their respective boundaries within their states. In the cadastral utopias that were envisaged from the seventeenth century on, the courts would dispose of the information they needed to settle land disputes quickly and

[15] Josef W. Konvitz, *Cartography in France, 1660–1848: Science, Engineering, and State-craft* (Chicago: University of Chicago Press, 1987), 2–31; David Turnbull, "Cartography and Science in Early Modern Europe: Mapping the Construction of Knowledge Spaces," *Imago Mundi* 48 (1996): 14–16.

easily; central governments would have a complete picture of the lands and resources of the kingdom; and, not the smallest consideration, land taxation would be greatly facilitated. If all the land within a state could be apprehended within the uniform spatial coordinates that the scientific philosophy proclaimed as the fundamental reality, subject and monarch alike would prosper. According to James C. Scott, cadastres served to appropriate local knowledge of the land for the purposes of the state: "Land maps in general and cadastral maps in particular are designed to make the local situation legible to an outsider." Scott adds that cadastres played a central role in property formation: "The cadastral map added documentary intelligence to state power and thus provided the basis for the synoptic view of the state and a supralocal market in land."[16]

What Scott presents as an accomplished fact, I see as a utopian aspiration, at least as far as the early modern period is concerned. A few regions on the periphery of western Europe could boast systematic cadastres by the end of the seventeenth century: Finland and Swedish Livonia being the foremost examples; there was a cadastre in the duchy of Savoy (later part of France) as of 1738. But in the large imperial countries, there was nothing of the sort. Louis XIV and his chief minister Jean-Baptiste Colbert aimed to map all the properties in France, but they had to settle for a survey of royal forests. (One of the many obstacles to the project was the bewildering diversity of units of measurement; reformers tried to come up with a uniform unit of length and surface area, without success before the Revolution.)[17] Work on a national cadastre finally began under Napoleon in 1808 but was completed only in 1850. James I of England ordered a "Great Survey" of Crown lands and forests in 1607, but no maps were produced; the revolutionary Parliament tried again in 1649, but ended up with only a written description of state lands, and nothing on private holdings. There were various attempts to establish systematic property mapping and registration in England throughout the nineteenth century, none of them entirely successful.[18]

---

[16] James C. Scott, *Seeing like a State: How Certain Schemes to Improve the Human Condition Have Failed* (New Haven, Conn.: Yale University Press, 1998), 39, 45.

[17] Jean-Robert Armoghate, "Un seul poids, une seule mesure: le concept de mesure universelle," *Dix-septième siècle*, no. 213 (2001): 631–40; Michèle Virol, "De l'usage politique de la mesure: l'exemple de la lieue carrée," in *La juste mesure: quantifier, évaluer, mesurer entre orient et occident, VIIIe-XVIIIe siècle*, ed. Laurence Moulinier (Saint-Denis: Presses universitaires de Vincennes, 2005), 159–73.

[18] Marc Bloch, "Les plans parcellaires," *Annales d'histoire économique et sociale* 1 (1929): 63; R. J. P. Kain and Elizabeth Baigent, *The Cadastral Map in the Service of the State:*

In this context, Ireland appears as a revealing special case. A subjugated polity where lands were repeatedly confiscated and reassigned, it was also the site of much precocious property mapping. In Elizabethan times, the Munster Plantation involved the careful laying out of lands to accommodate Protestant settlers. Dispossession and reallocation on a grand scale occurred later, following a Catholic uprising and Oliver Cromwell's bloody reconquest of Ireland in 1649. As part of the program of confiscating rebel holdings and regranting them to English soldiers, Sir William Petty undertook a survey of unprecedented ambition, called the "Down Survey," covering five million acres in twenty-nine counties. A member of the Royal Society and a pioneer of "political arithmetick," Petty supervised the creation of large-scale maps that both measured holdings and evaluated their agricultural value. Much about the Down Survey seems to foreshadow the transformation of indigenous American territories. "Petty's survey, which reduced the Irish estates to standard units of size and gradations of value, and whose progress fed speculation in land debentures, commodified Irish land," observes one modern study; "Colonization and commercialization went hand in hand."[19] Here again, however, we have to take note of the gap between early modern aspirations to precise measurement and uniform recording and the more modest on-the-ground achievements of the period. Petty's field-workers, mostly untrained ex-soldiers working in the midst of hostile local populations (eight surveyors were slaughtered by insurgents), produced maps of uneven quality. Not as precise as expected, the Down Survey covered only selected regions and confiscated lands; it had none of the comprehensiveness of a true cadaster. In spite of these imperfections, it did nevertheless foster speculation in Irish lands; William Petty himself was foremost among those who accumulated fortunes by that means.[20] Though it facilitated the "commodification" of land, the Down Survey did not actually succeed in reducing the Irish landscape to geometry.

A History of Property Mapping (Chicago: University of Chicago Press, 1992), 68, 71, 210–13, 236, 249–55; Alain Pottage, "The Measure of Land," *Modern Law Review* 57 (1994): 374–83.

[19] Ted McCormick, *William Petty and the Ambitions of Political Arithmetic* (Oxford: Oxford University Press, 2009), 117.

[20] R. J. P. Kain, "Maps and Rural Land Management in Early Modern Europe," in Woodward and Harley, ed., *Cartography in the European Renaissance*, 706–8; Mary Poovey, *A History of the Modern Fact: Problems of Knowledge in the Sciences of Wealth and Society* (Chicago: University of Chicago Press, 1998), 120–43; McCormick, *William Petty*, 90–118.

In the realms of European art and science, it might be fair to speak of a "spatial revolution," beginning in the second half of the sixteenth century and extending through the seventeenth. New ways of construing the world, of measuring the Earth and of representing it through maps and paintings came to the fore, transforming medieval understandings of space. These novel conceptions were implicated in a shift toward a more territorial approach to political authority. They even played a part in inspiring global exploration and the pursuit of overseas empire. Finally, they suggested a revolutionary new way to construe landed property as geometrically measured surface areas. These spatial reconfigurations sought to impose a kind of mathematical perfection on land and society. It was a utopian vision, powerfully compelling but impossible of realization.

SPACES OF EMPIRE

At times it seems that a certain mathematization of space was central to the colonization of America and the dispossession of its indigenous peoples. However, the links between scientific/philosophical breakthroughs and contemporaneous imperial expansion are rather difficult to pin down. Scholars have long speculated about ways in which the overarching idea of "discovery" – the notion that truly unprecedented knowledge can be acquired – connected the disparate spheres of overseas exploration and philosophical/cosmological inquiry. Climbing down from these speculative heights to the realms of empirical history, we can say that the new spatial technologies of cartography and navigation played an important part in enabling Europeans to travel to America and to begin laying claim to territory there. Charts, rutters, compasses and cross-staffs all played their part, both in the sea voyages and in the representation and recording of the coasts, rivers and inlets of the "new" continent. Even so, it is easy to exaggerate the technological and "scientific" dimensions of these enterprises; we should remember that Columbus himself was basically an intuitive navigator: "He relied on celestial navigation by astrolabe and quadrant from time to time, but on the whole he trusted his abilities as a dead reckoning navigator."[21]

On the one hand, European diplomacy and nascent international law began to project abstract boundaries onto the world, invoking latitudes, longitudes and measured distances: from the Treaty of Tordesillas (1494)

---

[21] Delno West, "Christopher Columbus and His Enterprise to the Indies: Scholarship of the Last Quarter Century," *William and Mary Quarterly* 49 (1992): 264–65.

that divided a Spanish from a Portuguese sphere at 370 leagues west of Cape Verde, to various seventeenth-century colonial charters that mentioned the Tropic of Cancer, the Arctic circle and various degrees of latitude. On the other hand, it proved impossible to locate the Spanish-Portuguese dividing line on South American soil;[22] North American imperial frontiers proved equally elusive when the French and the British clashed. Empires extended out across real terrain and through populous nations; they used mathematical spatial technologies mostly for strictly tactical purposes, rarely as a means of defining sovereign territory.

From the time of Columbus on, *mappemundi* and atlases provided Europe's elite with a picture of the world that, more than the highly stylized world maps of the Middle Ages, seemed to invite travel and to show the way to the most distant lands. Some scholars read into these representations of the Earth an impulse to possess and control. Only within limits, however, can they be said to embody a mathematization of space. The great repositories of geographical knowledge that the Spanish accumulated in their *Casa de la Contratación* and the Portuguese in Lisbon's *Casa da Mina* were mainly composed of portolan charts. The latter were drawings produced by mariners from direct observation of coastlines; they gave indications of direction, but not of distance. Lines radiated out in all directions on such a chart and a navigator chose the one that best corresponded to his route and then sailed until he struck land. "Portolan charts," writes David Turnbull, "were not based on the techniques of coordinate geometry, perspective, calculation and the notion – central to our notions of science and rational action – of a mathematically and logically consistent plan or set of rules. Instead, portolan charts were based in a different set of techniques for assembling local knowledge. Their heterogeneous components were not assembled by rendering them equivalent through quantification, measurement and calculation."[23] Reviving an idea first proposed by Ptolemy, Gerardus Mercator devised a technique for projecting geographical information onto a grid of latitude and longitude lines as of 1569, but it would be two centuries before the Cassinis and their collaborators would succeed in finally situating places precisely within Mercator's projection. Until then,

---

[22] Herzog, *Frontiers of Possession*, 25–69.

[23] Turnbull, "Cartography and Science in Early Modern Europe," 9. See also Edgerton, *The Renaissance Rediscovery of Linear Perspective*, 95; Antonio Barrera-Osorio, "Empiricism in the Spanish Atlantic World," in *Science and Empire in the Atlantic World*, ed. James Delbourgo and Nicholas Dew (New York: Routledge, 2008), 177–202.

maps would be based on close observation of terrain, aided by rudimentary instruments, but they hardly represented the incorporation of the
Earth into an abstract geometry of mathematical space.

The Spanish managed to conquer and colonize Mexico with essentially
no help from "scientific" geography. The first attempt at a systematic
description of New Spain occurred in the 1570s, long after the country
had come under effective European control. It began with a questionnaire
sent out from the center of the empire to local administrators across
Spanish America, asking for information on each of the Spanish and
Indian communities, their population, resources, history and so on, in
their respective jurisdictions. The approach was more textual than cartographic, though many localities submitted maps. In many respects,
the methods of the *Relaciones Geográficas* project mimicked those of
the Casa de la Contratación: it was a matter of collecting and compiling
local knowledge from local residents.[24] Of the maps that have survived,
most seem to have been drawn by natives in a distinctively indigenous
style; the submission from Culhuacan, for example, shows footprints that
are the Nahua symbol indicating travel (Figure 8.3). Far from imposing
abstract coordinates that would integrate Mexico into a universal spatial
pattern, the *Relaciones Geográficas* represent the appropriation of indigenous knowledge in its "raw" form: Nahua geography in Nahua forms,
to be stored up in the archives of empire.

At the beginning of the next century, French and English explorers
brought what seemed to be more advanced geographical techniques as
they charted the coasts and rivers of northeastern North America. The
maps they produced have every appearance of fully European productions; some even displayed inset images of calipers and compass crests as
emblems of "scientific" cartographic methods. These embellishments are
a bit misleading, however, as even the most famous explorers and map-
makers of the period had only minimal recourse to mathematical concepts
and scientific instruments. Samuel de Champlain, whose maps of New
France and New England are still widely admired for their accuracy,
seems to have been a self-taught cartographer with little or no knowledge
of geometry or trigonometry (though he could do simple triangulation).

[24] See Serge Gruzinski, *The Conquest of Mexico: The Incorporation of Indian Societies into
the Western World, 16th–18th Centuries*, trans. Eileen Corrigan (Cambridge: Polity
Press, 1993), 70–97; Barbara Mundy, *The Mapping of New Spain: Indigenous Cartography and the Maps of the Relaciones Geográphicas* (Chicago: University of Chicago
Press, 1996), 180–208.

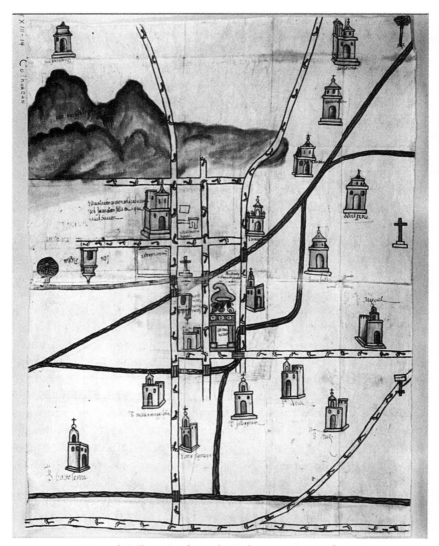

FIGURE 8.3 Map of Culhuacán, from the *Relaciones Geográficas*, 1580. This map, apparently the work of an indigenous artist and very much in the native Mesoamerican style, formed part of an inquiry, launched from the imperial center, to gather systematic information about Spain's New World dominions.

Source: Relaciones Geográficas Collection, Nettie Lee Benson Latin American Collection, University of Texas at Austin. Courtesy University of Texas Libraries.

His method for mapping coasts and ports was to sail past in a small vessel, monitoring speed by counting the fathom-spaced knots in a rope attached to a floating anchor as they unspooled; by keeping track of the hours that passed, he could determine the distance from point to point. For mapping on a small scale, Champlain essentially drew what he saw. Inland, he cultivated relationships with the native people who guided his travels and sketched for him the features of more distant countries he did not himself reach. Champlain's maps are all based on local knowledge: his own personal observations and those of his indigenous associates. Although he did use an accurate astrolabe to determine latitude, he basically drew the land rather than measuring it.[25] His famous 1632 map of New France (Figure 8.4) is covered in lines, but these do not represent the latitude–longitude grid of a Mercator projection; instead, the lines radiate out from a central point in the North Atlantic and they extend only over water. They are rhumb lines, basically sailors' compass bearings, and they are characteristic of portolan charts. Like most early maps of North America, Champlain's is essentially a sea chart with land added.

More or less the same could be said of the cartography of Champlain's English contemporary, John Smith. As a follow-up to his *Map of Virginia*, published together with a book describing the country and promoting colonization, Smith published a similar map of New England (1616), along with an accompanying text[26] (Figure 8.5). Neither of the major Smith maps displays signs of mathematical spatial procedures; both have maritime rhumb lines, though the New England map, like Champlain's New France, devotes more space to the sea than does the Virginia map. Whereas the inland portions of the New France map were constructed on a combination of Champlain's personal observations and borrowed native cartography, Smith did not penetrate beyond the coast of New England. However, his explorations in Virginia were similar to Champlain's further north; Smith's Virginia map actually indicates, by little crosses marked on the rivers he ascended, where his personal observations end and his reliance on indigenous geography begins. These early

[25] Conrad Heidenreich and Edward H. Dahl, "La cartographie de Champlain (1603–1632)," in *Champlain: la naissance de l'Amérique française*, ed. Raymonde Litalien and Denis Vaugeois (Québec and Paris: Les éditions du Septentrion and Nouveau monde éditions, 2004), 312–32.

[26] John Smith, *A Description of New England* (London: Robert Clerke, 1616); John Smith, *A Map of Virginia. With a Description of the Countrey, the Commodities, People, Government and Religion* (Oxford: Joseph Barnes, 1612).

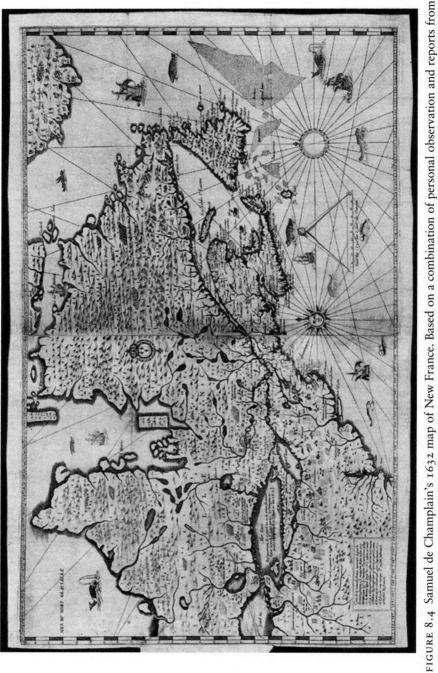

FIGURE 8.4 Samuel de Champlain's 1632 map of New France. Based on a combination of personal observation and reports from indigenous collaborators, this map displays the character of a sea chart more than of a mathematical representation of space. *Source:* "Carte de la Nouvelle France," in *Les voyages de la Nouvelle France occidentale, dicte Canada, faits par le Sr de Champlain* (Paris: chez Louis Sevestre, 1632). Courtesy Bibliothèque et Archives nationales du Québec.

FIGURE 8.5 John Smith's map of New England, 1616. As in Champlain's map of
New France (Figure 8.4), rhumb lines for maritime navigation are a prominent
feature of this map. John Smith bestowed the name "New England" on the region.
Source: John Smith, *A Description of New England* (London: Robert Clerke, 1616).
Courtesy University of Nebraska at Lincoln Digital Commons.

maps are doubly hybrids, mixing traditional navigational techniques with
a dose of up-to-date spatial technology, while also combining European
observation and appropriated native geographical knowledge. It could
hardly be said that the French and English explorers simply incorporated
eastern North America into a mathematical spatial grid.

Champlain's and Smith's maps bear all the marks of the presumptuous
imperialist chutzpah that we expect of European overseas geography in
this period. They suggest a privileged and globally qualified observer
encompassing far-flung lands, waterways and nations into a unified, all-
knowing gaze. Royal insignias hover over both New France and New
England and sailing ships ply the Atlantic, suggesting commercial and
political connections between Old and New France/England (though
some of Champlain's and Smith's other maps do depict native people).

Furthermore, the two explorers engage in the game of "naming and claiming," assigning toponyms that assert an additional connection to their respective home countries. Smith actually engaged the assistance of the heir to the English throne to help him "change their Barbarous names, for such *English*," and so, in deference to the prince's vanity, the Massachusets River became the Charles River.[27] Smith himself assigned the name "New England" to the whole region. These two toponyms stuck, as did "New Plimouth" and "Salem," but most of the explorer's other names – "London," "South Hampton," "Cape James" – did not. The impulse to assert toponymic control was strong, the ability to enforce conformity somewhat less impressive. Such preliminary mapping may have stimulated imperial dreams – it may even have facilitated colonizing enterprises – but it did not do much to transform American space.

Nor did the early coastal maps and inland surveys amount to a mathematical representation of space. Eventually, colonization would come to be cast within the grid lines of mathematics, but that development occurred quite late in the day. The British East India company, borrowing the methods the Cassinis pioneered in France, would undertake, mostly in the first half of the nineteenth century, a systematic geodetic survey from one end of the Indian subcontinent to the other.[28] Meanwhile, the Continental Congress's Land Ordinance of 1785 had established the parameters for a square grid of townships, each subdivided into forty-nine sections, that was to be the pattern for land allocation over much of North America.[29] The plan involved a carefully surveyed baseline across Ohio, serving to orient further surveys along north–south and east–west axes. Western lands were then to be laid out systematically and in advance of settlement. The township/section pattern was adopted in Canada as well and something similar was later introduced into Australia and New Zealand. Measurement errors, the wrinkly topography of the land and the resistance of native peoples combined to ensure that boundary lines were never perfectly straight, while the curve of the Earth precluded exactly square angles. Parts of the North American plains would indeed bear a resemblance to a massive checkerboard, serving as a visible symbol of the utopian ambitions of Enlightenment colonization

---

[27] Smith, *A Description of New England*, 3.
[28] Matthew H. Edney, *Mapping an Empire: The Geographical Construction of British India, 1765–1843* (Chicago: University of Chicago Press, 1997).
[29] Bill Hubbard, *American Boundaries: The Nation, the States, the Rectangular Survey* (Chicago: University of Chicago Press, 2009), 183–233.

planning, but geometric perfection always proved elusive. Only since the late twentieth century, with the advent of satellite technologies and global positioning systems, can the Earth's surface really be treated as instances within a mathematical grid.

PLACES

Rather than space, scholars discussing the relationship of indigenous peoples and the environment are more inclined to speak of "place." Place has been defined as "a location in the environment as contrasted with a point in space ... Places can be named, but they need not have sharp boundaries."[30] It has to do with landscape in relation to human communities. People inhabit places: they experience them with their bodies and indeed form part of what a place is. Place is land as local knowledge, the lived experience of its inhabitants, rather than as abstract space. Furthermore, place implies time as well as location. In the words of the philosopher Edward S. Casey: "Rather than being one definite sort of thing – for example, physical, spiritual, cultural, social – a given place takes on the qualities of its occupants, reflecting these qualities in its own constitution and description and expressing them in its occurrence as an event: places not only *are*, they *happen*." Observing that modernists accord priority to abstract, absolute space, Casey argues that place is actually the more fundamental reality. Newtonian space, for all its prestige, never erased other modes of experiencing the world. Though place is often associated with "primitive societies," we in the "modern west" continue to inhabit a world of places.[31]

The anthropologist Keith Basso is among those who have written most compellingly about Native American places and sense of place, on the basis, in his case, of extensive research with the western Apaches of Arizona. Basso evokes a landscape in which streams, buttes, trails and rock formations all have names richly evoking ancestors, spirits and

---

[30] J. J. Gibson, *The Ecological Approach to Visual Perception* (1979), 33–36, as quoted in Tim Ingold, "Territoriality and Tenure: The Appropriation of Space in Hunting and Gathering Societies," in *The Appropriation of Nature: Essays on Human Ecology and Social Relations* (Manchester: Manchester University Press, 1986), 147.

[31] Edward S. Casey, "How to Get from Space to Place in a Fairly Short Stretch of Time: Phenomenological Prolegomena," in *Senses of Place*, ed. Steven Feld and Keith H. Basso (Santa Fe, N.M.: School of American Research Press, 1996), 13–52 (quotation at 27). See also Edward S. Casey, *Getting Back into Place: Toward a Renewed Understanding of the Place-World* (Bloomington: Indiana University Press, 2009).

significant events. Places are meaningful to the indigenous inhabitants; the land reveals itself to them, providing them with bodily and spiritual sustenance. Their identities and histories are bound up in the earth's features. Far from being external observers, the Apaches in their very embodied selves form a part of their homeland, according to Basso.[32] In a similar vein, Peter Nabokov makes this general observation about indigenous American geography (and by implication, property):

> For many American Indian peoples, the land was often its own best map and demanded knowing first on its own terms, almost as if the topography itself possessed some sort of volitional authority. Before representing it, for instance, some native traditions expected you first to listen to its stories and learn its names, to follow it with your feet or to find a way to dream at its most propitious locations. Only after practicing a range of such knowledge-engendering practices *with* the landscape might you be able to truly depict it on a flat surface. This was often the reverse of the non-Indian process of appropriating space by first naming and drawing it, and only then by striding over or settling what was thereby already your own(ed) conception.[33]

Humanity, from this perspective, is not above and outside the natural world. It is instead a living part of a living land.

For all the richness of its insights, the work of scholars such as Nabokov and Basso on the intimate relationship between native people and the land should not blind us to the fact that a sense of place has never been exclusively indigenous. Europeans also lived in places as, for that matter, did Euro-American colonists. Indeed, colonial property formation (and therefore native dispossession) developed to a significant degree through place making, the attachment of specific landscapes to human communities and vice versa. Abstract constructions of space were involved, though, as I have argued, far less centrally than is usually assumed. To imply that colonization was a matter of geometry displacing human places is not only at odds with historical reality, it runs the risk of veering toward a sentimentalized version of the old savagery/civilization dichotomy, the one in which natives are assimilated to Nature while Europeans represent Culture.[34]

---

[32] Keith H. Basso, *Wisdom Sits in Places: Landscape and Language among the Western Apache* (Albuquerque: University of New Mexico Press, 1996).

[33] Peter Nabokov, "Orientations from Their Side: Dimensions of Native American Cartographic Discourse," in *Cartographic Encounters: Perspectives on Native American Mapmaking and Map Use*, ed. Malcolm G. Lewis (Chicago: University of Chicago Press, 1998), 242.

[34] In a related objection to anthropologists' habit of associating "natives" and "places," Appadurai argues that it implies a confined and confining definition of "native," one that attributes mobility and wider horizons to the outside observer alone, while ignoring or

As earlier chapters have shown, settler property-making in early New Spain, New France and New England was largely a matter of "striding over or settling" terrain, often in the wake of roaming herds of grazing livestock, but usually before allotments had been mapped. When he speaks of "the non-Indian process of appropriating space by first naming and drawing it," Peter Nabokov probably has in mind the grand gestures of early explorers who claimed whole continents in their monarch's name and rebaptized coastal features accordingly. But the early voyages of reconnaissance did not usually involve real appropriation of territory. Expansive claims, preliminary mapping, grandiloquent "ceremonies of possession" such as the erecting of a cross or flag or the reading of a proclamation[35] were all expressions of imperial ambition and warnings to competing European empires, but by themselves, they had little effect on indigenous control over lands. American space would be genuinely transformed when colonists occupied it and made it into places for themselves.

How could it be otherwise? Europe itself was then a continent of places where land was richly meaningful to its inhabitants, where properties were deeply embedded within particular communities and specific landscapes; even the boundaries dividing neighboring kingdoms were largely determined at the local level, rather than through diplomatic negotiations over map coordinates; and kingdoms were typically composed of an amalgam of fiefs, dependencies and autonomous towns. The countries that sent colonists to the New World were thickly populated with *lieux de mémoire*: villages, mountains, fountains, forests, fields, ponds, paths and highways, all of them constitutive of communal identities and most of them largely unknown and unknowable to learned outsiders.[36] William Christian's research on sixteenth-century Spain reveals a world of magical springs, uncanonized local saints and unauthorized cults and pilgrimages associated with specific sites. Generations of Annales School historians have made broadly similar points about the French countryside.[37]

---

downplaying these qualities among the indigenous. Arjun Appadurai, "Putting Hierarchy in Its Place," *Cultural Anthropology* 3 (1988): 36–49.

[35] See Patricia Seed, *Ceremonies of Possession in Europe's Conquest of the New World, 1492–1640* (New York: Cambridge University Press, 1995).

[36] Pierre Nora, ed., *Realms of Memory: Rethinking the French Past*, trans. Arthur Goldhammer, 3 vols. (New York: Columbia University Press, 1996).

[37] William Christian, Jr., *Local Religion in Sixteenth-Century Spain* (Princeton: Princeton University Press, 1981); Robert Mandrou, *Introduction to Modern France, 1500–1640: An Essay in Historical Psychology* (New York: Holmes & Meier, 1976).

England too, desacralized somewhat by the effects of the Reformation, still remained a land of deeply meaningful local places.[38] Property was fully embedded within this infinitely varied constellation of local places. At least until the nineteenth century, when ordinance survey mapping and systematic cadastral registration allowed the state's mathematically calibrated vision to penetrate into the rural landscape, the living memory of peasant communities would remain the most important record of property rights and boundaries.

Viewed from one angle, the colonization of North America consisted in settlers appropriating landscape, investing it with meaning and, in effect, making it into a set of colonial places.[39] Whether or not longitude, latitude and compass orientation had been established in advance, colonists had to come to terms with the soils, the waterways, the flora, fauna and landforms of the region they had come to inhabit. They transformed the environment in many areas, through forest clearance, irrigation and plowing, but they also inserted themselves into the landscape and became a part of it. "Science" and spatial measurement were not entirely foreign to that process, but the accretion of experience, and surely even a certain sympathy with the land, were at least as important. Settler local knowledge of the environment grew; it was not entirely unlike the native local knowledge alongside of which it developed, because it was of course often built largely through appropriation of that indigenous knowledge of place.

Like natives, settlers gave places names, and these were always evocative and meaningful. Colonists frequently borrowed indigenous place names, sometimes translated them into a European language, sometimes not (Canada, Coyoacan, Connecticut); names recalling a European origin (and therefore a sense of cultural connection) were also common: Nuevo Leon, Boston, Ipswich. (It would be interesting to explore the question of why such names were so much more popular in New England than in New Spain and New France.) Also favored were names commemorating a colonial founding figure (most rural communities in New France bore the name of their first seigneur). In Connecticut, colonists named some places in honor of local fish and game resources: Turkey Hills and Salmon Brook

---

[38] Keith Thomas, *Religion and the Decline of Magic* (New York: Scribner, 1971); Oliver Rackham, *The History of the Countryside* (London: J. M. Dent, 1986).
[39] See Paul Carter's path-breaking spatial analysis of the colonization of Australia: *The Road to Botany Bay: An Essay in Spatial History* (London: Faber, 1987).

are two examples.[40] Other toponyms described landscape features or historical events: the Canadian parish of Les Éboulements, site of a landslide occasioned by the earthquake of 1663, evoked both topography and history. Saints' names and other religious toponyms suggested connections with the Old World, with the distant past and with the cosmic order. All these names, whether of settlements, colonies, rivers or landscape features, remind us that the most basic aspects of colonization took place on a local level and at a human scale; space was appropriated largely through the creation of colonial places: beside, on top of and in place of indigenous places.

If native peoples inhabited a sacred landscape, so too did settlers. New England townships were organized around meeting houses, the site of religious services, and their initial membership coincided (largely if not perfectly) with membership in a church; even the names of some towns (Providence and Concord, for example) proclaimed a Christian identity. Much more than the dour Puritans of New England, the founders of New Spain and New France made a point of infusing a religious identity into the lands they colonized. Catholic toponyms were strewn far and wide, sometimes in conjunction with indigenous names. There was place and place-name aggression, as when Spanish conquerors erected churches over the sites of demolished Aztec temples and when they built the city of Mexico on the ruins of Tenochtitlán. There was also more complex melding and merging, as when a shrine to the Virgin of Guadalupe arose on a spot where a Nahua Catholic convert had witnessed a vision of Our Lady. This location had been venerated in pre-Hispanic times, and even after it had been thoroughly Christianized, it attracted both native and Spanish pilgrims.[41] By the seventeenth century, New Spain was dotted with a network of holy sites and points of pilgrimage, most of them displaying some combination of indigenous and European Christian antecedents. A recent study of Jesuit writings of this period refers to the "sacred geography" of colonial Mexico.[42] A similar term might be applied to the more modest network of holy places that developed in New France, starting with the miraculous

---

[40] Peter Benes, *New England Prospect: A Loan Exhibition of Maps at the Currier Gallery of Art, Manchester, New Hampshire* (Boston: Boston University for the Dublin Seminar for New England Folklife, 1981), 82.

[41] William Taylor, "Mexico's Virgin of Guadalupe in the Seventeenth Century and Beyond," in *Colonial Saints: Discovering the Holy in the Americas, 1500–1800*, ed. Allan Greer and Jodi Bilinkoff (New York: Routledge, 2003), 277–98.

[42] Jason Dyck, "The Sacred Historian's Craft: Francisco de Florencia and Creole Identity in Seventeenth-Century New Spain," PhD dissertation, University of Toronto, 2011.

shrine of Sainte-Anne-de-Beaupré.[43] Native people were, in many instances, active participants in the colonial reconfiguration of landscape, integrating Christian elements into their own sense of place. The fact remains that the settlers – absorbing native concepts even as they infused the land with significations of Old World origin – were also experiencing the American environment as spiritually meaningful.

The spatial practices of property-making played out within the context of these emergent colonial places. Even when the techniques of geometric surveying were deployed to allocate plots, settlers still treated land as a socially defined entity with natural and supernatural dimensions. We see signs of this in the ceremonies by which *mercedes* were enacted in New Spain. A land grant was not valid until the grantee, accompanied by a local judge, had trudged its length and width, ritually breaking twigs, uprooting plants and throwing stones along the way.[44] Similar ceremonies, featuring physical manipulation of the land and the marking of boundaries, accompanied the sale of land. Thus when a Spanish Franciscan bought a small tract from two Nahua brothers in 1738, the notary recorded the words of the local judge who, having examined the site and investigated the sellers' title, summoned Antonio Gonzalez, the buyer, "and with the power of the king our lord I introduced him into possession; he threw stones, mashed down the grass, and strolled about on his purchased land signifying that he took possession properly; no one disputed it, there was acceptance."[45] Such ceremonies were public and clearly they served to provide an opportunity for community members to register objections as to the boundaries of, or title to, the land in question. At the same time, they were insistently physical; as a complement to written deeds, these public performances of ownership rooted

---

[43] Mary Corley Dunn, "The Miracles at Sainte-Anne-Du-Petit-Cap and the Making of a Seventeenth-Century Colonial Community," *Canadian Historical Review* 91 (2010): 611–35.

[44] Hanns J. Prem, *Milpa y hacienda: Tenencia de la tierra indígena y española en la cuenca del Alto Atoyac, Puebla, México (1520–1650)* (Wiesbaden: Steiner, 1978), 122; Malcolm Ebright, "New Mexican Land Grants: The Legal Background," in *Land, Water, and Culture: New Perspectives on Hispanic Land Grants*, ed. Charles L. Briggs and John R. Van Ness (Albuquerque: University of New Mexico Press, 1987), 22; Brian Owensby, *Empire of Law and Indian Justice in Colonial Mexico* (Stanford, Calif.: Stanford University Press, 2008), 91.

[45] Arthur J. O. Anderson, Frances Berdan, and James Lockhart, *Beyond the Codices: The Nahua View of Colonial Mexico* (Berkeley: University of California Press, 1976), 107. Similar Spanish-inflected rituals of possession as practiced in native communities are mentioned in Gruzinski, *The Conquest of Mexico*, 119–20.

property in a particular spot on the face of the land and they did so in the presence of a living community.

Somewhat similar performative practices surrounded property in early New England. There it became customary to "beat the bounds," as freemen from one town met their counterparts from the next town and walked in procession along their common boundary.[46] This was an annual event and people made a point of bringing along children so as to instill in the younger generation a physical memory of the local property geography, thus assuring a living, nondocumentary record of the land that would continue into the future. Private perambulations were also common, one proprietor calling on a neighbor to walk their common boundary and verify its landmarks. Medieval English traditions of Rogationtide perambulation lay behind these colonial practices, ceremonies in which local clergy would lead parishioners on a procession through the fields, pausing at landmarks and boundaries, often reciting a psalm or saying a prayer to ask for God to ensure fertility in the soil and peace in the community. In Virginia, the ceremony of "beating the bounds" retained its religious character, but the New England Puritans secularized this custom (as they did weddings and funerals). It remained, in Alegra di Bonaventura's words, a "performative, memorial experience,"[47] similar in that respect to New Spain's essentially secular ceremonies of possession.

Natives living under colonial rule incorporated some of these European rituals of possession into their own practices of property. An incident recorded in southeastern Connecticut in the early eighteenth century illustrates this point. A member of the ubiquitous Winthrop family, Major John Winthrop, great grandson of his illustrious namesake, sought to confirm the bounds of a large property he owned, adjacent to native land (unspecified, but probably Mohegan). He took along a party of "bounders" that included an elderly settler woman, Goodwife Houghton, who "led the party through the landscape, pointing out signifying boundary features."

Playing a role parallel to Goodwife Houghton's was an "old Indian," a leader among the Native bounders. This old man represented indigenous memory, affirming to Winthrop "in Indian": "Yes, Old Houghton's

---

[46] Allegra Di Bonaventura, "Beating the Bounds: Property and Perambulation in Early New England," *Yale Journal of Law and the Humanities* 115 (2007), 115–48.

[47] Ibid., 135. On this topic, see also Jack R. Stilgoe, "Jack-o'-Lanterns to Surveyors: The Secularization of Landscape Boundaries," *Environmental Review* 1 (1976): 14–31; Edward T. Price, *Dividing the Land: Early American Beginnings of Our Private Property Mosaic* (Chicago: University of Chicago Press, 1995), 352.

daughter knows the bounds well." ... When Goodwife Houghton led to "the bound on the river," the "Old Indian" said, "So it is" and put his stick that he had in his hand down into said little brook where it run through the sandy beach ...[48]

In central Mexico, says James Lockhart, land transactions were surrounded by ritual since before the conquest, but under colonial rule, Nahuas readily incorporated Spanish practices into their repertoire of land-related ceremonies. "The Spanish manner of having the principal officer present take the new possessor by the hand and lead him over the property, while the latter carried out symbolic destructive acts showing his full rights (pulling off twigs and throwing stones), seems to have become deeply embedded in Nahua practice."[49]

"Sense of place" was not a monopoly of aboriginal peoples in North America. Settlers too experienced the land at a local level, on the ground and as a bodily experience; they too invested topographical features with cultural meaning and historical memory. Settler place was built partly through the appropriation of native place, but native place in turn absorbed elements of colonial place. These versions of meaningful landscapes, populated with humans, animals and spiritual forces, were neither static nor monochromatic nor entirely exclusive; Goodwife Houghton and "the Indian" could agree on where a boundary was located and how it should be signified. Yet at the same time there was, inevitably, an underlying current of antagonism in the confrontation of these different, overlapping versions of space. And surely it was in this zone of contention, where the land was symbolically marked with cultural meaning and where property situated itself, that settler property formation and native dispossession ultimately occurred.

TERRITORIES WITHOUT BORDERS

Is it possible to conceive of territory without reference to boundaries and outer edges? In the endless forests of the Canadian Shield, stretching from

---

[48] Di Bonaventura, "Beating the Bounds," 127, quoting deposition of John Post, New London County Court Records, Files, Box 153, File of 1700, Connecticut State Library.

[49] James Lockhart, *The Nahuas after the Conquest: A Social and Cultural History of the Indians of Central Mexico, Sixteenth through Eighteenth Centuries* (Stanford, Calif.: Stanford University Press, 1992), 169. See also Blanca Jiménez Padilla and Samuel Villela Flores, "Rituales y protocolos de posesión territorial en documentos pictográficos y títulos del actual estado de Guerrero," *Relaciones: estudios de historia y sociedad* (Zamora, Mexico) 24 (2003): 93–112.

the St. Lawrence Valley north to the Arctic tundra, there were no real boundary markers. And yet this was not, as the cliché would have it, a "trackless wilderness": the region was veined with an intricate network of rivers, streams, lakes and ponds that served as tracks for mobile hunter-gatherers. For half the year, canoes plied their waters, while in the winter their frozen, snow-covered surfaces formed a roadway for snowshoe and toboggan travel. Waterways traced lines of travel and hunting, and they functioned as the axes of a property system derived from these activities. By the same token, rivers were not suitable as border markers in a land where waterways were at the heart, rather than at the edge, of hunting grounds. Even in the absence of outer lines of demarcation, however, territories were nonetheless real and the exclusions of property consequential. That much becomes clear when we catch a glimpse, thanks to a rare set of documents from the colonial archives, of a conflict between rival claimants to hunting rights.[50] The trouble arose from the movement of peoples and the commercialization of beaver hunting, which had led to challenges to Innu territories. With Iroquois, Hurons and Abenakis moving into the rich hunting grounds north of the St. Lawrence in ever-greater numbers around the turn of the eighteenth century, the small bands of Innu were feeling squeezed out. The conflicts that ensued both tested the resilience of established property claims and illustrated how these worked in a hunter-gatherer context.

In March 1705, Guillaume Chische, Joseph Marachualik and François 8cachy,[51] along with three other Innu, were encamped somewhere on the extensive domain where they hunted for beaver (a commercial product) and moose (a source of food and of hides to make clothing and for a variety of other purposes). These were probably descendants of the Innu

---

[50] France, Archives nationales d'outre-mer, colonies (hereafter ANOM), C11A, vol. 25, fol. 27–36, Requête du Sr. Hazard à Jacques Raudot, 3 August 1706, plus attached documents. See also ibid., 25: 82–87v, Déclaration à Messieurs les directeurs general de la Compagnie de la colonie de Canada, 19 June 1705; ibid., 25: 76v; Petition of Sr. Hazeur to Govr. Vaudreuil, 4 November 1705; ibid., 27: 55v, Hazeur to Pontchartrain, 5 November 1707. This material is discussed in Toby Morantz, "Colonial French Insights into Early 18th-Century Algonquians of Central Quebec," in *Papers of the Twenty-Second Algonquian Conference*, ed. William Cowan (Ottawa: Carleton University, 1991), 213–24; Sylvie Savoie and Jean Tanguay, "Le noeud de l'ancienne amitié: La presence abénaquise sur la rive nord du Saint-Laurent aux XVIIe et XVIIIe siècles," *Recherches amérindiennes au Québec* 33 (2003): 36–41; Nelson-Martin Dawson, *Feu, fourrures, fléaux et foi foudroyèrent: les Montagnais: Histoire et destin de ces tribus nomades d'après les archives de l'époque coloniale* (Sillery: Septentrion, 2005), 182–84.

[51] In their attempts to record indigenous American languages, the French Jesuits frequently used "8," probably a "u" on top of an "o," to represent the sounds "ou" or "woo."

who had been driven from the eel fisheries of Sillery half a century earlier. They made their summer quarters at this time on Lac St-Jean and they traded at the Saguenay River post of Chicoutimi. Subsequent events suggest that they had traveled west to reach their winter camp, pulling their toboggans up one of the many rivers that flow into Lac St.-Jean. One day in March 1705, they sighted footprints in the snow near their camp – many of them. Having had a run-in a year earlier with a large group of Abenakis, in the course of which they had been "pillaged" of their furs and skins by the stronger party, the Innu must have been alarmed by this discovery. Their forebodings were soon confirmed when a party of six men led by the Abenaki chief, François Thék8érimat, strode into the camp. As in the previous incident, there was no violence and no direct threat of force; yet a great disparity in numbers was clearly evident. The Abenakis took care to organize a delegation that put them on a numerical par with the Innu, an approach that suggests diplomatic – or even "judicial" – intentions: forceful but restrained. They had come to talk. It seems that the people involved knew one another personally. They spoke different, but related, languages: communication was possible. "Thék8érimat told us that the lands of Lac St-Jean belonged to the Abenakis and that they had come to hunt on them," the Innu later testified. In calling them "the lands of Lac St-Jean" the Innu may have been distorting their opponents' words; the Abenakis certainly claimed that particular location, but they probably did not recognize it as lying within the Lac St-Jean watershed. Only many months later would the Innu be able to challenge the Abenakis' territorial assertion; at the time they were too intimidated to resist. Knowing what his guests expected, Joseph Marachualik handed over six moose hides "to save us from pillaging," as he put it.

There were probably many such confrontations in the northern woods around this time, but in this case alone, we have a fairly detailed written account. That is because the interests of François Hazeur, a merchant to whom the government leased the "King's Posts," a regional trade monopoly, were affected and he was determined to seek redress. Hazeur's agents had outfitted the Innu on credit and, in the wake of two successive pillagings, debts were unpaid and the hunters' starving families had to be supported. Behind the Abenakis' intrusions, Hazeur discerned the machinations of rival traders based in Three Rivers, but rather than try to sue his competitors over an indirect and unprovable violation of his monopoly privileges, he instead persuaded the Innu hunters to lodge an official complaint. They went to the intendant, the highest judicial officer in New France; using his magistrate's power, the intendant instituted a formal inquiry. In keeping with French judicial procedures, questions were prepared in advance and, speaking through an interpreter, Chische, Marachualik and 8cachy replied; a clerk recorded their words, using the third person where they would have spoken in the first person. In order to hear the other side of the dispute, the intendant summoned Louis, the son of the Abenaki chief François Thék8érimat, to give his version of events through a separate interrogation. Thus, representatives of the two contending parties that had struggled for control of a remote stream in the Canadian Shield now faced one another once again in the intendant's palace at Quebec where a different kind of judicial procedure unfolded. It was an unusual episode, since in striking contrast to New Spain, indigenous people rarely made use of the courts of New France, especially for a dispute with other natives.[52] Even if the proceedings went to court in furtherance of the business interests of François Hazeur, we still learn much from the testimony about Algonquian hunting customs and territorial property practices.

Louis Thék8érimat's account does not really contradict the Innu version of events, except for his crucial insistence that the confrontation occurred on lands "which belonged to his father." He and five companions had visited the Innu camp, he said, to lodge a protest. "They complained that the Innu were hunting on their lands, and that they had so thoroughly destroyed the animals on it, that they could find no food, to the point where they had had to make canoes in order to return [to St. François]." It seems that the allusion to making canoes was meant not literally, but as a metaphor indicating material injury, for he added, "they did not know why they should not pillage them," i.e., take the Innu goods as compensation. Joseph Marachualik, according to the Abenaki witness, immediately offered them six moose hides, saying, "here, take this to make canoes." The Abenakis spent the night in the Innu lodge, and in the morning, the intimidated hosts revealed their food caches and stood by while the Abenakis helped themselves. They even took – or as Thék8érimat told it, the Innu gave them – toboggans to take away their loot.

This was not an act of war. Older Innu would have retained painful memories of a time when enemy Mohawks had descended upon the region, pouncing without warning upon sleeping encampments, killing men, burning lodges and carrying off women and children into

---

[52] Jan Grabowski, "French Criminal Justice and Indians in Montreal, 1670–1760," *Ethnohistory* 43 (1996): 405–29.

captivity.[53] Indigenous warfare in the northeast was normally about killing and capturing enemies rather than conquering territories. In the diplomatic alignments of the period, the Abenakis, Algonquins and Innu were actually allies, united over the course of the seventeenth century by a common antagonism toward the Mohawks. This was a clash between peoples bound by a historic alliance relationship, a connection that was obviously not devoid of tensions. Nor was this encounter simply a robbery. There were words of justification. "Pillaging" was spoken of as an act of justice on the part of people who were convinced their property rights had been violated. The Innu seem to have understood and accepted the legitimacy of the procedure, even as they denied the Abenaki claim to that specific location. A colonial judicial officer later asked them "if it is not a rule among them never to hunt without permission on the lands of another"; the Innu affirmed that, "it is a rule for us that each hunter hunts on his own lands."

The Abenakis subscribed to the same principle. Casting the smaller band in the role of trespassers and as such subject to confiscation, they proceeded to hunt and trap without restraint on the contested terrain. For the Innu, this was the most grievous injury inflicted by the intruders. The Abenakis killed all the moose they could find, including those "which we had raised and conserved." Even more shockingly, they slaughtered "all the beavers, large and small, going so far as to destroy their lodges." As a result, there would be no game when the Innu returned the following year. These revelations of wanton destruction seem at first glance to lend credence to the views of those ethnohistorians, impatient with sentimental myths about "ecological Indians," who argue that natives could be wasteful hunters.[54] Was this a case, as others might have it, of natives undergoing a spiritual crisis after suffering the effects of epidemics and rapid cultural change and "making war on the beaver" as a pathological response?[55] The Abenakis do appear to have engaged in the sort of overhunting that would impair the ability of moose and beaver to reproduce in this particular area, but there was deliberation in their actions. This was hardly a routine trapping expedition: it was an assertion of ownership over a disputed zone. Rather than proving that the Abenakis

[53] Madeleine Rousseau and Jacques Rousseau, "La crainte des Iroquois chez les Mistassins," *Revue d'histoire de l'Amérique française* 2 (June 1948): 13–26.

[54] Shepard Krech, *The Ecological Indian: Myth and History* (New York: W. W. Norton, 1999).

[55] See Calvin Martin, *Keepers of the Game: Indian–Animal Relationships and the Fur Trade* (Berkeley: University of California Press, 1978).

had no thought for the future survival of game animals, it suggests that their intention was to ruin the hunt for their rivals.

Perhaps more striking than the scorched-earth tactics of the Abenakis are the normal hunting practices implied by the Innu when they complained about the destructive actions of the intruders. Beaver lodges, they suggest, should not be dismantled and care should be taken to distinguish adult from juvenile animals, sparing the young. As for moose, the hunters speak of them almost as though they were livestock to be managed and culled selectively. Of course, everything we know of modern Innu attitudes toward animals as subjects with their own personalities and intentions clashes with the stock-raiser's mentality, more inclined to treat animals as objects; yet this brief phrase – "raised and conserved," imperfectly translated though it may have been – speaks to norms that were conservationist in their practical thrust.[56] We are reminded of the Innu property term *tipenitam*, with its connotations of both an obligation to manage and a right to exclude outsiders. The Abenakis, speaking a related language and sharing a similar view of territory, deliberately violated norms of stewardship, within a strictly delimited zone, for punitive purposes.

Zeroing in on the fundamental issue, the intendant of New France asked Thék8érimat straight out: did the Abenakis usually hunt in this area? "Replied that they go there whenever they want and that no one has ever opposed them. Being presently numerous, they have been obliged to go and seek their livelihood where they could and the land in question belonged to his grandfather who in turn gave it to his father. In killing all the animals that were in this place, the said Innu have, in effect, killed the Abenakis themselves."[57] There is equivocation here: Thék8érimat seems to be asserting both time-honored rights and the necessity to secure new

---

[56] Similar approaches to moose hunting have been recorded in other times and places: "They did not kill more Moose than was necessary to supply themselves with provisions," a Nova Scotia official wrote of the Mi'kmaq in 1801, "as they considered them as their own property." Quoted in William Craig Wicken, *Mi'kmaq Treaties on Trial: History, Land and Donald Marshall Junior* (Toronto: University of Toronto Press, 2002), 32. For a description of modern native approaches to moose hunting, see Hugh Brody, *Maps and Dreams* (Vancouver: Douglas & McIntyre, 1981), 103–9, 182–88.

[57] ANOM, C11A, vol. 25, fol. 33–36, record of interrogation, signed Raudot, 27 October 1706. "... a répondû qu'ils y vont quand ils veulent qu'on ne leur a jamais empeché, et qu'estant présentement un grand nombre ils sont obligez d'aller chercher leur vie ou ils peuvent et que la ditte terre appartenoit a son grand pere qui l'a donné a son pere et que les dits montagnais ont comme tué les Abennaquis en tuant touttes les bestes qui estoient en cest endroit-là."

resources for a burgeoning population. The intendant seems to have been at a loss as to how to adjudicate the conflicting claims; at any rate, it was doubtful from the start that he could exercise effective jurisdiction over the Innu and Abenakis. He therefore stuck to New France traditions and confined himself to ordering new regulations for the King's posts monopoly.[58]

What is most striking in all the evidence presented in the course of this trial is the complete absence of any reference to boundaries. Territorial claims were front and center; encroachment had led to very serious consequences on the ground and the subsequent judicial investigation was focused on determining whose property rights were legitimate. Yet neither the Innu nor the Abenaki witnesses supported their positions with assertions about landmarks or topographical features. They each asserted simply that the conflict occurred on "their" land, with no indication as to whether the encounter took place within the Lac St.-Jean watershed or that of the St.-Maurice. In the absence of mountains or abrupt changes in elevation in this part of the world, the transition point between watersheds is not obvious, particularly when ice and snow cover the land. It is quite plausible that both the Innu and the Abenakis honestly thought they were in the right, working on their own territory. As it happens, the latter formed the stronger party and so they took action to secure what they regarded as their rights.

Relations between these two Algonquian-language peoples were actually complex, ambiguous and shifting. Mostly they were allies, joined in alliance with the French, with one another and with the Algonquins; their diplomatic agreements spoke of shared hunting territories, adopting the metaphor of a single spoon drawing nourishment from a common pot. The Innu were not necessarily averse to sharing the land with friendly newcomers; their own numbers were depleted in the second half of the seventeenth century and they felt the need for support, particularly when Iroquois enemies threatened. In practice, there was much jostling for hunting grounds, especially after the Great Peace of 1701 had ensured basic military security. There appears to have been a happy sequel to the confrontation and pillaging of 1705. Though the incident had baffled French judicial authorities, the Innu and Abenaki seem to have worked things out among themselves. The ethnic boundaries dividing the two nations were as indistinct as those marking their hunting grounds, and far

---

[58] Jean Tanguay, "Les règles d'alliance et l'occupation huronne du territoire," *Recherches amérindiennes au Québec* 30 (2002): 31.

more permeable. In spite of occasional conflicts, they were actually connected by personal links of kinship, marriage and friendship.[59] Kin and kin-based alliances were what defined territorial possession in this culture and so the solution to disputes over hunting grounds lay not in negotiating borders but in redefining personal identities and relationships.

ESTABLISHING PERIMETERS

The anthropologist Tim Ingold has written insightfully about land tenure and spatial practices among hunting-gathering peoples.[60] These are best understood, he argues, in zero-dimensional terms (places or sites) and one-dimensional terms (paths or tracks). "Tenure in hunting and gathering societies," he writes, "is not of surface area, but *of sites and paths within a landscape*. In agricultural societies, on the other hand, two-dimensional tenure does come into operation." Land defined by surface area and outer boundaries Ingold sees as a "consequence of agricultural production."[61] Applying a similar perspective to summarize the contrast between indigenous and European approaches to cartography, another scholar speaks of a transition "from mapping the territory according to its interior spaces to mapping according to intersections of outer boundaries."[62] With these observations in mind, it is tempting to see the spatial dimension of property formation in early modern North America as essentially a matter of imposing a pattern of land delineated by outer perimeters where territory had previously been defined by inner sites and lines. A lot of nuances and qualifications have to be inserted to bring this formulation into line with actual historical realities, but Ingold's dichotomy of ideal types does provide a fruitful tool for analysis.

We need to begin by recognizing that purely "agricultural" and purely "hunting-gathering" societies are rather rare. The Innu of northern Quebec seem to come closest to the latter type, but even in their case, spatial practices of tenure varied somewhat with the seasonal cycle of subsistence activities. Winter hunting grounds were defined by the lines of waterways that formed their spines, but summer eel-fishing and fowling sites may have been allocated on the basis of outer edges. As far as the

---

[59] Alice Nash, "Odanak durant les années 1920, un prisme reflétant l'histoire des Abénaquis," *Recherches amérindiennes au Québec* 32 (2002): 17–33; Savoie and Tanguay, "Le noeud de l'ancienne amitié," 29–43; Dawson, *Feu, fourrures, fléaux et foi*, 178–84.

[60] Ingold, "Territoriality and Tenure," 130–64.   [61] Ibid., 153, 148.

[62] Margaret Wickens Pearce, "Native Mapping in Southern New England Indian Deeds," in Lewis, ed., *Cartographic Encounters*, 169.

Ninnimissinuok of southern New England are concerned, their fishing, hunting and farming pursuits implied quite varied spatial forms. Cultivated areas had rather well-defined boundaries, as did shellfish beds. Hunting grounds, on the other hand, were not clearly bounded. Something similar might be said of the Nahua people of central Mexico, seemingly quintessential cultivators. Though they marked off and measured their fields with great precision, the Aztecs and their neighbors also made use of extensive spaces without definite boundaries to hunt, forage and gather fuel, reeds and building materials. In this basic respect, the settler communities of North America were not all that different. Fields for tillage were indeed defined in two dimensions – with fences, walls or hedges typically forming concrete barriers at their outer edges – but outer commons for foraging and grazing were usually either unbounded or at least vaguely delineated and porous. Thus, it seems that most indigenous and settler tenures combined a variety of different spatial practices that corresponded to different productive activities and that defined land in zero, one or two dimensions. (Including mining grants might lengthen that list to include three-dimensional spaces.)

Of course, in contexts of competition and conflict, space had political and military significance, as well as economic meaning, for Europeans and for natives. While the concept of precisely defined sovereign territory with consistently defended borders was beginning to take hold in Europe in this period, it seems to have been largely absent in pre-Columbian North America. It is difficult to be definitive on this point, since the evidence is negative, but there is no indication that indigenous polities were defined spatially by precise outer boundaries. Even in densely populated Mesoamerica, where cities and fields were carefully and geometrically laid out, it seems that the neighboring *altepeme* were separated not by sharply defined borders but by broad, mostly uninhabited buffer zones; hills or swamps typically marked the transition from one *altepetl* to another.[63] Wars and other contests in that period centered on relations of tribute and subjugation, rather than on any realignment of boundaries. Something similar might be said of the chiefdoms of southern New England. Contestation between, for example, Narragansett and Wampanoag sachems revolved around the question of who would be

---

[63] William B. Taylor, *Landlord and Peasant in Colonial Oaxaca* (Stanford, Calif.: Stanford University Press, 1972), 84; John F. Richards, *The Unending Frontier: An Environmental History of the Early Modern World* (Berkeley: University of California Press, 2003), 343.

tributary to whom, rather than over the exact location of a dividing line between their respective territories. We should not overdraw the contrast between colonizers and indigenous peoples in this connection, for European imperial claims were not usually precisely territorial either.

Colonization was another matter, however. Because it was so expansive and invasive, natives were compelled to set limits and defend these to the best of their ability. As the reforming New Spain official Alonso de Zorita put it: "The Spaniards have taken their lands, pushed back their boundaries, and put them to an endless labor of guarding their fields against the Spaniards' cattle."[64] With livestock, settlers and government pressing at the edges of their lands, indigenous communities that had been somewhat casual about outer edges in the past were increasingly compelled to establish defensive perimeters and defend them as best they could: their survival was at stake.[65] In a context of expanding Spanish *haciendas* and indigenous depopulation, not to mention the general disruption associated with colonization and productive of competition for space among neighboring native communities as well as between Indians and Spaniards, it was vital to protect pueblo lands by all possible means. We have already seen (Chapter 4) how "primordial titles" (*titulos primitivos*) proliferated in the seventeenth century as natives did their best to adapt their strategies to the Spanish obsession with written documents. The primordial titles, together with the associated rituals by which pueblos sought to protect their lands, paid special attention to spatial boundaries. Written in the voice of ancestral elders, the *titulo* of Cuijingo addressed later generations, explaining that its purpose was to enable them "to be able to know how to speak and answer to defend your lands."[66] Some *titulos*, especially those from recently founded *congregación* villages, recounted a solemn procession, lasting days in some cases, during which the inhabitants walked the entire perimeter of their new territory, setting up boundary markers. "We made with our hands two mounds," reads the title of San Bartolomé Capulhuac, "... with stones [we placed here] a stone serpent ... a stone face that we carved ..." There were ritual encounters with delegations from adjacent pueblos, festive banquets and solemn masses. These were stories of place

---

[64] Alonso de Zorita, *Life and Labor in Ancient Mexico: The Brief and Summary Relation of the Lords of New Spain*, ed. and trans. Benjamin Keen (New Brunswick, N.J.: Rutgers University Press, 1963), 109.

[65] Jonathan D. Amith, *The Mobius Strip: A Spatial History of Colonial Society in Guerrero, Mexico* (Stanford, Calif.: Stanford University Press, 2005), 76.

[66] Quoted in Gruzinski, *The Conquest of Mexico*, 100.

and identity, but they focused on the tracing of perimeters.[67] They suggest that territory, as defined by outer limits and as inscribed in official documents, was becoming a matter of the highest importance for indigenous communities in this threatening colonial setting.

In a somewhat similar fashion, the Ninnimissinuok of New England found themselves having to attend more closely to outer boundaries as they struggled to keep English livestock out of their gardens and clam beds and to stem the advancing tide of settlement. Whereas settlers initially occupied small, delimited enclaves, their spatial practices soon became so expansive that it was, ironically, the natives who eventually tried to insist on territories marked by clear and stable boundaries. Thus we read of Mohegans trying (unsuccessfully, as it turned out) to secure recognition of a rock by the side of the Thames River in Connecticut as an outer limit to the settler advance (see Chapter 6).

In addition to the practical impulse to establish and defend perimeters on the ground, natives were also driven to define their lands more in terms of surface areas with specified boundaries simply because the use of such terms facilitated communication with colonial officials. When power relations precluded direct physical resistance, it often made sense to appeal to the colonizer's sense of justice and legality and that meant adapting as much as possible to his conceptions of property and space. The central processes of colonization involved the consolidation of zones of colonial property and jurisdiction, and here space was construed as bounded areas, very much in line with the "agricultural" ideal type. Magistrates, governors and missionaries generally understood land rights in terms of a geometry of outer edges, and if natives wished to appeal to these leaders' sense of justice, they had to make their case accordingly. *Titulos primitivos* formed part of that strategy in the Mexican case. In New England, the Puritans' penchant for Indian deeds and commercial rectitude set the tone, establishing a property idiom that Ninnimissinuok sometimes adopted in order to secure whatever small advantages they could in the face of advancing dispossession. That meant that sachems had to present themselves as much as possible in the guise of landed proprietors. Since there were many sachems and would-be sachems in the region, it was important to insist on a definite territory with clearly delineated borders.

---

[67] Ibid., 119–21. See also Ethelia Ruiz Medrano, *Mexico's Indigenous Communities: Their Lands and Histories, 1500–2010*, trans. Russ Davidson (Boulder: University Press of Colorado, 2010), 109–14.

In areas such as northern Canada, where indigenous people remain numerically predominant to this day, anthropologists find that natives have had to develop a special idiom for "speaking to the white man" about land, especially where courts and officialdom are involved. It is a matter not only of linguistic translation, but also of converting a whole constellation of hunter-gatherer spatial practices into the alien terms of agricultural societies organized into territorial states. Natives are disadvantaged since much is lost in translation, but they have no alternative: to protect their territories and their way of life, they need to express themselves in the language of sovereignty, property and bounded spaces.[68] Something fundamentally similar occurred in colonial times in the three areas of North America examined in this book.

In the Anglo-American sphere of colonization, indigenous people were particularly constrained to conform to the colonizers' spatial expectations. The monolithic English approach to landed property forced natives to represent their respective countries as precisely bounded estates; that was the case in New England in the seventeenth century and also in areas further to the west in the eighteenth. Thus, the historical record contains innumerable statements like this one, from a Wyandot spokesman during treaty negotiations at Fort McIntosh in 1785: "Brothers, You wish to know our line. We will inform you of it. It begins at the Little Miami, and runs from thence across to the Great Miami. Farther than this our line does not extend. The lands beyond it belong to the different nations."[69] Following the Royal Proclamation of 1763 (see Chapter 10), Anglo-American colonists tended to speak about indigenous lands in terms of a "Proclamation Line" or a "Property Line," and natives of the Northwest had apparently adopted the vocabulary of "lines" for negotiating purposes.[70] Such adaptations did not always work to the natives'

---

[68] Colin Scott, "Property, Practice and Aboriginal rights among Quebec Cree Hunters," in *Hunters and Gatherers*, vol. 2: *Property, Power and Ideology*, ed. Tim Ingold, David Riches and James Woodburn (Oxford: Berg, 1988), 35–51; Paul Nadasdy, "'Property' and Aboriginal Land Claims in the Canadian Subarctic: Some Theoretical Considerations," *American Anthropologist* 104 (March 2002): 247–61; Paul Nadasdy, "Boundaries among Kin: Sovereignty, the Modern Treaty Process, and the Rise of Ethno-Territorial Nationalism among Yukon First Nations," *Comparative Studies in Society and History* 54 (2012): 499–532.

[69] Anthony F. C. Wallace, "Political Organization and Land Tenure among the Northeastern Indians, 1600–1830," *Southwestern Journal of Anthropology* 13 (1957): 314.

[70] Allan Greer, "Dispossession in a Commercial Idiom: From Indian Deeds to Land Cession Treaties," in *Contested Spaces of Early America*, ed. Juliana Barr and Edward Countryman (Philadelphia: University of Pennsylvania Press, 2014), 89–91.

advantage, however, for there were always land speculators prepared to coopt the language of bounded, two-dimensional property rights, the better to get possession of their lands. When it suited their purposes, these speculators would insist that indigenous property, like English property, was clearly bounded and alienable.

Increasingly, in the era of the American Revolution, indigenous nations would have to contend with lines of sovereignty as well as lines of property. The comparatively open-ended imperial geography of the early modern period gave way in many areas to more precisely bounded territorial states. The general transition from "borderlands" to "bordered lands"[71] was of course deeply threatening to the independence and to the territorial practices of indigenous nations; they felt the pressure to define perimeters of their own to salvage what they could of what was theirs. Some even challenged the trend at a more fundamental level. On the question of bounded spaces, the last word belongs to Tecumseh, the Shawnee war chief who knew how to talk to colonizers, but who also was bold enough to reject their territorial assumptions:

These lands are ours: no one has a right to remove us because we were the first owners; the Great Spirit above has appointed this place for us, on which to light our fires, and here we will remain. As to boundaries, the Great Spirit above knows no boundaries, nor will his red people acknowledge any.[72]

[71] Jeremy Adelman and Stephen Aron, "From Borderlands to Borders: Empires, Nation-States, and the Peoples in between in North American History," *American Historical Review* 104 (1999): 814–41. See also Nancy Shoemaker, *A Strange Likeness: Becoming Red and White in Eighteenth-Century North America* (New York: Oxford University Press, 2004), 23–28; Juliana Barr, "Geographies of Power: Mapping Indian Borders in the 'Borderlands' of the Early Southwest," *William and Mary Quarterly* 68 (2011): 5–46.

[72] Tecumseh, message to President Thomas Jefferson, 1807, as quoted in George Snyderman, "Concepts of Land Ownership among the Iroquois and Their Neighbors," in *Symposium on Local Diversity in Iroquois Culture, No. 2*, ed. William A. Fenton (Washington, D.C.: Government Printing Office, 1951), 30.

9

A Survey of Surveying

THE UPSTART ART

At the time of the initial colonization of North America, surveying was both an ancient practice and a novel technique in Europe. On the one hand, almost every agricultural civilization has had some sort of system for laying out fields in two dimensions and for marking boundaries; on the other hand, new procedures emerged in the early modern period for measuring and representing land, with the effect that topography, property and maps could stand in for one another. Thus an English publication of the early seventeenth century could refer to surveying as "an upstart art found out of late, both measuring and plotting."[1] The discrepancy arises partly from historical shifts in the meaning of the word "survey" and its Spanish and French equivalents. More fundamentally, talk of surveying, in the present as well as in the early modern past, encompasses a variety of quite distinct operations as though they were all one thing. A twentieth-century manual defines land surveying as consisting, among other things, of the following:

1. Rerunning old land lines to determine their length and direction ...
3. Subdividing lands into parcels of predetermined shape and size.
4. Setting monuments to preserve the location of land lines ...

---

[1] John Norden, *The Surveiors Dialogue* (1607), as quoted in Sarah S. Hughes, *Surveyors and Statesmen: Land Measuring in Colonial Virginia* (Richmond: Virginia Surveyors Foundation and Virginia Association of Surveyors, 1979), 28. See also Bernhard Klein, *Maps and the Writing of Space in Early Modern England and Ireland* (New York: St. Martin's Press, 2001), 42–60.

6. Calculating areas, distances, and angles or directions.
7. Portraying the data of the survey on a land map.
8. Writing descriptions for deeds.[2]

Verifying and measuring existing property spaces is one thing that surveyors do, setting out new property spaces on the land is another. Inscription is also a central aspect of surveying: tracing property onto the face of the earth by setting up markers ("monumentation"), but also inscribing property cartographically and textually. The production of property maps ("plats") and written reports has become every bit as crucial to land surveying as the placing of pins and monuments. Such documentation connects the profession to the edifice of the law and makes property surveying in that sense a legal practice. These distinct geometric, environmental, textual, cartographic and legal components came together to form the modern definition of land surveying through a historical process that was gradual and uneven.

To foreshadow some of this chapter's themes, we might note at the outset that, even though European expertise and knowledge were imported into North America at an early stage of colonization, surveying was, in important respects, quite different here than in the Old World. The divergence is partly due to the presence – at least in Mesoamerica – of well-developed indigenous spatial practices. It also reflects the fact that surveying generally served different purposes in a colonial setting where the objective was to remake the property landscape rather than to record and preserve existing arrangements. Whereas geometric surveying was deployed quite selectively in Europe, mainly to verify and map existing properties, in America it was mostly a matter of creating new properties ("subdividing lands into parcels"). Some sort of surveying in this latter sense was almost universal on the property-making frontier of North America, whereas the majority of lands in Europe were never measured until after the end of the early modern period. On the other hand, surveying in Europe at this time involved refined measurement, property mapping and textual description, features that were far from universal in America at the same time. As background to an examination of surveying in New Spain, New France and New England, we need to start with a brief look at Old World land measurement, both as traditional practice and as "upstart art."

---

[2] Raymond E. Davis and Francis S. Foote, *Surveying: Theory and Practice*, 3rd ed. (New York: McGraw-Hill, 1940), 6.

Monumentation is the most ancient of the operations now associated with surveying. "Cursed *be* he that removeth his neighbour's landmark. And all the people shall say, Amen," says one of the oldest books of the Judeo-Christian Bible. There is ample evidence of boundary marking in ancient China, Greece and the Roman Empire, not to mention Meso-america. In the *Metamorphoses*, Ovid assigns surveyors a central role in his account of the decline in human happiness from the Golden to the Silver to the Bronze Age. "The land that was once common to all, as the light of the sun is, and the air, was marked out, to its furthest boundaries, by wary surveyors."[3] The Romans recognized *agrimensores* as experts in the art of measuring precise right angles; they used an instrument with plumb lines called the *groma*, but basically relied on line of sight over flat, open ground. "The original function of the *agrimensores* was to define the layout and the limits of newly founded towns and military camps, as well as to distribute land to campaign veterans."[4] From an early date, it seems, surveying in this generic sense of the term was associated with conquest and the appropriation of land for colonists.

After the fall of Rome, there was little call in Europe for any precise measuring of land surfaces. Terrain was occupied by peasant commun-ities, each of which worked out intricate local customs to regulate land use and access; seigneurs and territorial overlords claimed revenues from estates defined as much in human as in topographical terms. Hedges, fences and stones indicated the limits of fields and, in open-field areas, individual strips were inscribed into the earth by the patterns of plowing. The complex local geography of commons and individual holdings in a given locality would be fully known only to the people who had lived there all their life. In such a setting, landlords depended on the services of expert "surveyors" to ensure that their interest in the land was preserved and their revenues protected. Until the seventeenth century, the English terms "survey" and "surveyor" had little or nothing to do with geometric measurement. "The work of surveying involved the 'engrossment,' or writing up in detail, of all the legitimate, customary uses of a piece of land, a process of verbal interview and 'auditing' which did not

---

[3] Deuteronomy 27:17; Ovid, *The Metamorphoses*, trans. Anthony S. Kline, Book 1, lines 125–50, "The Bronze Age," in "The Ovid Collection," online resource, http://ovid.lib .virginia.edu/index.html.

[4] Uta Lindgren, "Land Surveys, Instruments, and Practitioners in the Renaissance," in *The History of Cartography*, vol. 3: *Cartography in the European Renaissance*, ed. David Woodward and J. B. Harley. (Chicago: University of Chicago Press, 2007), 478.

particularly prioritize measurement."[5] A 1523 English surveying manual does not even mention measurement: "It is necessary that euery great estate bothe men & women of worship that haue great possessyons of landes and tenementes shulde haue a Surueyour that can extende but and bounde and value them. And therof to make a boke in parchement bearyng a certayne date . . . that the lorde his freholders copyeholders nor tenauntes shall neuer lose landes nor rentes customes nor seruyces."[6] ("Extend, butt and bound" means to describe a tenant's plot of land by specifying the tenancies that adjoin it.) This definition of the duties of a surveyor corresponds to a strictly textual procedure for recording property claims. The "terrier," the medieval estate roll listing tenants and their obligations, was his chosen instrument. In addition to bounding lands, surveyors in this pre-modern setting might also estimate their rental value. They were men of legal and agricultural expertise and landlords turned to them for advice on improving productivity through drainage and manuring.[7]

For certain types of land, English surveyors of the early modern period were required to provide a figure for acreage, but according to one study based on published manuals of the time, "it was very usual to estimate rather than to measure these acreages, perhaps by merely counting the strips."[8] But then, what would be the point of exact measurement at a time when the acre had no precise, agreed-upon size? In a general sense, an acre was the amount of land that could be plowed by a team of oxen in a single day, a definition that left plenty of room for variation in the length of the day, the strength of the oxen, the heaviness of the soil, and so on. In the Middle Ages, an acre was often assigned a particular shape, its length ten times its width, in keeping with plowing customs. Some attempts were made in the period to standardize the acre, setting it at forty by four perches (or "poles"), but a perch could vary in length from twelve to twenty-eight feet.[9] Perceptions of the size and value of any tract of land were firmly situated in a particular natural environment and in the human community that lived and worked on it. Surveyors made their estimates accordingly.

[5] Jess Edwards, *Writing, Geometry, and Space in Seventeenth-Century England and America: Circles in the Sand* (New York: Routledge, 2006), 25. See also Klein, *Maps and the Writing of Space in Early Modern England and Ireland*, 43–44.

[6] John Fitzherbert, *The Boke of Surveyeng and Improvmentes* (London: R. Pynson, 1523), as quoted in A. Sarah Bendall, *Maps, Land and Society: A History, with a Carto-Bibliography of Cambridgeshire Estate Maps, c. 1600–1836* (Cambridge: Cambridge University Press, 1992), 77–78.

[7] E. G. R. Taylor, "The Surveyor," *The Economic History Review* 17 (1947): 122–24.

[8] Ibid., 123.   [9] Ibid., 127–28.

The story of the acre actually fits into a broader pattern of European measures that, until the advent of the metric system in the 1790s, remained inconsistent and variable. In this respect, as in many others, there was always far more regional diversity in early modern France than in England. Even by the mid-eighteenth century, when many local differences had been eliminated, the author of the *Encyclopédie* article on land measurement complained of the confusion of units. "*Arpent, journal, acre, setier, saumée*, &c. are the terms used in speaking of surveying: but these names are all different and the measures and quantities they express are no less so. Moreover, the same term does not always signify the same thing: for example, the *arpent* can be more or less large, depending on the different customs [regional laws], which changes the practice of surveying and makes it more difficult."[10] Another French writer of that period drew attention to metric diversity even within a particular region: "In Normandy, plowlands and meadows are measured by the acre, forests and woods by the *arpent* and vineyards by the *quartier*."[11] To an Enlightenment encyclopedist, steeped in modern conceptions of abstract space and committed to the project of integrating landed property into a uniform geometric grid, the metric diversity of *ancien régime* France was a scandal. Then as now, modernizers could only see what the older measures were not – that is, they were not universal and mathematically consistent – but had little interest in what they were. It might therefore be useful to attempt to grasp the logic of the measuring practices that prevailed in Europe at the time of the colonization of North America.

Consider just two of the units mentioned in the *Encyclopédie*, the *arpent* and the *setier*: the first was perhaps the most widely used in the kingdom. (It was also adopted in New France.) The *arpent* was originally defined, like the acre, as the land that could be tilled in a day, and, again like the acre, it varied in size; standardized to some extent in the eighteenth century, the *arpent* was set at 100 square perches, smaller than the English acre

---

[10] Faiguet de Villeneuve, "Terres, Mesure des," *L'Encyclopédie*, vol. 16: 176. ARTFL Encyclopédie Project, encyclopedie.uchicago.edu. (my translation) "... *arpent, journal, acre, setier, saumée*, &c. sont des termes usités en parlant d'arpentage: mais si ces noms sont differens, les mesures ou les quantités qu'ils expriment ne le sont guere moins; il y a plus, c'est que le même terme ne signifie pas toujours la même chose; par exemple, l'arpent est plus ou moins grand, suivant les differentes coutumes, ce qui fait varier la pratique de l'arpentage, & la rend même plus difficile."

[11] Quoted in Claude Boudreau, *La cartographie au Québec, 1760–1840* (Quebec City: Presses de l'Université Laval, 1994), 54. (my translation) "[En] Normandie, les terres et les près se mesurent par acre, les bois et bocages par arpent et les vergers par quartier."

(140 square perches). (A different "acre" altogether was employed in French Normandy.) Other common units of area were the *setier* and the *boisseau*; these terms also doubled as units of volume for measuring grain (comparable to the English bushel). In theory, a *setier* of land was the area that would be sown with one *setier* of seed. Of course, seed grain was distributed more or less densely, depending on the quality of the soil. Thus, the geometric size of a *setier* or a *boisseau* varied from place to place, which, of course, is the point: pre-metric land measurement tended to be localized and calibrated according to human labor and agricultural productivity. Acres and *arpents* measured work, while *setiers* and *boisseaux* measured seed input, and therefore, indirectly, crop output. These two quite different principles of land measurement actually interconnected in practice. Early English surveyors sometimes estimated acreage on the basis of seeding quantities and French notaries sometimes made adjustments for soil quality when calculating property shares in inheritance arrangements. "An eighteenth-century French manual on the compilation of estate inventories clarifies the matter well, if schematically," reports Witold Kula: "for soils of middling quality, the proper measure is one-fifth as large again as for good soils, whereas for poor soils, it is larger by a sixth; the reason for the difference, says the author, is that the seed is sown relatively thickly on good soils and sparsely on poor soils."[12]

The metric landscape of early modern Spain was no less varied than that of France.[13] The most common units of distance were the league ("*legua*") and the yard ("*vara*"), but both varied across regions; the *vara de Burgos*, proposed as the standard for the entire kingdom, never became truly universal. Surface measurements included the *obrada*, a measure rooted in plowing and analogous to the acre and the *arpent*; it too implied different areas depending on the region. The *fanega*, originally a specific volume of grain, was also applied to designate the area of land on which that much seed would be sown. Many other, strictly local, units were used to measure land in the component regions of Spain, all of them illustrating Witold Kula's general conclusion about early modern European land measurement:

To sum up: all pre-metric systems of agrarian measures, despite their many differences, were systems of representational measures that "signified." Of the

---

[12] Witold Kula, *Measures and Men*, trans. R. Szreter (Princeton, N.J.: Princeton University Press, 1986), 29–42 (quotation at 31); Taylor, "The Surveyor," 127.

[13] Antonio López Ontiveros, "El Catastro de ensenada y las medidas de tierra en Andalucía," *Revista de Estudios Regionales*, no. 53 (1999): 191–206.

various characteristics of any piece of land, that of its square dimensions was the least taken into account, and qualitative aspects were of major importance ... The real task was therefore to agree on measurable criteria for nonmeasurable values.[14]

Into this early modern context of local measures geared to plows, furrows, seeding and harvesting stepped a new breed of surveyor promising to map and measure on a uniform scale, treating lands as surface areas. Innovative techniques based on recent advances in applied mathematics, cartography and military engineering were available to landowners as early as the second half of the sixteenth century, though they were used quite sparingly until the eighteenth (Figure 9.1). New-style surveyors used a variety of ingenious devices for measuring elevations and horizontal angles, as well as for marking off distances. Rulers, compass dividers and protractors enabled them to plot their measurements on paper, while geometric analysis and basic arithmetic allowed them to calculate areas; many surveyors also used trigonometry, aided by handy trigonometric tables published in the back of popular surveying manuals of the seventeenth and eighteenth centuries. Increasingly the surveyor was becoming an expert in plane geometry rather than in agriculture.

Geodaesia, a widely used English handbook published in 1688 by John Love, offered instruction in the use of various field instruments, including the Gunter's chain, its 100 brass links stretching out 66 feet.[15] While the surveyor ensured that they followed a straight line, his two assistants (chainmen) would alternately anchor the trailing end and walk forward with the advancing end until it was taut. A magnetic compass with a mounting and notched sights could be used to get an orientation and measure angles; Love referred to compass readings finely calibrated in degrees and minutes, though most colonial surveyors of the time relied on much cruder devices. There were also theodolites, "semi-circles" and other instruments, some with built-in compasses, all designed to indicate angular arcs; they all used notched sighting mechanisms, for telescopic "verniers" were introduced only in the second half of the eighteenth century. Love also describes a method for measuring angles with chain measurements alone, though this worked only in open fields. Another device for measuring and mapping clear terrain was the "plane table." Setting up a table with a sheet of paper in the middle of a field, a surveyor

---

[14] Kula, *Measures and Men,* 42.
[15] John Love, *Geodaesia: Or, the Art of Surveying and Measuring of Land, Made Easie* (London: John Taylor, 1688).

FIGURE 9.1 A sixteenth-century surveyor, with compass and chain. These two devices formed the essential equipment for surveyors in New France and other early modern colonies. Unlike the theodolite, the compass measures angles only in a horizontal plane.
Source: Charles Étienne and Jean Liébault, *L'Agriculture et maison rustique* (Paris: Chez Jacques du Puys, 1583), 291. Courtesy Bibliothèque nationale de France.

could sight corners and angles and inscribe them directly onto his paper; chaining from table to angles provided a scale for the emerging rough map. John Love, who had experience surveying in Britain's American colonies, warned that some approved methods, including the use of the plane table, were useless in a wooded colonial setting. In such conditions, he recommended that the surveyor circumnavigate the property, chaining distances and recording angles as he went. With all the relevant data recorded in a field book, the practitioner could then perform his calculations and prepare his report and plat back at his own desk. Love's manual is exceptional in its recognition of the divergent objectives and methods of colonial and European surveying. It provides a sense of professional standards as of the late seventeenth century, standards that colonial surveyors rarely attained in practice.

In Britain and on the European continent land measurement practices seem to have been much more careful and more exact than in America; they were also much less widespread in our period. The new approach to surveying caught on very gradually, not only because it was expensive, and not only because the absence of universally accepted units of measure posed practical obstacles. The problem was that, as Witold Kula points out, precise measures of surface areas were not necessarily particularly meaningful in the real world of agrarian Europe. In special circumstances, it might make sense to reduce a variegated rural landscape into a homogeneous space that could be subdivided and reassembled at will, as when enclosure was on the agenda – which is to say, when established patterns of local possession and use-rights were to be blown up. Some landlords found that geometric surveying could also be useful for less drastic readjustments. For example, a new-style surveyor might discover that a particular farm or field was of greater acreage than the lease or rent-roll indicated and so the rent could be increased. (If the survey produced the contrary result, no one needed to be the wiser!) This was of particular interest to English landlords at a time when leaseholds were becoming more common in that country (continental landlords generally lacked this incentive to measure). Unsurprisingly, English farmers and peasants were almost always hostile to surveying. John Norden published a promotional tract in favor of the new methods in 1607; he used the dialogue form to enumerate common objections to surveying, the better to refute them. One of Norden's antagonists in *The Surveiors Dialogue* was "the farmer," who voiced his concerns in these terms: "I have heard much evill of the profession, and to tell you my conceit plainly I think the same both evill and unprofitable . . . and oftentime you are the cause that men lose their land and sometimes they are abridged of such liberties as they have long used in mannors."[16]

---

[16] John Norden, *The Surveiors Dialogue* (1607), as quoted in R. H. Tawney, *The Agrarian Problem in the Sixteenth Century* (London: Longmans 1912), 349. See also Kula, *Measures and Men*, 16.

This popular opposition was hardly irrational, for geometric surveying, like enclosure, implied a radical redefinition of landed property. It attempted to draw sharp lines across the land in a setting where gradients had previously prevailed, where individual and collective claims followed agrarian activities, where zones of exclusion overlapped with areas of shared use and where many claims (for example, to gleaning and stubble pasturing) were seasonal rather than timeless and absolute. The transformation implied by the new surveying would never be completed during the early modern period when entrenched custom and the active resistance of resident rural folk slowed the progress of property mapping to a very uneven crawl. Surveying became common and widespread in Europe only as of the nineteenth century. But in the meantime, it would be taken up on a much broader scale in the North American colonies, as part of another program to reconstitute property and space, though even there it was never universal and never uniform. The peculiarities, hesitations and anomalies of colonial land measurement form the subject of the rest of this chapter.

INDIGENOUS LAND MEASUREMENT

The starting point has to be indigenous spatial practices, which were very much mathematically inflected in Mesoamerica. Whereas the outer edges of indigenous polities (*alpeteme*) in central Mexico were somewhat indistinct, individual fields were definitely marked off and measured, for tribute payments were a function of the size of these agricultural holdings. Mesoamerican peoples, like agriculturalists in other parts of the world, delineated their fields on the ground, set up boundary markers and threatened human and divine punishment to anyone who disturbed the latter.[17] They also measured plots precisely and recorded their size, shape, location and ownership in systematic fashion. There is no specific indication in the surviving records of how exactly lands were measured and mapped; we do not know what instruments, if any, were employed for these purposes. In fact, there is hardly any direct evidence at all from the pre-Hispanic period. However, scholars have at their disposal a wealth of Nahuatl language land records from the decades following the conquest that reflect long-established practices with every appearance of antiquity. The language itself was stocked with a rich and varied vocabulary for

[17] S. L. Cline, *Colonial Culhuacan, 1580–1600: A Social History of an Aztec Town* (Albuquerque: University of New Mexico Press, 1986), 126.

classifying lands according to soil quality and legal status; of special interest are all the words and glyphic symbols related to measurement and calculation.

As in Europe, units of length and area were standard within a given locality, but they varied from place to place: "it is clear that each sub-region or altepetl had its own version of a refined system of standard units capable of handling both large and small dimensions."[18] In post-conquest Coyoacan, notaries used the possessive form of the Nahuatl term for measurement when they wrote up land transactions: *totlatamachihual*, which means essentially "our measurement." Frequently, documents simply give numbers with units implied, and presumably well understood by all interested parties. When units of measure were specified in land records, *quahuitl* was the most common; it meant "stick" or "rod," and, as in early modern England or France, the reference was to a physical measuring pole that, depending on the locality, might be somewhere between ten and twelve "feet" long. For fractions of a *quahuitl*, there was a smaller unit, called a *tlacxitl* in some *altepeme*.[19] Such units were useful for relatively small areas, such as a house lot, but for lands of large dimensions, a cord was used. A single term, *mecatl*, meant a rope, a linear measure (equal to twenty "units") and a surface area twenty units square; James Lockhart speculates that this may have been the size of a traditional standard family allotment.[20] Aside from the rod and the cord, Mesoamerican measures were mostly derived from human body dimensions. There was the *matl*, which seems to have been the length of a man's outstretched arms; Spaniards had a measure, the *braza* (fathom), with a similar derivation, but the *matl* was generally longer and so the Spanish in Mexico would distinguish between their unit and a *"braza de indios."* There were also Nahuatl terms corresponding to the distance from the elbow to the wrist, from the outstretched thumb to little finger, the length of the foot, and so on. Many of these units had European counterparts. What differentiates Mesoamerican from European land measurements is

---

[18] James Lockhart, *The Nahuas after the Conquest: A Social and Cultural History of the Indians of Central Mexico, Sixteenth through Eighteenth Centuries* (Stanford, Calif.: Stanford University Press, 1992), 144. See also Serge Gruzinski, "Sistemas de medición españoles e indios en el México del siglo XVI," in *Metros, Leguas y Mecates. Historia de los Sistemas de Medición en México*, ed. Hector Vera and Garcia Acosta (Mexico City: Publicaciones de la Casa Chata, 2011), 67–78.

[19] Rebecca Horn, *Postconquest Coyoacan: Nahua-Spanish Relations in Central Mexico, 1519–1650* (Stanford, Calif.: Stanford University Press, 1997), 129.

[20] Lockhart, *The Nahuas after the Conquest*, 145.

the apparent absence of units defined by seed quantities and cultivation. The nature of indigenous agriculture readily explains that divergence: the land was hand tilled in places rather than being plowed in sections; and seeds were carefully planted in hills rather than being broadcast over an area. Nevertheless, the two systems of measuring land had much in common, both at the level of detail (*quahuitl* and *braza* as rough equivalents) and at the general level: measures on a human scale that were rooted in local communities.

In addition to setting boundaries and measuring lengths, widths and areas, Mesoamerican land practices also involved systems of inscription. Scholars have identified two exceptionally complete cadastral registers relating to land-holdings in the pueblo of Tepetlaoztoc, near the city of Texcoco in the Valley of Mexico. Though these seem to date from the early 1540s (that is, a generation after the Spanish conquest), everything about them (except for the paper on which they are written) is indigenous: the mapping conventions, the glyphic symbols and the numerical information all clearly continue well-established pre-Hispanic customs of recording. The geographer Barbara Williams has been studying these documents for decades, in collaboration with different colleagues in anthropology and mathematics.[21] The more closely these scholars examine the Tepetlaoztoc land records, the more indications they find of precise, meticulous measurement and recording. Knowing that most Nahuatl writings of all sorts were lost or destroyed during the conquest period, it seems reasonable to suppose that these isolated cadastres are representative of a large corpus of such material, now lost forever. Certainly, they show us what native Mesoamericans were capable of.

The most interesting and most fully analyzed of the Tepetlaoztoc documents, known as the "Codex Vergara," is held at the Bibliothèque nationale in Paris.[22] It consists of fifty-five paper folios and covers all the

[21] Barbara J. Williams, "Mexican Pictoral Cadastral Registers: An Analysis of the Códice de Santa María Asunción and the Codex Vergara," in *Explorations in Ethnohistory: Indians of Central Mexico in the Sixteenth Century*, ed. H. R. Harvey and Hanns J. Prem (Albuquerque: University of New Mexico Press, 1984), 103–25; Barbara J. Williams and H. R. Harvey, "Content, Provenience, and Significance of the Codex Vergara and the Codice de Santa Maria Asuncion," *American Antiquity* 53, no. 2 (1988): 337–51. Dr. Williams credits her late husband, the anthropologist H. R. Harvey, with initiating this extended inquiry into Nahua geometry (personal communication to the author).

[22] Bibliothèque nationale de France, manuscrits mexicains, 37–39, document cadastral ou codex Vergara. Digital images available through the BNF's Gallica website: ark:/12148/btv1b84528032. A published facsimile is also available: Barbara J. Williams and Frederic Hicks, eds., *El Códice Vergara: edición facsimilar con comentario: pintura indígena de*

households of five small localities within the *alteptl*, each of them enumerated three times in three separate lists. First comes a census, with glyphs representing the heads of family members, each classified by sex, age group and civic status, and each linked by lines to the household head. Following that, the same households are listed again, each one displayed horizontally, usually five to a page, but this time the entries concern their respective land-holdings. Diagrams of the plots come complete with symbols indicating the dimensions of the various pieces of land held by each family. Finally, a third section shows these same land holdings once again, but now each has a small tag at the upper right corner where a numerical glyph is inscribed, different from the linear length and width measures in the second section. Williams and her collaborators eventually determined that these numbers refer to the surface area of each plot. The juxtaposition of numerical data on outer dimensions and area gave these researchers a golden opportunity to check up on Nahua mathematical ability.

The two entries from the Vergara Codex shown in Figure 9.2 both concern the same lands belonging to the pictured householder. His house lot appears first on the left, as indicated by the special sign placed above it. The top row gives a better sense of the shape of the plots (though not their locations), while the lower row, meant to record surface area, shows them as stylized rectangles. Every tract has a symbol in the center that designates the quality of the soil. Most of the linear measurements along the lengths and breadths of the lots above represent numbers, with the local unit (a Texcocan version of the *quahuitl* or "rod") understood. These are given in standard Nahuatl glyphs, with a line standing for one – these were bundled into groups of five – and a black dot standing for twenty. (Central Mexican arithmetic used a base-twenty system.) Since the dimensions did not all come out to an exact number of standard units, the plans all contain smaller measures, added to enhance precision. There is a "heart" at the upper left corner of the first two plots and in the bottom left of the third, as well as a "hand" on the right side of the last plot. A "heart," nominally the distance from the middle of a man's chest to the fingertips of his outstretched hand, stood in Tepetlaoztoc for two-fifths of a standard unit, or rod, while a "hand,"

casas, campos y organización social de Tepetlaoztoc a mediados del siglo XVI (Mexico City: Universidad Nacional Autónoma de México; Apoyo al Desarrollo de Archivos y Bibliotecas de México, A.C., 2011).

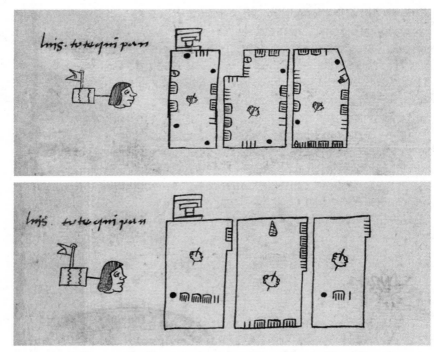

FIGURE 9.2 Two entries from a cadastral register of the pueblo of Tepetlaoztoc, ca. 1540. Both relate to the lands held by the individual represented here. The upper image records the outer dimensions of his three irregular-shaped plots, while the lower image shows their respective surface areas.
Source: Bibliothèque nationale de France, manuscrits mexicains, 37–39, document cadastral ou codex Vergara. Courtesy Bibliothèque nationale de France.

meaning the distance from fingertip to fingertip with arms outstretched, amounted to three-fifths of a rod.[23]

In the bottom row of this image, as in all the other entries in that section of the Tepetlaoztoc cadaster, the plots are shown as regular rectangles. Though their purpose is to indicate surface area, these rectangles are not drawn to scale; instead, they display numbers. The numerical indicators here are, to all appearances, the same as those used above for linear dimensions – mostly symbols for one or twenty units – and, as with the French *arpent,* the unit of surface area was a square with sides of one basic unit of linear distance. What is not at all obvious is how exactly

[23] Barbara J. Williams and Maria del Carmen Jorge y Jorge, "Aztec Arithmetic Revisited: Land-Area Algorithms and Acolhua Congruence Arithmetic," *Science* 320, no. 5872 (2008): 74.

these area glyphs are to be read. There are numbers in the small tabs and numbers at the bottom or in the middle of each plot; none seems to be a correct area measurement for the outer dimensions recorded in the upper images. In attempting to decode the notation system at work here, Williams and her collaborators came to the conclusion that the position of the glyphs was part of their meaning. "Numbers positioned in the tab represent units from one to 19. The lower margin and the middle positions of the rectangle record multiples of 20 ... One dot, when placed in the middle position of the rectangle, carries the value of 1 (20 × 20) = 400, and five dots 5 (20 × 20) = 2,000."[24] This was a very important finding. Mathematical notation that combines numerals and positionality – for example, when we write "248," we know that the "2" represents 200 and the "4" means 40 simply because of where these symbols appear – is a major intellectual achievement. It is not something the Romans practiced, nor did Europeans in the Middle Ages. The Mayans are famous for their invention of the concept of zero in ancient times; it seems that the Nahua surveyors of central Mexico had a similar device for aiding calculation.[25]

Barbara Williams's first publication on "Aztec arithmetic" in 1980 had concluded its critical analysis of Tepetlaoztoc cadastral sources with the observation that "Overall this implies not only accurate measuring and careful record-keeping, but also sophisticated methods to compute areas."[26] More recently, she joined forces with a team of Mexican mathematical researchers led by María del Carmen Jorge y Jorge to subject the Vergara Codex data to more refined and exacting mathematical tests. Analyzing data on 386 fields, of which 122 were right-angled rectangles (like the first field depicted in Figure 9.2) and 264 were of irregular shape (like the other two in the figure), they found the area calculations on the regular rectangles to be 100 percent correct. Checking the irregular shapes was more challenging; since both the exact shape of the fields and the calculation of surface area were at issue, the mathematicians had to devise tests to measure the degree of plausibility of each of the results. They found evidence of a few mistakes in recording dimensions, as well as some imperfections in calculation, but their overall assessment was that

[24] Williams and Harvey, "Content, Provenience, and Significance of the Codex Vergara," 338.
[25] H. R. Harvey and B. J. Williams, "Aztec Arithmetic: Positional Notation and Area Calculation," *Science* 210 (1980): 499–505.
[26] Ibid., 502.

the indigenous surveyors had done their job remarkably well: the area measures were "reasonably to very accurate." The margin of error, they point out, is comparable to that found in tests of an English map drawn in 1613 with the aid of geometric surveying instruments, and much better than that found in the rather sloppy property mapping of early colonial North America. Indeed, in the context of the time, it is not clear that anyone anywhere measured and calculated land surface area with more precision than the Nahua surveyors of Tepetlaoztoc.[27]

Careful practices of land measurement endured among the indigenous peoples of central Mexico long after the Spanish conquest. Land rods and cords were kept in every pueblo to verify measures. When remnant populations were gathered into new communities through the procedures of *congregación*, natives used these instruments to lay out lots on the land.

NEW SPAIN

As far as land measurement is concerned, it was all downhill for the better part of two centuries after the Spanish took over Mexico. Indigenous communities generally continued to rely on their accustomed techniques for laying out, measuring and recording individual plots, even as they adopted some Spanish legal vocabulary and even as they struggled to mark off and defend outer perimeters of their pueblo territories. Early Spanish *pobladores* laid out their towns with cords and stakes in a somewhat similar manner, but without the careful surface area calculations and systematic recording that characterized Nahua practice. With native populations declining rapidly and settlers streaming into New Spain, the colonial regime increasingly had recourse to land grants (*mercedes*). Authorities immediately faced a number of issues, not only in relation to the basic question, covered earlier in this book, of how to accommodate Spaniards while preserving Indian property, but also about how exactly to allocate grants in zones deemed open to settlement. How large would the tracts be and what would be their shape, what metrics would apply, how would they be measured and bounded, what records would be kept, and how would boundary conflicts be settled? In a

---

[27] Maria del Carmen Jorge, Barbara J. Williams, C. E. Garza-Hume and Arturo Olvera, "Mathematical Accuracy of Aztec Land Surveys Assessed from Records in the Codex Vergara," *Proceedings of the National Academy of Sciences of the United States of America* 108 (2011): 1–5.

sixteenth-century context, before Europe's "spatial revolution" had fully emerged, none of these mundane technical questions had an obvious answer. Temporary expedients and makeshift solutions ensued, and the results added a substantial layer of confusion to the general chaos of the colonial transformation of central Mexico.[28]

Initially, land-granting procedures worked out on the West Indian island of Hispaniola were transferred to the newly conquered Mesoamerican mainland. As noted in Chapter 4, comparatively large grants designated for the mounted conquistador elite – *caballerías* – soon came to predominate. The Caribbean *caballería* was originally designed to provide both land and labor and it was usually defined in terms of the hillocks (*montones*) that the Taino people used to plant their staple crop of manioc. A *caballería* comprised 100,000 *montones*, sufficient for the subsistence and exploitation of a community of 250 people.[29] This unit, like the acre and the *arpent,* had its origin in productive agricultural operations and no doubt it too varied in geometric extent, depending on terrain and soil fertility. Like their European counterparts, struggling at the time to impose consistent land measurements, Spanish American authorities tried to translate the *caballería* from a variable operational measure into a unit of standardized dimensions. (And again as in the Old World, their task was complicated by the uncertainty and variability of linear measures.) In its migration from Hispaniola to Mesoamerica, the *caballería* lost its association with indigenous agriculture and became the unit for distributing what was supposed to be vacant land to Spanish settlers. A *caballería* was intended to provide more than enough land for the subsistence needs of a household, but its exact size was not entirely clear. Official documents sometimes referred to agricultural

---

[28] On the topic of land measurement in New Spain, see the following works: Manuel Carrera Stampa, "The Evolution of Weights and Measures in New Spain," *Hispanic American Historical Review* 29 (1949): 19–23; Hanns J. Prem, "Con Mesa, Agujón y T; Trángulo filar. Die Kolonialzeitliche Grenze zwischen Huejotzingo und Tlaxcala," *Ibero-Amerikanisches Archiv* 7 (1981): 151–68; Herbert J. Nickel, *Landvermessung und Hacienda-Karten in Mexico* (Freiburg: Arnold-Bergstraesser-Institut, 2002); Nadine Béligand, "L'agrimenseur, le juge et le roi: mesure et appropriation de l'espace en Nouvelle Espagne," in *Connaissances et pouvoirs: les espaces impériaux (XVIe-XVIIIe siècles: France, Espagne, Portugal,* ed. Charlotte de Castelnau-L'Estoile and François Regourd (Bordeaux: Presses universitaires de Bordeaux, 2005), 101–25; Miguel Aguilar-Robledo, "Contested Terrain: The Rise and Decline of Surveying in New Spain, 1500–1800," *Journal of Latin American Geography* 8 (2009): 23–47.

[29] Francisco de Solano, "Introduction," in *Cedulario de tierras: Compilación de legislación agraria colonial, 1497–1820,* ed. Francisco de Solano (Mexico: Universidad Nacional Autónoma de México, 1991), 31.

capacity – enough land to grow a certain amount of wheat or to support a given number of pigs or cattle – and sometimes to measured dimensions. The notion was that a *caballería* would be rectangular in form, its length double its width. As of the mid-sixteenth century, the most common definition of a *caballería* set its size at 1104 by 552 *varas*; but then, the *vara* was not a fully standardized linear unit at that time and field surveying was never an exact science in colonial Mexico. Thus, in spite of the air of precision conveyed by much of New Spain's land-granting legislation, the *caballería* and other units of area were always quite approximate.[30]

One of the interesting features of the term "*caballería*" is that it designated both a type of land grant and a unit of surface area. Other kinds of grants emerged alongside the *caballería* – the *suerte*, for example, was a smaller area designed for orchards, while very large *sitios de ganado* designated areas for livestock raising – and these words too had that double meaning; each referred to both a kind of grant, with a specific set of legal conditions governing land use, and a particular area measurement. A second New Spain peculiarity worth noting is that all of these measurements originated in America. English and French settlers measured their lands according to Old World units, but not so the Spaniards, who, though they imported some European units of weight and length, made up their own colonial land measures. And one final observation in this context: *caballerías*, *suertes* and *sitios de ganado* were exclusively for the Spanish sector of New Spain. Indians did not normally receive grants of this sort and their lands were not measured in these units. Some Spanish linear units, such as the *braza*, did make their way into native usage, but the units and procedures for measuring land remained basically indigenous. Two quite distinct systems, each with its own way of inscribing property on the land and of determining the size, shape and topographic meaning of plots, emerged in Mexico; this divergence mirrored (and indeed contributed substantially to the construction of) the fundamental division of New Spain into *indio* space and *español* space.

With the rise of ranching, the *sitio de ganado* made its appearance alongside the *caballería* and other agricultural land grants. As described

---

[30] On the *caballería*, see Carrera Stampa, "The Evolution of Weights and Measures in New Spain," 19–21; "Ordenanzas de tierras," 26 May 1567, in Solano, ed., *Cedulario de tierras*, 205–8. On the variability of linear measurements such as the *vara*, see Aguilar-Robledo, "Contested Terrain," 25–28, 36–37. A *real cedula* of 1 December 1581 attempted to impose the Castillian *vara* in Spanish America, this in response to "los pacificadores y pobladores de las Indias," who "... ponían pesos y medidas a su arbitrio." Solano, ed., *Cedulario de tierras*, 260.

in Chapter 7, such grants were originally little more than a license to make use of a portion of the common rangelands and to build corrals and simple structures to shelter animals and herdsmen. A *sitio de ganado mayor* or *ganado menor* was hardly a bounded piece of property: in the early colonial period, it was literally a "site," a place for huts and corrals that opened out onto a wide, unfenced range. It bore some resemblance to the hunting grounds of northern hunter-gatherers in that it was a space defined by a center rather than by a perimeter. And yet sixteenth-century legislation does actually specify precise measures: *sitios de ganado mayor* were usually set at 5000 by 5000 *varas* (sometimes expressed as one league by one league); *sitios de ganado menor* at 3333 *varas*. However, these distances seem to have had more to do with the spatial distribution of ranching sites than the delineation of outer boundaries.

Typically, a source of water lay at the center of each *estancia*, where the corrals and buildings were located,[31] and it was from this point that a cord could be run out half a league (2500 *varas*) in any direction to suggest an outer limit. The distances were considerable and the *juez* in charge of the *vista de ojo* would not have had the expertise, the instruments or the time and inclination to establish precise boundaries. It would be enough to ensure that the center of a *sitio* was sufficiently removed from the next ranch and from any indigenous pueblos. According to some sixteenth-century official documents, as well as a certain number of *estancia* sketch maps produced as evidence in lawsuits (see Figure 9.3), the granted lands were literally circular in shape.[32] This might seem an absurd way to lay out property, since a field of circles that touched at their edges would leave unallocated areas outside their boundaries, but in an open-range grazing landscape, these shapes were, in fact, purely notional.[33] In the absence of fences, nothing would have stopped sheep or cattle wandering into the interstitial spaces.

This might be the moment to return to Tim Ingold's categories of zero-, one- and two-dimensional spaces, mentioned in the previous chapter.

---

[31] Chantal Cramaussel, *Poblar la frontera: la provincia de Santa Bárbara en Nueva Vizcaya durante los siglos XVI y XVII* (Zamora: El Colegio de Michoacán, 2006), 326. Recall that "*estancia*" designates the stock-raising operation, whereas "*sitio*" means the land grant upon which it sits.

[32] Juan Cercillo, "Explicaciones sobre las medidas que deben tener las estancias de ganado mayor y menor" (1575), in Solano, ed., *Cedulario de tierras*, 228–30. Additional images of circular *sitios de ganado* can be found in Aguilar-Robledo, "Contested Terrain," 28; Nickel, *Landvermessung und Hacienda-Karten*, 11–13.

[33] Gisela Von Wobeser, *La formación de la hacienda en la época colonial: el uso de la tierra y el agua* (Mexico City: Universidad Nacional Autónoma de México, 1989), 29.

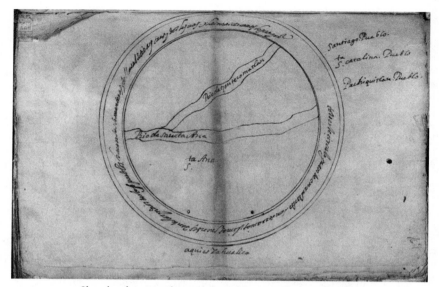

FIGURE 9.3 Sketch of a *sitio de ganado* (exclusive pasture) depicted as a circle.
Source: Archivo General de la Nación (Mexico), Fondo Hermanos Mayo, concentrados
sobre 563, Mapa 2029. Courtesy Archivo General de la Nación (Mexico).

If the cultivated fields of indigenous pueblos and the arable *caballerías*
granted to Spanish settlers were configured in two dimensions and defined
by their outer edges, the early ranching lands of New Spain were more in
the nature of a zero-dimensional central point, together with its
surroundings. Pastoralists, neither hunters nor farmers, form territories
in a variety of different ways, most of them reflecting a mobile way of life;
seasonal migrations (transhumance) or more erratic movements in search
of fodder are typical. In colonial Mexico, livestock did tend to wander,
changing ecologies and playing havoc with native subsistence as they
went, but the logic of the government's land-granting policy suggests an
attempt to limit the size of herds and to anchor them to specific locations,
all in order to control their potential to disrupt settled agriculture. As
we have seen, this strategy was not entirely effective, especially where
native lands were concerned. However, it does seem to have encouraged
estancia owners to accumulate more and more *sitios*, extending and
consolidating their holdings in order to ensure adequate grazing, while
simultaneously intensifying their control over territory. The interests of
the ranchers drove them to claim more land – which meant more cattle or
sheep – and more exclusive possession: to transform, as far as possible,
grazing licenses into landed estates. In Figure 9.4, we see a zone of circular

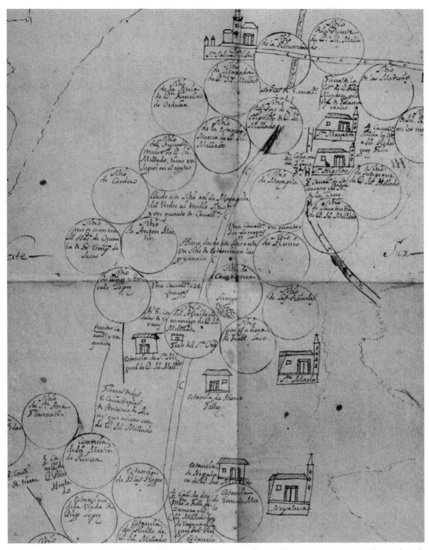

FIGURE 9.4 Notionally circular *sitios de ganado* (exclusive pasture). These land grants, depicted ca. 1610, formed the basis for the extensive San José Ozumba hacienda, owned by the Jesuit college of Puebla.

Source: Herbert J. Nickel, *Die Hacienda San José Ozumba (Puebla). Bilddokumente Zu Hacienas Im Zentralmexikanischen Hochland* (CD-ROM) (Freiburg, Germany: Arnold-Bergstraesser-Institut, 2012). Courtesy Herbert J. Nickel.

sitios, interspersed with *caballería* grants around Ozumba in the region of Puebla, as these properties were configured around 1610. The Jesuits of the College of Espiritu Santo acquired most of these grants and, by 1757, when the government conducted an investigation of titles, had consolidated their holding, occupying the spaces between circles in the process, to create a hacienda covering 6828 hectares.[34]

Over time, as New Spain haciendas evolved from enterprises with grazing rights on the commons to something more like landed estates with exclusive control over territory, they also changed their shape. Straight lines replaced circles as multiple *sitios* were absorbed into giant holdings, the latter defined increasingly by outer boundaries. Through the institution of the *"composicion,"* the imperial state played a crucial role in enabling *hacendados* to transform notionally circular grants into rough squares and rectangles of enlarged surface area (see Chapter 10). It was by this means that Jesuit title to the Ozumba *hacienda* was legitimated.

One might imagine that a general shift from round to squarish lots would play havoc with maps and property records, but these developments took place in a colonial setting where the quality of surveying and property mapping remained at a low ebb. Outside the indigenous pueblos and the zones of settler agriculture that surrounded the major cities, modern surveying instruments were seldom seen until the nineteenth century.[35] When, for legal purposes, land-holdings had to be depicted on paper, the images were crude and schematic, as in Figure 9.3. New Spain's spatial practices of property were shot through with "irregularities" and illegal occupation: so said the imperial government when it stepped in to tidy things up (for a price) through the judicial procedure of the *composicion*, and historians tend to echo this verdict, leaving the impression that the colonial regime was geographically and mathematically incompetent, not to mention generally "backward." However, the confusion was partly strategic and deliberate. Mexico actually boasted the oldest university in North America and as early as 1537 instruction was being offered in Euclidean geometry and cartography.[36] The latest concepts of space and the new technologies of measurement were

---

[34] Herbert J. Nickel, *Die Hacienda San José Ozumba (Puebla)*, CD-ROM in the series Bilddokumente Zu Hacienas Im Zentralmexikanischen Hochland (Freiburg i.Br., Germany: Arnold-Bergstraesser-Institut, 2012), introduction, p. 7.

[35] Raymond B. Craib situates the emergence of national cartography in the second half of the nineteenth century: *Cartographic Mexico: A History of State Fixations and Fugitive Landscapes* (Durham, N.C.: Duke University Press, 2004).

[36] Aguilar-Robledo, "Contested Terrain," 33.

available, but these were rarely put to use in the field where property was being created. Especially where livestock-raising was concerned, the vast distances and proportionally elevated expense of geometric surveying go a long way to explaining this striking absence. There was more to it than that, however. Beyond their natural aversion to spending money, *hacienda* owners generally had a horror of surveying because of the way it could expose past appropriations of land and place limits on future expansion of their domains. Spatial indeterminacy had a way of working to the advantage of powerful proprietors, such as the Jesuits of Espiritu Santo, as they assembled vast land holdings.

One fascinating document, an unpublished manual of practical geometry and surveying written about the year 1700 by Joseph Sáenz de Escobar, sheds a good deal of light on the spatial practices of property in New Spain.[37] Sáenz was actually a lawyer and magistrate, seemingly without training in mathematics or surveying, but driven to take up his pen by a sense that the landowners and legal personnel that he dealt with on a daily basis had a woefully defective knowledge of basic geometry.[38] Approaching his mathematical self-education as a humanistic project, Saenz studied sixteenth-century treatises in Latin and Italian, but unfortunately he does not seem to have mastered the subject fully. The German scholar Herbert J. Nickel checked his calculations for determining the area of irregular shapes and found several flagrant errors.[39] Furthermore, when he attempts to find the area of circles (a peculiar requirement for colonial Mexican surveyors), Sáenz resorts to the unpromising method of "squaring the circle." It may be just as well, then, that his book was never

---

[37] Joseph Sáenz de Escobar, "*Geometría Práctica y Mecánica*" (Mexico City, ca. 1700). Though never published, this work was frequently copied and quoted. Five manuscipt copies are known to exist, held in libraries in Mexico, Spain and the United States. I made use of the copy housed at the Archivo del Universidad Interamericana in Mexico City, transcribed in a hand other than the author's in 1749. For further information on Séanz de Escobar and his book, see Herbert J. Nickel, "Joseph Sáenz de Escobar y su tratado sobre Geometría Prática y Mecánica: un manual sobre geometría aplicada para personas no cualificadas en la materia, escrito en Nueva España (México) alrededor del año 1700," *Historia y Grafía* 15 (2000): 241–67; Nickel, *Landvermessung und Hacienda-Karten in Mexico*, 45–89.

[38] Among other indications of the depth of the ignorance he felt he faced is a lengthy and labored passage in Sáenz's book demonstrating that a square with sides of half a *vara* was not actually half the area of a one-*vara* square, but rather one-quarter. Sáenz de Escobar, "Geometría Práctica y Mecánica," fol. 67v–68.

[39] Nickel, "Joseph Sáenz de Escobar," 252–56. Nickel points out that careless copyists might be responsible for these errors.

printed for distribution to field practitioners, but its technical shortcomings do not detract from its value as historical evidence.

Sáenz de Escobar examines surveying from the viewpoint of a magistrate dealing with litigation over land boundaries. Mexican courts, he notes, face two or three cases per week arising out of problems in land measurement. He seems to take for granted that the magistrate's job is to make his way to the site in question and carry out the measurements and calculations needed to settle matters. In New England or New France, attention in such situations would focus on boundary lines and markers, but this being pastoral New Spain, the first task is to identify the *center* of the land. Sites granted a century ago (i.e., the late sixteenth to early seventeenth century), Sáenz observes, were generally well marked with a proper stone and mortar monument ("*mojonera*"), but standards have declined in recent decades, such that center points are indicated only by wooden crosses or mere notches on a tree.[40] And what apparatus should the well-equipped investigator take with him to the field? Sáenz's list of instruments is short: a ruler, a compass, a set-square and a standard-length cord. For measuring long distances, the author recommends relying on a mule of steady pace together with an accurate clock to time the journey from center to periphery.[41] Here the reforming geometer seems to be lowering his standards for a moment as he adapts to customary practices of measuring territory in the ranching zones of Mexico. A *sitio de ganado mayor* was supposed to measure 5000 *varas*, or one league, from edge to edge; Sáenz reveals in passing that, out in the country, the vernacular meaning of the term "*una legua*" is understood to be "the distance that a mule walks, going at a good pace, in an hour." That, at least, is one conception of a league; cowboys have a different measuring protocol, he adds: "the vaqueros maintain that a league is how far a horse can run at a gallop in one hour"![42]

From plodding mules to galloping horses: it begins to seem that the "confusion" that reigned in Mexican land measurement may have had its origins in something less innocent than ignorance of the rules of Euclid. New Spain is a vast country, Sáenz observes, and there are *haciendas* here composed of multiple *caballeriás* and *sitios de ganado*, estates more extensive than entire provinces of Spain. He reports that almost all

---

[40] Sáenz de Escobar, "Geometría Práctica y Mecánica," fol. 7v.   [41] Ibid., fol. 6–6v.

[42] Ibid., fol. 16v. (my translation) "... la distancia que andan en una mula de buen paso en una hora, y los Baqueros tienen por legua lo que corren en una hora en un caballo a el galope ..."

properties are bigger than they should be. When there was doubt as to the shape of a grant or as to the units of measurement or the methods of calculating area – and there was always ambiguity on these points – *hacienda* owners habitually resolved matters in their own favor. And when a *hacendado* was told that he was occupying more land than he was entitled to (Sáenz seems to be writing on the basis of personal experience), he would always adopt a stance of baffled innocence.[43] The author makes these observations in passing, all the while maintaining an air of naive earnestness as he promotes the cause of mathematical enlightenment; however, his remarks suggest that the indeterminacy of property boundaries and measurement in colonial Mexico was not due to purely technical deficiencies. Powerful landowners looking for opportunities to expand their estates had little interest in the mathematization of the spaces of property.

NEW FRANCE

To all superficial appearances, New France seems the opposite of New Spain where land measurement is concerned. From the beginning of colonization here, surveying was an integral part of property formation. Unlike the other colonies, and in striking contrast with *ancien régime* France itself, almost all settler properties were laid out with measurements on the ground; markers indicated boundaries and there was a standardized written record. The latter, known as a "*procès-verbal d'arpentage*," served as an important element in establishing title to a seigneurie or a *roture*. The survey was supposed to be conducted and the documentation drawn up and signed by an official "*arpenteur juré*," a state-licensed professional with a legal standing similar to that of a notary. Through most of its history, New France had a recognized geometry expert with overall authority over the profession. A succession of individuals beginning with Jean Bourdon, "engineer and surveyor-general of the colony" (ca. 1635–68), examined the competence of prospective surveyors.[44] Succeeding Bourdon in this role was Martin Boutet, a layman who taught mathematics and hydrography at the Jesuit College in Quebec. Between

---

[43] Ibid., fol. 17–19.

[44] J.-Edmond Roy, "La Cartographie et l'arpentage sous le régime français," *Bulletin des recherches historiques* 1 (1895): 17–20, 33–40, 49–56; Don W. Thomson, *Men and Meridians: The History of Surveying and Mapping in Canada*, vol. 1: *Prior to 1867* (Ottawa: Queen's Printer, 1966), 48–81.

the Jesuits and the naval/military establishment of the colony, there was usually at least one individual in Canada at any given time to provide instruction and credentialing in navigation and surveying. The close association of these two disciplines in a colony where settlement hugged the shoreline was no coincidence. Notable also is the government's active role in promoting and regulating surveying. In addition to ensuring mathematical competence, it demanded of all applicants for surveyor licenses a "certificate of good morals," basically a religious test proving that the subject was a good Catholic.

Aiming at metric as well as religious conformity, the state settled as early as the 1630s on the *"arpent de Paris"* as the standard unit of distance (58.4 meters), with the league (*lieu*) (3.89 kilometers) serving to measure large distances (such as the dimensions of a seigneurie), and the *perche* ("rod" or "pole," one-tenth of an *arpent*) for shorter lengths.[45] The *arpent*, originally an area measure, served also as a linear measurement defined as the length of each side of a square measuring one superficial *arpent*. The calculation of area from outer dimensions was therefore quite easy in New France. More important, there was never any variation or confusion about standards of measurement here, as there was in most of the countries of Europe and their American colonies. Colonial legislation also decreed a uniform orientation for property lines, a matter of central importance in New France surveying as will soon become clear. Finally, the colonial régime insisted that seigneurs must see to the surveying of all lands as these were granted to settlers.[46] Repeated exhortations to this effect testify to the government's commitment to uniform land measurement, but of course they also suggest that practices on the ground fell short of legislated standards. Indeed, as we look more closely at surveying in New France, the initial impression of professionalism, spatial consistency and strict regulation begins to appear somewhat misleading. Here as in other early modern colonies, slapdash procedures were the rule; surveying that was supposed to be entirely professional actually coexisted with vernacular

---

[45] Marcel Trudel, *Les débuts du régime seigneurial au Canada* (Montreal: Fides, 1974), 156; Louise Dechêne, *Habitants and Merchants in Seventeenth-Century Montreal* (Montreal: McGill-Queen's University Press, 1992), 289; Boudreau, *La cartographie au Québec, 1760–1840*, 54.

[46] Arrêt du conseil souverain, 13 April 1669, in *Jugements et délibérations du conseil souverain de la Nouvelle-France*, 6 vols. (Quebec City: Imprimerie A. Coté, 1885–91), vol. 1: 554–55.

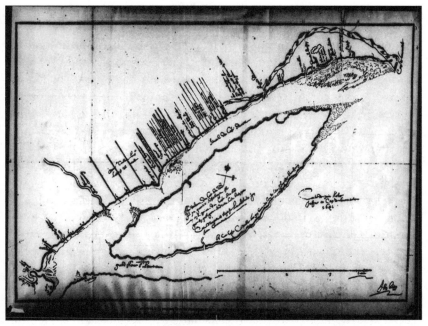

FIGURE 9.5 Jean Bourdon, "Carte depuis Kébec jusqu'au Cap de Tourmente," 1641.

Source: Bibliothèque nationale de France, ark:/12148/cb40681088n. Courtesy Bibliothèque nationale de France.

practices; and the utopian notion that lots should be laid out before settlers arrived to occupy and modify the land turned out to be unrealizable.

To get a basic sense of the geography of property here, we need to picture parallel lines, New France's signature configuration. An early map by Jean Bourdon of the settlements northeast of Quebec shows boundary lines looking like the teeth of a ragged comb (see Figure 9.5). No fully bounded spaces are represented on this cartographic image; instead, narrow allotments extend inland from the banks of the St. Lawrence with the long dimensions unspecified and the rear boundaries completely open. Bourdon was a protégé of Samuel de Champlain, and like those of the great explorer-colonizer, his maps have a nautical flavor. With a starting point anchored on the shore, his property lines pierce the land in such a way as to specify direction, but not distance. (Later property maps usually indicated rear boundaries, even though these were rarely laid out on the ground; Bourdon's 1641 map was unusually honest in its indeterminacy.) French Canada began as a riverfront settlement (seigneuries were often called "coasts" (*côtes*) in the early years[47]) and its surveying practices, hinging as they did on points and angles, always maintained a certain affinity with the techniques of maritime navigation. A good surveyor, like a good mariner, had to find the right compass bearing and stick to it as he charted a course into the forest. The terminology of surveying in New France always retained a nautical flavor: the sources invariably refer to the alignment of property lines as the "*rhumb de vent*," a phrase that expresses directions in relation to the north, south, east and west winds. No wonder that, at the highest levels of official expertise, hydrography and land measurement tended to converge.

After some initial experimentation with other forms, the elongated parallelogram had emerged, rather spontaneously, as the predominant shape for both fiefs and *rotures* in New France.[48] The St. Lawrence was the principal transportation corridor; its waters provided early settlers with eels and other fish, while its tidal edges were in many places perfect for pastures and meadows; moreover, especially around Quebec, the valley of fertile soils was fairly narrow: for all these reasons, it made perfect sense to maximize the number of settler farms fronting the river. There was nothing particularly "feudal" or "seigneurial" about this configuration of properties. Similar long lots were laid out in non-seigneurial North American settlements, including parts of New England, Texas and Louisiana.[49] Rows of long lots were also a favored pattern in the "frontier" zones of forest clearance in medieval Europe, for it quickly opened up ribbons of sun-drenched ground as neighbors worked in parallel to fell trees from the fronts of their respective lots.[50] There was an additional advantage in the Canadian case: in contrast to the sinuous Mississippi, the St. Lawrence follows a rather straight course,

---

[47] Trudel, *Les débuts du régime seigneurial*, 169–74.

[48] Certainly, there were exceptions to this rule, many of them imposed by topography. Some of the earliest grants of seigneuries specified greater breadth along the river than depth; others had irregular shapes. See R. Cole Harris, *The Seigneurial System in Early Canada: A Geographical Study* (Madison: University of Wisconsin Press, 1966), 23–24; Trudel, *Les débuts du régime seigneurial au Canada*, 11–14.

[49] Donald William Meinig, *The Shaping of America: A Geographical Perspective on 500 Years of History*, vol. 1: *Atlantic America, 1492–1800* (New Haven, Conn.: Yale University Press, 1986), 103, 243; Edward T. Price, *Dividing the Land: Early American Beginnings of Our Private Property Mosaic* (Chicago: University of Chicago Press, 1995), 50–54, 289–300, 307–8, 325–26.

[50] Marc Bloch, "Les plans parcellaires," *Annales d'histoire économique et sociale* 1 (1929): 68–69; Allan Greer, *Peasant, Lord, and Merchant: Rural Society in Three Quebec Parishes, 1740–1840* (Toronto: University of Toronto Press, 1985), 26.

in a northeasterly direction, from the outlet of Lake Ontario to the sea. Thus it provided surveyors with a very rough baseline that seemed to invite them to trace fief and *roture* boundaries at right angles to its course.[51]

Land grants (*concessions*), whether of fiefs accorded by the Company of New France or *rotures* granted by seigneurs to settlers, always specified two dimensions. Seigneuries came in many sizes, but their sides were usually given in leagues: the seigneurie of Sainte-Croix, for example, awarded to the Ursuline nuns in the 1630s, was set at one league by ten. Typical *roture* grants were two, three or four *arpents* in width by twenty or thirty in depth, meaning that they were supposed to stretch back from the river more than a kilometer, and in many cases closer to two kilometers. To survey these lots fully in all dimensions would have been hugely challenging. Over rough terrain and through dense bush, surveyors would have had to hack their way inland, chaining distances and leaving landmarks along the way. Such expensive precision was out of the question at a stage when settlement was just beginning and lands cleared only to a short distance back from the river. Accordingly, surveyors measured linear frontages and then, relying exclusively on their compasses, gestured toward what would eventually emerge as lateral boundaries. Much later, when all the riverfront land in a seigneurie had been granted and as habitants continued to expand their clearings back into the interior, the seigneur would open up a new row of *rotures* along an artificial "coast" (*côte*) behind the riverfront strip. Only at that point, with the surveyor brought in to lay out the new line parallel to the river, would the original lots finally be fully bounded (while the new *côte* remained open-ended).

The initial, and very basic, allocation of property usually took place without the intervention of a professional surveyor. As in other colonies of the period, land measurement was supposed to precede settlement, but actually tended to follow it; and as in those other jurisdictions, something of a mess ensued, to the exasperation of colonial authorities. The sovereign council of New France considered the problem in a 1669 ruling, only one in a series of attempts to legislate better surveying practices:

---

[51] Although topography generally favored parallel lines and long lots, there are numerous irregularities, including the large islands of Montreal and Orléans. Also complicating the picture are the places where settlement extended up tributaries. Highlighting these irregularities, Sylvie Dépatie argues that the property landscape of New France was hardly a model of geometric regularity. Sylvie Dépatie, "Le régime seigneurial, la structure agraire et le paysage de la vallée laurentienne," *Cap-Aux-Diamant* (June 2011), 9–12.

The seigneurs of the Quebec region and elsewhere, having neglected up to the present to see to the surveying of lands by them granted, it has recently become apparent that, because of the alignments made [on these lands], several possessors, working in good faith and with the metes and bounds indicated in their contracts, have cleared portions of their neighbors' lands; the latter claim these areas and wish to enter into possession of the same; all of which causes a large number of lawsuits and could lead to very serious problems ...[52]

In spite of all the appearances of professionalism and rigorous geometry, it seems that the laying-out of lots in seigneurial *censives* was often a do-it-yourself affair. A document from the archives of the Jesuit seigneurie of Batiscan provides a rare glimpse at procedures that were probably quite typical. When they first opened up their seigneurie to settlers in the 1660s, it seems that the Jesuits simply handed a surveyor's chain to the new *censitaires* and told them to measure off two *arpents* each along the riverside and begin creating farmsteads.[53] Starting from a stake driven in at the edge of the water, it seems, the settlers gradually expanded their clearings, establishing de facto side boundaries as they worked their way into the interior. In a setting where forested land was not in short supply, one imagines rough line-of-sight procedures and neighborly negotiation guiding the progressive tracing of fence lines. Clearly, there was a strongly vernacular dimension to New France surveying, particularly in the early years of settlement in a given locality.

Things turned sour in Batiscan in 1668 when a surveyor showed up to establish lateral boundaries. As was becoming the custom in New France, the seigneur arranged and ordered the professional survey, but the *censitaires* were on the hook for the costs. Perhaps the Jesuits were anticipating the sovereign council ordinance referred to above, which would make that arrangement mandatory: "All those [seigneurs] who shall in the future grant concessions are enjoined to ensure that they are measured, surveyed, and that the alignments are traced ten *arpents* in depth, ... at the expense of those who receive them ..."[54] The habitants of Batiscan, furious at their seigneurs' interference in their spatial procedures, and all

---

[52] Arrêt du conseil souverain, 13 April 1669, in *Jugements et délibérations du conseil souverain*, 1: 554–55 (my translation).

[53] Unsigned, undated memorandum from the Batiscan seigneurial collection, Bibliothèque et Archives nationales du Québec (hereafter BANQ), Biens des Jésuites, E21, S64, SS5, SSS10. On this incident, see Colin Coates, *The Metamorphoses of Landscape and Community in Early Quebec* (Montreal: McGill-Queen's University Press, 2000), 33.

[54] Arrêt du conseil souverain, 13 April 1669, in *Jugements et délibérations du conseil souverain*, 1: 554–55 (my translation).

the more so as they were expected to foot the bill, organized meetings and sent off letters of protest. We know about their views only indirectly, since the protest has been lost and our source is a Jesuit memorandum refuting them, but it seems that the seigneurs were accused of every sort of dishonesty and malevolence. One habitant complaint was that the surveyor had done his work discretely, if not in secret ("à la sourdine"). The Jesuits were at great pains to refute this "calumny": the surveyor is an honorable man, they protested, and he traced the alignments publicly, with a large number of local residents witnessing the operation. Here then is further evidence of a vernacular dimension to early Canadian surveying: even when a professional was employed, he normally worked under the watchful gaze of local landowners. Other sources suggest that the local chainmen who always assisted surveyors were more than mere porters and bushwhackers: they seem to have provided a good deal of information about local land practices as well. Settler place-making therefore coexisted, in some degree of tension with, but not entirely in opposition to, official attempts to rationalize space.

It is apparent that the Batiscan clash between vernacular lot-laying and professional surveying was hardly an isolated case. The wording of the 1669 sovereign council ordinance implies that after-the-fact surveys routinely uncovered discrepancies between the land that settlers were occupying and that which their respective title deeds indicated. The problem was almost always one of "alignment," that is to say, the orientation of side boundaries. The council announced a policy (perhaps derived from habitant practices of arbitration) for correcting such problems: if, in good faith, a settler cleared and cropped land beyond what turned out to be his property line, he could continue to make productive use of this excess for six years, as a recompense for his land-clearing labors; at the end of six years, it had to be restored to the "rightful" owner.

While the 1669 ordinance was premised on the belief that alignment issues were caused by an absence of proper procedures, it turned out that such problems came up even when professional surveyors were employed. In requiring that side boundaries be "traced ten *arpents* in depth," the sovereign council did not set the bar very high; indeed, their ruling reflects the current, rather crude, procedures of Canadian surveyors in the field. In laying out a row of *roture* lots, practitioners would check frontage measures, referring to concession deeds and local informants. Along the riverbank, they would mark the point where two lots met (in Batiscan, that would be every two *arpents*), driving a cedar stake into the ground after burying a deposit of crushed brick and clinkers on the spot. (The subterranean marker was in case someone later tampered with the stake. More high-class markers (*bornes*) were reserved for urban surveys and for the boundaries of a seigneurie: a stone pillar with a lead tablet, sometimes inscribed with the seigneur's coat of arms, and some coins or religious medallions buried underneath along with the brick and clinkers.) The next step was the trickiest part of the operation: the surveyor placed his trusty compass at the *borne* and sighted the correct *rhumb de vent*, using the instrument's notched sighting device. Then, following this orientation away from the river, he and his chainmen would measure a straight line ten *arpents* into the interior, slashing their way through the underbrush as they went. Another stake would mark that spot. They did not continue on to the end of the property, but only marked a point along its lateral boundary as a means of indicating its direction (see Figure 9.6). The problem is that even the most careful sightings, especially with seventeenth-century compasses, can never be perfectly exact, and with the exceptionally long lots of New France even a small error in alignment at the water's edge would be magnified as the line advanced inland. This is why proper surveying practice, as prescribed in John Love's *Geodaesia* and every other manual of the period, required that all outer boundaries be measured: chaining across the back was the way to ensure that the long lines of the parallelogram were exactly parallel. Without such a check, the side boundaries were bound to wobble. Small wonder then that alignment disputes continued to crop up, even when boundaries were professionally surveyed with compasses.

Beyond the problem of seigneurs' tardiness in bringing in surveyors, and in addition to the rather approximate methods that the latter employed, there was yet another source of inconsistency: the magnetic variation of compass readings. Most early survey records indicate that lateral lines ran northwest-southeast, but increasingly over the course of the seventeenth century, *procès-verbaux d'arpentage* would indicate that the lines actually ran "nord-ouest quart de nord," suggesting that the surveyor had followed a magnetic northwest bearing, which was really halfway between northwest and north-northwest. At the time, Canadian compass roses were marked with 32 divisions, a far cry from Love's 360-degree compass with intervals of ten minutes, effectively 2160 divisions of the circle. By the early eighteenth century, they were more precisely calibrated with 360 degrees (still no minutes), and so a typical *procès-verbal* from the south shore of the St. Lawrence recorded a bearing of

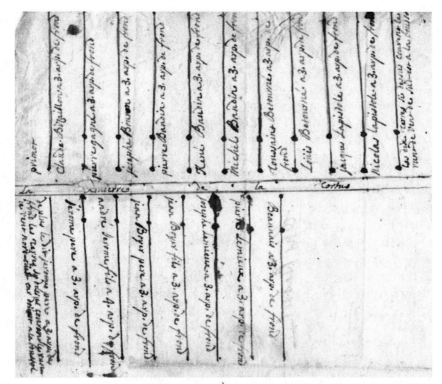

FIGURE 9.6 Surveyor's plat from the seigneurie of La Prairie, October 1719. This rough sketch map – apparently a working document – shows lots laid out along a tributary of the St. Lawrence. It uses dots to indicate the placement of "bornes" (markers) at the riverfront and a fraction of the distance toward the back of each lot. Their purpose is to indicate alignment without fully enclosing the long lots, which remained unmeasured along their longest dimension.

Source: Charles Basset, procès-verbal d'arpentage, 30 October 1719, Bibliothèque et Archives nationales du Québec, fonds des arpenteurs, CA601-6. Courtesy Bibliothèque et Archives nationales du Québec.

"northwest southeast thirteen degrees south."[55] In theory, all the properties in New France followed the same alignment – documents used the definite article when referring to *"le rhumb de vent"* – and the authorities took care to establish one uniform angle for the colony. (Though, in fact,

---

[55] Trudel, *Les débuts du régime seigneurial*, 16; "procès-verbal d'arpentage d'une terre de Jean Guie," 30 June 1727, Sorel seigneurial papers, Library-Archives Canada, MG8, F89, 2110. Large assemblages of survey records can be found at the BANQ (CA601, greffes des arpenteurs) as well as in various seigneurial collections at the BANQ and Library and Archives Canada.

there were many local exceptions to this rule.) A 1676 sovereign council decree ordered the professor of mathematics Martin Boutet to install four pillars at Quebec City to define the *rhumb de vent* for the whole colony. Additionally, all surveyors had to submit their compasses to Boutet so that he could check the calibration.[56] It seems, however, that many properties had already been surveyed without taking account of magnetic variation. By the late seventeenth century, it was becoming clear that there were, in effect, two standard property line orientations, and that they differed by thirteen degrees. As clearing progressed further inland and as land values rose, this discrepancy became more consequential.

Neighborly compromise relying on some version of the six-year cropping rule described in the 1669 sovereign council ordinance probably solved most problems as they came to light. However, the court records show that some landowners insisted on demanding all the lands their deeds entitled them to, even if some of it had been cleared and brought into production, however inadvertently, by a neighbor. Two of New France's oldest seigneuries, Beauport and Notre-Dame-des-Anges, the latter owned by the Jesuits, were initially bounded on a roughly northwest-southeast line. In the early eighteenth century, when this area had been fully settled, the seigneur of Beauport lamented that he had lost half his seigneurie because the Jesuits, always sticklers when exactitude gave them an advantage, insisted on a resurvey along the then official *rhumb de vent*.[57] Another case from the same period involved *censitaires* rather than seigneurs. The village notary of Rivière Ouelle, Étienne Janneau, launched a suit after almost coming to blows with the local captain of militia, Jean Gagnon, whose *roture* lot lay next to his. A survey line had been run between the two properties in 1711, but three years later, claiming that the original survey had failed to take magnetic variation into account, the notary brought in a new surveyor who relocated the boundary well within Gagnon's field. Janneau had a new fence built on this corrected line and Gagnon promptly demolished it. The two parties soon found themselves pleading their cases before the intendant of New France. In his judgment, the latter leaned in the direction of the militia captain: the fence would stay down and the boundary line would

---

[56] Règlements de police, 11 May 1676, *Ordonnances, commissions, etc., etc., des gouverneurs et intendants de la Nouvelle-France, 1639–1706*, ed. Pierre-Georges Roy, 2 vols. (Beauceville, Quebec: L'Eclaireur, 1924), 1: 199–200.

[57] Pierre-Georges Roy, *Inventaire des concessions en fief et seigneurie, fois et hommages et aveux et dénombrements conservés aux archives de la province de Québec*, 6 vols. (Beauceville, Quebec: L'Éclaireur, 1927), 5: 123–31.

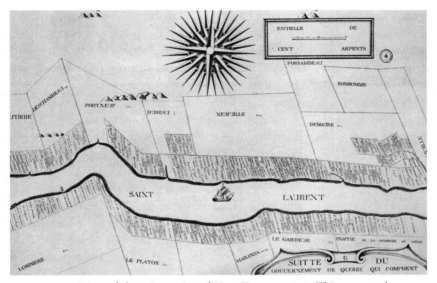

FIGURE 9.7 Map of the seigneuries of New France, 1709. This excerpt from a large and comprehensive property map of the St. Lawrence settlements shows the fiefs and *rotures* of a stretch of the river west of Quebec City. Here properties followed the official orientation ("*rhumb de vent*") fairly closely.
Source: Gédéon de Catalogne and Jean-Baptiste de Couagne, "Suitte du gouvernement de Québec," 1709. Bibliothèque et Archives nationales du Québec, G/3451/G46/1709/C382/1921. Courtesy Bibliothèque et Archives nationales du Québec.

return to where it had been pending an agreement between the two parties to undertake a new survey at their joint expense. In New France as in other colonial settings, officials were inclined to favor actual possession and productive use of land over geometric rectitude.[58]

In 1709, a pair of military engineers/cartographers, Gédéon de Catalogne and Jean-Baptiste de Couagne, mapped all the seigneuries in Canada, showing every constituent *roture* along the settled portions of the St. Lawrence and its tributaries (Figure 9.7).[59] Their maps give the

[58] Ordonnance de Michel Bégon, 14–15 June 1721, BANQ, fonds intendant, E1, S1, P1279–1280. Faced with another case, this one involving several properties on the island of Montreal where lines had been incorrectly drawn, a different intendant decreed that, however misaligned, the existing boundaries would stand in order to avoid future lawsuits and other difficulties. Ordonnance de Duchesneau, 31 July 1680, in Roy ed., *Ordonnances, commissions, etc., etc.*, 1: 278.

[59] Gédéon de Catalogne and Jean-Baptiste de Couagne, "Carte du gouvernement de Québec" (three sheets) and "Carte du gouvernement des Trois-Rivières" (two sheets), G/3451/G46/1709/C382/1921. The sheets covering the district of Montreal have not been found. See Raymonde Litalien, Jean-François Palomino and Denis Vaugeois, *La*

impression of a rather neat and tidy pattern of parallel strips, and yet Catalogne's judgment was that the property geography of New France was a mess: "The early seigneurs and habitants settled the land in good faith, but the lands were laid out by surveyors of little intelligence, and today there is nothing but disputes as everyone wants to follow the terms of their respective contracts, which in most cases is impossible."[60] He happened to have carried out his survey at a moment – the early eighteenth century – when litigation over boundaries peaked. With most of the accessible riverfront property occupied and population expanding, good land had become valuable. Inconsistent surveying in the previous century had left a residue of contestable boundaries and now there was an incentive as well as an opportunity for landowners who felt slighted to demand their due. The fact remains that professional surveying, for all its imperfections, was almost universal in early French Canada, something that could not be said of New Spain or New England or, for that matter, *ancien régime* France.

NEW ENGLAND

Whereas the historian has to look closely at the New France sources to discover the presence of vernacular surveying, this quality is front and center in the records of early New England. Professional surveyors had made an early appearance in the Chesapeake colonies, largely because the "headright system" entitled newly arrived colonists to a specified number of acres as a direct grant from the government; an officially authorized agent had to lay out the land and verify its size. In New England, on the other hand, most allocations were distributed through the intermediary of a township and it was up to the town to establish boundaries. Through most of the seventeenth century, townships tended to rely on local residents, elected annually as "lot layers." Like fence viewers or overseers of the poor, lot layers were basically townsmen serving the community on a temporary basis. Inevitably, their efforts were empirical and ad hoc.

This is not to suggest that the Puritans were indifferent to property bounding; to the contrary. An English tract, republished in Boston in

---

mesure d'un continent: atlas historique de l'Amérique du nord 1492–1814 (Sillery, QC: Septentrion, 2008), 134–35.

[60] Gédéon de Catalogne, "Report on the Seigniories and Settlements in the Districts of Quebec, Three Rivers, and Montreal, November 7, 1712," in *Documents Relating to the Seigniorial Tenure in Canada, 1598–1854*, ed. William Bennett Munro (Toronto: Champlain Society, 1908), 148 (my translation).

1709, made the marking of land into a religious metaphor, with overtones suggestive of the confrontation between civilization and barbarism:

> *Husbandmen* divide and separate their lands from other mens, they have their Landmarks and Boundaries by which property is preserved. So are the People of God wonderfully separated, and distinguisht from the People of the earth. It is a special act of Grace, to be inclosed by God out of the Waste Howling Wilderness of the World.[61]

According to this vision, it is the husbandmen themselves who "divide and separate" properties, while carving a godly space out of the "Howling Wilderness." And so it was in early New England where townships saw to the dividing of the land, with the colonial governments largely standing aside. Government attempts in New France to institute and regulate geometric surveying may have been flawed and inconsistent: in early New England they were essentially nonexistent. When the Massachusetts General Court ordered in 1634 that every town appoint five men to "make a surveyinge of the howses backeside, corne feildes, moweing ground, & other lands," it clearly had in mind the older, nonmathematical sense of "survey": a textual description or mere listing of properties. Actual boundary marking only comes up in the Massachusetts records thirteen years later, and then it concerns lines dividing townships, rather than bounds between individual holdings; the General Court required representatives from adjoining towns to meet and agree on their mutual border and mark the line with a "greate heap of stones, or a trench." In 1682, long after most of its territories had been thoroughly colonized, the Bay Colony did finally require "that no countrey grants of land shall hencforth be laid out but by some knowne, able, and approved person, whom this Court shall appoint"; the same law ordered authorized surveyors to produce a written record and a plat of every plot laid out.[62] In striking contrast to New France, there was really no state-sanctioned system of property bounding through the first two

---

[61] John Flavel, *Husbandry Spiritualized* (Boston, 1709), as quoted in J. B. Harley, "New England Cartography and the Native Americans," in *The New Nature of Maps: Essays in the History of Cartography*, ed. Paul Laxton (Baltimore: Johns Hopkins University Press, 2001), 190. On the prevalence of metaphors of boundaries and fences in early New England public discourse, see David Thomas Konig, *Law and Society in Puritan Massachusetts: Essex County, 1629–1692* (Chapel Hill: University of North Carolina Press, 1979), 132.

[62] Nathaniel Bradstreet Shurtleff, ed., *Records of the Governor and Company of the Massachusetts Bay*, 5 vols. (Boston: W. White printer to the Commonwealth, 1853), 1: 116; 2: 210; 5: 374–75.

generations of Massachusetts settlement; and notwithstanding the General Court's intervention, vernacular practices continued to predominate in much of New England until the eighteenth century.

For this reason, there are no great collections of surveying records in the archives of seventeenth-century New England, though we do get occasional glimpses of the processes of land allocation in the court records, town records and personal diaries of the period. These sources suggest that informality and common sense were the rule; topography rather than geometry guided the setting of boundaries. A lot in early Salisbury was described as "two acres more or less of meadow lying between the meadow lots of John Hoyt and John Clough, butting upon the great creek and the great neck."[63] Lengths, when they were actually measured, were expressed as "poles," "rods" or "perches" (apparently synonyms), implying both an instrument and a unit of measurement. I find no mention of chains in the seventeenth-century record, though that was the approved device for surveyors in England (and in New France) to measure distances along the ground. Simple compasses were sometimes used though these lacked fine calibration in degrees. I did not come across references to theodolites – again the norm in Europe, though these were not common anywhere in the New World at this time. As compared with their counterparts in New Spain, New England land measurers had the advantage of recognized standard measures: the pole/ rod/perch for length and the acre for area. However, it seems that measurements could be elastic. In a document associated with a court case in Essex County, Massachusetts, an Ipswich lot-layer testified that he and his fellow lot-layers measured out 100 acres for "Goodman Brodstreet," but when the latter complained that the lot did not contain enough good meadowland, they promptly added four acres, still calling the total one hundred.[64]

In the early decades of settlement, lot-laying seems to have been extremely rudimentary; moreover, "records" were lodged mainly in human memory and community tradition. Thus, when a major boundary dispute in Ipswich township came before the courts in 1659, there were no drawings or documents to guide the magistrates; instead, a series of

---

[63] Quoted in Konig, *Law and Society in Puritan Massachusetts*, 42.

[64] Archie N. Frost, ed., *Verbatim Transcript of the Records of the Quarterly Courts of Essex County, Massachusetts, 1636–1694*, 57 vols. (typescript held at the Phillips Library, Peabody Essex Museum, Salem, Mass., 1936–39), vol. 2: 2-12-2, Presentment, Ipswich, 4th mo., 1651.

middle-aged and older men was called in to testify about the original tracing of lines twenty-four years earlier. The area at issue ran from a tidal marsh up through an upland crowned by a ridge. Tenants and proprietors as of 1659 generally relied on ditches in the lowland meadow areas to indicate the edges of lots where they mowed hay; in the uplands, fences marked the boundaries. In this case, however, one colonist, Jonathan Wade, became concerned when he noticed "crookedness in the ditches where they meet"; he worried that this might "cause a question to some of my land." Wade was not alone in thinking that there was something wrong with the fence- and ditch-lines in this part of Ipswich; soon his anxieties had unleashed a series of lawsuits aimed at settling property lines in the area. Among the protagonists were members of the elite of Ipswich society, including Major Daniel Denison and Samuel Symonds, both of whom had substantial properties ("farms" in seventeenth-century usage). The town had granted them this land when it was first founded and felt the need to attract influential colonists into their midst; these farms were rented out to tenants. The neighbors who sued one another in 1659 were not necessarily bitter enemies; indeed, it was common in early New England to use cooperative litigation to clarify uncertain boundaries and solidify titles.[65]

At any rate, the case proceeded in the Essex County court through a series of depositions sworn by witnesses who knew something of the original establishment of lines in the area under dispute. They harked back "23 or 24 yeares or there about," meaning 1635 or 1636, which would have been only a few years after the town was founded. A significant fact was never mentioned in these court cases: the sachem of the Agawam people only "sold" these territories in 1638; thus, the laying out of colonists' farms constituted an important aspect of the primary appropriation of indigenous land. A quarter-century later, the day of lot-laying was instead remembered as the occasion when an earlier

---

[65] Frost, ed., *Records of the Quarterly Courts of Essex County*, 5-18-1 to 5-22-2, Denison v. Symonds, Ipswich, September 1659. On related boundary disputes, see also ibid., 5-23-2 to 5-25-3, Fellows v. Bennett, Ipswich, September 1659. On early Ipswich, see Edward Spaulding Perzel, "*The First Generation of Settlement in Colonial Ipswich, Massachusetts, 1633–1660*," PhD dissertation, Rutgers University, 1967. On land litigation in Massachusetts, see David Thomas Konig, "Community Custom and the Common Law: Social Change and the Development of Land Law in Seventeenth-Century Massachusetts," *American Journal of Legal History* 18 (1974): 137–77; Konig, *Law and Society in Puritan Massachusetts*; Jonathan M. Chu, "Nursing a Poisonous Tree: Litigation and Property Law in Seventeenth-Century Essex County, Massachusetts – The Case of Bishop's Farm," *American Journal of Legal History* 31 (1987): 221–52.

grant to John Winthrop, Jr., one of Ipswich's founders, was bounded and, following that, other large "farms," as well as several ordinary settlers' plots, were laid out on adjacent ground.

As one of the proprietors entitled to a lot in the new division, Samuel Hall had taken part in the proceedings. He named John Gage and Richard Jacob as the official lot-layers, though he thought there might have been others. Though these township officers were nominally in charge, Hall gives the impression that others were present, himself included; far from passive observers, these townsmen discussed the proceedings and helped out with the work. "This deponent marked severall trees in or nere the line," Hall noted. Lot-laying seems to have been very much a community exercise. Note also the heavy reliance on trees to mark boundaries. At one crucial point, in a treeless meadow, they did drive in a stake. "And so run from the stake in the medow by Mr. Wades ffarme unto a great white Oake yt was a bound tree [i.e., a boundary marker] att ye upp end of Mr. Winthropps ffarme." Hall continues his account, describing a "head line from the breadth of the farm"; this seems to mean a perpendicular line, though nowhere in any of the testimony is there mention of instruments or procedures other than naked-eye dead-reckoning for determining a square angle. The line ended at "a Creeke called the Labor in Vain," leaving Governor Winthrop's farm bounded on three sides only: "the East end of itt was not mesured but was to run straight upon a line from the stake where they began to mesure unto the Labor in Vain." There was one final boundary to mark, and here the party, possibly tired at the end of a long day, decided on a short-cut that would trouble the peace of a later generation. They chose a distinctive-looking "crotched" tree in the distance as their marker and, without actually notching its bark, they packed up and went home. Samuel Hall claimed he knew better at the time. "This depont to the best remembrance saith that hee moved that that tree should bee Marked, & they answered that itt was so obvious that there was no neede."[66]

By 1659, the landmark was no longer obvious. Robert Roberts had been employed making hay and herding cattle on Major Denison's farm for many years and "he never heard of any crotched or forked tree to be any bounds." Instead, he thought the line ran from the walnut tree "through the glade or hollow of the Eagles nest running neere a rocke in the sd hollow where the fence now standeth." Roberts added that he

[66] Frost, ed., *Records of the Quarterly Courts of Essex County*, 5-20-1, Denison v. Symonds, Ipswich, deposition of Samuel Hall, September 1659.

thought he was present when the lots were laid out, "though it bee long since & some things may have slipped my memory." A long-time tenant on one of the farms bounded by the line in question told the court that he had always been told that "a tall straight tree standing in the hollow of the Eagles nest" marked the boundary – that is, "till Mr Eps felled it"! Seven men then came forward to swear that they had gone that morning to "the place where the wallnuttree stood in" (had that monument also been felled?) and "did from thence aparantly [i.e., visibly] see the body of that tree that is cald a cracht tree or forked tree ... and the sayd tree stands very faynt to be seene from hense as a marke." Four other men recalled that, one day the previous July, "standing about the fence neare William Fellowes house where they say the walnut tree stood which was the bounds of these farms wee observed plainly a faire glade or hollow on the Eagles nest and with all diligence viewing to see a forked tree tho it were pointed to and a ditch in the meaddow guided us to look directly thither, yet wee could not in the least perceive any forked or crotched tree ...." There was just no agreement on trees, standing or fallen, though these were supposed to be the monuments that defined the shapes of properties. How the court decided this thorny, crotched case is not known, but the documentation it generated sheds ample light on the lot-laying practices of the 1630s. Witness depositions reveal completely non-professional procedures, with townsmen visually lining up landmarks, usually trees that might or might not be visible in later years, and inscribing the results not on paper, but in the living memory of the community.[67]

Finally, one further source of confusion needs to be mentioned: lot-laying in this part of Ipswich actually proceeded by stages. Most testimony in the 1659 trials focused on the first day of property bounding, but it appears that the lot layers returned on a later occasion to trace out other plots and they did not hesitate at that point to make a few adjustments to earlier arrangements. John Gage admitted that there had been an initial running of lines for Jonathan Wade's property, with all neighboring proprietors present, but that later, "when mr wades farme was layd out afterward we altered that Line, thinking we had power soe to doe."[68]

[67] Ibid., 5-22-1, Denison v. Symonds, testimony of Robert Roberts, September 1659; 5-21-1, testimony of Richard Brabrooke, 27 September 1659; 2-21-3, deposition of Jonathan Wade, George Giddings, John Daues, Thomas Bishop, Simon Tomson, Daniel Houey and Thomas Burnum, 27 September 1659; 5-19-3, deposition of Eldar Whipple, Mr. John Appleton, Theophilus Willson and Richard Brabrooke, 27 September 1659.

[68] Ibid., 5-25-3, Fellows v. Bennett, deposition of John Gage, 27 September 1659.

All this testimony shows that the early colonists of Ipswich were closely engaged with the land itself. In a group, the elected lot-layers at their head, they walked its surface, examined its contours and evaluated its marshes and uplands for their agricultural potential. The farms they laid out were bounded in relation to this topography, rather than to mathematical concepts of space. They etched property lines in the first instance into living nature: memorizing the positions of trees, rocks and streams, cutting away patches of bark and, at one point, driving a stake into the earth. As the years passed and the land was gradually transformed into pastures and grain fields, fences and ditches were arranged so as to follow and reinforce the boundaries sketched out earlier. Something went wrong in this particular part of Ipswich, with its uncertain "bound trees," but other early ventures in boundary making were probably less confused and controversial. The point is not that early lot laying was necessarily "inaccurate," but rather that it was basically a vernacular folk procedure that connected settlers to the land, even as it transformed landscape into property. In the midst of what was hitherto Agawam space, the colonists of Ipswich were making a *place* for themselves.

The New England tradition of electing lot-layers was not entirely incompatible with the emergence of professional expertise. The same individuals were often called on to fill that office year after year, particularly if they had some talent or education in applied mathematics. The diary of Thomas Minor, an early settler of Stonington, Connecticut, contains many references to surveying, interspersed with the usual pioneer record of plowing, firewood cutting and haying: "Captaine Gookin was heare this weeck we laid out walter palmer his land" (1661); "the first snow fell I came whome from laying out land" (1667); "we laid out 300 ackres of land ministrie" (1668); "laid out 600 acres for Elihu Cheeseborough" (1673) and so on. His son, Manasseh Minor, also kept a diary and it too is punctuated with brief entries, from 1699 to 1715, noting occasional lot-laying. There is no indication that either of the Minors was equipped with any special training or instruments for surveying, but they seem to have developed a certain practical expertise that led fellow-townsmen to rely on them.[69]

---

[69] Thomas Minor, *The Diary of Thomas Minor, Stonington, Connecticut, 1653–1684*, ed. Sidney H. Miner and George D. Stanton (New London, Conn.: Day Publishing Company, 1899), 45, 60, 79, 81, 87, 120; Manasseh Minor, *The Diary of Manasseh Minor, Stonington, Conn., 1696–1720*, ed. Frank Denison Miner and Hannah Miner (1915), 36, 79, 91, 103, 122. Virginia Anderson has made excellent use of the elder Minor's diary to paint a portrait of agrarian life in mid-seventeenth-century New England. The fact that

In the second-generation Massachusetts town of Billerica, residents habitually turned to Jonathan Danforth when it came to dividing a common field or tracing a boundary with an adjacent township. Danforth was a leading figure in the community, and though fellow-townsmen recognized his expertise, they never appointed him to work alone. A 1659 entry in the town record book announces that "the Comitte apoynted to goe alonge with Jonathan danforth to goe ronde the Land yt is Alotted for a coman field to meshre the Land are George ffarley, Henery Jests, James Paterson." In 1660, Danforth was elected selectman and he and Jests were chosen "surveires for the yere insewing." The next year, he and John Parker contracted with the town to survey ("lay out") 4000 acres recently granted Billerica by the General Court. The pair would "be at all Charge about it returninge a record of the buttings and boundinges of the same with a faire platt of it to the Generall Courte for there Confirmation of the same," in return for which service they would be allowed 1000 acres for themselves. Danforth functioned both as a local official and as a practitioner/entrepreneur. He was frequently referred to as an "artist," though surveying and mapping were never his exclusive pursuit. The records provide some clues as to the procedures he and his collaborators followed. The first two "divisions" of common fields (1659) involved tracing parallel lines to create allotments in the form of strips; measurements seem to have been taken with a pole. When Danforth supervised the tracing of a township boundary between Billerica and Woburn, he ran the line "two point and half Easterly of ye North," which suggests the use of a thirty-two-point compass, comparable to the equipment that guided licensed surveyors of the time in New France.[70]

One early New England surveyor whose career has received some attention from historians is William Godsoe, "surveyor for the Town of Kittery [Maine]," from 1694 to 1715. Though he enjoyed a kind of semi-official local status, Godsoe was still elected and reelected every year. His biographer makes no mention of professional training or credentials, though Godsoe does seem to have served previously as a minor legal officer. Like Thomas Minor and Jonathan Danforth, he appears to have

---

she makes no mention of the diarist's surveying activities only serves to confirm the impression that he was a rather typical colonist who turned his hand to surveying as one of the many tasks performed on behalf of his household and his community. Virginia Anderson, "Thomas Minor's World: Agrarian Life in Seventeenth-Century New England," *Agricultural History* 82 (fall 2008): 496–518.

[70] Massachusetts Historical Society, Ms. N-1845, Billerica (Mass.) Records, 1658 [*sic*]– 1816, passim.

grown into the job of surveyor. He was famous for inserting attractive drawings of buildings into his plats, though the latter are rather crude where property boundaries are concerned. In addition to laying out lots in newly opened portions of the settlement, Godsoe also surveyed boundaries in connection with property disputes and inheritance issues.[71]

Over the course of the eighteenth century, surveying finally emerged in New England as a recognized profession, independent of local public office. Mathematical training and up-to-date instrumentation became the norm, as they were in other colonial jurisdictions. Surveyors measured angles in degrees and produced precise plats for their clients. These developments occurred at a time when land had acquired considerable value and speculation was becoming common. Surveyors now operated in the vanguard of property-making, tracing property lines through the forests of Maine and northern New Hampshire, well in advance of actual settlement. In some of these frontier regions, there were experiments with a rectangular grid pattern, more than half a century before it was imposed on the Midwest in the wake of the Northwest Ordinance of 1787.[72] The connection between more abstract spatial definitions of property and speculative land dealings is quite apparent.

---

[71] Richard M. Candee, "Land Surveys of William and John Godsoe of Kittery, Maine: 1689–1769," in *New England Prospect: Maps, Place Names, and the Historical Landscape*, ed. Peter Benes (Boston: Boston University Press, 1982), 9–46.

[72] Richard Judd, *Second Nature: An Environmental History of New England* (Amherst: University of Massachusetts Press, 2014), 78; Jerald E. Brown, *The Years of the Life of Samuel Lane, 1718–1806: A New Hampshire Man and His World*, ed. Donna-Belle Garvin (Hanover, NH: University Press of New England, 2000).

10

Empires and Colonies

One of the themes of this book concerns the intimate connection between state formation and property making. So far the focus has mainly been on the emergence of colonial quasi-states extending their territorial reach in New Spain, New France and New England. Land grants as well as the regulation and registration of property were fundamental functions of these colonial regimes; their respective judicial apparatuses were centrally concerned with disputes over property claims and boundaries, as well as the inheritance and sale of lands. Colonial governments helped make property and property helped make colonial governments. Along with waging war, negotiating peace and defining and suppressing criminality, property formation was one of the principal processes through which they constructed territorial sovereignty. Of necessity, they defined and regulated space while situating diverse colonial peoples and individuals under a superior authority. Of course, such property/state-making was not fully coherent nor was it ever entirely finished; it was always an ongoing work in progress, a matter of deepening the ramifications of property and extending its reach over widening territories, even as the regime worked to repair, reform and buttress a property edifice that never seemed fully stable.

In Europe itself, as well as in the overseas sphere, the processes of state formation and property formation went hand in hand. The seventeenth century saw major developments in European state-making with the growth of standing armies and all the other apparatus of centralized monarchical rule. Meanwhile, in many jurisdictions land was coming increasingly to be bounded and commodified. In Perry Anderson's words, "the enhancement of private property from below was matched by the increase of public authority from above, embodied in the discretionary power of the royal ruler."[1] The trend was for jurisdictions, sovereignties and particular claims to the Earth's resources to be expressed in spatial terms ever more precisely and emphatically; borders and territorial states came to the fore in the political realm, while surveys, enclosed and consolidated holdings and cadastral maps were beginning to transform the nature of land holding.[2] Whereas rule had once been based mainly on jurisdiction, defined in human rather than territorial terms, European rulers began to redeploy the Roman concept of *dominium*, traditionally associated with land ownership, to justify their authority spatially. "Gradually sovereigns transferred the idea of *dominium* from private to public law," writes James Sheehan, "turning it into claims to make and enforce the rules over a group of people and, increasingly, over a bounded territory."[3] In complementary and ultimately interconnected ways, sovereignty and property were being inscribed upon the ground in Europe.

And in Europe's overseas empires. As Jane Burbank and Frederick Cooper have noted, even as the kingdoms of Europe strove to establish homogeneous authority within a neatly bounded territory "at home," they were simultaneously advancing vague and unbounded territorial claims over portions of the New World. "Empire," they state, "always implied governing different people differently."[4] We might add that it also implied governing different *spaces* differently. The expansive and unbounded claims that European monarchies asserted in America represented something of a throwback in contrast to the increasingly defined territories of sovereignty that were then being constructed in early modern Europe. The approach overseas recalled that of the ancient Romans when their empire was in its expansive phase, aspiring to rule the world and recognizing no boundaries to limit Roman sovereignty, only *limes*, "a temporary stopping place where the potentially unlimited expansion of the Pax Romana had come to a halt."[5] But the Romans had also founded

---

[1] Perry Anderson, *Lineages of the Absolutist State* (London: NLB, 1974), 28.

[2] On state formation as a spatial phenomenon, see Henri Lefebvre, *The Production of Space* (Malden, Mass.: Blackwell, 2004).

[3] James J. Sheehan, "The Problem of Sovereignty in European History," *American Historical Review* 111 (February 2006): 5.

[4] Jane Burbank and Frederick Cooper, *Empires in World History: Power and the Politics of Difference* (Princeton, N.J.: Princeton University Press, 2010), 181–84.

[5] Friedrich Kratochwil, "Of Systems, Boundaries, and Territoriality: An Inquiry into the Formation of the State System," *World Politics* 39 (1986): 35–36.

colonia on the edges of their empire, enclaves with outer boundaries and internally divided into individual allotments; these were fully subject to Roman law and effective sovereignty. North America as claimed by European powers in the sixteenth and seventeenth centuries had an analogous geography of sovereignty, with broad, unbounded and frequently overlapping realms that kings aspired to rule and, within each of these, smaller zones of colonization and effective sovereignty. As at the time of the Roman Empire, landed property played a crucial role in defining these latter spaces.

State-making and sovereignty construction was thus going forward in several distinct, though interconnected spheres: within Europe, territorial states were taking shape; overseas, European empires were forming with very different spatial characteristics; and in parts of North America, colonial quasi-states were emerging, simultaneously components of empire and rudimentary versions of the European states that sponsored them. Sovereignty was being asserted and constructed in "Spain," in the Spanish Empire and in New Spain; France, the French Empire and New France; England/Britain, the British Empire and New England. There were both convergences and tensions: the sovereignty of the Spanish Empire was constructed and expanded in New Spain largely through the agency of the government of New Spain, but the sovereignty of New Spain was, in practice, not completely subordinate to that of Spain; it could, on occasion, act in ways that were obliquely at odds with the authority of the empire (likewise New France and New England). Action provoked reaction as imperial states struggled to maintain control over their American domains. This chapter is about some of the ways in which the impulse to bolster imperial sovereignty, seconded by a desire to tap into colonial revenues, led the Spanish, French and British Crowns to intervene in the property-making affairs of their respective colonies.

From the point of view of conventional political theory, this may seem an absurd way of construing things: sovereignty is normally understood to be indivisible, the supreme authority in a given territory. But when sovereignty is considered historically, James Sheehan argues, it has to be understood "as both a doctrine and a set of activities, a way of thinking about politics and a form of political action. As a doctrine, sovereignty is usually regarded as unified and inseparable; as an activity, however, it is plural and divisible." Sheehan goes on to note some similarities linking sovereignty and property as spatial practices: "Like property, territorial sovereignty is never as solid and simple as it sometimes appears. Property and sovereignty are both baskets of claims, whose extent is continually being tested and limited by competing claims."[6] From this angle of vision, it is perfectly reasonable to see states constructing themselves on different levels and territorial sovereignties emerging in overlapping fashion.

Colonial regimes did indeed exercise delegated authority and therefore, in theory, colonial state/property formation should have been completely in harmony with imperial state/property formation. The legal and political theories of early modern imperialism insisted that it was the crowned heads of Europe who stood as the fount at the origin of legitimate claims to the lands of the New World (with the exception of native lands under the Spanish Crown). Spaniards, French and English who occupied American enclaves and established jurisdictions and institutions of government usually announced that they did so in the name of their respective monarchs. Of course, it was never that simple in practice. As powerful interests became established in the colonies – conquistadors, settlers, Creoles – they exercised a great influence over state making and property formation. This was most visibly apparent in the New England case, where colonies enjoyed a high degree of autonomy through most of the seventeenth century. However, even in New Spain, ruled over by a viceroy sent from Spain to represent the king, and even in New France, where governors and intendants also came from Europe with responsibility for implementing policies dictated by monarch and minister, colonial interests remained formidable, particularly where land and property were concerned. Except at its highest levels, the colonial judicial and administrative apparatus tended to be controlled by seigneurs, *hacendados* and their friends. Plenipotentiaries dispatched from Europe to reform colonial administration had the greatest difficulty overcoming pervasive resistance, all the more so when the interests of landholders were at issue. Property-making in early modern North America seemed constantly in danger of escaping the effective control of European sovereigns.

The practical business of dispossessing natives and remaking American space as colonial property and state had fallen to Europeans on the spot: explorers, conquerors, priests, administrators, settlers, magistrates, soldiers and others who came and gave tangible meaning to the concepts of "New Spain," "New France" and "New England." By and large, it was they who constructed colonial jurisdictions, distributed land and developed tenure practices within their respective enclaves; they also expanded those enclaves, eating ever further into indigenous territories.

---

[6] Sheehan, "The Problem of Sovereignty in European History," 2, 6.

The distant king provided an essential touchstone of legitimacy, not to mention occasional military assistance in the face of native resistance and the depredations of rival imperial powers. The natural tendency of the colonial elite to pursue its own interests even when they diverged from those of the metropolitan government presented a basic challenge to the rule of empire, one that European authorities had been acutely aware of starting from the time of Columbus. Among the many strategies they devised to reassert control from the center were various measures designed to insert the imperial state more directly into the processes of colonial property formation. The case studies that follow are all instances of European monarchies attempting to "tidy up" imperial rule in that specific area. The kings of Spain, France and England had somewhat different motives and objectives, but all seem to have felt a need to strengthen their *dominium* over their North American possessions by injecting monarchical authority into colonial property titles.

NEW SPAIN: *COMPOSICIÓNES DE TIERRAS*

In 1591 Philip II issued a series of orders ushering in a new era in land policy for Spain's New World colonies. There would be a thorough investigation of titles, they announced, and anyone found to be illegally occupying land rightfully belonging to the Crown would be required to pay for the privilege of having their holdings legitimated. The legal instrument invoked was a medieval Spanish procedure known as *composición*. Originally devised to reconcile a conflict when the judicial order had been affronted, *composición* involved the payment of a sum to the Crown – not exactly a fine, more a peace offering – in order to terminate the discord.[7] Philip's motives were frankly fiscal: the king needs money, the edicts announced, to rebuild his fleet – this was shortly after the Spanish Armada had come to grief off the coasts of Britain – and he is determined to make his subjects pay for usurping his lands in America.[8] When his successors initiated a subsequent round of *composición* half a century later, they earmarked the proceeds for the reconstruction of the "armada de Barlovento," the Caribbean squadron that protected Spanish territories and shipping from English, French and Dutch pirates. Military

---

[7] José María Ots Capdequí, *El Régimen de la tierra en la América española durante el período colonial* (Ciudad Trujillo: Universidad de Santo Domingo, 1946), 71–73.

[8] Francisco de Solano, *Cedulario de tierras: Compilación de legislación agraria colonial, 1497–1820* (Mexico: Universidad Nacional Autónoma de México, 1991), 43–49, 269–77.

expenditures, including expensive naval shipbuilding, generally formed the weightiest item in the budgets of early modern governments, and, together with the scramble for revenue that these occasioned, they acted as a basic driving force in the process of state formation.[9] In the Spanish case, the landed wealth of New World colonies emerged in the late sixteenth century as a significant target in the unending search for revenues.

Through most of the sixteenth century, the hand of imperial Spain had lain rather lightly over the lands of Mexico. "The Spanish Crown," writes Anthony Pagden, emphasizing the contrast with English claims to New World territory, "... only ever made claims to exercise property rights in several limited areas which were described as being under 'the King's head,' or *cabeza del rey*."[10] Indigenous lands were to remain Indian property, subject only to the sovereign authority of Spain. In theory, the king claimed ownership rights over all precious metals, whether from mines or buried treasure. Since direct exploitation of subsoil rights was impractical, this meant that, in practice, the Crown levied a tax, the *quinto real*, on the gold and silver production of licensed mines. Unoccupied land and estates left vacant when lineages died out (*tierras baldias*) were also supposed to revert to the king. As indigenous communities were decimated by disease and pushed from one location to another, considerable territory – supposedly "abandoned" – passed into the category of Crown lands. However, the monarchy lacked the means to verify, locate and manage this royal estate, which had the effect of opening the door to land-grabbing colonists. All in all, while the Spanish monarchy made efforts to regulate access to the land's resources in the sixteenth century, it did not generally comport itself as the country's ultimate landlord; only to a limited extent – and hardly at all in those vast areas of New Spain already possessed by natives – did the king pose act as the source of legitimate property rights.

---

[9] Charles Tilly, *Coercion, Capital, and European States, AD 990–1990* (Cambridge, Mass.: Basil Blackwell, 1990), 67–95; Jan Glete, *War and the State in Early Modern Europe: Spain, the Dutch Republic and Sweden as Fiscal-Military States, 1500–1660* (London: Routledge, 2002). Even as the Spanish monarchy was devising ways to tap into the wealth of "the Indies" by way of an assertion of Crown land rights, it was also extracting revenue from Iberian lands by selling off the *baldíos* that traditionally formed a national commons. David E. Vassberg, *Land and Society in Golden Age Castile* (Cambridge: Cambridge University Press, 1984), 172–76.

[10] Anthony Pagden, "Law, Colonization, Legitimation, and the European Background," in *Cambridge History of Law in America*, vol. 1: *Early America (1580–1815)*, ed. Michael Grossberg and Christopher Tomlins (New York: Cambridge University Press, 2007), 9.

Evolving circumstances, not least of these the straitened financial circumstances of the Spanish monarchy, combined to provoke a change in attitude toward colonial land in the late sixteenth century. With the decline in the conquest tribute economy and the rise of mining, agriculture and ranching, the land's resources became an ever more valuable prize. Powerful ranchers competed with one another for control over rangelands, even as they wrested territory from indigenous communities. And before long, the imperial government was looking for ways to extract revenue from the boom. The conquistadors and their descendants had been exempted from the direct taxes that applied in Iberian Spain.[11] With so many of them accumulating vast fortunes at a time when Spain faced a deteriorating fiscal situation, the land seemed to offer an ideal target. The prevailing atmosphere of disorder where land granting was concerned gave the state ample justification for moving to stabilize title and punish "usurpations," while the profitability of farming and ranching created interesting possibilities for using the regulation of land tenure to drain private wealth into government coffers. The dormant royal claim to *tierras baldías* provided the legal basis for bringing colonists to heal.

Initially, attention focused on the Marquesado del Valle, the feudal enclave controlled by the heirs of Hernan Cortés; successive *marqueses* had appropriated and then profited by the sale of estates left vacant through the extinction of native lineages. Backed by the imperial government, successive viceroys had fought to suppress this fiefdom and lay claim to its lucrative *tierras baldías* on behalf of the Crown. A series of special commissions and lawsuits culminated finally in the deployment of the *composición* of 1591, which not only swept away the marquesado, it asserted effective Crown ownership over all "vacant" and illegitimately occupied lands across New Spain and Spanish America.[12] The notion was that property titles would be investigated and that unlawfully occupied land would revert to the Crown unless the claimant paid a specified sum to "settle" (*componer*) his dispute with the king. By this means, irregular occupation would be regularized, the possessor would receive legal title and the state would collect valuable revenue. The initial *composición* order of 1591 was not effectively carried out across New Spain, but it did herald a major shift in the way in which property in land was

---

[11] John H. Elliott, *Empires of the Atlantic World: Britain and Spain in America* (New Haven, Conn.: Yale University Press, 2006), 139.

[12] Rebecca Horn, *Postconquest Coyoacan: Nahua-Spanish Relations in Central Mexico, 1519–1650* (Stanford, Calif.: Stanford University Press, 1997), 176, 189–91.

construed. Later waves of *composición* in the seventeenth century would produce more in the way of tangible effects, restructuring colonial tenure and property relations while refiguring the place of the Spanish imperial state in relation to its colonial subjects, Spanish and indigenous.

Under that first *composición*, investigations were conducted and when it was found that land was held without proper title – as was usually the case – the property in question was subject to forfeiture. The government's objective being to squeeze occupants rather than evict them, a price was set for regularizing possession, its value dependant on the value of the tract in question and on whether all or only part of it was held illegitimately. In many cases, investigators determined that a possessor had a proper land grant, but that the area held exceeded the limits prescribed in the *merced*. A *composición* could then be purchased for the excess area, known as "*demasias*." Whether for an entire tract or for *demasias* only, an official document would be forthcoming (the paper, like the procedure from which it derived, known as a "*composición*") that would henceforth constitute legal title to the land. In keeping with the established principle that native property rights pre-dated the Spanish conquest, *indios* were exempted, at this initial stage of *composición*, from the requirement to provide proof of title for the lands they occupied.[13]

If Philip II was hoping to extract vast wealth from Mexican landowners by means of the *composición* of 1591, he must have been disappointed. The sums charged for regularizing possession were indeed steep – one-quarter of the market value of the tract in some areas[14] – but implementation and enforcement were spotty. Landowners, abetted by local governments and by colonial officials sympathetic to their plight, evaded the procedure or dragged their feet. In the absence of adequate administrative agencies to carry out a systematic investigation of titles, it was difficult to overcome this resistance. Money poured into royal coffers more readily in the 1630s and 1640s when the government, pressed for funds to rebuild the naval fleet at the time of the Thirty Years' War, instituted a new round of *composiciónes*. This time they allowed "collective *composiciónes*,"[15] a variant version of the early modern procedure of tax farming. Basically, the landowners of a given area would negotiate a

---

[13] Solano, *Cedulario de tierras*, 43–45.
[14] Tomás Jalpa Flores, *Tierra y sociedad: la apropiación del suelo en la región de Chalco durante los siglos XV–XVII* (Mexico City: Instituto Nacional de Antropología e Historia, 2008), 166.
[15] Solano, *Cedulario de tierras*, 51–57; Jalpa Flores, *Tierra y sociedad*, 167.

lump-sum payment for a blanket *composición*. By this means, the state could collect its money, perhaps at a lower rate than a full, case-by-case investigation would have netted, but without the trouble, expense and delays of the official procedure. The landowners, for their part, gained greater control over the process, paying for the collective *composición* through a local property assessment.[16] With local *hacendados* deciding property claims in this way, Indians – for whom *composición* was rarely good news – were left largely at the mercy of the very Spaniards who had occupied their lands and who now sought to legitimize their possession.

A new *composición* edict emanating from Spain in 1643 ensured that revenues continued to swell by providing for new procedures and more effective enforcement mechanisms. Henceforth, Mexico would be provided with a corps of specialized magistrates and "masters of geometry" to survey and measure the areas involved. Under the new legislation, some collective *composiciónes* were revisited and additional payments imposed on individuals judged to have gotten off too lightly in the past. Besides improving enforcement and administration, the 1643 law enhanced the flow of revenues by transforming the very nature of *composición*. Previously a procedure for verifying title and sanctioning illegitimate occupation, *composición* now became a device for legalizing almost any de facto possession without investigating original title.[17] *Hacendados* sometimes secured *composiciónes* for lands they had not even occupied. What mattered was the money: *composición* began to resemble a simple sale of what were now considered Crown lands, pure and simple. The result, Brian Owensby writes, was that it became "the chief means by which Spanish owners acquired land between 1600 and 1700."[18]

Composiciónes, imperial authorities proclaimed, were not supposed to dispossess Indians. A royal *cédula* of 1646 reiterated traditional policies designed to safeguard native lands and called on New Spain officials to take active steps to prevent *composicónes* being used to sanction usurpation. "To further favor and protect the Indians and to ensure that they are not harmed, we order *composiciónes* not be issued for land acquired from the Indians in violation of our royal decrees and ordinances."[19] Such

---

[16] Ots Copedequí, *El régimen de la tierra*, 149–50.
[17] Hanns J. Prem, *Milpa y hacienda: tenencia de la tierra indígena y española en la cuenca del Alto Atoyac, Puebla, México (1520–1650)* (Wiesbaden: Steiner, 1978), 125.
[18] Brian Owensby, *Empire of Law and Indian Justice in Colonial Mexico* (Stanford, Calif.: Stanford University Press, 2008), 20.
[19] Real cédula of 30 June 1646, Solano, *Cedulario de tierras*, 352–53. "Para más favorecer y amparar a los indios y que no reciban perjuicio mandamos que las composiciones de

pious ideals, though by no means without effect, ran counter to the imperative to maximize revenue. Natives were particularly vulnerable in cases of collective *composición*, but even where individual *composiciónes* are concerned, officials' sense of their duty to protect Indian lands was rarely a match for the opposing pressures exerted by fellow colonizers, by the avidity for official fees and by the need to secure government revenues. No wonder that indigenous Mexicans of the seventeenth century came to regard *composición* as a transaction among Spaniards to sell their lands.[20]

With more and more territory escaping their control in the seventeenth and eighteenth centuries, and with colonial courts tending to favor documented title over traditional occupation, natives searched with increasing desperation for legal protection for their lands. Colonial authorities were less and less inclined to take their word for it that a given tract had been theirs since pre-Hispanic times. In Oaxaca, says William Taylor, "Ancient ownership declined as a legal argument in the seventeenth century, when the composiciones de tierras initiated by the Crown confirmed what were considered to be valid titles of primitivo patrimonio. Afterwards, evidence of this composición served as a substitute title, and in most cases claims of primitivo patrimonio were no longer accepted."[21] Hence, the various measures, mentioned in Chapter 4, that pueblos resorted to in order to secure their lands: *titulos* and *lienzos* of indigenous manufacture and protective court orders known as "*amparos.*" An *amparo* was better than nothing, but it did not provide the kind of strong title that a *composición* did.[22] The original *composición* law of 1591 had exempted native lands from the requirement to prove title, but as *composición* evolved over the course of the seventeenth century from a punitive investigation into an opportunity to acquire land with a solid title, the exemption of native property began to seem more like exclusion than privilege. Even when natives were finally allowed to purchase *composiciones* in the eighteenth century, few could afford the high price. Whereas Indian tenure differed from nonnative tenure in many ways, it was progressively assimilated to a

tierras no sean de las que los españoles hubieren adquirido de indios contra nuestras cédulas reales y ordenanzas ..."

[20] Jonathan D. Amith, *The Mobius Strip: A Spatial History of Colonial Society in Guerrero, Mexico* (Stanford, Calif.: Stanford University Press, 2005), 96.

[21] William B. Taylor, *Landlord and Peasant in Colonial Oaxaca* (Stanford, Calif.: Stanford University Press, 1972), 79.

[22] Owensby, *Empire of Law*, 20; Ots Copedequí, *El régimen de la tierra*, 74–76.

new colonial norm in one important respect: property would depend increasingly on documents issued by the state.[23]

A final phase of *composición* began with the law of 1692, establishing a bureaucracy in Spain to administer colonial lands directly from Madrid.[24] Henceforth, *composición* would be a routine procedure for verifying and documenting title, rather than an occasional investigation of wrongdoing. More than in the past, the accent was on using land policy to foster agricultural "improvement," encouraging the productive use of the soil and extracting revenue for the benefit of the imperial state. Moreover, in asserting that all lands, claimed by any individual, corporation or ethnic group, came within its purview, the 1692 *composición* legislation implied a great extension of the Crown's eminent domain property rights as compared with sixteenth-century practice. Finally, by making use of tribunals answerable to Iberian authorities and by largely bypassing the viceregal state, this new property regime represented a major step in imperial centralization.

By and large, these developments were bad news for natives, representing the culmination of a seventeenth-century trend to reduce the earlier commitment to protect Indian property and to recognize it as primordial. Explicitly targeting all properties and all varieties of proprietor "without exception," the new *composición* legislation dragged indigenous communities toward a situation where land-holdings depended on official documentation and money, two assets they generally lacked. The conquest-era notion that natives had a right to their traditional lands had shrunk by the late seventeenth century to a residual commitment to maintain a modest 600-*vara* perimeter of protected land around every pueblo. That arbitrary figure of course took no account of terrain, soil quality, agricultural practices or population. The fact is that native populations were rebounding in the seventeenth century: even as indigenous lands were being hemmed in ever more narrowly, subsistence needs were generally on the rise. Communities were therefore desperate to hold on to their lands and to expand them if possible. Some pueblos actually bought land from neighboring *haciendas* in the early eighteenth century and others acquired ranching *sitios* through grants from the government. The problem is that

[23] Nadine Béligand, "L'agrimenseur, le juge et le roi: mesure et appropriation de l'espace en Nouvelle Espagne," in *Connaissances et pouvoirs: les espaces impériaux (XVIe-XVIIIe siècles: France, Espagne, Portugal*, ed. Charlotte de Castelnau-L'Estoile and François Regourd (Bordeaux: Presses universitaires de Bordeaux, 2005), 125.

[24] Solano, *Cedulario de tierras*, 60–67; Mariano Peset and Margarita Menegus, "Rey propietario o rey soberano," *Historia Mexicana* 43 (1994): 588–89.

any terrain beyond the 600-*vara* perimeter, whether newly acquired or claimed from time immemorial, was subject to the rules of *composición*, meaning that title remained uncertain until and unless it was verified by the appropriate tribunal, for a price. An edict of 1711 gave Indians what looked like favorable consideration for their "excess" lands: approaching the tribunal with whatever documentation they had, they could make a "free contribution" (*donativo gracioso*) – presumably less than the cost of *composición* – to the royal coffers and receive formal recognition of their property. That was the theory, but in practice native pueblos found that they had to secure a proper *composición*, at the full price, if they wanted full protection from encroachment and legal challenges.[25]

The thrust of *composición* varied greatly over time and from region to region as laws were modified and administrative apparatus grew and as Spaniards and Indians in farming areas, ranchlands and frontier zones adapted to the constraints and opportunities the procedure offered. Some basic common effects nevertheless stand out in the seventeenth-century history of *composición*. First, it went a long way toward transforming the spatial definition of property, proposing a geometry of outer boundaries in place of a landscape that had been defined in large parts of New Spain by central places and radiuses. It was not for nothing that "geometers" (surveyors) formed a part of the team charged with establishing title, though surveying techniques remained rudimentary. In ranching regions, where *sitios* had been conceived in circular form, *composición* mainly took the form of payment for "*demasías*," that is, additional territory adjacent to an earlier grant; these usually took the form of four rough triangles that expanded a circle into the square or rectangle of dimensions corresponding to its diameter. "In the province of Santa Bárbara," writes Chantal Cramaussel, "the total size of haciendas grew quite substantially ... and enormous latifundios began to make their appearance."[26] Where previously there had been islands of private control in a

---

[25] Sergio Eduardo Carrera Quezada, "Las composiciónes de tierras en los pueblos de indios en dos jurisdicciones coloniales de la Huasteca, 1692–1720," *Estudios de Historia Novohispana* 52 (January 2015): 29–50. See also María Cristina Torales Pacheco, "A Note on the Composiciones de Tierra in the Jurisdiction of Cholula, Puebla (1591–1757)," in *The Indian Community of Colonial Mexico: Fifteen Essays on Land Tenure, Corporate Organizations, Ideology and Village Politics*, ed. Arij Ouweneel and Simon Miller (Amsterdam: CEDLA, 1990), 87–102.

[26] Chantal Cramaussel, *Poblar la frontera: la provincia de Santa Bárbara en Nueva Vizcaya durante los siglos XVI y XVII* (Zamora: El Colegio de Michoacán, 2006), 325. "En la provincia de Santa Bárbara, las superficies globales de las haciendas aumentaron así sensiblemente ... y enormes latifundios comenzaron a aparecer." See also Joseph Sáenz

sea of vaguely delineated territory, a full geometry of property was taking shape: henceforth every space was supposed to have a proprietor.

Second, *composición* had the effect of reducing a variety of particular and sometimes overlapping use rights to a singular and much more exclusive form of land ownership.[27] Spatially defined by outer edges, land was also more intensively owned under the sign of *composición*. In some ranching areas, fences were erected to keep out intruding livestock, and perhaps as a sign to humans.[28] Moreover, *hacendados* now had greater legal justification for their efforts to claim all the resources within their estates, securing the dependence of native workers by barring independent access to the land. Third, *composición* provided a more uniform system of title in place of the preexisting welter of grants, traditional claims and undocumented possession. More exclusive property rights spread across the Mexican landscape and sank more deeply into its soil. Since *composición* generally benefited "Spaniards" at the expense of "Indians," it functioned as a prime instrument of colonial dispossession, but it did so through a fundamental transformation in the nature of property in land.

At the same time, the massive issuance of *composiciónes* implied a major change in colonial and imperial governance. Driven by the Spanish Crown's thirst for revenues, the *composición* laws of the late sixteenth and seventeenth centuries tended to construct a property regime in which title and legitimate property derived from the state. Government had always claimed a role as arbiter and guarantor of property rights, but *composición* made it a much more active and potent creator of property. Measuring, judging and mapping territory, documenting and archiving title, taxing land, the state made property even as property made the state. Moreover, it was increasingly the metropolitan state that drove this operation; relying at first on viceroys and audiencias to perform the legal operations involved, the Spanish monarchy moved eventually to centralize control of the bureaucracy in the Iberian kingdom itself.

---

de Escobar, *"Geometría Práctica y Mecánica"* (ca. 1700), Archivo del Universidad Interamericana, Mexico City, 63–64v; Álvarez, "Latifundio y poblamiento," 161–64.

[27] François Chevalier, *Land and Society in Colonial Mexico: The Great Hacienda* (Berkeley: University of California Press, 1963), 276.

[28] Miguel Aguilar-Robledo, "Formation of the Miraflores Hacienda: Lands, Indians, and Livestock in Eastern New Spain at the End of the Sixteenth Century," *Journal of Latin American Geography* 2 (2003): 102.

NEW FRANCE: *PAPIER TERRIER*

Like the Spanish Hapsburgs, the French Bourbons woke up to find that New World property was being created in their name, but largely beyond their control. But whereas the Spanish response was to stamp out the feudal pretentions of the Cortés clan in Mexico, while deploying an enhanced doctrine of Crown land to extract revenue from landowners, the Bourbons accepted the basically feudal nature of property in Canada. Instead of posing as the full proprietor of some colonial lands, willing – for a price – to cede their claims to colonists, the French kings claimed continuing feudal overlord rights over all colonial seigneuries. With the attributes of sovereignty and property tending to coincide at the top, monarchs and their agents intervened in different ways to regulate seigneurialism, combining the Crown's powers as superior landlord with its powers as sovereign. Partly the aim was to maximize revenues, as in the New Spain case, but since there was very little real estate wealth to tap in New France, the objectives were generally more "political": a matter of promoting colonial development and keeping seigneurs in line. Imperial state intervention took a variety of forms. One of the most important of these, a procedure that nicely illustrates the conjunction of state-making and property formation, was the creation of a *papier terrier* for New France.

The *terrier*, sometimes known as estate roll in England, emerged in medieval France as a written inventory of a feudal estate, with a description of the lands held, the size and quality of each and the dues and services owed, and the identity of each vassal and tenant. As notaries were increasingly called on to draw up *terriers*, these came to be recognized as legal documents, an element of the title by which both the lord of the manor and the lord's tenants held their respective properties.[29] Eventually, a valid *terrier* would require authorization in advance from a court; as of the early modern period, that authorization had to come from a royal court and thus it represented an exercise of the king's power and authority.[30] Fiscal considerations were driving the state to assert control

[29] Ghislain Brunel, Olivier Guyotjeannin and Jean-Marc Moriceau, eds., *Terriers et plans-terriers du XIIIe au XVIIIe siècle. Actes du colloque de Paris (23–25 septembre 1998)* (Rennes: Association d'histoire des sociétés rurales - Ecole nationale de Chartes, 2002).

[30] Claude-Joseph de Ferrière, *Dictionnaire de droit et pratique contenant l'explication des termes de droit, d'ordonnances, de coutume et de pratique avec les jurisdictions de France* (Paris: Bauche, 1771), 311–12.

over the creation of *terriers*. By the seventeenth century, seigneurial obligations that once took the form of labor service and various payments in kind were increasingly being translated into money payments. In many instances, for example, when a feudal estate was sold, the king might be entitled to a payment by virtue of his position as superior lord; hence the growing interest of the revenue-hungry monarchy in monitoring the affairs of fiefs, seigneurs and tenants. Additionally, *terriers* were of interest in the context of tax assessments since, in the absence of a national land registry system, they provided the most complete record of land holdings. Little wonder then that Louis XIV's chief minister, Jean-Baptiste Colbert, specialist in all things financial and administrative, embarked on a vast effort to assemble copies of all the *papiers terriers* from the thousands of seigneuries across the kingdom.[31] No longer simply the "private" record of a personal estate, the *terrier* had become by the 1660s a state document. Feudal tenures, traditionally associated with fragmented sovereignty, were being drawn into the information-storage facilities of a centralizing, rationalizing, bureaucratic monarchy. The tangled welter of overlapping fiefs, contending jurisdictions and inconsistent provincial laws tended to frustrate attempts to construct a complete property archive in France, but in the colonies conditions were more propitious.

The occasion for the first Canadian *terrier* of 1667–68 was the transfer of New France from the Company of New France to the Compagnie des Indes Occidentales. The new company wished to take stock of its landed estates, assert its proprietary rights and assess current and potential future revenues. Just as important, Colbert wanted a full picture of colonial property for his own developmentalist purposes. The 1660s and early 1670s, a peaceful interlude between expensive European wars, was a time of massive government investment and restructuring in the colonies, part of a larger overhaul and reinvigoration of the French economy. Presiding over that process from the imperial center was Jean-Baptiste Colbert, who, along with his many other functions, acted as Louis XIV's minister in charge of colonies and of the navy (*ministre de la marine*). Colbert dispatched troops and immigrants to New France, as well as a corps of officials answerable directly to him as minister. His principal agent in Canada was Jean Talon, who occupied (1665–68, 1670–72) the position most closely associated with royal "absolutism" in seventeenth-century

---

[31] Marie-Thérèse Lalague-Guilhemsans, "Le dépôt des terriers de la chambre des comptes de Paris," in Brunel, Guyotjeannin and Moriceau, eds., *Terriers et plans-terriers*, 151–66.

France, that of intendant.[32] Colbert, dubbed "the information master" in a recent study,[33] had an approach to state-building that emphasized the systematic collection and archiving of massive amounts of data and he gave Talon some specific orders in this area: the intendant was to gather information on Canada's economic potential, conduct a nominal census and, in cooperation with the Compagnie des Indes Occidentales, prepare a *papier terrier*.

From the outset, Jean Talon complained of what he perceived as a basic contradiction in his instructions. On the one hand, Colbert wanted him to establish royal control over New France and to encourage the settler population and stimulate economic development; on the other hand, the minister had given feudal property rights over New France to a commercial corporation.[34] Over the years of his intendancy, Talon worked quietly and relentlessly to sideline the Compagnie des Indes Occidentales where land was concerned. By the late 1660s, Talon was granting seigneuries (subinfeodation) in the king's name, without mention of the company.[35] By the time Louis XIV dissolved the company and took over direct control of New France in 1674, the colony was already effectively a royal fief administered by the Marine ministry. However, none of this had been settled by 1667 and so the *papier terrier* was drawn up in the company's name, even though the process was driven by the royal administration.[36] In typical *ancien régime* fashion, there were no definite boundaries separating the corporation, the state and the feudal lord.

---

[32] André Vachon, "Jean Talon," *Dictionary of Canadian Biography* (Toronto: University of Toronto Press, 1966–), 1: 614–32.

[33] Jacob Soll, *The Information Master: Jean-Baptiste Colbert's Secret State Intelligence System* (Ann Arbor: University of Michigan Press, 2009).

[34] Talon to Colbert, 4 October 1665, in "Correspondance échangée entre la cour de France et l'intendant Talon pendant ses deux administrations dans la Nouvelle-France," in *Rapport de l'archiviste de la province de Québec pour 1930–1931* (Quebec: Rédempti Paradis, 1931) (hereafter *RAPQ*, 1930–31), 34; Colbert to Talon, 5 January 1666, in *RAPQ*, 1930–31, 43.

[35] Marcel Trudel, *La seigneurie de la compagnie des indes occidentales, 1663–1674* (Montreal: Fides, 1997), 115; William Bennett Munro, *The Seigniorial System in Canada: A Study in French Colonial Policy* (New York: Longmans Green, 1907), 34.

[36] The main tribunal, at Quebec, was presided over by the chief judge of the Quebec *prévôté* court, Louis-Théandre Chartier de Lotbinière, and the *procureur fiscal*, Jean-Baptiste Peuvret Demesnu. Another tribunal sat at Three Rivers. As for Montreal, where the Sulpician order held the entire island as a single fief, Talon administered that part of the colonial terrier personally in 1666. Trudel, *La seigneurie de la compagnie des indes occidentales*, 114; Talon to Colbert, 13 November 1666, *RAPQ*, 1930–31, 55.

The bulk of the work was completed between October 1667 and July 1668. Even though the colony was small and the number of estates quite limited, it turned out to be a protracted affair because more was involved in a seventeenth-century *papier terrier* than a simple inventory of lands. It involved an investigation of title, the administration of an oath of allegiance and a detailed description of holdings. By means of a written notice attached to every church door, vassals from the Quebec region were summoned to the governor's palace where each was to present his or her titles for verification.[37] Most land within the city and in its immediate vicinity (*banlieue*) was held directly from the company in small lots by ordinary colonists who owed a small annual *cens*. These direct tenants presented their documents and described their respective holdings, the dimensions of the lot, the size of the house and outbuildings. Most could produce a written grant signed by a representative of the old company, but on paying a small fee to the notary, they went away with a renewed, and more solid title deed. In the countryside, almost all land had been subinfeodated, and it was only the seigneurs of these rural fiefs who had to make their appearance, to present their titles and to enact a performance of submission. Each seigneur, bareheaded and without sword, had to drop to one knee and pledge allegiance (*foi et hommage*) to the Compagnie des Indes Occidentales. *Censitaires*, that is, the colonists who held land from these seigneurs, were not directly involved, but each seigneur was supposed to submit a list of all the *censitaires* who held land within their seigneurie, specifying the size of each *roture*, the extent of cleared land and the number of houses and barns. This seigneurial inventory, known as an *aveu et dénombrement*, theoretically formed part of a *terrier*, but the authorities did not insist on that level of documentation in 1667.[38]

Creating a *terrier* involved an investigation of title reminiscent of the early *composiciónes* of New Spain, but the purpose was generally more political than financial. Jean Talon was under specific orders to make sure that the instruments by which the old company had granted fiefs contained no clauses that might be "to the prejudice of the rights of sovereignty." Similarly, he was to examine the seigneurs' grants of land to settlers and ensure that these deeds "require nothing that might injure the

---

[37] Pierre-Georges Roy, ed., *Papier terrier de la compagnie des indes occidentales, 1667–1668* (Beauceville, QC: L'Eclaireur, 1931).

[38] Marcel Trudel, *Le terrier du Saint-Laurent en 1663* (Ottawa: Éditions de l'Université d'Ottawa, 1973), 3–4.

rights of the Crown regarding the subjection that is due to the king alone."[39] New France might have feudal lords, but the vigilance of the colonial administration, armed with procedures that included the *papier terrier*, would ensure that these would not be allowed to interfere with the king's sovereign authority. Memories of the Fronde, the troubled period (1650–53) of Louis XIV's minority when feudal grandees and provincial *parlements* challenged the monarchy, remained fresh when instructions on the *terrier* and other aspects of New France land policy were drawn up. The final paragraph is very explicit on this point; since obedience and loyalty are more endangered in countries distant from the person of the prince,

It would be prudent, in establishing the nascent state of Canada, to avert any unfortunate revolution that might turn it from a monarchical into an aristocratic or democratic regime, or by some balance of power and authority among its subjects to divide and dismember it, as was the case in France where sovereignties were elected in the kingdoms of Soissons and Orléans and in the counties of Champagne and elsewhere.[40]

The drawing up of the *terrier* also provided an opportunity for the company and the colonial administration to rationalize and standardize tenures in the colony to some extent. As with the *composiciónes* of Spanish America, Talon and his fellow-panelists felt authorized to reject some property claims and to change the size or the terms of tenure of others.[41] Peculiarities that had crept into some of the deeds granted to

---

[39] "Sur la distribution des terres du Canada et des concessions faites et à faire avec leurs clauses [1667]," in Pierre Georges Roy, *Ordonnances, commissions, etc., etc., des gouverneurs et intendants de la Nouvelle-France, 1639–1706*, 2 vols. (Beauceville, QC: l'Éclaireur, 1924), 1: 55–64. "... au préjudice des droits de souveraineté ... ils n'ont rien exigé qui puisse blesser les droits de la couronne en ceux de la subjection dûs seulement au Roy."

[40] Ibid., 63–64. "Posant toujours le même principe que l'obéissance et la fidélité dûes au prince souffrent plutôt altération dans les pays de l'état éloignés que dans les voisins de l'autorité souveraine, résidant principalement en la personne du prince et y ayant plus de force et de vertu qu'en tout autre, il est de prudence de prévenir, dans l'établissement de l'état naissant du Canada, toutes les fâcheuses révolutions qui pourroient le rendre de monarchique aristocratique ou démocratique, ou bien, par une puissance et autorité balancée entre les sujets, le partager en ses parties et donner lieu à un démembrement tel que la France a vu par l'élection des souverainetés dans les royaumes de Soissons, d'Orléans, comtés de Champagne et autres." Though undoubtedly conditioned by more recent threats to the integrity of the monarchy, this author dredged up very ancient historical precedents. The allusion to the kingdoms of Soissons and Orléans seems to refer to the breakup of the Frankish empire on the death of its first king, Clovis, in 511. My thanks to Professor William Beik for his advice on this point.

[41] Trudel, *La seigneurie de la compagnie des indes occidentales*, 329–30.

seigneurs, and particularly deviations from the laws of the Custom of Paris, were eliminated. Some seigneuries were suppressed because they were too large – the previous company had granted a few fiefs the size of a European principality to relatives of its own shareholders – others because they had not been developed.[42] Though many negligent seigneurs got off with a warning, some discovered, to their cost, that formal grants of "perpetual" property issued by the Company of New France counted for little when representatives of the new regime were empowered to decide on property claims.

After Louis XIV took direct control of New France, colonial intendants would be ordered on repeated occasions to renew the *terrier* and to keep it updated. Beginning in the 1720s, under Louis XV, a concerted effort finally produced an almost complete and much more elaborate archive of property, complete with *aveux et dénombrements* recording all the *rotures* within every seigneurie in the colony. These inventories included the names of all *censitaires,* the size and location of their lands, the number of houses and outbuildings, the extent of cleared plowland and meadow within each lot, together with the annual seigneurial rent owed. *Aveux et dénombrements* for the majority (135) of seigneuries were submitted between 1723 and 1726; a further 55 dribbled in between 1731 and 1745; in the end, only a handful of fiefs was left out.[43] The initial impulse to complete this more ambitious *papier terrier* came from the *Domaine d'Occident*, a tax-farming corporation that leased the right to collect, among many other revenue sources, the king's feudal income from Canadian lands. The revenues were in fact quite paltry, but perhaps the tax farmers hoped for better returns in the future.[44] However, the

---

[42] *RAPQ*, 1930–31, 79, 96; Louis Lavallée, *La Prairie en Nouvelle-France, 1647–1760: étude d'histoire sociale* (Montréal: McGill-Queen's University Press, 1992), 50–51.

[43] Jacques Mathieu and Alain Laberge, *L'Occupation des terres dans la vallée du Saint-Laurent: les aveux et dénombrements, 1723–1745* (Sillery, QC: Septentrion, 1991), xii–xvii.

[44] The Crown – and therefore the *domaine d'occident* in practice – was entitled to the *droit de quint*, amounting to one-fifth of the purchase price, whenever a fief within New France was alienated; generally, seigneurs were given a one-third discount on the *quint*. By virtue of the *lods et ventes*, it could also collect one-twelfth of the price of any of the urban and suburban lots in Quebec City and Three Rivers held directly from the Crown if these were sold outside the holder's lineage. Given the low value of properties and the difficulties of collection, these revenue streams remained minuscule, averaging 1100 *livres* per year, 1723–33. François-Joseph Cugnet, *Traité de la loi des fiefs qui a toujours été suivie en Canada depuis son établissement, tirée de celle contenüe en la coûtume de la prevôté et vicomté de Paris, à laquelle les fiefs et seigneuries de cette province sont assujettis, en vertu de leurs titres primitifs de concession, et des édits, reglemens, ordonances et declarations*

naval ministry had other motives in ordering colonial officials to bend all their efforts to completing the new and improved *terrier*: financial considerations aside, the imperial state wanted data on land use as part of its drive to promote development of the colony. Versailles had already issued the Edicts of Marly (1711) ordering that unoccupied *rotures* be repossessed by seigneurs and that undeveloped seigneuries be repossessed by the government. Sensitive to the fact that French Canada was being outpaced economically and demographically by the English colonies, authorities in France were convinced that too much land had been granted in the St. Lawrence Valley and that seigneurs, habitants and colonial officials were all neglecting their duty to ensure that every *arpent* of that property be put into agricultural production. They wanted detailed information on the progress of land clearance, cultivation and occupation in order to verify their suspicions and penalize those at fault. The feudal institution of the *papier terrier* provided them with a legal vehicle for what might otherwise be considered a thoroughly modern socioeconomic inquiry. There is no evidence that this exercise in disciplinary fact-gathering had the desired effect on the Canadian agricultural economy, but the *terrier/aveu et dénombrement* procedures certainly ensured that the archives would bulge with documentation to further solidify the colonial property regime.

Dispossession of natives was not the stated purpose of the New France *terriers*, any more than it was an objective of the *composiciónes* of New Spain; yet the drive to impose tenure uniformity proved detrimental to indigenous lands. One of the anomalies that the 1667–68 commissioners came upon was the fief of Sillery, which had been granted the Christian Innu in 1651 (see Chapter 3). This was the occasion on which intendant Talon and his colleagues revoked what they called the "ridiculous" grant of a seigneurie to "savages," and placed Sillery directly in the hands of the Jesuits.[45] Other small plots of land that had come into native possession were also confiscated and given to the missionaries. Thus, the *terrier* of

---

de sa majesté très chrétienne, rendus en consequence; et des diferens jugemens d'intendans rendus à cet égard, en vertu de La loi des fiefs, et des dits edits, reglemens, ordonances et declarations (Quebec City: G. Brown, 1775), 8–11; Jacques Mathieu, Alain Laberge, Renald Lessard and Lina Gouger, "Les aveux et dénombrements du régime français (1723–1745)," *Revue d'histoire de l'Amérique française* 42, no. 4 (1989): 548.

45 "Estat de ce qu'il plaise a messieurs de La Compagnie des Indes Occidentalles regler et faire ensuitte des ordonnances, incluses en leur papier terrier composé par assises tenues par le lieutenant general en leur justice le Sieur Chartier," [1667], ANOM, C11E, vol. 11: fol. 12.

1667–68 can be seen as an important step in the construction of a tenure regime for native lands within the St. Lawrence colonized zone that subjected these territories to the legal preeminence of the missionary orders. Even though indigenous residents never recognized the Jesuits and Sulpicians as seigneurs and never paid them rent, this development would have important consequences. Late in the history of New France, the missionary-seigneurs would use their dubious legal powers to transfer lands intended for natives into the hands of rent-paying settlers (Chapter 5). The metropolitan drive to tidy up an inconsistent colonial tenure regime thus had the effect of facilitating the dispossession of New France's indigenous people.

At one level, France's interventions into Canadian tenure practices can be seen as fostering a superficial legal uniformity, notably by vesting indigenous lands in fiefs held by Jesuits or Sulpicians and resembling, in their legal outward appearances, any other New France fief. At another level, however, as we learned earlier, these were not at all like the seigneuries intended for white *habitants*. The *aveux et dénombrements* that accompanied the *terrier* of the 1723–45 period vividly differentiate native tenure and settler tenure. Whereas the entries for most seigneuries comprise dozens of pages, with a paragraph devoted to describing each constituent *roture*, the *terrier* sections concerning "mission" seigneuries occupied by natives are cryptic and perfunctory. Out of the 233 pages devoted to the *aveux et dénombrements* of the Jesuit seigneuries, the entire village of Kahnawake (fief of Sault St.- Louis) merits only a single sentence: "On this land, the said Iroquois are settled, in conformity with the said grant, and they might have an area of about two hundred and fifty arpents of cleared land which they use to grow their corn."[46] There is, of course, no mention of individual allotments or of seigneurial rents, for these lands were actually held according to Iroquois tenure practices. Even as it imposed a rough uniformity among New France fiefs, when it came to lands held for actual use (*domaine utile*), the *terrier* process had the effect of accentuating the differentiation of settler tenure and native tenure.

DOMINION OF NEW ENGLAND

As in New Spain and New France, the impulse to build and reinforce imperial authority expressed itself in seventeenth-century New England

[46] BANQ, E21, S64, SS5, SSS1, D283, Registre des aveux et dénombrements des seigneuries des R.P. Jésuites, 17 January 1733.

through efforts to remake colonial land tenure. Movements in that direction were detectable as early as the 1660s but they came dramatically to the fore during the reign of James II with the creation of the short-lived Dominion of New England. Assembled between 1685 and 1688 out of formerly chartered colonies now brought under royal rule, the Dominion of New England was presided over by the autocratic governor Edmund Andros. The heavy-handed Andros regime provoked vigorous resistance from within a settler society accustomed to a high degree of self-government; uprisings roughly coinciding with England's Glorious Revolution brought it down in 1689. High on the opposition's list of grievances was the land question, that is to say, Andros's controversial and largely unsuccessful, though far from inconsequential, attempt to reform and overhaul New England tenure.[47]

Throughout the Restoration period, there had been a growing tendency within imperial circles to focus on the potential of New World lands to contribute to state finances; earlier, the focus had been almost exclusively on colonial commerce as the means of enriching the mother country. This shift paralleled, though at a remove in time, a similar change in emphasis in Spanish thinking about the political economy of empire. Both political and financial impulses were at work: the basic idea seems to have been to make use of quitrents and other charges to underwrite the costs of royal government, and by so doing to obviate the need for colonial assemblies. It would therefore not have been a great surprise to well-informed colonists that Edmund Andros came to Boston in 1686 with instructions to clean up supposedly disordered colonial tenures and use land to finance a more authoritarian government. With a mission not unlike those assigned to viceroys of New Spain and intendants of New France (indeed James II was accused of trying to impose a French style of rule on the colonies), Andros was supposed to examine land titles and make sure they were not at odds with the king's position as sovereign and ultimate landlord.[48]

Once installed in the colonies, Andros discovered that hardly any New England titles conformed to his standards of legality. In Massachusetts, only the Massachusetts Bay Company had been authorized by the Crown to grant lands and so he recognized no title except that derived from deeds

---

[47] An old book remains the standard work on this topic: Viola Florence Barnes, *The Dominion of New England, a Study in British Colonial Policy* (New Haven, Conn.: Yale University Press, 1923).

[48] Ibid., 188.

that bore the company's seal and that conferred land directly on an individual. But the colony's proprietors had distributed land mainly through the intermediary of townships, with the result that the great majority of colonists held their respective lots not from the Bay company directly, but from a town, making their title entirely spurious in the eyes of Edmund Andros. Accordingly, the governor announced that proprietors must come forward, apply for a patent, pay a quitclaim and receive proper title in the king's name; otherwise, their ownership would not be recognized.[49] Investigating title, correcting tenurial "disorder," collecting revenue and imposing Crown ownership: Andros was embarked on an enterprise that had much in common with a Spanish *composición*.

It was not a very successful campaign, however. Although there were some applications, especially from frontier regions of Maine and New Hampshire where a deed issued by the governor might be of use in an environment of uncertain and contested claims, Andros's call for renewed title fell on deaf ears in the more settled parts of New England. "The generality of the people are very averse," wrote Samuel Sewall in 1688, "from complying with any thing that may alter the Tenure of their Lands."[50] An anti-Andros pamphlet from the period recounts an argument that pitted Rev. John Higginson of Salem against the governor when the latter visited that town. The lands of New England, Andros maintained, were originally the king's and with the revocation of Massachusetts's charter, they reverted to the Crown. Higginson, a Puritan minister who seemed to speak for many fellow-colonists on this point, replied that the land belonged not to the king but to his American subjects, and this by virtue of two considerations: first, "by a right of just occupation," since settlers had "subdued and replenished" the earth; second, "by a right of purchase from the Indians." (For Higginson, as for hundreds of other Anglo-American apologists for colonization over the years, these two lines of justification somehow complemented rather than contradicted one another.) His arguments simply infuriated the governor and his companions, one of whom was heard "vilifying the Indian title, saying, they were brutes." Another Massachusetts interlocutor quoted in the pamphlet, Joseph Lynde of Charlestown, reported on his

[49] Richard Bushman, *From Puritan to Yankee: Character and the Social Order in Connecticut, 1690–1765* (Cambridge, Mass.: Harvard University Press, 1967), 46.

[50] Quoted in John Frederick Martin, *Profits in the Wilderness: Entrepreneurship and the Founding of New England Towns in the Seventeenth Century* (Chapel Hill: University of North Carolina Press, 1991), 263.

unavailing efforts to convince Andros of the validity of his title. "At another time after shewing him an Indian deed for land, he said, that their hand was no more worth than a scratch of a bear's paw, undervaluing all my titles, though every way legal under our former charter government."[51]

Notwithstanding their proto-Lockean tendency to ground property rights in the act of cultivating and "subduing" the land, New England's early colonists had come to rely on "Indian deeds" to document title. No wonder then that Edmund Andros unleashed a storm when he pronounced Indian deeds "no more worth than a scratch of a bear's paw." Rev. John Higginson would have been particularly distressed to hear the governor dismiss the notion that natives ever owned the land in the first place. His town, Salem, was one of several in Massachusetts that, in anticipation of the new regime, had hastily concluded a late-in-the-day Indian purchase to strengthen its ownership claims and those of its inhabitants. On the eleventh of October 1686, representatives from Salem had found nine natives from the praying town of Natick who agreed, in consideration of the sum of twenty pounds, to sign a very elaborate parchment document that conveyed to the township all the lands within its boundaries, lands that by then had been occupied by colonists for almost sixty years. Similar deeds were concluded about the same time on behalf of Lynn, Beverly, Marblehead and other towns.[52] It was a windfall for a few lucky native survivors of King Philip's War – and the episode speaks volumes about the strange legal logic underlying the New England practice of "Indian purchases." However, Salem and the other towns had wasted their money: Governor Andros was supremely unimpressed with these retroactive deeds.

Not only did the governor reject Indian deeds; he did not recognize New England townships as legitimate legal actors. This really was the nub of the conflict. Whereas the chartered colonies were, by and large, legally empowered to grant lands to individuals, they had chosen to subgrant the bulk of their domains to self-organized townships; these in turn

---

[51] *The Revolution in New-England Justified, and the People There Vindicated from the Aspersions Cast upon Them by Mr. John Palmer, in His Pretended Answer to the Declaration Published by the Inhabitants of Boston, and the Country Adjacent, on the Day When They Secured Their Late Oppressors, Who Acted by an Illegal and Arbitrary Commission from the Late King James*, (Boston: Reprinted and sold by Isaiah Thomas, 1691), 18–19, 21.

[52] Sidney Perley, *The Indian Land Titles of Essex County, Massachusetts* (Salem, Mass.: Essex Book and Print Club, 1912), 64–92.

distributed some of their land to settlers in severalty, held some of it as an agricultural commons and saved some to be distributed to later generations of colonists. However, as Edmund Andros saw it, townships had no corporate standing in law and so properties they had granted to individuals lacked validity.[53]

Impractical though they found it to force all affected proprietors to take out new patents, the Andros administration did mount a partially successful assault on the "undivided commons," lands held in reserve within a given township for eventual allocation to the rising generation of settlers. The governor considered that lands not in the possession of any individual reverted to the Crown; in some notorious cases, he issued grants to applicants who petitioned for unoccupied land within a township. Edward Randolph, one of his closest advisors, claimed 700 acres from the commons of Lynn as well as other tracts in Massachusetts and Rhode Island.[54] Protests and legal opposition prevented Randolph from gaining clear title to the lands he had been awarded before the fall of the Andros regime, but the threat to township control was serious enough to send shock waves through New England society. Actually, it had been apparent even before the Dominion of New England was established that undivided commons were vulnerable to a legal challenge. Anticipating Andros's assault on township ownership, the Connecticut General Court had in 1685 ordered townships to take out patents in the name of the "proprietors inhabitants of the Towne."[55] Though no change was intended in the actual management and distribution of township commons, the effect was to vest ownership in each inhabitant as a fee-simple estate rather than in the township as a corporation.[56]

Quite apart from Edmund Andros's hostility to townships, undivided township commons were emerging as a genuine problem in the second half of the seventeenth century. As we saw in Chapter 6, there had long been uncertainty as to who exactly was entitled to share in these lands – all township residents or only the original township grantees? – and this due to ambiguities inherent in the New England tenure system. It was in the decades immediately preceding the establishment of the Dominion of New England that many townships were declaring themselves "closed" in

---

[53] Richard R. Johnson, *Adjustment to Empire: The New England Colonies, 1675–1715* (New Brunswick, N.J.: Rutgers University Press, 1981), 80.
[54] Barnes, *Dominion of New England*, 195–99; Martin, *Profits in the Wilderness*, 265–66.
[55] Quoted in Martin, *Profits in the Wilderness*, 267.
[56] Bushman, *Puritan to Yankee*, 46.

the sense that newcomers who acquired a lot by purchase or grant would not be entitled to share in future divisions of the town commons. It is also apparent that the land policies pursued by Governor Andros gave a big boost to this movement in the direction of restricted ownership. John Frederick Martin identifies the years between 1685 and 1720 as "the era of dramatic change for New England towns," for it was then that, in the majority of cases, a corporation of proprietors came into existence separate from the township as a local political institution.[57] Connecticut's defensive legislation, passed in 1685 to head off the anticipated assault on town commons, had the effect of freezing the then-current ownership of each township. "Before 1685 the town inhabitants held common lands as a group and distributed them to admitted inhabitants, while after 1685 the undivided lands belonged to the individual proprietors as their fee-simple estates. Title was vested in the specific persons named or implied in the patents and not in the members of the town corporations."[58] Such changes affected not only who could claim township land, but also how it would be owned. Township proprietors could sell their shares in the commons, even to nonresidents. This was an important step in the direction of commodification, providing unprecedented opportunities for accumulation and speculation as the price of land rose.

It would be an exaggeration to treat these changes as a great rupture with the New England past touched off by Andros's reform attempts. Even by the end of the seventeenth century, colonial property-making continued to be dominated by the subsistence and reproductive needs of settler households. There were nevertheless significant shifts in the direction of speculation and a growing tendency to treat land as interchangeable with money. The colony governments and the British Empire itself were at the forefront of this movement as they, like the rulers of the Spanish empire, were turning to land as a source of revenue. In the wake of the Dominion of New England interlude, town proprietors were increasingly looking to land sales as a source of revenue, while the colonies themselves were following suit. By the beginning of the eighteenth century, the colony of Connecticut was drawing revenue from the disposal of public lands to finance military expenditures and to pay for the construction of a new state house.[59] Money-making was never a central objective of land policy during the colonial period, but by the

---

[57] Ibid., 276.   [58] Ibid., 46–47.   [59] Ibid., 74–75.

end of the seventeenth century there were advance signs of a tendency that would fully take hold a century later (see Chapter 11), to fiscalize the granting of land. The Edmund Andros regime did not act alone to bring about these changes, but it did make its contribution to accelerating that important shift in the nature of property in land.

American historians are accustomed to seeing this and associated mid-colonial transformations in a strictly New England/US field of vision, whether as a symptom of spiritual "declension," as an aspect of the triumph of individualistic over communitarian values or, to borrow Richard Bushman's memorable phrase, as a shift "from Puritan to Yankee."[60] Such a national framing of the subject, along with a tendency to favor explanations emphasizing an internal dialectic of mental states, attitudes and values, lend themselves to a narrative of national identity in formation. But when we consider the affinities between changes in landed property within the New England context and roughly contemporaneous developments in New France and New Spain, and when we note the general pattern of linkages connecting property formation and imperial state building, the reconfiguration of New England land holding begins to look more like an instance of something much larger, an evolution that took place at the level of the Atlantic world. In their very different but nonetheless convergent ways, the governments of England, France and Spain made efforts to dig into North American soil, building territorial states overseas, asserting metropolitan rule and establishing colonial tenures deriving from their respective monarchies.

THE ROYAL PROCLAMATION OF 1763

Though Edmund Andros's plan to establish imperial control over New England land titles collapsed, the British Empire did not abandon its efforts to give practical meaning to its claim to eminent domain in America. In the mid-eighteenth century, the focus shifted to property formation on the trans-Appalachian frontier. At that time, the region was emerging as both a magnet for colonization and a dangerous flash point for conflict with the French Empire and its indigenous allies. The Board of Trade therefore took charge of Indian relations through the appointment of two Superintendents, one for the north and one

---

[60] Bushman, *From Puritan to Yankee*. See also Perry Miller, *The New England Mind*, 2 vols. (Cambridge, Mass.: Harvard University Press, 1939, 1953).

for the south, in 1754.[61] A dispute over the Ohio Valley quickly led to a major conflagration, during the course of which Canada was invaded and New France ceased to exist. The native nations of the West remained unconquered, however, and with settlers beginning to cross the mountains into the rich lands of the Ohio and Mississippi watersheds and with the British maintaining military posts they had promised to abandon, a renewed conflict threatened in 1763. It was in this emergency context that Britain issued a Royal Proclamation in October of that year establishing Canada as a British colony while restraining and regulating the procedures of colonization and property formation in the indigenous territories west of the Appalachians. Meanwhile, the terrible, and entirely predictable, conflict known as Pontiac's War had broken out in May 1763. The hope of averting the conflagration by stemming the settler invasion proved vain (and not only because the Proclamation reached America too late to make a difference). Yet the edict would nevertheless have lasting consequences, invoked in later centuries in discussions concerning sovereignty and aboriginal title. Whatever the substantive provisions of the Royal Proclamation did or did not say, the important fact in the present context is that this attempt to regularize colonial property formation had come from the European center of empire.

Though historians sometimes focus on the way the Proclamation tried and failed to erect a settler-proof dam along the ridge of the Appalachians, it is clear that its main thrust was to set down basic guidelines regarding settlement, property and jurisdiction – in other words, to regulate procedures of dispossession – rather than to trace a permanent boundary between colonial and indigenous domains.[62] The framers of this document casually assume that the western interior is already subject to British sovereignty, but consider it "just and reasonable" that "the several Nations or Tribes of Indians" there should not "be molested or disturbed" in their possession of unceded lands. These lands are reserved,

---

[61] Daniel K. Richter, "Native Peoples of North America and the Eighteenth-Century British Empire," in *The Oxford History of the British Empire*, vol. 2: *The Eighteenth Century*, ed. P. J. Marshall (Oxford: Oxford University Press, 1998), 364–65.

[62] The text can be consulted in *Documents Relating to the Constitutional History of Canada, 1759–1791*, ed. Adam Shortt and Arthur G. Doughty (Ottawa: King's Printer, 1918), 163–68. On the Royal Proclamation and the context in which it was conceived and promulgated, see Gregory Evans Dowd, *War under Heaven: Pontiac, the Indian Nations, and the British Empire* (Baltimore: Johns Hopkins University Press, 2002), 177–79, 233–36; Colin Calloway, *The Scratch of a Pen: 1763 and the Transformation of North America* (New York: Oxford University Press, 2006), 92–100.

"under our Sovereignty, Protection and Dominion, for the use of the said Indians." Noting that "great Frauds and Abuses have been committed in purchasing Lands of the Indians," the king forbids unauthorized "Purchases or Settlements." Dispossession is by no means ruled out, however. "If at any time any of the said Indians should be inclined to dispose of the said Lands, the same shall be Purchased only for Us, in our Name, at some public Meeting or Assembly of the said Indians."[63] As Pontiac's War was drawing to a close, Sir William Johnson and other officers of the Crown distributed copies of the Proclamation to the western nations and gave them assurances in the course of peace negotiations that Britain would not take their lands without consent.[64]

In many respects, the Proclamation represents continuity with the Anglo-American past. Its commitment to upholding the ideal of land cession by voluntary contract harks back to the days of Roger Williams, while the assertion of a state monopoly over native purchases recalls seventeenth-century General Courts' attempts to regulate such transactions. Much about the Royal Proclamation represents a new departure, however.[65] Rather than merely requiring colonists or townships to secure official permission to conclude "Indian deeds," it insists that only agents of government could negotiate territorial cessions. Under the regime it envisions, property would never pass directly from natives to settlers. Between the processes of land surrender and property reconfiguration stood the state in its capacity as direct proprietor *pro tem*. Though colonies, as represented by their royal governors, had an important role to play in the new system, a crucial feature of the Proclamation is the active role it assigns to the Crown. This was an imperial enactment boldly asserting centralized imperial control over "Indian affairs" and therefore over frontier lands, and in that respect, it represents a culmination of sorts of earlier initiatives in the Spanish, French and British Empires.

---

[63] *Documents Relating to the Constitutional History of Canada, 1759–1791*, 167.

[64] John Borrows, "Wampum at Niagara: The Royal Proclamation, Canadian Legal History, and Self-Government," in *Aboriginal and Treaty Rights in Canada: Essays on Law Equality, and Respect for Difference*, ed. Michael Asch (Vancouver: UBC Press, 1997), 167–68; J. R. Miller, *Compact, Contract, Covenant: Aboriginal Treaty-Making in Canada* (Toronto: University of Toronto Press, 2009), 72–73; William Johnson, *The Papers of Sir William Johnson*, 14 vols. (Albany: State University of New York, 1921), 4: 332.

[65] There were indeed precedents foreshadowing most provisions of the Proclamation, but as a general statement on colonial property formation, it does mark a real turning point. See Stuart Banner, *How the Indians Lost Their Land: Law and Power on the Frontier* (Cambridge, Mass.: Harvard University Press, 2005), 85–95.

This intervention from the center of empire did not sit well with colonists, particularly with those who hoped to make money from western lands. Ordinary settlers, brushing past the Proclamation Line of exclusion and "squatting" on reserved indigenous territory without regard to formalities of title, were not the main source of complaint. Rather, it was the eastern speculators who coveted native lands purely as a lucrative investment who objected most loudly. Land speculation was, of course, nothing new at this time, but it had entered a new phase as of the mid-eighteenth century. Men with access to capital and political influence had begun organizing themselves into associations, such as the Ohio Company, which through grants and purchases accumulated claims to vast tracts with the sole purpose of later extracting a profit from settlers.[66] Several future revolutionary heroes such as Patrick Henry and George Washington were among the most active speculators. They bided their time during the "French and Indian Wars" when western expansion was blocked, eagerly anticipating spectacular profits once peace returned and rustic hordes crossed the Appalachians, ready to buy land. The Royal Proclamation frustrated the speculators' designs, for they, more than the settlers, required clear legal title; that really was all they would have to sell.[67] The British administration stood accused of, in effect, stealing land from Americans; the 1763 edict infringed on both the colonists' freedom to buy lands and the natives' natural freedom to sell. In denouncing the proclamation, land speculators and their allies posed as defenders of both colonial liberty and indigenous rights. "Suddenly," writes Robert Williams, "even the most hardened land-market capitalist assumed the mantle of zealous advocate of the Indians' natural-law right to engage in unregulated real-estate transactions." Colonists' grievances over the Royal Proclamation merged with other issues and eventually found expression in the Declaration of Independence.[68]

[66] Bernard Bailyn, *Voyagers to the West: A Passage in the Peopling of America on the Eve of the Revolution* (New York: Alfred A. Knopf, 1986), 355–58; Daniel K. Richter, *Before the Revolution: America's Ancient Pasts* (Cambridge, Mass.: Harvard University Press, 2011), 369–73.

[67] Woody Holton, *Forced Founders: Indians, Debtors, Slaves, and the Making of the American Revolution in Virginia* (Chapel Hill: University of North Carolina Press, 1999), 3–38.

[68] Robert A. Williams, *The American Indian in Western Legal Thought: The Discourses of Conquest* (New York: Oxford University Press, 1990), 271–80 (quotation at 272); Banner, *How the Indians Lost Their Land*, 85–111; Holton, *Forced Founders*, 35.

North of the future United States, the Proclamation of 1763 would have a very different, but equally consequential impact. The edict divided what had been New France into its component parts, creating a colonial space in the St. Lawrence Valley – what the French called Canada, now rechristened the "Province of Quebec" – and an imperial/indigenous space, the zone the French called the "pays d'en haut." Since Canada remained within the British Empire, the Proclamation, and especially its provisions regarding the acquisition of native territories, entered the legal canon there. Whereas the settler elite of the Thirteen Colonies had seen the proclamation as a provocative extension of British authority over colonial property formation, a different reading came to prevail in Canada. There it would eventually be incorporated into a specifically English-Canadian national myth of peaceful and orderly fair dealing between settler regimes and native nations. Idealizing the proclamation's commitment to procedural justice, its insistence that land surrenders must be based on voluntary negotiation tied to material compensation, some writers go so far as to present the Royal Proclamation as the foundation stone for a national tradition of conducting indigenous-nonindigenous relations in "a collaborative spirit"[69] – as though the French had never respected native territory before 1763, and as though the British Empire and its Canadian successor state assembled a national territory through truly voluntary negotiations and treaty agreements that were honored.

Native people, in Canada especially, developed a third reading of the Royal Proclamation, beginning not long after 1763 and continuing to the present day. The printed copies of the document that were distributed to indigenous communities as tokens of a British commitment to just treatment were carefully preserved, along with wampum belts that memorialized words spoken by imperial officials when they gave assurances that lands would not be appropriated without negotiations and compensation. There is evidence from the 1830s of Quebec Algonquin and Nipissing bands bringing forward yellowing copies of the Proclamation as part of their (largely unsuccessful) protest against settler encroachments on their hunting grounds.[70] Over the years, as colonization pressed in ever more insistently and as indigenous people fought back, the latter would

---

[69] Greg Poelzer and Kenneth Coates. *From Treaty Peoples to Treaty Nation: A Road Map for All Canadians* (Vancouver: UBC Press, 2015), 5.

[70] Alain Beaulieu, *La question des terres autochtones au Québec, 1760–1860* (Varennes, QC: Ministère de la Justice et Ministère des Ressources naturelles du Québec, 2002), 306–12.

frequently cite the proclamation's provisions for orderly dispossession. The principle that land surrenders must be voluntary and tied to material compensation, the implication that indigenous peoples negotiate as independent nations, the requirement that their dealings be with the highest level of imperial authority: all these provide recourse and legal leverage to peoples subject to colonial power. The fact that the Proclamation's promise of procedural justice was so often violated over the years does not detract from its importance as a legal resource to remedy historic wrongs and to ward off current threats. In sharp contrast to the self-congratulatory settler-national view of the 1763 document as a landmark of mutual respect, the indigenous approach tends to treat it as an opportunity to hold the colonizers to account for deviations from their own stated principles.

In the immediate historical context of 1763, however, the Royal Proclamation looks less like a charter of indigenous rights than a bold assertion of British sovereignty. Any rights it conferred derived from the assumption that the British Empire possessed a superior authority over the indigenous nations of the Great Lakes/Ohio Valley region, at that point free agents and unconquered proprietors of their respective territories. The proclamation's claim to control over land cessions should be understood mainly in the context of ongoing struggles between the metropolitan center and the colonies over the processes of colonial property formation. Considerations of military security urged the British to take prompt and decisive action to restrain the destabilizing intrusions of settlers and speculators in the wake of the Seven Years' War, but the longer strategy was to reinforce imperial authority over this crucial aspect of territorial expansion. In approaching relations with indigenous nations as a problem of territories and boundaries, one that revolved around procedures devised for transforming land into settler property, the Royal Proclamation appears as a culmination of sorts to the earlier history of colonial-era dispossession.

PART III

CONCLUSION AND EPILOGUE

Property and Dispossession in an Age of Revolution

THE ELUSIVE IDEAL OF ABSOLUTE OWNERSHIP

In the late-eighteenth century age of Atlantic Revolution, property emerged as a question of the highest importance. As established sovereignties were broken down and reconstructed on new foundations, there were searching reconsiderations of the nature and legitimacy of property in land, property in human beings, property in the structuring of family relations, property as a constituent of personal identity and civic standing and property as point of connection between society and state. In the general program of sweeping clean the accumulated detritus of history, there would be ambitious efforts to establish property anew. The plurality of property practices across the Atlantic World, their flagrant ambiguities and internal inconsistencies, were to be done away with in favor of a simple, rational system of property, clearly inscribed in law and universally applicable. The ideals of private property and absolute ownership shone as beacons of hope in the midst of a general effort to make the world anew. In his influential global study, *Birth of the Modern World 1780–1914*, C. A. Bayly writes that "this setting of universal standards for the holding of property was one of the most important changes of the whole era."[1]

Standards were indeed set, property was redefined and universality was proclaimed in the Age of Revolution; without a doubt, major transformations occurred in the realm of landed property. What is far less clear,

---

[1] C. A. Bayly, *Birth of the Modern World 1780–1914: Global Connections and Comparisons* (Oxford: Blackwell, 2004), 112.

however, is whether or not the clean-sweep revolutionary rhetoric of the period accurately describes what happened on the ground and in the different European countries and overseas possessions affected by the bracing atmosphere of the time. Sometimes the wording of theoretical pronouncements and legal enactments can obscure as much as they elucidate about the real nature of historical change, especially where empires and colonialism are concerned. In a study of nineteenth-century Egypt, Timothy Mitchell makes a point about law and property that may be applicable to the Atlantic world in the Age of Revolution. "The law of property," Mitchell writes, "gains its power by appearing as an abstraction. It seems to stand as a conceptual structure, based not on particular claims or histories but on 'principles true in every country,' in the words of a British colonial administrator."[2] In what follows, it will be important to keep in mind the distinction between the abstract categories of public discourse about property and the actual practices of property formation and dispossession that took place on North American ground.

At one level, it is clear that "property" was a concept that fired imaginations in the late eighteenth and early nineteenth century as never before. Typically, the term was equated with private property and frequently it was coupled with the notion of fundamental "rights." In legal circles, William Blackstone's hyperbolic view of property as "that sole and despotic dominion which one man claims and exercises over the external things of the world, in total exclusion of the right of any other individual in the universe,"[3] commanded assent because it seemed to capture an essential truth about how entitlements *ought* to work. Property also occupied a prominent place in the works of the Classical Economists of the time: their analyses of agricultural rent posited a simplified world, far removed from the actual tenure conditions prevailing in François Quesnay's France or Adam Smith's Scotland, peopled by pure proprietors and pure tenants whose relations were regulated by the market rather than by ancient customs backed by political power.[4]

---

[2] Timothy Mitchell, *Rule of Experts: Egypt, Techno-Politics, Modernity* (Berkeley: University of California Press, 2002), 11.

[3] William Blackstone, *Blackstone's Commentaries on the Laws of England in Four Volumes* (London: Cavendish, 2001), book 2, ch. 1, p. 2.

[4] François Quesnay, *Quesnay's Tableau Économique*, ed. Marguerite Steinfeld Kuczynski and Ronald L. Meek (London: Macmillan, 1972); Adam Smith, *An Inquiry into the Nature and Causes of the Wealth of Nations* (New York: Random House, 1937); Robert L. Heilbroner, *The Worldly Philosophers: The Great Economic Thinkers* (London: Allen Lane, 1969), 16–101; Keith Tribe, *Land, Labour and Economic Discourse* (London:

The philosophers Kant and Hegel wrote of property as a basic constituent of human personality and individual liberty.[5] All these intellectual currents tended both to exalt property as a basic organizing principle in society and politics and, at the same time, implicitly to call for a massive overhaul of existing property relations.

The American and French Revolutions enshrined property as a right that the state had an imperative obligation to protect; ironically enough, both revolutions were also the occasion for ambitious attempts to remake property in land, guaranteeing tensions between the impulse to rationalize property and the obligation to preserve existing rights. From an early stage of the trans-Atlantic property revolution, Thomas Jefferson emerged as an influential and uncompromisingly radical voice. His 1774 pamphlet, *A Summary View of the Rights of British America*, dismissed the entire edifice of English land tenure then prevailing in the American colonies as an illegitimate contrivance of Norman conquerors, one that imposed "feudal burthens" derived from "the fictitious principle that all lands belong originally to the king."[6] Rather than freehold or any other version of tenure ("tenure," after all, meant "holding," and "holding from" an individual or even a state implied a hierarchy of property claims), Jefferson believed in "allodial" property as an absolute and primordial claim to land, prior to any state enactment. Over the course of the revolutionary period, he would insist that private property so constituted provided the foundation of liberty and served as the proper basis for citizenship.[7] Unsuccessful in his attempt to have his version of allodial ownership inserted into Virginia's state constitution, Jefferson did manage to get statutes passed in 1779 abolishing quitrents and tenures and instituting "absolute and unconditional property."[8] Unqualified property rights, widely distributed among white men, were central to

---

Routledge, 1978); Margaret Schabas, *The Natural Origins of Economics* (Chicago: University of Chicago Press, 2005).

[5] Alan Ryan, *Property and Political Theory* (Oxford: B. Blackwell, 1984), 73–90; Jeremy Waldron, *The Right to Private Property* (Oxford: Oxford University Press, 1988), 266–78, 343–90; Peter Garnsey, *Thinking about Property: From Antiquity to the Age of Revolution* (Cambridge: Cambridge University Press, 2007), 204–33.

[6] Quoted in David Konig, "Legal Fictions and the Rule(s) of Law: The Jeffersonian Critique of Common-Law Adjudication," in *The Many Legalities of Early America*, ed. Christopher L. Tomlins and Bruce H. Mann (Chapel Hill: University of North Carolina Press, 2001), 114.

[7] Christopher M. Curtis, *Jefferson's Freeholders and the Politics of Ownership in the Old Dominion* (New York: Cambridge University Press, 2012).

[8] Ibid., 53.

Jefferson's democratic vision for America, but things did not work out entirely according to his plans; indeed, how could they? As long as "unconditional ownership" included unfettered power to alienate land and to pledge it against debts, proprietors would be in perpetual danger of losing their land, and along with it their liberty and civic status. The omnipresence of debt and the dynamic forces of the market economy proved too unstable a foundation for an ownership democracy, with the result that Jefferson and his contemporaries were soon hedging "absolute" property with various restrictions.[9]

Jefferson's commitment to absolute private property did not come out of nowhere. No doubt it formed part and parcel of a broader ideology of white male equality; together with his campaign against entail, it meshed with the anti-aristocratic, anti-monarchical thrust of the revolution. And yet there is surely significance in the fact that the revolutionary's views on the subject were forged in the specific context of public controversy over property formation in the trans-Appalachian West. Son of a founder of the Ohio Company, Jefferson matured in a Virginia political milieu where land company investors and their allies fiercely objected to the Crown's attempts to limit access to the indigenous lands they coveted. The Royal Proclamation of 1763 was the first in a series of objectionable measures. Later came the Dartmouth Plan, designed to impose systematic control over the granting of Crown lands, and the Quebec Act of 1774, which placed the Ohio country under Canadian jurisdiction, measures that provided the immediate stimulus for Jefferson to write *A Summary View*.[10] The colonial elites that Jefferson claimed to speak for might be divided over which colonies and which circles of speculators should have precedence in the West, but they tended to agree on some basic points: native peoples have a right to alienate their lands, colonists have a right to acquire the same, and the king of England has no right to stop them.[11] A concept of hard and unambiguous property rights, grounded in nature rather than gifted by the sovereign, appeared as a welcome theoretical foundation for this viewpoint.

---

[9] Ibid., 86, 233; Claire Priest, "Creating an American Property Law: Alienability and Its Limits in American History," *Harvard Law Review* 120 (2006): 449–56.

[10] Curtis, *Jefferson's Freeholders*, 44.

[11] Robert A. Williams, *The American Indian in Western Legal Thought: The Discourses of Conquest* (New York: Oxford University Press, 1990), 271–80; Andrew Fitzmaurice, *Sovereignty, Property and Empire, 1500–2000* (Cambridge: Cambridge University Press, 2014), 194–99.

Questions of property were at the heart of the French Revolution as well. The "Declaration of the Rights of Man and the Citizen" (1789) lists property as one of the basic "natural and imprescriptible rights of man." It goes on to describe it as "an inviolable and sacred right."[12] The liquidation of feudal privileges, together with the confiscation and redistribution of church lands, were central elements in the wider drama that brought down the *ancien régime*. In place of the bewildering jumble of seigneurial privileges – lucrative rents and monopolies, as well as jurisdiction rights – that overlay almost all land holdings in France, revolutionaries aimed to institute a pure and simple form of individual land ownership. The thrust of their project was to introduce clear distinctions, in Rafe Blaufarb's words, "between the political and social, state and society, sovereignty and ownership, the public and private."[13] On the short term, frustration was inevitable, if only because the revolutionary state, having staked its faltering finances largely on estates confiscated from the Church and from counterrevolutionary emigrés, much of it in the form of seigneuries, became the greatest feudal landlord in the country. Beyond that issue lay the more fundamental question of whether state and society, public and private, etc. could ever be fully disentangled.

It was under the regime of Napoleon Bonaparte that French property law was systematically recast as a rational and comprehensive set of rules. The civil code, promulgated in 1804, seems to echo Blackstone's and Jefferson's uncompromising view of ownership. "Property," it proclaims, "is the right to make use of and dispose of things in the most absolute

---

[12] "Declaration of the Rights of Man and Citizen," in Georges Lefebvre, *The Coming of the French Revolution* (New York: Random House, 1947), 189. See also Garnsey, *Thinking about Property*, 221–25; Joseph Comby, "L'impossible propriété absolue," in *Un droit inviolable et sacré. La propriété*, ed. Catherine Chavelet (Paris: ADEF, 1991), 9–20. Comby notes that the 1789 text actually uses the plural "properties," implying a commitment to protecting existing entitlements from arbitrary power. Over the course of the revolutionary years, the plural would be changed to the singular, indicating a shift to a more radical impulse to transform property into a uniform system.

[13] Rafe Blaufarb, *The Great Demarcation: The French Revolution and the Invention of Modern Property* (New York: Oxford University Press, 2016), 14. Note that while Blaufarb brings out the tangled and often contradictory nature of the transformation, he argues that the revolutionary period really did see a fundamental "transition from a system of real estate based on hierarchical tenure to one based on independent ownership" (ibid., 12). See also Rafe Blaufarb, "Propriété, politique et délimitation des groupes sociaux: le débat sur les rentes foncières, 1789–1811," *Annales historiques de la Révolution française*, no. 358 (January 2010): 119–40; Hannah Calloway, "Property and Its Contents in Revolutionary France," paper delivered at the annual meeting of the Western Society for French History, San Antonio, Texas, November 2014.

manner, provided that nothing is done contrary to the laws and regulations,"[14] setting the tone for civil law regimes as subsequently established across much of Europe and Latin America, as well as former French colonies such as Quebec and Louisiana. More clearly than is the case in the English common law tradition, absolute ownership rights stand at the center of civil law property doctrine. However, the very sentence that asserts those supposedly "absolute" rights ends in a clause that subordinates them to state legislation. The Napoleonic Code certainly favored strong property rights, but the word "absolute" was strictly a rhetorical flourish.

In the third great Atlantic World revolution, the Haitian Revolution, the property form centrally at issue was of course slavery. However, although the ownership of humans never lost the saliency it acquired when slave insurrections broke out in 1791, later stages of the revolution brought the question of land to the fore. Even after slavery had been formally abolished, Toussaint Louverture and his successors tried to keep the sugar plantations intact, which meant forcing ex-slaves to continue working for those agroindustrial enterprises. Plantation workers fought back, however, carving out garden plots for their own subsistence from the large estates. Eventually they prevailed: the plantation system collapsed and independent Haiti emerged as a land of independent peasants supporting themselves on smallholdings. As Carolyn Fick puts it, "A personal claim to the land upon which one labored and from which to derive and express one's individuality was, for the black laborers, a necessary and an essential element in their vision of freedom."[15] Widely recognized as the most profound of the revolutions that shook the Atlantic World in the late eighteenth century because it destroyed slavery while securing national independence, the Haitian Revolution might well qualify as the most radical as far as actual changes to landed property are concerned. It was in Haiti that self-emancipated black people transformed the property regime most directly and concretely. In the realm of property, the American and French Revolutions, long on rhetoric and declarations of principle, seem by comparison more uncertain and less coherent.

---

[14] Code civil, article 544. www.legifrance.gouv.fr. My translation. "La propriété est le droit de jouir et disposer des choses de la manière la plus absolue, pourvu qu'on n'en fasse pas un usage prohibé par les lois ou par les règlements."

[15] Carolyn E. Fick, *The Making of Haiti: The Saint Domingue Revolution from Below* (Knoxville: University of Tennessee Press, 1990), 249. See also Robert K. Lacerte, "The Evolution of Land and Labor in the Haitian Revolution, 1791–1820," *The Americas* 34 (1978): 449–59; Laurent Dubois, *Avengers of the New World: The Story of the Haitian Revolution* (Cambridge, Mass.: Harvard University Press, 2004), 162–65, 185, 239–40.

Hispanic America experienced its revolutionary moment a little later than France, Haiti and the United States, but here too property emerged as a core issue. It was a crisis at the imperial center touched off by Napoleon's invasion of Spain that provoked political upheavals in New Spain and all around the Hispanic world. With most of the country occupied by French forces, representatives from across the kingdom, as well as from Spanish America, met as a national *cortes* in the besieged city of Cádiz, 1810–14, to reconstruct a government of resistance for Spain and its empire. They were determined to rebuild the national/imperial state along modern lines and to that end they promulgated the liberal Cádiz Constitution of 1812, proclaiming citizenship and equal rights for all.[16] Two crucial provisions of that document – the abolition of racial categories and the reform of municipal institutions – would have a lasting influence on Mexico, even as the country fought free of Spanish rule and established itself as independent empire, later republic. The Cádiz constitution declared an end to the legal distinction between "Indians" and "Spaniards," a fundamental feature of the colonial order; in effect, it accorded full citizenship to natives. Henceforth, there would not be separate "republics" for "Spaniards" and "Indians," each with its distinctive land tenure and local administration. The *cortes* also decreed that unoccupied lands and surplus town commons be broken up and sold as private property. Leading Mexican politicians of the early independence era would follow the lead of the Cádiz regime as they attempted to eliminate Old Regime "privileges" rooted in the *mano muerta* ("dead hand") that blocked the sale, and thus the free circulation, of land belonging to the Church, municipal *ejidos* and Indian pueblos. Where land was concerned, their aim was fundamentally similar to that of other revolutionaries of the period: institute a uniform regime of transferable private property. They were no more successful than their counterparts in other parts of the Atlantic World.

In Mexico, as in France, the United States and elsewhere, the liberal ideal of absolute ownership turned out to be, in the words of the legal historian Joseph Comby, "a mirage briefly encountered along the road."[17] No sooner had the French revolutionaries proclaimed private property a "sacred right" than they began to hedge it round with

[16] Jaime E. Rodríguez O., *The Independence of Spanish America* (New York: Cambridge University Press, 1998), 82–92.
[17] Comby, "L'impossible propriété absolue," 17. My translation. "Cette propriété absolue qui fut un mirage rapidement croisé sur la route."

restrictions and regulations. In the revolutionary period, there was legislation on access rights to waterways for transportation and fishing, prohibitions against leaving agricultural lands to waste, state claims to subterranean mineral rights, hunting rights and common pastures. In later centuries such "servitudes" only became more numerous since modern economies, especially in cities, depend on urban planning and a host of utilities and transportation facilities that have to take precedence over proprietors' rights. The economic value of property, he notes, depends on such infringements on absolute ownership.[18] Morton J. Horowitz detects a similar pattern where property in the early American republic is concerned. His thesis is that, following the Revolution, courts tended to favor economic development over strict property rights, with the result that, to take one example, dams for industrial purposes could interfere with fishing and flood farmlands and the landowners affected would have less recourse than in the past.[19] Regulatory and judicial practice on both sides of the Atlantic was busily undermining the absolute property that ideological discourses continued to exalt.

According to another legal historian, Robert Gordon, the principle of absolute property was not simply at odds with actual practice, it was an essentially incoherent concept, impossible of realization.[20] Using evidence from eighteenth-century Britain and revolutionary America, Gordon focuses on, among other issues, the problem of family property and inheritance. Revolutionaries like Jefferson were keen to eliminate entail as a restriction placed by the dead on the property rights of the living, but they had no difficulty with wills, a device for transmitting estates favored in English law since the sixteenth century. Wills allow owners – almost always men – a great deal of control over the disposal of property, though unlike entail, that control operates one generation at a time. More fundamentally, property, even as it empowers an owner, disempowers everyone else, "and so invariably restricts freedom while creating it." He goes on: "Absolute dominion is paradoxical at the core. The freedom to do anything one likes with property implies the freedom to create restraints on it, and thus to bind one's own hands or the hands of one's transferees."[21]

---

[18] Ibid., 16–20.

[19] Morton J. Horwitz, *The Transformation of American Law, 1780–1860* (Cambridge, Mass.: Harvard University Press, 1977).

[20] Robert W. Gordon, "Paradoxical Property," in *Early Modern Conceptions of Property*, ed. John Brewer and Susan Staves (London: Routledge, 1996), 95–110.

[21] Ibid., 102.

The fact that pure private property did not and could not exist did not prevent it becoming a potent ideal.

Deeply significant changes took place in North American property relations in the late eighteenth to early nineteenth century, transformations profound enough to merit the term "property revolution." But these changes were not what they appeared to be. Slogans from the period about the "sacred rights of property," programs to rid the world of feudal vestiges and traditional privileges and to replace these with "absolute" ownership of land: these were important ideological developments, but they cannot be taken as objective descriptions of what actually happened. The liberal absolutist property project nevertheless had ominous implications from the point of view of indigenous property and independence. The extension of colonial sovereignty had, in the past, left spaces of various sorts for native residence and subsistence. The nineteenth century would bring increasing impatience with the uncertainties and indeterminacies that indigenous peoples had worked with to ensure their survival.

AFTER NEW FRANCE

The Age of Revolution begins in North America with a false dawn over a defeated New France. During the Seven Years' War (1756–63), the feudal colony of Canada, together with the imperial networks radiating out from it, fell into the hands of a conquering and expanding British Empire, confident of the superiority of its constitution and laws, soon to be regarded as a model for the world. Just around the time when Blackstone was proclaiming the absolutism of private property, and when the Royal Proclamation instituted a policy of orderly negotiated surrenders of native lands to the Crown, the upheavals of war and conquest gave the British an unparalleled ascendancy in North America and seemed to invite them to remake New France in their own idealized image. Would this turn out to be the moment when private property would prevail in the Laurentian colony and when procedures for dispossessing indigenous peoples would at last acquire a uniform and systematic character? Not at all: in fact, more or less the opposite occurred. Seigneurial tenure was instead reinforced in the riverine regions where it had spread under French rule, while English tenure would be introduced in adjacent parts of Canada. Here, the Royal Proclamation's promise of just and transparent land cessions was neither recognized in principle nor observed in practice. Instead, procedural bricolage ensured that tenurial diversity and legal pluralism would prevail even more than they had under French rule. The Age of Revolution in Canada turned out to be mainly an age of counterrevolution.

Among the circumstances shaping property formation under British rule were the property provisions of agreements negotiated at the time New France surrendered. These covenants were multiple, as natives and French made peace with the invaders separately. With Quebec lost and three armies bearing down on Montreal, the last bastion of French power in Canada, Governor Vaudreuil on 8 September 1760 surrendered the colony on the explicit understanding that the property of "seigneurs" and "all other persons" would be respected. The agreement with the British commander also provided that the "Indian allies of his most Christian Majesty, shall be maintained in the Lands they inhabit."[22] This last clause was redundant, for those native allies had already come to terms with the British. Only a week before the fall of Montreal, representatives of the "Seven Nations of Canada," meaning the Kahnawake Iroquois, the St. François Abenaquis and other indigenous communities of the St. Lawrence Valley, had met with the invaders at Oswegatchie, west of the city, to conclude a separate peace. The Oswegatchie treaty was one in a series of such agreements that British officers had negotiated as part of a vast diplomatic offensive aimed at dismantling New France's native alliance system in the last years of the war. The Laurentian villages, long the key to New France's military power,[23] were among the last to go over to the enemy. In seeking out talks, they were driven not only by the urgent need to come to terms with an unstoppable force that threatened their destruction; they also had political motives. If the British were to be the dominant power – and by the summer of 1760 that outcome was not in doubt – the Seven Nations needed to take the initiative to assert their independence and avoid being treated as mere colonial subjects whose persons and lands could be transferred from one empire to another. In a retrospective declaration in 1795, the council of the Seven Nations made all this explicit. "We beg you to observe," a spokesman said, "that we were never conquered by the French; on the contrary, we were always the protectors of the white skins ..." As to lands, the declaration continued,

---

[22] "Articles of Capitulation, Montreal," *Documents Relating to the Constitutional History of Canada, 1759–1791*, ed. Adam Shortt and Arthur G. Doughty, 2nd ed. (Ottawa: J. de L. Taché, King's Printer, 1918), 18–19, 33.

[23] Jean-François Lozier, "In Each Other's Arms: France and the St. Lawrence Mission Villages in War and Peace, 1630–1730," PhD dissertation, University of Toronto, 2012.

these had been given to them by the Maker of Life and they had been pleased to share them with the French.[24]

Handling negotiations for the British side at Oswegatchie was Sir William Johnson, the Superintendant of Indian Affairs, drawing on his deep knowledge of native diplomatic customs and his strong Iroquois connections. No written transcript of the treaty was kept, but Johnson's correspondence basically concurs with the natives' wampum record, as interpreted in subsequent confrontations with government officials, though we need to make allowance for the usual "creative misunder-standings" that, according to Richard White, characterize such agree-ments. Johnson reported that the Seven Nations "submitted" to the British, whereas the native accounts indicate a mutual agreement, one in which the two parties undertook to cease hostilities. The native side thenceforth referred to the British commander/governor as "father," but as is now well understood, such language implied alliance, arbitration and gifts rather than surrender and obedience.[25] It is clear from all accounts that William Johnson promised the Seven Nations secure possession of their lands and the same rights they enjoyed under French imperial rule. Similar undertakings were central to other treaties negotiated around the same time. These are the covenants the indigenous communities of the St. Lawrence Valley would refer to in the future, not to any agreement between representatives of the king of France and his Britannic majesty.[26]

Initially, the new rulers of Canada expected a flood of Anglo-American immigrants to drown the French-Canadian and indigenous populations; accordingly, they made plans to introduce English law and tenure prac-tices. Instructions to the first British governor in 1763, for example, called for land grants in the form of townships, with quitrents, surveying and

---

[24] Quoted in Denys Delâge and Jean-Pierre Sawaya, *Les traités des Sept-Feux avec les Britanniques: droits et pièges d'un héritage colonial au Québec* (Montreal: Septentrion, 2001), 229. My translation. "Vous prient d'observer que nous n'avons jamais été conquis par les françois, qu'au contraire nous avonts toujours été: protecteur des peaux blanche [*sic*] ..."

[25] Richard White, *The Middle Ground: Indians, Empires, and Republics in the Great Lakes Region, 1650–1815* (Cambridge: Cambridge University Press, 1991).

[26] On the Oswegatchie treaty and its context, see Alain Beaulieu, "Les guaranties d'un traité disparu: le traité d'Oswegatchie, 30 août 1760," *Revue juridique thémis* 34 (2000): 369–408. See also Delâge and Sawaya, *Les traités des Sept-Feux avec les Britanniques*, 47–54; Alain Beaulieu, "'Under His Majesty's Protection: The Meaning of the Conquest of New France for the Aboriginal People," in *The Culture of the Seven Years' War: Empire, Identity, and the Arts in the Eighteenth-Century Atlantic World*, ed. Frans De Bruyn and Shaun Regan (Toronto: University of Toronto Press, 2014), 95–97.

title registration.²⁷ In the event, the anticipated influx of American settlers never materialized, since, in the wake of the Seven Years' War, population movement was westward across the Appalachians rather than northward into Canada, and so the colony that had been at the heart of New France remained predominantly French-Canadian space, interspersed with islands of native ground. With no significant Anglophone population to force them to do otherwise, British governors of the new "province of Quebec" generally favored the preservation of French and native property and property forms, as much for tactical political reasons as out of respect for the solemn undertakings concluded at the time of the surrender. The outbreak of Pontiac's War, followed by growing tensions between the Thirteen Colonies and the empire, gave Quebec governors ample reason to placate French and native Canadians where land and tenure were concerned. The upshot was that the St. Lawrence Valley remained a land of fiefs, *rotures* and autonomous indigenous villages.

No new seigneuries would be granted after 1763 and seigneurial courts were abolished, but otherwise the tenure regime was preserved, complete with the laws of the Custom of Paris as regards inheritance, marital property and landed security for debt.²⁸ In the cities, there was some confusion and uncertainty about law and property during the first decade of British rule (settled finally by the Quebec Act, which formally confirmed French private law), but in the countryside habitants continued to pay *cens et rentes* and other charges, much as before the conquest. Notwithstanding the conqueror's assumptions about the superiority of English tenure, many British military officers and merchants were pleased to acquire seigneurial estates (in some cases purchased from emigrating Canadian nobles). Perhaps because they came from a country where landlords had a freer hand to set the terms of tenure in ways that allowed them to take full advantage of market forces, these new seigneurs tended to be quite demanding seigneurs, setting the pace in a postwar trend toward heavier seigneurial exactions.²⁹ A general tendancy in the

---

²⁷ "Instructions to Governor Murray [7 December 1763]," Shortt and Doughty, *Documents Relating to the Constitutional History of Canada, 1759–1791*, 194–95. For the general context of these measures, see A. L. Burt, *The Old Province of Quebec*, 2nd ed., 2 vols. (Toronto: McClelland and Stewart, 1968), 1: 66–89.

²⁸ Benoît Grenier, *Brève histoire du régime seigneurial* (Montréal: Boréal, 2012), 140–49.

²⁹ Lieutenant-Colonel Gabriel Christie exemplifies the grasping British seigneur (though many French-Canadian seigneurs were also part of the trend). See Jan Noel, *The Christie Seigneuries: Estate Management and Settlement in the Upper Richelieu Valley, 1760–1854* (Montreal and Kingston: McGill-Queen's University Press, 1992).

direction of more rigorous estate management had already been apparent under the French régime, but it accelerated during the agricultural boom of the late eighteenth century. Generalized prosperity muted the reactions of the habitants, but the latter's long-term interests were imperiled by the way seigneurs were claiming increased timber rights and greater control over their unconceded domains. Seigneurs had long been accustomed to push against limits to their privileges in such areas, but under British rule the bias of the courts and the government gave them greater latitude. On the whole, a landlord in Britain enjoyed a much higher degree of proprietary control over the lands within his estate than did a Canadian seigneur, and the unconscious tendency within officialdom and the judiciary was to assimilate the latter figure to the former. The fief was favored over the *roture* in a hundred subtle respects, with the ironic result that the St. Lawrence Valley arguably became more feudal under British rule than it had been under the French.[30]

Transformative change of a sort came in 1791, at what might be considered a peak year of the Age of Revolution. Responding both to the migration into Canada of Loyalist refugees from the American Revolution (the first major influx of anglophones) and to the early stages of the French Revolution, Britain divided the province of Quebec in two, designating the western part ("Upper Canada") for Loyalists, with the eastern part ("Lower Canada") remaining predominantly French. The two new colonies were fitted out with elective institutions on a broad franchise. Upper Canada embarked upon a pattern very different from that of its sister province for dispossessing natives and instituting colonial tenure. There land would be acquired from natives through treaty negotiations before being formed into townships and granted out to settlers on the "free and common soccage" tenure that had long prevailed in the Thirteen Colonies. Within Lower Canada, seigneurial tenure and the Custom of Paris continued in force in the St. Lawrence Valley, while

---

[30] William Bennett Munro, *The Seigniorial System in Canada: A Study in French Colonial Policy* (New York: Longmans Green, 1907), 204–7; Fernand Ouellet, "Le régime seigneurial dans le Québec (1760–1854)," in *Éléments d'histoire sociale du Bas-Canada* (Montreal: Hurtubise, 1972), 91–110; Allan Greer, *Peasant, Lord, and Merchant: Rural Society in Three Quebec Parishes, 1740–1840* (Toronto: University of Toronto Press, 1985), 122–39; Christian Dessureault, "L'évolution du régime seigneurial canadien de 1760 à 1854: essai de synthèse," in *Le régime seigneurial au Québec 150 ans après. Bilans et perspectives de recherches à l'occasion de la commémoration du 150e anniversaire de l'abolition du régime seigneurial*, ed. Alain Laberge and Benoît Grenier (Quebec City: Centre interuniversitaire d'études québécoises, 2009), 23–37.

beyond the limits of fiefs previously granted by the French, land would now be granted to settlers under free and common soccage, complete with English private law. The 1790s saw large tracts granted to American and British immigrants in areas close to the US border and known henceforth as the "Eastern Townships." The effect of this tenure partition was to establish the St. Lawrence Valley as a kind of French-Canadian reservation, subject to feudal tenure and French law, and punctuated by some indigenous enclaves. Native hunting grounds north and south of the Laurentian seigneurial zone would be colonized mainly by British and American settlers and subjected to English law and soccage tenure.[31]

Native lands constituted yet another tenure form within Lower Canada, actually several others. Each of the seven indigenous villages situated within the seigneurial zone had a fairly clearly bounded (though frequently encroached upon) home territory. Each also controlled extensive hunting grounds in the forested hinterlands, mostly north of the St. Lawrence Valley. As noted in Chapters 4 and 8, these latter lands had remained largely beyond the ken of the French colonial state, but they nevertheless formed an integral part of the resource base on which the Laurentian native communities depended.

In the years preceding the fall of New France, the indigenous villages of the St. Lawrence Valley were already struggling to defend their territories from land-hungry settlers and opportunistic missionary-seigneurs. With good lands close to Montreal, Kahnawake was the most vulnerable to encroachment. The Iroquois there protested against the Jesuit practice of granting portions of their land to rent-paying French Canadian habitants; in 1750, under pressure from the natives, the governor had intervened to put an end to that practice. No sooner had the French been defeated, however, than the Jesuits, claiming seigneurial rights that the natives had never recognized, seized the opportunity to distribute fifty lots to colonists under *censive* tenure.[32] The outraged Mohawks of Kahnawake took the matter to court in 1762 and won a decisive victory. This was at a

---

[31] While pointing to a general legal/linguistic/ethnic spatial bifurcation in Lower Canada's settler zone, I would like to distance myself from the conspiratorial view put forward by some historians of the 1970s to the effect that British authorities aimed to confine French Canada territorially and hobble its economic development. See Maurice Séguin, *La "nation canadienne" et l'agriculture (1760–1850): essai d'histoire économique* (Trois-Rivières, Quebec: Éditions Boréal Express, 1970).

[32] Alain Beaulieu, *La question des terres autochtones au Québec, 1760–1860* (Varennes, QC: Ministère de la Justice et Ministère des Ressources naturelles du Québec, 2002), 101–2.

time – between the surrender of Canada and the final cession to Britain – when the colony was under military occupation, with justice administered by British officers. As governor of the district of Montreal, General Thomas Gage heard this important case. Gage had every reason to placate the Kahnawake Mohawks, still a formidable fighting force with diplomatic influence extending far and wide across the indigenous northeast, and little cause to sympathize with the Society of Jesus, abominated by Protestants and, in any case, headed for oblivion in France at that moment. Accordingly, he ruled against the Jesuits' claim to be legitimate seigneurs of Sault St-Louis and in favor of the Mohawks, who had argued that the seigneurie belonged to them.[33] This legal victory allowed the Mohawks of Kahnawake to manage their affairs as the corporate seigneur of their village lands, setting up a grist mill, collecting rents from the habitant farmers the Jesuits had admitted and defending their interests in colonial courts.

Other native communities in the Laurentian Valley did not fare so well in their struggle to preserve their lands against settler encroachment. The Mohawks and Algonquins of Deux-Montagnes (Oka) lived on land that, according to their wampum records, had been guaranteed to them by the governor of New France in the name of the king. Deux-Montagnes was also a seigneurie for which the Sulpician order held the title. Though their seigneurie had been granted exclusively for the use of the natives, the Sulpicians began granting lands to settlers in the 1780s, rapidly reducing the territory available to indigenous villagers to a small fraction of their domain. When the latter applied to the governor, asking him to stop this alienation of their territory, they discovered that their oral and wampum records counted for nothing against the priests' written documents. In spite of repeated protests, the depredations continued.[34] Other native communities of the St. Lawrence Lowlands held their seigneurial-zone lands on different terms, some of which commanded greater respect than others from the colonial courts and government.

Inland hunting territories were another matter. To the consternation of the natives, who considered these an integral part of their land holdings, and therefore subject to the solemn guarantees the British had announced at the time of the conquest, the new masters of Canada generally brushed

[33] Ibid., 102–4; Arnaud Decroix, "Le conflit juridique entre les jésuites et les iroquois au sujet de la seigneurie du Sault Saint-Louis: Analyse de la décision de Thomas Gage (1762)," *Revue Juridique Thémis* 41 (2007): 279–97.
[34] Beaulieu, *La question des terres autochtones au Québec*, 110–14.

aside their claims to these tracts. As of the 1790s, Lower Canadian authorities were issuing land grants covering vast portions of the Abenaki domains (now the Eastern Townships); timber contractors were at the same time receiving authorization to invade, and effectively lay waste to, Algonquin and Nipissing hunting territories on tributaries of the Ottawa River. These and all other areas outside the seigneurial zone were treated as lands of the Crown, though no formal surrender of aboriginal rights was ever concluded. Natives living within the colonized portions of Lower Canada, and therefore in most respects subject to colonial jurisdiction (many voted in parliamentary elections), were continually frustrated when they called on the provincial government to honor its historic commitment to protect their lands.[35]

What about the Royal Proclamation of 1763, with its requirement of orderly negotiations and material compensation as the basis for any cession of indigenous title? Procedures along those lines would be followed in Upper Canada (with the usual instances of coercion and misrepresentation).[36] There, in return for payments or annuities, natives ceded title to large tracts, retaining small enclaves for their own use, but nothing of the sort took place in Lower Canada.[37] Strictly speaking, the Royal Proclamation did not apply in this province, or within the seaboard British colonies. However, for propaganda purposes, copies of the proclamation had been distributed to the native communities of the St. Lawrence, leading indigenous leaders to conclude, quite reasonably, that these printed documents reinforced the verbal undertakings of British officials during the Seven Years' War to the effect that indigenous territories would be respected.[38] Moreover, regardless of the legal geography implied by the Proclamation of 1763, there was nothing to stop colonial administrators from offering treaties, for voluntary, publicly negotiated agreements were, according to current British thinking, the proper way to extinguish aboriginal title. However, legal experts advised succeeding governors of Lower Canada that native lands already belonged to the Crown by right of conquest from the French. The government of New France, they asserted, "was in the practice of granting away the Country

---

[35] Ibid., 218–80.

[36] J. R. Miller, *Compact, Contract, Covenant: Aboriginal Treaty-Making in Canada* (Toronto: University of Toronto Press, 2009), 66–92.

[37] Alain Beaulieu, "'An Equitable Right to Be Compensated': The Dispossession of the Aboriginal Peoples of Quebec and the Emergence of a New Legal Rationale (1760–1860)," *Canadian Historical Review* 94 (2013): 1–27.

[38] See Beaulieu, "Under His Majesty's Protection," 103.

with a perfect disregard of any supposed prior title in the Indians."[39] This was, of course, a tendentious reading of French regime practice, which had neither recognized indigenous title (exceptional cases like Sillery apart) nor erased it.

Even in the absence of treaty negotiations under the Royal Proclamation, Lower Canada's indigenous peoples did push back against dispossession, never renouncing their right to control their historic territories. Through court actions, petitions and face-to-face meetings, they had some success on specific points, more so during periods of war when their military services were most highly valued. But they never succeeded in forcing government to undertake broad treaty negotiations like those that occurred in Upper Canada and nearby parts of the United States. Alain Beaulieu, who has examined these issues thoroughly, warns us against fetishizing the procedures, theories and justifications surrounding the refusal of formal land treaties.[40] I might go one step further and note that colonial recognition of aboriginal title and commitment to treaty formalities did not necessarily protect indigenous peoples in other parts of North America from arbitrary dispossession. Where actual outcomes are concerned, the natives of New France/Lower Canada/Quebec generally seem to have fared better than their counterparts in other jurisdictions.

UNITED STATES

To find an appropriate sequel to the history of property-making in colonial New England, we need to widen the aperture and look at the American Revolution and its aftermath, across the thirteen original states and in the western territories they quickly annexed. In three distinct ways, this was a watershed era in the history of American landed property. First of all, the last quarter of the eighteenth century witnessed indigenous dispossession on an unprecedented scale, involving mainly the trans-Appalachian West. Second, a real estate market formed, very rapidly, making land a fungible asset as never before. Third and finally, the ideology of private ownership took hold of the national imaginary.

---

[39] Report of a committee of the executive council, 13 August 1787, quoted in Alain Beaulieu, *La question des terres autochtones au Québec*, 167. An additional argument used to justify appropriation without treaty agreements was that, in continuing the French regime practice of making annual presents of merchandise to native allies, the British were, in effect, offering "just compensation" for any loss of lands. See Beaulieu, "An Equitable Right to Be Compensated," 23.

[40] Beaulieu, "An Equitable Right to Be Compensated," 26–27.

None of these developments was without precedent in the colonial period, but on all three fronts – massive dispossession, commoditization and ownership ideology – change went deep and moved fast.

For the indigenous nations that lived just beyond the edges of British-era colonization – among many others, Creeks and Cherokees in the southeast; Delawares, Shawnees and other Algonquian peoples in the lands drained by the Ohio River; the Iroquois nations close to Lake Ontario; and Abenakis in the northeast – the last quarter of the eighteenth century was a time of massive and relentless invasion. First came thousands of settler families, armed and dangerous, erecting log shanties, clearing and tilling patches of ground, while sending livestock out to forage in the woods; their presence undermined native livelihoods over wider and wider regions. Colonists had been seen in these parts before 1775, but native resistance, bolstered by the Royal Proclamation and other imperial constraints, had tended to limit the flow. Demographic pressure in the seaboard colonies built up, however, and as the practical power of the British Empire collapsed, the effect was almost like that of a dam bursting. "In the late colonial period," writes Edward Countryman, "European/African society crept westward. In the early republic, it surged."[41] Migration and land grabbing peaked during the Revolution itself, and this was partly due to the progress of white male democracy, which transferred political power into the hands of settlers and speculators. Reconstituted state legislatures were highly responsive to these sectors of the population.[42]

State assistance included, most notably, military aid. The settler incursions into the West were accompanied by armed skirmishes, massacres and atrocities, and in several locations, state militias hastened to the rescue of beleaguered fellow citizens. This led many indigenous nations to forge alliances with British forces and before long their countries had become a major theater of the war. The violence came to a climax with General John Sullivan's 1779 invasion of Iroquoia, in the course of which

[41] Edward Countryman, "Indians, the Colonial Order, and the Social Significance of the American Revolution," *William and Mary Quarterly* 53, no. 2 (1996): 348. See also Alan Taylor, *Liberty Men and Great Proprietors: The Revolutionary Settlement on the Maine Frontier, 1760–1820* (Chapel Hill: University of North Carolina Press, 1990), 5; Eric Hinderaker, *Elusive Empires: Constructing Colonialism in the Ohio Valley, 1673–1800* (New York: Cambridge University Press, 1997), 187–225.

[42] Stuart Banner, *How the Indians Lost Their Land: Law and Power on the Frontier* (Cambridge, Mass.: Harvard University Press, 2005), 120.

forty villages were razed.⁴³ Such frontier violence had been common throughout the colonial period, but now it occurred on a broader scale. It was also framed, more explicitly than in the past, as a struggle for land, the latter now coming to be seen as an economic asset for both governments and individuals. "As the war continued," Stuart Banner observes, "the conquest of Indian land came to be a primary reason for fighting."⁴⁴ Throwing off the imperial yoke, the settler republic was fighting for independence and a free hand to carry out dispossession on its own terms.⁴⁵ Natives fought for survival, and when the powers arrayed against them were overwhelming, they pursued diplomacy with the same purpose in mind. In attempting to secure peace and coexistence, they often found that a *modus vivendi* was not necessarily what the Americans had in mind. Where the latter secured the upper hand, they required natives to vacate huge territories as the price of a cessation of hostilities. Moreover, during the Revolutionary War and in its aftermath, there was little of the usual pretense of voluntary consent and just compensation. The problem with the treaties of this period is that natives could not rely on them to protect even the vestigial lands guaranteed by the conquerors. Cherokees and Iroquois went to extraordinary lengths to accommodate settlers, decreasing their footprint by adapting to the agricultural way of life themselves and leasing out their reserved lands to settlers, but they still experienced dispossession – and in the Cherokee case, deportation – regardless. In the northwest, an alliance formed to wage war against American expansion into the future state of Ohio and adjacent regions (1792–94); successful for a time, it too was eventually defeated. For the indigenous nations bordering the original thirteen states, the entire period was one of settler invasion, destructive warfare and dispossession, interrupted by deceptive and one-sided agreements that provided little security against further incursions.

Having brushed aside, in the heat of war, the Anglo-American tradition of formalizing dispossession with notionally voluntary treaties of cession, the young republic soon resurrected the theoretical principles embodied in the Royal Proclamation of 1763. The Northwest Ordinance, passed by Congress in 1787 declared (in all apparent

⁴³ Alan Taylor, *The Divided Ground: Indians, Settlers, and the Northern Borderland of the American Revolution* (New York: Knopf, 2006), 97–99.
⁴⁴ Banner, *How the Indians Lost Their Land*, 121.
⁴⁵ Ibid., 113, 121–25; Anthony F. C. Wallace, *Jefferson and the Indians: The Tragic Fate of the First Americans* (Cambridge, Mass.: Harvard University Press, 1999), 54–60, 163; Hinderaker, *Elusive Empires*, 187–225.

seriousness) that "The utmost good faith shall always be observed towards the Indians; their lands and property shall never be taken from them without their consent; and, in their property, rights, and liberty."[46] Desirous of securing powers previously claimed by the British Empire, the government of the United States asserted a monopoly over the dispossession of indigenous nations. After the Constitution had strengthened the national government, a 1790 act prohibiting the purchase of Indian lands unless "made and duly executed at some public treaty, held under the authority of the United States," was still only partially effective.[47] States, most notably New York and Georgia, would continue to challenge the federal government's monopoly over the acquisition of indigenous title, while on the ground settlers and speculators still made private arrangements to acquire land from indigenous leaders. Gradually, however, the United States managed to impose something approaching full authority in this realm, thanks in large measure to its growing military predominance on the frontier.

The United States sought to impose its sovereignty vis-à-vis the states, but also in relation to neighboring European empires, specifically the British and the Spanish. By the terms of the 1783 Treaty of Paris, Britain had ceded territories from the Gulf of Mexico to the Great Lakes and as far west as the Mississippi. The United States accordingly claimed sovereignty over that entire domain, even though the western half was mostly owned and controlled by independent indigenous nations. In the context of the history of European imperialism, there was nothing unusual about such an essentially groundless claim to territorial authority; empires had always run ahead of themselves, expressing aspirations to rule and warning off rival empires. What distinguished American imperialism in this respect was the way its spatial claims were expressed mainly through reference to vendible landed property. The United States made its case in terms of the legal concept of "preemption," a keyword that came to the fore just at the time of the revolution.[48] It was a term that applied to property rights at a number of different levels, but in the current context,

---

[46] Quoted in Peter S. Onuf, *Statehood and Union: A History of the Northwest Ordinance* (Bloomington: Indiana University Press, 1987), 63.

[47] Banner, *How the Indians Lost Their Land*, 135.

[48] On preemption, see Paul W. Gates, *History of Public Land Law Development* (Washington, D.C.: Zenger, 1968), 219–47; Banner, *How the Indians Lost Their Land*, 135–36, 160ff.; Michael Albert Blaakman, "Speculation Nation: Land and Mania in the Revolutionary American Republic, 1776–1803," PhD dissertation, Yale University, 2016, ch. 5, 384–474.

preemption designated the national government's exclusive right to acquire land from natives. In formulating territorial sovereignty over the west primarily as a real estate monopsony, the Americans were taking to a kind of logical extreme a tendency that had emerged in eighteenth-century British colonial practice.[49] To a remarkable degree, they attempted to reduce the complex processes of colonization and imperial expansion to a matter of land purchasing. Perhaps the predominance of lawyers and land speculators among the Founding Fathers helps to explain this unprecedented instance of "state simplification." More likely, the key to understanding the sudden commodification of territorial sovereignty lies in the pressing fiscal needs of the young republic.

With their finances in a shambles during the war and its aftermath, both the states and the federal government looked to western lands as a potential treasure chest. They also drew on that source to discharge their obligations to military veterans, typically rewarding the latter with paper entitlements to unspecified plots. Under British rule, the general pattern had been for colonial governments to distribute all land wrested from native control as free grants to settlers (theoretically subject to annual quitrents, but without initial purchase price); similarly in New Spain and New France, land grants were essentially free. The point of land grants had always been to encourage European immigrants and their offspring to establish themselves in America and especially to contribute to the expansion of imperial control by strengthening the colonial presence at its outer edges. Consolidating sovereignty and developing the economic potential of "new" regions went along with the transformation of indigenous terrain into colonial real estate. However, as of the Revolution, the American republic embarked on a policy of selling lands.[50] The monetization of uncolonized land represented another major break with precedent and it would have far-reaching consequences. When Philip II had imposed *composición* on his New World subjects, and when French and British monarchs had attempted to tap in to American landed wealth, they targeted established and developed properties within the colonized zone, skimming off a portion of the income the latter produced for their private owners. The US federal government and the states hoped instead

---

[49] The importance of the shift is not always apparent in a historical literature where land surrender treaties and purchase rituals tend to be naturalized. See Allan Greer, "Dispossession in a Commercial Idiom: From Indian Deeds to Land Cession Treaties," in *Contested Spaces of Early America*, ed. Juliana Barr and Edward Countryman (Philadelphia: University of Pennsylvania Press, 2014), 69–92.

[50] Gates, *History of Public Land Law Development*, 47, 61.

to extract revenue from forested tracts that were still under the contested control of indigenous nations and only marginally integrated into a market economy.

In their financial desperation, the new republics wanted to eradicate all the intermediate steps of property formation through which native territory became settler real estate. Their strategy entailed some legal sleights-of-hand and could succeed only through the workings of a speculative market. It of course made a mockery of the commitment to "good faith toward the Indians." Making the whole business even more artificial was the fact that governments frequently sold, not estates in fee simple, but rather preemption rights, which is to say claims to lands that had not even been ceded by native proprietors. (See below.) In order to finance their own operations while avoiding direct taxation, states and the US government were cashing in on indigenous lands and playing a central role in creating a highly speculative frontier real estate market.

"Land" per se is not inherently a fungible asset: it has to be legally constructed as alienable property and it needs investment (or at least investment potential) to render it valuable as a commodity. In their haste to financialize indigenous territories, governments of the period were trying to conjure up valuable real estate by legal enactment alone. In fact, neither they nor the vast majority of western settlers possessed the capital necessary to make good on the economic promise of these vast forested tracts. Most of the families who actually built the frontier farmsteads likely aspired to the kind of householder's "competency" that seventeenth-century settlers of New England and New France prized, but the land policies of the early republic period undermined the prospects for stable householding. Settlers were forced to immerse themselves, far more completely than their ancestors in the colonies had, into the volatile world of the market economy. State and national government placed a price on formal land title, and it was not a trivial amount. With the US government giving natives either nothing or a cent or two an acre to cede their territories, the Land Ordinance of 1785 authorized the federal state to auction that same land with a minimum price, set in 1796 at $2 per acre, with no consideration for the wide variation in the productive potential of particular locations.[51] The result was the rapid monetization

[51] Elizabeth Blackmar, personal communication, 12 September 2016; Gates, *History of Public Land Law Development*, 68–73; Francis Paul Prucha, *American Indian Treaties: The History of a Political Anomaly* (Berkeley: University of California Press, 1994), 229; Banner, *How the Indians Lost Their Land*, 127.

of land at inflated prices, more so on the margins of the national economy than in its eastern heartland. Settlers on the western frontier moved their families with amazing frequency, buying, selling and renting land as they went. Concludes Elizabeth Blackmar: "Government action in effect organized the first wholesale land market in the United States."[52]

To the extent that the federal state was able to capture control of the processes of frontier dispossession and settler property-making, it instituted a new form of landed property, known as the "public domain." This was territory where native title had been cleared but where settler tenure had not yet been established.[53] The republican "public domain" bore some resemblance to Crown land rights of colonial times, except that the latter – at least in the Spanish American case – constituted a more diffuse and pervasive claim to empty and neglected spaces within the zone of colonization, whereas the former was construed as a distinct and bounded space of state property.[54] Unlike the larger area, still in native possession, over which the United States claimed sovereignty and "preemption rights," the public domain was treated as government property. Lawmakers cherished the ideal of an orderly and regulated process of colonization, from native land cession, through surveying to sale, deeding and settlement (even as they subverted the process by selling land that had not been ceded!). With the Land Ordinance of 1785, Congress tried to impose spatial as well as economic order over its western holdings. Henceforth, territory where native title had been extinguished would be surveyed in advance of settlement, following a rigidly geometric east–west/north–south grid, with townships six miles square (John Winthrop's 1635 norm for a churchgoing pedestrian community still applied), subdivided into 36 lots of 640 acres.[55] A version of the grid survey would eventually prevail, across western America as well as much of Canada,

---

[52] Elizabeth Blackmar, "Six (or Sixty) Questions about the Relation of Land and Capitalism in the Early U.S. Republic," unpublished paper presented at "The Problem of Land in North American History, c. 1700–1850" conference, University of Montreal, April 2011, 4.

[53] See Gates, *History of Public Land Law Development*, 251, 260. Gates emphasizes the role of state and federal military land bounties in creating the legal category of "public domain."

[54] In Canada, the term "Crown Land" would come in the nineteenth century to serve as a synonym for the US term "public domain." See H. V. Nelles, *The Politics of Development: Forests, Mines and Hydro-electric Power in Ontario, 1849–1941* (Toronto: Macmillan 1974), 1–47.

[55] Onuf, *Statehood and Union*, 22–24; Bill Hubbard, *American Boundaries: The Nation, the States, the Rectangular Survey* (Chicago: University of Chicago Press, 2009), 186–94.

but in the republic's early decades, colonization and dispossession were hardly orderly processes, whether viewed at the spatial, economic or legal level.

Land grabbing in the wake of the Revolution was basically unregulated, chaotic and frequently violent. As in late colonial times, but now at a more frenzied pace, "squatters" surged ahead of the government's attempts to secure native cessions and to ensure geometric surveying and proper titles. Their claims to land by virtue of occupation clashed with the claims of speculators who brandished various kinds of legal documentation. Some of the large land corporations of the late colonial period had by now disappeared, but new speculative concerns, large and small, were springing up in their place. In the governments' haste to get revenues flowing, they were inclined to sell large blocks of land to anyone with the resources to offer money up front. Corruption was rife at every level of government. Prospective settlers often encountered "land offices" offering lots for sale, and it was not always clear whether these operations were run by government agents, private speculators, or some strange combination of the two.[56] After a tour of the west in 1784, George Washington expressed his anxieties about the dangers of unbridled expansion:

Such is the rage for speculating in, and forestalling of Lands on the No. West side of Ohio [River], that scarce a valuable spot within any tolerable distance of it, is left without a claimant. Men in these times talk with as much facility of fifty, a hundred, and even 500,000 Acres as a Gentleman formerly would do of 1000 acres. In defiance of the proclamation of Congress, they roam over the Country on the Indian side of the Ohio, mark out lands, Survey and even settle them. This gives great discontent to the Indians, and will unless measures are taken in time to prevent it, inevitably produce a war with the western Tribes.[57]

Orderly property formation was, as always, a pipe dream, but the governments' desperate need for money did provide a certain focus in the actual workings of land policy. The emphasis on revenue had an integrating effect, in that it tended to impose the rules of the marketplace, making settler property formation, much more than in the past, a business.

---

[56] See J. M. Opal, *Avenging the People: Andrew Jackson, the Rule of Law, and the American Nation* (New York: Oxford University Press, 2017), ch. 2. My thanks to Prof. Opal for sharing his work with me in advance of publication.

[57] Washington to Jacob Read, 3 November 1784, quoted in Francis Paul Prucha, *The Great Father: The United States Government and the American Indians* (Lincoln: University of Nebraska Press, 1984), 45.

Western natives, by no means blind to what was going on, felt the devastating effects of the commercialization of their countries most directly. However, settlers did not benefit fully or equally from the new system of property formation. When they occupied land without formal title, they did enjoy some protection through the operation of "preemption" of a different sort, a kind of "first refusal" right by which squatters could purchase their holdings at a moderate price.[58] Secure title still required money, however, and frontier settlers rarely had much of that. In the confusing welter of government auctions, military entitlements, land-jobbers and preemption rights, the sharpest dealers with the best political connections tended to win out (though not always for long: the instabilities of the system ensured that fortunes were won and lost quickly). In the scramble for advantage, many ordinary settlers became indebted and marginalized. "By 1810," writes Eric Hinderaker, "only about 45% of Ohio's adult males owned land, while almost a quarter of its real estate was held by 1% of taxpayers." He goes on to conclude: "Ohio Valley lands exposed everyone, wealthy, middling, or poor, well-connected or obscure, to the risks and opportunities of the market."[59] Thomas Jefferson dreamed of an egalitarian society of small-scale owner-producers, but the republic he founded had, thanks to its reliance on western lands to finance the national debt, impelled frontier property formation in a different direction.[60]

In the established settler societies of the eastern seaboard, as well as on the western frontier, land was being transformed into a market commodity in the late eighteenth century. Mortgages, it seems, became more common and they were used for new purposes in the early republic. Previously, mortgages served mainly to facilitate land purchases: sellers took them on merely to protect their interests as they waited for buyers to pay off the sale price in annual installments. After the Revolution, land was more likely to be mortgaged to raise capital for improvements and even for commercial purposes; at the same time, lenders were showing an interest in mortgages as secure but lucrative investments.[61] Legislation in the 1780s, by reducing the role of equity law in this area, seems to have streamlined mortgaging.[62] This was a significant step in reinforcing

[58] Gates, *History of Public Land Law Development*, 219–47.
[59] Hinderaker, *Elusive Empires*, 249–50.
[60] On this point, I am indebted to the unpublished scholarship of Elizabeth Blackmar.
[61] Blackmar, "Six (or Sixty) Questions," 2–3.
[62] James Sullivan, *The History of Land Titles in Massachusetts* (Boston: I. Thomas and E. T. Andrews, 1801), 95–108. On this topic, see also Morton J. Horwitz, *The Transformation*

land/money equivalency. Another aspect of the monetization of landed property lay in the area of inheritance law. It became more common at this time to merge land and chattels in the process of liquidating assets to satisfy heirs and creditors after a death (the tradition in Europe as well as most parts of colonial America was to keep land separate from movable goods, only the latter being reducible to a monetary value).[63] Such changes had the aggregate effect of placing landed property firmly within the realm of an emergent market economy. Especially where western lands are concerned, the gyrating waves of speculation were largely unconnected to the agricultural economy and so the booms tended to go bust, taking the speculators down with them. A real estate market had indeed emerged and, whether that change is labeled "capitalistic" or not, it does seem justified to speak of a "property revolution" in the late eighteenth-century United States.

Is this what Jefferson and other ideologues of the age had in mind when they hailed the establishment of "absolute private property"? Certainly, the power freely to buy, sell, bequeath and otherwise alienate (for example, through mortgage), one of the attributes associated with private property, was greatly enhanced in the late eighteenth century. Vendibility was still not really "absolute," however, for a number of reasons that were enumerated earlier in this chapter. More to the point, the property that could now be bought and sold with so little friction hardly rested on anything like an exclusive and unmediated connection – Blackstone's "sole and despotic dominion" – between proprietors and land. To the contrary, the emergent real estate market dealt in partial, uncertain and often overlapping entitlements to certain portions of the Earth.

The extensive monetization of preemption rights illustrates this point nicely. We have noted that "preemption" acquired different, but related meanings: the sovereign's exclusive right to acquire title from natives at one level, squatters' right to buy the land they occupied at another level. It is time now to focus on a third sense in which that keyword was employed around the time of the American Revolution. State and national governments sold provisional title, known as "preemptions," to land that had

---

of American Law, 1780–1860 (Cambridge, Mass.: Harvard University Press, 1977), 265–66.

[63] Elizabeth Blackmar, "Inheriting Property and Debt: From Family Security to Corporate Accumulation," in *Capitalism Takes Command: The Social Transformation of Nineteenth-Century America*, ed. Michael Zakim and Gary John Kornblith (Chicago: University of Chicago Press, 2012), 96–97.

not been ceded by natives and that did not therefore really belong to the public domain.[64] Tracts held under preemptions could be occupied, developed and sold, even though legally they represented not so much a firm title as "contingent future interests in land still owned by the Indians."[65] What gave them value was the firm conviction, shared by settlers, investors and governments, that native "rights of occupancy" constituted only a temporary impediment to colonization. Natives, it was assumed, would soon be driven from the land. Competition and confusion over the division of powers between state and national governments had the effect of spurring on the market in preemption rights, states granting land without regard to the federation's authority over Indian affairs. There were cases in which the senior government would negotiate a reserved area for natives, while the state was busy granting these same lands to settlers and speculators. An English visitor to Albany, New York, in the mid-1790s was astonished at the intensity of the land speculation he witnessed, and all the more so as much of it concerned preemptions: "American jurisprudence holds valid many such airey sales and purchases as this." He added, ominously, that the contingent nature of such title gave investors a pecuniary interest in genocide. Referring to the indigenous nations whose resistance stood between preemption and clear title, he wrote: "Their destruction is perused with remorseless perseverance and their annihilation spoken of with atrocious pleasure."[66]

AFTER NEW SPAIN

Dreams of private property and uniform territorial sovereignty hovered over the independence movement in Mexico, as much as that of its northern neighbor. And as in the early history of the United States, the protracted process of forging a territorial nation-state revolved to an important degree around the issue of natives and native lands. But whereas the United States and, in somewhat more ambiguous fashion, Canada developed as expansive settler nations during the century following the American Revolution, progressively colonizing indigenous lands and relegating their original inhabitants to confined spaces, the

---

[64] On this form of preemption, see Banner, *How the Indians Lost Their Land*, 160–68; Blaakman, "Speculation Nation," 384–474.

[65] Banner, *How the Indians Lost Their Land*, 163.

[66] William Strickland, *Journal of a Tour in the United States of America, 1794–1795*, quoted in Banner, *How the Indians Lost Their Land*, 161.

formation of a Mexican territorial state confronted natives and native lands more as an "internal" matter. To Mexican state-makers, indigenous communities appeared as a municipal/land tenure anomaly at the heart of the nation's territory. Islands of indigenous control and land tenure would also take shape within the United States and Canada in the form of reservations, but the initial emphasis in those northern settler-states was on incorporating independent indigenous spaces into the settler sphere. Nineteenth-century Mexico was not expansive in this way: indeed, its national territory actually shrank. Whereas New Spain had conquered and incorporated extensive territories, subjecting natives from Central America in the south to California and Texas in the north to tributary status, the Mexican federation lost its northernmost territories to the United States during the decades that followed independence. And rather than subjugating distant "barbarous" nations as in the past, the country fell victim to a Comanche "empire" that, for many years, routinely exacted people and goods captured in raids on its northern provinces.[67]

Indigenous people were by no means on the periphery of the popular upheavals, political contests and military campaigns that led to Mexican independence in 1821 and then to the constitution of a federal republic in 1824. Whereas the North American revolutionary struggle had combined a war of conquest in the trans-Appalachian West with an anti-imperial conflict in the East, Mexico's fight for independence saw native involvement at the center of the emergent nation-state. The Hidalgo Revolt of 1810, usually seen as the first blow for national independence, was almost entirely an indigenous affair. At later stages, Indians would fight in royalist as well as in republican armies, acquiring military and political experience that helped them assert themselves more effectively in the innumerable local conflicts over land that arose in that turbulent time. Natives were not an enemy to be pushed back from the edges of white settlement, but rather an integral part of the revolutionary process in all parts of the country.[68]

---

[67] Pekka Hämäläinen, *The Comanche Empire* (New Haven, Conn.: Yale University Press, 2008).

[68] On the Independence period, see Timothy Anna, "The Independence of Mexico and Central America," in *The Cambridge History of Latin America*, vol. 3: *From Independence to c. 1870*, ed. Leslie Bethell (Cambridge: Cambridge University Press, 1984), 51–94; John Tutino, *From Insurrection to Revolution in Mexico: Social Bases of Agrarian Violence, 1750–1940* (Princeton, N.J.: Princeton University Press, 1986); Peter F. Guardino, *Peasants, Politics, and the Formation of Mexico's National State: Guerrero,*

That, of course, had much to do with the simple force of numbers. Toward the end of the colonial period, the indigenous population formed a majority within New Spain and its numbers had been growing since their nadir in the early seventeenth century. Indian pueblos remained a major presence within the colonized zone at the heart of New Spain/ Mexico. Self-governing, culturally and linguistically distinct from the ambient Hispanic world of Creoles, *mestizos* and other racial categories, native communities held land and used its productive resources in their own distinctive ways. The barriers separating native and Hispanic spheres had blurred considerably over the centuries of Spanish rule. Native workers had been detached from traditional communities and integrated into *haciendas*, especially in the north; *ranchos* (small farms) operated mainly by *mestizos* were insinuating themselves into the edges of pueblo lands; on their own lands, many individual natives were raising crops and livestock for external markets. Little wonder then that they felt implicated in the struggles for Mexican independence. And yet at the same time, they remained apart, thousands of communities, each with its own autonomous administration and with its lands, held under complex tenures harking back to pre-conquest times and shaped by centuries of colonial rule.

Poor, agrarian, localized and exploited, indigenous Mexicans struggled to maintain a place for themselves in the emergent new order. Many natives labored as peons on *haciendas*, while those who persisted on pueblo lands faced difficult times; even in the absence of traditional tribute and labor service, they were still subject to the heavy exactions of church tithes and state taxes. As in the past, communities had to be vigilant to prevent outsiders from encroaching on their lands, lands that were all the more precious at a time when growing populations were putting pressure on their agricultural base. There were instances where pueblos, trying to reclaim rental lands and convert them to subsistence purposes, found themselves powerless to evict nonnative ranchers; the tenants would not vacate and the courts would not force them to go.[69] On the other hand, the upheavals of the independence era also brought new

---

1800–1857 (Stanford, Calif.: Stanford University Press, 1996); John Tutino, "The Revolution in Mexican Independence: Insurgency and the Renegotiation of Property, Production, and Patriarchy in the Bajío, 1800–1855," *Hispanic American Historical Review* 78 (1998): 367–418; Rodríguez O., *The Independence of Spanish America*.

[69] Guardino, *Peasants, Politics, and the Formation of Mexico's National State*, 34. For a succinct overview of the situation of natives more generally in the first half of the nineteenth century, see Robert M. Carmack, Janine Gasco and Gary H. Gossen, *The*

opportunities for indigenous communities to defend, and even to expand, their respective land bases. The civil strife of the period weakened the *haciendas* economically and politically, with the result that some were willing to sell land to natives. At the same time, the indigenous population, mobilized for violent conflict from the time of the Hidalgo Revolt of 1810, was emboldened to take action at the local level when its interests were threatened. Historians combing through local records find multiple instances of micro-rebellion in the 1820s and 1830s, including land invasions by which native pueblos managed to seize terrain from large estates.[70]

That kind of strengthening of indigenous communities is not what the liberal visionaries attempting to steer Mexican independence had in mind. As they knocked the props out from under the colonial Old Regime and set about constituting an integrated modern state, the founders of Mexico confronted their "Indian problem." In the process, they translated the issue of national homogeneity from an ethnic register into a question of land and local administration. Working very much in the theoretical realm of legal and constitutional principles, they settled on what they understood as the generous ideal of civic equality. Following in the wake of Spain's 1812 liberal constitution, they abolished tribute and labor service and decreed full citizenship for indigenous people. (This last measure occurred in Mexico at least a century before Canada or the United States admitted any such formal equality.) Gone would be the legal distinctions that underlay the colonial order, dividing a "Spanish republic" from "Indian republics," the latter burdened with tribute and characterized by its special land tenure and local government.[71] Again taking their cue from the Cádiz Constitution of 1812, Mexico's leaders

Legacy of Mesoamerica: History and Culture of a Native American Civilization (Englewood Cliffs, N.J.: Prentice Hall, 1996), 196–237.

[70] Tutino, "The Revolution in Mexican Independence"; Michael T. Ducey, "Liberal Theory and Peasant Practice: Land and Power in Northern Veracruz, Mexico, 1826–1900," in *Liberals, the Church, and Indian Peasants: Corporate Lands and the Challenge of Reform in Nineteenth-Century Spanish America*, ed. Robert H. Jackson (Albuquerque: University of New Mexico Press, 1997), 67.

[71] Among the many works treating this subject, see Robert J. Knowlton and Lucrecia Orensanz, "El ejido mexicano en el siglo XIX," *Historia Mexicana* 48 (1998): 71–96; Brian Hamnett, "Los pueblos indios y la defensa de la comunidad en el México independiente, 1824–1884: el caso de Oaxaca," in *Pueblos, comunidades y municipios frente a los proyectos modernizadores en América latina, siglo XIX*, ed. Antonio Escobar Ohmstede (San Luis de Potosi, Mexico: Colegio de San Luis; Centro de estudios y documentación latinoamericanos, 2002), 189–205.

did away with separate Spanish and Indian *cabildos*, establishing in their place a new, nonracial institution of municipal government, the *ayuntamiento*. Since the latter was organized on a larger scale than the former, many small pueblos found themselves folded into a bigger unit and dominated by a neighboring village. In some regions, the new municipal councils tried to lay claim to rental income from the common lands of their constituent communities.[72] What ensued was an intensified struggle on the part of many subordinated communities to emancipate themselves from the rule of local centers (*cabeceras*).[73] To make matters worse, municipal voting qualifications were no longer defined in ethnic terms, which left open the possibility of nonnatives capturing local office even in majority Indian *ayuntamientos*. Communities used all means at their disposal, including direct action, lawsuits, petitions and powers of attorney, to maintain their coherence and autonomy and their control over pueblo lands. Notwithstanding the nation-makers' general hostility to local and ethnic particularisms, natives generally managed to preserve the essential.

In their attempts to abolish the special status of Indians, Mexico's liberal-minded parliamentarians and ideologues, like their counterparts in Europe in relation to their own peasantries, thought they had the best interests of the natives at heart. With racial distinctions supposedly eradicated, natives (and their lands) were to join in the forward march of freedom and prosperity. Needless to say, this emancipatory vision was not created through any consultation with real indigenous people: it referred to an imagined figure, the native who had been freed from the isolation and ignorance that the colonial regime and the Catholic Church had perpetuated and who would consequently embrace the opportunity to function as a citizen and an individual economic actor. Villagers who would once have been called "Indians" were now generally known as "peasants"; notaries drawing up contracts would even refer to "those who were previously called Indians."[74] A leading liberal intellectual of the

---

[72] Guardino, *Peasants, Politics, and the Formation of Mexico's National State*, 104–6.

[73] Such local conflicts were common in the colonial period as well, but the shake-up of municipal geography in the independence era served to increase their frequency. Luis Alberto Arrioja Díaz Viruell, *Pueblos de indios y tierras comunales. Villa Alta, Oaxaca: 1742–1856* (Mexico City: El Colegio de Michoacán, 2011), 142–44 and passim.

[74] Robert J. Knowlton, "Dealing in Real Estate in Mid-Nineteenth-Century Jalisco: The Guadalajara Region," in Jackson, ed., *Liberals, the Church, and Indian Peasants*, 22–23. (my translation) "... los que antes se llamaban indios." On the tendency to substitute class for ethnic designations in public discourse on rural communities in Mexico, see also

Independence era, José María Luis Mora, proposed that the term "indio" be extirpated from public discourse: "The Indians," he declared, "should not continue to exist."[75]

All Creole factions tended to see actual existing indigenous communities and their aspirations to maintain their integrity as utterly benighted and backward, an obstacle to progress and improvement. Those who rallied to the Liberal banner in the mid-nineteenth century were convinced that this cultural/economic backwardness was essentially a legal problem, rooted in the separate status of Indian communities and their peculiar land tenure.[76] (Conservatives, typically whites who profited from cheap indigenous labor, were generally less optimistic about the prospects for transforming natives into "*gentes de razon.*") Under liberal auspices, the campaign to assimilate natives found expression in property terms. Public discourse focused not on indigenous culture, but on "communal" lands. Modern historiography perpetuates this deethnicizing of identity, such that whereas studies on the New Spain period refer to "natives" or "Indians," those devoted to the nineteenth century are more inclined to speak of "peasants." It is as if indigeneity had already been eradicated, leaving only an issue of land tenure.

More fundamentally, the liberal commitment to the ideal of private property implied the liquidation of indigenous pueblos. Breaking up pueblos into private holdings, one statesman declared in 1824, would benefit natives economically and would raise them to the status of "genuine citizens, free of any tutelage."[77] The state of Veracruz passed a law in 1826 ordering that "all community lands of the natives, forested or not, shall be reduced to private property, divided up with equality to every person belonging to the community."[78] Legislation tended to be vague and inconsistent, however, with the result that local officials charged with

---

Frans J. Schryer, *Ethnicity and Class Conflict in Rural Mexico* (Princeton, N.J.: Princeton University Press, 1990), 245–56.

[75] Quoted in Donald J. Fraser, "La política de desamortización en las comunidades indígenas, 1856–1872," *Historia Mexicana* 21 (1972): 619. (my translation) "Los indios no deben seguir existiendo." On Mora, see Charles A. Hale, *Mexican Liberalism in the Age of Mora, 1821–1853* (New Haven, Conn.: Yale University Press, 1968), 215–47; Enrique Krauze, *Siglo de caudillos: biografía política de México (1810–1910)* (Barcelona: Tusquets Editores, 1994).

[76] Ducey, "Liberal Theory and Peasant Practice," 73–75; Hale, *Mexican Liberalism in the Age of Mora*, 224–34.

[77] Quoted in Fraser, "La política de desamortización," 621. (my translation) "verdaderos ciudadanos sin ningún tutelaje."

[78] Quoted in Ducey, "Liberal Theory and Peasant Practice," 74.

implementing these measures were not sure what exactly was required in concrete terms.[79] Officialdom tended to simplify the complexities of pueblo tenure, distinguishing only between *tierras de repartimiento*, meaning individual plots that could be inherited but not sold outside the community, and "commons," which designated land that was either used collectively or rented out for the benefit of the community. Convinced that such rental revenues were either squandered on useless festivals or dedicated to "harassing the neighboring landowners with suits,"[80] state politicians wanted to have the common lands in question privatized or at least placed under nonnative municipal control. However, these initiatives generally came to naught, partly because the new regime was weak in the countryside. Local representatives of the state, themselves enmeshed within local societies, could not always square generic legislation with concrete local realities; besides, they knew that drastic measures might well provoke violent native resistance.

In legal terms, the upshot was that, through most of the nineteenth century, "Indian polities retained their personalidad juídica [corporate standing in law], at least in principle, and Indian village lands – notwithstanding the sporadic efforts of some state governments – remained for the most part entailed, still a collective patrimony protected from legal alienation."[81] One essential feature of native tenure carried over from the colonial period, the key to preserving the integrity of the community as a unit of residence and subsistence, was the prohibition on alienating land to outsiders. For liberals, this situated Indian land in the same category as Church land: it was *mano muerta*. After decades of ineffectual attempts at the state level to promote alienability, the national government took more forceful steps under the Liberal regime of President Benito Juaréz. The Ley Lerdo of 1856, its provisions later incorporated into the Mexican constitution of 1857, ordered the immediate disentailment (*desamortización*) of all lands held by corporate bodies (essentially ecclesiastical and native holdings).[82] Where such lands were leased out, they would have to be either sold to their current tenants or auctioned off.

---

[79] Guardino, *Peasants, Politics, and the Formation of Mexico's National State*, 104–6.

[80] Ibid., 106.

[81] Emilio Kourí, "Interpreting the Expropriation of Indian Pueblo Lands in Porfirian Mexico: The Unexamined Legacies of Andres Molina Enriquez," *Hispanic American Historical Review* 82 (2002): 81.

[82] Willem Assies, "Land Tenure and Tenure Regimes in Mexico: An Overview," *Journal of Agrarian Change* 8 (2008): 38.

The blunt wording of the Ley Lerdo, and the liberal enthusiasm that surrounded its passage, give the impression of a decisive break with the past through the establishment of universal private property. In this respect, it resembles earlier pronouncements and manifestos associated with the American and French Revolutions, as well as with the Spanish and Spanish-American awakenings earlier in the century. And like these other property revolutionaries, the liberal legislators of Mexico's Reforma cherished the democratic ideal of a society of independent smallholders; they therefore saw themselves as emancipating Indians from the "slavery" of corporate tenure. Historians are divided and uncertain as to the extent to which the Ley Lerdo actually affected indigenous communities and their lands. Most suggest that the disintegrating effects of *desamortización* came to be widely felt only toward the end of the nineteenth century, if at all.[83] They cite native resistance, facilitated by the civil strife that weakened the Mexican state between 1857 and 1876. To these historical factors accounting for the failure to implement a universal regime of private property, I would add a more basic impediment: the inherent impossibility of bringing land as a socially embedded object into line with the abstract idea of property as a freely circulating commodity. The politicians of the Reforma, like the Jeffersonians dreaming of a republic based on absolute ownership or the French revolutionaries imagining doing away with feudal tenure at one fell swoop, could not make social reality conform to liberal dogma.

Historical discussion of the issues at stake in the nineteenth century are not well served by a tendency to frame matters in terms of a communal-versus-private-property dichotomy. The term "communal" as applied to native land practices is just as abstract and reductive, and therefore misleading, as the concept of "private property" used to designate the nonindigenous alternative.[84] Nineteenth-century pueblos typically encompassed a variety of lands, each held in different ways. Michael Ducey enumerates the property elements found within pueblos in the region of Huasteca (Veracruz state) in the following terms:

The *fundo legal* consisted of the original "six hundred *varas*" square that served as the town site. Closely related to the *fundo*, *ejidos* served as common pastures and forest lands also located near the town. The two most important categories of land

---

[83] For a listing of studies on the topic, see Kourí, "Interpreting the Expropriation of Indian Pueblo Lands in Porfirian Mexico," 70 n 2.

[84] See Raymond B. Craib, *Cartographic Mexico: A History of State Fixations and Fugitive Landscapes* (Durham, N.C.: Duke University Press, 2004), 94–95.

for the towns in the Huasteca consisted of the *propios* and the *tierras de repartimiento*. Communities owned the *propios* and rented the land out as a source of municipal revenue. The *tierras de repartimiento* were the most important lands for the Indian peasants. Peasant agricultural production actually occurred on these lands. The communities divided up these lands among the members of the villages and farmed them in family plots. A certain sense of ownership developed among the indigenous peasantry since sons inherited the family plots from their fathers.[85]

Pointing up the dominance of some wealthy villagers, Ducey makes it clear that these were not egalitarian societies in which all shared equally. Nor were their lands unaffected by the ways of the market economy: "Evidently, community members bought, sold, rented, and even mortgaged usufruct rights, which made the accumulation of wealth within the community possible."[86] The real world of rural Mexico was not the site of a monumental confrontation between communal and private property; rather, it was a place where native villagers, by no means economically or politically united, struggled over very specific local land issues, among themselves and with neighboring pueblos and nonnative outsiders. Using municipal institutions and local courts, they did their best to preserve their communities and secure whatever advantages the simplified categories of the law allowed.

The crisis for indigenous pueblos and their lands came during the period known as the "Porfiriato" (1877–1910) when, under the relatively stable authoritarian rule of President Porfirio Díaz, capitalist development hit Mexico full force. Railroads, industry, export-driven agriculture (notably cotton) and ranching were the most visible signs of the new era, but it also involved a thorough transformation of property arrangements. New legislation to nationalize and then privatize supposedly unoccupied lands (*baldías*) allowed foreign corporations to gain control of huge tracts, some of it claimed by natives. An ambitious program of surveying and mapping, largely carried out by corporations on behalf of the Mexican state, was part of this reconfiguration of national space.[87] With less fanfare but more effectiveness than the liberal reforms of earlier decades, the Díaz regime also managed to eliminate the entail on native *tierras de repartimiento*, with the result that many poor and endebted peasants sold out to *haciendas*, the main beneficiaries of land reform in

[85] Ducey, "Liberal Theory and Peasant Practice," 70. Cf. Kouri, "Interpreting the Expropriation of Indian Pueblo Lands in Porfirian Mexico," 77, 80.
[86] Ducey, "Liberal Theory and Peasant Practice," 72.   [87] Craib, *Cartographic Mexico*.

many parts of the country.[88] Natives pushed back with varying degrees of success, thereby preventing the complete liquidation of indigenous property, but the Porfiriato was nevertheless a time of severe dispossession.[89]

TOWARD THE RESERVATION

Three large territorial states developed in nineteenth-century North America, growing spatially over the course of the century and consolidating their hold over lands and people until, among them, they claimed sovereignty over every inch of the continent. (The fact that one of these countries, Mexico, actually shrank rather than expanded, and that another, Canada, formed part of the British Empire, can be overlooked for the moment as we focus on their common features as territorial polities.) This was an unprecedented development with cataclysmic implications for the indigenous peoples of America. Colonization and dispossession had, by this time, been proceeding incrementally for some three hundred years, but up until the second half of the nineteenth century wide portions of the continent had still remained under the effective control of indigenous nations. As the United States, and then the Dominion of Canada, occupied territories stretching "from sea to sea," fully independent native space shrank drastically.

Yet indigenous communities and indigenous lands did not disappear. Natives had resisted the settler onslaught, and when they could not hold back the tide, they resisted integration into the settler nation-state. However small the territorial enclaves left to them when the wave of colonization had passed, they did their best to hold on to these and to maintain their own version of land tenure and governance, maximizing their margin of independence and preserving the integrity of their communities. When colonial expansion had reached its natural limits – the "end of the frontier" as this transition was often called – the indigenous presence became an "internal" issue within the settler state. In that respect, Canada and the United States came to resemble Mexico, where native communities had taken the form of enclaves within the national space (as opposed to unconquered territory beyond the reach of the settler-state) from the time of independence. The continuing indigenous presence posed

---

[88] Schryer, *Ethnicity and Class Conflict in Rural Mexico*, 96–101.

[89] Ethelia Ruiz Medrano, *Mexico's Indigenous Communities: Their Lands and Histories, 1500–2010*, trans. Russ Davidson (Boulder: University Press of Colorado, 2010), 151; Assies, "Land Tenure and Tenure Regimes in Mexico," 38.

(and still poses) a fundamental challenge to the basic principles on which these modern nation-states had been founded, namely, private property and uniform territorial sovereignty. All land was supposed to belong to someone – tracts that were not privately held being deemed government property (the "public domain" in US parlance) – and every bit of it was considered to be subject to state authority in the same way. Indigenous lands, a vestige of the colonial and pre-colonial past, did not fit in this conception of space.

Under the colonial "old regime," property formation had proceeded through a process of bricolage involving all sorts of improvisations and tactical compromises between European and indigenous ways. Empires grew and deepened their territorial claims through the creation of different kinds of legal spaces for settlers and natives. The result was a set of thoroughly unsystematic property "systems" in New Spain, New France and New England, each of them shaped by a long and eventful history of colonization. Laws were confusing, surveying and title registration uncertain, claims to a given tract frequently multiple and contested. In such settings, there was almost always a place and a space for natives, though it might be tenuously held and vulnerable to further dispossession. Tenure difference implied political/juridical separateness: New Spain had its *"republicas de indios,"* while colonial New England and New France had analogous indigenous spaces, less fully elaborated in law. Crucially, the native/settler tenure divergence existed within a generally variegated property landscape in which land was held in many different ways and in which there was usually a place for indigenous tenures. However, when revolutionaries proclaimed that property was unitary and universal, that the power it conferred on proprietors was full, exclusive, and even absolute, native ways of holding land came to be seen as a disturbing anomaly.[90]

The predominant response on the part of the statesmen, legal authorities and national ideologues who shaped the destinies of the North American nation-states was willfully to forget the history that had left undigested chunks of indigenous land in the midst of their national

---

[90] It is true that European theorists, including John Locke and Emer de Vattel, had long before contested the legitimacy of indigenous claims to property in land. The arguments mostly focused on natives' supposed reliance on hunting and gathering and in their practical implications they seemed to authorize settler property formation and native dispossession, rather than require it. What was new in the wake of the Age of Revolution was the sense that indigenous lands – even those under cultivation – constituted a threat to the integrity of the national territory.

territories. The US Supreme Court led by Chief Justice John Marshall issued a series of decisions that stand as prime examples of the radical denial of history in the interests of squaring the reality of indigenous possession with the doctrines of indivisible sovereignty and full and exclusive property.[91] *Johnson v. M'Intosh* (1823) established the novel position that "Indians" had no right to sell their lands, but could only cede them to the government; as though this doctrine did not fly in the face of the pre-revolutionary American tradition of regulating the buyers, rather than the sellers of native lands, the court pretended it was simply applying a timeless principle. Indians it characterized as "an inferior race of people, without the privileges of citizens, and under the perpetual protection and pupilage of the government."[92] Government owned the land, native peoples merely "occupied" it. Marshall's opinion on the issue, a fundamental text in American legal history and one that would exert an influence in Canada and other settler-colonial nations, includes a long fable on the history of European empires in America. From the moment of "discovery" by representatives of a European power, the Chief Justice declared, the land belonged to the European sovereign rather than to the natives who lived there. Along the way, "discovery" somehow becomes tantamount to conquest and the assertion of imperial claims over distant lands implies actual ownership. Since Britain, by the 1783 Treaty of Paris, ceded all claims to North America between Florida and Canada and as far west as the Mississippi, the United States was consequently the rightful owner of this territory (not merely its sovereign), something the British had never dared claim. This assertion served to bolster the doctrine of preemption,[93] while aligning the law with the prevailing assumption that both sovereignty and property are unitary (except insofar as federalism requires a sharing between the several states and the union). British, French and Spanish monarchs had indeed (though not always) asserted sovereignty claims that included *dominium* as well as *imperium*, but they never denied in anything like this blanket fashion that natives too were proprietors of the land. The point about the Marshall

---

[91] On the Marshall rulings, see Hinderaker, *Elusive Empires*, 265–67; Banner, *How the Indians Lost Their Land*, 168–90; Lindsay G. Robertson, *Conquest by Law: How the Conquest of America Dispossessed Indigenous Peoples of Their Lands* (New York: Oxford University Press, 2005). The text of the opinion ("*Johnson & Graham's Lessee v. McIntosh*, 21 U.S. 8 Wheat. 543 (1823)") can be found on the Justicia website: https://supreme.justia.com/cases/federal/us/21/543/case.html, accessed 8 September 2016.

[92] Quoted in Hinderaker, *Elusive Empires*, 265.

[93] Banner, *How the Indians Lost Their Land*, 182.

opinion is not that it transformed the practices of dispossession – settlers, speculators and officials were already acting as though natives had no legitimate property rights – but the way that it illustrates the drive to force history and theory into conformity with the platonic ideals of absolute property and unitary sovereignty.

In other settings and in different ways, the nation-builders of the early nineteenth century tried to cut the Gordian knots of complexity and inconsistency that the centuries of colonial rule had left behind. If native peoples on native lands clashed with the modern vision of a unified national space, the tendency was to wish away the whole "Indian problem." José María Luis Mora of Mexico put it explicitly in a phrase quoted earlier – "The Indians should not continue to exist" – but he was surely not the only liberal visionary in North America who harbored such thoughts. Writing in 1783, George Washington predicted that "the gradual extension of our Settlements will as certainly cause the Savage as the Wolf to retire."[94] By "retire," Washington meant, "withdraw to the West," foreshadowing the Indian Removal Act of 1830 and the expulsion of most natives from states east of the Mississippi River.[95] Removal, of course, only delayed the day when advancing colonization had left nowhere in the continental United States for natives to be "removed" to. (Canada and Alaska present a different story: there extensive regions still remain as essentially indigenous territory.) Genocidal impulses seem to lurk in the language of both Mora and Washington, impulses that might well be linked to the wars, massacres and policies of starvation that mark the nineteenth-century history of North American colonization.[96] However, it is worth recalling that episodes of murderous violence can be found throughout the long history of colonialism and empire-formation – think of the conquest of Mexico and King Philip's War – and are not specific to the era that concerns us here. A more characteristically nineteenth-century expression of the impulse

---

[94] Quoted in Onuf, *Statehood and Union*, 37.
[95] There were similar, though much less effective, attempts to relocate Upper Canadian Natives. See Roger L. Nichols, *Indians in the United States and Canada: A Comparative History* (Lincoln: University of Nebraska Press, 1998), 174–205.
[96] For examples of such atrocities, see Karl Jacoby, *Shadows at Dawn: An Apache Massacre and the Violence of History* (New York: Penguin Books, 2009); James Daschuk, *Clearing the Plains: Disease, Politics of Starvation and the Loss of Aboriginal Life* (Regina, Saskatchewan: University of Regina Press, 2013); Benjamin Madley, *An American Genocide: The United States and the California Indian Catastrophe, 1846–1873* (New Haven, Conn.: Yale University Press, 2016).

to sweep away the "Indian problem" was a combination of cultural assimilation and bureaucratic administration.

Nation-builders like Mora and many of his North American counterparts liked to think that the "Indian problem" was at its heart a matter of the legal status of land. The habit of imagining native peoples out of existence as culturally distinct, self-governing societies, while trying to break up pueblo lands into alienable fragments, became ingrained in nineteenth-century Mexico. Somewhat similar half-fantasies of eliminating native communities by privatizing and allotting their lands arose in the United States and Canada as well. In contemplating a better future for natives, President James Madison pointed to "divided and individual ownership" as the "true foundation for a transit from the habits of the savage to the arts and comforts of social life." A Canadian parliamentary commission of 1844 diagnosed the problem in similar terms: "Owing to the peculiar title under which the Indians held their lands and their incapacity to alienate them, they continue as in their uncivilized state to hold them in common."[97] As indicated earlier in this chapter, the binary opposition of "private" and "common" ownership was a misleading simplification. The quality Madison and the parliamentary commission objected to was actually an artefact of colonialism: in negotiating territory, the state dealt with "tribes" and "bands," rather than individuals. This was a holdover from the basic colonialist stance that treated natives as foreigners. Similarly, the "incapacity to alienate" land was a continuation of colonial protective measures. Across North America, natives generally resisted privatization, which they rightly saw as an attempt to undermine the integrity and the autonomy of their communities and thus to eliminate their distinct societies and cultures.

The "reservation" (US) or "reserve" (Canada) system that emerged in the mid-nineteenth century, around the time when the United States had at last occupied a transcontinental territory and natives were rapidly running out of places to "remove" to, may be seen as another attempt to resolve the conflict between the absolutist approach to property and sovereignty and the disturbing persistence of native communities. "An island of Indian territory within a sea of white settlement," as Stuart Banner calls it,[98] the reservation was a "zone of exception" that would

---

[97] Quoted in Banner, *How the Indians Lost Their Land*, 260; and in William B. Henderson, *Canada's Indian Reserves: Pre-Confederation* (Ottawa: Research Branch Indian and Northern Affairs, 1980), 11.

[98] Banner, *How the Indians Lost Their Land*, 228.

play a central role in defining "Indian" as a legal identity and "Indian lands" as something outside the new national property regime. Just at a time when Mexico was doing its best to abolish the distinction between *indios* and others by breaking up pueblos and integrating their lands into the national real estate regime (Ley Lerdo, 1856), the United States and Canada were segregating natives and their "islands" of territory. The contrast is not as stark as it seems at first glance, however, as officials in the northern nations always envisioned reservations/reserves as a temporary expedient to accommodate a "doomed race." Reservations from that point of view were to serve as instruments of assimilation and vehicles for the orderly transfer of additional lands from natives to settlers.[99]

For indigenous peoples, on the other hand, reservations became homelands. Whether the latter took the form of a small fraction of a once-extensive plains hunting domain or a place of exile at the end of the "trail of tears," as was the case for many eastern nations removed to the future state of Oklahoma, these constrained territories were what was left to them under the new order. Since that was what they had to support themselves, maintain their communities and preserve a margin of political independence, they were likely to prize the reservation and to defend its territorial integrity, contesting the government's designs to use it as an instrument of assimilation and dispossession.

The nineteenth-century reservation in many respects represents the culmination of tendencies established during the so-called colonial period. From the early stages of the colonization of New Spain, protective legislation tried to preserve indigenous community lands and keep encroaching Spaniards at bay. Something vaguely similar to the *"republica de indios"* developed in New France and New England: enclaves of indigenous space within the colonized zone, with their own distinctive forms of land tenure and community organization. Christian missions were a typical feature of these colonized communities, and French Jesuits, Spanish Franciscans and Puritans like John Eliot assumed a supervisory role that foreshadowed that of nineteenth-century Indian agents. Notionally foreign elements in colonies where settlers and settler land tenures predominated, these native communities managed their lands and their

---

[99] In the Canadian legislation governing Indian reserves, more clauses are devoted to the selling of reserve land to nonnatives, as well as to the leasing out of timber rights and mining rights, than to any other topic. See especially the Indian Act of 1876. Indigenous and Northern Affairs Canada, "An Act to Amend and Consolidate the Laws Respecting Indians": www.aadnc-aandc.gc.ca/eng/1100100010252/1100100010254.

community life largely as they saw fit. The continuing presence of independent indigenous peoples and territories beyond the frontier of settlement provided a possible alternative if the colonial regime became so oppressive that people wished to leave. The reservation system represented a break with these traditions in that it left natives virtually nowhere to hide. More than its colonial-era analogues, it increasingly displayed the characteristics of a "total institution." By the last quarter of the century, natives in western Canada and the United States were being forcibly confined to reservations that were starting to function as places of incarceration.[100]

The term "reservation" had first arisen in the seventeenth century, and as Stuart Banner explains, it originally denoted nothing more than a condition inserted into a real estate transaction, whether settler-to-settler or native-to-settler. By the terms of early Indian deeds, Ninnimissinuok negotiators often "reserved" a specified tract within the territory being surrendered (together with usufruct rights over wider areas); as a result of the "reservation" clause in the deed, that land remained theirs.[101] Following the American Revolution, when the United States was insisting that it already owned the territory over which it claimed sovereignty, the word acquired a different legal meaning, suggestive of territory allocated by government rather than retained by natives. Such "reservations" were typically associated with treaties: at the point when natives surrendered their "right of occupancy," the government would assign a tract for their use. Even if natives considered the reservation as retained sovereign territory and community property, the state construed it legally as government property where Indians were allowed to live. In both Canada and the United States, the reservation model spread beyond the areas covered by treaties. A notable example of this extension would be the case of Quebec, a jurisdiction where there were no significant land surrender treaties until the 1970s. The Canadian government (like its US counterpart in the extensive parts of the country where no treaties were ever negotiated) unilaterally created reserves for northern hunters. It also tried to reduce the villages of the St. Lawrence Valley, some of them native-held seigneuries, to the status of reserves, the better to bring the diversity

---

[100] Nichols, *Indians in the United States and Canada*, 206–25; Banner, *How the Indians Lost Their Land*, 240; Sarah Carter, *Aboriginal People and Colonizers of Western Canada to 1900* (Toronto: University of Toronto Press, 1999), 140–49, 161–68.
[101] Banner, *How the Indians Lost Their Land*, 229.

created by history into conformity with the standardized bureaucratic culture of "Indian administration."[102]

Though not all people who considered themselves indigenous by virtue of their culture and ancestry lived on reservations – far from it – the American and Canadian states nevertheless tended to treat these territories and the people who inhabited them as synonymous. To be an "Indian," to live on a reservation and to be part of an administered community came down to more or less the same thing in the second half of the nineteenth century. Reservation/reserve land could not be sold or mortgaged by those who occupied it, though individual allocations were usually heritable. At a time – the nineteenth century – when the ideal of universal private property predominated, the tenure assigned to natives represented not merely a deviation from a norm, but rather something more like its antithesis: Indian land appeared, in this sense, as anti-property. By the same token, "Indians" were people who were subject to the state's sovereignty, but who were not citizens. Vacillating like all colonial regimes between incorporating and distancing colonized peoples,[103] Canadian and American governments treated natives and their assigned lands as foreign objects within the national territory and then tried to integrate them both into the nation. Thus Canada's "Gradual Civilization Act" of 1857, which encouraged indigenous men to become citizens and proprietors by allowing them to carve out a portion of their respective reserves to hold as private property. (Natives refused the bait, however, and the program was a failure.)[104] The United States went a step further with the Dawes Act (1887), which instituted mandatory "allotment" of reservation lands; in this instance as well, private property and citizenship were intimately connected.[105] These attempts to "solve the Indian problem" served partly as cover for further

---

[102] Alain Beaulieu, "La création des réserves indiennes au Québec," in *Les Autochtones et le Québec: des premiers contacts au plan nord*, ed. Alain Beaulieu, Stéphan Gervais and Martin Papillon (Montreal: Presses de l'Université de Montréal, 2002), 135–51.

[103] Ann Laura Stoler, *Carnal Knowledge and Imperial Power: Race and the Intimate in Colonial Rule* (Berkeley: University of California Press, 2002), 83–84.

[104] *An Act to Encourage the Gradual Civilization of Indian Tribes in this Province, and to Amend the Laws Relating to Indians* (Toronto: S. Derbishire & G. Desbarats, 1857); John L. Tobias, "Protection, Civilization, Assimilation: An Outline History of Canada's Indian Policy," in *As Long as the Sun Shines and Water Flows*, ed. Ian A. L. Getty and Antoine Lussier (Vancouver: UBC Press, 1983), 13–30; J. R. Miller, *Skyscrapers Hide the Heavens: A History of Indian-White Relations in Canada*, 3rd ed. (Toronto: University of Toronto Press, 2000), 110–14.

[105] Banner, *How the Indians Lost Their Land*, 257–90.

dispossession (reservation lands were much reduced under the Dawes Act), but native resistance foiled the attempt completely to liquidate their homelands. The basic thrust of these privatizing measures, like the construction of reservations in the first place, nevertheless serves to illustrate how closely civic integration and private property in land were linked in this era of liberal nation-building.

Since the beginning of the colonial era, property-making and sovereignty-making had been closely associated, but as of the Age of Revolution, the notion had taken hold that property in land should be unitary, private and even absolute. Indigenous communities and their lands then became not just a variant form of social organization and tenure, but rather a fundamental exception that helped to define the dominant norm. The nineteenth century was also a period that saw the consolidation of racism. Scholars have noted that "race" and racism developed on different tracks in North America, depending on whether the denigrated identity was construed as "black" or "Indian."[106] This study suggests that, in Canada and the United States at least, the category "Indian" developed in intimate relation to the processes of dispossession and property formation. At a time when property tended to function as a defining feature of citizenship, an "Indian" was quintessentially someone subject to the state's power, but unqualified to own land.

CODA

As I write these lines, the Standing Rock Sioux, joined by thousands of indigenous supporters from across North America, have mounted a protest against the construction of the Dakota Access oil pipeline that would intrude on their ancestral lands and endanger their community water supply. A "Peace Caravan" is making its way across Canada in an effort to stop the construction of a hydroelectric dam in northern British

---

[106] Patrick Wolfe's seminal essay, "Land, Labor, and Difference: Elementary Structures of Race," *American Historical Review* 106 (2001): 866–905, forms the starting point for any discussion of settler-colonial racism. At the same time, it has to be noted that the scope of Wolfe's interpretation is narrower than it seems, since its vision rarely extends beyond the nineteenth-century Anglosphere. The legal scholar Laura Brace is also worth consulting on questions of property, race and citizenship. "Property rights in land," she writes, "are central to nationhood in terms of both territory and identity. They work as a means of defining who may control valuable objects and the conditions under which this power may be exercised." Laura Brace, *The Politics of Property: Labour, Freedom, and Belonging* (Edinburgh: Edinburgh University Press, 2004), 208–9.

Columbia; the dam would flood much of the remaining hunting grounds of the West Moberly and Prophet River First Nations. Meanwhile, *ch'ol* members of the *ejido* of Tila in the southern Mexican state of Chiapas have demolished the town hall that houses the rival municipal government, dominated by nonindigenous *pobladores*. Disputes over land tenure and local government in Tila reached a peak in recent months with the intervention of units of the Mexican armed forces and the murder of two young men by machete-wielding paramilitaries. Anyone willing to look beyond the front pages of the major outlets can find news of similar episodes connected with property and indigenous dispossession across North America virtually at any given time.[107]

These incidents remind us that colonization, dispossession and resistance have not ended, though they have taken new forms in the twenty-first century. Native communities still have to struggle to preserve both the lands that have been left to them after centuries of colonization and the margin of political independence that goes along with their territorial enclaves. Indigenous lands were a major target of the global surge in corporate "land grabs" that marked the opening decade of our century and that has not yet subsided.[108] Speaking generally, the principal threat now comes more from resource extraction corporations – above all, the mining, forestry, nuclear and petroleum industries – rather than agrarian settlers.[109] (The Chiapas case may be an exception to this generalization.) As always, however, these conflicts cannot be understood in narrowly economic terms. Questions of sovereignty and autonomy are at stake as much as issues of resources and environmental protection. Along with

---

[107] "Occupying the Prairie: Tensions Rise as Tribes Move to Block a Pipeline," *New York Times*, 23 August 2016; "First Nations Leaders Decry Site C Approval," *Globe and Mail*, 13 September 2016; "Commicado Ejido Tila," 6 September 2016, komaniel.org/2016/09/08/communicado-ejido/tila/, accessed 18 September 2016; "Chiapas: Tila Ejido Reports Violent Murder of Two Youths in Its Territory, Intended to Destabilize Its Assertion of Autonomy," https://sipazen.wordpress.com, accessed 20 September 2016.

[108] In Africa and Asia, huge tracts of land have been taken over for the use of large-scale agricultural enterprises, such as palm oil plantations. Mining, ranching and commercial forestry are the main drivers of land grabs in South America. See "The Surge in Land Deals: When Others Are Grabbing Their Land," *The Economist*, 5 May 2011; Fred Pearce, *The Land Grabbers: The New Fight over Who Owns the Earth* (Boston: Beacon Press, 2012); "'Our Land, Our Lives': Time Out in the Global Land Rush," Oxfam International Briefing Notes, October 2012.

[109] See, for example, Terri Hansen, "Eight Hottest Environmental Battlegrounds in Indian Country," 27 August 2013, http://indiancountrytodaymedianetwork.com/2013/08/27/eight-hot-environmental-battlegrounds-indian-country-151054, accessed 20 September 2016.

indigenous communities and resource companies, governments are the third major actor in every important confrontation. As in the distant colonial past, states are caught between the paternalistic impulse to protect indigenous communities from exploitation and the imperatives to assert state authority and facilitate economic development.

The flare-up in Chiapas is particularly interesting as an illustration of just how durable centuries-old approaches to the questions of property, dispossession and sovereignty have proven to be. The *ejido* (local commons) of Tila owes its modern existence to the Mexican Revolution of 1910–17. Thanks to the successes of the peasant movement led by Emiliano Zapata, article 27 of the revolutionary constitution of 1917 gave natives (and others) the right to hold land collectively as village *ejidos*, a development that allowed them to rebuild communities dismantled under the rule of Porfirio Díaz.[110] The post-revolutionary restoration of indigenous community lands was abruptly reversed in 1992, however, when President Carlos Salinas de Gortari engineered a constitutional amendment to eliminate article 27 with the aim of breaking up the commons (*ejidos*) and privatizing community property. The imminent establishment of the North American Free Trade Agreement, part of a broader movement of globalization under neoliberal auspices, provided the immediate impulse to this drastic measure. Although the legislation did not mention ethnicity, it was clearly aimed principally at indigenous lands. It looked forward to continental – and eventually global – integration, bringing Mexico's property regime into closer alignment with that of the United States, but it looked backward as well, to the familiar nineteenth-century project of liquidating native communities by eliminating their distinctive land tenure. In the predominantly indigenous southern state of Chiapas, an insurrectionary movement, the Zapatista Army of National Liberation, rose up to oppose this renewed attempt to "modernize" natives out of existence.[111]

The confrontation at Tila has to be seen as a late manifestation of the Zapatista uprising, twenty-two years after that movement burst onto the scene. Defending pueblo lands and resisting globalization of a very contemporary sort, the Tila *ejidatarios* are also engaged in a contest for local power that stems from the municipal rearrangements set in motion at the

---

[110] Assies, "Land Tenure and Tenure Regimes in Mexico," 39–44. On the Mexican Revolution more generally, see Alan Knight, *The Mexican Revolution* (Cambridge: Cambridge University Press, 1986).

[111] June Nash, "The Reassertion of Indigenous Identity: Mayan Responses to State Intervention in Chiapas," *Latin American Research Review* 30 (1995): 7–41.

time of Mexican independence. While the native majority of Tila adheres to the *ejido* as the voice of the community and collective holder of land rights, a state-recognized *ayuntamiento* dominated by mestizos (and backed, according to the *ejido*, by drug dealers) claims to be the legitimate local municipality. It was the violent confrontation of these two institutions of local government, one heir to a centuries-old tradition of self-governing indigenous pueblos, the other embodying nineteenth-century notions of municipal modernization, that provoked the Mexican government to send in the marines.

In their conflicts with governments and corporations, indigenous peoples can usually count on some support from sympathetic elements within the settler population and the state, but they still have to contend with policies and attitudes rooted in the nineteenth-century era of state-building. With depressing frequency, voices are still raised in favor of the privatization of reservation lands in the name of modernization and economic efficiency. The tendency to reduce issues of territoriality, sovereignty and community survival to purely economic considerations remains as strong. "Prosperity is built on property rights," proclaims a *Forbes* magazine article, "and reservations often have neither. They're a demonstration of what happens when property rights are weak or non-existent." Why are so many Native Americans poor? Because of legal and cultural obstacles to entrepreneurialism: "The vast majority of land on reservations is held communally. That means residents can't get clear title to the land where their home sits, one reason for the abundance of mobile homes on reservations."[112] The positive connotations of the term

---

[112] John Koppisch, "Why Are Indian Reservations so Poor? A Look at the Bottom 1%," *Forbes*, 13 December 2011; see also Naomi Shaefer Riley, "One Way to Help Native Americans: Property Rights," *The Atlantic*, 30 July 2016. For a more scholarly version of this line of thinking, see Tom Flanagan, Christopher Alcantara and André Le Dressay, *Beyond the Indian Act: Restoring Aboriginal Property Rights* (Montreal: McGill-Queen's University Press, 2010). Though rooted in late eighteenth/early nineteenth-century liberal thought, this position is more immediately inspired by the neoliberal vision of private property advocate Hernando de Soto: *The Mystery of Capital: Why Capitalism Triumphs in the West and Fails Everywhere Else* (New York: Basic Books, 2000). On de Soto, see Timothy Mitchell, "The Work of Economics: How a Discipline Makes Its World," *European Journal of Sociology* 46, no. 2 (August 2005): 297–320. For a critical response to Flanagan, Alcantara and Le Dressay, see Jessica Dempsey, Kevin Gould and Juanita Sundberg, "Changing Land Tenure, Defining Subjects: Neo-Liberalism and Property Regimes on Native Reserves," in *Rethinking the Great White North: Race, Nature, and the Historical Geographies of Whiteness in Canada*, ed. Audrey Kobayashi, Laura Cameron and Andrew Baldwin (Vancouver: UBC Press, 2011), 233–58.

"rights" are linked here to the ideal of property in land that is vested in individuals (not "held communally"): all will be well as indigenous land is absorbed into the Euro-American "mainstream" and indigenous people disappear into oblivion. It is as though the Age of Revolution, with its utopian settler ambitions and property delusions, had occurred yesterday.

Index